CONTEMPORARY COMMUNICATION THEORY

DOMINIC A. INFANTE
Kent State University

ANDREW S. RANCER
University of Akron

THEODORE A. AVTGIS
West Virginia University

D1158730

Kendall Hunt
publishing company
4050 Westmark Drive • P O Box 1840 • Dubuque IA 52004-1840

Book Team

Chairman and Chief Executive Officer   Mark C. Falb
President and Chief Operating Officer   Chad M. Chandlee
Vice President, Higher Education   David L. Tart
Director of National Book Program   Paul B. Carty
Editorial Manager   Georgia Botsford
Senior Editor   Angela Willenbring
Vice President, Operations   Timothy J. Beitzel
Assistant Vice President, Production Services   Christine E. O'Brien
Senior Production Editor   Mary Melloy
Permissions Editor   Renae Horstman
Cover Designer   Jenifer Chapman
Web Project Manager   Sheena Reed

Cover image © Terry Chan, 2009
Used under license from Shutterstock, Inc.

Kendall Hunt
publishing company

www.kendallhunt.com
Send all inquiries to:
4050 Westmark Drive
Dubuque, IA 52004-1840

Printed in the United States of America
10 9 8 7 6 5 4 3 2 1

DEDICATION

Dedicated to our wonderful wives

Sandy, Kathi, Mary

BRIEF CONTENTS

CONTENTS

CHAPTER 7

Verbal Behavior Approaches   185

CHAPTER 8

Nonverbal Behavior Approaches   215

PART III

Theory Building in Communication Contexts   249

CHAPTER 9

Interpersonal Contexts   251

PREFACE

This book is designed to introduce college students to theories in the field of communication. Theory courses are offered at many levels in the curriculum. If a course in communication theory is the only communication course a student takes, it is important that the material present a fairly detailed picture of the current thinking in the discipline. The different approaches taken to understanding human communication, major theories within the structure of each approach, and representative research conducted to test the validity of theory building are all important areas to emphasize.

The possibility that students using this book might become more than casual observers of communication was very much on our minds as we wrote. We attempted to reveal the importance of the field, the value of its teachings, and the richness of the discipline's thinking. We have tried to give equal treatment to the areas in which people specialize so that we do not influence the student to specialize in one area of the field instead of another. We intend this book to be used by communication majors or minors as a springboard to discover for themselves their strongest interests. It would be nice if equal treatment resulted in some students liking the major areas of the field equally. However, the current composition of the discipline suggests otherwise. Generalists are rather rare in the communication field; as in other disciplines, specialists are more the rule. A more realistic expectation might be that the first course in communication theory would provide a would-be specialist in organizational communication, for example, with an understanding and appreciation of the major tenets of other areas of the field.

There are six distinctive features of this book that we would like to highlight. First, the book emphasizes the complementary relationship of theory building and research in the communication discipline. Gary Cronkhite has explained persuasively that the focus and scope of the communication discipline is defined by human symbolic activity. This book utilizes Cronkhite's conceptualization and rejects earlier models based on the "you cannot not communicate" notion. As a result, there is a strong emphasis on human symbolic activity. This turns our attention more to researchers in the field of communication and less to scholars in other disciplines who, although interested in communication, give it attention only insofar as communication enhances understanding of broad social processes such as risk taking, cooperation, apathy, violence, and prejudice.

A limited amount of work by scholars in fields such as social psychology will be discussed in this book. In the 1960s, there was so little original theory building in the discipline that textbook writers in the communication field had little choice other than to "import" theories from related disciplines. However, that condition began shifting in the 1970s with Berger's uncertainty reduction theory and McCroskey's model of communication apprehension and then changed markedly in the 1980s. It will be evident to the reader that there is now no shortage of theory building in communication. If communication journals have reflected sufficient interest in theories from outside the field (Petty and Cacioppo's work, for example), we have used that criterion to include some theories from outside the discipline. The fact that this book is able to rely so heavily on the work of communication scholars may be viewed as a sign of the maturity of contemporary communication theory.

A second feature of this book is that the coverage of theory is selective. Books that attempt to survey an entire field are limited to a brief mention of many theories because of the vast amount of theory and research in each area. At the other extreme, if too few theories are covered, a sense of the scope of theorizing is lost. We chose an intermediate position in order to emphasize how contemporary scholars build on past theory and research. We hope this will be more intellectually satisfying than reading a "handbook" of statements about theories. In selecting this middle course, we have included a sufficient number of theories to present an overview of the different theory-building approaches in each area. Our main concern has been to highlight the *development* of theory building rather than a particular set of theories.

A third feature of the book is the presentation of the trait approach to studying communication. In terms of sheer quantity of research, this approach is probably the major one taken by researchers during the past twenty-five years or so. A trait approach involves discovering what is characteristic of a person's communicative behavior—what regularities are consistent across situations. Researchers in the communication field tend to be either trait or situationist in terms of orientation. Situationists believe the factors in a given communication situation overwhelm characteristics of the individual so that the nature of the situation best explains communicative behavior. More and more contemporary theorists are emphasizing the interaction between traits and situational factors.

Interestingly, some introductory textbooks in communication include little or no discussion of the findings from trait research. This is puzzling because much of our current knowledge of communication involves traits. One of the most thoroughly researched topics in the history of the discipline is communication apprehension, yet some books do not address this topic. What is the explanation? Although a large portion of recent research has been conducted by trait researchers, many of the textbooks have been written by situationists or rhetoricians who conduct a very different kind of research. We have included both trait and situational research and delineate the usefulness of each.

A fourth distinguishing characteristic of this book is that the student is taught how theories are tested. To complement the theories presented, we discuss how each has been studied by communication researchers. Lawrence

Frey and Carl Botan emphasized the interdependence of theory and research and question "whether undergraduates are learning the research methods needed to fully appreciate and understand communication theory" (1988, p. 250). We agree with Frey and Botan's concern. We would question how deeply a student understands a given communication theory if the student has no idea how to test the theory.

The fifth area of emphasis is the discussion of important new areas of research. We devote a chapter to intercultural, family, political, and health communication. In addition, the intercultural communication context provides an opportunity to trace differences and similarities in the communication process. We examine basic communication concepts in a variety of different contexts. For example, Berger's uncertainty reduction theory is first presented in the interpersonal chapter, and its extensions are discussed in the intercultural section. This approach illustrates what we feel is one of the most important aspects of theory: theorists often build on previous work and extend applications of particular approaches to new areas.

A sixth distinguishing feature of this book is the emphasis on what is called the social scientific, quantitative, or behavioral science approach to the study of communication. Other approaches—often termed human action, rules, systems, qualitative, or humanistic—are not ignored in this book. For instance, we present the major concepts from rhetorical theory, constructivism, and symbolic convergence theory. However, we believe the social science approach is particularly valuable and should constitute a primary way of studying communicative behavior. As you will see in this book, a scientific approach emphasizes the orderly and highly rigorous accumulation of knowledge by developing theories that can be tested empirically. Quantitative analysis establishes a degree of confidence in ideas and often results in a progression of research questions for further study that arise from a given research project. This is the type of research conducted extensively by your authors who have devoted their careers to the social scientific approach to studying communication. Some of their research will be discussed in this book.

This book is divided into three parts. The first part provides an introduction and foundation. In these four chapters, we conceptualize communication as a symbol-using activity, discuss the nature of theories, review the historical development of communication theory, and explain the laws, rules, and systems perspectives on communication. The second part of the book focuses on several major approaches to understanding human communication: communication traits, persuasion, verbal behavior, and nonverbal behavior. The third part of the book looks at communication theory building contextually. A good deal of the literature in the field pertains to the set of circumstances where communication takes place—the context. Five chapters cover theory building in the interpersonal, group, organizational, and mass media contexts, followed by the intercultural/health/political/family chapter. The Appendix contains a chapter on the methods used to test communication theories.

We have believed that a book was needed that emphasized the theoretical contributions of communication scholars in the communication discipline. Completing *Contemporary Communication Theory* crystallized our beliefs that the discipline is able to stand by itself, its posture is rather impressive, and we are proud of it.

As we wrote this book, we were reminded of the excitement scientists feel as they create theories and conduct research to test them. Theory building is an exploratory process designed to extend the frontiers of knowledge. We hope this text will convince the reader of the importance of building theory and will lead to shared enthusiasm for theory building in communication.

STUDENT-ORIENTED PEDAGOGY

Because we recognize the importance of assessing student learning, we have included the following features to facilitate students' understanding of the concepts.

Chapter Introduction—offers an overview of the material highlighted in the chapter

Running Glossary—provides a quick definition of key terms within the text

Figures and Tables—further illustrate theories visually

Chapter Summary—effectively reviews chapter elements presented

Key Terms—lists important concepts for each chapter

Glossary—includes all key terms found throughout the text

References—a comprehensive list documenting the extensive research cited

INSTRUCTIONAL ONLINE ENHANCEMENTS

Look for the web icon in the page margins of the text to direct you to various interactive tools, accessed through the web code included in the textbook. The online materials are integrated chapter-by-chapter with the textbook to enrich students' learning.

Student Web Content

Video interviews—showcase experts' explanations of theory

Review games—provide extensive concept review in game formats

Flash cards—offer an interactive version of the key terms

Exercises, research projects, activities—various tools encourage active learning and understanding of the material

Instructor Web Content

Chapter outlines—highlight central ideas for each chapter and can serve as lecture notes

Comprehensive test bank—offers different question formats to better assess student knowledge

PowerPoint slides—illustrate important chapter concepts and can be made accessible to students

ACKNOWLEDGMENTS

We would like to thank Brian R. Flynn, Kimberly Straight, and Nikki Loy of West Virginia University as well as Gregory A. Divins-Stoll for their help with the text. We would also like to thank three individuals at Kendall Hunt who were instrumental in conceiving of this project and whose guidance assisted us greatly in bringing it to fruition—Paul Carty, Angela Willenbring, and Mary Melloy. We also appreciate the constructive comments of the colleagues who reviewed the content. They include:

Alicia Alexander
Southern Illinois University Edwardsville

Carolyn M. Anderson
University of Akron

Michael Irvin Arrington
University of Kentucky

Susan Avanzino
California State University Chico

Nathan Baxter
Gordon College

Monica Brasted
SUNY Brockport

Sakile Camara
California State University Northridge

David Carlone
The University of North Carolina at Greensboro

Debbie Chasteen
William Jewell College

Kathleen D. Clark
University of Akron

Leda Cooks
University of Massachusetts

Andrew Jared Critchfield
The George Washington University

Linda Czuba Brigance
SUNY Fredonia

John Dahlberg
Canisius College

Lucian F. Dinu
University of Louisiana at Lafayette

Norbert Elliot
New Jersey Institute of Technology

Celeste Farr
North Carolina State University

G.L. Forward
Point Loma Nazarene University

Merry E. George
Pikeville College

Jodi Hallsten
Illinois State University

Heidi Hamilton
Emporia State University

Mary Beth Holmes
Marywood University

Mark E. Huglen
University of Minnesota–Crookston

Laura Janusik
Rockhurst University

John Katsion
Multnomah University

William W. Kenner
University of Michigan Flint

Anastacia Kurylo
Marymount Manhattan College

Kara Laskowski
Shippensburg University

Susan Leggett
Westfield State College

Kristin Lindholm
Trinity International University

Hsin-I Liu
University of Incarnate Word

Tina McCorkindale
Cal Poly Pomona

Courtney Miller
Elmhurst College

Nancy Morris
Temple University

Anne Nicotera
George Mason University

Margaret Z. Ostrenko
Saint Leo University

Shara Toursh Pavlow
Florida Atlantic University

Barbara Penington
University of Wisconsin–Whitewater

Amber Peplow
Wright State University

Thomas E Ruggiero
University of Texas at El Paso

Brian Simmons
Cascade College

Sherry S. Strain
Keystone College

Yan Tian
University of Missouri-St. Louis

Beatriz Torres
Keene State College

Bill Wallace
Northeastern State University

John Warren
Southern Illinois University

Dennis L. Wignall
Dixie State College

MJ Woeste
University of Cincinnati

Edward Woods
Marshall University

ABOUT THE AUTHORS

Dominic A. Infante (Ph.D.—Kent State University, 1971) is Emeritus Professor of Communication Studies at Kent State University, Kent, Ohio. He is living in Alliance, Ohio, during his retirement. Among his awards and honors, he is particularly proud of receiving the President's Medal from Kent State University, being named a Centennial Scholar by the Eastern Communication Association, and being identified in a published study of research productivity as the Seventh Most Productive Scholar in the Communication Discipline during the Twentieth Century. He is the author of numerous books, chapters in books, and research journal articles in communication, psychology, sociology, business administration, and business education.

Andrew S. Rancer (Ph.D.—Kent State University, 1979) is Professor of Communication in the School of Communication, University of Akron, Kolbe Hall 108, Akron, Ohio, 44325-1003. He has served as editor of *Communication Research Reports* (1999–2001) and the *Massachusetts Communication Journal* (1981). Among several honors, he is the recipient of the Eastern Communication Association's Past Presidents/Officers Award (1989) and Distinguished Research Fellow Award (1997) and was a member of ECA's Committee of Scholars (1989–1990). In 2009 he received a Centennial Scholar of Communication Award from the Eastern Communication Association. He has published articles in *Communication Monographs, Human Communication Research, Communication Education, Communication Quarterly,* and *Communication Research Reports,* among others. He is the co-author of four books, including *Argumentative and Aggressive Communication* (2006).

Theodore A. Avtgis (Ph.D.—Kent State University, 1999) is Associate Professor of Communication in the Department of Communication Studies, West Virginia University, 108 Armstrong Hall, PO Box 6293, Morgantown, West Virginia, 26506. He is the Coordinator of the graduate program in corporate and organizational communication (2006–present) and currently serves on the editorial boards of *Argumentation and Advocacy, Communication Research Reports,*

Human Communication, and *Journal of Intercultural Research,* among others. Among several awards, he was recognized as one of the Top Twelve Most Productive Scholars in the field of Communication Studies (between 1996–2001) and recognized as a member of the World Council on Hellenes Abroad, USA Region of American Academics. He was also named as a Centennial Scholar of Communication by the Eastern Communication Association. Dr. Avtgis has published articles in *Communication Education, Management Communication Quarterly, Communication Research Reports,* and the *Journal of Intercultural Communication,* among others. He is co-author of four books, including *Argumentative and Aggressive Communication* (2006). He is also co-founder of *Medical Communication Specialists.*

THEORY BUILDING IN COMMUNICATION

To introduce you to theory building in the field of communication, we will explore the following topics: What is the nature of communication? How do theories function? How has theory building in communication developed over time? What approaches have been used in building communication theories?

Chapter 1 describes communication as a transactional process: people interact and relate to each other by exchanging messages. There are many different definitions of communication, and each one explains communication from a different focus. One of the central issues of difference is whether a message must be intentional to be considered communication. Another is whether we should use the term *communication* to describe all verbal and nonverbal expression. We believe definitions that claim all behavior is communicative obscure the significance of communication. After defining communication, we discuss several characteristics and points of controversy about communication.

Chapter 2 defines and explains theories. What is a theory? Are theories of communication different from other types of theories? Why do humans—both scientists and laypersons—invent theories? Theories are dynamic creations; they develop and change; they are seldom stagnant. Testing theories allows us to see how they can be changed to make them better. The testing process basically provides a theory with the opportunity to fail or to prove itself wrong. Evaluation of theories is an essential process. Without it, we would be unable to tell a good theory from a bad one. We will look at the criteria for a good communication theory and the criteria used in evaluating theories in general.

Chapter 3 reviews how theory building in communication has developed over time. We will first examine the major ideas from rhetorical theory, which is the approach to communication taken by the ancient Greeks and Romans. We will focus particularly on the ideas of the great Greek philosopher Aristotle and the famous Roman politician and educator Cicero. Their conceptions of rhetoric had a major influence on nearly all theorists throughout the history of the field, well into the twentieth century. Descriptive models of communication from the mid-twentieth century, which had an effect on subsequent theorizing, will be explained. We will then review some of the early theories and research programs that directly influenced many of the later theories covered in this book. Among the early influences were the Yale University communication studies, information theory, Berlo's process model, cognitive dissonance theory, symbolic convergence theory, and Burke's dramatism.

Chapter 4 presents an overview of the four major perspectives of theory building in communication. The laws perspective is the approach that emphasizes the discovery of regularities or laws through empirical observation. Basically, this is the model of the physical sciences as applied to the social sciences. The focus is on modeling and testing causal relationships. The human action perspective stresses the human aspect of free will. This approach emphasizes studying how people make choices, how they interpret and react to events, their intentions, their goals, the rules they follow, and the rules they violate. The systems perspective examines how parts of something function interdependently in seeking to attain certain goals. This approach emphasizes studying patterns of communication, inputs and outputs, and how the system maintains a state of equilibrium. The communibiological perspective claims that why we communicate in the ways that we do is explained mainly by biology. There is a genetic basis for most of our communicative behavior; we inherit temperaments. The focus is especially on brain activity responsible for particular temperaments.

Introduction to Studying Communication

As we shall see in this book, building useful communication theories is important for many reasons. Perhaps none is more significant than the idea that communication is vital to individuals, groups, and organizations in a democratic society.

What is unique about a free society? One distinguishing characteristic has been termed the "marketplace of ideas" (Cronkhite, 1976). People who have ideas are free to express them. If the ideas have merit, they will survive the competition with other ideas. This means freedom of speech is highly prized and protected from any possible erosion. It is assumed that people in the marketplace have the ability to select the best idea. Freedom of speech is crucial to ensure that there will be a wide variety of ideas available. This increases the probability that a very good idea will be present in the group of available ideas.

Communication is particularly prominent in *selecting* an idea from the marketplace of ideas. Aristotle believed that communication, especially persuasion, enabled people to discover what was good for society at a particular time and place. Public deliberation occurs when advocates and opponents for various ideas or proposals attempt to persuade people. If all proposals are not represented by competent advocates, the best proposal may not survive. The consequences of proposals must be clearly understood if the best decision is to be made. Advocates of an inferior proposal may deceive the audience by misrepresenting the superior proposal's advantages or potential disadvantages. If there were no competent spokespersons for the superior proposal, the audience might select the inferior proposal. People will do their best to make a good decision on an important matter. If awareness of the issues has been reduced by deception or incompetence, even the best ideas can go unnoticed. This is why effective communication is so important in our society. People will select the best candidate, approve worthy issues by referendum, or support good changes in the status quo—if the communication is of such quality that the significant issues are understood. This idea, of course, is not new. It was central in the thinking of both Aristotle and the writers of our Constitution. A major goal of the field of communication has been to prepare students to be effective participants in a democracy. The study of communication is more extensive in the educational system of the United States than in any other country in the world. This is no accident. It is difficult to find a country that has more freedom of expression than the United States. Our very existence depends on people making good decisions. As we have said, that is very unlikely without effective communication.

Despite the fact that our society is so advanced, we have not achieved complete equality of opportunity. Although there may be greater opportunity in the United States and the laws protect against discrimination, your sex, race, religion, or national origin may affect your achievements. However, communicative ability is an equalizer; our society rewards people who are effective communicators. For example, doors open for members of minority groups that would have remained closed if it were not for communication skills. Our society is not perfect, but that does not mean you cannot succeed. It is exciting to be part of the communication discipline; we commonly observe people "getting ahead" because of improvements made in their communication skills. As you study the material in the rest of this book, it is important to keep in mind the vital role of communication in our private and public lives. Because communication is so important, building the best possible communication theories and models is perhaps the most important activity scholars in our discipline can undertake.

When you take your first course in a discipline, you are sometimes completely unfamiliar with the subject matter. In your first chemistry course, for example, you probably had no knowledge about covalent and ionic bonding of elements. In other courses, you probably recognized some of the elements of what the discipline studies, but the knowledge was only superficial. For instance, if you took a course in meteorology, you would be acquainted with basic terms like weather, climate, or storms. The course would introduce you to new aspects of familiar phenomena. You might learn that a stationary high-pressure system in the Pacific Ocean west of the state of Oregon can direct the jet stream northward, creating a return flow of cold air to the northern states—resulting in unusually harsh weather.

Your first course in communication falls in the second category; you are already familiar with the subject matter. Because of personal interactions and what you have experienced through the mass media, there are few, if any, communication behaviors you have not encountered. As in our meteorology example, you probably expect to learn about the "whys" of the phenomena. For instance, why are some people more easily persuaded than others? Why are some people predisposed to communicate? How can you reduce your level of speech anxiety? What are the characteristics of a person who can talk effortlessly about any topic? How does the image people have of us influence how they react to our messages? How does your gender influence your verbal behavior? What nonverbal messages do we send to others?

We will begin to understand these and many other concepts as we examine *theory* in this book. A **theory** is a set of related statements designed to describe, explain, and/or predict reality. As we shall observe in the next chapter, there are several types of theories of communication, and all are useful in providing explanations. It is important to realize that theories are useful guides for behavior. They are not just abstract concepts; they provide a basis for practical application. For instance, a theory about communication in organizations might suggest that particular tasks require different communication skills. In practice, this theory would indicate that managers should be trained to communicate one way and that salespeople should be encouraged to communicate in other ways to make the organization more productive.

Theory A set of related statements designed to describe, explain, and/or predict reality

ISSUES IN UNDERSTANDING COMMUNICATION

Basic Components and Concepts

In this section, we will review some terms essential to your study of communication. As with our meteorology example, you have at least some familiarity with these concepts. Before we enter the complex area of defining communication, we will start with the somewhat easier, and less controversial, definitions of key elements in the process.

Source. A **source** designates the originator of a message. Some communication scholars have differentiated between the concepts of "source" and "sender." A sender is one who transmits messages but does not necessarily originate them. An example of a sender could be a radio announcer reading an ad for the program sponsors. A source could be a single person, a group of people, or even an institution.

Source Designates the originator of a message

Message. A **message** is the stimulus that the source transmits to the receiver. A message may be verbal, nonverbal, or both. Tone of voice, gestures, and facial expressions are all examples of nonverbal messages. Usually, both verbal and nonverbal messages are conveyed human communication transactions.

Message The stimulus that the source transmits to the receiver

Channel. A **channel** is the means by which the message is conveyed from source to receiver. Channels may be air waves, light waves, or even laser beams.

Channel The means by which the message is conveyed from source to receiver

Any of the five senses of human perception may serve as channels in the communication process. The number of channels being used by an individual can affect the accuracy of a given message. For example, in which case could a job applicant present more information about himself or herself—on a telephone or in a face-to-face interview? In the latter instance, the applicant would be using more sensory channels to convey his or her message, and the interviewer would be doing the same in receiving that message. Using more than one channel in conveying a message increases the **redundancy** (repetition) and, to a point, the accuracy of that message. Excessive redundancy, on the other hand, could be viewed by the receiver as insulting. When there is conflicting information presented over the verbal and nonverbal channels during a communication transaction, people may place a greater emphasis on the nonverbal cues. We will discuss this in greater detail in Chapter 8.

Receiver Decodes and interprets the message sent

Receiver. As the destination of a given message, the receiver decodes and interprets the message sent, whereas the source/sender encodes a message and transmits it. *Encoding* is defined as the process of taking an already conceived idea and getting it ready for transmission. *Decoding*, on the other hand, is the process of taking the stimuli that have been received and giving those stimuli meaning through individual interpretation and perception. In human communication transactions, the stimuli are signs and symbols. It is important to note that all individuals function as source and receiver. Because humans perform both the functions of encoding and decoding, they have been labeled "transceivers."

Noise Any stimulus that inhibits the receiver's accurate reception of a given message

Noise. Noise is any stimulus that inhibits the receiver's accurate reception of a given message. Noise is often classified as physical, psychological, or semantic. Examples of *physical noise* would be the thunder of a jet airplane overhead, car horns blowing, or the blaring of a stereo system next door. *Psychological noise* occurs when an individual is preoccupied and therefore misses or misinterprets the external message. As you are sitting and listening to a lecture in class, you may be thinking of what you are going to eat for dinner or about the quarrel you had this morning. If this activity prohibits the accurate reception of the professor's lecture, then psychological noise has occurred. *Semantic noise* occurs when individuals have different meanings for symbols and when those meanings are not mutually understood. For example, semantic noise occurs when you do not understand a particular word being used by another communicator or when the particular word or symbol used has many denotative or connotative meanings. When one of the authors moved to the midwest and ordered "soda," he received an ice cream soda—not the carbonated beverage he thought he had ordered! Semantic noise occurred here. It is important to note that some element(s) of noise are always present in human communication transactions.

Feedback. Like all communication messages, feedback may be verbal, non-verbal, or both. Feedback is often called positive or negative. Positive feedback consists of responses perceived as rewarding by the speaker, such as applause or verbal/nonverbal agreement. Negative feedback consists of responses perceived as punishing or not rewarding. In interpersonal or public communication situations, frowns or whistles are examples of negative feedback. Even a complete lack of response on the part of the receiver could be perceived as negative feedback because the source would have no cues by which to gauge the effects of the message produced. Thus, without feedback, a source would have no means of assessing how a message was being, decoded, and subsequent inaccuracies might never be corrected. Because negative feedback implies that changes should be made, it is especially useful in helping us to send messages more effectively.

Feedback Allows a source to have a means of assessing how a message is being decoded

Defining Communication

There have been numerous attempts to define communication. In fact, nearly every book on communication offers its own definition! No author seems satisfied with other authors' definitions, and the proliferation goes on and on. Why is this? You would think if we know what communication is, we should be able to agree on a definition. We reach this predicament because there is no *single* approach to the study of communication; there are many. Definitions differ on matters such as whether communication has occurred if a source did not intend to send a message, whether communication is a linear process (a source sending a message in a channel to a receiver who then reacts), or whether a transactional perspective is more accurate (emphasizing the relationships between people and how they constantly, mutually influence one another). Another factor in the lack of agreement on definitions is that the study of communication is not a precise science.

Measurement in communication research, as well as in other social sciences, is inexact. In sciences such as chemistry, there is very little error in measurement. In the measurement of weight, accuracy can be achieved to 1/10,000 of a gram (about 1/4,500,000 of a pound). We cannot achieve the same accuracy in the measurement of persuasion. For instance, we are not able to determine the precise impact a certain television commercial will have on buying behavior.

Because people have free choice and active minds, some theorists believe that predicting human behavior is qualitatively different from predictions about other phenomena. These theorists believe that we will never be able to make predictions about communication behavior that are as accurate as predictions about the physical world, no matter how sophisticated our theories become or how accurate our measuring instruments are. These theoretical differences will be discussed in more detail in Chapter 2.

What this discussion means in terms of defining communication is that people disagree on definitions of communication because they disagree on the nature of communication. This seems to be an unavoidable condition when a science is less precise. If something is clearly understood, it is possible to formulate a universally acceptable definition. For instance, a triangle is an enclosed, three-sided figure with three internal angles whose sum equals 180 degrees. Students of human behavior would assert that there is little hope of achieving an understanding of communication that equals the clarity of our understanding of the triangle. Communication has more properties than the triangle. Thus, an understanding of communication must be vastly more complex. The prospects for a universally accepted definition of communication are not good, at least not in the immediate future. The many definitions raise a number of issues about the nature of communication. One important question is, "What makes human communication so powerful and distinctive?" If theorists can determine the answer, they can agree on what topics communication scholars should study. Table 1.1 presents five different definitions of communication.

Each definition emphasizes a slightly different aspect of communication. The first definition emphasizes the response made by someone who receives a stimulus. Berelson and Steiner focus our attention on the transmission of symbols; Dance's and Cronkhite's definitions combine the receiver's response with symbols chosen by a sender. Miller includes the ideas of symbolism and receiver's response, but he also emphasizes the intentional nature of communication.

The fact that we have no universally accepted definition of communication is not a debilitating problem. In fact, such a state of affairs is to be expected, given our current level of understanding. What is important is that we continue studying communication, learning as much as we can about this very significant set of human behaviors. The more we learn, the more precisely we

Table 1.1   **SOME DEFINITIONS OF COMMUNICATION**

- "Communication is the discriminatory response of an organism to a stimulus." (Stevens, 1950)

- "the transmission of information, ideas, emotions, skills, etc., by the use of symbols— words, pictures, figures, graphs, etc." (Berelson & Steiner, 1964)

- "the eliciting of a response through verbal symbols." (Dance, 1967)

- "Communication has as its central interest those behavioral situations in which a source transmits a message to a receiver(s) *with conscious intent to affect the latter's behaviors.*" (Miller, 1966)

- "Human communication has occurred when a human being responds to a symbol." (Cronkhite, 1976)

will be able to define communication. At any time in our study we can stop and redefine. The definition would simply represent our present thinking. As we learn more, we surely would change our definition. As you read this text, you might try defining communication at the end of each chapter. The chances are you will feel a need to redefine communication as you progress. The more you learn, the more you will see the inadequacies in your earlier definitions.

Your authors have chosen to define communication as follows:

> *Communication occurs when humans manipulate symbols to stimulate meaning in other humans.*

Our definition differs from those above in that it emphasizes both sender and receiver. It also calls attention to the symbolic and intentional nature of communication. The next section presents some of the characteristics your authors believe communication exhibits: it is a social, symbolic process that occurs in a context. Some characteristics of communication are more controversial than others. After we present our position on the nature of communication, we will discuss three issues of controversy among scholars.

Characteristics of Communication

1. Communication Is a Symbolic Process. Human symbolic activity is the very essence of communication and therefore should be the focus of the communication discipline. Cronkhite (1976) clarified this idea by differentiating three types of signs. A **sign** can be thought of as something that stands for another thing. A **symptom** is one type of sign. For instance, sneezing is a symptom of having an allergy. A **symbol** is a second type of sign. It is created to stand for something else. A symbol is arbitrary in that the creator is not limited in what can be used to represent something else. The idea is for the symbol to stimulate awareness of a particular thing when the symbol is used. Thus, for example, if you were an inventor who invented something, you would want to give it a unique name (i.e., a symbol) so that when the name is used, your invention would come to mind. A third type of sign is a **ritual**. This is a combination of being naturally produced, as in the case of a symptom, and being arbitrary or created, as would be a symbol. Many nonverbal behaviors are examples. For instance, grimacing in pain when we bump our elbow is a symptom. However, grimacing a certain way (e.g., with an accompanying laugh) because we are being observed and want to be seen as "tough" or impervious to pain is a ritual. Thus, a ritual involves *stylizing* a symptom so that it also becomes somewhat symbolic. It shows something natural, such as a sign of pain, but does it in a way that says something about the individual who exhibits the symptom.

We agree with Cronkhite that symbolic activity represents what is and is not communication. Many academic disciplines study human symbols. However,

Sign   Something that stands for another thing

Symptom   One type of sign

Symbol   A second type of sign created to stand for something else

Ritual   A third type of sign that is a combination of being naturally produced and being arbitrary or created

the communication discipline is unique in that it gives primary attention to the human activity of using symbols.

2. **Communication Involves Socially Shared Meaning.** Our definition asserts that communication occurs when people use symbols to stimulate meaning in other people. This emphasizes that communication is a social process and involves more than simply perception of another person. Perception of another person at times might not involve communication, for instance, perceiving a person taking a nap in the library. If symbolic activity is not responsible for the perception, then communication did not occur. In the case of a nap, there may be no symbols or rituals involved. All the behavior may be symptoms. Perception is an important product of the communication process. But perception is produced by processes besides communication. These are studied by cognitive psychologists as individual processes. Communication is not an individual process, but a social one that involves symbolic activity of at least two people.

Because we are from the same culture, we share meaning for symbols. That does not suggest that the meanings that you and a friend have for a given concept, such as "freedom of speech," are identical. What is suggested is that your meanings overlap so that you can discuss the concept with some common understanding. As a result of discussion, individuals might influence one another on what it means to have freedom of speech. Meanings are represented by symbols, and symbols can be used to change meanings in people. This emphasizes the idea that communication is a social process involving socially shared meaning.

3. **Communication Occurs in a Context.** A fundamental characteristic of communication is that it is highly contextual. To understand communication usually means taking into account the **context** in which it occurs. A communication context may be thought of as a particular type of communication situation. There is general agreement on the types of contexts. Most contemporary communication theory books present chapters on the various types.

Context   A particular type of communication situation

> **Interpersonal**—communication between two people
> **Small Group**—communication between about three to fifteen people
> **Organizational**—communication within and between organizations
> **Public**—a speaker addressing an audience
> **Mass Communication**—print or electronically mediated communication
> **Intercultural**—communication between people representing different cultures
> **Family**—communication in the family setting
> **Health**—communication between and among health-care providers and receivers
> **Political**—communication that involves persons governing our society

Communication tends to be influenced greatly by the context. For example, a negative assessment of a person's intelligence might be viewed as humorous in a family context but mean spirited in a small-group work setting, even though the very same words are used in both situations. Contexts vary on basic attributes, and that affects response to messages. For instance, because there is less immediate feedback in mass communication as compared to organizational communication, it could take longer for negative evaluations of a TV news anchor to lead to replacement than it would to replace a negatively evaluated work supervisor.

POINTS OF CONTROVERSY ABOUT COMMUNICATION

To understand the nature of communication and the characteristics that make it so complex and powerful, it is important for you to understand some key areas of disagreement among communication scholars. The following section will discuss three interesting questions currently disputed by communication theorists: Is communication intentional? Is communication **planned**? Is communication **transactional**?

Intentional Knowingly influencing the receiver of the message

Communication and Intent

Has communication occurred if the source, the message sender, had no intention to influence the receiver of the message? Let us say Jan overhears Joe telling someone to take a particular course because Professor Smith is interesting. Jan then registers for that course. Should we say communication occurred between Jan and Joe? Certainly, meaning was stimulated in Jan's mind by the verbal behavior of Joe. Does communication always occur whenever meaning is stimulated? If Jan told Professor Smith that Joe mentioned how interesting the class was, and Smith then approached Joe and said, "Thanks for talking so favorably with Jan about my course," Joe would probably be very puzzled and would think, "I don't remember talking with Jan about the course." Suppose you read an article that discusses pupil dilation as an indication of favorable feelings (and you do not know there is controversy among researchers as to the meaning of pupil dilation). You then approach a potential romantic partner. As you are talking, you notice the person's pupils are dilating. Should you assume the other person sent you a message communicating attraction? Once again, meaning was stimulated, but was it stimulated intentionally? Clearly not in this case, because pupil dilation is an involuntary response. If intentionality is not required to designate behavior as communicative, then mere existence is all that is needed. Thus, if you were to observe a patient lying in a hospital bed in a deep coma, we would have to say you were "communicating" with the person.

Some people argue that if a message is sent, then communication occurs, regardless of the intended recipient. The central issue is whether there actually is a message. When the other person is unaware he or she is influencing you and you ask the person to repeat the "message," you would get only a confused look. If you read a message into another person's unintentional behavior, you act as both the message creator and message consumer.

This issue illustrates a trend by some people to claim "everything is communication." Certainly communication is pervasive, but is it everywhere—all the time? That view dilutes the significance of communication. There is an old saying that if something is everything, it is nothing. Such exuberance in staking out territory is not necessary. If we consider communication to occur when humans manipulate symbols to stimulate meaning in other humans, the territory is vast enough to justify a field of study. This view of communication is neither too narrow nor too restrictive. It allows for the complexity of human interaction but avoids the task of accounting for unintentional behavior. Humans unknowingly stimulating meaning in other humans is interesting, yet it is not the same as humans knowingly doing so. An important point is that we are not claiming it is always possible to determine intentionality. At times, we cannot tell whether Sue sent a message to Anne or whether Anne both created and consumed a message about Sue. The issue is whether Sue sent a message. If Sue did so intentionally, communication occurred—regardless of Anne's reaction to the message.

Another reason for limiting communication to intentional behavior is to distinguish it from perception. **Perception** is a process through which individuals interpret sensory information. You might perceive that the walls of your classroom are painted "institutional green" or "institutional beige," but it would seem strange to say that you are communicating with the walls. Again, you might say that the painters communicated with you through the choice of color, but if you asked them to repeat their message, they would be puzzled if no message was intended. Instead, you observed and drew inferences from sensory data. Although perception is an essential part of the communication process because it enables us to receive and interpret messages sent by others, not all perception involves communication. Human communication requires at least two people who intend to send and to receive messages; communication is a social rather than an individual process.

Figure 1.1 illustrates our position. If the sender intends to communicate *and* the receiver recognizes the intention, *communication has occurred.* This situation is an example of what Brant Burleson (1992) terms a paradigm case, a case in which virtually everyone would agree that communication occurs. Burleson believes that face-to-face conversation is a paradigm case of communication behavior. Other situations are not so clear. What if you are walking

Perception   A process through which individuals interpret sensory information

	Sender intends to send a message	Sender does not intend to send a message
Receiver recognizes sender's intent	1. Communication occurs	2. Communication attributed
Receiver does not recognize sender's intent	3. Communication attempted	4. Perception, but not communication, occurs

Adapted from Burgoon & Ruffner (1978).

Figure 1.1

Communication and intention

down the street, notice a friend, and assume the friend is deliberately avoiding you? Suppose the friend did not see you. This event is attributed communication. Your friend did not intend to communicate with you, but you believed he or she intended to send a message about avoiding you. When a sender attempts to send a message, but the message is not received, this is an attempted communication. An example would be shouting to a friend who could not hear you because of traffic noise. No communication occurs in the fourth situation. If questioned, neither person would state that a message was sent or received. This situation might apply to behavior such as swatting at a fly that has settled on your book in class. Both you and another person in the room (the perceiver) are aware that you swatted at the fly, but neither inferred that a message was sent. This situation is an example of perception but not communication.

The axiom, "You cannot not communicate," was presented in the book, *Pragmatics of Human Communication* (Watzlawick, Beavin, & Jackson, 1967). For years after the publication of the book, this idea was embraced by many scholars in the communication field. Although the notion that everything is communication had a certain appeal, after a while other scholars began questioning whether everything about a person actually does represent a communicative message. This led to the issue of what exactly is a message, and what are the necessary conditions to declare that a message exists? The view emerged over time that symbolic activity was a necessary condition for communication to have occurred.

The controversy over what is and what is not communication was exemplified by the exchange between Motley (1990a, 1990b) and Andersen (1991). Motley postulated that for communication to have occurred, the behavior must have four features. It must be interactive, involve encoding, involve the exchange of symbols, and range in quality from high to low. Thus, when a person sneezes, it is not communication because it really does not have any of the four features (i.e., it does not meet any of the four necessary conditions for communication). This is because a sneeze is not a symbol but instead is a symptom of something such as an allergic reaction to tree pollen.

Andersen disagreed with Motley's position and asserted that types of symptomatic behavior constitute communication because attributes of a person such as body shape, body odor, and race are considered to have message value, they say something, they inform. Also, Andersen considers "informative communication" to have occurred if meaning is derived from observing things such as a person's height, gender, relaxation, or energy levels. In these instances, no intention to communicate may exist, yet receivers may believe there was intent and develop meaning accordingly. Andersen was particularly concerned that many symptomatic nonverbal behaviors occur along with symbols and are a part of the total meaning derived from a situation. He believed that excluding such symptoms would distort understanding of what happened in a situation. For instance, to ignore a person's coughing while explaining something would distort the fact that the person was trying to be helpful, even though he or she was sick.

Motley (1991) defended his position by emphasizing that communicative behavior always is encoded and symbolic. Andersen's idea that the minimum necessary condition for communication is the perception of some form of human behavior is defective because the process of perceiving a person's sneeze, for example, is not different from perceiving an animal's sneeze. This nondifferentiation of human and nonhuman behavior devalues the message source as an active part of the communication process. Allowing symptoms to stand as communication does not establish what is and what is not human communication. Certainly meaning might be stimulated by a sneeze, but that does not make it communication.

Motley's postulates and ideas are consistent with our definition—*communication occurs when humans manipulate symbols to stimulate meaning in other humans.* This conceptualization provides active roles for the message source and the message receiver, covers both verbal and nonverbal symbolic behavior, considers the receiver's perceptions, and focuses on highly conscious symbolic behavior while also allowing for and recognizing behavior encoded at a very low level of awareness.

Communication as Planned Behavior

Communication plans offer answers to the issues raised in the previous section about intentionality, what constitutes a message, and when symbols are actually manipulated. Viewing communication as planned behavior, in essence, makes it clear that intentions are a necessary element of the communication process. The notion of communication plans defines when human behavior represents communication and when it does not.

Communication plan A set of behaviors that the person believes will accomplish a purpose

A **communication plan** is a set of behaviors that the person believes will accomplish a purpose. You might have a general plan to graduate from college, to get a good job, to raise a family, and to retire comfortably. Some plans are more specific: take the car to the garage the first thing tomorrow. The plans we form are controlled by our beliefs, attitudes, and values; plans are hierarchically arranged (Cronkhite, 1976). "If I don't graduate from college, I will work in my father's store."

There are two types of communication plans: verbal plans and nonverbal plans (Infante, 1980). A verbal plan is what you plan to say in a specific or general communication situation. A plan for a specific situation might be: "When Joan congratulates me on my award, I will tell her she helped me greatly." A plan for a general situation could be: "Whenever people congratulate me, I will act humble and thank them for whatever assistance they provided." This assumes human communication behavior is *volitional.* People say what they plan to say. Some verbal plans are formed well in advance of the utterance, whereas others are created and spoken immediately. For example, you may decide what to say when asked about your future profession years before you actually respond to an inquiry. However, you may form a plan to express your feelings about a particular presidential candidate only seconds before you speak. A verbal plan may resemble a topical outline where only the main ideas are specified. For instance, "Generally, I think education should be funded at the state level." Or a verbal plan may contain specific details and precise wording. For example, "The next time John loses his temper I will say, 'You're acting like a jerk again; I'm leaving.'"

Verbal plans vary in terms of how frequently they are used. Some are used only once or a few times. Others are used in recurring situations. For a large portion of our communication behavior, we recycle the same verbal plans. They work well, so we continue to use them. You can probably identify a large number of verbal plans you use habitually. When someone asks you what you think about college, do you have a standard reply? Once we determine a verbal plan, execute it, and decide it accomplishes the desired purpose, we reuse it in future situations with slight modification when necessary. We revise verbal plans from time to time. What we say in a given situation usually represents a verbal plan that has evolved over a period of time. For instance, you may have a verbal plan for telling another person you do not want to date him or her again. After using it, you decide, "Well, I could have said that better." So you revise your original plan, and the next time you are in a similar situation, you decline future engagements more tactfully.

Nonverbal plans sometimes precede or follow the execution of verbal plans, but usually they are formed along with our verbal plans. An example of a non-verbal plan preceding verbal behavior might be, "I'll get that person to come over and meet me by looking interested." Many nonverbal plans are formed along with verbal plans: "When I talk with my boss today, I'll display calm and confidence." As with verbal plans, nonverbal plans can be general or specific, formed well in advance or formed at the moment, used once or habitually, revised or unrevised.

In order to understand and predict communication behavior, it is necessary to understand and predict a person's communication plans. Research indicates that people learn to associate and/or anticipate consequences regarding their plans. How those consequences are perceived by the person permits a prediction of what the person will say. *Human communication represents the execution of the individual's most recently adopted communication plan* (Infante, 1980).

The idea of communication plans provides a way to address the issue of whether communication has occurred if one person is unaware that his or her behavior is stimulating a response in another person. Under the communication plans framework, we would say communication has occurred if we can trace the individual's behavior to a plan. If not, communication did not occur, even though meaning may have been stimulated in another person's mind. For instance, a student might purchase a sweatshirt with the school's logo to communicate her support for the school's athletic teams. Let us suppose that another student sees her (she is unaware of him) wearing the sweatshirt at a basketball game and says to himself, "She's a loyal fan!" According to the communication plan perspective, that would be an example of communication. When it is not possible to attribute behavior to a communication plan, we would say no communication has occurred. Meaning might have been perceived, but there was no communication. Of course, it is not always easy to determine whether a communication plan stimulated behavior. Plans, like other forms of knowledge, are usually discoverable. The only limitations are the ingenuity and resourcefulness of the researcher.

Messages molded and energized by communication plans are symbolic behaviors. This emphasizes the intentional versus the accidental nature of human communication. Messages are expressed with verbal and nonverbal symbols. Plans, of course, are also composed of symbols. However, the symbols in a plan are not necessarily the same ones that will appear in a message. Human judgment and volition transform plans into action. Plans can be modified and adapted to the given situation. For instance, suppose you have a plan for refusing to drink beer when it is offered to you. What you say might vary according to the situation. You could say it is "sinful" when talking with religious people or "unhealthy" when talking with physical fitness enthusiasts. The transformation process allows for revisions of a communication plan. This complex human ability presents a formidable obstacle for attempts to simulate human communication through the use of computers.

According to a communication plans framework, communication does not always entail a great deal of thinking by the people involved. If we do not have a plan for a situation, then substantial thinking is involved. However, much of our communication behavior is *habitual* in the sense that we prefer to place ourselves in familiar situations where we have communication plans that are very dependable—they always seem to work for us. Life would be difficult if we had to examine each situation thoroughly to determine what to say. Instead, we form plans that are as robust as possible and cover as many circumstances as feasible. It is easier to talk if we have reliable plans.

This notion is similar to Ellen Langer's (1989) concept of "mindlessness." The idea is that people prefer to avoid cognitive activity because a restful state is more desirable than expending effort. Thus, people prefer familiar situations because they have already developed plans that have worked in the past. Having a dependable plan means the person may go on "automatic pilot" and not have to think much about the situation. According to this analysis, much human behavior is neither unique nor novel; it is repetitive and therefore predictable. If Langer is correct, theories of human behavior and awareness that depict people as always alert, forever thinking, and cognitively active rather than passive are suspect. Indeed, many theories may be subject to this criticism. Moreover, this conception challenges one of the most accepted ideas in the communication field—Berlo's (1977) notion of communication as **process**. Berlo's idea is that communication is a continual stream of unique behavior that is unrepeatable. The concepts of plans and mindlessness suggest that such a dynamic depiction of communication may be misleading. According to Berlo's model, predicting communication seems nearly impossible. However, in view of the framework in this section, much communication may be highly predictable because it is based on plans that people use and reuse, even if each situation itself is unique.

Transactional Nature of Communication

The fact that communication is planned helps us recognize that communication is a transactional process. By that we mean communication involves people sending each other messages that reflect the motivations of the participants. People expect others to react to their messages; in turn they expect to respond to the messages of others. When we communicate, we attempt to affect our environment. We understand that others also communicate to exert such influence. We anticipate a "give and take" in communication—an interaction of human motivations. A simple linear process (a one-thing-leads-to-another description) does not adequately explain the communication situation. For instance, if we learn that Joel asked Rob for fifty cents for the candy machine, we don't have very much information. If Joel says, "I asked for two quarters and got only a frown," the statement is more revealing because it describes a reaction to the request. In this case, Joel frowned because he just learned that his sister is dating Rob. Because Rob has a reputation for "breaking hearts," Joel is afraid his sister will be hurt. We could present more details, but the point should be clear. Communication is a process of mutual influence in which participants' motivations interact. Often, a linear description does not even identify the most important meaning in a communication situation. Not getting the money certainly was not the most significant meaning in this interaction. To identify a single message source, a single message receiver, and a single effect of a message may be accurate for a very limited period of time—at best. The

Transactional process Communication involves people sending each other messages that reflect the motivations of the participants

thinking of the people involved in a communication situation, their characteristic traits, the factors in the physical and social environments, and how all
these things interact are necessary for a more complete understanding of communication in the particular situation.

The transactional nature of communication means each communication
situation is unique, to a degree. A communication situation occurs with particular people, in particular physical and social circumstances, and during a
particular period of time. Because what a person wants changes from one point
in time to the next and, because the physical and especially the social environments are rarely if ever the same, we recognize that each of our communication experiences is at least somewhat unique. We are able to distinguish among
communication situations, even though the people and places may be the same.

Communication involves both *content* and *relationship* dimensions
(Watzlawick, Beavin, & Jackson, 1967). When we communicate, we present
information and points of view, and we also tell the other person about our
perceptions about the relationship. Sometimes we verbally describe the relationship dimension; often, however, we use our tone of voice, gestures, posture, or the physical situation to carry the relationship message. For instance,
the relationship message in "please sweep the floor" is different, depending on
whom you are addressing. If you were a supervisor talking to a subordinate,
the relationship would be different than if a wife asked her husband to sweep
the floor. With the subordinate, the unspoken relationship part of the message
would be "do this because I am your boss." With the husband the message
would be "do this because we are equals and it's your turn." Sometimes there is
conflict between people not because of the content of a message but because
of disagreement on the relationship dimension. For example, your subordinate may agree the floor needs sweeping but may not want to do it because he
or she may believe you are going beyond your authority by issuing orders about
floor sweeping.

The Functions of Communication

Even though communication scholars disagree on the points of definition discussed earlier, most would agree on uses or functions of communication. The
Roman orator Cicero believed the basic purposes of a speech were *to entertain,
to inform,* and *to persuade.* In recent times, the purpose *to stimulate* has been
added. The distinction made between persuading and stimulating is that persuading involves changing a listener from accepting to rejecting the speaker's
proposal (or the reverse), whereas stimulating means moving a person who
already approves, for example, to become even more intensely supportive.
These purposes have been applied mainly to public speaking. Some contemporary theorists have explored other perspectives on the functions that communication fulfills for humans.

Clark and Delia (1979) developed the idea that three basic objectives are present to varying degrees in all communication situations. Instrumental objectives refer to the speaker's intention to entertain, inform, stimulate, and/or persuade people on the topic of the message. Interpersonal objectives pertain to the relationship that the speaker desires with the message receiver. For instance, a closer personal relationship might be wanted. Identity objectives refer to the image the communicator wants others to have of him or her. For example, a person might want to be seen as very eager and ambitious. These three objectives vary according to the situation in terms of how much they matter. Thus, they are not necessarily always or even often equally important.

Dance and Larson (1976) suggested that human communication has three functions that are realized without conscious effort. The functions are inherent, operating automatically for the individual. The **linking function** establishes relationships between the individual and the environment. Thus, individuals might be very friendly to encourage others to include them in activities. The **mentation function** stimulates the development of higher mental processes. Mental growth is enhanced by communication. For example, using symbols encourages the development of displacement, the ability to move mentally from the present moment and circumstances to the future, to the past, or to solve problems in the immediate situation by going to a high level of abstraction. Displacement is a higher mental process that stimulates the child to move from egocentric (seeing self at the center of everything) to non-egocentric speech. Selecting symbols appropriate for a given receiver causes the source to consider the perspective of the other, an activity that is decidedly nonegocentric. The **regulatory function** develops as the individual is influenced by persons and other things in the environment. During this period of dependency, the child learns what behaviors are acceptable. After internalizing these rules, the child/adult will use the same methods to influence the behavior of other people. Humans need to influence their environment, and communication fulfills this need well. When we feel we are not able to influence events satisfactorily, a sense of helplessness can develop that can have very serious consequences in terms of mental health.

Instrumental objectives
Refer to the speaker's intention to entertain, inform, stimulate, and/or persuade people on the topic of the message

Interpersonal objectives
Pertain to the relationship that the speaker desires with the message receiver

Identity objectives
Refer to the image the communicator wants others to have of him or her

THE IMPORTANCE OF COMMUNICATION

Creating Cooperation

Because communication performs the functions discussed earlier, it plays a vital role in each of our lives. Humans are very interdependent. The arrangement of society is such that each of us depends on others to provide what we need. Communication is very important in enabling people to coordinate their efforts and to produce a variety of goods and services, which would be impossible if people were to work independently. Beyond this macroscopic view, there are many examples in our individual lives when we use communication to enlist the cooperation of others. We ask people for directions when we are lost. We want our friends to support us when we take a stand on a controversial issue. We suggest a division of work to our colleagues when assigned a time-consuming task. It is probably accurate to say that we do not live a day without asking for the cooperation of others and also cooperating with requests made by others.

Of course, some people get more cooperation than others. Communication skill is an obvious factor to explain this discrepancy. If people do not cooperate with us as much as we would like, it may be our communication behavior that is at fault. We have a need for control in our interpersonal relations (Schutz, 1958). If this need is not satisfied, we tend to feel powerless and view ourselves as relatively helpless—dependent on the whims of others. It is possible to desire too much control. When this happens, others view us as burdensome and prefer not to cooperate. We can ask too much of people. To be well adjusted interpersonally, we must learn what it is reasonable to ask of others and what we should reasonably give.

Erich Fromm's (1947) theory of character provides insights into certain kinds of cooperative communication behavior. There are four nonproductive character orientations. Each views cooperation differently and will communicate in distinctive patterns to enlist cooperation. The *receptive orientation* describes individuals who believe that good things are only received from others. Because this type of person depends on others to receive what is worthwhile and does not feel he or she has anything of value to give, relationships are one-sided. This person behaves pleasantly and acts favorably to maximize the chance that others will cooperate, but he or she is unable to reciprocate. If you were dealing with such a person, you would feel you were giving but not receiving. In a romantic relationship, you would feel you were not loved in return for the love you were giving. Whereas the receptive orientation looks for gifts, the *exploiting orientation* thinks it is necessary to take things from others by force or cunning. Individuals with this orientation generally employ subtle or even overt threats when asking for cooperation. Deception is also a common tactic. The person may misrepresent a situation to get something from you. The source of what is good changes with the *hoarding orientation*. This type of person believes he or she possesses what is good and wants to save, hoard, and protect it. Such individuals value orderliness and security above all. They will cooperate if they believe cooperation will help fortify their position and will not involve intrusion. They will ask for cooperation and give it on matters that involve restoring order or putting things back in their proper place. The *marketing orientation* also centers around the belief that the individual possesses what is good. Unlike the hoarding orientation, this person views himself or herself as a commodity with exchange value. An engaging personality and attractive physical appearance are prized because such characteristics make an effective package for the "product." This individual's communication behavior reflects a desire to barter or to get ahead by "delivering the goods." When you ask such an individual to cooperate with you, you may get the feeling that you are going into debt and that the person will later expect something of you. As we said earlier, these four character types are seen as unproductive. More desirable and satisfying cooperative communication behavior would indicate sincere respect and concern for the other person, a desire to realize one's potential, and a sense of how one's behavior will enhance his or her environment. Productive character orientation will be discussed in more detail in the section on entertainment.

Acquiring Information

The second key role of communication is to help us acquire information. Information or knowledge is probably our greatest possession. Humans have always accumulated information; knowledge is power. At the international level, nations that have the most information also have the most economic power and prestige. Information is no less important at the microscopic level. For various reasons, we need a vast amount of information in our lives. We want facts about candidates to reach a decision when we go to the polls. Information about the weather affects our plans for the day. The principles of gardening are necessary to produce vegetables in our backyard. If we want to be bankers, we need a knowledge of finance. Other information satisfies our sense of curiosity with no apparent utility value. We read about the Bushmen of the Kalahari Desert because we are interested in extraordinary examples of survival. We listen to a lecture about black holes in space because we find the idea fascinating. We read a biography about a composer simply because we like his or her music. The cliché states that people thirst for knowledge: that the thirst is unquenchable seems to be a permanent condition of being human.

Communication plays a very important role in acquiring information. Other than in cases of direct experience with our physical environment, information without communication is rare. Here is an example of purely physical information, which you technically could acquire without communicating with other people. Let us say that you have just moved to another region of the United States and you wish to know where to catch a lot of fish. To do this independently, you would have to roam the countryside and search for lakes and streams. You would have to stay off highways because they contain signs, refrain from asking anyone about fishing waters, and reject consulting a map because all of these involve communication. Suppose you succeed in locating twelve lakes in a 15-mile radius from your new home without the benefit of communication. Would you have accomplished your goal of catching a lot of fish? Because not all bodies of water contain ample fish populations, your quest has only narrowed slightly.

Suppose you realize this and decide to communicate just once to find out which of the lakes contains the most fish. You ask a local expert; he names the best lake. Can you now proceed to accomplish your goal without further communication? Perhaps, but if the lake is large, you could spend the entire year there and not catch many fish. Even if you found the productive parts of the lake, there still is the matter of how to catch the fish. What bait, lures, and techniques work on this lake? You might catch a lot of fish without any human assistance. However, unless you are unusually lucky, it would take a very long time. Communication would not make the task easy, but it would make it simpler. Just find an experienced local fisherman and talk! Communication is vital in acquiring whatever information you need.

In this process of acquiring information, we have learned it is necessary to have a system of beliefs about the sources of information. According to Rokeach (1960), we have a set of beliefs about which sources are credible (believable) and which are not. Because we need information, we must know whether information is dependable. We have positive beliefs about highly credible sources and negative beliefs or disbeliefs about sources with low credibility. Consider the following piece of information: "Evidence indicates that OPEC has been instrumental in manipulating the supply of oil to ruin the economies of free nations." Whether you believe that information will depend heavily on the source. If it is announced on the CBS evening news, and if CBS is a credible source for you, you probably would see this as a very plausible possibility. However, if the source is a group you distrust, you probably would dismiss the idea as highly implausible and as further proof of the "conspiracy mentality" of extremists.

Forming Self-Concept

The third area in which communication is useful is in forming our self-concepts. A commonly accepted principle of communication is that how we perceive ourselves greatly influences our communication behavior. If you believe you are worthwhile and a success, you say this in many ways and on many occasions. Your verbal messages reflect optimism and an unpretentious confidence in yourself. Nonverbally, your posture, gestures, tone of voice, and facial expression say you have positive beliefs about yourself.

People sometimes exude too much confidence. This communication behavior is also revealing. This type of individual may be uncertain about his or her self-worth and is attempting to convince others that he or she is productive and valuable. Such attempts at social influence may be termed *ego-defensive* communication behaviors. The person finds his or her unfavorable self-concept psychologically uncomfortable and seeks to remedy the condition by obtaining esteem from others. "My fears about myself must be wrong; how could I be a failure if people treat me like I am a success?" Of course, such self-deception is seldom sufficient to convince the individual of his or her worth, so the exaggerated communication behavior continues. This is not the only pattern of behavior that communicates an unfavorable self-concept. Other people say quite clearly in their verbal messages that they are pessimistic about their future or that they are helpless in their environments. Perhaps as a way of asking for help, people sometimes use facial expressions to say they are depressed, a message that is also communicated by their tone of voice and by posture and gestures.

Does communication influence who we think we are? That is, how does communication operate in the formation of our self-concepts? One theory claims our self-concept is a reflection of how we see ourselves in the responses of other people to us (Cooley, 1902). We communicate; others observe our communication behavior and react to it; we observe these reactions, and they become the basis for deciding who we are. Hence, the combination of our communication behavior and the communication behavior of others toward us controls our self-concepts. All of this is a very hopeful perspective about the idea of self-concept. It means we are partially responsible for the way we view ourselves because we stimulate the responses of others that result in our particular self-concept. There is hope because we can continue to communicate with people and obtain responses from them. People are discriminating. They respond differently according to the stimulus.

This is another way of saying you can change people's responses to you. You are partially responsible for and in control of your interpersonal world. This perspective says it is not valid for you to claim, "People do not show an interest in me or in what I am doing, so I must not be an interesting person." Instead, this orientation to self-concept would want you to conclude, "People do not show an interest in me because I do not encourage them to; I do not show an interest in them." The explanation for this would lie in your communication behavior. You probably do not ask many questions about others' interests when you talk. You give little if any positive verbal and nonverbal reinforcement to others when they show an interest in you. What could you do, according to this perspective? You could develop sincere interest in others—ask questions and show positive reactions to their responses to your questions. When people reciprocate by inquiring about your interests, you could show them that you are happy they asked. This should become an established pattern in your interpersonal relations, not something you try only once.

The point we are trying to make is that communication has been important in the formation of your self-concept, and communication can be used to change your self-concept. We can change our communication behavior, and that will cause people to react differently to us, The new responses toward us will cause us to perceive ourselves differently. There is considerable reason for adopting this "communication orientation" to self-concept. We are happier in life if we have a favorable self-concept. We are not happy if we believe others have not treated us fairly or have not given us what we deserve. We are happier when we believe in the communication process—that communicating to the best of our ability will produce results. They may not always be exactly what we wanted, but they will be satisfying nevertheless because of our active involvement in the process.

Communication as Entertainment

The previous discussion of the importance of communication gives the impression that humans are serious, goal-oriented, information seekers proceeding through life in search of sober contentment. As we know, humans and other advanced animal species have a strong inclination toward entertainment. Once basic survival needs like safety and nourishment have been satisfied, it seems quite natural to occupy our time with less-serious matters. Sometimes this sequence of survival-then-entertainment is not followed exactly. Some college students, for example, have even been known to place entertainment before survival in college. Some of our students have said if it were not for entertainment, they could not survive in college. The point is that entertainment is necessary.

Recall the discussion of Fromm's unproductive and productive character orientations. Fromm (1947) said the productive character orientation involves a pattern of alternating between work and rest. We are more productive if we learn how to relax away from our work. Our diversions may be related to our work. For instance, if you are a comedian, you might enjoy going to comedy clubs when you are not working. The important issue is to find an enjoyable balance between work and play. Fromm emphasizes the idea of balance; if either work or play becomes disproportionate, the individual will not be as happy as when the two are in balance.

Communication is vital for the entertainment side of the productive character orientation. True, some of our diversions seem to involve no communication. We might paint in a private place and never discuss our paintings with anyone. However, most entertainment involves communication. Movies, plays, books, and magazines are some obvious examples. It has been said that entertainment is the main purpose of the mass media. While that claim may be debated, there seems little doubt that mass media provide us with much of our entertainment.

We sometimes find entertainment in the way a person communicates. We often watch a particular television talk show not so much for the guests, but because we like listening to and watching the host. Talk show host Jay Leno's nonverbal behavior—the way he moves his eyes after a line and uses his voice to give additional meaning to words—adds to the entertainment value of the actual words. We like the way he says things and do not tire of his verbal and nonverbal mannerisms. The jokes told by comedians may not be as important as how they are told. Often leaders seem to be selected because of the way they express their ideas, even though the ideas may be rather commonplace.

Social conversations represent one of the most common forms of entertainment through communication. For many of us, this is our chief form of relaxation. We enjoy talking with people. Such conversations may have no serious purpose. We may not want to accomplish anything other than to enjoy ourselves. The topics may be trivial and the talk may be shallow because the purpose is pleasant diversion. Rational dialogue is also entertaining. Some of us find arguing a source of entertainment. We perceive an argument over a controversial issue as an exciting intellectual challenge—a verbal game of chess. The issue argued may not even be important to us; what matters is the activity.

Returning to Fromm's conception of the productive character orientation for a moment, we should emphasize further the importance of balancing work and rest. If all of our communication behavior is task oriented, we are conveying a less-than-desirable impression of ourselves. Most people feel uncomfortable with someone who is totally production oriented. People also find it difficult to rely on someone who takes the opposite extreme, a preoccupation with entertainment. We may instinctively realize the validity of Fromm's notion; the healthy, productive person is one who alternates between work and rest. Our more favorable impressions are probably formed of people who have such an orientation.

In the Evolution of Ideas

Cronkhite (1976) discussed the important role that communication plays in the evolution of ideas. We explored this briefly at the beginning of the chapter with the concept of the "marketplace of ideas in a democracy." We will elaborate a little more on this now. This process of how ideas evolve is seen as parallel to evolution as it operates in the physical world. That is, besides plants and animals, ideas also change in response to what is going on in the environment and reflects a "survival of the fittest" dynamic in operation. Three processes are involved: **variety**, **selection**, and **retention**. An example with animals would be that competition for food may result in certain animals with longer necks being better able to get adequate food. Those animals would be more likely to survive, mate, and pass on to their offspring the gene for longer necks. Each successive generation then would favor long necks for survival value, and after many, many, generations, the animal would come to be recognized by what we know today as a giraffe.

For this outcome to happen there must be a variety in the species. Some animals must have a somewhat longer neck to reach the vital food, otherwise the outcome would be extinction. The selection process would involve the longer necked animals feeding and surviving while the others eventually would die out. Retention pertains to how nature institutionalizes the change in the species. Genetics plays a key role here as a certain gene structure passes from generation to generation.

Cronkhite's (1976) insightful analysis proposed a similar process for ideas. When our environment creates a need for something, for example, a need for universal health-care coverage, it is necessary to have a *variety* of ideas that have the potential for solving the problem. To achieve such variety of ideas, freedom of speech is essential for making everyone aware of the possible ideas for a solution, even if some of the ideas are offensive or seem really bad. As with our animal example, without adequate variety, extinction is possible. Extinction in the case of our health-care system could mean the system collapsing into a very undesirable state of chaos.

Communication then plays a crucial role in the selection process. Here argumentation is essential. People would argue in favor of some ideas and against others. With rigorous debate, the bad ideas would be weeded out and after a while one idea would remain, reflecting "survival of the fittest" for ideas, not unlike what happens with plants and animals. Argumentation, one of the central parts of the communication discipline since antiquity, is the major part of the selection process for ideas.

The retention part of ideational evolution pertains to institutionalizing what is adopted. The idea for health-care coverage in this case could result in a law and a bureaucracy created to administer the law. Communication is vital also in this process and would involve what is called "organizational communication." A good deal of the communication would be informative in nature along with a public relations effort to convince us that the program is good and is working well. Chapter 11 will explain organizational communication in considerable detail.

THE INTERDISCIPLINARY APPROACH TO COMMUNICATION

The 1960s produced a number of changes in the communication field. One of the most far reaching was the emergence of the behavioral science method to study communication. This scientific approach has produced most of the theories presented in this book. However, the production of communication theories by communication researchers was slow in developing because of the emergence of another trend in the 1960s when communication scholars declared that the study of communication was *interdisciplinary*.

Some of the leading scholars proclaimed that communication was central to the subject matter of many other disciplines. Because so many disciplines (e.g., sociology, psychology, anthropology, business administration, political science) were interested in communication, it was thought a joint venture would be more productive because it would eliminate duplication of effort and would result in more systematic study. Each of the other disciplines would bring particular strengths, and the sum of those strengths would represent a formidable research force. Progress would be maximized by a coordinated effort of attacking problems of mutual interest.

Although this sounds sensible, the idea never really developed. Although leaders in the field of communication declared that the discipline was an interdisciplinary field of study, other fields ignored the invitation to cooperate and continued their discipline-specific research. Despite this rejection, communication researchers acted as if there were an interdisciplinary approach. They borrowed theory freely from other disciplines such as psychology and sociology. Thus, communication researchers presented theories from other disciplines as if they were communication theories by scholars in the communication field. The borrowing of theories and treating them as though they originated in the communication field greatly hindered theory building. An assumption was made that there was no need to develop new theories because there were already a sufficient number. This condition has been corrected in recent years. This book presents numerous theories about communication developed by researchers who are members of the communication discipline.

We will present a few theories from other disciplines such as psychology that have been especially influential in communication research. When we do this, we identify the discipline so that you will have a clear understanding of the origin of the theory. Books in the communication discipline have (some still do) discussed theories from other disciplines without identifying them as such. Regrettably, for a significant part of the past thirty years students have completed courses in communication departments and left thinking that scholars such as Festinger, Hovland, Heider, Bem, Fishbein, Homans, Taylor, McGregor, Hall, Cartwright, Dewey, Shannon, McGuire, Kelman, and Goffman were professors in communication departments. In reality, these scholars were primarily psychology or sociology professors.

Why was an interdisciplinary approach promoted? One possible explanation lies in the tenor of the 1960s, an era when individualism was challenged by movements that espoused collectivism as a central value. Individualism would assert, "We need to develop our own field," while collectivism would counter, "We are all in this together so let's join hands." The past three decades—which gave rise to most of the theories in this book—could be characterized as the return to individualism in the field of communication. There is abundant evidence that numerous communication scholars are intent on carving out a place for communication in the broader academic community by engaging in the activity that forms the basis for this book—building communication theory.

SUMMARY

Studying communication means acquiring a deeper understanding of familiar phenomena, such as the symbolic nature of communication. Communication is a transactional process that involves both content and relationship dimensions. We reviewed the reasons for a lack of agreement on a single definition of communication and then explained our position that communication involves humans manipulating symbols to stimulate meaning in other humans. We addressed the issue of intentionality by considering communication as planned verbal and nonverbal behavior.

Communication is influenced by the situation, the most familiar contexts being: interpersonal, small group, organizational, public, mass, intercultural, family, health, and political. We looked at the functions of communication from several perspectives: as purposes of public speeches (inform, entertain, stimulate, persuade); as basic objectives of any communication (instrumental, interpersonal, identity); and as inherent functions of speech communication (linking, mentation, regulatory). The importance of communication was discussed in terms of creating cooperation, acquiring information, forming self-concept, communication as entertainment, and in the evolution of ideas. We concluded our discussion by looking at past efforts to incorporate the findings from other disciplines. As you explore the process of theory building in this text, we hope you develop an appreciation for the wealth of information communication researchers have painstakingly constructed about communication behaviors. We hope their work inspires you to reconceptualize behaviors you took for granted and to acquire a "communication mind-set" that enhances your own communication and provides new perspectives on the communication of others.

KEY TERMS

channel
communication plan
context
feedback
identity objectives
instrumental objectives
intentionality

interpersonal objectives
message
noise
perception
receiver
ritual
sign

source
symbol
symptom
theory
transactional process

Perspectives on Communication Theory

Theory building is bound by the perspectives and biases of the people who develop them. A person can only make sense of an event based on their previous experience. Throughout this book you will be exposed to some theories that were developed solely within the communication discipline and other theories based on ideas imported from other disciplines such as psychology, sociology, and anthropology. This chapter will present elements that all theories have in common and focus on the criteria necessary for sound communication theory development.

Psychologist Kurt Lewin is attributed with the saying, "*There is nothing so practical as a good theory.*" This statement is echoed by Hoover (1992) in that "knowledge is socially powerful only if it is knowledge that can be put to use. Social knowledge, if it is to be useful, must be communicable, valid, and compelling" (p. 6). These arguments highlight the importance of systematic thought necessary for theory building in aiding our understanding of ourselves and our world.

As mentioned in the introduction of this book, the authors take a social scientific approach to contemporary communication theory. Given this, we must answer the question, "What is scientific theory?" The scientific approach is based on principles developed in fields such as medicine, chemistry, physics, and engineering. According to Hoover (1992), "Science is a mode of inquiry that is common to all human beings" (p. 5). Heider (1958) believed that human beings are naïve scientists who seek certainty in our environment. "The need to understand what is happening around us and to share experiences with others makes systematic thought and inquiry essential" (Hoover, 1992, p. 6). Karl Popper, who is believed to be the most influential philosopher of natural science in the twentieth century did not believe that the aim of science is to simply establish correlations between observed events. Instead, he believed that the aim of science is to discover undiscovered worlds beyond the world of ordinary experience (Popper, 1996). In other words, to hear the unheard, see the unseen, speak the unspoken, and touch the untouched.

It is our innate curiosity to constantly discover new things about ourselves and our environment that has made science the hallmark of "truth" throughout the world. Given that science can be considered a living and breathing entity in that it is ever changing, Thomas Kuhn (1970) argued that "science is the constellation of facts, theories, and methods collected in current texts" (p. 1). The words *current texts* are important because what is contained in the latest texts in any given discipline is based on the most up-to-date research information. As such, theories contained throughout this book represent an up-to-date *constellation of communication theory.* Communication theorist Ernest Bormann offered a very general definition of theory by defining it as an "umbrella term for all careful, systematic, and self-conscious discussion and analysis of communication phenomena" (1980, p. 25).

THE SCIENTIFIC METHOD

social scientific method
Using the concept of systematic thought and the application of scientific principles

The concept of systematic thought and the application of scientific principles are the key to the social scientific method. All scientists, whether in the hard sciences or the social sciences, have to agree on a systematic way to investigate any given construct or concept. By agreeing on a particular method of inquiry, any doubt about the validity of a particular finding or study can be verified by conducting another study using the same systematic steps (Hoover, 1992). Replicating a study to assess any given theory building effort is crucial in science. Such a systematic method prompted Albert Einstein to remark, "Development of Western science is based on two great achievements: The invention of the formal logic system and the discovery of the possibility to find out causal relationships by systematic experiment" (MacKay, 1977, p. 51).

Hoover (1992) argued, "The scientific method seeks to test thoughts against observable evidence in a disciplined manner with each step in the process" (p. 33). Therefore, science can be considered reality testing where we take our theoretical assumptions about how a phenomenon works then seek to find objective and observable evidence. According to Hempel (1965), a scientific explanation for any given theory is one that could be thought of as deductive argument. For example, a deductive argument may take the form of the following:

Major Premise:	*All humans need oxygen to survive*
Minor Premise:	*You are human*
Conclusion:	*Therefore, you need oxygen to survive*

Theory Building through Deductive and Inductive Approaches

The scientific approach to theory building makes certain assumptions about reality. **Ontology** concerns what it is the theorist is examining, what he or she considers the exact nature of reality as well as the most basic measuring units of reality. For the social scientific approach, it is assumed that reality exists beyond our human experience. For example, if you ask a scientist the classic question that students struggle with in any introductory philosophy course, "If a tree falls in the forest and no one is there to hear it, does it make a sound?" The scientist, given the ontological assumptions about reality would probably respond, "Of course it does." Whether or not we are there to hear the tree fall does not affect the physical reality of the tree striking the ground and all the sights and sounds that go along with such a natural event. Another important assumption concerns how we come to know knowledge as well as how the theorist investigates the theory. This is known as **epistemology**. Scientists believe that true knowledge can only be discovered via the scientific method, by empirical observation and empirical evidence collected in an objective manner. The third set of assumptions concerns what constitutes findings that are valuable, important, and worthy for us to study as scientists, what values guide a theorist to build theory, and how theory contributes to the overall body of knowledge and practice. For the scientist, this concerns **axiology**, the discovery of worlds beyond the obvious, and how these worlds contribute to the overall quality of human experience. Given that one of the foundational assumptions of science is that of objectivity, can scientists truly be objective? Are they motivated by their preferences for doing research in particular way or during the process of observing a phenomenon, does the researcher influence the phenomenon in any way? Although these questions are more ethical and aesthetic in nature, they are important for theorists to keep in mind when developing theories, as arguably we cannot escape our human condition even when we are engaged in the practice of science.

The scientific method is comprised of five systematic steps that any study, to be considered valid, must move through in logical progression.

Identifying Variables to Be Investigated

The first step concerns identifying the specific behaviors that you want to observe and measure. When we use the term **variable**, we are speaking of characteristics of the thing under study. The variables that you identify are abstract in nature, whereas measurement is tangible or something you can experience with one of your five senses. For example, in their theoretical model of argumentativeness, Infante and Rancer (1982) argued that people have two competing motivations when it comes to arguing. First, there is a motivation to approach arguments with other people and a motivation to avoid arguments

ontology What it is the theorist is examining and what is considered the exact nature of reality and the most basic measuring units of reality

epistemology how we come to know knowledge as well as how the theorist investigates the theory

axiology The discovery of worlds beyond the obvious and how these worlds contribute to the overall quality of human experience

variable Abstraction referring to a class of things; a term often used at the level of measurement

with other people. The two motivations comprise a person's general tendency to argue (see Chapter 5 for a complete discussion of argumentativeness). To provide **empirical** (i.e., information or data gathered by observation) evidence for their model, they had to develop questions that actually assess the approach and avoidant behaviors used when faced with an argumentative situation. An example of items to assess the motivation to approach arguments include: "Arguing over controversial issues improves my intelligence" and "I am energetic and enthusiastic when I argue." Motivation to avoid arguments is assessed through items such as "Once I finish an argument, I promise myself that I will not get into another" and "I prefer being with people who rarely disagree with me." These items are examples of how argumentative motivations can be made observable through asking people questions about their behavior.

Development of Hypotheses

The second step of the scientific method concerns the development of specific hypotheses that make predictions about possible relationships between variables. A **hypothesis** is generally considered an educated guess as to what the probable result will be when you measure your variables. According to Hoover (1992), "A hypothesis is a sentence of a particularly well-cultivated breed" (p. 27). In the Infante and Rancer (1982) example mentioned earlier, they hypothesized that as a person's argumentativeness scores increase, so too would the person's desire to participate in debate (H1: Argumentativeness will be positively related to desire to participate in debate). What if these researchers were not sure of the direction of the relationship between the variables? What if there was no previous evidence suggesting that scores on the argumentativeness measure were linked to a desire to approach other people in argumentative communication? In this case, we would utilize a **research question**, or statements that do not predict relationships but inquire as to whether or not the variables are related (RQ1: Is there a relationship between argumentativeness and a desire to participate in debate?). Simply put, hypotheses predict associations in particular directions where research questions inquire whether the variables are in any way related.

It is important to distinguish assertions/questions of science versus other types of propositions that people pose. People generally pose three types of assertions/questions, those of fact, value, and policy. **Assertions/questions of fact** concern whether something is or isn't, occurred or didn't occur, will or not will occur. Examples would include, "Does vitamin C decreases susceptibility to the influenza virus?" Factual assertions/questions are considered *scientific* in nature because they can be tested using the scientific method that assumes objectivity and is empirical in nature. **Assertions/questions of value** concern whether something is good or bad or favorable or unfavorable. Examples of

empirical Information gathered by observation

hypothesis Tentative statement about the relationships between concepts of a theory; a statement of prediction about the relationships between variables

research question Question guiding investigation; usually used when a hypothesis is not warranted

assertions/questions of fact Concern whether something is or isn't, occurred or didn't occur, will or will not occur

assertions/questions of value Concern whether something is good or bad or favorable or unfavorable

value-based assertions would include "abortion is wrong" or "restricting a woman's right to choose is immoral." According to Infante (1988), "People often differ considerably in what they believe is right or wrong, good or bad, valuable or worthless, desirable or undesirable when individuals apply their value standards . . . they come up with very different conceptions of whether the thing is favorable or not (p. 35). Values are idiosyncratic and specific to each person. Therefore, there is no way to form an assessment of value that is objective in nature and as such not considered scientific in nature. **Assertions/questions of policy** concern whether or not something should or shouldn't be done. For example, "Should the United States immediately withdraw all troops from Iraq?" or "The government should institute mandatory military service for all Americans under 35 years of age." The fact that assertions/questions of policy are based on what people should or shouldn't do is considered a subjective question (as opposed to objective) and, as such, cannot be considered scientific in nature.

assertions/questions of policy Concern whether something should or shouldn't be done

Conduct an Empirical Investigation

The third step in the scientific method is conducting an empirical study. As stated earlier, the word *empirical* means to use observation in assessment of any given phenomena. According to Hoover (1992), "Science is the art of reality testing or taking ideas and confronting them with observable evidence drawn from the phenomena to which they relate" (p. 11). There are four methods through which theories can be empirically tested. These consist of experiments (measure the effects of the independent variable on the dependent variable), survey research (interviews or questionnaires), field research (observing something in its natural setting), and available data research (observing things from the past such as letters, artifacts, or e-mails). The method chosen is determined by the type of hypothesis that is derived in step 2 of the scientific method. Please refer to the Appendix for a detailed discussion of these different research methods.

Compare Results to the Original Hypothesis

Once the data collection from your observation of the phenomena is complete, you must then evaluate the results to determine if the theoretically derived hypotheses are supported (either fully or partially) or rejected. If the hypothesis is rejected, we conclude that your theory (based on the results of your study) was not supported, and we must continue to accept the status quo. If, however, we find that our hypothesis is supported, then we accept our new finding as being supported, not proven (this will be discussed in more detail later in this chapter).

Assess Theoretical Significance of the Findings and Identify Threats to Validity

The final step in the scientific method is to assess the theoretical significance of the findings. When we use the word *significance,* we are referring to two different concepts. First, theoretical significance means the empirical findings either support or do not support the theory. Second, statistical significance reflects whether the results are due to chance. To say that a finding is statistically significant is not necessarily saying it is theoretically significant and vice versa (see the Appendix for a discussion of theoretical and statistical significance). Although the scientific method ensures a process that should lead to the development of quality theory development, it does not guarantee it.

theoretical significance
The empirical findings either support or do not support the theory

statistical significance
Reflects whether the results are due to chance

CONSTITUTIONS OF QUALITY COMMUNICATION THEORY

Throughout this book you will be exposed to many theories that seek to describe, explain, predict, or control one or more particular aspects of communication. Some of these theories, as you will come to know, will have greater utility than others. A question that inevitably comes to a person's mind when considering any theory is, "How do I know if this theory is of any use?" If not for specific scientific guidelines, this question would be difficult to answer. However, theorists have compiled a list of criteria that serve to evaluate the worth of any given theory. These constitutions of quality theory building include the need for theories to be testable, falsifiable, heuristic, parsimonious, logically consistent, and pleasing to the mind.

One of the major premises of the scientific method to theory building is the ability to test empirically the effectiveness of a theory to determine if it accounts adequately for the communication phenomena that it seeks to explain, predict, and/or control. Therefore, a theory must be empirically testable. A theory that cannot be tested can never be scrutinized to debate based on observation and, thus, is of very little utility to social scientists. By being able to test a theory based on agreed-upon steps (i.e., the scientific method) we can (a) conclude the utility and thoroughness of the theory, (b) determine whether the theory should be rejected or supported in its entirety, or (c) determine whether elements of the theory that are underdeveloped should be modified and then, once modified, retest the new theory. The concept of testing should not be thought of as a one-time event. As society and technology change, constant testing should be conducted to account for such changes. Therefore, any study should be replicable. Study replication allows researchers to design a study similar to an earlier study to determine if the results of the original study are similar to those results observed in the replication

testable   Quality of a good theory; capable of being disproved or falsified

replicable   A study similar to an earlier study which determines if the results of the original study are similar when repeated study. Throughout your college career you will read many scholarly journals reporting on one phenomena or another. For example, you may read studies reporting on marital satisfaction, depression, math anxiety, or intellectual aptitude. All these studies will contain similar elements in terms of the information they provide the reader. That is, information such as who was involved, what was assessed, when it was assessed, and how it was assessed are usually contained within the article. The reason that researchers are required to include this information is so that any reader will be able to replicate the study in its entirety. The ability to replicate the test of a theory is critical to good science. The standards for constituting good research and theory are stringent by nature to ensure that particular systematic procedures are followed.

Not only should a quality communication theory be testable, but those tests should also conclusively reveal either support or lack of support for the theoretical assumptions under examination. Thus, the pursuit of **falsification** is one that the scientist should take extremely seriously because a theory that cannot be tested and objectively found to be supported or falsified is of no utility to science. Phillip Kitcher (1982) argued, "There is surely something right in the idea that a science can succeed only if it can fail" (p. 45). The importance of theory falsification can also be seen in Popper's (1963, 1996) process of falsifying theory through systematic observation. Further, falsification should serve as the demarcation determining what is and what is not considered scientific theory in that only if the theory is falsifiable can it be considered scientific. Similarly, Hawkings (1996) believed that "any physical theory is always provisional, in the sense that it is only a hypothesis; you can never prove it. No matter how many times the results of experiments agree with some theory, you can never be sure that the next time the result will not contradict the theory. On the other hand, you can disprove a theory by finding even a single observation which disagrees with the predictions of the theory" (p. 15). The concept of falsification (as opposed to theoretical confirmation) is so important to quality theory building that Popper (1963) proposed the following seven elements that good theorists need to consider when engaging in theory building:

falsification To find a theory to be false

1. Confirming and verifying theory is easy to obtain for almost any theory, if the scientist looks for confirmation.
2. Confirmation of a theory should only be counted if the confirmation is that of a risky prediction, that is, a prediction that would have potential to refute the theory.
3. To be considered a good scientific theory, there needs to be a level of prohibition. The more a theory prohibits certain events from happening, the better the theory.
4. Any theory that cannot be refuted must be considered nonscientific. The refutability of any theory should be considered a theoretical virtue with irrefutability a theoretical vice.

5. Whenever a theory is tested, a valid test is always geared toward falsifying the theory, not confirming it.

6. When a theory is confirmed through testing, it should be discounted unless the test was indeed designed to try to falsify the theory.

7. Theories, when found to be false, may still be argued as true by their admirers and developers. However, such blind allegiance to a theory's scientific application is greatly diminished if not destroyed.

For theory to be of any use, it should solve or explain some problem. The **heuristic value** of a theory lies within the theory's ability to solve problems or provide solutions that are the closest to the "best solution." For example, in George Polya's (1945) classic text, *How to Solve It*, he identifies some of the most common heuristics, some of which you may be very familiar with: *Look to the unknown; if you are having a problem understanding something, draw a picture; if you can't find a solution, work backward; solve the more general problems first*. One common business heuristic is know as K.I.S.S., which is an acronym for *keep it simple stupid*. As these examples illustrate, heuristics are valuable for all types of theory-building efforts. In Chapter 6 we present Robert Cialdini's persuasive heuristics, which explain various reasons why people behave the way they do. Upon reading about the persuasive heuristics, you will get a better understanding as to the intuitive appeal they have in explaining behavior such as conformity and commitment.

Another attribute of theory is that it should be reduced to its simplest form possible or demonstrate **parsimony**. Perhaps one of the most popular examples of a parsimonious theory is Albert Einstein's *theory of relativity* (Stachel, 1989), which was reduced into two postulates. A **postulate**, also known as an **axiom**, is a proposition that is not proven or demonstrated, but simply considered true in nature.

- POSTULATE 1: The laws of physics are identical for all observers in uniform motion relative to one another.

- POSTULATE 2: The speed of light in a vacuum is the same for all observers, regardless of their relative motion or of the motion of the source of the light.

Einstein also reduced, among other elements of his theory, the equivalent relationship of energy and mass into the mathematical formula: $E = mc^2$. As this example illustrates, great theories are not necessarily those that are comprised of overly elaborate or ornate propositions but those that are expressed in the most concise and direct ways. Further, theories should contain as few assumptions as possible, yet be comprehensive enough to explain fully the phenomenon. For example, uncertainty reduction theory (URT) (Berger and Calabrese, 1975) assumes that when we first meet a person, people seek to

heuristic value   A theory's ability to solve problems or provide solutions that are the closest to the "best solution"

parsimony   Reducing a theory to its simplest form possible

postulate   A proposition that is not proven or demonstrated, but simply considered true in nature

axiom   A proposition that is not proven or demonstrated, but simply considered true in nature

reduce uncertainty. Therefore, this theory seeks to explain the process people go through when reducing uncertainty in initial interactions (see Chapter 9).

Another term used to represent the precision of theoretical explanation is known as **Occam's razor** and is named after the fourteenth-century English logician William of Ockham. He argued, "*Entia non sunt multiplicanda praeter necessi tatem,*" which loosely translated means, "Entities must not be multiplied beyond necessity." The idea of simplicity comes from reductionist philosophy or the need to reduce units or concepts of a theory down to their simplest parts.

Occam's razor Term used to represent the precision of theoretical explanation; stresses simplicity

The idea that theory should be **logically consistent** is based on the application of formal logic to theory building. Whether a theory is derived from inductive or deductive reasoning, all theory building is based on principles that are consistent and related to one another. Consider the following objects and identify which of them do not belong: (a) suntan lotion, (b) towel, (c) swimsuit, (d) sunglasses, and (e) hacksaw. It is not too difficult to determine that one of these items does not belong with the others, as a hacksaw has no logical reason to be included with the other elements of our "theory of going swimming." Given this, the propositions within a theory should serve to logically relate to one another, not contradict one another. For example, uncertainty reduction ttheory (URT) (see Chapter 9) contains many axioms and theorems explaining how communication is used to reduce the uncertainty we experience when we encounter another person. Using the following two propositions as an example, all the axioms and theorems contained in URT are logically related to one another.

logistically consistent Theory building based on principles that are consistent and related to one another

- **URT AXIOM 4:** High levels of uncertainty in a relationship lead to less sharing and emotional intimacy. Low levels of uncertainty allow for more sharing and emotional intimacy.

- **URT AXIOM 5:** High levels of uncertainty lead to more symmetrical question exchanges in interaction. As uncertainty decreases, so does the need for an equal exchange of talk.

Another attribute of good theory building is the notion that any theory should be **pleasing to the mind**. That is, it should have intuitive appeal and be eloquently simple. Many theorists rely on diagrams or pictures when presenting complex ideas in an effort to pictorially represent theoretical models (see for instance, the early models of communication in Chapter 3). For example, in the next chapter you will be exposed to David Berlo's *Source, Message, Channel, Receiver* model of communication. The pictorial representation of this model simply "makes sense" to the everyday person. There is little cognitive work required to understand the assumptions of the model.

pleasing to the mind Has intuitive appeal and is eloquently simple

The constitutions of communication theory discussed earlier represent both the desired and necessary characteristics that allow the field of communication studies to further its exploration of human interaction. Scholars that are engaged in theory building efforts will forward theories that may include all these characteristics or only a select few. As a general rule, when developing communication theory, a scholar should be aware of all the characteristics associated with good theory building and seek to make sure that their theory contains elements of each.

COMMUNICATION THEORY DEVELOPMENT

Theories are ever changing as a constant evolution must take place for any given theory to maintain the ability to describe, explain, predict, and control human events. Consider the annual drafting procedure of the National Football League (NFL). Each spring, the NFL evaluates the top college football athletes at an annual competition known as the NFL Combine. Each of the 32 professional football teams will send representatives to evaluate the performance of each athlete. In the early days of the combine, athletes were assessed on speed, strength, and jumping ability. Therefore, the development of a theory as to what made a successful professional football player was somewhat simple (i.e., how strong, how fast, how high). However, as professional football began to gain popularity and included lucrative product endorsement deals, increased celebrity, and other perquisites, the NFL began to experience players who had exceptional speed, strength, and jumping ability, yet did not perform well at the professional level. When enough evidence indicating a theory's lack of explanatory or predictive power has amassed, the theorist should alter or discard the theory for one that better accounts for the phenomenon. In terms of our NFL Combine example, today's theories of what predicts successful performance at the professional level includes a host of physiological as well as psychological test factors that include dexterity, flexibility, intelligence, and psychological stability among others. Therefore, the theory of what makes a good NFL football player has had to evolve as the game, society, and the athletes have evolved. We cannot assume that once we explain and/or predict things effectively that explanation/prediction will forever be satisfactory. Recall the earlier discussion about statistical and theoretical significance. The vast majority of NFL theories concerning professional football prospects explains a very small percentage of success in the NFL; however, in this case, a theory that is correct one out of ten times would be considered a pretty good theory.

extension Process in which a theory grows by adding knowledge and new concepts

intention Process in which a theory grows by developing a deeper understanding of the original concepts and variables

How do theories grow and change? Theories can change through the process of **extension** or **intention** (Kaplan, 1964). The process of extension reflects the growing ability of a theory to describe, explain, and predict an ever-growing number of concepts and situations. For example, in Chapter 12 we discuss the social information processing theory (SIPT) of computer-mediated communication. According to Walther (2008), SIPT "explains how people get to know one another online, without nonverbal cues, and how they develop and manage relationships in the computer-mediated environment" (p. 391). This theory of mediated communication is believed to be a more comprehensive explanation of how people use technology than theories developed earlier (i.e., Cathcart & Gumpert, 1983) because it accounts for newer technologies such as e-mail and instant messages that were not in existence when earlier theories were developed. As new communication technologies emerge, theorists will probably try to apply SIPT to explain the how people communicate via the new technology. Thus, SIPT will experience theoretical growth by extension. However, when theories grow by intention, they do not seek to further explain new concepts but seek a deeper understanding of the concepts that the theory already explains. An example of theoretical growth by intention is the development of information reception apprehension (IRA) (see Chapter 5). According to Wheeless, Preiss, and Gayle (1997), IRA is "a pattern of anxiety and antipathy that filters informational reception, perception, and processing, and/or adjustment (psychologically, verbally, physically) associated with complexity, abstractness, and flexibility" (p. 166). IRA was an extension of receiver apprehension, which sought to explain why some people become anxious when receiving communicative messages in general. However, IRA specifies the following types of factors that comprise the construct: listening apprehension, reading anxiety, and intellectual inflexibility. Therefore, the development of IRA was not necessarily intended to explain any new information as much as to provide a greater understanding of the different facets of anxiety associated with receiving information.

Regardless of the way that communication theories develop and evolve, all theory seeks to investigate the various phenomena and events that occur in nature. In the next section, we will cover the underlying functions and goals that are served/pursued by theory.

FUNDAMENTAL FUNCTIONS AND GOALS OF COMMUNICATION THEORY

Theory building efforts seek to contribute to the further understanding of our world. They also serve as a continuing benchmark from which we are constantly updating our understanding of new events and occurrences in our world. For example, in attending college, students are exposed to an incredible amount of information that will inevitably change their way of thinking and perceiving the world. Students would probably not be able to have this new way of thinking about things had it not been for the exposure to the new ideas and concepts. With this concept in mind, theory serves as the vehicle through which we are able to further our ideas about our environment and about ourselves.

Marvin Shaw and Philip Costanzo (1970) forwarded four main functions of theories. First, theories serve to organize our experience. Every day we are

organizational function
A sense-making process that aids us in interpreting an event that allows us to process the information effectively

knowledge extension function An enhanced learning process by utilizing what we already know to proceed to learn more about it

anticipatory function
Reflects the theories' ability to develop expectations or hypotheses about events that we have yet to encounter

stimulating further research Reflects the development of new experiences that then need to be organized and understood

bombarded with stimuli (e.g., media, messages, people) that need to be processed and made sense of. The organizational function of theory represents a sense-making process that aids us in interpreting the event that allows us to process the information effectively. For example, once we are able to make sense of and organize our experience of the event, we can then proceed to extend our knowledge about the event. That is, utilizing what we already know about the event, we can then proceed to learn more about it. This enhanced learning process is known as the knowledge extension function. Once we have organized and acquired detailed knowledge of an event, we can then move to the anticipatory function of theory, which reflects the theories' ability to develop expectations or hypotheses about events that we have yet to encounter. For example, scientists have developed elaborate theoretical models about human survivability on the planet Mars. These calculations and models have been primarily based on atmospheric and astronomical knowledge. Although we have actually never tested these survivability models, they remain our best interpretation of the knowledge base used in their calculation. Theory can also serve the function of stimulating further research, which reflects the development of new experiences. These new experiences then need to be organized and understood. As Figure 2.1 indicates, each function of theory influences the other functions of theory. Thus, the four functions of organization, extension, anticipation, and stimulation are circular in that any one of these functions is necessary for the others to occur (Shaw & Costanzo, 1970). Consider the seasons of the year, spring, summer, fall, and winter. The types of environmental events during any one season will directly affect the other seasons. For example, a snowy winter, dry spring, hot summer, and cold fall will affect the other seasons in terms of their severity, average temperature, and so forth.

Figure 2.1

The four functions of theory.

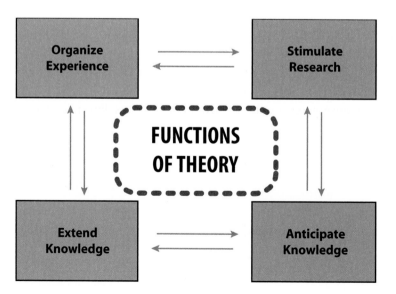

Fundamental Goals of Theory

There are particular goals that scholars pursue about any given event and use theory as a vehicle to achieve these goals. The four major goals of theory are to predict, explain, describe, and control. All these goals are central in determining the relative value of a theory.

The goal of prediction, the concept of knowing what events will occur in the future, is something that is vital to the survival of humankind as well as nature at large. Whether it is a tornado on the horizon, an oncoming recession of the economy, or an impending global war, our ability/need to predict events is a vital function that can be satisfied by theory. In his book *A Brief History of Time,* Stephen Hawking (1996) argued, "A theory is a good theory if it satisfies two requirements: It must accurately describe a large class of observations on the basis of a model which contains only a few arbitrary elements, and it must make definite predictions about the results of future observations" (p. 15).

The need to predict future events is a need that transcends science and is found in our everyday ways of thinking and explaining the world. For example, consider a time when you were walking home late at night on a dark street, and you see a couple of people up ahead walking toward you. Most people would theorize (not scientifically but based on their own personal experience) that this situation has the potential to have adverse circumstances such as being robbed or physically assaulted. As such, you decide to cross the street based on the prediction that this street-crossing behavior will result in reducing the probability of being in an altercation with the oncoming strangers.

For communication theorists, one of the most important aspects of a theory is the ability to predict communicative behavior. Many scholars develop models and theoretical frameworks designed to forecast a person's behavior in an expected way. For example, in Chapter 8 we present interaction adaptation theory. This theory is designed to predict how people will behave by accounting for, among other things, the communicator's requirements, expectancies, and desires. Several empirical investigations have supported the two propositions of IAT in terms of its ability to predict communication behavior. As will become evident in the later chapters of this book, some of the theories presented possess greater predictive powers than others. For many communication researchers, the degree of predictability of any theory is a direct translation of the overall quality of that theory.

The explanation goal of theory concerns understanding how a phenomenon or event occurs. To explain a communication phenomenon is vital to theory building in that to organize experience, which is one of the functions of theory explained earlier, we need to be able to explain how a communication process works. An example of the theories that do a particularly good job at satisfying the explanatory theoretical goal is coordinated management of meaning, discussed in Chapter 9, and the theory of groupthink (a.k.a. the

prediction The concept of knowing what events will occur in the future

explanation Understanding how a phenomenon or event occurs

groupthink hypothesis), discussed in Chapter 10. These theories are extremely effective in explaining the rules engaged in any given interpersonal conversation and a faulty decision-making process, respectively. However, although these theories are very effective at explaining different types of interaction and interaction outcomes, they are both considered post facto theories (that is, they are able to explain the past), as they have very little predictive power in terms of the future. Therefore, theories that have been developed to explain a communication phenomenon may lack in the other goals of description and prediction.

description Focuses the attention of scholars on particular parts of an event or phenomenon

The **description** goal of theory serves to focus the attention of scholars on particular parts of an event or phenomenon. For example, family communication scholars have long debated the definition of the word *family*. This debate has only become more complicated in light of reproductive technologies, same-sex unions, and other issues that confound the definition. However, once we are able to describe a particular phenomenon, scholars can then move to assess the efficacy with which a theory explains and predicts aspects of the thing being studied. Theories are designed to represent a phenomenon or event. The ability to describe the phenomena under investigation provides a blueprint with which the theory can be applied to other situations.

The importance of the descriptive function of theory can be illustrated in the parable of *the blind men and the elephant.* Once upon a time, a king summoned his servant and ordered him to gather up all the blind men in the village. The king presented the elephant to each man. To one man he presented the elephant's head, to another the ears, to another the tusks, to another the trunk, to another the foot, to another the back, to another the tail, and to the last man the tuft of the tail. He told each man that this was an elephant. The man who was presented the head described the elephant as a pot, the man presented with the ear described the elephant as a winnowing basket, the man presented with the tusk described it as a ploughshare, the man presented with the trunk believed the elephant was a plough, and so on and so forth. The men began to quarrel shouting things such as, "Yes it is!" "No, it is not!." This quarrel continued until the men came to blows. The king, delighted to see this scene shouted, "Just so are these preachers and scholars holding various views blind and unseeing . . . In their ignorance they are by nature quarrelsome, wrangling, and disputatious, each maintaining reality is thus and thus." This parable illustrates the need for a theory to describe in direct and clear terms exactly what it is the theory is addressing. By making sure everyone experiences the same concept of "what is an elephant," we can then have a description of an event that is understood by others.

control The ability to alter elements in the present to achieve a specified outcome given certain situational factors in the future

The goal of **control** is made possible by our ability to predict, explain, and describe any given phenomenon or event. The explanation function of theory seeks to understand why events occur, whereas control concerns under what situations events will occur. When we use the term *control,* we are referring to the ability to alter elements in the present to achieve a specified outcome given certain situational factors in the future. For example, marketing and advertising professionals are aware of the theories of nonverbal communication and psychology regarding how humans react to color and the color spectrum. When advertising new products (whether be on a Web page, magazine, or television commercial), marketers and advertisers will utilize the color red when they want the reader/viewer to attend to a message. Research indicates that the color red activates the human brain in different ways than other colors and that this activation has resulted in increased product sales. Knowing what we do about the influence of color on the human brain allows us to control the types of messages (in terms of color choice) that we want people to attend to.

The goals and functions of theory discussed in this section transcend all disciplines. Whether we are developing theory based on biology, chemistry, physics, engineering, psychology, or communication, we all strive to satisfy these fundamental functions and goals.

How Many Theories Are Enough?

This book presents dozens of theories across all contexts and aspects of human communication. There has long been a debate on the necessity of so many communication theories contrasted with other theorists who believe that we have too few. Berger (1991) presented a number of issues related to theory building in communication. First, was the lack of a theoretical paradigm, or touchstone theory. Instead, contemporary theory has its roots in many disciplines, including sociology, psychology, English, linguistics, and philosophy. Second, Berger believed that there is a scarcity of theory-building efforts throughout the entire field of communication studies. Berger argued that "we are hardly in danger of being buried under an avalanche of original communication theories" (p. 103). This critique was rebutted by Purcell (1992), who suggested that "there is a paucity of communication theories only if one assumes that theory construction began in the twentieth century" (p. 94), citing the contribution of pre-twentieth-century philosophers and scholars such as Decartes, Bacon, Blair, Campbell, and Whately. In sum, "the field of communication would be well served by communication theorists who attempt to bridge the broad span between interpersonal communication theory and classical rhetorical theory with covering communication theories" (Purcell, 1992, p. 97). The different perspectives of Berger and Purcell highlight the fundamental distinctions of what does/doesn't constitute contemporary communication theory.

Burleson (1992) offered yet another perspective on the number of communication theories. He rejected the question, "Why are there so few communication theories?" and rephrased the question to ask, "Why are there so few theories of human communication?" He argued that theorists have primarily been concerned with the content and uses that people put on communication rather than the development of a "philosophy of communication." A philosophy of communication should treat human communication holistically, providing a "characterization of the overall process of communication" (Burleson, 1992,

p. 84). Such a philosophy should be general, leading to theories that transcend culture and context or are etic in nature (i.e., true to all people and cultures).

Still another unique perspective was offered by Craig (1993). He pointed out the paradox in communication theory building in that even though there have been numerous and much more complex theories forwarded, "confusion, uncertainty, implicit dissention, and to a lesser degree, explicit controversy about the proper foci, forms, and functions of communication theory have markedly increased" (Craig, 1993, p. 26). In fact, Craig also reframed the original question of, "Why are there so few communication theories?" to ask, "Why are there not so many communication theories?" He believes that although description, explanation, prediction, and control are fundamental goals of science, science should simultaneously advance moral and political objectives. In sum, he advocates that the field of communication studies be viewed as an integrative, practical discipline where all traditions (social science, critical, and interpretive methods) be used in any contemporary communication theory building.

METATHEORETICAL CONTRIBUTIONS TO COMMUNICATION THEORY

metatheory Theorizing about theory

Perhaps one of the more difficult concepts for communication theory students to grasp is that of **metatheory**. Simply put, metatheory means *theorizing about theory.* Throughout this text you will be exposed to many theories and critiques of those theories. Can these different traditions and perspectives coexist? Or will there be further division and splintering of these perspectives?

One of the most significant theoretical developments in recent years was the metatheoretical framework forwarded by Robert Craig's (1999) practical theory approach. This framework provides a way to value all different perspectives when it comes to communication theory building. What is it that theorists seek to examine? What constitutes the basic unit of reality? and What is the nature of reality? These questions reflect those of ontology discussed earlier in this chapter. Craig and Muller (2007) believe that theorists, regardless of their perspective, cannot agree as to whether any phenomena or event can exist objectively. Simply put, if you assume that there is a world outside our own experience, then it is true in nature. However, if you do not believe that there is a world beyond our own experience, then you believe that the phenomenon or event is a social construction of the individual observer and, as such, should be socially interpreted. There are, however, theorists in between these two positions that assume reality is both objective and subjective in nature (see Rancer & Avtgis, 2009).

Just as ontology concerns the nature of reality, epistemology explores how theorists investigate any given phenomena. Simply put, epistemology asks,

"How do we know what we know?" Given that this text is heavily influenced by the social scientific approach to theory building, the epistemological assumption is empirical in nature, and as such, people who theorize from this perspective are known as **empiricists**. That is, they believe theory-building efforts are based on observation and objectivity. Another influence on social scientists concerns the value of studying or developing particular theories and how those theories will stimulate the overall body of knowledge and practice. Asking questions concerning the value of a particular theory and the amount of contribution that theory affords to the overall body of research is known as axiology. Some theories have much more axiological value than others.

> **empiricists** Those who believe theory building efforts are based on observation and objectivity

Throughout the development of the communication studies discipline, there has been much debate as to the value of any one perspective or theoretical paradigm (Craig & Muller, 2007). The first approach, and the approach from which this text is heavily influenced by, is the empirical **social scientific approach**. The main function of this approach is to provide prediction, explanation, description, and control of and for communication behavior. Further, theory and research follow a universal sequence known as the scientific method. Basically, hypotheses are developed or deduced, tested, then either supported or rejected. Another approach is the **philosophical normative approach**. From this perspective, rational and abstract principles are tested, with results providing methods for the evaluation and practice of communication.

> **social scientific approach** Provides prediction, explanation, description, and control of and for communication behavior

> **philosophical normative approach** Rational and abstract principles are tested, with results providing methods for the evaluation and practice of communication

More recently, in an attempt to find common ground for theorizing about real-world communication behavior, Craig (1999) developed the **Constitutive Metamodel of Communication Theory**. The main assumption of this approach is that communication should be conceptualized as a means to fixing practical problems. That is, it allows for debate on which perspective best addresses the everyday communication problems found in society (Craig, 2007).

> **Constitutive Metamodel of Communication Theory** Assumes that communication should be conceptualized as a means to fixing practical problems

Until Craig's model, scholars have primarily divided conceptualizations and approaches of communication theory building by context (e.g., interpersonal, small group, mass), by how we explain communication behavior (e.g., empirical, critical), by epistemological assumptions (e.g., trait, cognitive, affective), and by discipline (e.g., psychology, social-psychology, rhetoric). The constitutive model is a radical departure from traditional ways of organizing theory, as it organizes theory based on underlying assumptions each tradition has about the practice of communication. Craig (2006) argued that his model "situates communication theory within the societal communication process that constitutes and regulates communication as a social practice" (p. 127).

SEVEN THEORETICAL TRADITIONS

There are seven theoretical traditions in the constitutive model consisting of the sociopsychological tradition, the cybernetic tradition, the rhetorical tradition, the phenomenological tradition, the sociocultural tradition, the critical

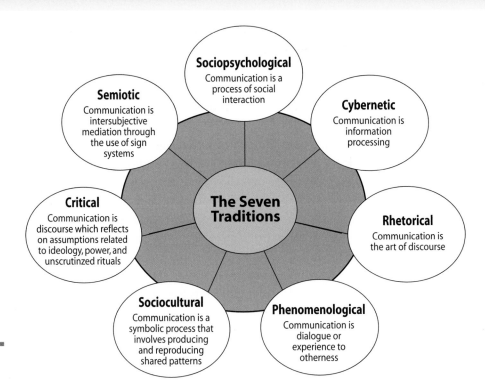

Figure 2.2

The seven theoretical traditions.

tradition, and the semiotic tradition. These seven traditions and the interaction among them provides a comprehensive description of contemporary communication theory building (see Figure 2.2). That is, "each tradition is characterized by a unique definition of communication, conceptualization of communication problems, metadiscursive vocabulary (terms for talking about communication), and metadiscursive commonplaces (everyday assumptions about communication)" (Craig, 2006, p. 129). As the field of communication continues to develop, Craig (2007) believes that there may be more traditions developed as long as they: (a) are comprised of a unique and large body of evidence not found in other traditions, and (b) have a distinct perspective on communication problems, have a unique metadiscursive vocabulary, and have commonplace beliefs that are either embraced or rejected (Rancer & Avtgis, 2009).

The Sociopsychological Tradition

sociopsychological tradition Assumes that communication is a process of social interaction

The **sociopsychological tradition** is one of the newer traditions of communication theory building. Developed in the early 1900s, the sociopsychological tradition assumes that communication is a process of social interaction (Craig, 1999). The validation of theories from this perspective relies on the scientific method and the use of experimental designs in an effort to reveal cause-and-effect relationships along with control mechanisms to regulate these cause-and-effect relationships. Due to its reliance on the scientific method, some scholars refer to this as "communication science" (Berger & Chaffee, 1987).

Because this perspective focuses on the process of social interaction, theory building within this tradition has been contextual in nature (e.g., interpersonal, group, organizational, health) with further subdivision of each context (e.g., within-organizational communication we may examine aggressive communication within the workplace). Even though the term *communication* existed in the early 1900s, it wasn't until the 1940s that psychologists overtly used communication as a focus in experimental research design (Hovland, 1948). Carl Hovland was the first person who advocated that all the social sciences (i.e., anthropology, psychology, political science, and sociology) utilize the scientific method to investigate communication. The sociopsychological tradition has been widely integrated into the field of communication studies and will continue to be one of the most prominent traditions for the foreseeable future. According to Craig (1999), this tradition views communication as "situations requiring manipulation of causes of behavior to achieve specified outcomes" (p. 133). The metadiscourses used in the sociopsychological tradition include vocabulary such as *attribute, behavior, cognition, effect, emotion, interaction, perception, personality,* and *variable* (Craig, 1999).

The Cybernetic Tradition

The cybernetic tradition treats communication theory building as information processing and concerns analyzing communication problems such as "noise; overload; a malfunction or 'bug' in a system" (Craig, 1999, p. 133). The vocabulary utilized in this metadiscourse includes feedback, function, information, network, noise, receiver, redundancy, signal, and source (Craig, 1999). This tradition was developed in the mid-twentieth century by researchers such as Claude Shannon and Warren Weaver (Heims, 1991) (see Chapter 3 for a discussion of Shannon and Weaver's information approach to communication).

cybernetic tradition
Treats communication theory building as information processing and concerns analyzing communication problems in a system

Theories that are developed in the cybernetic tradition focuses on the flow of information and includes noise, information overload, and incongruity between function and structure (Craig, 1999). Norbert Weiner (1948) originally coined the word *cybernetics* and was concerned with how human and machines communicate. Weiner's principles were adapted to human relationships by Gregory Bateson (1972) as well as Paul Watzlawick, Janet Beavin, and Donald Jackson (1967). The systems perspective, which is widely used in communication studies, was developed from the cybernetic tradition. This tradition considers the larger context within which communication interactions occur.

The Rhetorical Tradition

The rhetorical tradition conceptualizes communication as the art of discourse (Craig & Muller, 2007). Theory building from this tradition looks at the direct relation to problems encountered within the sociohistorical context in which

rhetorical tradition
Conceptualizes communication as the art of discourse

they occur. For example, consider Plato's critique of rhetoric as the art of deception, Aristotle's exploration of *logos,* and Burke's idea that all language is rhetorical (Craig & Muller, 2007). Craig (1999) believes that the rhetorical tradition "challenges the commonplaces that mere words are less important than actions, that true knowledge is more than just a matter of opinion, and that telling the plain truth is something other than strategic adaptation of a message to an audience" (p. 136). The rhetorical tradition approaches problems of communication as "social exigency requiring collective deliberation and judgment" (Craig, 1999, p. 133). Metadiscourse use in this tradition includes vocabulary such as *art, audience, commonplace, communicator, emotion, logic, method,* and *strategy* (Craig, 1999).

The Phenomenological Tradition

phenomenological tradition
Views communication as dialogue or experience to otherness

The **phenomenological tradition** views communication as dialogue or experience to otherness (Craig & Muller, 2007). Craig (1999) argued that theorists operating from this perspective are concerned with "the necessity, and yet the inherent difficulty—even, arguably, the practical impossibility—of sustained, authentic communication between persons" (p. 139). Unlike some of the other traditions, the phenomenological tradition does not treat objectivity and subjectivity as mutually exclusive. Instead, both objectivity and subjectivity are believed to be necessary to understand the human experience. In terms of problems with communication, Craig (1999) believes that theorists treat problematic communication as "absence of, or failure to sustain, authentic human relationship" (p. 133). Metadiscourse common to this tradition includes vocabulary such as *dialogue, experience, genuineness, openness, other, self,* and *supportiveness* (Craig, 1999).

In terms of practical implications, phenomenological theorists assume that people experience events in very different ways and that we need to respect experiential differences as well as make good-faith efforts to seek common ground (Craig, 1999). Furthermore, there are practical applications in pursuing the goal of an ideal dialogue while simultaneously acknowledging problems associated with achieving the ideal dialogue.

The Sociocultural Tradition

sociocultural tradition
Addresses problems of diversity and relativity as well as cultural change

The **sociocultural tradition** reflects a "symbolic process that produces shared sociocultural patterns" (Craig, 1999, p. 144). Communication problems that are addressed by this tradition are problems of diversity and relativity as well as cultural change. Simply put, the sociocultural tradition views problematic communication as "conflict; alienation; misalignment; failure to coordinate" (Craig, 1999, p. 133). Metadiscourse common to this tradition contains vocabulary such as co-construction, culture, identity, practice, ritual, rule, socialization, society, and structure (Craig, 1999). It is believed that this tradition is the most diverse, as it includes theory building at the macro sociocultural level (e.g., functionalism and structuralism), at the micro sociocultural level (e.g., symbolic interactionism and ethnomethodology), or a combination of both (e.g., structuration). Edward Sapir and Benjamin Whorf are believed to be the pioneers of this tradition (Rancer & Avtgis, 2009). The theories contained in this tradition are diverse and include coordinated management of meaning (Pearce & Cronen, 1980), social action media theory (Schoening & Anderson, 1995), and more contemporary approaches to rhetorical theory (Ehninger, 1968). Further, in terms of practical use of this traidition, Craig (1999) believed

> Sociocultural theory is plausible from a lay point of view in part because it appeals rhetorically to the commonplace beliefs that individuals are products of their social environments, that groups develop particular norms, rituals, and worldviews; that social change can be difficult and disruptive; and that attempts to intervene actively in social processes often have unintended consequences. (p. 146)

The Critical Tradition

The **critical tradition** has its origins in Plato's development of the Socratic dialectic (Craig, 1999). Communication is conceptualized as a discursive reflects or discourse that freely reflects on assumptions that can be related to ideology, power, and unscrutinized rituals (Craig & Muller, 2007). The overarching goal of the critical tradition is to expose hidden elements that distort communication and to advocate efforts to resist the use of power by these elements. Problems with communication are seen as "hegemonic ideology; systematically distorted speech situation" (Craig, 1999, p. 133). Metadiscourse within this tradition includes vocabulary such as *consciousness-raising, dialectic, emancipation ideology, oppression,* and *resistence* (Craig, 1999). The contemporary critical tradition includes the writings of Karl Marx and Jürgan Habermas. More recently, current communication theories developed from this tradition involve political economy, critical cultural studies, feminist theory, postcolonial theory, and queer theory (Craig & Muller, 2007). Craig (1999) argued that the real-world application of the critical tradition lies in the commonplace belief of injustices and conflict that is ubiquitous in contemporary society. Further, this tradition serves to call into question the neutrality and objectivity assumed in science and technology.

critical tradition　Goal is to expose hidden elements that distort communication and to advocate efforts to resist the use of power by these elements

The Semiotic Tradition

The final tradition is that of the **semiotic tradition**, and it can be traced back to the late seventeenth- to early eighteenth-century writings of John Locke, who is considered the father of modern ideas of treating communication as

semiotic tradition conceptualizes communication as intersubjective mediation by signs

transmission (Peters, 1989). This tradition conceptualizes communication as intersubjective mediation by signs, or "a process in which language and other sign systems come to have shared meanings and thereby serve as a medium for common understanding between individuals (subjects)" (Craig & Muller, 2007, p. 163). The semiotic tradition views communication problems as issues of transmission and representation that serve to reduce effective meaning exchange or misunderstandings or gap between subjective viewpoints (Craig, 1999, p. 133). Metadiscourse common to this tradition includes vocabulary such as *code, icon, index, language, meaning, medium, misunderstanding, referent, sign,* and *symbol* (Craig, 1999).

According to Craig (1999), the future of organizing communication theory as an interrelated yet distinct tradition is based on the continued pursuit of new traditions that offer practical metadiscourse about practical problems associated with everyday interaction (Craig, 1999). As with any metatheoretical approach, new problems emerge as theory-building efforts continue in all traditions. Craig believes some of these problems include "the problem of strategy versus authenticity . . . , the problem of intentionality versus functionality . . . , the problem of proving the effectiveness of techniques . . . , the problem of instrumental reason as ideological distortion" (p. 130). With regard to the addition of new traditions in the future, Craig (1999) believes that a feminist tradition (if theorized as connectedness to others), an aesthetic tradition (if theorized as embodied performance), an economic tradition (if theorized as exchange), and a spiritual tradition (if theorized as communication on a mystical plane of existence) all hold interesting possibilities for the adaptation and addition to the constitutive metamodel of communication theory. The partitioning of communication theory into distinct traditions, yet also serving as a common ground by focusing theories on the task of explaining and rectifying everyday communication problems, serves as an innovative perspective that may reduce the splintering of approaches common to the communication discipline.

Theory-building efforts from scholars within the critical, cultural, and interpretive paradigms, as well as the postmodern tradition, have increased in recent years. Theorists and researchers from the social scientific tradition (such as the authors of this book) may find this trend of some concern because of the movement away from behavioral science. However, we readily acknowledge the contribution of these perspectives in increasing our understanding of human communication. According to Rancer and Avtgis (2009), "It is our contention that contemporary communication theory building efforts from all paradigmatic perspectives and theoretical traditions will simultaneously serve to fragment the discipline, yet unite it, based on the simple truth that we are all theorizing about the same phenomena—*communication.*"

SUMMARY

The material presented in this chapter is designed to expose you to the fundamental concepts, challenges, and procedures that every scholar must consider when engaged in theory-building efforts. Although some of these concepts may seem quite complex, whereas others appear quite simple, each concept is crucial to the integrity and foundation of quality theory-building efforts.

The scientific method and the steps that are associated with it provide a road map through which theories can be tested and modified. As evidenced in the chapter, theories that lack the ability to describe, explain, predict, and control are of little utility for scholars as well as researchers and practitioners. As society demands more problem-centered communication theories from the field of communication studies (i.e., theories that make a marked difference in the lives of people), adherence to the scientific method serves as a quality control process through which good theory can be rigorously developed and be applicable to the everyday communication problems that people face.

The final material in this chapter reflected Craig's constitutive metamodel that focuses on the utility that all traditions of communication theory building serve to alleviate everyday problems associated with or caused by problematic communication. This approach assumes that whatever the particular theory-building perspective, focusing on alleviating problems is a common thread that all communication theorists and theories can share.

KEY TERMS

Anticipatory function
Assertions/questions of fact
Assertions/questions of policy
Assertions/questions of value
Axiology
Axiom
Constitutive Metamodel of Communication Theory
Control
Critical tradition
Cybernetic tradition
Description
Empirical
Empiricists
Epistemology
Explanation

Extension
Falsification
Heuristic value
Hypothesis
Intention
Knowledge extension function
Logistically consistent
Metatheory
Occam's razor
Ontology
Organizational function
Parsimony
Phenomenological tradition
Philosophical normative approach
Pleasing to the mind

Postulate
Prediction
Replicable
Research question
Rhetorical tradition
Semiotic tradition
Social scientific approach
Social scientific method
Sociocultural tradition
Sociopsychological tradition
Statistical significance
Stimulating further research
Testable
Theoretical significance
Variable

The Development of Approaches to Communication

THE RHETORICAL TRADITION IN THE DEVELOPMENT OF COMMUNICATION THEORY

This first part of the chapter will provide some background from the history of the field on which the communication theories that are presented in this book are based. The communication discipline has existed in an unbroken line that goes back to the fifth century BC in ancient Greece, where it was called **rhetoric**. The study of rhetoric was mainly concerned with the various forms of oratory, or persuasive speech making. This was an important part of the educational system in ancient Greece and ancient Rome, and it continued as a central part of the educational curriculum in the Middle Ages and the Renaissance, where it was one of the three liberal arts along with grammar and dialectic. The interest in rhetoric then persisted into modern and contemporary times, where it developed into departments of higher education and was called, at various times, rhetoric, speech, and more commonly today, communication, or communication studies.

rhetoric Communication study beginning in ancient Greece, mainly concerned with the various forms of oratory, or persuasive speech making

There have been many influences on the study of rhetoric that have affected its nature. The political climate in a culture is a particularly important influence, as it affects the types of speeches students are permitted to deliver. For instance, as Rome changed from a republic to an empire, freedom to criticize the government was severely restricted. Rome as a republic permitted criticism, but when Rome became an empire, few emperors tolerated criticism. Students were limited to declamations on frivolous and otherwise politically neutral topics such as, "Does a ship captain have the right to keep treasure he found while his ship was hired to recover a shipment of tools lost in a shipwreck?" Freedom of speech in a culture influences rhetorical practices to a considerable degree.

The needs of society have been determinants of what is taught. Although the major emphasis through the centuries has been on teaching persuasive speaking, the art of letter writing was a focus of rhetorical training, especially in the Middle Ages and the Renaissance. Letter writing was a major method of persuasion when face-to-face communication was not possible or practical. This led to the modern and contemporary practices of using rhetoric to teach written composition. Thus, rhetoric today is taught in English as well as communication departments. There also has been a close connection between rhetoric and religion. From at least the time of St. Augustine (354–430) rhetoric has been used to teach pulpit oratory. This ecclesiastical context has endured because many individuals who wrote books on rhetoric and taught rhetoric were also theologians. There has been little doubt that success from the pulpit can be enhanced greatly by eloquent oratory and a good grasp of the principles of persuasion.

We will review in this chapter the essential parts of what has been termed *rhetorical theory* throughout its long history in Western education. We will not attempt even a brief history of rhetoric. A fairly comprehensive history of this topic can be found in several sources (Conley, 1990; Golden, Berquist, & Coleman, 1978; Horner, 1990; Kennedy, 1963; Murphy, 1974). Our concern here will be with the major concepts that make up rhetorical theory.

We need to first emphasize that "rhetorical theory" is a bit of a misnomer. Rhetorical theory is not a theory in the sense of what is considered a theory in this book. That is, it does not conform to what we have specified in Chapter 2 as the essential characteristics of a theory. Of particular importance, rhetorical theory does not constitute a systematic explanation of the domain of public speaking, nor does it provide a set of testable predictions that can be empirically verified. It does not seem possible to falsify rhetorical theory, and as discussed in Chapter 2, being falsifiable is a necessary condition for any scientific theory. If it is not possible to prove something wrong, then it is not a theory, but something else such as a value, or a policy, or mysticism, or a set of utilitarian procedures.

rhetorical pedagogy   A set of utilitarian procedures for teaching oratory, eloquence, or simply public speaking

What has been termed rhetorical theory is actually **rhetorical pedagogy**, a set of utilitarian procedures for teaching oratory, eloquence, or simply public speaking. Teaching procedures, of course, can be based on theory. However, one does not have to have a theoretical framework to develop effective ways of teaching something. Simple trial and error can provide a valuable approach to pedagogy.

The field of communication has not always been clear on this. At times it has been claimed that communication theories such as those covered in this book represent a direct development from the rhetorical concepts of the past two thousand years or so. In part, this has been done to promote unity in the communication field where rhetoricians take an approach to communication that is very different from the social scientific approach, which characterizes most of the theories presented in this book. Once we explain the basic concepts of rhetoric, and once you study the theories included in this book, it will be clear that although some of the theories here are related to some of the ideas from rhetoric, most also have their roots in the social sciences, especially personality, social psychology, sociology, management, anthropology, and linguistics. Contemporary communication theory in a sense has evolved uniquely from several academic disciplines.

Basic Rhetorical Concepts

Hundreds of books on rhetoric were written from the time of ancient Greece to the present (see Conley, 1990, for a good review). This along with the emphasis on rhetorical training in education illustrates the importance people have attributed to persuasion in human society. Principles of persuasion were derived by the ancient Greeks and Romans, and methods were developed for teaching those principles to students. The great Greek philosopher Aristotle (384–322) and the Roman philosopher, politician, and lawyer Cicero (106–43) wrote books on rhetoric that exerted major influences from ancient times, through the Middle Ages, the Renaissance, and into the modern era. Aristotle and Cicero may be viewed as the major figures in the history of rhetoric.

Aristotle's *Rhetoric* is probably the most insightful book on persuasion ever written. Here he defined rhetoric as the faculty for determining in any situation what the available means are for persuasion. Many of his ideas about persuasion have remained core ideas about rhetoric and will be discussed here. You will notice his influence in Chapter 6 on persuasion. Cicero probably was even more influential than Aristotle in terms of his effect on the many rhetoricians who followed over the centuries. Cicero was greatly influenced by Aristotle's ideas and wrote several books on rhetoric that had a great impact on Roman education and on the civilizations that followed. Although many of Cicero's ideas originated with Aristotle, Cicero's formulations of those concepts are responsible for much of the popularization and endurance of what has been termed rhetorical theory.

From the early years in ancient Greece, rhetoric was seen as comprising five separate arts, usually called the Canons of Oratory: (1) **inventio** (invention), (2) **dispositio** (arrangement), (3) **elocutio** (style), (4) **pronuntiatio** (delivery), and (5) **memoria** (memory).

inventio   Invention

dispositio   Arrangement

elocutio   Style

pronuntiatio   Delivery

memoria   Memory

INVENTIO/INVENTION

Inventio was concerned with the discovery of arguments that pertained to the particular object of persuasion in the situation. This involved knowing the subject matter relevant to the oration, analyzing the audience to determine what mattered most to them concerning the topic, what the relationships were among the elements of topic information, and what issues were in dispute for the topic of the oration. An issue is a point of contention or question that must be dealt with to win audience acceptance.

It was generally recognized that there were three types of oratory, each having its own unique set of possible issues that must be dealt with to persuade. For **forensic speaking**, which was courtroom oratory, common issues were fact (what occurred), definition (what was the act, murder, self-defense . . .), and quality (was the act harmful, helpful). **Deliberative speaking** pertained to political oratory. The central issues to be addressed usually were problem (what is wrong that would justify changing the status quo), blame (what are the causes of the problem, is the status quo to blame), solution (how may the problem be solved), and consequences (what are the good and bad consequences of the solution). **Epideictic oratory** was typified by commemorative speaking such as funeral orations or holiday speeches. The common issues to be addressed were concerned with what needed to be praised or blamed, what values needed to be emphasized.

Once the issues were determined for a persuasive attempt, the next step was to develop arguments about the issues. There were different types of arguments such as inductive and deductive (several forms of each). Of particular importance to developing arguments were the **topoi** or lines of argument, which Aristotle explained and which constitute one of his important contributions to the study of persuasion. Aristotle's conception of the **koinoi topoi** and the **eide topoi**, along with his three universals of argument, represent a unique paradigm of rhetorical invention.

The *eide topoi* are beliefs, values, and attitudes held by listeners that may be stated in propositional form and used for major premises in arguments. An example, for a speaker attempting to oppose military aid to developing countries, might be: "If military aid to developing countries increases the likelihood of war, it should not be provided." Often the speaker will derive an argument from this premise that justifies a conclusion: "Increased military aid will increase the chance of war with unfriendly neighbors." This would lead to the conclusion the speaker wants to establish: "Military aid should not be provided." Often the speaker will not actually verbalize all three premises, but will intend on the listener realizing the unspoken premise and therefore actively participating in the argument by supplying part of it. The implied or unspoken premise is often the *eidos topos* (the major premise of the argument). Aristotle termed this type of argument an **ethymeme**, a kind of argument that stimulates the listener's cognitive activity so that the listener feels he or she arrived fairly independently at the conclusion. Thus the speaker should build arguments within the conceptual system of receivers to create a sense of "persuading oneself." Persuasion is usually most effective, Aristotle explained, when listeners feel they reached a conclusion themselves (i.e., self-persuasion).

Whereas the *eide topoi* are material topics because they concern specific matter (e.g., beliefs, attitudes, values) that can be developed into arguments,

forensic speaking Courtroom oratory

deliberative speaking Political oratory

epideictic oratory Commemorative speaking

topoi Lines of argument

koinoi topoi Formal topics in that they represent forms or ways of presenting materials for arguments

eide topoi Beliefs, values, and attitudes held by listeners that may be stated in propositional form and used for major premises in arguments

ethymeme A kind of argument that stimulates the listener's cognitive activity so the listener feels he or she arrived fairly independently at the conclusion

the *koinoi topoi* are formal topics in that they represent forms or ways of presenting materials for arguments. Aristotle provided twenty-eight of these in the *Rhetoric.* These forms are important for the speaker because listeners tend to understand and respond accordingly when materials are placed in these forms. In other words, the *koinoi topoi* are molds into which arguments are cast. Some examples are an effect is produced by a cause, parts are related to the whole, the concept of opposites, some things are related but do not cause each other, and some things are incentives, others deterrents. These are forms that can be applied to a variety of materials.

The *eide* and *koinoi topoi* need to be considered along with three universal arguments that occur with such regularity that listeners usually want them answered especially in deliberative rhetoric. They are (1) fact past and future (what has happened in the past and what does this suggest about the future), (2) possibility–impossibility (what is the likelihood of future facts happening), and (3) degree (how good or bad is each fact). By considering how listeners would answer the three universals (this is the process of audience analysis), the speaker is able to formulate *eide topoi,* the major premises for arguments, and decide which *koinoi topoi* can be used as forms for the arguments.

This brief account of some of Aristotle's ideas on invention illustrates that he developed a system of analysis for persuasion designed to assist the orator in discovering the available means of persuasion. Many other early writers also conceptualized invention. However, Aristotle, along with Cicero's later renditions, were the most sophisticated and influential.

A related part of Aristotle's rhetorical theory was his conception of the three forms of proof in persuasion: **logos**, **pathos**, and **ethos**. *Logos* has been termed *logical proof* but is more clearly thought of as proof resulting from the speaker building arguments, especially enthymemes, within the predispositional fields of the listeners. That is, arguments seem logical because some of their premises are beliefs, attitudes, and values held by the listeners. That is the purpose of using *eide topoi* as major premises for our arguments.

Pathos at times has been interpreted as emotional appeals. However, Aristotle meant a little more than that. He said *pathos* involved causing listeners to experience emotions that reinforce the object of persuasion. Aristotle went to great lengths explaining what causes people to feel various emotions. Audience analysis is a crucial part of this type of proof because it involves understanding the listeners to determine what emotions should be aroused and how to increase the probability of persuasion.

Ethos as a form of proof refers to the way listeners perceive the speaker. *Ethos* can be a very potent form of proof if the speaker is perceived favorably on what Aristotle said are the three components of *ethos*: character, competence, and goodwill. Listeners are more easily persuaded when they believe the speaker has good character (often this means similar to their own character), has expert knowledge of the speech subject, and has goodwill toward listeners

logos Proof resulting from the speaker building arguments within the predispositional fields of the listeners

pathos Causes listeners to experience emotions that reinforce the object of persuasion

ethos Character, competence, and goodwill

by being sincerely concerned for their well-being. In contemporary communication theory, as you shall see later in this book, especially Chapter 6, *ethos* is discussed as "source credibility" and is considered of primary importance in persuasion. In fact, most of Aristotle's ideas about persuasion have survived the many centuries and to this day affect how we think about persuasion.

Although these ideas about invention were formulated over two thousand years ago in ancient Greece and Rome, an important part of the invention process did not actually get clarified until 1828, when an Anglican bishop, Richard Whately, published a treatise on argumentation. Whately noted in discovering arguments the direction one looks depends on what the persuader is attempting to accomplish and what the expectations are for the persuasive goal. Persuaders in different situations have different obligations, and those obligations exert a powerful influence on invention.

Whately explained that the arguments one creates depends on whether the persuader has the **burden of proof** or the **benefit of presumption**. An initial step in preparing arguments is to realize which of these states applies to your speech. For instance, the burden of proof is always on the person who would change the status quo. The status quo is assumed to be adequate unless shown otherwise. Thus, the status quo always has the benefit of presumption. In court the benefit of presumption is with the accused; the person is presumed innocent until proven guilty. The burden of proof is with the prosecution who must prove guilt. There is a very real difference in having to prove you are innocent as compared to claiming you were not proven guilty. For a deliberative issue such as adopting a nationalized health-care system, the burden of proof is on the person who advocates such a system. The rhetorical obligation would be to show that the status quo, our current health-care system, is inadequate, is fatally flawed, and needs to be changed to a system that corrects the problems and results in significant benefits with reasonable costs. Once this type of analysis is accomplished, a rather clear direction is provided for the kinds of arguments that need to be invented. In essence the burden of proof and the benefit of presumption guide the invention process. Whately's ideas had a great impact on rhetorical theory throughout the nineteenth century, and that influence continues today, nearly two centuries later.

DISPOSITIO/ARRANGEMENT

The second canon of oratory is *dispositio* or arrangement. The focus here was on taking the arguments from the invention phase and arranging and organizing them to form a case to be presented to listeners. Audience analysis also was a crucial part of this process. On the basis of the concerns of the listeners, what materials should be placed first and last, which should be amplified, and which should be de-emphasized? Early writers gave a good deal of attention to the parts of an oration. There was considerable variation in what was claimed to be

burden of proof
Obligation to show status quo should be changed.

benefit of presumption
Assumption that the status quo is adequate.

the number of necessary parts to an oration. Cicero, in his book *De Inventione,* discussed a typical six-part arrangement for a Roman oration: exordium (getting attention by using a device such as a story); **narratio** (a general overview of one's case); **partitio** (an announcement of the main points or headings of the case to be discussed); **confirmatio** (arguments that confirm and support the case); **refutatio** (arguments that refute the arguments against your case); and **peroratio** (the per oration, which typically presented a summary of the case, a conclusion based on the arguments, and a final appeal, which could take a number of forms, such as a plea, a challenge, or a story).

The teachings on *dispositio* have not changed much over the centuries. Today the parts of a speech are termed *introduction, body,* and *conclusion,* which incorporates each of the parts identified by Cicero. For instance, the introduction often includes an *exordium, narratio,* and *partitio.* The body includes the *confirmatio* and *refutatio,* whereas the conclusion in today's speech performs the functions of the *peroratio.*

ELOCUTIO/STYLE

The third canon of oratory is *elocutio,* or style. This canon was also written on extensively, and students spent a good deal of time developing the art of language style. On a general level, three levels of style were taught: plain, middle, and grand. As you might suppose, one's level of education and class influenced how the styles were identified, defined, and evaluated. The plain style emphasized simple expressions, limited use of sophisticated vocabulary, and straightforward explanations. The other styles varied accordingly in terms of more complex expressions, more sophisticated vocabulary, and more abstract and complex explanation, along with more flowery and ornate language. Training emphasized grammatical accuracy, what was considered correct and incorrect usage, and rhythm, which involved selecting language where sounds harmonized, where words seemed to go together such as alliterations, where the last sounds of words do not clash with the first sounds of other words, and on choosing words that are appropriate for the occasion.

Literary figures of speech were taught. For instance books on rhetorical style discussed dozens of figures of speech such as antithesis, maxim, definition, hyperbole, and allegory and also figures of thought, such as understatement, division, simile, comparison, and conciseness. Students were given examples of each for study, composed speeches that utilized the figures, and focused on various applications. Students typically spent a good deal of time practicing the use of metaphors, tropes, language vividness, and word choice, along with Aristotle's ideas on energia or energy in language. Another major element in studying style was the extensive use of what were called "commonplaces." These were cleverly worded ideas, pithy sayings, and memorable and unique wordings of ideas that could be worked into one's oration. Some

exordium Getting attention by using a device such as a story

narratio A general overview of one's case

partitio An announcement of the main points or headings of the case to be discussed

confirmatio Arguments that confirm and support the case

refutatio Arguments that refute the arguments against your case

peroratio A summary of the case, a conclusion based on the arguments, and a final appeal

energia Energy in language

writers and teachers emphasized fairly large numbers of commonplaces because of their believed usefulness.

The study of style often was linked to the three basic functions of discourse identified by Cicero: to inform, to please (or entertain), and to persuade. Thus, word choice is to be guided by the speech purpose. Language that is meant more to inform, for instance, could be a poor choice when the speech purpose is to please or entertain.

PRONUNTIATIO/DELIVERY

The fourth canon of oratory is delivery or *pronuntiatio*. Delivery received considerably less attention than invention, arrangement, and style in ancient Greek and Roman rhetorical theory. As we shall see shortly, the canon of delivery was developed extensively and emphasized in more modern times. The Greeks and Romans instructed students to deliver orations with a graceful vocal style. They were told to regulate voice and gestures to produce pleasing tones and movements by varying rate, volume, and pitch and by using gestures that were not overly dramatic or too subdued. The great Greek orator Demosthenes (ca. 385–322) was held as an ideal. Born with a weak voice, he was said to have developed his vocal abilities by practicing his speeches with pebbles in his mouth, speaking into the roar of the surf on a beach. This developed power in his voice and gave him the ability to control vocal qualities of tone, rate, volume, and pitch.

It was not until the eighteenth century, however, that the canon of delivery was developed in great detail. In England, writers on rhetoric such as Thomas Sheridan recognized an increased need for well-spoken English in the pulpit, parliament, and the bar. It was noted that although the vocal effectiveness of Demosthenes was greatly admired by the ancients, they gave very little attention to the analysis of delivery. The "elocutionists," as they came to be known, corrected this neglect by going into great detail in analyzing the human voice and gestures. For instance, many ideas were developed for improving vocal control. If a person had a rate of speech that was too fast, they were directed to read a passage from a book or speech with a much slower rate than required. Thus, a greatly exaggerated methodical tone is established firmly in one's mind as to what represents "too slow," and then the rate gradually increased until it falls naturally between "too fast" and "too slow."

Bodily movements also were subjected to extremely detailed analysis. Gilbert Austin published a treatise in 1806 on bodily movement that was influential for an extensive period of time in Europe and America. Austin went into great detail with descriptions and drawings of the positions of the feet and lower limbs, the head, the eyes, shoulders, and hands for expressing numerous emotions and ideas. Systems of notation were developed to systematize delivery and aid in having students express themselves in particular ways. Unfortunately, at times this led to students appearing mechanical in their delivery, and this produced a reaction opposing the elocutionary movement. This eventually resulted in other approaches to delivery that appeared more spontaneous, such as "conversational delivery" and "think the thought" (rather than follow the notation). We should note that this detailed analysis of bodily movements represents the beginning of what is known today as the study of nonverbal communication. We will examine this area of the communication field in Chapter 8.

MEMORIA/MEMORY

Although delivery was emphasized much more in modern times than long ago, the fifth canon, *memoria,* or memory, experienced exactly the opposite pattern of emphasis. The ancient Greeks and Romans gave considerable attention to memory as part of rhetorical training. Modern and contemporary rhetorics have almost completely ignored memoria. The ancients viewed memory as an essential part of the oratorical process where once a speech was written it needed to be committed to memory and then delivered.

The way students were taught to memorize involved a system based on associating the material to be memorized with vivid mental images. A principle that was discovered in these ancient times was that unusual, absurd, ridiculous images were particularly memorable, and what was associated with such images was easily recalled. Contemporary self-help books and courses on memory enhancement are all based on this idea. For instance, on remembering the names of people you meet, you might be instructed, "Let us say you are introduced to a Mr. Pendergrass who happens to have a beard. Think of him with grass growing out of his face instead of a beard, and a pen clipped to the grass on his chin." At a later date, then, you would remember his name because seeing him would stimulate the ridiculous image just described and the two prominent parts of the image, pen in the grass, would remind you of his name, which you would reassemble from the image as Pendergrass.

A common method for having students in ancient Greece or Rome memorize a speech was to have them associate the material in the speech with images of things in different rooms of their house. The entrance foyer might be used for the first part of the speech, the exordium. For example, a speech that advocates the need for more police control in dangerous parts of the city might begin with a story of a crime victim in that part of the city. Images of key parts of the story (a young man, a knife, a robbery, a stabbing) might be associated with one or more objects in the foyer. The young man could be visualized lying on the welcome mat, a knife seen as hanging on the clothes tree, the robber hiding behind a chair, and so on. Then the next part of the speech would move the imaging to another room in the house. Perhaps the next room in the house is the dining room. This is then where the images for the *narratio* or overview of the case would be associated with different things in the room. Each of the

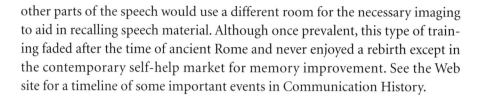

other parts of the speech would use a different room for the necessary imaging to aid in recalling speech material. Although once prevalent, this type of training faded after the time of ancient Rome and never enjoyed a rebirth except in the contemporary self-help market for memory improvement. See the Web site for a timeline of some important events in Communication History.

DESCRIPTIVE MODELS OF COMMUNICATION

In reading this book, it will become clear that there is no single comprehensive theory of the domain called communication. Not only is there no overall theory of communication, but there is also little agreement as to what should and should not be considered a communication theory. What we do have are numerous theories about the communication process. There are, for example, theories about how people persuade one another, the stages of relationship development, the apprehension that people experience when engaged in communication, organizational leadership, group communication and problem solving, and violence in the media. This book will introduce you to many of these theories, which might be thought of as "partial theories" of communication because they deal with parts of a whole.

Although there are no comprehensive theories of communication to provide us with an overall view of the communication process, there are several descriptive models of communication that permit at least a "peek" at the overall process. The descriptive models that follow were created during the modern era, roughly the middle of the twentieth century, to conceptualize the communication process. These models represent one development in a long line of developments communication scholars have advanced for understanding communication. The major difference between a descriptive model and a theory is that a theory provides not only a description of the area of interest but also an explanation for what occurs. This allows prediction about what will happen if certain conditions are created. Descriptive models do not provide an explanation or predictions. Instead, descriptive models identify relevant components of the process and attempt to describe how they operate. Often, the model only identifies the relevant parts. Despite the fact that they are extremely limited in what they tell us about communication, several models are worth examining because they help us begin thinking critically about communication, which is a necessary early step in theory building.

The Schramm Model of Communication

Wilbur Schramm has been called by many the founder of the contemporary discipline of communication (Chaffee & Rogers, 1997). In 1954, Wilbur Schramm created one of the first models of the communication process. It is a nonlinear model, and it is diagrammed in Figure 3.1.

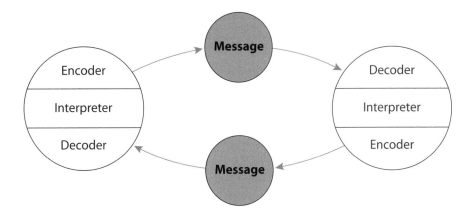

Figure 3.1

The Schramm model.

Schramm's key point in this model of communication is the concept that we as communicators act as *both* source and receiver, encoder and decoder, in a given communication interaction. **Encoding** is defined as the process of taking an already conceived idea and getting it ready for transmission. **Decoding**, on the other hand, is the process of taking the stimuli that have been received and giving those stimuli meaning through your own individual interpretation and perception. In human communication transactions, the stimuli are signs and symbols.

Employing Schramm's model of communication, Person A encodes and transmits a message to Person B, who then decodes it, interprets its signs, symbols, and meanings, and encodes another message as a result of Person A's initial transmission. Person A then acts as the receiver and decoder, and the entire system repeats itself. The message from Person B to Person A we call feedback. Feedback is included in the Schramm model of communication because we, as communicators, act simultaneously as both source and receiver. His model depicts the concept of communication as a process more accurately than some earlier models. The inclusion of feedback helps illustrate this process of communication. As we suggested earlier, feedback is an essential component in the communication process because, as he stated over a half century ago, "It tells us how our messages are being interpreted" (Schramm, 1954, p. 9).

We cannot underestimate the contribution of Schramm's model to our understanding of communication. However, although the first to introduce several new elements concerning communication (e.g., encoding, decoding, feedback), it might be considered too limited for us to fully understand human communication as a *process*. Although it identifies many key variables, several were omitted. The noise element, for example, is missing. Further, Schramm's model does not inform us about the channel of communication.

encoding   The process of taking an idea and getting it ready for transmission

decoding   The process of giving meaning to a message that has been received

Berlo's SMCR Model of Communication

David Berlo was another early leader of the social science orientation in communication theory. His groundbreaking book, *The Process of Communication* (1960), introduced his model of the communication process. Berlo's Model of Communication goes into greater depth than previous models on certain key components. The concepts of source and receiver are expanded, and his treatment and representation of the channels of communication are different from that of other communication models. See Figure 3.2 for Berlo's Source-Message-Channel-Receiver (SMCR) model of communication.

The SMCR model examines four of the key variables that make up many of the models of communication: source, message, channel, and receiver. The unique way Berlo defined channels of communication should be noted here. Berlo was the first researcher to treat the five senses as channels of communication. In addition, he expanded greatly on the concepts of source and receiver. Under the source dimension, Berlo listed such components as communication skills, attitudes, knowledge, social system, and culture. These same components are part of the receiver's profile. They can either create noise in the system or increase accuracy and understanding in the communication encounter, depending on the individuals and the context at hand. However, noise is not

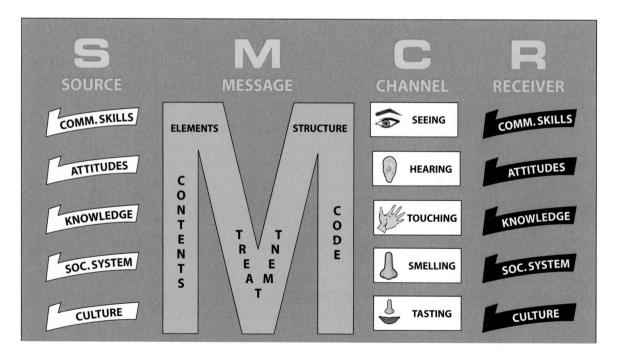

Figure 3.2

Berlo's SMCR model of the ingredients in communication.

explicitly labeled in this model, and feedback is also absent. Because Berlo's book stresses that communication should be viewed as a process, the omission of feedback is especially noteworthy. At a minimum, the model should have included a feedback loop (an arrow going from receiver back to source). This omission was later corrected when he explicitly incorporated feedback into the communication process (Berlo, 1977).

The McCroskey Model of Communication

James C. McCroskey is recognized as one of the most prolific scholars in contemporary communication theory. Early in his career, he offered his own unique model of communication. The McCroskey model (1968) expanded the concept of noise to include the encoding and decoding process in the source and receiver, in the primary channel, and in the feedback channel. The McCroskey model also notes that noise may be evident prior to the communication act and after the communication act. This concept is often referred to as intrapersonal noise. The McCroskey Model of Communication is represented in Figure 3.3.

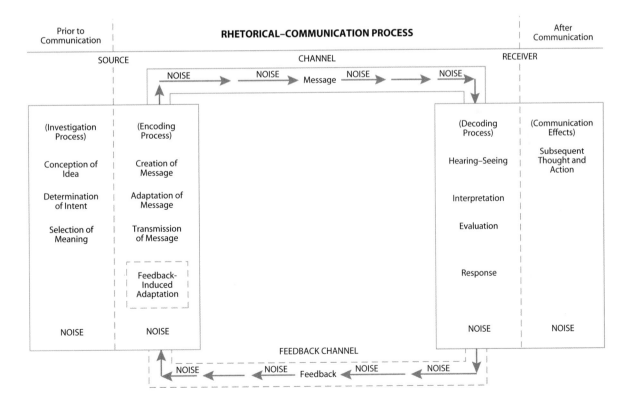

Figure 3.3

The McCroskey model.

The McCroskey model shows the intentional aspect of human communication and includes the terms *feedback* and *feedback-induced adaptation.* Feedback-induced adaptation means that a source can adapt to a receiver's feedback by altering his or her subsequent messages and responses. In comparison to earlier models, the McCroskey model represents a more complete model of the communication process.

The Ruesch and Bateson Model of Communication

The Ruesch and Bateson Model of Communication set forth in 1951 is concerned less with the traditional components of the communication process (source, channel, message, and receiver) than with four specific communication functions: evaluating, sending, channeling, and receiving. The Ruesch and Bateson Model of Communication is found in Figure 3.4.

The receiver can evaluate the source in two ways: through the content of the message and nonverbally through vocal cues, facial expression, physical distance, and body motion and movement. The source can evaluate the receiver in the same manner. In human communication, this evaluating as set forth in the Ruesch and Bateson model closely corresponds to the concept of feedback-induced adaptation mentioned in the McCroskey model. In public speaking and mass communication contexts, a source can also evaluate a receiver or receivers. This is usually accomplished prior to the delivery of the message by

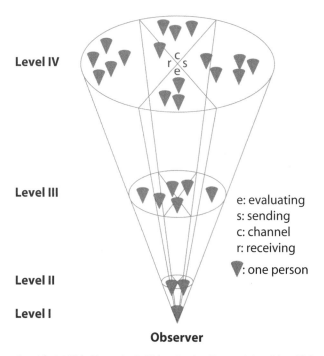

Figure 3.4

The Ruesch and Bateson model.

the technique of audience analysis. Through audience analysis, the source attempts to find out the feelings, attitudes, beliefs, and values of the group she or he will be addressing.

> **audience analysis** An attempt to find out the feelings, attitudes, beliefs, and values of the group being addressed

Sending is the act of transmitting a message to a receiver or group of receivers. Channeling is the selection of an appropriate channel or channels through which to transmit your message. Receiving is the act of obtaining and decoding messages.

The process of communication for Ruesch and Bateson occurs at the same time at four different levels of analysis. Level 1 represents the intrapersonal level, or communication within the individual. Level 2 represents the interpersonal level, or communication between two people. Level 3 is the group interaction level between many people, and Level 4 is the cultural level, which joins large groups of people.

One of the most important functions of the Ruesch and Bateson model is that it shows overlapping fields of experience. Any one person can, and usually does, operate on more than one level of communication at any one time. Think of the classroom situation. You are sitting in class, and you are thinking to yourself about some material just described by the instructor. This is an example of Level 1 in the model. Something about that material puzzles you, so you turn to your classmate on the left and ask her about it. Level 2 in the model is representative of this type of interpersonal communication. Finally, the entire class tries to discuss the concept, and there is great interaction between the class members. This is represented by Level 3 in the model, the group interaction level. Thus, in this example, the communication process was represented by three different levels of analysis.

The Westley-MacLean Model of Communication

The Westley-MacLean model of communication (1957) was designed specifically to explain the process of communication in a mediated or mass communication context. However, the model of communication designed by Westley and MacLean can also be adapted to explain communication in other contexts as well. The model is diagrammed in Figure 3.5.

A key concept that the Westley-MacLean model includes is the intermediary in the communication process. Between the original source of the communication (A) and the ultimate receiver of the communication (B), there is often another person or persons (C), who might intervene or intrude on the communication process and encode the original source's communication for the receiver. The intervening person or persons in this process are referred to as a gatekeeper. An example of a gatekeeper in the mass media is the editor of a newspaper, magazine, news program, Web page, or even blog, who intervenes between the reporter/writer and the ultimate audience. The editor may alter the content in some manner by intensifying certain parts or by deleting other

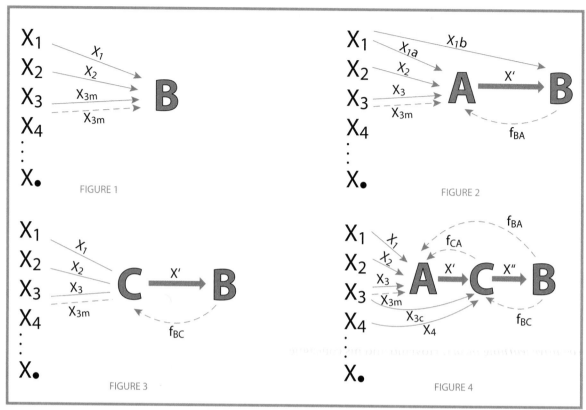

Figure 3.5

The Westley-MacLean model.

parts. The editor thus fulfills the role of the gatekeeper or "filter" between the reporter/writer and the ultimate receivers of the story. Even the Web site *YouTube* employs gatekeepers to ensure that videos on their Web site do not violate copyright laws. Examples of gatekeepers in interpersonal contexts include the neighborhood gossip who relays the news of the day to a friend or the person we ask to relay bad news to a third party.

The variable of feedback in the Westley-MacLean model is extremely important. There is a feedback channel not only between the ultimate receivers (B) and the gatekeeper (C), but also between the gatekeeper (C) and the source (A), as well as between the receivers (B) and the source (A).

An important concept becomes apparent in the model. Between the ultimate receiver of communication and the objects of orientation in one's sensory field, a constant process of filtering and abstraction occurs. Communication is always being shaped and altered due to individuals' own perceptions of reality; their attitudes, beliefs, and values; and their past experiences and biases. We all see and interpret things differently. There could be a vast difference between the actual object of orientation and the ultimate receiver's interpretation, perception, and decoding of a message about that object.

MAJOR APPROACHES IN THE DEVELOPMENT OF CONTEMPORARY COMMUNICATION THEORY

Shortly after World War II, Carl Hovland, Irving Janis, and Harold Kelley developed a research program to investigate factors associated with attitude change and persuasion. This systematic research continued for more than a decade. The major findings were summarized in their text, *Communication and Persuasion* (1953). Because the bulk of the experimental work was conducted at Yale University, the research is commonly referred to as the Yale communication research program.

The Yale Studies on Communication

The Yale approach to persuasion and communication was largely based on *cognitive learning theory.* Hovland and his colleagues believed that individuals who are exposed to persuasive messages may change their attitudes through a type of learning process. The bulk of the Yale studies is classified into four major headings, each examining one major component in the communication process.

The first component examined the role of the *source* in communication. The researchers believed that the potential success of a persuasive effort depended on the credibility of the source (a concept similar to Aristotle's *ethos*). The Yale studies examined a communicator's perceived expertise and trustworthiness (credibility) as factors that influence the acceptance of a persuasive message. The research suggested that if we view a communicator to be highly expert and trustworthy, there is a greater likelihood we will accept his or her positions. (The Yale studies identified several factors that influence the relationship between source credibility and persuasion; see Chapters 6 and 7 for more detail.)

The second component, the *content* of the message, describes efforts to identify the primary variables that influence attitude change and persuasion. The researchers sought to identify certain types of motivation appeals that stimulate a receiver's emotions. They found that emotional appeals could assist in the change of attitudes. In particular, the influence of fear-arousing messages was studied.

The Yale studies examined the *organization* of persuasive messages in the third component of the research. Some of this research will be examined in Chapter 6. Hovland and his colleagues felt that the order of persuasive appeals could influence attitude change and persuasion. Other factors, such as implicitly or explicitly stating a conclusion, the presentation of one side versus two sides of an issue, and the ordering of arguments (i.e., primacy-recency, or placing the strongest argument first or last), could influence persuasion.

The nature of the *receiver* and audience predispositions/characteristics comprised the fourth component. The Yale studies examined the influence of group membership or group affiliation as factors in the resistance to a persuasive message. Individual personality factors associated with receivers' susceptibility to persuasion were also considered. Level of ego-involvement and initial attitudes toward a message were investigated. The relationships between intelligence, self-esteem, aggressiveness, and social withdrawal were explored to determine their influence on persuasion. Changes in a person's overt verbal behavior in response to persuasive messages were also studied. Do individuals willingly and voluntarily express or verbalize a newly acquired opinion or attitude? How long does a person retain the newly acquired attitude?

CONTRIBUTIONS

The Yale studies had a major impact on the development and advancement of communication theory. As Delia (1987) stated, "Hovland's emphasis on attitude change through communication . . . served to bring these topics to center stage for communication researchers" (p. 64). The Yale studies stimulated almost two decades of research on attitude change and persuasion, much of it conducted by contemporary communication researchers such as Gerald R. Miller, James C. McCroskey, John W. Bowers, and their colleagues.

Many scholars now credit the Yale studies with moving the communication discipline into the social scientific approach (McGuire, 1996; Sypher, Davenport-Sypher & Haas, 1988). Importing social psychological research methods into the communication discipline helped bring other constructs such as interpersonal attraction, leadership, and group decision making to the attention of communication theorists and researchers. Delia stated, "By 1970, American communication research was utterly dominated by social psychological approaches" (1987, p. 65).

Hovland and his colleagues acknowledged that the topics of their concern closely paralleled Harold D. Lasswell's formula of who (the source) says what (the message) to whom (the receiver) with what effect (the consequence) (Smith, Lasswell & Casey, 1946). This focus led to the development of Berlo's frequently cited model of the communication process. The Yale communication research program has been said to have *heuristic value* because it stimulated numerous research studies on the influence of communication in persuasion.

LIMITATIONS

Although the Yale approach to communication contributed greatly to the development of communication theory, critics argue that the program suffered from several limitations. Some communication scholars have argued that the Yale researchers were incorrect in their assumption that learning and attitude change are related. The approach has also been classified as **atheoretical**— lacking a theoretical framework to draw on. Critics challenge the Yale studies' reliance on cognitive learning theory to provide explanations of *why* changes in attitudes lead to changes in behavior (Smith, 1982).

atheoretical   Lacking a theoretical foundation

Communication theorists who advocate a rules approach to understanding communication also challenge the findings of the Yale studies with the very paradigm on which they were based. One characteristic of the Yale approach was its reliance on the law-governed, causal model of inquiry. The majority of Yale results were obtained from experimental research conducted under controlled conditions (see Appendix A). Communication rules theorists such as Smith argue that the findings are limited in that they "focus on what messages 'do to' people rather than what people 'do with' messages" (1982, p. 236). Despite these possible limitations, the Yale approach to communication had a tremendous influence on the development of contemporary communication research.

An Information Approach to Communication

Claude Shannon (scientist at the Bell Telephone Laboratory) and Warren Weaver (professor of mathematics) published two papers jointly referred to as *The Mathematical Theory of Communication* in 1949. Their work is frequently referred to as the information theory of communication. Concepts such as channel and noise (discussed earlier) were brought to the attention of the communication discipline through **information theory**.

information theory Shannon and Weaver's effort to discover the systematic and mathematical foundations for communication

In an effort to discover the systematic and mathematical foundations for communication, Shannon and Weaver sought to identify the quickest and most efficient way to get a message from one point to another. Their goal was to discover how communication messages could be converted into electronic signals most efficiently, and how those signals could be transmitted with a minimum of error. To do this, Shannon and Weaver had to quantify the information contained in messages. They also had to determine the amount of distortion, or *noise,* in the channel used to transmit the messages (Hawes, 1975). According to the theory, transmission of the message involved sending information through electronic signals. A word of caution: "Information," in the information theory sense of the word, should not be confused with "information" as we commonly understand it. Conventionally, information is thought of as what we know; we think of information in terms of meaning. However, information theorists view information quite differently. According to Shannon and Weaver, information is defined as "a measure of one's freedom of choice when one selects a message" (p. 9). Hawes suggested that information "refers not to the content contained in a message but to all possible messages that could be transmitted" (1975, p. 87).

uncertainty Occurs when you are unsure about something

information Refers to the degree of uncertainty present in a situation

To understand this concept of information, we must consider another concept, uncertainty. Uncertainty occurs when you are unsure about something—when you do not know exactly what will happen in a given situation. In information theory, information and uncertainty are closely related. Information refers to the degree of uncertainty present in a situation. Uncertainty also relates to the concept of predictability. When something is completely predictable, it is completely certain. Therefore, it contains very little, if any, information. For example, the letter *U* almost always follows the letter *Q* in the English language. Thus, the letter *U* is almost completely predictable in words that start with *Q*. If you were playing the television game *Wheel of Fortune*, you could easily guess that the second letter of a word beginning with a *Q* must be *U*. You would not need to spend money to buy a vowel. If another player revealed that the second letter in the word was *U*, you would know nothing more than you had previously known. You would have gained no information. One way to understand information in terms of this theory is to think of it as potential information, or as all possible knowledge that you do not yet have with regard to a subject.

A related term, *entropy,* is also important in information theory. Entropy refers to the degree of randomness, lack of organization, or disorder in a situation. A situation that is highly random, or unpredictable, is characterized as highly entropic. Thus, the more entropy in a system, the less predictability. The less predictability, the greater the potential information. Because you need more messages to predict the outcome of a complex situation than a simple one, the complex situation is said to contain more information.

bit A measure of the actual amount of information in a message

Information theory introduced a concept to our vocabulary, which is heard with great frequency today—bit. A bit is a measure of the actual amount of information in a message. Bit comes from the condensation of the term *binary digit*. In the binary system, there are only two digits, 0 and 1. Computers make use of the binary code. Every piece of "information" that a computer receives or transmits is reduced to a pattern of electrical impulses like those controlled by a light switch. On is represented by a 1, and off is represented by a 0. The American Standard Code for Information Interchange (ASCII) has converted all the letters of the alphabet, both upper- and lowercase, and all the numerals from 0 through 9 into combinations of zeros and ones.

redundancy Repetition; something that adds little, if any, information to a message

Redundancy is another concept that has emerged from the information theory to communication. Redundancy is the opposite of information. Something that is redundant adds little, if any, information to a message. Redundancy is important because it helps combat *noise* in a communication system. If a professor is asked to repeat something in class because a student was daydreaming, the statement that is repeated does not add any information for those students who heard it the first time. The repeated message is totally redundant. However, the message may serve as a reinforcement. The repetition provides confirmation that the message was recorded accurately. Redundancy adds little to the amount of information transmitted but a great deal to reinforcing messages sent. Some research indicates that reinforcement is related to attitude change and persuasion (see Chapter 6). This may help explain why we hear commercials repeated with such frequency in the media.

The language of information theory is symbolic, and its symbols are those of mathematics (Hawes, 1975). Information theory concepts do much to challenge our conventional understanding of the concept of information. Information theory has, however, contributed to the clarification of certain concepts such as noise, redundancy, and entropy. These concepts are inherently part of the communication process. Indeed, the information theory concepts have been applied to many other information-related fields, including banking, airline reservations, and weather forecasting (Rogers, 1994).

Critics of the information theory approach to communication argue that the theory has limited utility when applied to human communication. One major criticism of the theory is that it does not deal with meaning, and meaning is most important in the context of *human* communication. According to information theory, a message may contain a great deal of information and still contain little meaning. The definition of communication as the stimulation of meaning in another is clearly not addressed by the information theory approach. Information theory concentrates on the transfer of electronic signals, not on the meaning generated when receivers interpret those signals. The information theory approach to communication has provided us with a rich set of concepts and propositions. These concepts are especially useful for theorizing about message transmission using computers and the electronic media. Indeed, the information theory approach still emerges as useful when our discipline examines human–machine interaction.

Berlo's Process Approach to Communication

At about the time that information theory was developed, a new group of scholars in communication emerged. David Berlo and his contemporaries were firmly rooted in speech and rhetorical studies. At the same time, they were strong advocates of adopting a behavioral science approach to studying human communication. This new generation of communication scholars developed research programs designed to explore the traditional problems of speech performance and speech training. They also studied other issues such as the process of persuasion, small-group decision making, and language.

In 1960, David Berlo published *The Process of Communication*. Communication definitions that describe communication as the process of exchanging symbols or a process in which many interrelated variables influence each other reflect Berlo's contribution. His process approach to communication theory argues that events and relationships are dynamic, continuous, and constantly changing. All the factors involved in a process are in continuous interaction with each other; all the variables affect and influence each other. An example from biology illustrates the concept. The digestive process is a complex procedure involving many variables that work together to break down food into chemicals, nutrients, and wastes. Berlo argued that communication also was best conceived as a process in which variables act on each other concurrently to influence the direction, flow, and outcome of an interaction. Communication cannot be isolated or separated from other events, either internal or external.

The concept of process has been used by communication theorists in several ways. When asked to define communication, many scholars claim that it is not definable because it is a *process.* That is, attempts to define communication would render it static, whereas communication is dynamic. In this context, communication is referred to as a process without a distinct beginning, end, or set of boundaries. This view assumes that everything is related to everything else (similar to the systems approach to communication, see Chapter 4). Process has also been viewed as a "complex organization of an individual or group of individuals" (Berlo, 1977, p. 13). This approach suggests that relationships should be the unit of analysis in communication. Process, therefore, is seen as the "organization of relationships." Others view process as a change over time. Process is also seen as an activity, as in information *processing.* Berlo argued, "Communication processes are subsets of information processes in that they consist of symbolic informational activity" (1977, p. 23).

Imagine sitting in your 11:00 A.M. class. The instructor is lecturing and asking a series of questions of the class members. What are some of the variables that are influencing the flow, direction, and outcome of this interaction? We can use Berlo's process approach to examine some of them. How dynamic and interesting is the professor when she delivers the lecture? What is her mood that morning? What is the topic of the lecture? How interested are you and the other class members in the topic? How technical or abstract is the material? How much jargon is used in conveying the information? How prepared is the class to respond to the questions posed by the instructor? Does one class member dominate the interaction? What about the time of day? Are you hungry and thinking about lunch? Are you tired because you stayed up late the previous night? Are you thinking about the upcoming semester break? Are you assessing and processing the dispute you had with your roommate the night before? What is the temperature of the classroom? Is this a course which was required, or is it an elective?

These are a few of the factors that affect the process of communication in the classroom. If we spent a great deal of time and effort, we probably could not list all the variables that comprise the communication process in that context. Each of these factors is important in its own right, and each influences the others. If you are tired and hungry, then you may miss some of the concepts presented. Obviously, the process of communication is quite complex. We can list the individual ingredients, but we must not forget that it is the simultaneous *interaction* of these variables that makes up the process of communication.

Style-Specific or Special Communication Theories

Communication theorist Ernest Bormann has offered a useful distinction in the way in which we can classify communication theory. Bormann (1980) argued that scholars have confused theories that deal with specific communication practices of particular groups with more general propositions accounting for broad classes of events covering many groups. Bormann labeled the former **style-specific**, or *special,* communication theories and the latter **general theories** of communication. These two kinds of theories represent different kinds of knowledge and serve different functions.

Special theories concern communication styles or practices of given rhetorical communities. A rhetorical community is a "group of people who participate in a rhetorical style and share common rhetorical visions from within the perspective of that style" (Bormann, 1980, p. 61). **Rhetorical communities** are groups of people engaged in interaction in which the participants understand the rules, customs, and conventions of "appropriate" or "correct" communication. Individuals in rhetorical communities understand the rules, customs, and practices regarding what is deemed "appropriate" communication.

These special theories guide the actual practice of communication within the group according to a predetermined, normative style. Style-specific or special communication theories are bound by time and space. That is, the theory is primarily useful to particular groups of people in a particular time frame. Several style-specific communication theories will be noted here. Earlier in this chapter we discussed the canon of rhetoric called *pronuntiatio,* or delivery. During the eighteenth century, this method of delivering speeches, involving prescribed ways of speaking, dressing, and gesturing, developed and became known as the elocution movement. As we stated earlier, during the elocution period, public communication or public speaking was extremely stylized, rigid, and formal by today's standards. Most phrases and words have a "correct" pronunciation and a precise delivery style. If a speaker were to utter the phrase "the brilliant sun shone upon the city," the speaker would be taught the "correct" pronunciation of each of these words and the "correct" body posture and gestures used to accompany each word. Elocution can be considered one example of a style-specific or special communication theory.

Try to imagine how strange it would seem to us today if our politicians or public speakers communicated under the rubric of elocution theory. Every phrase and manner of delivery would be "scripted" for the speaker. Today, this style of public address would appear exceedingly rigid and unnatural at best.

style-specific Theories that deal with specific communication practices of particular groups

general theories General propositions accounting for broad classes of events covering many groups

rhetorical communities Groups of people who share a rhetorical vision and style

Observing a public speaker delivering a message under the stylized practices of elocution theory would conjure images of the robotlike figures one observes in amusement parks like Disney World. The usefulness of any style-specific theory diminishes considerably if you observe it in a different time frame or if it is used by a different group of people.

Another special communication theory relates to the authentic relationship style of interpersonal communication popular in the 1960s. This theory advocates that communicators create social awareness and growth and establish authentic and meaningful relationships with each other. Communicators are urged to create a warm, trusting communication climate. To do so, they must engage in such behaviors as risk taking, self-disclosure, and openness. People are encouraged to respond to another's messages with emotion. Sensitivity groups and encounter sessions were created to teach people how to communicate in this style, just as elocution classes were created to teach people how to communicate in that style.

Style-specific theories are also culture bound. This means that the style is appropriate primarily for the given culture or group that practices it. To extend the theory beyond that culture might be inappropriate and even counterproductive. For example, our Western theories of argumentation are style specific and primarily relevant to our Western culture. Western theories of argumentation suggest that opinions of others on controversial issues should be verbally attacked with data, warrants, and claims if we disagree with them. These theories explain how to construct arguments and counterarguments during conflict situations. Courses dealing with these theories are offered at many colleges, often under the title "Argumentation" or "Argument and Advocacy: Theory and Practice." The Theory of Independent-Mindedness (see Chapter 11) would be considered a style-specific theory of communication, as it was developed and considered bound primarily by Western culture.

The argumentative approach to social conflict is highly culture bound and Western in cultural orientation. That is, the norms and rules of other cultures, specifically Eastern cultures, do not endorse or advocate an attack-and-defend orientation for managing conflict. In Eastern cultures, a verbal attack on another person's position on an issue, delivered publicly, might be considered a violation of social etiquette. Thus, special communication theories such as theories of argument apply only within a particular culture.

GENERAL THEORIES OF COMMUNICATION

According to Bormann (1980), general theories are universal explanations that account for broad classes of events. General theories are similar to the theories developed in the natural and physical sciences. General theories attempt to provide accounts of human communication behavior based on generalizable regularities. General theories describe features or aspects of communication common to many different rhetorical communities. Because general theories are not culture bound, the propositions that undergird these theories may be applied to many different people and cultures. That is, a general theory has as much usefulness in predicting and/or explaining the communication behavior of an American as it does an Australian, or a Japanese person. As general theories are not time bound, the propositions that undergird the theory might be as true today, or fifty years from now, as they were fifty or one hundred years ago.

Cognitive Dissonance

Festinger's (1957) theory of cognitive dissonance (a greater treatment of this theory is presented in Chapter 6) has been identified as a general theory that developed from the cognitive consistency approach to persuasion. Cognitive dissonance theory suggests that individuals who hold two contradictory ideas or ideas contradicted by their behaviors (for example, saying, "Smoking is unhealthy," and then lighting up a cigarette) will experience psychological discomfort called dissonance. This discomfort motivates people to change their attitudes, their behaviors, or both. Cognitive dissonance reflects an attempt by scientists to construct a general theory. It suggests that, like gravity, feelings of cognitive dissonance may be experienced by many people at many different times across human history. Bormann (1980) stated, "The assumption is that the cognitive dissonance phenomenon is an unvarying human drive that can account for Julius Caesar's crossing the Rubicon as well as predict the behavior of a cigarette smoker in the future who reads of new evidence of the danger of smoking" (p. 171).

cognitive dissonance
Suggests that individuals who hold two contradictory ideas or ideas contradicted by their behaviors will experience psychological discomfort called dissonance

Symbolic Convergence

Another general theory that has been useful in applied communication research is called symbolic convergence. It deals with the general human tendency to interpret and to give meaning to signs and symbols. Convergence refers to the way people try to unite their own private symbolic "worlds" to achieve what has been described as a "meeting of the minds." When individuals communicate in such a way that their own private symbolic "worlds" begin to come together, they begin to share symbol systems. During this convergence process, people share their individual fantasies, dreams, and meanings; they begin to interpret signs and symbols in similar ways.

symbolic convergence
Deals with the general human tendency to interpret and to give meaning to signs and symbols

Some theorists believe that the process of symbolic convergence occurs when individuals share group fantasies (Bormann, 1980). This process can occur in small-group encounter sessions, in focus groups, or in an audience during the delivery of a public speech or the viewing of a television show or movie. Sylvester Stallone's iconic films *Rocky* and *Rambo* include images, symbols, dramatizations, and narratives that tend to draw audience members together into a common "symbolic world." The group fantasies that emerge create common dreams, goals, and values for the audience. Typically, this type of film depicts "underdogs" overcoming humble or difficult beginnings, fighting against the establishment and winning—thereby triumphing over the injustices of the world. As Bormann (1972) suggested, when group members share a number of fantasies over a period of time, they begin to share the same heroes and villains, and they applaud the same actions. These group fantasies make it easier for individuals to communicate with each other.

Symbolic convergence theory also suggests that people often share a particular fantasy type. This involves sharing the same story but with different characters and slightly different events. Bormann (1980) compared a fantasy type to a recurring script in the group's culture. Political parties are held together by common fantasy types. Bormann suggested that members of the Republican Party often emerge with the same fantasy type: a conception of Democrats as too liberal, fiscally irresponsible, and the creators of inflation, imbalanced budgets, and economic chaos. Democrats, on the other hand, often emerge with a fantasy type that depicts the Republicans as too conservative, swayed by big business and corporate interests, and unsympathetic to the working person and the poor. Bormann argued that symbolic convergence theory represents a general theory of communication because it transcends rhetorical communities and various communication contexts. The sharing of group fantasies is "assumed to include all human collectives in the past, now, and in the future, regardless of cultural differences and rhetorical style" (p. 54).

Burke's Theory of Dramatism

The final general theory to be discussed is Burke's rhetorical theory called dramatism. Kenneth Burke has been a major influence in the development of contemporary communication theory. His works span the literature of the humanities and social sciences, and he has been cited by scholars in the fields of philosophy, sociology, theology, psychology, and literature.

Burke (1966) recognized that human beings are symbol-making, symbol-using, and symbol-misusing animals. The ability to create and manipulate symbols is what distinguishes human beings from other animals. Humans alone, Burke argued, use symbols and are reflexive creatures. That is, human beings can communicate, and they can communicate about their communication. For example, we can deliver a presentation in our speech class and can then talk about this presentation with others. Dogs, on the other hand, can bark, but they cannot bark about the nature of barking. Burke argued that symbols influence behavior because motives are an inherent part of human communication. "Motives and language are so closely associated that by analyzing a rhetorical artifact, we can discover a rhetor's underlying motives"

(Foss, Foss, & Trapp, 1991, p. 184). The motivation for the rhetoric is synony-mous with the structure of the examples, experiences, and values comprising the rhetoric. In other words, persuading, a communicative action, fits Burke's definition of a motive. The rhetoric produced and the motive for producing it are inextricably linked. Burke is interested in how motives influence commu-nication behavior. He believes that if we understand the motives of individu-als, we are better able to understand their perceptions of reality.

Burke's notion of dramatism is at the core of his theory, a theory grounded in the symbolic nature of communication. Because most of human action is symbolic, the theory provides a means of analyzing human action. Dramatistic theory has been called a "communication theory of human behavior" (Stewart, Smith, & Denton, 1994, p. 165). A key concept in dramatistic theory is identifi-cation. Burke believes that an important goal of communication is identifica-tion. When we communicate, we try to develop a "common bond" with our audience. When we attempt to persuade an individual or group, we try to estab-lish a sense of rapport or similarity with them. Burke (1950) argued, "You per-suade a man only insofar as you can talk his language by speech, gesture, tonality, order, image, attitude, idea, identifying your ways with his" (p. 55). To create identification with an audience, several options are available to a communica-tor. You can participate in or observe the actions and behaviors of the group. For example, if you wanted to persuade the members of your college class to elect you class president, you could participate in social functions sponsored by the class. You could try to dress like the class members. Adopting and under-standing the language of the group helps foster identification. Using group expressions, if done honestly and adroitly, will increase identification. Using examples that are easily understood by the audience and emphasizing shared experiences between you and the audience also create identification. For exam-ple, in your quest for the class presidency, you may suggest that as a dormitory resident, you, too, are troubled by the lack of space, privacy, and decent meals.

Burke's dramatistic theory has been extremely useful to scholars attempt-ing to explain and predict human communication behavior. The dramatistic approach has been used to understand and explain a wide variety of commu-nication events ranging from analyzing the inherent characteristics of formal organizations (Tompkins, Fisher, Infante, & Tompkins, 1975) to assessing the rhetorical dimensions of a multiple murder and suicide (Fisher, 1974).

CONTEXTUAL APPROACHES TO COMMUNICATION

During the early development of the discipline, the focus of communication theorists was much narrower than it is today. Primary emphasis was placed on studying message effects. As Berger and Chaffee (1987) noted, the study of communication was dominated by the study of public and mass persuasion.

As the communication discipline grew in size, it also grew in scope. One-way, linear models were abandoned in favor of process models of communication. Interest in the role of communication in developing social and personal relationships grew. Alternative methodologies and paradigms for building communication theory were adopted. Research emphasis broadened to include both applied studies and attempts to build general theories. Communication scholars no longer primarily depended on other disciplines such as social psychology to create theories. With increasing frequency, communication theories were being advanced by scholars trained primarily in the communication arts and sciences.

Concomitant with this growth has been the development of contextual approaches to the study of human communication. Developing an all-encompassing, general theory that explains a wide range of communication behavior across contexts is a daunting, perhaps impossible, task. During the past four decades, communication theorists have been attempting to build theories that have greater utility when applied to specific *communication contexts.* It is our belief that this contextual approach marks the current state of theory building in our discipline. Communication associations (e.g., the National Communication Association, the International Communication Association, the Eastern Communication Association, the Central States Communication Association, the Southern States Communication Association, the Western Communication Association, as well as many others) have created interest groups and divisions for scholars interested in research and theory building in specific communication contexts.

Some scholars argue that the contextual approach to communication may encourage fragmented research. They suggest that because communication occurs in a great many different contexts, "there is the possibility for confusion and overlap in theory and research efforts" (Berger & Chaffee, 1987, p. 538). These cautions, however, are balanced by the many powerful and useful theories developed by communication scholars employing a contextual approach. The explanatory power and practical value of contextual theories indicate that the trend toward developing our knowledge of communication processes in specific contexts will continue well into the twenty-first century.

SUMMARY

This chapter has attempted to trace the history of the study of communication with two goals in mind: (1) to trace the development of the questions and problems that concern communication theorists today, and (2) to indicate the rich educational heritage in which students participate through the study of rhetoric and communication. From the earliest development of Western philosophy to contemporary research on media and advertising, rhetoric and persuasion have been a central focus of communication studies. Around 400 to 300 BC, sophists such as Gorgias and Protagoras traveled from city to city to prepare students to argue cases in the law courts and political assemblies. Plato and Aristotle developed theories of rhetoric firmly grounded in the philosophical tradition of their time, yet designed to aid those who wished to study the practical art of rhetoric. In the first century AD, Roman rhetoricians such as Cicero and Quintilian classified rhetorical topics and styles and set forth a system for educating orators that maintained its influence on universities through today. In the fourth century AD, Augustine developed a theory of rhetoric for training Christian preachers and teachers.

Various segments of the classical traditions were emphasized from the time of Augustine until the 1700s, when a philosophy of logic led some scholars to develop modern rhetorical theories and others to limit rhetoric to the study of delivery alone. Since the beginning of the twentieth century, a renewed interest in the classics has strengthened the traditional strain of rhetoric. The influence of classical rhetoric today intertwines with the study of communication, including mass communication, by social scientists. As this chapter has shown, the field called communication has a long and rich tradition as well as an adaptive and energetic modern focus. Although rhetoric and communication theories have been developed by scholars from different traditions using different methods, their complementary focus provides both breadth and depth to help scholars better understand an important phenomenon in the lives of all human beings. As a student of communication, you are participating in an ancient and honorable, yet exciting and very modern enterprise.

This chapter also functioned as an introduction to the study of human communication by presenting several early models of human communication that influenced the development of the discipline and helped shape several theories of communication. Studying communication means acquiring an understanding of familiar phenomena. This is accomplished by examining theory building. Descriptive models of communication were reviewed because they provide an overall view of the communication process. Basic components of the models were source, message, channel, receiver, noise, and feedback. Five descriptive models, which varied in how these components were depicted, were examined.

The chapter introduced you to important developments in the history of theory building in communication. The Yale Studies on Communication were instrumental in the empirical investigation of attitude change and persuasion and contributed to the communication discipline's interest in the psychology of social influence. Shannon and Weaver's information theory not only gave the discipline one of its first models of communication, but also introduced key concepts such as information, entropy, bit, and redundancy. Berlo's process approach to communication theory reinforced the notion that communication is dynamic, continuous, and constantly changing with all variables acting on each other to influence the outcome of an interaction. Bormann's distinction between style-specific (or special) and general theories of communication helps us understand which theories are designed to explain the communication practices of particular groups (i.e., style-specific theories) versus broader theories (i.e., general theories) that span time, space, and culture.

Three general theories were also introduced in this chapter. Cognitive dissonance theory has been, and still is, a popular theory that explains attitude change and persuasion. Symbolic Convergence Theory deals with the general tendency to interpret and give meaning to signs and symbols. Convergence is important for it helps individuals communicate in ways in which they attempt to share their symbolic worlds and symbol systems. Burke's Theory of Dramatism is another theory that emphasizes human symbolic activity. Because most human action is symbolic, the theory provides a means of analyzing human activity. Finally, the contextual approach to studying communication was introduced. Rather than attempting to build all-emcompassing general theories of communication, many theories you will encounter in this text have been developed to help explain and predict communication behavior in specific communication contexts (e.g., family, organizational, intercultural). The contextual approach appears to mark the current state of theory building in communication.

KEY TERMS

atheoretical
audience analysis
bit
cognitive dissonance
confirmatio
decoding
deliberative speaking
dispositio
eide topoi
elocutio
encoding
energia
enthymeme

epideictic oratory
ethos
exordium
forensic speaking
general theories
information
information theory
inventio
koinoi topoi
logos
memoria
narratio
pathos

partitio
peroratio
pronuntiatio
redundancy
refutatio
rhetoric
rhetorical communities
rhetorical pedagogy
style specific theories
symbolic convergence
topoi
uncertainty

Paradigms and Communication Theory

Theories in communication and other fields tend to cluster in families, or paradigms. Theories are grouped together when they reflect the same perspective; that is, they adopt the same assumptions about what is important and how it can best be discovered. In the past, a particular theoretical perspective would be so well developed and enjoy such widespread support that the vast majority of researchers would use that paradigm or worldview. When a sufficient amount of evidence accumulated to question the core assumptions of that paradigm, new paradigms were introduced to try to account for discrepancies. If enough evidence was found for the superiority of one model over another, a **paradigm shift** took place. One paradigm eclipsed another in adoption and support. Soon, the "new" paradigm became the dominant one. Today, several paradigms are operating simultaneously. In this chapter we will learn that some families of theories are better at explaining and others at predicting.

paradigm shift Situation in which one theoretical paradigm replaces another in popularity among a group of scientists

PARADIGMS AND COMMUNICATION THEORY

In Chapter 2 we introduced the concept of paradigms. **Paradigms** are "grand models" or sets of theoretical assumptions shared by many theories. Individuals use paradigms as guides to develop and to test questions about the phenomena they are studying. Usually scientists, including communication scientists, tend to favor one paradigm over another. When a communication scholar adopts a particular paradigm or **theoretical perspective**, that paradigm defines both the questions to be asked and often the methods of discovering answers to those questions. To a lesser although significant degree, the theoretical perspective chosen may also help define what are acceptable answers to the questions posed.

paradigms "Grand models" consisting of theoretical assumptions a group of scientists uses to guide their research

theoretical perspective By adopting a particular paradigm, the questions to be asked and the methods of discovering answers are defined in this way

Each model has an inherent set of assumptions that provides questions to ask about communication behavior, methods to try to discover answers to those questions, and even some "established" answers. Although each of the theory-building perspectives we will explore has a different set of assumptions, none of the paradigms has achieved total dominance in our field. Because human communication is such a complex and multifaceted phenomenon, contemporary communication scientists seek the theoretical perspective they believe will best help them answer a specific research question. Although communication scholars may have a preference for one paradigm over another when they conduct their research, the critical review process of our field encourages researchers to be open to several perspectives when conducting scientific inquiry.

We will describe four theory-building perspectives and provide examples of communication research illustrating the four models for inquiry. As you examine each perspective, you may find that one particularly appeals to you. Remember that each paradigm outlined has been used by communication scholars to generate much outstanding research; each has strengths and weaknesses, friends and enemies. Each model has helped provide answers to very complex questions about human communication behavior. The four paradigms are the covering laws perspective, the communibiological perspective, the rules perspective, and the systems perspective.

THE COVERING LAWS PERSPECTIVE

covering laws perspective
Developed from logical positivism, a theoretical paradigm that asserts the true nature of reality is contained in regular, observable, natural patterns

This perspective, sometimes referred to as the *classical* model or the logical positivist model, is the oldest and most frequently used in contemporary communication theory and research. The **covering laws perspective** was a frequent method of inquiry in the communication arts and sciences when our discipline incorporated a behavioral science orientation during the early 1960s. This pattern of discovery has also been widely used in other social science disciplines such as psychology. The laws perspective did not originate in the social sciences. Theorists and researchers from the physical sciences (biology, chemistry, physics, for example) used the covering laws model (logical positivist thought) well before psychologists and communication scholars embraced it.

logical positivism
Philosophical position that events can be explained by laws that have the formal structure of deductive reasoning

To understand fully the covering laws perspective, we should examine its underpinnings in logical positivism. **Logical positivism** represents one particular way of knowing. It asserts that we can only know something in two ways: (1) we can see, taste, touch, smell, or hear it—we gather information through our senses; or (2) we can discover it through some type of logical derivation or mathematical modeling. For example, physicists and astrophysicists used high-level mathematical modeling to discover the forces that create weightlessness long before we had the capacity to experience the effects during space travel.

The concept of "weightlessness" was uncovered through this logical discovery and modeling process before anyone actually felt the effect.

A third crucial premise of logical positivism suggests that there are certain regularities in nature that can be observed and/or discovered. These regularities are called "laws." Laws are universal. Once established, that law transcends time and space. The physical sciences have provided us with many law-governed regularities such as, "At 100 degrees Celsius, water will boil," or, "With the proper velocity, mass, acceleration and wind, an airplane will fly." Of course, these law-governed regularities do not eliminate the possibility that human error might create havoc with our plans! We will address this point again later in the chapter.

laws Regularities involving behavior

As with the preceding examples, the underlying structure of a law generally follows this form:

If X, then Y

If X (some antecedent condition) exists, then Y (some consequent effect) will occur. The existing law predicts that X will *cause* Y.

We have now articulated a concept that is crucial to our understanding of the covering laws model: causation or **causality**. The inherent assumption of the laws approach to communication is that we can understand human communication behavior if we uncover the antecedent conditions that cause consequent effects. The laws approach emphasizes cause-and-effect relationships. People communicate the way they do because some prior condition caused them to respond to a message in certain ways. Advocates of the covering laws model of communication are continually seeking to discover what preceding conditions will cause people to respond in various ways. If we discover those conditions, then we can re-create them and have people respond the way the law-governed generalization indicates they will. In this way, we can better **explain** our environment, predict outcomes, and ultimately control our environment.

causality Relationship in which previous (antecedent) events produce later (consequent) effects

explain To make understandable; to give the reason for or cause of

Prediction is another important characteristic of the law-governed perspective in human communication. Advocates of this approach try to use their knowledge about antecedent conditions to predict how people will respond or behave in communication situations. Researchers in the fields of advertising and marketing are particularly interested in discovering the conditions that *cause* people to react to packaging and advertising. If research had found that the color red is more eyecatching than other colors and that red creates more psychological arousal, then we could predict with accuracy that people would generally be more responsive to a product packaged in red.

prediction To use knowledge about antecedent conditions to predict how people will respond or behave in communication situations

We have just made a lawlike proposition involving human behavior. Stating it another way, if X (packaging is red), then Y (the product may be more easily seen and more psychologically arousing). In addition, we have alluded to another important aspect of the covering laws perspective, the **generalizability** of lawlike statements. Proponents of the laws approach probe for lawlike

generalizability Lawlike statements that hold true across many situations and many different time periods

generalizations that hold true across many situations and many different time periods. This is what we meant when we stated that laws transcend time and space. If an antecedent condition is found to be the cause of a consequent effect today, the law predicts the same effect will occur a month from today, a year from today, perhaps even several decades from now! In addition, if the lawlike generalization holds true for one group of people, then it should also hold true for many different groups of people as well.

Earlier we mentioned one of the law-governed generalizations regarding the temperature at which water will boil. There are certain conditions that falsify our example. Water will boil at 212 degrees Fahrenheit—if we have the water at sea level. If we are at the top of a very high mountain, the water will boil at a lower temperature (one degree lower for every 555 feet above sea level). The law-governed statement has been found to be true—but there may be qualifiers in the prediction. We are suggesting, therefore, that laws exist under certain conditional constraints.

Positivistic versus Probabilistic Conception of Laws

According to the framework of the logical positivist tradition, laws cannot be broken. That is, if certain antecedent conditions cause a certain consequent effect, once those conditions have been introduced, the consequent effect will *always* result. *Every* time X occurs, Y will always follow. In fact, the logical positivist approach believes that the consequent effect will occur 100 times out of 100 if the antecedent conditions are in effect. Under the appropriate environmental conditions, every time a sodium (Na) atom is introduced to a chlorine (Cl) atom, they will join to form NaCl or salt. This result will be observed 100 times in 100 trials. The "laws" of chemistry prevent any other consequent effect from occurring. The sodium and/or chlorine atoms are not free to choose whether they want to be joined (bonded) in any given situation. The strict logical positivist or mechanistic approach to laws works quite well in the fields of chemistry and physics. Although we trust our lives to the laws of physics that an airplane will *always* take off and fly, many communication theorists and scholars would agree that human beings do not act in the same fashion as atoms or molecules. Most contemporary communication theorists would admit that the human being differs from those particles because we have some choice in how we respond to stimuli in our environment. Human beings have volition and can, to some degree, exercise their choices even in the presence of certain *antecedent* conditions that have a strong causal relationship to some consequent outcomes.

Communication theorists who advocate this particular view of laws and causality are called probabilists. Miller and Berger (1978) have suggested that most communication theorists advocating the covering laws approach to building communication theory today have rejected the strict mechanistic view of laws and have opted for a probabilistic orientation. The probabilistic view of laws asserts that given a certain antecedent condition (X), the outcome or consequent effect (Y) will occur with (P) degree of probability, under certain conditions. Consider an example of a communication "law" regarding the use of evidence in persuasive communication. Stated in its most basic law-governed fashion, "Using evidence in a persuasive message will cause listeners to accept that message more than they would a persuasive message without evidence." The probabilistic view of laws might suggest that using evidence in a message will produce more persuasion "70 percent of the time."

Further, probabilistic law-governed communication theorists would establish certain conditions that must exist in order for that law to hold true even 70 percent of the time. In the example earlier, they might state that the evidence must be timely and current because extremely old evidence might be more harmful than no evidence at all. Second, they might suggest that the evidence must be new to the listeners. Third, they might suggest that the evidence should come from expert and trustworthy sources who are believable to the audience. Probabilistic law-governed communication theorists recognize that human beings do have choice or volition even when confronted by extremely strong causal relationships. These scholars also recognize that some laws or regularities in nature regarding communication behavior exist only under certain specific conditions.

Discovering Certain "Laws" of Communication

For the last forty years, communication theorists and scholars have attempted to uncover some "laws" or regularities involving human communication behavior. Much of this research activity has centered around the area of persuasion or attitude change. One of the earliest attempts was conducted at Yale University (see Figure 4.1).

The Yale communication research team was essentially interested in discovering certain conditions that would make individuals more susceptible to the persuasive influence of others. The use of propaganda in World War II and the Korean War, the introduction and rapid diffusion of commercial television and the worldwide increase in advertising focused attention on persuasion and social influence. Through a series of systematic research studies, the team sought to discover the many source, message, channel, and receiver characteristics that would enhance such influence. They found that certain characteristics of a message source increased that source's persuasive impact on an audience. The higher the source's perceived credibility (believability, expertise, trustworthiness), the more likely an audience member would be persuaded. They also observed that physical appearance affected persuasion. In general, the more physically attractive the message source, the more the source persuaded the audience.

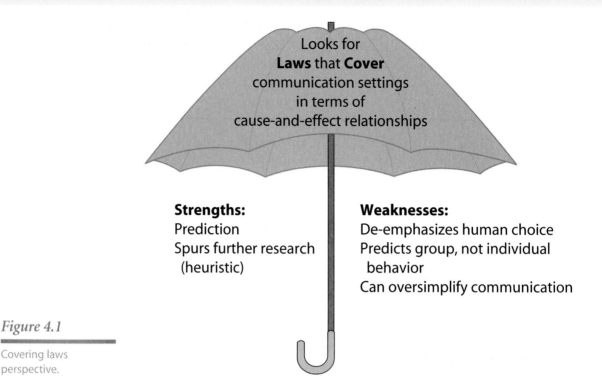

Figure 4.1

Covering laws
perspective.

Regarding characteristics of the message itself, the Yale communication researchers discovered that well-organized messages were more persuasive than disorganized messages. Messages with more evidence or testimony had more impact than other types of messages. Messages containing modest amounts of information designed to frighten a receiver into believing or doing what the persuader wanted (fear appeals) had more impact than messages that did not contain any fear-arousing information.

Characteristics of an audience were also investigated. Educational level, sexual composition, and level of self-esteem were a few of the audience/receiver characteristics that received research attention in the Yale studies on communication. One interesting finding that emerged was that two-sided messages (messages that contain both your position and a few arguments from the opposing side, which you refute) worked best with more educated audiences.

More recently, certain lawlike generalizations have been discovered in the area of interpersonal attraction. The question of what makes people like each other has received considerable attention from theorists in communication and social psychology. Certain factors have been discovered that contribute to attraction or liking between people: attitudes in common, similar backgrounds, and physical resemblance. Examples of lawlike generalizations in the area of interpersonal attraction might include: "People are more likely to be attracted to others with similar rather than different attitudes" and "Physically attractive people are more likely to develop relationships with others who are also physically attractive." Several studies have indeed found that relationships between two people, one of whom is highly attractive and the other is highly unattractive, are unusual. There are many more lawlike generalizations that have been discovered in the area of interpersonal attraction and relationship development during the last several years. These findings will be presented in Chapter 9.

"Tools" of the Law-Governed Communication Researcher

As we have stressed, the concept of causality is central to the law-governed approach to communication. In an effort to demonstrate causal relationships between communication variables, researchers use a very important method or set of tools, the experimental model. The experimental model is used by researchers to create controlled situations to test the effect of antecedent conditions on subsequent outcomes. The experimental model is the only method researchers can use to establish *causal* relationships between communication variables.

To illustrate the use of the experimental paradigm, consider a person's general tendency to argue or to defend his or her beliefs—trait argumentativeness. Two of the authors decided to explore this topic. They wanted to investigate whether individuals who like to argue would behave differently when arguing with people who hesitate to voice their opinions than with people who quickly express their opinions. Similarly, would individuals who avoid argument behave differently when talking to people who like to defend their beliefs versus people who try to avoid disputes?

experimental paradigm
Used by researchers to create controlled situations to test the effect of antecedent conditions on subsequent outcomes

Four experimental situations were created. In one, individuals high in argumentativeness were led to believe that they would have to argue informally with another person who was also very argumentative. In the second, high argumentatives thought they were going to argue with an opponent dissimilar to themselves, a low argumentative individual. In the third experimental condition, participants were low argumentatives who thought they were going to argue with someone similar to themselves. In the fourth condition, low argumentatives thought they would argue with someone dissimilar, a highly argumentative adversary. The results of this experiment revealed that high argumentatives were more motivated to argue than low argumentatives. In addition, it was discovered that highly argumentative individuals were most motivated when they expected to argue with another high argumentative. This experiment demonstrated that motivation to argue is influenced not only by a person's own underlying tendency but also by expectations about the adversary. Highly argumentative individuals were especially likely to be influenced by expectations about their partners.

Strengths of the Laws Perspective

predictions Indications in advance on the basis of observation, experience, or scientific reason

1. The laws approach to communication seems especially useful in helping us make **predictions** about human communication behavior. This approach to communication has uncovered many causal relationships between communication variables. For example, many of the findings of the Yale studies on communication continue to receive support. The use of evidence to help persuade an audience under certain conditions (see Chapter 6) is one such relationship.

2. Theory building in communication is strengthened by utilizing findings from studies conducted using the laws approach. Our understanding of communication apprehension (fear or anxiety associated with communication), for example, has been greatly enhanced by nearly two decades of research that has tested the many factors associated with this trait and has painstakingly constructed new predictions based on previous results (see Chapter 5). Our knowledge about this subject increases with each additional effort.

Weaknesses of the Laws Perspective

1. Critics suggest that the laws approach, especially the positivist tradition, does not place enough emphasis on human choice, free will, and interpretation of stimuli. They suggest that the primary tool used in laws research, the experimental model, is best left to researchers and theorists in the physical sciences who do not have to be concerned with issues of human choice and interpretation.

2. The laws approach can help us make predictions about how people will behave *in general.* Critics state that the laws approach cannot, with any degree of certainty, help us predict how any single individual will behave. For example, research suggests that messages designed to frighten an audience somewhat (moderate fear appeals) are effective in a persuasive speech. If you used moderate fear appeals in your message, you might conclude that some percentage of one hundred audience members would change their minds and vote for your proposal. However, the laws approach would not help you determine the specific individuals likely to change their minds. The focus is on the group, not the individual.

3. Other critics of the laws approach maintain that breaking down communication events into separate parts does not contribute to theoretical advancement. They claim that this method, often referred to as *variable analysis,* oversimplifies human communication. Jesse Delia (1975) said variable analysis "fails to reflect the interwoven texture of the processes

participating in human communication" (p. 2). Critics suggest that studying only one variable at a time misleadingly reduces a very complex event to a very simple one.

THE COMMUNIBIOLOGICAL PERSPECTIVE

The most recent paradigm for communication research was introduced by Michael Beatty and James McCroskey (1997; 1998; Beatty, McCroskey, & Heisel, 1998). Until the introduction of the communibiological perspective, the field of communication was almost universal in its support of nurture in the debate of "nature versus nurture." The belief was that people are born with what some philosophers term a *tabula rasa,* a "blank slate." People develop differences because of the varying impressions made on their minds (the blank slates) by their universe of experience. That is, the environment shapes people; they are *nurtured* to behave one way or the other. People have goals, make choices from the options present, and are shaped by the rewards and punishments experienced because of the choices. To understand communicative behavior, you need to understand how it was nurtured.

communibiological perspective Approach to explaining communication that claims there is a genetic basis for most communicative behavior

The communibiological perspective takes the opposite position—that most human behavior is due to nature. People are born with a set of biologically determined temperaments that are consistent across life. Temperaments are expressed as what we have come to know as traits, behavioral tendencies that differentiate people. This position maintains that much human behavior is genetically determined (i.e., it is inherited). To claim that your temperaments or traits are inherited does not mean that you are simply a copy of your biological parents. Genetically determined traits skip generations; some of your traits may be more like those of your great-grandparents than those of your parents. Also, the genes of one parent can interact with genes of the other parent, and this can produce some unique combinations. Furthermore, genes can become damaged, for instance, by a parent's substance abuse or exposure to harmful environmental conditions.

temperaments Traits with a biological basis that differentiate people

The communibiological perspective is receiving serious attention particularly because of Beatty and McCroskey's claim, based on a review of research, that about 80% of the variability in communication behavior may be due to biology, while perhaps 20% at most is due to environmental influences. Some of the evidence on which this claim is based was conducted with identical and nonidentical twins. Identical twins have the same set of genes, whereas nonidentical twins are no more similar genetically than are other pairs of siblings in a family. Comparing the two types of twins on a trait such as shyness and finding a much higher correlation for the identical as compared to nonidentical twins is a direct test of the idea that genes are the basis for behavior. Some of the research examined both types of twins in terms of whether they were raised together or whether they were separated at birth and raised apart. Results here showed that identical twins became more alike as they grew older, regardless of whether they lived together or apart. However, nonidentical twins did not become more alike as they grew older. Particularly strong evidence has been observed in studies comparing adopted children's personalities to those of their adoptive parents and also to those of their biological parents. The adoptive parents represent the "nurture" condition because they raised the children from shortly after birth, whereas the biological parents constitute a nature condition because they provided the children's genes. Results here have shown that adopted children's traits were more correlated with those of their biological parents than with those of their adoptive parents, even though the children lived with their adoptive parents.

The claim that 80% of the variation in communication behavior is attributable to biology needs to be examined very carefully. If correct, then we might conclude that we have been wasting our time with models of how the environment shapes behavior. Such models may be based on wishful thinking—that people have a great deal of control over their behavior when that may not be the case. As we explained at the beginning of this chapter, paradigm shifts occur in a field of study when researchers realize that the old paradigm does not fit the data as well as the new paradigm. That would be the case if 80% of communicative behavior is accounted for by biology while only 20% is explained by environmental influence. If this idea were accepted, then the data (communication behaviors) would be seen as fitting better with a biological model.

Let's examine the five propositions of the communibiological perspective advanced by Beatty and McCroskey (1998). The first is, "All psychological processes—including cognitive, affective, and motor—involved in social interaction depend on brain activity, making necessary a neurobiology" (p. 46). They emphasize, for instance, that the many cognitive operations on which researchers have speculated must be identified in terms of whether they are neurologically possible; otherwise there is nothing but mere speculations about what goes on in individuals' heads.

The second proposition is, "Brain activity precedes psychological experience" (p. 47). This pertains to the idea of whether people have nonbiological consciousness that directs brain activity. An important example of this is free will. Beatty and McCroskey do not support the free will position and challenge those who do to specify the brain circuitry and other biological mechanisms that at least make such a process possible. So, if there is no identifiable brain activity, there is no basis for claiming that an actual choice existed and was acted on.

The third proposition is, "The neurobiological structures underlying temperament traits and individual differences are mostly inherited" (p. 48). Based on research evidence, this proposes that the biological structures are inherited and result in traits. However, not all of the behavior of interest necessarily will be explained by the genes involved in the relevant traits. There could be some small amount of social learning. Also, there could be some other biological influence involved that has an impact on behavior, such as poor nutrition. So, it is unlikely that genetics will ever predict 100% of communicative behavior.

Proposition 4 is, "Environment or 'situation' has only a negligible effect on interpersonal behavior" (p. 50). The idea here is that we have "set points" for traits, and when the situation does manage to cause a fluctuation in behavior, it is merely a temporary change from a stable set point. For instance, suppose a person's trait set point in terms of a happy–sad trait is "moderately sad." Now if the person wins some money while on a trip to Las Vegas, the person would experience a deviation from the set point, perhaps all the way to "extremely happy." However, before long the individual's feelings would return to where they have been most of his or her life, the set point of "moderately sad," and over the course of time the measurable impact of the Las Vegas experience would be negligible or very small.

Beatty and McCroskey's fifth proposition is, "Differences in interpersonal behavior are principally due to individual differences in neurobiological functioning" (p. 52). The authors identified the parts of the brain involved in three major behavioral systems that produce many of our traits. They are (a) the **behavioral activation system**, (b) the **behavioral inhibition system**, and (c) the **fight-flight system**. Identifying these systems anatomically makes it possible to test hypotheses about which regions of the brain should show activity for certain behaviors, such as, for example, a highly aggressive person flying into a rage when receiving a very mild insult from another person. This proposition also involves the idea that at times it is most difficult to predict a given behavior because of conflicting traits in the situation. For instance, will a highly aggressive person fly into a rage over a mild insult if he or she has a strong need for affiliation, and the person who delivered the mild insult is a member of a group the aggressive person wants to join, and members of the group are present? Other competing drives could be involved, such as a potential romantic interest being present. Advocates of this approach would attempt to identify the relevant neurobiological activity and then formulate a prediction about what the person will do based on that information. Obviously, the process could get quite complicated.

The ideas associated with these five propositions have been applied to two areas of communication research to provide an explanation for why people engage in certain communication behaviors. We will review these efforts in the next chapter when we discuss the traits of communication apprehension and verbal aggressiveness.

The communibiological perspective has some important implications for communication education. If traits have an inherited biological basis and if the environment minimally influences behavior, then classroom instruction

behavioral activation system System used in the communibiological perspective to explain communication by identifying the brain circuitry activated by desire for a reward

behavioral inhibition system System used in the communibiological perspective to explain communication by identifying the brain circuitry that results in anxiety about behavior

fight-flight system System used in the communibiological perspective to explain communication by identifying the brain circuitry involved in response to a threat

will have little impact on behavior. For example, it may not be possible to move a person from being quite high in communication anxiety to being very low on such a trait through teaching. This does not mean, however, that no change in skill level is possible. Although people may be very fearful of public speaking, they can be taught to write a good speech and how to deliver it effectively. They may not like the activity, but they can be coached to do it well. This is also true for argumentation. They may not enjoy the activity, and you may not get them to try out for the college debating team, but individuals can be taught how to construct an argument and how to present it effectively. If the communibiological perspective is correct, another implication would be that communication education should help individuals understand their temperaments and how to manage their lives so that they generally avoid uncomfortable and troublesome situations and learn how to place themselves in situations that are more satisfying.

Strengths of the Communibiological Perspective

1. The communibiological approach is particularly strong in generating explanations of communication that rely on objective criteria such as whether a region of the brain is activated. This is a unique strength. In the past, most explanations have rested on speculation without a reliable means of observing whether what was supposed to have happened actually did happen. The communibiological perspective identifies regions of the brain and circuits that must be activated to have a particular type of communication. Activation can be detected and measured by instruments such as the electroencephalograph. Utilizing more objective criteria should move the communication field toward greater scientific rigor.

2. This approach has the potential for generating greater scientific precision if the conceptualization is expanded to utilize more fully the science of genetics. With this science it should be possible to calculate the probability that a given trait will occur in a particular generation. For instance, it may be possible to state the probability that an individual will have the trait of communication apprehension by looking at the level of the trait in family members such as parents or grandparents. It may be that genetics researchers will discover a gene or combination of genes that control certain communication behaviors. Genetic explanations very well could be a part of our understanding of communication in the future. At the present time, however, the communibiological perspective deals with genetics in a very general manner by asserting that traits are inherited, that traits can skip a generation, and that the genes inherited from parents can interact. The genetic formulas for the occurrence of these events have not yet been specified.

3. This approach to studying communication might result in an important diagnostic tool and suggest a medical basis for changing highly destructive behaviors and increasing the rate of highly desirable behavior. For instance, if a brain circuit that is activated for a particular destructive behavior is identified, a pharmaceutical approach would be to develop a medication that suppresses activation of that circuit. On the other hand, increasing the occurrence of a desirable behavior might involve a medication that stimulates a particular brain region and/or circuitry. Gene therapy may be possible in the future to modify behavior with an identified genetic basis. Of course, serious and extensive discussions of ethical issues should accompany theoretical and medical development. They might be similar to the discussions of ethics that have been going on for some time regarding prescribing the drug Ritalin for hyperactive children. It should be mentioned also that drug therapies currently are being used with success to influence communication in a favorable manner. For example, the drug Paxil is used for controlling social anxiety. Should it be used to alleviate stress for people with communication apprehension? Is the risk of pharmaceutical dependency balanced by improved well-being?

Weaknesses of the Communibiological Perspective

1. A possible impediment to the approach being widely adopted is that the field's researchers will have to acquire new methodological tools. A certain amount of retooling will be necessary because to use the communibiological perspective, a rather detailed understanding of the brain and genetics will be needed. Getting people to change the way they have been doing things and learn a new approach can be challenging. Whether the methodology of the field will move in this direction is difficult to predict. In the 1970s a need for understanding multivariate statistics (analyzing several variables together) was articulated. There was very little resistance to this requirement. Before long graduate students in communication were taking multivariate statistics courses. A similar movement for the teaching of the biology of communication will be needed for this new perspective to thrive.

2. What this perspective means for the future of communication education needs to be explained more thoroughly. Because scholars most frequently use the social learning model to explain why we communicate the way that we do, it is understandable that some people are skeptical of the communibiological approach. If our traits are inherited, is there any room for learning? Will students conclude, "What is the use in trying to change because I was born this way? There is nothing I can do about that!" The extent to which behavior can be changed to a meaningful degree needs to be addressed. In the context of that issue, the role of communication

education should be delineated. It may well be decided, as mentioned earlier, that although trait behavior cannot be changed much, specific skills are very amenable to improvement.

3. The ethical implications of a communibiological perspective need to be identified. As suggested earlier, because this approach could lead to the use of medications and perhaps gene therapy, the ethical issues need to be answered satisfactorily. It is not too much of a stretch of the imagination to suppose, for example, that the biological control could be identified for a trait that predisposes the individual to argue against the status quo. Pharmacology might then develop a medication for suppressing the brain region and brain circuitry involved. A government might try to use the medication to achieve a population that is not prone to attack the status quo (i.e., a population that accepts the current system). Such a scenario can be avoided by thoughtful discussions of ethics and policies drafted to protect individual rights.

THE RULES PERSPECTIVE

It may not be a coincidence that the rules approach (sometimes referred to as the *Human Action Perspective*) emerged during the early 1970s, a time of great social upheaval and change in society. During this period, individuals challenged what they perceived as constraints on freedoms and advocated for casting aside limitations they felt were imposed on them by American society.

The rules approach to communication theory building was a reaction by some scholars against the prevailing and dominant paradigm at the time, the law-governed view of human communication behavior. Critics became disenchanted with the laws perspective because they perceived it as viewing communication behavior being largely mechanistic and determined by outside forces. Instead of being inextricably bound by the notion of causality and the stimulus-response orientation, which are essential tenets of the covering laws perspective, rules theorists believe that human communication behavior is the result of practical regularities or norms observed in society.

A major assumption of the rules approach to communication is that communication behavior is largely volitional, under one's control, and not dictated by outside forces, which "compel" people to behave or communicate in certain ways. In other words, rules theorists argue that individuals have a great deal of freedom to choose their communication behavior within situations to achieve goals and intentions. Several communication scholars are recognized as early developers and advocates of the rules approach, among them Professors Vernon E. Cronen, Donald P. Cushman, Robert Nofsinger, W. Barnett Pearce, Gerald Philipsen, Richard L. Wiseman, and Gordon C. Whiting.

Pearce and Wiseman (1983) suggested that the rules perspective became popular in the communication discipline for three reasons: (a) efforts to identify "laws" of human communication behavior were failing, and a new generation of communication researchers were becoming disenchanted with this dominant paradigm; (b) the behaviorist approach to understanding and developing communication theory was waning, and a viable alternative to this approach was "action theory," a perspective more closely aligned with a rules approach; and (c) the rules perspective was already established in other disciplines (e.g., cognitive psychology, sociolinguistics, ethnomethodology) and thus, had "an instant intellectual heritage" (Pearce & Wiseman, 1983, p. 80). Susan Shimanoff (1980) offered a fourth reason for its early popularity and adoption, which speaks to the essence of the rules approach: The rules perspective views human beings as having a great deal of freedom to make choices about their actions and behavior, and many of these choices are made on the basis of rules.

Although the "rules approach" generated a great deal of interest among scholars in its initial presentation, the advocates of this perspective differed greatly in how they defined it, described it, and studied it. At that time, Pearce and Wiseman (1983) even stated "The rules perspective as it currently exists in the communication discipline is dysfunctionally diverse, with substantive disagreements about the most basic concepts" (p. 80). In an effort to bring some clarity, Shimanoff (1980) offered a productive definition of a rule as "a followable prescription that indicates what behavior is obligated, preferred, or prohibited in certain contexts" (p. 57).

Rules can be considered "norms," which inform us about appropriate behavior in communication situations. Where do these rules come from? Rules are largely determined by the society or culture you function in, your family, and other reference groups you belong to. Parents often make rules for their children to follow (e.g., "You must be home by midnight during the week"), and your own teachers and professors often make rules for the specific classes they teach (e.g., "To participate in this class, you must raise your hand and be acknowledged"). These rules are considered explicit in that they are formally stated regulations that have been imposed by a person in an authority position (in the preceding examples by parents and teachers).

Some rules are implicit, in that they may have been learned by inference, that is, by observing behaviors of others in the reference group or culture. You obtain knowledge of these rules by observing normative verbal and nonverbal behavior as practiced by members of your culture. An example of an implicit rule functioning in many families might be, "Do not discuss family finances and income with others outside the family." Individuals also acquire knowledge of implicit rules by observing the consequences that occur when people violate a rule. For example, a nonverbal "rule" that operates in our culture is,

"One must dress professionally and/or appropriately when going for a job interview." Even if this rule was not explicitly told to you, it is likely that you acquired knowledge of this rule by observing how others dress during job interviews, or by not getting a second interview when you dressed unprofessionally or inappropriately during the employment interview process.

Rules state what we should do (i.e., how to behave) and what is deemed appropriate in certain situations. The rule governing a particular type of nonverbal kinesic (i.e., body motion) behavior of females in this culture, "Women are to sit with their knees together," might have been learned implicitly by observing how most women sit. However, many females also learned this rule by being explicitly told how to sit, especially if they violated that rule (e.g., "Kim, sit properly!" "Girls do not sit with their knees apart!"). Other examples of rules for "proper" communication behavior are, "If someone calls your name and you hear it, you should respond to the person," and "If you want to begin talking, you should wait until your conversational partner has finished his or her turn; you must not interrupt another speaker."

Rules are said to possess the following characteristics:

1. *Rules must be followable*—rules are associated with actions, and individuals can choose to perform, or not perform those actions. This suggests that rules, unlike laws, "are breakable." This characteristic helps discriminate between laws and rules, as "Scientific laws differ from rules in that there is no choice whether one can or cannot follow them; they (i.e., laws) cannot be broken" (Shimanoff, 1980, p. 39).

2. *Rules are prescriptive*—if an individual knows the rule, they can be held accountable if they break the rule (e.g., "Do not use profanity when speaking with your parents)." Some theorists have described this prescriptive quality of rules as "practical necessity" (e.g., Pearce and Cushman, 1977), whereas others prefer to describe it as "prescriptive force" (Shimanoff, 1980). Either way, communicators use rules to achieve goals.

3. *Rules are contextual*—rules apply in certain situations, but not all situations. That is, rules occur within, or interact with, the context of communication. The context includes people in the situation, the setting (where the interaction takes place), the channel that is being used to communicate (e.g., face-to-face, by phone, mail, e-mail, text messaging), and the purpose of the interaction (i.e., the goal of the interaction). For example, in some classes, instructors have instituted a "rule" that to speak in class, one must raise a hand and be acknowledged by the instructor. In other classes, no such rule exists, and students are free to simply speak up whenever they wish. Rules that are imposed on the communication situation are referred to as "imposed rules." Understanding the elements of a given situation helps determine appropriate

rule use. Thus, understanding these situational elements, followed by a correct response to them, allows individuals to present themselves as competent rule users.

Different perspectives emerged among advocates of the rules approach, which helped shape the type of rules theory that was developed. Depending on the perspective of the rules theorist, rules can take several different forms. One perspective suggests that rules take the general form: "If X, then Y is obligated (preferred or prohibited)" (Shimanoff, 1980, p. 76). Another way of stating this is: If X, then Y (must be done, should be done, or should not be done). At first glance, this seems similar to the underlying structure of a covering law, "If X, then Y." However, unlike in the covering laws perspective, causality is not assumed and does not exist.

A second perspective, called the **rule-following approach** to communication behavior, comes closest to the law-governed approach, as it views individuals acting with some degree of regularity. From this perspective, the form of the rule is, "If X, then people usually do Y; X occurs; Therefore, this person will probably do Y" (Pearce & Wiseman, 1983, p. 82). A third perspective, called the **rule-governed approach** to communication behavior, views rules as an "individual's belief about what should be done or what probably will occur as a consequence of his or her action" (Pearce & Wiseman, 1983, p. 83). From this perspective, the form of a rule is: "Person A wants Y; Person A knows that he or she must do X if Y is to occur; therefore, Person A prepares to do X" (Pearce & Wiseman, 1983, p. 83).

rule-following approach Views individuals acting with some degree of regularity

rule-governing approach Views rules as an "individual's belief about what should be done or what probably will occur as a consequence of his or her action"

Research from an applied communication perspective has used the rules approach. Here are two studies that might be considered exemplars of the rules approach to understanding communication behavior in two contexts. One explores the notion of family rules for media use, whereas the second study identifies organizational rules that guide employee judgments of organizational communication competence.

James Lull (1982) used the rules approach to investigate media (television) use and interpersonal communication activity within the home. Perhaps you can recall examples of "rules" that existed in your own home regarding television viewing behavior (how many hours you were allowed to watch TV daily, what types of programs you were allowed to watch, and what behaviors were, or were not, acceptable during family viewing hours). For example, you may have been subjected to the explicit rule of "No TV until all your homework is done." Another implicit rule "learned" through observing the consequences of violating the rule might have been, "When watching TV with other members of the family present, one does not change the channel without first asking permission."

In his research, Lull (1982) identified three classes of rule behavior for family TV viewing. **Habitual rules** were typically nonnegotiable, usually

habitual rules Typically nonnegotiable, imposed by those in positions of authority, and yield negative consequences if violated

imposed by those in positions of authority (e.g., parents), and yielded negative consequences (or punishments) if they were violated. Habitual rules usually dealt with the amount, time, or content of TV viewing (e.g., "You cannot watch an R-rated HBO program unless approved by a parent").

parametric rules Patterns of action considered appropriate within certain mutually understood boundaries; usually stated verbally by an authority figure and somewhat negotiable

Parametric rules describe patterns of action considered appropriate within certain mutually understood boundaries. Parametric rules are frequently, but not always, stated verbally, usually dictated by an authority figure in the family, and somewhat negotiable. That is, they provide opportunities to choose from a range of acceptable behaviors. The negotiation of TV program preferences or times for TV viewing are examples of parametric rules for family viewing behavior. "Extended talk is to be done only during commercial breaks" might be an example of a parametric rule of family TV viewing.

tactical rules Used to achieve some type of personal or interpersonal objective

The third type of rules were deemed **tactical rules**, or rules used to achieve some type of personal or interpersonal objective. An example of a tactical rule would be to "give in" to your significant other's TV viewing preference to maintain relational harmony. With the advent of TiVo and other digital recording options, a few of the family TV viewing rules identified by Lull have become somewhat moot, as we can now easily record one program while simultaneously watching another. However, the importance of Lull's study is that it underscores that powerful rules are indeed constructed not only at the societal level, but at the family level as well. As far as TV viewing is concerned, many families still construct rules dealing with the selection of programming, the activities that accompany the viewing of programs, and even the consumption of goods and services that are shown on television.

Another study identified components and "rules" of organizational communication competence from a rules perspective (Wellmon, 1988). Through the use of the "critical incident interview technique," examples of how individuals adhered to or broke organizational rules were collected, thus eliciting examples of rule-generated behavior for competent as well as incompetent organizational communication behavior. Among the findings that emerged from the study was the rule for organizations that perceptions of competence are based on: the ability of individuals to listen well, project a friendly and personable communicator style, do their share of the work, maintain a professional "business" demeanor, understand the rules of social "chitchat," exhibit a proper verbal style, and possess a working knowledge of the politics within organizations.

Strengths of the Rules Perspective

1. The rules perspective views people as having a great deal of choice and free will on how to communicate and behave. Thus, they believe that a person's communication behavior is not predetermined or dictated by underlying "laws" in nature.

2. The rules approach allows us to understand more fully *why* people communicate the way they do. Because interpretation is a key element in this perspective, rules researchers and theorists may probe more deeply than law-governed researchers on why someone communicates or behaves the way they do.

Weaknesses of the Rules Perspective

1. The rules perspective excels in the goal of explanation (i.e., understanding and identifying why do people communicate or behave in a particular way in a given situation), but it is much weaker regarding helping us make predictions about individuals' future behavior.

2. Although the rules approach generated a substantial amount of research during the 1970s and early to mid-1980s, during the last two decades the amount of research generated from this perspective has diminished considerably. Although this is not necessarily a condemnation of this perspective, it suggests that the questions contemporary communication researchers and theorists are asking may not be appropriately or adequately addressed by this perspective.

THE SYSTEMS PERSPECTIVE

The **systems perspective** was introduced in 1968 by Ludwig von Bertalanffy, a biologist, in an attempt to find principles common to all types of systems. Von Bertalanffy believed that science is unified so that all types of systems—biological, physical, and chemical, for example—have common properties. Although systems theory as a communication perspective is not an attempt to find properties common to all systems, communication scholars have found some of the principles von Bertalanffy developed to be useful in studying communication.

systems perspective A theoretical paradigm whose followers believe that the true nature of reality is contained in systems—interdependent units that work together to adapt to a changing environment

Systems theory is somewhat different from the laws and rules perspectives in that systems theorists do not advocate a particular "way of knowing." A system could be held together with laws, with rules, or with both laws and rules. The contribution of systems theory is a set of concepts that helps us understand communication as an integrated process—not as an isolated event.

A system is a set of interdependent units that work together to adapt to a changing environment. An organization is one type of system and a good one to use as an example in discussing communication systems. Communication systems are **open systems**—they interact with their environments. An organization communicates with customers, suppliers, the government, and other groups of individuals or institutions that form its environment. If it were a

open system System that interacts with its environment, interchanging inputs and outputs

closed system System that has little or no interaction with its environment; system that is not open to new information

subsystems Smaller units within a system

suprasystems Larger units that make up a system; suprasystems are composed of subsystems

nonsummativity Characteristic of a system that states the system is more than the contributions of each individual part. The interactions of the parts also contribute to the system; changing one part causes changes to the entire system

cybernetic systems Open systems that are self-regulating

homeostasis Process of self-regulation by which a cybernetic system maintains an equilibrium

closed system that did not communicate with its environment, it would die. Closed systems tend toward entropy, chaos, or total disorganization. Organizations receive inputs such as raw materials from their environment, transform those inputs in some way (such as using research information to create an advertising campaign), then send outputs back to the environment. During the transformation process, different departments of the organization may send outputs to each other for further processing.

A system is hierarchical. The system can be broken up into smaller units called **subsystems** or combined with other systems to form larger **suprasystems**. The personnel department of an organization is a subsystem of the larger organization, which may itself be a subsystem of a multinational corporation, the suprasystem. The fact that the suprasystems and subsystems are interdependent leads to the systems property called **nonsummativity**. The whole system is more than the sum of the contributions of each individual part. Brent D. Ruben (1983) provides an example of nonsummativity, "System is the term used to label any entity or whole that is made up of interdependent parts in a relationship, such that the entity as a whole has properties and functions distinct from those of the separate components. A simple example of a system is a cake. The ingredients of a typical cake are sugar, flour, salt, eggs, butter, vanilla, and baking soda. When combined and heated, the result is a finished product that is much different than any of the parts themselves" (pp. 133–134). Frequently, a system functions more effectively as a whole rather than merely as the sum of its parts. We are sure that you have heard of the legendary and iconic band, the Beatles. The individual members of the Beatles, John Lennon, Paul McCartney, George Harrison, and Ringo Starr were, and are, recognized as extremely proficient and extraordinary musicians on their own. However, when their separate talents were combined as the group the Beatles, they became something much greater than they were individually.

If you take away or change one individual part, the entire system is affected. If the sales department of an organization has problems, the entire organization may lose profits. Perhaps the production department will have to make fewer cars or even lay off workers on the assembly line because of a problem in a completely different department.

The more individual parts in a system, the more relationships, and therefore the more complex the communication. Changing one part of the system—for example, firing an employee or a child leaving the family to live away from home for the first time—changes all the other parts because each other part previously interacted with the one that is now removed. Because systems are so intricate, coordinating or managing them is a very complex and very important task. The smallest of changes creates a chain reaction that reverberates throughout every part of even the largest system.

Cybernetic systems try to maintain a balance with their environments through a process called **homeostasis**, or self-regulation. After a change in the environment, the system adapts to maintain an equilibrium. It may not be the same equilibrium point as before the change, but the system comes to some balance point. For example, many U.S. manufacturing companies laid off workers during the last recession. When times got better, many—but not all—workers were rehired. The system maintained a balance, but the balance resulted in fewer jobs than the equilibrium point before the recession.

One of the most interesting system properties is called **equifinality**. Equifinality means that there are many different ways by which a system may reach the same end state. Systems are **teleological**; they are designed to reach specific end states or goals. If an organization has a goal of increasing profits, it may reach the goal by increasing sales, by decreasing labor or materials costs, by increasing prices, or by adapting in other ways. Because of equifinality, researchers looking at an organizational outcome cannot know immediately what has caused the outcome. If profits increased, researchers would have to study the system closely to discover which of the many factors just listed contributed to raising profits. Organizational communication researchers concerned with a decrease in workers' morale must examine many possible causes to recommend an appropriate solution.

> **equifinality** Concept that there are many different ways by which a system may reach the same end state
>
> **teleological** Property of open systems that indicates they try to reach specific end states or goals

The systems perspective on communication is complex, reflecting the complicated nature of communication. It encourages communication students to be concerned about the environment. Many of the terms applied to other types of systems are useful in shedding light on communication in our complex society, especially communication in organizations. Due to its "holistic" orientation, the attraction of using the systems approach to the study of human communication is strong. Our definition of a system (a set of interdependent units working together to adapt to a changing environment) conjures up thoughts of at least two communication systems that are well suited for scholarly investigation from this perspective—organizations and families. Indeed, these two types of systems have received the most attention from communication theorists operating from a systems perspective. Many studies have focused on the exchange of information and the development and maintenance of relationships among the members of a system.

Let's examine one type of system common to all of us—the family. The relationships and interactions of various members are the materials that actually constitute the family. Four discrete, noninteracting, noncommunicating individuals, although they may live under the same roof, do not necessarily constitute a family. In employing the systems perspective to study a family, you will not be able to identify the essence of the family—their relationships and interactions—if you simply study each member in isolation. The systems perspective requires that you focus attention on the whole family and that you see each individual member only in the context of the whole family. Even when members of a family are spread far and wide over several geographic locations, communication and, interaction form bonds that hold the system together.

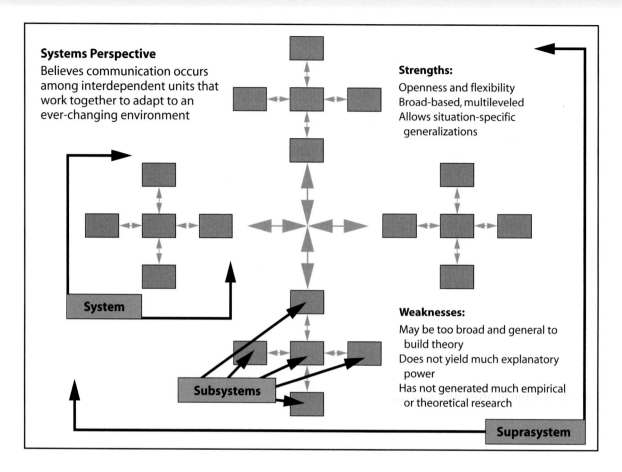

Figure 4.2

Systems perspective.

As previously stated, open systems are characterized by a great deal of exchange and interaction with their environment. Because families could not exist in isolation from others and their environment, families are considered open systems. The boundaries of the family are open to interactions with many others: neighbors, friends, and colleagues, to name but a few. A single family may also exist in the context of a much larger extended family, which can be considered an environment (Bavelas & Segal, 1982). This type of environment would consist of several nuclear families. Each nuclear family would contain subsystems consisting of spouses, children, grandparents, cousins and the like. It is also possible to identify the environment in a much broader fashion when discussing family interaction from a systems perspective. The environment could be taken to mean a given culture and/or climate in which the family exists. You may recall that one characteristic of a system is the attempt to maintain a balance with its environment through homeostasis or self-regulation.

How does a family system attempt to adjust communicatively to changing environmental conditions? How is family communication affected by a change in the environment? Two communication students were interested in examining how a change in the environment—poor economic conditions leading to the unemployment of the family provider—caused a change in family interaction and communication patterns (Bellefontaine & Florea, 1983). The students were specifically interested in examining how the unemployment of the family provider affected how frequently family members communicated, shared personal feelings, and argued, and how the self-esteem of the family members changed. Four families agreed to participate in the study. In each family, the husband/father was unemployed for a period of between 1 to 6 months. Using several methods to gather data (surveys, interviews with family members, observations), the researchers discovered that several changes in family communication patterns did indeed occur.

With the provider more accessible and available during the period of unemployment, communication between the family members increased. Husbands and wives reported a slight increase in overall disclosure of feelings to each other. Understandably, the husbands' feelings of self-esteem decreased. However, in several of the families studied, the wives reported increases in feelings of self-worth and self-esteem. Finally, all families noted increases in the frequency of conflict. As one father stated, "As a consequence of being laid off, I was home more often and saw things I normally didn't have to deal with. Consequently, there were more areas of conflict."

This study of family interaction helps illustrate several key concepts of the systems perspective as applied to communication. It demonstrates the concept that a system is a set of interdependent units all working together. When the main provider was laid off, the other members of the system tried to find jobs to keep money flowing into the system. The study also demonstrated the systems maxim that a change in one part of a system of necessity creates changes in other parts of the system. In this case, when the husband/father became unemployed, the other family members were affected financially and communicatively. However, each system tried to maintain a balance through self-regulation. If possible, the wife went to work, and the husband assumed more of the domestic responsibilities. Increased communication resulted from the need for all members of the system to get used to the new family arrangement. The other adjustments noted by the researchers, such as changes in social conflict and levels of self-esteem, reflect the complex and interactive nature of the family system.

Strengths of the Systems Perspective

1. The systems approach is a flexible and open perspective from which to study human communication. Advocates of this approach state that it does not impose a series of perceptual constraints or biases on researchers to force them to focus only on certain elements in a communication situation. Laws theorists focus on trying to identify causal relationships among communication phenomena, whereas rules theorists focus primarily on trying to

identify social norms or individual interpretive patterns that guide communication behaviors in various contexts. Systems theorists attempt to focus on all aspects of interactions and relationships within a communication event.

2. Human communication is such a complex phenomenon that it requires a multileveled investigatory schema. For example, many factors contribute to the breakup of a marriage and family. If one were to interview just the husband, or the wife, or the children alone, a partial and incomplete picture would result. The systems approach opts for studying the effects of all the factors involved—alone *and* in interaction. Advocates of the systems perspective feel that the laws and human action approaches are too narrow to investigate fully the complex interaction of the large number of factors that make up a communication event.

3. Advocates of the systems perspective state that this perspective utilizes *situation-specific* generalizations and thus is a more appropriate perspective to employ than the laws approach, which uses universal generalizations. Many communication theorists feel that communication is culture specific. If communication is culture bound, then the universal generalizations identified by the laws approach are not truly universal. Rather, they apply only to the culture of the scientists or research participants. Systems theorists do not attempt to make universal generalizations.

Weaknesses of the Systems Perspective

1. Critics suggest that the systems perspective is too broad and too general to be useful in building theory in applied contexts. If everything can be described as a system, then looking at phenomena as systems is not useful because this way of theorizing does not add insight. Instead, systems theory just makes explicit concepts that we intuitively understand from observation of the world around us. If it is equally valid to draw the boundaries of an organizational system around a work group, a department, a manufacturing plant, and an entire company, what benefit is gained by examining a department as a subsystem rather than as a suprasystem? If both are equally valid, it should make no difference which approach we take. It would be impossible to test which level of observation was best.

2. Although uncovering many important interactions and relationships involving communication in human systems, many feel that the systems perspective does not yield a great deal of explanatory power. Cahn (1981) suggested that the systems approach fails to explain events previously unexplained—it does not shed light on *why* things happen the way they do. An advocate of the systems approach, Monge (1973) noted that scientists developed theories that predicted the motion of planets before they had one that explained it. Perhaps future researchers may be able to develop systems theories with greater explanatory power.

3. Critics state that although the systems approach has many advocates, it has yet to generate much empirical or theoretical research. This criticism may reflect our discipline's desire to conduct research and publish findings rapidly. Investigating the interrelationships and interactions of the many parts of a system is not only costly but also very time consuming. Examining all possible interactions between units of the system requires a relatively long-term research focus. Many communication scholars simply cannot acquire the necessary resources—particularly the time and money—required to engage in an all-encompassing research study of changes in a system over time.

4. A final criticism of systems theory is that it focuses so much on interactions that it overlooks the importance of the individual. This criticism is similar to the logic that one cannot simultaneously view a scene from distant and close-up views. One must use either a bird's-eye or a worm's-eye view; it is impossible to take both perspectives at once. Because systems theory might be described as taking a bird's-eye view, or panoramic perspective, critics argue that it does so at the expense of fully understanding individuals or individual parts. For example, a researcher taking a systems approach to an organizational communication problem would focus on interactions between parts of the system. Although the researcher would also consider the parts individually, there would be little time or energy to explore parts as deeply as a human action researcher might, for example. If there was a sudden change in an employee's performance, a systems researcher might look at the records of everyone in the employee's department. Has the performance of others with the same job title been affected? Has there been a change in interactions (relationships, procedures, computer or telephone connections, to name just a few interaction types) between the employee and others with whom he or she must interact to accomplish tasks? Have changes in other parts of the system affected the employee or the employee's work group? The systems researcher would not have the time and would have little inclination to interview each employee individually because the systems emphasis is on interactions between system units. However, a rules researcher might immediately ask the employee to list possible reasons for the change in performance. If the answer happens to be that the employee is having serious personal difficulties with family members, the rules researcher would be the first to discover this type of cause; a systems researcher might return to discover it only after ruling out organizational or group changes as possibilities. A systems theorist tends to view employees with the same job title as very similar organizational units rather than as distinct individuals with many idiosyncrasies. Thus, the trade-off for gaining a way to analyze complex interactions through the systems perspective is some loss of individual and personal perspective.

SUMMARY

In this chapter we have examined four perspectives on communication theory: covering laws, communibiological, rules, and systems. As you have learned, scientists from different perspectives make different assumptions, ask different questions, study the questions in different ways, and are interested in different types of answers. Researchers operating from the covering laws perspective emphasize cause-and-effect relationships; communibiological researchers emphasize the role of biology in predicting behavior. Rules or human action researchers emphasize choice and the creation of individual and social rules. Systems theorists emphasize the interactions between the parts of an interdependent system and de-emphasize the role of individuals.

Your own experience has probably led you to feel more comfortable with one of these perspectives. If not, perhaps you will be tempted to adopt the perspective favored by your instructor. As you read the chapters in the next section of the book, try to imagine why your authors believe a particular theory is an example of a given perspective. For example, ask yourself, "Why is this theory an example of the laws approach? What cause–effect relationships does it propose? Might rules or systems provide a better explanation of the communication behavior being studied? How would theorists from other perspectives approach this research question?"

KEY TERMS

behavioral activation system
behavioral inhibition system
causality
closed system
communibiological perspective
covering laws perspective
cybernetic systems
equifinality
experimental paradigm
explain

fight–flight system
generalizability
habitual rules
homeostasis
laws
logical positivism
nonsummativity
open systems
paradigms
paradigm shift

parametric rules
prediction
rule-following approach
rule-governed approach
subsystems
suprasystems
tactical rules
teleological
temperaments
theoretical perspective

THEORY BUILDING IN MAJOR APPROACHES TO COMMUNICATION

II

Part II introduces four major lines of communication research that have been investigated without being tied to a specific context: communication traits, persuasion, verbal behavior, and nonverbal behavior. Ideas concerning persuasion, for instance, are assumed to apply in some form, regardless of the specific situation in which the persuasion occurs. Part III will discuss theory building in particular communication contexts.

Chapter 5 examines an extensively researched approach to communication. The concept of communication traits began with the study of personality by psychologists. We discuss four types of communication traits. Apprehension traits cover feelings of fear and anxiety about communication. Presentation traits comprise ways or styles of presenting verbal and nonverbal messages. Adaptation traits concern the different ways individuals adjust or adapt to the people with whom they communicate. Aggression traits involve tendencies to use force; these can be either constructive or destructive to communication. The theories presented in chapter 5 provide excellent illustrations of the covering laws approach.

Prior to the current line of research on communication traits, persuasion was probably the most popular research area. Chapter 6 conceptualizes persuasion as changing one's attitude about a proposal. We consider persuasion research on several variables: personality traits, message variables, and the source credibility approach to persuasion are discussed in some detail. Next we examine several covering laws theories of persuasion: cognitive dissonance, ego-involvement, reasoned action, theory of planned behavior, elaboration likelihood, compliance-gaining message selection, and persuasive heuristics. We conclude with a brief look at preventing persuasion.

Chapter 7 focuses on verbal behavior theory and research, a consistently popular area of study for the past several decades. First we discuss basic concepts such as symbols, meaning, and perception. Next we examine research on how language communicates power and status. Then we review areas of verbal behavior research in some detail: communication accommodation, conversational and discourse analysis, and language expectancy theory.

Nonverbal communication has emerged as one of the most popular areas of research in the communication field and has also generated a great deal of general public interest. Chapter 8 contrasts the effectiveness of verbal and nonverbal codes and discusses the influence of context, intentionality, emotional leakage, and the functions of nonverbal communication. We then examine nonverbal immediacy, cognitive valence theory, expectancy-violation theory, interpersonal deception theory, and interaction adaptation theory in detail because they have guided a good deal of nonverbal communication research and theory building.

Trait Approaches

W hat is a communication trait? The concept originated in personality theory. "Personality is an abstraction or hypothetical construction from or about behavior. . . . a [personality] trait is a construction or abstraction to account for enduring behavioral consistencies and differences" (Mischel, 1968, pp. 4–5). Our interest is in communicative behavior—when individuals manipulate verbal and nonverbal symbols to stimulate meaning in others. The study of personality encompasses this and much more, for instance, traits such as compulsiveness, masochism, tolerance for ambiguity, richness of fantasy, and rigidity. Although these traits certainly might affect *how* we communicate, they do not constitute communicative behavior per se.

Communication traits are personality traits related specifically to human symbolic behavior. Communication traits thus represent a subset of the larger set of personality traits. An adaptation of Mischel's definition to make it more communication-oriented would be: *A communication trait is an abstraction constructed to account for enduring consistencies and differences in message-sending and message-receiving behaviors among individuals.*

Communication traits are hypothetical constructs. A hypothetical construct represents reality by structuring and giving meaning to experience. The traits we will examine in this chapter have an appeal because they appear to give meaning to certain communication behaviors and provide explanations that would not otherwise exist. It is important to note that a hypothetical construct in the social sciences is invented to represent and characterize something scientists cannot absolutely prove by observing it empirically with the five senses. For instance, the most prominent hypothetical construct in

communication trait
An abstraction constructed to account for enduring consistencies and differences in message-sending and message-receiving behaviors among individuals.

the history of the social sciences is probably *attitude.* An attitude is usually defined as a predisposition to respond favorably or unfavorably. This seems clear, for example, when we think of how favorable our feelings are toward a particular food. To say we have a favorable attitude toward that food makes sense. Remember, however, that "attitude" is a hypothetical construct, an invention to explain behavior. No one has actually ever seen an attitude. Likewise, we do not know that a given trait is "real." Researchers assume that if it is real, the data from a study will take a certain form. If it does, the researcher essentially says, "I'm right so far; the data don't contradict my assumptions. Now let's gather some different data to see if there is further proof." This process never really ends because somewhere along the line it will be possible to invent a different construct that explains the data better.

A major criticism of trait approaches is that they "beg the question." For instance, it is not very helpful to say some people argue a lot because they are high in trait argumentativeness. Using a label for one aspect of a trait as an explanation for behavior does not say much. However, the criticism is a "straw man" argument (describing and then refuting a position no one actually holds). Trait researchers do not use the label to explain the behavior. Instead, a theoretical framework is used. The label "high in argumentativeness" is a description of people who engage in arguments frequently. That label does not explain *why* they argue. The last section of this chapter will present a theoretical explanation that addresses competing motives and how people's perceptions interact with those motives to cause them to argue in a particular situation.

One of the reasons for interest in traits such as assertiveness, openness, friendliness, attentiveness, and aggressiveness is that it is easy to think of people whose personalities are defined mainly by one or another of these traits. Communication traits provide a basis for what to expect from others in various situations. It is useful to know in advance (at least to have an idea) how others will respond to us. Becoming more familiar with communication traits may provide an acceptable basis for predicting how others will respond in various communication situations.

CONTEXTS, TRAITS, AND STATES

contextual view Behavior is consistent within contexts but varies across contexts.

Distinctions are sometimes made between contextual, trait, and state behaviors. A **contextual view** of communication behavior contends that behavior is consistent within contexts but varies across contexts. Some examples of contexts would be family, school, and work. In this view, how one communicates on the job is not a good predictor of how one communicates at home. Communication competence is sometimes claimed to be contextual. For instance, being a competent communicator in public speaking situations does not mean one will be a competent interviewer or conversationalist. Similarly, a good interpersonal communicator may be a poor public speaker. The contextualist position is contrary to that of a trait theorist, who would expect someone who is very competent in one communication situation to be highly competent in all situations.

Trait behavior is assumed to be consistent across contexts and specific situations within particular contexts. That is, one's behavior regarding a trait is expected not to vary greatly from one situation to the next, nor from one point in time to the next. This does not mean that there should be no variability in trait behavior. Rather, types of behavior are usually predictable and reasonably consistent. Thus, a person who is assertive in one situation tends to be assertive in another. A person who is unassertive at age 13 tends to be unassertive at 23, 33, 43, and so forth. This does not mean that a given context or specific situation exerts no influence on behavior. Particular circumstances might, for instance, stimulate an unassertive person to speak up for his or her rights. In general, trait approaches maintain that there is a fairly high degree of consistency in trait behaviors across contexts, time, and situations. This idea has sparked a good deal of controversy, which we will review in the next section.

> **trait behavior** Behavior is assumed to be consistent across contexts and specific situations within particular contexts.

A state differs from trait and context in that state behavior varies from one situation to another within the same context. Trait communication apprehension predicts that a uniform level of fear will be associated with real or anticipated communication situations (McCroskey, 1970). State communication apprehension fluctuates with different circumstances. At times your fear might vary from your general trait behavior. You might normally be relatively free from fear about communicating (low in trait apprehension) but might experience a good deal of state apprehension in a specific situation. For example, a student who had usually been confident in the public speaking context trembled and was almost speechless when she had to recite a prayer in front of three thousand people at her graduation. She reported that if she had not written the prayer out beforehand, she would have been too afraid to think of a single word!

> **state behavior** Behavior that varies from one situation to another within the same context.

Trait behavior, as we noted earlier, can be expected to vary somewhat across contexts and situations within those contexts. In fact, exhibiting precisely the same communication behavior regardless of the situation might indicate that a person is neurotic with obsessive-compulsive symptoms (Infante, 1987b). Trait theorists do not deny that the situation influences behavior. The question is how *much* does the behavior vary? Are situations basically different from one another, and do their varying characteristics force us to behave in ways that are unique to the given situation? Or, do we tend to place ourselves in contexts and specific situations that we view as functionally equivalent, thus enabling us to repeat familiar behaviors?

THE CROSS-SITUATIONAL CONSISTENCY FRAMEWORK

The issue of the stability of behavior across situations has been the subject of much debate in the field of psychology. The most recent controversy began with personality theorist Walter Mischel's (1968) analysis that a correlation of about .30 seems to be the limit of the relationship of behavior in one situation to behavior in another situation. Thus, if we were to observe how *sociable* a group of people appeared to be in one situation by noting the number of smiles and then observed the same people in a different situation, the correlation would be rather low. A 1.00 correlation represents a perfect relationship; behavior in one situation could be predicted with perfect accuracy from behavior in another situation. In our example, if the rank order of the individuals in terms of the number of smiles were exactly the same in the first situation and the second, the correlation would be 1.00. Joe Smith smiled the most in both situations, Sally Jones was second in both, etc. A .30 correlation is low; it indicates considerable variability in smiling behavior from the first to the second situation. Joe Smith ranked first in smiling in situation one but ranked tenth in situation two. Whereas a 1.00 correlation means perfect consistency, .30 means there is some but not much consistency between two sets of observations.

Those who support this idea have been termed **situationists**. In the social sciences, a situationist believes situations primarily determine behavior because situations are unique and present different demands on the individual. People experience these demands and try to adapt their behavior to the environment. Therefore, behavior is shaped by situations. Because situations are seldom the same, behavior is not consistent. Basically, this position maintains that personality is overwhelmed by the situation. For instance, a person may not be as sociable in one situation as compared to another because one situation is more task oriented and the participants simply do not have as much time or opportunity to act sociably.

Situationists also argue that stability in behavior across situations may be more in the mind of the observer than in the subject's actual behavior. That is, we may want to see consistency in the behavior of others because this reduces uncertainty in our lives. We want others to be predictable and dependable because it is easier to deal with reliable behavior than with unreliable behavior. Perhaps due to wishful thinking, we see people as cross-situationally consistent even if they are not; we distort the .30 relationship and make it closer to 1.00. Traits, according to this view, are more in the minds of perceivers than in the behavior of social actors.

The **trait position** maintains that there are broad predispositions to behave in a particular manner. Trait theorists argue that a major reason why some research has failed to find consistent behavior across situations is that the studies were conducted in laboratory environments that placed people in unrealistic positions. Artificial situations cannot test the consistency or inconsistency of individuals in real life. According to the trait view, our personality traits predispose us to seek certain situations that allow us to "be ourselves," to behave characteristically, or to act in ways that reflect our uniqueness. If studies are not designed to permit people to select the situations in which they communicate, then the trait approach is not being fairly tested by researchers.

situationist Approach to understanding communication that emphasizes the impact of situational variables.

trait position Approach to communication that maintains there are broad predispositions that account for behavior.

A trait approach to personality assumes that there are "ways of behaving" that we associate with the people in our lives. You have probably heard someone say, "That is just like her to do that," or "I knew he would do that." We tend to think of people in terms of a cluster of *central traits*. One person might be known for being assertive, dominant, and competitive, whereas another person might be shy, polite, and anxious. All traits are not equally important to everyone's personality. For a given trait, some people will show stronger patterns than others across situations, depending on how important the trait is in the makeup of that individual's personality. For example, the person described as shy, polite, and anxious might be consistently shy but might not show strong patterns regarding other traits.

According to trait theorists, another major reason why low cross-situational consistency has been noted is that too few behaviors have been observed in studies. A behavior such as smiling in one situation may not be related to smiling in another because situations can influence behavior to some extent. The idea of a trait is not that behavior in *two* situations should be consistent, but that there should be a pattern across *many* situations. A person who is very sociable (high in the sociability trait) might be friendly in one situation but not in another. However, in looking at the person's sociability behavior across a large number of situations, a distinct pattern should emerge. For example, behavior might be characterized as sociable in 35 out of 40 situations. A person who is not very sociable (low in the trait) might be sociable in Situation 1 and Situation 2, yet he or she may not be very sociable over time. Sociable behavior might occur in only 8 out of 40 situations.

The **interactionist position** emerged from the conflict between trait and situationist theorists. Interactionists maintain that behavior in a partitular situation is a *joint* product of a person's traits and of variables in the situation. To ignore either of these influences on behavior results in less understanding of a person's actions. The interactionist position represents an attempt to integrate

interactionist position
Assumes that behavior in a particular situation is a joint product of a person's traits and of variables in the situation.

Three Positions on the Cross-situational Consistency Issue

SITUATIONIST:
Situation *primarily* determines behavior

TRAIT THEORIST:
Traits *primarily* determine behavior

INTERACTIONIST:
Traits and situation interact; the interaction *primarily* determines behavior

trait and situationist positions—to show they are compatible and not inherently antagonistic. According to an interactionist approach, trait and situational variables interact with one another to produce behavior. This means they influence one another and thereby create something that is unique—behavior that cannot be explained by the person's traits alone or by the situation alone. For instance, to predict whether a person will ask someone to turn down loud music, we must know not only whether the person has an assertive personality trait but also important characteristics of the situation. Is the loud music interfering with study for final exams? If the music is not blocking an important goal such as passing a difficult course, even an assertive person may say nothing. The interactionist position emphasizes the need to consider both trait and situational factors in predicting behavior.

Communication theories tend to be either trait or situationist in nature. It has been recommended that communication research should take an interactionist approach instead of the more fragmented approach of examining only traits or situations (Andersen, 1987; Infante, 1987a). Ignoring one factor leads to less than complete knowledge of communication. In the final section of this chapter we will examine a theory of argumentativeness that takes an interactionist approach.

The cross-situational consistency debate in psychology has been important for the field of communication because it has caused scholars to realize that there are trait and situationist approaches to communication. Unlike the field of psychology, trait and situationist researchers in communication have largely ignored one another. The situationist models of communication are inadequate because they cannot explain the many results found in trait research. Trait models are lacking because they cannot account for differences in behavior due to the situation. It seems obvious that combining the trait and situationist approaches would be desirable; taking an interactionist approach is a promising way for researchers to do so.

This debate in psychology has also been valuable because it has largely answered the question of how consistent behavior is across situations. Research indicates that behavior is consistent when enough relevant situations are considered. In addition to demonstrating cross-situational consistency, the research has suggested other areas for study. The focus on consistency has revealed that inconsistency occurs and also that scientists do not yet adequately understand why it occurs. Models need to be developed to account for differences in behavior. Is a given difference due entirely to occurrences within the situation? Why is someone very sociable at parties but very quiet when working as a librarian? Is there a trait that predicts whether sociable individuals will choose jobs in which sociable behavior is appropriate? Are unexpected, novel, and creative communicative behaviors even more revealing than regularities in communication?

The research examined in this chapter is from a laws perspective. The idea of traits—that behavior is cross-situationally consistent—is compatible with the assumptions of a laws approach and the communibiological perspective. Systems and human action researchers, on the other hand, have tended to be more situationist in terms of their study of communicative behavior. Thus, they have shown little interest in communication traits.

We will examine four classes of communication traits in this chapter: apprehension, presentation, adaptation, and aggression.

Apprehension Traits

COMMUNICATION APPREHENSION

Due to the ambitious research program of James C. McCroskey and his associates, **communication apprehension** is probably the most thoroughly researched topic in the history of the communication discipline (for a good overview of the research see Richmond & McCroskey, 1985). Hundreds of studies have been conducted over the past three decades. As a result, an impressive body of knowledge exists today. In 1970 McCroskey defined communication apprehension as "a broadly based anxiety related to oral communication" (p. 270). This definition was expanded in later work to "an individual's level of fear or anxiety associated with either real or anticipated communication with another person or persons" (McCroskey, 1977, p. 78).

> **communication apprehension** A broadly based anxiety related to oral communication.

There are four types of communication apprehension (CA). *Traitlike CA* is the relatively stable degree of anxiety a person experiences across communication contexts (public speaking, meetings, interpersonal and group communication) and over time. Traitlike CA reflects a personality orientation and has been the major focus of study.

For some people, communication apprehension varies across contexts; this is termed *context-based CA*. For instance, some people are more fearful of speaking before a large crowd than of taking part in a group discussion. Other people have little fear of giving speeches but are uncomfortable talking with people on a one-to-one basis. Thus, it is meaningful to consider the context when studying CA.

Audience-based CA is fear experienced when communicating with certain types of people regardless of the time or context. The particular audience members trigger the fear reaction. A person who is apprehensive about communicating with parents, for instance, will experience CA when giving a speech if parents are in the audience even though the person has little fear of public speaking. The person experiences fear similar to that felt when talking with the parents interpersonally.

Situational CA is the degree of fear experienced in talking with people in a given situation. This is the apprehension created by variables unique to a particular situation. People who are high in CA are not always fearful, and low CAs sometimes do experience fear. What accounts for this inconsistency with one's trait? Variables in the given situation probably best explain such discrepancies. For instance, a person who is low in CA might become apprehensive if the person is told a great deal depends on a superior performance. Pressure can result in even very confident people "choking" in terms of performance.

There is basically only one internal effect of CA: The person feels psychologically uncomfortable. There are physical manifestations of this uncomfortable feeling, including "butterflies" in the stomach, shaking hands and knees, dry mouth, excessive perspiration, elevated heart rate, increased respiration rate, and increased blood pressure. What does it mean for someone to experience this internal effect on a regular basis? The research is striking in terms of how debilitating it is to be apprehensive about communication. For instance, people with high CA have less academic success, take jobs with lower communication requirements, are less satisfied with work, are not viewed as leaders, and are seen as less friendly and less attractive than people with low CA. Richmond and McCroskey (1985) concluded that the more talkative, low CA person "is perceived to be more competent in general, more communicatively competent, less anxious about communication, more composed and extroverted, more assertive and responsive, generally a leader and an opinion leader, more friendly and sociable, and more attractive" (p. 60).

There are several speculations about what causes CA. A *low self-esteem* explanation posits that people fear communication when they have an unfavorable concept of self and therefore anticipate that they will do poorly. A *parental reinforcement* model predicts that when children are positively reinforced for communicating, they communicate more and develop less CA. On the other hand, when children are negatively reinforced by being told not to disagree with adults or are inconsistently reinforced by being allowed to talk at the dinner table one day but not another, they learn to withdraw from communication and therefore become apprehensive about it because they have learned to expect punishment. An *inherited trait* explanation suggests that traits such as sociability are inherited. Persons who inherit a low sociability trait are especially susceptible to developing CA if their communicative behavior is not positively reinforced.

Three additional causes are linked to methods for reducing CA. *Excessive activation* refers to fear of communication as a result of a physiological overreaction to an event—trembling, difficulty in swallowing, or temporary loss of memory. If the person is taught to control the overreactions, CA for all practical purposes is reduced. A method of therapy, *systematic desensitization,* is based on this assumption and appears to work very well. This involves learning to relax while thinking about various kinds of anxiety-producing communication events. *Inappropriate cognitive processing* posits that what high CA and low CA people experience physically is very similar, but, what they "think" they experience is very different. The physical sensation of "butterflies in the stomach" may be perceived by low CA individuals as a mild, normal, stimulating reaction to public speaking, whereas high CA people interpret it as a major loss of control. Thus, to change CA, one needs to change one's mind about communication. *Cognitive restructuring* is a therapy method employed for this. It involves identifying and changing irrational beliefs about self and also formulating new positive beliefs. The *inadequate communication skills* model of CA maintains people are apprehensive about communication because they know they are not very good at the activity. Fear is a normal and predictable response to a situation that one does not know how to deal with competently. The treatment approach for this is *communication skills training.* This is a very popular approach exemplified by speech and communication courses in educational institutions.

Beatty, McCroskey, and Heisel (1998) claimed that none of these speculations about what causes CA has been firmly established in research. They then offered an explanation based on the communibiological perspective (see Chapter 4). They believe CA has a biological origin because it is determined by "genetically inherited thresholds of neurobiological structures" (p. 198). That is, the extent to which certain parts of the brain are activated controls the extent to which a person experiences CA. The biology involves neurobiological brain mechanisms, which, when activated, stimulate certain cognitive and emotional activity and subsequent patterns of behavior.

The authors identified parts of the brain and the neurological circuits that connect them as constituting the behavioral inhibition system (BIS). People who are habitually anxious have overactive BISs, whereas less anxious persons have underactive BISs. According to Beatty, McCroskey, and Heisel, high CAs have overactive BISs and experience anxiety more often because they have a low tolerance for stimulation to their BIS. All communication situations produce at least a minimal degree of stimulation. That is a problem for high CAs because most communication situations provide what turns out to be the minimal degree of stimulation necessary in these persons to trigger their BIS and thus produce feelings of anxiety.

The authors also explain the brain biology of the behavioral activation system (BAS) and discuss why occasionally a low CA, for instance, will avoid making an oral presentation, whereas a high CA might not avoid the situation (even though you would probably expect it would be the high CA, who would not speak because of his or her normally high level of anxiety). If the low CA is unprepared for the presentation, this could activate his or her BIS. However, a situation in which there is a large reward for a successful oral presentation might activate the BAS of the high CA but not trigger the BIS of the normally high CA individual. This example shows how and why traits do not always predict behavior.

The main point of their explanation is that the brain structures and circuitry involved in BIS and BAS are genetically determined, and the environment has very little to do with their biological development. Thus, this suggests that CA is based on one's genes and therefore not susceptible to a great deal of change. If you are a high CA, undergoing treatment for CA can reduce your CA, but not a great deal (such as going from a very high CA to a very low CA). It is much more likely, the authors say, that with some effort the high CA will learn how to live with the anxiety by acquiring coping methods such as relaxation techniques and learning how to avoid uncomfortable anxiety-provoking communication situations. It should be noted that this explanation represents a major departure from the social learning model, which has been used almost exclusively in previous attempts to explain CA. For example, social learning suggest children develop CA after being discouraged from talking at the dinner table. We expect the communibiological perspective will stimulate some interesting controversy in future research and findings.

RECEIVER APPREHENSION

Lawrence Wheeless (1975) maintained that CA is a multifaceted construct that includes dimensions pertaining to sending and receiving information in formal and informal contexts. The Personal Report of Communication Apprehension (PRCA) questionnaire developed by McCroskey (1970) focuses on fear of sending messages. A typical item on the scale is, "I look forward to expressing my opinion at meetings." If people are apprehensive about sending messages, it seems reasonable to speculate that they may also be anxious about receiving messages from others. According to Wheeless, receiver apprehension "is probably related more to fear of misinterpreting, inadequately processing, and/or not being able to adjust psychologically to messages sent by others" (p. 263). The Receiver Apprehension Test (RAT) was developed by Wheeless to measure this trait. His research suggests receiver and source apprehension appear to be two separate dimensions of CA. When dimensions are separate or independent, they are not related to one another. Thus, if you are high in source apprehension, you are not necessarily high in receiver apprehension.

For receiver apprehension, formal and informal communication contexts are not separate. This means the degree of receiver apprehension one feels in one context such as a public speech is similar to the degree experienced in other contexts, such as talking with a friend. Someone's level of receiver apprehension in one situation can be predicted from knowing about his or her receiver apprehension in another context. Wheeless's research suggests this is also true for source apprehension.

Wheeless' model of receiver apprehension is an example of theory building in communication because his conceptualization was influenced by work on communication apprehension. By building on earlier work, he expanded our understanding of the apprehension construct.

INFORMATIONAL RECEPTION APPREHENSION

Informational reception apprehension (IRA) is a relatively new trait that was developed from the trait of **receiver apprehension** (Wheeless, 1975). IRA is believed to be a secondary anxiety based on previous research on receiver apprehension (Wheeless, Preiss, & Gayle, 1997). IRA is defined as "a pattern of anxiety and antipathy that filters informational reception, perception, and processing, and/or adjustment (psychologically, verbally, physically) associated with complexity, abstractness, and flexibility" (Wheeless et al., 1997, p. 166).

The IRA construct is based on the idea that stimuli or message characteristics and cognitive processes interact with each other. Stimuli can vary in complexity, abstractness, and flexibility. Complexity reflects both the amount and details of the message, well as the cognitive capacity of the person receiving the information. Abstractness reflects how concrete the information is, as well as the capacity of the person receiving the message to think abstractly. Flexibility is "the demands of the external environment for openness, adaptability, change, etc., as well as the ability of a person to select, receive, and deal with such information" (Wheeless, Eddleman-Spears, Magness, & Preiss, 2005, p. 146).

Every person has a threshold for information processing that when crossed, results in an impairment in a person's ability to properly process information. For example, consider the following two situations. In the first situation your professor enters the classroom and says, "Tomorrow we will have a quiz on this material, but we will not be grading the quiz." In the second situation your professor walks into the classroom and says, "Tomorrow we will have a quiz on this material, and the resulting grade will be your grade for the entire semester." As the environmental demands change (i.e., ungraded quiz versus an entire course grade), some students may have severe informational reception apprehension when studying or attending to the lecture due to the magnitude of the final course grade in the second example.

Informational reception apprehension is believed to contain the three dimensions of **listening apprehension**, **reading anxiety**, and **intellectual inflexibility**. Listening apprehension is the fear associated with either anticipated or real listening situations. Reading anxiety refers to the degree of anxiety a person experiences when reading information. Intellectual inflexibility reflects the degree to which people are unwilling to consider different points of view. In a study looking at IRA and argumentative and aggressive communication, Paul Schrodt and Lawrence Wheeless (2001) found that both listening apprehension and intellectual inflexibility were predictors of both argumentativeness and verbal aggressiveness. That is, people reporting high levels of IRA also reported higher levels of verbal aggressiveness and lower argumentativeness.

Within the classroom, Schrodt, Wheeless, and Ptacek (2000) found that informational reception apprehension has an influence on student motivation and achievement. More specifically, both listening apprehension and the intellectual inflexibility dimensions were correlated with lower motivation and

informational reception apprehension A pattern of anxiety and antipathy that filters informational reception, perception, and processing, and/or adjustment (psychologically, verbally, physically) associated with complexity, abstractness, and flexibility.

receiver apprehension Fear of misinterpreting, inadequately processing, and/or not being able to adjust psychologically to messages sent by others.

listening apprehension The fear associated with either anticipated or real listening situations.

reading anxiety Refers to the degree of anxiety a person experiences when reading information.

intellectual inflexibility The degree to which people are unwilling to consider different points of view.

achievement in the classroom. They concluded that researchers should consider informational reception apprehension to better explain student motivation and achievement beyond what has been explained by only communication apprehension. The development of the IRA trait has significantly expanded our understanding of apprehensive communication specific to receiving stimuli in the environment.

Presentation Traits

COMMUNICATOR STYLE

communicator style The way a person verbally and paraverbally interacts to signal how literal meaning should be taken, interpreted, filtered, or understood.

Developed from a model by Robert Norton (1978, 1983), **communicator style** is concerned with how messages are communicated, not with the content of messages. According to Norton (1978) communicator style is "the way one verbally and paraverbally interacts to signal how literal meaning should be taken, interpreted, filtered, or understood" (p. 99). Style gives form to content and accumulates over time so that we develop a comprehensive, more global impression of a person's particular communicator style.

communicator image An overall impression of a communicator that is composed of at least ten traits.

Communicator style may be viewed as an overall impression, a **communicator image**, composed of at least ten traits: impression leaving, contentious, open, dramatic, dominant, precise, relaxed, friendly, attentive, and animated. The degree to which an individual possesses each of these traits contributes to the person's image. With ten traits, there are numerous possible combinations. Each configuration creates a different overall impression. For instance, a person who is dominant, animated, and friendly is perceived as very different from another person who is also dominant and animated but unfriendly. The unfriendly trait might be so prominent that impressions of this person's other prominent traits might be perceived more negatively when compared with the same traits in someone else. The unfriendly trait might lead to the dominant and animated traits being viewed as manipulative and untrustworthy. How a person's traits combine, therefore, is crucial to the overall image that is created.

impression leaving A dimension of communicator style that is a disposition to create a lasting image in the minds of the receivers.

We will briefly review the meaning of each of the ten traits. **Impression leaving** is the attempt to create a lasting image in the minds of receivers. Communicators are aware of this goal when talking with others. **Contentious** is a disposition to challenge others when disagreements occur, to argue with others. Whereas arguing constructively is a very positive trait (to be discussed later), contentiousness appears to be a somewhat negative trait because it involves arguing too much, getting "carried away" by the emotion in a situation, being unwilling to end an argument gracefully, and pursuing it to "the bitter end." **Open** is a predisposition to reveal feelings, thoughts, and personal information. The open person takes pride in being honest and in not hiding

contentious A disposition to challenge others when disagreements occur, to argue with others.

open A dimension of communicator style that is a predisposition to reveal feelings, thoughts, and personal information.

things from others. Dramatic style involves telling jokes and stories to illustrate points, exaggerating for emphasis, and generally creating the impression of "acting" when talking with people. Dominant denotes coming on strong, speaking frequently, taking leadership roles, and wanting to control social situations. Precise includes insisting that people document what they are saying and that they give definitions. Generally, a person with this trait tries very hard to be accurate and thorough. Relaxed means not having nervous mannerisms in speech or bodily communication; pride is taken in appearing relaxed in stressful situations. Friendly involves praising, encouraging, and expressing liking for others. Attentive is the tendency to listen carefully to people, to be able to repeat back what others say, and to act so that people know you are listening. Animated is a trait that signifies extensive use of eyes, face, and gestures to express meaning.

Dominic Infante and William Gorden (1981) used the communicator style model to investigate communication between superiors and subordinates in organizations. They explored how similarities and differences in the communicator styles of an employee and a boss related to the employee's satisfaction. Are there certain traits on which subordinates like to be similar to their bosses? Are there other traits on which subordinates like to differ? The study found employees were most satisfied when dramatic and animated traits were similar, but relaxed, open, and attentive traits were different. If a boss is much more dramatic and animated, the subordinate may be uneasy and perhaps feel somewhat inferior because the boss exerts so much more energy than the subordinate.

Another study investigated the communicator style traits of fashion innovators and fashion laggards (Gorden, Infante, & Braun, 1986). A fashion innovator was conceived as one who adopts recent fashion changes, whereas a fashion laggard was one who adopts a fashion change after a long time, or one who never adopts it. The study found that fashion innovators, when compared to fashion laggards, were higher on impression-leaving, dramatic, friendly, and animated traits. These traits comprise what has been called the "energy expenditure" dimension of communicator style. This finding supported the hypothesis that people who communicate at a high energy level would also "dress for the part." That is, they would wear more dramatic, attention-getting, and current fashions.

DISCLOSIVENESS

Self-disclosure, revealing intimate information about oneself, is a presentational trait that plays an important part in the development of close relationships. The general model is that trust is developed and strengthened when both persons self-disclose and show support for each other's disclosures. One person reveals something—a like, a fear, a secret goal. If the other person is

---

dramatic   A dimension of communicator style that involves telling jokes and stories to illustrate points, exaggerating for emphasis, and generally creating the impression of "acting" when talking with people.

dominant   A dimension of communicator style that reflects coming on strong, speaking frequently, taking leadership roles, and wanting to control social situations.

precise   A dimension of communicator style that includes insisting that people document what they are saying and that they give definitions.

relaxed   A dimension of communicator style that reflects not having nervous mannerisms in speech or bodily communication.

friendly   A dimension of communicator style that involves praising, encouraging, and expressing liking for others.

attentive   A dimension of communicator style and is the tendency to listen carefully to people, to be able to repeat back what others say.

animated   A dimension of communicator style which is a trait that signifies extensive use of eyes, face, and gestures to express meaning.

supportive, this revelation encourages more and more intimate disclosures. The other person may feel a need to reciprocate the disclosure, so the individuals might take turns sharing. It may be impossible to develop a close personal relationship without self-disclosure. In fact, not to self-disclose is probably a way of telling another person that you do not want the relationship to progress to a more personal or intimate level. Wheeless (1975a) developed a scale to measure the tendency to self-disclose as a trait. According to Wheeless, **disclosiveness** represents "a person's predilection to disclose to other people in general—his or her generalized openness in encoding" (p. 144). Wheeless's model specifies that persons high in disclosiveness must also trust others. People who are not very trusting will be especially cautious about revealing feelings to others.

The Disclosiveness Scale measures the trait of self-disclosure in terms of five dimensions. The **intent** dimension involves the degree of awareness that one is revealing information about self. Having intent to self-disclose may mean that the individual views disclosure as a strategy in relating to other people. **Amount** pertains to the frequency of disclosure relative to other types of messages in interpersonal communication. **Positiveness** is a subscale that measures the extent to which the information revealed about self is positive or negative. **Depth** refers to how superficial or intimate the information is. The **honesty** dimension involves the sincerity of disclosure.

Adaptation Traits

In contrast to the presentation traits just discussed, adaptation traits influence how we adapt to conversational partners. Five major categories of adaptation traits will be discussed in this section: communicative adaptability, rhetorical sensitivity, communication competence, interaction involvement, and cognitive flexibility.

COMMUNICATIVE ADAPTABILITY

The **communicative adaptability** trait was originally developed as a way of integrating several dimensions of communication competence. Robert Duran (1992) defined communicative adaptability as "the ability to perceive socio-interpersonal relationships and adapt one's interaction goals and behaviors accordingly" (p. 320). The basic premise is that the greater the person's repertoire of social skills, the more likely they will be able to engage in successful communicative performance. Therefore, communicative adaptability is a component of social communication competence.

Communicative adaptability consists of six dimensions that are closely related to aspects of communication competence. These six dimensions are **social composure**, **social confirmation**, **social experience**, **appropriate disclosure**, **articulation**, and **wit** (Duran, 1992). Social composure is the degree

---

disclosiveness   Personality trait that reflects a person's predilection to disclose to other people in general.

intent   A dimension of self-disclosure that involves the degree of awareness that one is revealing information about self.

amount   A dimension of disclosiveness that pertains to the frequency of disclosure relative to other people.

positiveness   A dimension of disclosiveness that measures the extent to which the information revealed about self is positive or negative.

depth   A dimension of disclosiveness that refers to how superficial or intimate the information is.

honesty   A dimension of disclosiveness that involves the sincerity of disclosure.

communicative adaptability   A trait that is the ability to perceive socio-interpersonal relationships and adapt interaction goals and interpersonal behaviors appropriately.

social composure   A dimension of communicative adaptability that reflects the degree to which a person is calm, cool, and collected in social situations.

to which a person is calm, cool, and collected in social situations. Social confirmation is the degree to which a person can affirm or maintain the other person's face or self-image while interacting. Social experience is the degree to which a person actually experiences, or is willing to experience, novel situations. Appropriate disclosure is the degree to which a person reveals personal information in the appropriate amount as dictated by any given social situation. Articulation is the degree to which a person is proficient or skilled in the expression of ideas. This involves the mastery of the language, which includes appropriate syntax and semantic elements. The wit dimension reflects the degree to which a person utilizes humor in appropriate situations to diffuse escalating aggressive communication exchanges. Thus, sociocommunication competence is comprised of psychological factors (i.e., social composure and social experience), sociological factors (i.e., appropriate disclosure and social confirmation), and communication factors (i.e., articulation and wit) factors.

The Communicative Adaptability Scale (CAS) (Duran, 1983) was created to assess the six dimensions of socioicommunicative competence. Initial testing revealed that the CAS is related to both communication traits and psychological traits. More specifically, communicative adaptability was found to be a causal factor in satisfaction in roommate relationships (Duran & Zakahi, 1988) and is related to interpersonal assertiveness (Zakahi, 1985). In a study looking at the role of communicative adaptability and attractiveness, Robert Duran and Lynne Kelly (1985) found that the more adaptive a person was, the more cognitively complex they were (i.e., possessed the ability to develop multiple categories for describing abstract as well as concrete ideas). Further, adaptability was also linked to greater levels of interaction involvement (i.e., another communication competence-based construct that reflects the degree to which people are cognitively and behaviorally engaged in interpersonal interactions; Duran & Kelly, 1988).

Focusing on the psychological trait of locus of control, Theodore Avtgis and Scott Myers (1996) found that people with an internal locus of control orientation (i.e., people who see outcomes in their lives as being a function of their own purposeful action) reported greater adaptability than people with an external control orientation (i.e., people who see outcomes in their lives as being due to chance, fate, or other people). More specifically, internally oriented people are much more socially composed and have more social experience than externally oriented people. Recall that the cognitive flexibility trait suggests that a person needs to believe that they have the control to successfully execute the behavior. We can conclude from the Avtgis and Myers study that the belief in control over the behavior (i.e., self-efficacy) is also an important part of communicative adaptability.

In terms of measurement issues, the CAS is highly interrelated with the Norton (1978) communicator style questionnaire. These two traits, when combined, form three "super traits." That is, all six dimension of the communicative

social confirmation A dimension of communicative adaptability that reflects the degree to which a person can affirm or maintain the other person's face or self-image while interacting

social experience A dimension of communicative adaptability that reflects the degree to which a person actually experiences, or is willing to experience novel situations.

appropriate disclosure A dimension of communicative adaptability that reflects the degree to which a person reveals personal information in the appropriate amount as dictated by any given situation.

articulation A dimension of communicative adaptability that reflects the degree to which a person is proficient or skilled in the expression of ideas.

wit A dimension of communicative adaptability that reflects the degree to which a person utilizes humor in appropriate situations to diffuse escalating aggressive communication exchanges.

adaptability trait and the eleven dimensions from the communicator style trait, when combined, form three larger dimensions of self-confidence, affect, and entertainment (Duran & Zakahi, 1984). More recently, the CAS can also be a valid measure when used by a third party (Hullman, 2007) to evaluate another person's communication adaptability (prior, the CAS was used exclusively as a self-report measure).

In an effort to determine if a genetic basis for communicative adaptability exists, Michael Beatty, Lenora Marshall, and Jill Rudd (2001) administered the CAS to both identical twins (i.e., monozygotic twin pairs) and fraternal twins (i.e., dizygotic twin pairs). It is believed that monozygotic twin pairs are genetically identical, whereas dizygotic twins average about 50% identical. The overall findings of this research indicate that the CAS dimensions of social composure is 88% heritable, wit is 90% heritable, and social confirmation is 36% heritable. The other dimensions did not have a genetic basis. These findings provide a strong endorsement for the communibiological paradigm discussed in Chapter 4, suggesting that communication adaptability may indeed have a genetic basis.

Communicative adaptability provides the field of communication studies with a generally stable trait that is conceptualized as a component of social competence. Although there is overlap with other competence-related and adaptive traits. Communication adaptability is unique in that it encompasses cognitive, affective, and behavioral dimensions of competence.

NOBLE SELF, RHETORICAL REFLECTOR, RHETORICAL SENSITIVITY

noble self A person who believes in expressing exactly what they think or feel. Noble selves do not value flexibility in adapting to different audiences.

Persons who are noble selves (Hart, Carlson, & Eadie, 1980) believe in expressing exactly what they think or feel. To do otherwise, they believe, betrays their "real self." Thus, a noble self who dislikes something feels compelled to express that dislike, even though other people might not want to hear such a negative assessment, or even though the negative comments might create difficulties for the speaker. Noble selves do not value flexibility in adapting to different audiences. Noble selves view the idea of presenting a message one way to some people and another way to other people as misrepresenting their true beliefs. They believe a message should be created to suit self, not others. Thus, the noble self tends to have a script for a given topic and uses that script, with little change, in all situations in which the topic is discussed. For instance, if a noble self has a script of critical views on the president's domestic policy, he or she says essentially the same thing when talking to the president's supporters as when talking with critics. No attempt is made to appease the listener, to put the message in more "acceptable" terms.

rhetorical reflector People who have the tendency to conceive their "selves" not as fixed entities, but as social "characters" who take on whatever role is necessary for the particular situation.

The rhetorical reflector (Hart, Carlson, & Eadie, 1980) is at the other end of this spectrum. Rhetorical reflectors conceive of their "selves" not as fixed entities, but as social "characters" who take on whatever role is necessary for the particular situation. "Self" is a servant of the person and is highly change-able and adaptable. Rhetorical reflectors take pride in seeing the type of per-son needed in a situation and then becoming that person. They see flexibility as a most important trait. They emphasize "telling people what they want to hear," expressing a position on an issue in terms of the attitudes, values, hopes, fears, and desires of the receiver. The rhetorical reflector believes in being the kind of person others want him or her to be. This does not mean being dis-honest. For rhetorical reflectors honesty is not the issue. Their concern is with the *requirements* of the situation. What type of person are people looking for, and what do they want to hear? As you would expect, the scripts of the rhetor-ical reflector are not as fixed as those of the noble self. Rhetorical reflectors probably have very general scripts for controversial issues and situations, which they adapt to the given situation.

Rhetorical sensitivity (Hart, Carlson, & Eadie, 1980) is intermediate with respect to the noble self and rhetorical reflector extremes. The rhetorically sen-sitive person believes there is no single self but a complex network of selves, such as father, husband, accountant, church member, golfer. Rhetorically sen-sitive persons do not adopt the constantly changing character of the rhetorical reflector, but neither do they agree with noble selves that individuals have only one immutable self. Rhetorical sensitives are flexible, but they neither sacrifice their values to please others nor ignore the needs of other people when com-municating with them. Rhetorical sensitivity avoids the rigidity of the noble self and the chameleon character of the rhetorical reflector. Whereas the rhetor-ical reflector sees messages as a means to please others, the rhetorical sensitive is more concerned with the function of messages in creating understanding. Thus, messages on a topic vary from audience to audience in terms of what it takes to make an idea clear and meaningful to people. The rhetorical sensitiv-ity trait involves an appreciation for the idea that communicating ideas and feelings to people need not be either rigid or overly accommodating.

A study of more than 3,000 college students (Hart, Carlson, & Eadie, 1980) found noble selves tended to be single, Democratic, liberal, living in cities in the eastern United States, from larger, lower-income families, and more likely to take pride in their ethnic origins. Rhetorical reflectors tended to be conservative, female, 21 years or older, married, academically noncom-petitive, conservative Protestants, regular churchgoers, and from low to mid-dle socioeconomic classes. Rhetorical sensitives were more likely to be male, competitive, from higher-income, upper-middle socioeconomic classes, low in ethnic identification, and Republican or politically independent. In other research Gorden and Infante (1980) found that freedom of speech was valued most by noble selves and least by rhetorical reflectors. Rhetorical sensitives were slightly less likely to value freedom of speech than noble selves.

rhetorical sensitivity A person who believes there is no single self but a complex network of selves. The rhetorical sensitive person is in between the noble self and the rhetorical reflector.

COMMUNICATION COMPETENCE

appropriateness
Dimension of communication competence where verbal and nonverbal communication results in no loss of face for the parties involved.

effectiveness A dimension of communication competence that refers to the speaker achieving communicative goals.

Communication competence is an adaptation trait that has received a good deal of attention by communication researchers (for instance see R. Rubin, 1982, 1985; Spitzberg & Cupach, 1984; Wiemann, 1977). Communication competence involves **appropriateness** and **effectiveness** and may eventually be found to involve other traits. Appropriateness means verbal and nonverbal communication that results in no loss of face for the parties involved. Effectiveness refers to the speaker achieving communicative goals. There is some controversy as to whether communication competence is a trait or whether it is contextual or situational. If communication competence is a trait, then it is context-free and is an attribute of the individual. Thus, if a person communicates competently in one context (at work), the person would also tend to communicate in a competent manner in other contexts (at school or at a party). Basically, as explained earlier, a trait approach maintains that there is considerable consistency in communication competency across a variety of situations.

A contextual approach maintains that our communicative behavior is influenced greatly by elements of context: the time, place, activity, and people involved. The nature of communication on the job, for instance, is greatly different from communication in the family. Therefore, contextual theorists maintain that having the skills to be good at one does not ensure that one will be good at the other. In other words, according to a contextual approach, you may be effective in getting subordinates to be more productive but might fail in motivating your children to work harder.

Unfortunately, there has been little research to resolve the trait versus contextual controversy. There is some intuitive appeal of a trait approach because we can usually think of some people who are such good communicators that they never appear to communicate inappropriately or ineffectively. On the other hand, there are some persons who never seem to measure up to the standards of competent communication. Thus, cross-situational consistency for some people seems high. However, such individuals may represent the extremes (high and low) of the distribution of people in terms of communication competence. People who are more moderate in communication competence may be much less consistent across contexts. That is, communication competence may be contextual for people who are neither extremely good nor extremely poor communicators. Thus, a person who is moderate in terms of trait communication competence might be very competent in some contexts such as work groups, low in others such as intimate relationships, and moderately competent in the remainder such as social functions.

There is a further possibility that communication competence contains a trait component but is also influenced by the context or situation. The real explanatory power of a trait aspect of competence may be the way the trait interacts with factors in the particular situation. The trait examined in the next section represents such a possibility.

INTERACTION INVOLVEMENT

Interaction involvement has been defined as "the extent to which an individual participates with another in conversation" (Cegala, Savage, Brunner, & Conrad, 1982, p. 229). Individuals who are highly involved tend to focus their attention on self, the other person, the situation, and the topic of communication. They are able to integrate their thoughts, feelings, and experiences with the interaction as it develops. People who are higher in interaction involvement are generally viewed as more competent communicators. Persons who are low in interaction involvement tend to be "removed" from the situation. They seem to be preoccupied with other things, to be distracted, and to have a difficult time remembering the content of conversations. Typically these individuals are judged as low in communication competence.

People can vary at times in how much involvement they experience. For instance, persons who are usually highly involved in conversations may occasionally find themselves experiencing low involvement. Despite such fluctuation there appears to be a characteristic level of interaction involvement that people prefer. Therefore, interaction involvement appears to be very traitlike. Cegala (1984) does emphasize an interactionist position—that factors in the given situation such as the degree of competitiveness can affect the amount of interaction involvement experienced.

Research suggests there are three aspects or dimensions of interaction involvement (Cegala et al., 1982). **Responsiveness** "is a tendency to react mentally to one's social circumstance and adapt by knowing what to say and when to say it" (p. 233). This reaction pertains to appropriateness and involves such aspects as alertness, judgment, and creativity. **Perceptiveness** "is an individual's general sensitivity to: (1) what meanings ought to be applied to others' behavior; and (2) what meanings others have applied to one's own behavior" (p. 321). Perceptiveness is concerned with social intelligence in the sense of assessing meanings important to the competent communicator. **Attentiveness** "is the extent to which one tends to heed cues in the immediate environment, especially one's interlocutor" (p. 321). Attentiveness reflects the individual's awareness of what comprises the environment.

Taken together, responsiveness, perceptiveness, and attentiveness are three tendencies that determine the individual's level of interaction involvement. Being high on all three or low on all three is an easy pattern to imagine. However, other combinations are possible. For instance, a person might be high on perceptiveness and attentiveness but low on responsiveness. Such a person is competent in terms of the cognitive aspects of communication competence but is unable to be responsive in terms of putting the knowledge into action.

Research has focused on how interaction involvement relates to other interaction traits such as communication apprehension, nonverbal communication, and leadership style. Cegala (1984) found that highly involved individuals could better process information and recall details of conversations. Also, they

interaction involvement The extent to which an individual participates with another in conversation.

responsiveness A dimension of interaction involvement that is a tendency to react mentally to one's social circumstance and adapt by knowing what to say and when to say it.

perceptiveness A dimension of interaction involvement and is an individual's general sensitivity to: (1) what meaning ought to be applied to others' behavior; and (2) what meanings others have applied to one's own behavior.

attentiveness A dimension of interaction involvement that is the extent to which one tends to heed cues in the immediate environment.

had stronger egos, felt more positive and friendly, prouder, and stronger than persons low in interaction involvement. For low-involvement persons, conversations with strangers may create uncertainty, which results in greater fear or anxiety. Similarly, a competitive situation represents a threat to low-involvement people, which also results in fear.

COGNITIVE FLEXIBILITY

cognitive flexibility
The degree to which a communicator considers options for behaving in different situations.

The communication trait of cognitive flexibility was developed by Matthew Martin and Rebecca Rubin (1995). They defined cognitive flexibility as the degree to which communicators are "able to adapt their communication to meet the demands of the situations, and perhaps more importantly, to consider options and alternative ways of behaving in different situations" (Martin, Anderson, & Thweatt, 1998, p. 531). It is believed that a person has an awareness of options and alternatives for behavior in any given situation, has a motivation to be flexible in any given situation, and believes that they have the ability to be able to adapt successfully to the situation. As such, someone who is high in cognitive flexibility will be able to identify and enact a variety of different behaviors as mandated by the situation. It is important to emphasize that a person not only needs to be aware that they have the options in terms of the way they behave, but that they also believe they can successfully enact those behaviors (i.e., self-efficacy).

Being flexible in any given situation is believed to be an important factor involved in competent communication (Parks, 1994). In fact, cognitive flexibility has been positively associated with communication competence (Rubin & Martin, 1994). In a study focusing on organizational relationships and the impact of cognitive flexibility, Paul Madlock, Matthew Martin, Leah Bogdan, and Melissa Ervin (2007) discovered that employees who were more cognitively flexible reported a more satisfying and greater quality relationship with their supervisor. There was a similar finding in that people who are more cognitively complex use more affinity seeking strategies (Martin & Anderson, 2001). Affinity-seeking strategies are the ways in which we get people to like us (Bell & Daly, 1984). More specifically, Martin and Anderson reported that cognitively flexible people: assume more control over the interaction, have more personal autonomy (i.e., independent and free thinking), listen more, give the impression that they are worthy of trust, and are less likely to concede control to the other person.

In terms of relating cognitive flexibility to argumentative and aggressive communication traits (discussed next in this chapter), Martin, Anderson, and Thweatt (1998) found that the trait of argumentativeness was positively related to cognitive flexibility. That is, the greater tendency a person has to approach arguments, the more flexible they are. Conversely, people who report greater trait verbal aggressiveness report less cognitive flexibility. This study clearly indicates that cognitively flexible people are more adept at cognitively creating arguments that are appropriate to the particular issue or situation and have less tendency to verbally aggress on another person. Investigating the influence that cognitive flexibility has on indirect interpersonal aggression, which is the "predisposition to harm other people without engaging in face-to face interaction" (Beatty, Valencic, Rudd, & Dobos, 1999, p. 105), Chesebro and Martin (2003) found that people who are highly flexible utilize indirect interpersonal aggression more than people who are low in flexibility. That is, high flexible people are more likely to spread rumors, withhold important information, and betray confidences. Highly cognitively flexible people may not resort to verbal aggression because of an awareness that they can reach their desired goals without resorting to a direct aggressive exchange. It is important to note that indirect interpersonal aggression is still within the realm of an aggressive personality (Rancer & Avtgis, 2006).

The trait of cognitive flexibility is a critical factor in the larger construct of communication competence (Parks, 1994). Similar to the Inventional System for generating arguments developed by Dominic Infante in 1988, cognitive flexibility concerns higher levels of thought (i.e., executive brain function) and greater ability to make appropriate and effective cognitive as well as behavioral alterations during the communication encounter. The cognitive flexibility trait will continue to aid researchers in understanding how people with higher-order cognitive function or greater critical thinking skills adapt to a variety of social and psychological situations.

Aggression Traits

Although not typical of the majority of our communicative behaviors, the final type of traits to be discussed is very important. A communicative behavior "may be considered aggressive if it applies force physically and symbolically in order, minimally, to dominate and perhaps damage or, maximally, to defeat and perhaps destroy the locus of attack. The locus of attack in interpersonal communication can be a person's body, material possessions, self-concept, positions on topics of communication, or behavior" (Infante, 1987b, p. 158). Thus, communication is aggressive when a person tries to "force" another person to believe something or to behave in a particular way. To force someone means to put such pressure on them that they do not really have much of a choice. According to this model of aggressive communication, force can be constructive or destructive in interpersonal relations. Aggression is constructive if it facilitates interpersonal communication satisfaction and enhances a relationship. Examples of physical aggression that can do this are sports, games, and playfulness such as mock assaults. Examples employing symbolic aggression might be defending one's rights without infringing on the rights of other people, as in persuading someone to cooperate on a new venture, On the other hand, aggressive communication is destructive when it produces dissatisfaction and reduces the quality of a relationship. Destructive types of physical aggression include violence against persons (for example, spouse beating) and violence directed at objects (for example, crushing someone's favorite hat). Examples of destructive symbolic aggression include insulting a person, swearing at someone, and expressing bitter resentment.

Infante's model of aggressive communication maintains that symbolic aggression is energized by a set of four personality traits. The idea is that the aggressive dimension of our personalities is not composed of a single trait but rather a complex combination of competing predispositions. Two of these traits are constructive, and two are destructive. The generally constructive traits are assertiveness and argumentativeness, whereas the usually destructive traits are hostility and verbal aggressiveness.

A recent book by Andrew Rancer and Theodore Avtgis (2006) presents a comprehensive review of aggressive forms of communication. In addition to reviewing the research on the various types of aggressive communication, which we are about to discuss here, the authors explained how aggressive communication is measured and how it functions in family, interpersonal, organizational, instructional, intercultural, mass media, and persuasion contexts. Rancer and Avtgis also gave attention to how a better understanding of aggressive communication and training in communication skills can result in desirable societal outcomes such as less-destructive physical aggression.

ASSERTIVENESS

Assertiveness is a person's general tendency to be interpersonally dominant, ascendant, and forceful. Alberti and Emmons (1974), who were influential in popularizing assertiveness training, said assertiveness involves people acting in their own best interests, defending their rights without undue anxiety, expressing honest feelings comfortably, and exercising their rights without denying others' rights.

Lorr and More (1980) developed a questionnaire for measuring assertiveness and discovered four major dimensions. **Directiveness** involves leadership: taking charge in group situations and seeking positions where one can influence others. **Social assertiveness** occurs when the individual is able to start conversations with strangers, feels comfortable around a wide variety of people, and is generally able to initiate desired relationships. **Defense of rights and interests** is a dimension of assertiveness that pertains, for example, to a person's willingness to return a defective purchase, to tell others when they are creating a disturbance, or to confront people who are taking advantage of others. **Independence** involves maintaining personal convictions, even when in the minority and receiving pressure from the majority to conform.

directiveness   A dimension of assertiveness that involves leadership: taking charge in group situations and seeking positions where one can influence others.

social assertiveness   A dimension of assertiveness that reflects an individual being able to start conversations with strangers, feel comfortable around a wide variety of people, and is generally able to initiate desired relationships.

defense of rights and interests   A willingness to confront others to protect rights and interests.

independence   A dimension of assertiveness and involves maintaining personal convictions even when in the minority and receiving pressure from the majority to conform.

Lorr and More's research suggests there are low to moderate relationships among the four dimensions. Thus, if you are very directive, for instance, you are not necessarily likely to be very socially assertive. With four dimensions a variety of combinations are possible, so that many people tend to be assertive in some ways but not in other ways. At the extremes, some people are assertive in all four ways, whereas others are not assertive at all.

Assertiveness training has been popular for a number of years. Its purpose is to teach people who are low in assertiveness how to behave assertively. The focus of this training has been primarily on the defense of rights and interests dimension, with some degree of attention paid to social assertiveness. A variety of assertiveness training programs have emerged. Some are designed for a particular group of people such as assertiveness training for women. Others constitute a form of psychotherapy. The programs vary greatly in length. An assertiveness "workshop" for nurses, for instance, might last an evening or weekend, whereas an assertiveness program in psychotherapy can be quite lengthy.

Assertiveness is conceived as a generally constructive aggressive trait. It is aggressive because it involves using verbal and nonverbal symbols to create a force that dominates in such ways as taking control of a group activity, getting what one deserves, or stopping violations of one's rights. Of course, dominance could be destructive if such actions are used to hurt other people, as in making a person seem foolish when you insist on your rights. If that happens, the trait of hostility, rather than assertiveness, is involved. Hostility will be discussed later in this chapter.

ARGUMENTATIVENESS

This is a subset of assertiveness because all arguing is assertive, but not all assertive behavior involves arguing. **Argumentativeness** is a person's tendency to present and defend positions on controversial issues while attempting to refute the positions others take. Argumentativeness includes two competing motives: the tendency to approach arguments and the tendency to avoid arguments. The person's argumentativeness trait is the difference between the approach and avoidance tendencies. The more the desire to approach exceeds the desire to avoid arguments, the more argumentative the individual tends to be.

Infante and Rancer's (1982) Argumentativeness Scale is a questionnaire that measures these tendencies. A person who is highly argumentative has strong approach and weak avoidance tendencies, whereas a person low in argumentativeness is low on approach and high on avoidance. There are at least two types of moderate argumentatives. A moderately argumentative person with **conflicting feelings** is high on both approach and avoidance. This person would like to argue often, but strong feelings of anxiety about arguing hold him or her back. This type of moderately argumentative person tends to argue only when the probability of success is high, such as arguing with someone

argumentativeness A person's tendency to present and defend positions on controversial issues while attempting to refute the positions others take.

conflicted feelings Experienced by a moderate argumentative person who is high in both approach and avoidance.

apathetic   Experienced by a moderately argumentative person who is low on both approach and avoidance.

who has little knowledge of the controversial issue. A moderately argumentative person termed **apathetic** is low on both approach and avoidance. This individual does not like arguing controversial issues, but does not really dislike the activity either. This type of moderately argumentative person argues mainly when the incentive for success is high—when there is something of importance to be gained by arguing.

Infante and Rancer's model of argumentativeness is an interactional model of personality because it suggests that a person's motivation to argue in a given situation is a function of both the person's argumentativeness trait and the influence of situational variables. The situation is represented in their model by the individual's perceptions of the probability and importance of success and failure in arguing. These perceptions of the situation interact with traits to produce one's motivation to argue in a given situation. This model can explain why a person who is high in trait argumentativeness does not always argue, or why a person who is low in the trait does argue at times. The model predicts that, in a given situation, high argumentatives will not argue if they perceive that failure is likely and important and that success is unlikely and unimportant. Further, there are situations in which persons low in argumentativeness do argue. This does not happen often. When it does, it is because these individuals perceive that arguing in the situation is likely to produce an important outcome and there is low likelihood that bad consequences will occur.

A good deal of research suggests that arguing produces valuable outcomes (Infante, 1987b; Infante & Rancer, 1996; Johnson & Johnson, 1979; Rancer & Avtgis, 2006). For instance, arguing has been shown to produce more learning by stimulating curiosity about the topics argued. Arguing is also related to greater social perspective-taking ability because arguing with others requires understanding their vantage points and engaging in less egocentric thinking and more mature reasoning. Arguing has been associated with enhanced credibility; when people argued more, they were viewed as more believable. Other research has found highly argumentative individuals to be more skilled and competent communicators, less easily provoked to use verbal aggression, leading to greater marital satisfaction and less marital violence. Argumentativeness has been linked with leadership and favorable assessments of supervisors by subordinates. Because arguing constructively can lead to so many positive outcomes, this basic skill should be taught to children early in their schooling. The inability to argue effectively is an unnecessary handicap because it is not difficult to learn how to argue well.

irritability   A dimension of hostility and is reflected in a quick temper in response to the slightest provocation, being generally moody and grouchy, showing little patience, being exasperated when there is a delay or something goes wrong, and being rude and inconsiderate of others' feelings.

HOSTILITY

Hostile people are often angry. Hostility, in terms of communication, has been defined as symbolic expression of irritability, negativism, resentment, and suspicion. **Irritability** is communicated by having a very quick temper in response to the slightest provocation, being generally moody and grouchy, showing little patience, being exasperated when there is a delay or something goes wrong, and being rude and inconsiderate of others' feelings. **Negativism** is expressed by refusing to cooperate, expressing unwarranted pessimism about the outcome of something when other people are very hopeful, and voicing antagonism concerning authority, rules, and social conventions. **Resentment** is a dimension of hostility that involves expressing jealousy and hatred, brooding about real or imagined mistreatment so that feelings of anger develop, and indicating that others do not really deserve success. **Suspicion** is communicated by expressing an unjustified distrust of people, expecting that others do not have goodwill, believing that others are planning to harm you, and treating people as if their characters are flawed.

Hostile persons might vary along these four dimensions. For instance, one hostile person might be high on resentment but low on the other three components. Another person might be high on suspicion and negativism and moderate on the other two dimensions. A person high on all four aspects would be particularly hostile.

As explained in the previous section for argumentativeness, an individual's perceptions of a situation can modify the behavior normally predicted by the person's trait. For example, a person who is very high on the negativism dimension of hostility might express no antagonism toward an authority figure in a particular situation and might cooperate readily. In the same situation, another person who is low in negativism might curse the authority figure and refuse to cooperate. In the first case the hostile urges toward the authority might be suppressed because the person has a stronger need, such as wanting a promotion. In the second case, the usually mild individual might behave in a hostile manner because of a belief that he or she was betrayed by the person in the position of authority.

One analysis of the hostile personality is particularly illuminating (Berkowitz, 1962). The hostile person is not one who is chronically angry; rather, the person has learned to behave aggressively, a trait that remains latent until aroused by frustration. Frustration stimulates anger. In time, merely thinking about a frustrating event can produce the anger. The frustration is sometimes generalized in the person's mind, so that even very ambiguous situations or events are seen as frustrating. For instance, a person who sees his or her father as frustrating might come to view all men that way. Hostile responses are learned. They can be influenced, for example, by the disciplinary method one experiences as a child. To a degree, a child learns from parents whether or not to behave aggressively. If a child is physically punished for not behaving in a particular way, and if the child then behaves as the parent desires, the lesson learned is, "Hitting someone must be a good way to influence people; it certainly worked on me!" Nonpunitive methods such as rewards for desired behavior can help children restrain hostile words and actions.

negativism   A dimension of hostility that is expressed by refusing to cooperate, expressing unwarranted pessimism about the outcome of something when other people are very hopeful, and voicing antagonism concerning authority, rules, and social conventions.

resentment   A dimension of hostility that involves expressing jealousy and hatred, brooding about real or imagined mistreatment so that feelings of anger develop, and indicating that others do not really deserve success.

suspicion   A dimension of hostility that is reflective of expressing an unjustified distrust of people, expecting that others do not have goodwill, believing that others are planning to harm you, and treating people as if their characters are flawed.

Encouraging people to talk about frustrations or to vent anger is not an effective way to limit aggression (Berkowitz, 1962). In fact, just the opposite happens. Talking about the hostile urge rekindles the anger. Because anger is the necessary prerequisite, aggression becomes more likely. Encouraging someone to talk about a frustration only facilitates the learning of the hostile response. This idea challenges the practice, sometimes popular in interpersonal communication courses, of encouraging students to "open up," to express their true feelings concerning their relations with others. Instead, the framework suggests that individuals should be taught nonhostile, rational methods for dealing with frustrating situations and should avoid mentally rehearsing hostile responses. Thus, if a husband and wife have bitter verbal fights over money, they could be taught methods of argumentation so that they can debate rather than fight about finances.

VERBAL AGGRESSIVENESS

verbal aggressiveness
Attacking the self-concepts of people instead of, or in addition to, their positions on issues.

As in the case of argumentativeness, which is a subset of assertiveness, **verbal aggressiveness** is a subset of hostility. That is, hostility is the more global trait of which verbal aggressiveness is a facet. As a subset of hostility, all verbal aggression is hostile. Verbal aggressiveness is defined as the trait of attacking the self-concepts of people instead of, or in addition to, their positions on issues (Infante & Wigley, 1986). Whereas a physically aggressive person tries to inflict bodily pain, a verbally aggressive person attempts to create mental pain. A verbally aggressive person tries to hurt others by making them feel badly about themselves. In a sense, a "verbal punch" is thrown at a person's self-concept.

There are many types of verbally aggressive messages. All are forms of insults: character attacks, competence attacks, personal background attacks, physical appearance attacks, curses, teasing, ridicule, profanity, threats, and nonverbal emblems. You probably recognize most of these and may have been the victim of some. The last on the list, nonverbal emblems, may seem to contradict the idea of "verbal" aggression. However, a nonverbal emblem is functionally equivalent to a word. Thus, to roll your eyes when someone says something can be a rather severe attack on the person's competence. An exaggerated look of disbelief would also be an insulting nonverbal emblem.

Verbal aggression produces a number of effects in interpersonal communication. The most fundamental effect is self-concept damage. A person can recover from many types of physical aggression such as being punched in the nose. Recovery from some forms of verbal aggression never occurs. The effects can last for a lifetime, for example, telling a child he has a "pig's nose."

Verbal aggression has both lasting and temporary effects on interpersonal communication. Hurt feelings, anger, irritation, and embarrassment may cause relationships to deteriorate. If those feeling subside, it may be possible to repair the damage. However, verbal aggression sometimes results in termination of the relationship. A very serious effect of verbal aggression, from a personal and a social perspective, is that verbal aggression can lead to physical violence. A good deal of research suggests murder, for example, is commonly preceded by verbal aggression in the form of threats, character attacks, or ridicule. Some research indicates that when there is verbal aggression in a marriage, physical assault is more likely. Verbal aggression also has negative effects in work situations. Verbally aggressive bosses are particularly disliked, whereas less success, lower motivation, and less credibility are also associated with verbal aggression on the job.

Four causes of verbal aggression have been posited (Infante, Trebing, Shepherd, & Seeds, 1984). Transference is a psychopathological basis for verbal aggression. People use verbally aggressive messages to attack persons who remind them of an unresolved conflict. For instance, childhood memories of humiliation by someone older might cause a person to project the undesirable characteristics of that particular older individual onto all persons "older." This transference from the unresolved conflict leads the person to feel justified and to derive pleasure when saying something verbally aggressive to any older person. Disdain is marked by the desire to communicate dislike for a person through verbally aggressive messages. Social learning serves as a cause for verbal aggression if people have been rewarded for such behavior in the past. For example, people laugh when one person "puts down" another person. We also learn things vicariously by observing someone "modeling' the behavior—seeing a "hero" on TV use verbal aggression. Verbal aggression sometimes results from an argumentative skill deficiency. If people do not know how to argue skillfully, they resort to attacking self-concepts because they are unable to attack positions on topics. This "misdirected" attack is less likely to occur when one is skilled at arguing positions.

It is difficult to say how much of the verbal aggression in society is due to each of the four causes. However, the first two causes are probably responsible for a rather small portion. That is, psychopathologies are not pervasive in the population, and we structure our lives so that we talk as little as possible with others we dislike. Social learning and argumentative skill deficiencies are probably responsible for more of the verbal aggression in society. If this is the case, there is hope that the destructiveness of verbal aggression can be reduced substantially. Education can be a solution. People, especially children, can be taught how to argue constructively and thus reduce the inclination to use verbal aggression. Children can also be taught constructive methods for dealing with verbal aggression when it does occur.

Michael Beatty and James McCroskey (1997) also have speculated on the causes of verbal aggressiveness. As they did for communication apprehension, they conceptualized verbal aggressiveness as an expression of inborn neurobiological structures. That is, verbal aggressiveness is a temperament that is inherited. Because there is a genetic basis for the trait, this does not mean simply

transference Cause of verbal aggression that involves using verbal aggression against people who remind one of unresolved sources of conflict and pain.

disdain Cause of verbal aggression that involves the desire to communicate dislike for a person through verbally aggressive messages.

social learning Cause of verbal aggression brought about by direct reinforcement of verbally aggressive behavior or by modeling the behavior after an esteemed person.

argumentative skill deficiency Cause of verbal aggression due to inability to argue skillfully; attack and defend needs are not satisfied.

that verbal aggressiveness is passed down from one generation to the next. As discussed in Chapter 4, traits can skip generations. Thus, you may inherit the verbal aggressiveness of one of your great-grandfathers. Moreover, because the genes of both of your parents are involved, there can be some rather complex genetic interactions. Like the color of your eyes, the influence of both parents can sometimes be found in personality traits such as verbal aggressiveness.

Beatty and McCroskey posit three neurological circuits that are the biological basis for verbal aggressiveness. In addition to the behavioral inhibition system and the behavioral activation system explained earlier in this chapter for communication apprehension, the authors specified the fight-or-flight system. This system involves response to a threat—either fleeing or staying and facing it aggressively. For each of the three systems Beatty and McCroskey identify the regions of the brain involved, the particular brain activity, and the chemical reactions. In doing this they have in essence identified the biology of aggression in general and verbal aggression specifically.

If Beatty and McCroskey are correct, then their efforts represent a major step toward understanding why people are verbally aggressive. What needs to be resolved, however, would be just how immutable the trait is. If a person is verbally aggressive, is there any hope of getting him or her to use fewer self-concept attacking messages? Interestingly, there is some research evidence that verbal aggressiveness can be lowered using educational activities (Colbert, 1993; Sanders, Wiseman, & Gass, 1994). If some change in aggressive communication is possible, quite a few educational activities have been suggested for this purpose (Infante, 1995).

Finally, we will examine two rather recently developed communication traits that pertain to aggressiveness. These provide additional ways to view conflict in human interaction.

TAKING CONFLICT PERSONALLY

The communication trait of Taking Conflict Personally (TCP) was developed by Dale Hample and Judith Dallinger (1995). This trait reflects "a negative emotional reaction to participating in a conflict" (p. 297). This negative emotional reaction constitutes low verbal aggressiveness. People who are high in this trait (i.e., take conflict personally) believe that conflicts are "antagonist, punishing interactions" in which the central goal of conflict communication is to purposely hurt the other person (Hample, 1999). TCP can take the form of either aggressive or avoidant behavior and is believed to bring about similar reactions from others with whom we are communicating.

The TCP trait is believed to be comprised of six dimensions of direct personalization, persecution feelings, stress reaction, positive relational effects, negative relational effects, and like/dislike valence. Direct personalization reflects the hurt a person experiences during the conflict episode. Persecution

Taking Conflict Personally A communication trait that reflects the degree to which we have a negative emotional reaction to participating in a conflict.

direct personalization A dimension of taking conflict personally reflecting the hurt a person experiences during a conflict episode.

persecution feelings A dimension of taking conflict personally and reflects the perception that other people are just seeking to pick a fight with you and purposely seek to engage in conflict.

stress reaction A dimension of taking conflict personally and reflects the level of physiological response one has when in a conflict episode.

positive relational effects A dimension of taking conflict personally that reflects the extent to which people feel conflict communication can be positive for both social and task relationships.

negative relational effects A dimension of taking conflict personally that reflects the extent to which people feel that conflict communication can have negative outcomes for both social and task relationships.

like/dislike valence A dimension of taking conflict personally that reflects the degree to which people enjoy engaging in conflict.

feelings reflects the perception that other people are just seeking to pick a fight with you and purposely seek to engage in conflict. It is believed that people who have feelings of persecution see conflict as a combative experience where there is a clear winner and a clear loser. Stress reaction is the level of physiological response one has when in a conflict episode (e.g., upset stomach, headache). Positive relational effects reflects the extent to which people feel conflict communication can be positive for both social and task relationships. Negative relational effects is the extent to which people feel that conflict communication can have negative outcomes for both social and task relationships. The final dimension of the TCP trait is that of like/dislike valence and is defined as the degree to which people enjoy engaging in conflict. Hample and Dallinger (1995) believe that like/dislike valence is very similar to the argumentativeness trait discussed earlier in this chapter but point out that argumentativeness is a person's intended behavior, whereas like/dislike valence reflects an emotional reaction.

The TCP trait is believed to be a product of both the situation and a person's predisposition to behave. Hample (1999) believes "TCP is a stable personality trait . . . permitting, among others, the simple generalization that some people are more predisposed toward personalization than others" (p. 173). People differ in their predisposition to be tolerant, trusting, self-interested, self-confident, generous in their attributions, and generally more or less easily hurt when involved in a conflict episode (Avtgis & Rancer, 2003).

Research findings using TCP revealed that people who are high in TCP (i.e., see conflict as punishing) tend to have a high motivation to avoid arguments, whereas people who think that conflict is productive reported a high motivation to approach arguments (Hample & Dallinger, 1995). Further, adult children with an internal conflict locus of control (i.e., see conflict outcomes as being under their control) reported less direct personalization, less persecution feelings, less stress reaction, less negative relational effects, and more positive relational effects than adult children with an external conflict locus of control (i.e., see conflict outcomes as being out of their control; Avtgis, 2002).

In a study comparing the United States, New Zealand, and Australia, Theodore Avtgis and Andrew Rancer (2003) found that Americans reported significantly less feelings of persecution, less direct personalization, yet greater stress reaction than either New Zealanders or Australians. The findings indicate that, overall, Americans have less tendency to interpret conflict behavior as a personal attack. Why, then, would Americans be higher in stress reaction? According to Avtgis and Rancer (2003), an "epidemic of incompetent communication permeates within the United States as well as between Americans and other cultures. Perhaps the lack of communication skills can be attributed to the arousal of stressful feelings in Americans when faced with conflict" (p. 115). Along with argumentativeness and verbal aggressiveness, the taking conflict personally trait will continue to prove to be a valuable tool in the explanation of conflict behavior. If society becomes ever increasingly hostile and segmented, looking at communication traits such as TCP will become important for theorists, researchers, and practitioners alike.

TOLERANCE FOR DISAGREEMENT

tolerance for disagreement A communication trait that reflects the amount of disagreement a person can tolerate before he or she perceives the existence of a conflict in a relationship.

disagreement Part of the tolerance for disagreement communication trait and reflects the difference of opinion on issues.

conflict Part of the tolerance for disagreement communication trait and reflects competition, suspicion, distrust, dislike, hostility, and self-perpetuation.

Tolerance for disagreement (TFD) is a communication trait that is defined as "the amount of disagreement an individual can tolerate before he or she perceives the existence of conflict in a relationship (Richmond, McCroskey, & McCroskey, 2005, p. 178). TFD was originally developed by James McCroskey and Lawrence Wheeless (1976) and later expanded (Knutson, McCroskey, Knutson, & Hurt, 1979). Most research on conflict relies on a unidimensional continuum that ranges from good conflict to bad conflict. McCroskey and Wheeless distinguished between **disagreement**, which is a difference of opinion on issues, and **conflict**, which involves competition, suspicion, distrust, hostility, and self-perpetuation.

Although TFD was originally conceptualized as something that is a product of the interaction and relationship specific, Knutson et al. (1979) argued that due to each individual's interpretation of what is considered disagreement and conflict, these interpretations are more cross-contextual and thus should be considered traitlike. More specifically, they argued that "the existence of an individual difference variable, which they labeled tolerance for disagreement (TFD), which they employed to explain why some people will perceive the presence of conflict much sooner than others will" (Teven, McCroskey, & Richmond, 1998, p. 210). The distinction between disagreement and conflict is very similar to the distinction between argument and verbal aggression, respectively (McCroskey, 2006). That is, argument (as well as trait argumentativeness) is considered constructive, whereas verbal aggression (as well as trait verbal aggressiveness) is considered destructive. All disagreement is considered constructive, and all conflict is considered destructive to the relationship.

The TFD trait is also influenced by situational factors such as a low degree of affinity (i.e., liking) between the people that is present in a disagreement on an issue. These situational triggers are similar to those situational triggers identified for verbally aggressive behavior (Wigley, 2006). Given that TFD is a joint function of the trait and situational cues, TFD is conceptualized from the interactionist trait perspective (Magnusson & Endler, 1977).

People who are high in TFD are relatively resistant to engaging in conflict, whereas people low in TFD are much more likely to engage in conflict across a wide range of relationships, regardless of the issue at hand. These differences are based on a person's threshold to which disagreement transforms into conflict. This consistency in the tendency to engage in either disagreement or conflict is rooted in the larger supertraits of assertiveness, which contains disagreement and hostility, which involves conflict.

Virginia Richmond and James McCroskey (1979) investigated the extent to which employee satisfaction was related to the employee's and supervisor's level of TFD. The findings indicated that employee satisfaction (which involves satisfaction with supervisor, work, and pay) were influenced more by the supervisor's TFD than that of the employee's TFD. Therefore, the greater supervisor tolerance for disagreement, the more satisfied the employee. Further evidence reveals that TFD is also related to cognitive flexibility and communication flexibility (Martin, Anderson, & Thweatt, 1998) in that "the flexible communicator appeared to be willing to argue and disagree with others. These individuals tend to approach arguments and do not avoid confrontations where there may be a difference of opinions" (Teven, McCroskey, & Richmond, 1998, p. 212).

In an effort to measure TFD, Jason Teven, James McCroskey, and Virginia Richmond (1998) developed a fifteen-item scale of TFD which was found to be a reliable and valid measure.

SUMMARY

This chapter explored trait approaches that have been taken to understand human communication. The approach has its origin in the study of personality from the field of psychology. Distinctions were made between trait, contextual, and state behaviors. The trait approach was contrasted with situationist and interactionist positions. The cross-situational consistency of behavior framework was reviewed because of its relevance to understanding traits. Four classes of communication traits were discussed: apprehension, presentation, adaptation, and aggression. In the apprehension traits category, we examined communication apprehension and receiver apprehension along with informational reception apprehension. The presentation traits presented were communicator style and disclosiveness. The category of adaptation traits included communication adaptability, rhetorical sensitivity, noble self, rhetorical reflector, communication competence, interaction involvement, and cognitive flexibility. The last class of communication traits explored consisted of aggression traits: assertiveness, argumentativeness, hostility, and verbal aggressiveness, along with taking conflict personally and tolerance for disagreement.

KEY TERMS

amount
animated
apathetic
appropriate disclosure
appropriateness
argumentative skill deficiency
argumentativeness
articulation
attentive
attentiveness
cognitive flexibility
communication apprehension
communication trait
communicative adaptability
communicator image
communicator style
conflict
conflicted feelings
contentious
contextual view
defense of rights and interests
depth
direct personalization
directiveness
disagreement

disclosiveness
disdain
dominant
dramatic
effectiveness
friendly
honesty
impression leaving
independence
informational reception
    apprehension
intellectual inflexibility
intent
interaction involvement
interactionist position
irritability
like/dislike valence
listening apprehension
negative relational effects
negativism
noble self
open
perceptiveness
persecution feelings
positive relational effect

positiveness
precise
reading anxiety
receiver apprehension
relaxed
resentment
responsiveness
rhetorical reflector
rhetorical sensitivity
situationist
social assertiveness
social composure
social confirmation
social experience
social learning
state behavior
stress reaction
suspicion
taking conflict personally
tolerance for disagreement
trait behavior
trait position
transference
verbal aggressiveness
wit

Persuasion Approaches

6

Persuasion was once the most frequently researched topic in the communication field. Scholars were enthusiastic about the prospect of unraveling the mysteries of social influence. People influencing one another is a basic process in society; to gain control over this process would be a monumental achievement. The scientific knowledge would allow people to predict and to control persuasion. The power inherent in this idea is staggering. In fact, you might be thinking it probably was best the feat was not accomplished! We are not implying that persuasion researchers were intent on discovering how to control masses of people. Prediction and control are, however, outcomes of successful scientific research. In some fields such as astronomy, researchers do not achieve control because they are unable to manipulate the objects of study. Research programs in persuasion were initiated to build knowledge so that a relatively complete understanding of the subject could be achieved.

In reviewing the history of persuasion research, it is clear that although communication researchers conducted numerous studies in the 1950s and 1960s, they did not develop new theories about the subject (see McGuire, 1969, for an excellent synthesis through the late 1960s). Persuasion theories were devised by social psychologists. Communication researchers typically based their research on these psychological models. If you were to examine, for example, the 1969 volume of *Speech Monographs,* you would find many more references to sources in social psychology than to communication sources. The number of persuasion studies began to decline in the early 1970s.

The lack of original theorizing, the heavy borrowing from other disciplines, and the abandonment of an area of research after a relatively short period of time may suggest that the communication field never really had a serious interest in the scientific study of persuasion. Actually, the focus has changed. "Traditional" persuasion research has been replaced by a broader model of influence. Earlier research focused on how a relatively formal speech or essay influences a person. More recent research examines how people try to influence one another in many ways: for example, how do we convince people to agree with us, how do we induce others to like us, how do we end an interpersonal relationship, what techniques should be used to control classroom behavior, what tactics are effective for resisting another's attempt to persuade us, what is the role of argument or verbal aggression in interpersonal relations? An examination of contemporary research suggests that the communication field's fascination with persuasion has matured into a more global interest in social influence. Moreover, if earlier research implied at least a tacit quest for laws that would enable prediction and control, the more contemporary research seems to have settled for prediction. The vast majority of recent social influence research in the communication discipline examines correlations between variables that affect social influence. Variables seldom are manipulated (as they once were) by scientists in controlled, laboratory situations to study what *causes* persuasion.

Conceptualizing Persuasion

persuasion Attitude change toward a source's proposal resulting from a message designed to alter a receiver's beliefs about the proposal.

attitude How favorably we evaluate something.

belief A perception of how two or more things are related.

At its most basic level, **persuasion** *may be thought of as attitude change toward a source's proposal that results from a message designed to alter beliefs about the proposal.* A proposal is a recommended course of action. For instance, "We should give a piece of land in our state back to Native Americans," or, on a more personal level, "Let's go to the movies tonight." **Attitude** is defined as how favorably we evaluate something. This is represented by feelings such as good versus bad, right versus wrong, nice versus awful, valuable versus worthless. An example of an attitude toward a proposal might be, "I feel giving that piece of land to the Native Americans is good and the right thing to do." A **belief** is a perception of how two or more things are related. In terms of persuasion, beliefs are perceptions of the consequences of a proposal. For instance, "If we return the land to the Native Americans, a number of farmers will have to be relocated."

If a persuader wants to influence a specific behavior, he or she must use messages to create a favorable attitude. If we want to influence someone to sign a petition, we need to address the individual's attitude toward the object of the petition. If the petition proposes returning a tract of land to Native Americans, persuasion involves presenting a message that will help the person form beliefs in support of giving land to a Native American tribe; for example, "A previous wrong would be corrected." If beliefs about the proposal are positive, the attitude toward the proposal will be favorable. Of course, if beliefs are negative, the attitude will be unfavorable. A mixture of positive and negative beliefs results in a moderately favorable or unfavorable attitude, depending on the proportion of positive to negative beliefs.

By persuading a person to favor a proposal, a persuader provides justification for the receiver to choose to behave in a particular manner. In order to have persuasion and not some other type of *social influence,* the receiver must feel free, not constrained, to choose. Thus, **perceived choice** is a distinguishing characteristic of persuasion. Persuasion uses symbols to modify an attitude to achieve a particular behavior. Attitude represents a predisposition to behave in a certain way. In persuasion the source is willing to let success depend on attitudinal influence.

In other types of social influence, the source is unwilling to allow behavior to be controlled by attitudes. Instead, the source applies force or pressure as a substitute for the motivation provided by attitudes. **Coercion** involves the use of physical aggression and verbal aggression (for example, threats, insults, ridicule, and profanity) as substitutes for attitudinal influence. If coercion is used, no choice is perceived: "The person is holding a gun to my head, so I must sign the petition."

coercion   Source applies force or pressure as a substitute for the motivation provided by attitudes.

Compliance involves more subtle forms of psychological pressure: "I (and/or others) will like you if you comply"; or "I (and/or others) will dislike you if you do not comply." There are many compliance-gaining strategies for each of these two forms. An example of the first is, "I will do something for you if you do this for me." "Our friends will be disappointed if you do not do this," illustrates the second. Instead of allowing the receiver's attitude toward the proposal to control the receiver's behavior, the source in a compliance situation implies that the desired behavior will make the receiver more socially accepted. An individual's attitude usually remains unchanged in compliance situations.

compliance   Social influence where the source implies that the desired behavior will make the receiver more socially accepted.

Placing persuasion within the framework **Belief Change → Attitude Change → Behavior Change** helps to verify whether *persuasion* or some other type of social influence took place. Isolating behavior change alone is not evidence of persuasion. For example, we might encourage a friend who dislikes fishing to go on a fishing trip by saying, "This trip is a chance to renew our friendship" (an example of compliance). If the person enjoys the experience (forms positive beliefs about fishing), the attitude toward fishing becomes more favorable. However, there was no persuasion in this situation because it was not a message from one person that caused the other to change an attitude. The fishing trip was not a message because it was not an intentional exchange of symbols. Catching a large fish on the trip was not symbolic activity; fish do not manipulate symbols to stimulate a feeling of exhilaration. Instead, engaging in the behavior produced an internal change in attitude. A message is required for persuasion to take place; no message about fishing was presented before the behavior. A person can be induced through coercion or compliance to behave in a certain manner that can lead to attitude change.

However, the steps involved in coercion or compliance are often the reverse of the belief-to-attitude-to-behavior model and are not examples of persuasion.

Six Dimensions of Persuasion Situations

It is apparent that the many situations we experience are not the same. But how do they differ? We can say that people differ physically in terms of height, weight, and body type. Can we be nearly as precise with persuasion situations? Because of research by Michael Cody and Margaret McLaughlin (1980), we are able to measure compliance situations. They identified six ways that one situation can differ from another. Although compliance is not the same as persuasion, the six dimensions are also relevant to persuasion situations. We will examine each briefly. Keep in mind that there are many other ways in which situations may differ. In terms of persuasion, however, these six dimensions are important.

The first dimension is *intimacy.* Situations vary in terms of how personal, meaningful, and perhaps intimate the source's relationship is with the receiver. The second is *dominance.* This involves how dominant or submissive each person is in the situation. The third is *resistance.* Situations vary in terms of how agreeable the receiver is to the object of persuasion. The fourth, *rights,* involves the justification that the source has for asking the receiver to do something, whether or not the source has reasonable grounds for the request. The fifth is *personal benefits.* This dimension includes what the source would gain by succeeding in the persuasion attempt and may also reflect advantages for the receiver in fulfilling the source's wishes. The sixth is *long-term consequences.* Situations vary in terms of whether the persuasion will have short-term or long-term consequences for the relationship between the source and receiver. When the relationship is an intimate one, the persuasion attempt could have very long-term consequences. However, persuasion between strangers usually will have only short-term relationship consequences.

Self-awareness and Persuasion

In studying persuasion, one can form the impression that the persuader is constantly thinking: analyzing the receiver, situation, and topic; composing the message a split second before delivering it; continually monitoring feedback from the receiver; and adjusting the message, along with delivery, to the feedback. The idea of the persuader as so completely alert and actively controlling the shape, content, and sound of the message is rarely the case (for a review see Roloff, 1980).

Individuals seem to follow a cognitive course of "least resistance" in communication, which leads them to rely on previously prepared communication plans. A plan is a meaningful sequence of events a person expects in a situation as either an observer or a participant. You may recall we discussed this concept in Chapter 1. A person may have found that a certain message was effective in a given situation. In a similar situation, the person simply recalls the message and repeats it, modifying perhaps a word or two. Persuaders often essentially rely on communication plans, reading from a previously prepared script. This requires very little effort and allows the source to communicate on "automatic pilot."

The idea that receivers are not very attentive, that their minds wander away from the message, is an ancient one. Add to it the recent notion of a source similarly preoccupied, and we have a model of persuasion where the source and receiver are physically present in the situation but mentally "in-and-out." This may be more the rule than the exception. One reason why this may be the case is that our personalities predispose us to prefer certain situations. Given a choice, we approach some situations and avoid others. Thus, we usually find ourselves in familiar situations. Because we are seldom in an unusual situation, we are seldom without a plan. That is, having been in certain types of situations virtually guarantees that we possess a plan that has enjoyed at least some previous success. Among other things, this suggests that we do not do much composing of original messages. We usually can recall a communication plan that is appropriate. If not, we revise one that is close to what is needed.

APPROACHES TO UNDERSTANDING PERSUASION

We will not attempt a comprehensive review of persuasion theory in this chapter (for more thorough treatments see Bostrom, 1983; Miller, Burgoon, & Burgoon, 1984). Instead, we will focus on several approaches and theories that have stimulated the most persuasion research in the field of communication. Then we will turn to theories explaining how to resist persuasion.

The Variable-Analytic Approach

A good deal of persuasion research, especially research from 1940 through 1969, explored specific variables in the persuasion process because they seemed to be important—not because they were part of a particular persuasion theory. Experiments targeted numerous variables relating to the source, message, channel, and receiver in persuasion. Much of the early research tried to determine how sources who are more and less believable (source credibility) influence attitude change and what factors influence source credibility (Andersen & Clevenger, 1963). Later in this chapter, we will examine three approaches to the study of source credibility.

There is a large body of research on the message in persuasion (for summaries, see Burgoon & Bettinghaus, 1980; Cronkhite, 1969). At least three categories seem relevant: message structure, message appeals, and language. The message structure research investigated such variables as whether the strongest argument in a message should be placed first (anticlimactic arrangement), last (climactic), or in the middle of the message (pyramidal) (Gulley & Berlo, 1956); whether two-sided messages are more persuasive than one-sided messages (Hovland, 1957); whether the opposition's argument should be refuted before or after presenting one's own case (Thistlethwaite, Kamenetsky, & Schmidt, 1956); and whether the speaker or receiver should draw conclusions from arguments in the speech (Tubbs, 1968). Message appeals explored were the use of fear or anxiety appeals, evidence, reward appeals (McCroskey & Wright, 1971), humor (Gruner, 1965, 1970), logic (Scott & Hurt, 1978), emotion (Ruechelle, 1958), and self-esteem (Spillman, 1979). Language variables included language intensity, use of qualifiers for arguments (Feezel, 1974), rhetorical questions (Zillman, 1972), opinionated language (Infante, 1975b), and obscenity (Bostrom, Baseheart, & Rossiter, 1973). We will examine some of the research in a later section of this chapter.

The channel in persuasion has received a limited amount of research. A major focus has been on comparing live, tape-recorded, and written messages for differences in persuasiveness (Knower, 1935; Wilkie, 1934).

The receiver in persuasion has been studied in a variety of ways: sex (Scheidel, 1963), ego involvement (Sereno & Bodaken, 1972), and attitude intensity. Probably the major way the receiver has been studied is in terms of personality. Some of the traits investigated have been persuasibility (Hovland & Janis, 1959), authoritarianism (Adorno, Frenkel-Brunswik, Levinson, & Sanford, 1950), dogmatism (Rokeach, 1960), self-esteem (Infante, 1976), richness of fantasy (Infante, 1975c), and tolerance of ambiguity (Infante, 1975a). Some of this research will be discussed in the next section.

These are just a sample of the persuasion variables that have been investigated. You might expect that numerous persuasion principles were discovered. However, that is not the case. Despite the vast amount of research, the conclusions are very tentative and subject to numerous qualifications. For instance, a message that tries to frighten the receiver will vary in its persuasiveness, depending on how important the topic is, how believable the source is, and how specific the solutions presented are. Thus, a high fear message can be more persuasive than a low fear message when the source is highly believable and the solution for the problem is very specific, but only if the topic is important to the receiver. The inability of this research to offer lawlike statements, such as "Intense fear is more persuasive than mild or no fear," has been viewed as a major criticism. Another criticism has been that because variable-analytic research investigates a variable without first developing a theory of persuasion, it does not advance theory building in persuasion. That is, critics claim that persuasion research should test persuasion theories.

Despite the rather serious criticisms, it is possible to find value in this research. Much of the research was done in an earlier era when there was little theory. The research served to "identify the territory"—to suggest what the important variables might be. The research stimulated thinking about persuasion (it had heuristic value). What began as relatively simple variable-analytic research sometimes resulted in a rather sophisticated theory of persuasion. For example, Burgoon, Jones, and Stewart's (1975) message-centered model of persuasion had its beginning in the language intensity research. An additional value of variable-analytic research is that its painstaking search for lawlike principles of persuasion revealed the complexity of persuasion. Time after time, the results of experiments had to be stated in the tentative, highly qualified manner of the fear appeal example presented earlier. If scientific research is supposed to reveal the nature of what is studied, variable-analytic research may have accomplished that rather well. We think of persuasion as a dynamic process involving numerous factors that can control differences in social influence. Little is static, and success is often equated with being able to adapt to the fluidity of the persuasion situation. It took many variable-analytic studies to bring this picture into semiclear focus. Now we at least have a better idea about what persuasion involves.

Personality Traits and Persuasion

Many communication studies have explored how personality influences communication, especially in persuasion situations. We will briefly survey some of the major personality traits that have been examined (for a review of this literature see Steinfatt, 1987).

PERSUASIBILITY

Research reported in the book *Personality and Persuasibility* (Hovland & Janis, 1959) suggests that a personality trait predicts how much a person is influenced by persuasion attempts—regardless of the topic, source, or situation. This idea appears to be valid. Some people seem easy to persuade. They rarely resist pressure to move in one direction or another. This willingness to change can be viewed as **persuasibility**. Also, other individuals seem consistently difficult to persuade. They rarely budge on any issue. In essence, they seem resistant to persuasion.

persuasibility Personality trait indicating willingness to be persuaded.

The idea of a persuasibility trait appears to be an uncomplicated way to explain susceptibility to social influence. However, conceptually the matter is not so clear. Is there such a trait, or are there other personality traits sometimes related to persuasion that create the illusion of a general persuasibility trait? In that regard, the traits that follow have been found to be related to persuasion.

The amount of persuasibility indicated by each trait, when viewed as a whole, could create the impression that there is a more global persuasibility trait.

SELF-ESTEEM

self-esteem How favorably the individual evaluates self is related to persuasion.

Self-esteem refers to how favorably the individual evaluates self and is a trait related to persuasion. When individuals have low self-esteem, they lack self-confidence in general, and they have little faith that their positions on controversial issues are valid. They tend to be high in persuasibility. When told by a speaker that their positions should be changed, they tend to believe the speaker: "The speaker must know what is right on this, for I certainly do not know." High self-esteem, on the other hand, is thought to be related to low persuasibility. When people feel very good about themselves, they are also confident about their positions on controversial issues because opinions are a part of one's identity. Satisfaction with oneself usually discourages change. Therefore, individuals with high self-esteem tend to resist persuasion.

DOGMATISM

dogmatism The individual's willingness to consider other belief systems.

Rokeach (1960) conceptualized dogmatism in terms of individuals' willingness to consider belief systems (what one associates with an object or issue) other than the ones they hold. Open-minded individuals are willing to consider other sets of beliefs, even if they feel very strongly about an issue. Dogmatic or closed-minded persons are unwilling to do so. They have a firm set of beliefs for an issue, and they do not want to be bothered by other belief systems.

Dogmatic people find it very difficult to separate a source from the source's message. Thus, if dogmatic people like a source, they tend to accept the source's message; if they dislike a speaker, rarely will the speaker's message persuade them. The open-minded person, however, has less trouble reacting differently to source and message—for example, "I can't stand the speaker, but he makes a good point." When the source is viewed as credible, dogmatism is associated with persuasion. This is especially true when the persuasion topic is not very important to the individual. Dogmatic people tend to be rather easy to persuade when given a credible source and a less important topic. This also suggests that open-minded persons are not necessarily easy to persuade. When the source is credible and the topic rather unimportant, open-minded people are more difficult to persuade than dogmatic individuals.

MACHIAVELLIANISM

Machiavellianism An orientation in which people believe that manipulating others is a basic strategy of social influence.

The trait of Machiavellianism refers to an orientation in which people believe that manipulating others is a basic strategy of social influence. Individuals who are high in Machiavellianism think it is ethical to tell people only what they want to hear, to use the receivers' doubts, fears, and insecurities to motivate action, and even to distort facts so they become more acceptable. Generally these people are willing to use whatever strategy works in persuasion; they are very pragmatic. High Machiavellians tend to act rather detached and to be less emotional than other people. They believe the end justifies the means. Persons with a high level of this trait have a strong need to influence others. They like leadership positions, and they are usually the dominant parties in their relations with other people.

Low Machiavellians, on the other hand, are very nonmanipulative in dealing with people. They want to avoid pressuring others, to allow others maximum freedom to decide for themselves. Low Machiavellians tend to have little need to dominate and influence others. They tend to be more emotional than high Machiavellians when discussing a controversial issue.

COGNITIVE COMPLEXITY

Cognitive complexity is sometimes conceptualized as a trait relating to our personal constructs. A construct is a bipolar pair of terms such as honest–dishonest or exciting–dull, which we apply to differentiate elements in our environment. People in a society learn a common core of constructs because of their shared culture, resulting in some fairly "standard" meanings. However, people also develop pairs of idiosyncratic constructs, opposites that are unique to the individual. The pair humorous–deadly would be an example of an unusual pairing. Individuals experience meaning in a situation depending on which constructs they apply and which pole of each construct they associate with the situation (for example, either *exciting* or *dull*). The basic idea is that people structure their reality based on their construct systems.

cognitive complexity   The complexity of one's construct system affects their persuasive ability.

Someone who is cognitively complex has a greater number of constructs that are both more abstract and more interconnected than someone who is cognitively simple. Cognitive complexity is related to a number of important communication processes. The greater one's cognitive complexity, the better one is able to imagine how *other* people view a situation. Perspective-taking ability is a key determinant of successful communication. With this ability one is able to understand another person's concerns by seeing things from his or her perspective. This means the more complex person is better able to adapt a message to a particular receiver. If a message is not adapted to the audience, it seems impersonal, generic, and less relevant. Because the probability of success in persuasion is usually lower if the message is not tailored to the likes and dislikes of the receiver, cognitively complex sources should be better persuaders.

NEED FOR SOCIAL APPROVAL

People vary in their **need for social approval** and the extent to which they fear social disapproval. According to this idea, a source who offers social approval or threatens social disapproval when the receiver has a strong need for approval

need for social approval   A person's need for approval from others influences how they react to persuasive messages implying approval-disapproval.

opinionated acceptance
Language that expresses a favorable attitude toward people who agree with the speaker.

opinionated rejection
Language that expresses an unfavorable attitude toward people who disagree with the speaker.

ought to be very persuasive. Various forms of opinionated language specified by Rokeach (1960) provide a way to test this relationship. **Opinionated acceptance** language expresses a favorable attitude toward those people who agree with the speaker—for example, "Intelligent and responsible people will agree that my proposal is needed." **Opinionated rejection** language states a negative attitude toward those who disagree with the speaker's position—for example, "Only a bigoted fool would oppose this plan." Opinionated acceptance language represents social approval, whereas opinionated rejection constitutes social disapproval. Baseheart (1971) found support for the idea that opinionated language leads to more persuasion when people have a strong need for social approval. In such a circumstance, opinionated rejection was as successful as opinionated acceptance in stimulating persuasion. Having a strong need for social approval probably heightens a person's sensitivity to language that suggests the speaker is evaluating the receiver in some way.

Research on Message Variables

Throughout the last four decades, communication theorists have identified several message variables that appear to influence our reaction to persuasive messages (Sussman, 1973). Two will be examined here: fear appeals and evidence.

FEAR APPEALS

The study of fear-arousing message content has its roots in antiquity. Aristotle discussed the use of fear and other emotions in the *Rhetoric.* Aristotle suggested that speakers must understand the emotional predispositions of their audience and then use that knowledge as one of the "available means of persuasion." Modern research considers fear appeals to be arguments that take the following form:

1. You (the listener) are vulnerable to a threat.
2. If you are vulnerable, then you should take action to reduce your vulnerability.
3. If you are to reduce your vulnerability, then you must accept the recommendations contained in this message.
4. Therefore, you should accept the recommendations contained in this message. (Boster & Mongeau, 1984, p. 371)

A typical fear appeal might be a variation on the following:

1. Smoking has been found to increase the chances for disease and death.
2. Because you do not want disease or death, you must do something to prevent them.
3. An effective way to prevent these outcomes is to stop smoking.
4. Therefore, you must stop smoking.

During an average evening, we may witness several fear-arousing messages in television commercials. From smoke detectors to life insurance, advertisers make frequent use of the fear appeal to influence consumers.

The contemporary study of fear in persuasion can be traced to the work of Irving Janis and Seymour Feshbach (1953). In their seminal study, high school students were randomly assigned to one of two experimental groups who heard messages on dental hygiene. For one group, a *moderate fear* appeal was used; for the other, a *high fear* appeal was created. A third group of students was also tested. They served as a *control group* and were exposed to an entirely different message on the structure and operation of the human eye. The high fear appeal urged dental care and recommended vigorous and proper brushing of the teeth; pictures of rotting gums and decaying teeth accompanied the message. In the moderate fear appeal, these pictures were omitted. Janis and Feshbach discovered that the moderate fear appeal was more effective than the high fear appeal in changing students' attitudes toward proper brushing and dental care.

These findings led to several decades of experimental research testing the relationship between the level of fear in a message and attitude change. Some studies discovered the opposite outcome: attitude change was more likely when a high fear appeal was used (Beck & Davis, 1978; see Miller, 1963, for a summary and analysis of the early research). Because experimenters sometimes arrived at different results when they studied fear appeals, scientists tried to reconcile these contradictions.

Boster and Mongeau (1984) reviewed six explanations of fear appeal effects. The *drive explanation* suggests that the fear aroused by a persuasive message creates a state of drive, which receivers find unpleasant. Individuals experiencing this state of drive are motivated to reduce it by changing their attitudes and/or behaviors. According to the drive explanation, the greater the amount of fear in a message, the greater the attitude change in the direction recommended by the message.

The *resistance explanation* finds that as perceived fear in a message decreases, individuals' attitudes and/or behaviors will move closer to those recommended in the message. The rationale is that receivers will pay attention to messages low in threatening content; they will resist more threatening messages. Low fear appeals are less threatening than high fear appeals. Thus, messages containing low fear appeals are more likely to be heard than messages containing high fear appeals.

According to the *curvilinear hypothesis,* when receivers are either very fearful or very unafraid, little attitude or behavior change results. High levels of fear are so strong that individuals block them out; low levels are too weak to produce the desired effect. Messages containing *moderate* amounts of fear-arousing content are most effective in producing attitudinal and/or behavior change.

The *parallel response explanation* suggests that fear-arousing messages activate fear control and danger control processes in listeners. *Fear control* is a coping process by which receivers strive to reduce the fear created by the message. *Danger control* refers to a problem-solving process in which listeners search for information on how to deal with the threat presented. These two processes interact to influence message acceptance. According to the parallel response explanation, when a fear-arousing message primarily activates the *danger control* process, a *high* fear appeal will most influence attitudes and/or behaviors. When a fear-arousing message primarily activates the *fear control* process, a *low* fear appeal is most influential.

The *protection motivation explanation* states that a receiver's attitude toward the topic is a result of the amount of "protection motivation" produced by the message. Protection motivation refers to receivers' drives to avoid or protect themselves from a threat. As protection motivation increases, conformity to attitudes and/or behaviors recommended in the message also increases. Thus, the greater the fear in a message: (a) the more likely a threat will occur; and (b) the greater the ability to deal with the threat by following the recommendations provided in the message; thus (c) the greater the attitude and/or behavioral change in the direction of the message.

The sixth explanation is labeled the *threat control explanation.* Reactions to fear appeals depend on logical, not emotional, factors. A fear-arousing message stimulates *response efficacy* and *personal efficacy* processes in listeners. Response efficacy refers to the receiver's perception of how effective the recommended attitudes or actions will be in reducing or eliminating the threat. Personal efficacy refers to whether or not the receiver is capable of taking the actions recommended by the message. These two responses combine to produce threat control. Threat control is a person's perceived probability of success in controlling the threat. This explanation suggests that, as threat control increases, listeners will adopt attitudes more closely corresponding to the recommendations of the message. As fear increases in a message, so too should the amount of attitude and/or behavioral change in the listener.

Boster and Mongeau concluded that all six explanations were less than adequate in explaining the results of experiments studying fear-arousing messages and persuasion. None of the six explanations was completely consistent with the evidence. Several problems were highlighted. First, researchers were not creating strong enough fear appeals. If manipulations of fear in messages were not strong enough to produce fear in listeners, then it was impossible for any relationship between fear and attitude or behavior change to emerge. Second, other demographic variables and personality traits interacted with fear appeals to affect attitudes and behavior. In particular, *age, trait anxiety* (see Chapter 5), and whether the participant *volunteers* for the study were offered as potential moderators of the fear–attitude relationship. Contrary to conventional wisdom, low-anxiety, older volunteers seemed to be more susceptible to fear appeals than high-anxiety, younger nonvolunteers.

Sussman (1973) similarly suggested the influence of mediating variables on the fear–attitude relationship. "Such variables as coping style, self-esteem, perceived vulnerability to danger, and chronic anxiety may mediate the response to a fear appeal" (p. 209). Despite the attention paid by researchers to understanding the fear–attitude relationship, additional theory and research are needed to uncover more satisfactory explanations. Because the use of fear appeals in messages is very common, the results of such research should be of interest both to applied communicators (for example, advertisers) and to scholars.

EVIDENCE IN MESSAGES

When we hear the term *evidence,* images of attorneys arguing cases come to mind. Television shows such as *Law and Order* depict the powerful effects of good evidence. Clearly evidence is a critical component in any trial. Evidence is also an important verbal behavior variable in less-formal communication contexts. When we become the target of a persuasive effort, we usually challenge our adversary to *prove* the case to us. When a new drug claims to prevent baldness, all but the most desperate or trusting of souls require some type of evidence before they spend huge sums of money on it.

Communication theorists beginning with Aristotle have focused on evidence as a determining influence on individual belief systems. Evidence consists of "factual statements originating from a source other than the speaker, objects not created by the speaker, and opinions of persons other than the speaker that are offered in support of the speaker's claims" (McCroskey, 1969, p. 170). A slightly different definition is "any statement of fact, statement of value, or definition offered by a speaker or writer which is intended to support a proposition" (Florence, 1975, p. 151). Contemporary communication courses, especially argumentation and public speaking, stress the relationship between evidence and persuasion. However, the findings of almost two decades of communication research do not appear to support a direct, positive association between evidence and persuasion. It has not been conclusively shown, for instance, that an audience will be more easily persuaded if more evidence is presented.

After reviewing over twenty studies on the influence of evidence in persuasion, James McCroskey concluded that several variables interact with evidence to produce changes in attitudes or increases in perceived speaker credibility: *evidence and source credibility, evidence and delivery effectiveness,* and *prior familiarity of evidence.*

There is a relationship between the use of evidence and the credibility or believability of the speaker. If a speaker is already perceived to be very credible, including "good" evidence will do little to change attitudes or enhance speaker credibility. However, speakers who are perceived as low to moderate in credibility may increase their credibility by employing evidence. This increase in perceived credibility may in turn increase attitude change.

In several studies on evidence and message topic, McCroskey believed that other factors were influencing the evidence–attitude change relationship. By interviewing participants after the experiments, he discovered that the quality of the delivery made a difference. To investigate the relationship further, he conducted several studies using live, audiotaped, and videotaped versions of a well-delivered and a poorly delivered presentation. The amount and type of evidence were the same for each version in each medium. From these studies, he found that: (a) including good evidence influences attitude change very little if the message is delivered poorly; and (b) including good evidence can influence attitude change and speaker credibility immediately after the speech if the message is well-delivered, the speaker initially has only low-to-moderate credibility, and the audience has little prior knowledge of the evidence. Because the results were consistent for all versions, he concluded that the medium of presentation has little effect on the use of evidence in persuasion.

McCroskey also believed that prior familiarity with evidence should be considered when assessing the evidence–persuasion relationship. Postexperimental interviews led him to conclude that "old" evidence does little to influence listeners. "Old" evidence has already been heard and processed cognitively. If any dissonance had been created by the message, it was already resolved or defense mechanisms were created to prevent a recurrence. These assumptions are consistent with explanations derived from information theories and cognitive dissonance theory (discussed later in this chapter). For evidence to affect listeners' attitude change or perceptions of the source immediately, McCroskey found that the evidence must be "new" to the listener. Including evidence has little, if any, impact on receivers if they are already familiar with it. McCroskey concluded that although considerable information has been uncovered about the influence of evidence in persuasion, communication theorists should continue their research efforts.

One researcher examined the theoretical foundations of previous research and reformulated the existing theories concerning evidence and persuasion (Florence, 1975). According to these findings, evidence influences persuasion only if the proposal, idea, or policy it supports is *desirable* to the audience. Both the credibility of a source of evidence and the evidence itself influence the desirability of a proposal. More recently, Dale Hample (1977, 1979, 1981) developed a theory of argument in which evidence plays a major role. In this theory, the relative power of evidence was measured. Hample argued that the power of evidence is one of the best predictors of attitude change. Because evidence is a key verbal message variable in the communication process, researchers will no doubt continue to examine its influence in persuasion.

The Source Credibility Approach

A great deal of research has been based on the idea that source credibility is important in explaining persuasion (for early summaries and analyses see Andersen & Clevenger, 1963). Generally, the research has failed to establish that source credibility is a necessary condition for persuasion. That is, some studies find that credible sources persuade more people, whereas other studies find no relationship between attitude change and source credibility. Such inconsistency seems strange, especially because the idea that credibility affects persuasion seems self-evident, hardly worth investigating. There are three major models of source credibility in the communication field: factor, functional, and constructivist.

THE FACTOR MODEL

The **factor model of credibility** has been dominant for the past 2,500 years. Aristotle promoted *ethos,* the Greek term for credibility, as one of the three major ways speakers persuade audiences. The others are *logos* (the words, ideas, and arguments in the speech) and *pathos* (arousing the audience's emotions and feelings). Aristotle believed there are three aspects of credibility: a source's competence or expertise, character, and goodwill toward the audience. Eventually, these three dimensions were viewed as factors of credibility. A factor is a cluster of perceptions—for example, perceptions of a source's intelligence, authoritativeness, and ability to inform—contributing to the source's perceived expertise.

> **factor model of credibility** Aspects of credibility are a source's expertise, character, and goodwill.

According to the factor model, source credibility is represented by how favorably the receiver judges the source on each of the factors of credibility. Thus, credibility exists in the mind of the receiver; it is not an actual characteristic of the source like eye color or hair color. If a source has an I.Q. of 160, is a published author on the subject of her speech, and presents an enormous amount of information on that topic, that does not mean that the audience will necessarily view her as an expert. One person may consider the source an expert on the topic, but another person may not. Credibility is strictly in the eye of the beholder.

Over the last thirty-five years, factor approach research has found that the expertise dimension appears to function independently from the character dimension. Thus, sources viewed as experts are not necessarily also thought to have good character. Some may be seen that way whereas others may not; one factor does not depend on the other. In the case of character and goodwill, however, the factors are not distinct. They work together. If we believe sources have our best interests in mind, we also perceive them as having good character. If we think they are trying to deceive us, we rate their character poorly.

A number of other variables may affect credibility: energy (dynamism), sociability, power, impact, mental balance, cultivation, and charisma. If credibility is a list of factors, critics wonder about the length of the list. Does a longer list imply a better understanding of credibility? This raises the issue of whether a "laundry list" of factors really tells us anything. Does each new factor increase understanding or cause confusion? Another criticism of the factor approach is that the model does not specify whether a receiver uses all the factors in assessing a source's credibility. A plausible expectation is that in some persuasion situations some factors matter more than other factors; some receivers will find certain factors more relevant than will other receivers. Thus, the characteristics used to judge the source's credibility can change with different sources, situations, and audiences. These and other criticisms of the factor model have led to the development of two additional models of credibility.

THE FUNCTIONAL MODEL

functional model of credibility Credibility is determined by the extent to which a source fulfills the receiver's needs.

The **functional model of credibility** views credibility as the degree to which a source satisfies the receiver's needs. Three simultaneous processes occur in a persuasive situation. First, the receiver becomes aware of the source's characteristics. Some, like height and voice quality, are observable; others, like education and social status, must be inferred. Second, the receiver determines criteria for judging the source in the situation. That is, the receiver becomes aware of the functions that the source could serve for the receiver (for example, to provide recent information, to entertain). Third, the receiver compares the characteristics with the functional criteria. An audience at a banquet might judge the extent to which a speaker has both informed and entertained them. The more needs that are fulfilled by the source, the more credible the source is. For example, the more the audience enjoyed the speech, the more credible they consider the speaker (Cronkhite & Liska, 1980).

Another group of researchers developed a method for measuring credibility according to the functional approach and then compared the functional model to the factor model to determine which explains persuasion best. The two models performed equally well in explaining differences, so the test was inconclusive. However, because the factors did not explain persuasion better than a general measure of credibility, the functional model was judged to be promising (Infante, Parker, Clarke, Wilson, & Nathu, 1983).

THE CONSTRUCTIVISTIC MODEL

constructivistic model of credibility How individuals use their personal construct systems to form, reinforce, and change impressions of sources.

Our earlier discussion in this chapter of constructivism and cognitive complexity as a trait related to persuasion is relevant to understanding the **constructivistic model of credibility**. The basic idea is that people use their personal construct systems to construct their reality. That is, reality is not something that exists where everyone experiences the very same thing. Two people viewing the same situation can have radically different conceptions of that reality because they have applied very different personal constructs to the situation. Personal construct systems involve bipolar judgments such as valuable-worthless. Some constructs are acquired from culture, others from family, friends, or school. Some constructs can be unique to the individual and highly idiosyncratic. For instance, an economically oriented person might see a situation mainly as having great potential for yielding investment profit, whereas a scholarly individual might mainly perceive how that situation could produce certain knowledge that will advance understanding of a problem.

These ideas can be applied to conceptualizing source credibility. Delia (1976) said understanding source credibility involves learning how individuals use their personal construct systems to form, reinforce, and change impressions of people in persuasion situations. Just as two people can have a very different conception of reality in viewing a given situation, they also can have very different impressions of the credibility of a given speaker. We need to determine which constructs the receiver of a message used in deciding to accept or reject the source's position on the object of persuasion. Although this seems to be a reasonable approach to understanding source credibility, a problem is that an appealing measurement model has not been developed. Whereas sets of rating scales have been used successfully for measuring credibility according to the factor approach, a comparable method of measurement has not been developed for the constructivistic approach. Research here typically has had the research subject write an impression of the communicator, which was then content analyzed later by researchers to determine the constructs used and how those identified constructs related to the degree of persuasion that took place (e.g., Delia, O'Keefe & O'Keefe, 1982). Not only is this a tedious, labor-intensive way to study credibility, but the results have not been promising enough to stimulate much further research. More progress in measuring source credibility is necessary, and if that is accomplished, it should have a very beneficial effect in stimulating future research.

Cognitive Dissonance Theory

Social psychologist Leon Festinger's cognitive dissonance theory (1957) is the most thoroughly researched of a family of cognitive consistency theories and therefore the one we shall discuss in this chapter (for a review of other consistency theories, see Kiesler, Collins, & Miller, 1969). Consistency theories of persuasion are based on the idea that inconsistency is psychologically uncomfortable. Inconsistency results when we believe A should have a certain relationship to B but does not, or when A has an unexpected, undesirable relationship with something. For instance, inconsistency would be felt if we see that a program to reduce poverty in our city is not reducing hunger among children as we had expected. Instead, the program is reducing hope and aspirations among poor people.

cognitive dissonance theory Assumes that two beliefs are related either in a state of consonance or dissonance.

Cognitive dissonance theory assumes that two beliefs are related either in a state of consonance or dissonance. A state of **consonance** is characterized by consistency: "I like my sorority, and my good friend likes my sorority." **Dissonance** is marked by inconsistency: "I like my sorority, but my good friend does not like it." The idea is that it would "bother" us (we would feel dissonance) if our friend did not also value what we value, and we would be motivated to get rid of the uncomfortable feeling. A central tenet of the theory is: The more the mental discomfort (dissonance), the more we are motivated to change something to make things comfortable.

The theory identifies a number of factors that influence the amount of dissonance experienced. Perhaps the most important one is whether the person's self-concept is involved in the dissonant relationship. If one belief is, "I just said that I liked a task that I really hate" ("I lied"), and a second belief is, "I am an honest person," the dissonance involves self-concept—our mental picture of the kind of person we are. What will be done to reduce dissonance? Research suggests individuals tend to change so that their attitude toward the task is more favorable, "I actually do like that task." This change in attitude permits consistency with the belief, "I am an honest person." We try to protect our self-concepts by rationalizing our actions and decisions so we do not "look bad" to ourselves. Changing the second belief to "I am dishonest" would also have restored consistency: "I lied" and "I am dishonest." However, we seldom reduce dissonance by changing a favorable belief about ourselves.

This principle can be used to explain the results of a classic study by Aronson and Mills (1959). To join a very dull discussion group, individuals were required either to recite a list of sexual terms (mild initiation) or to recite a list of "obscene" words (severe initiation). The research participants were then asked how much they liked the group. Did the severe or the mild initiation lead to greater liking for the group? In line with the theory's prediction, persons given the severe initiation liked the group more. Why? Because they experienced more dissonance. Their beliefs could be characterized as: "I am efficient," so "I just put forth a great effort, and I got something worthwhile." To conclude that the group was worthless would force the belief about self to be: "I am inefficient" because "I just put forth a great effort for little reward." Individuals who experienced the mild initiation did not distort their feelings about the group. "I am efficient," and "I got little benefit from the discussion, but I did not put much into it, so I have not lost."

Dissonance can be reduced in many ways besides changing beliefs, as in the preceding example. Attitude change toward a speaker's proposal and attitude change toward the speaker are two basic methods of resolving dissonance. Attitude change toward the speaker might involve criticizing the source of the

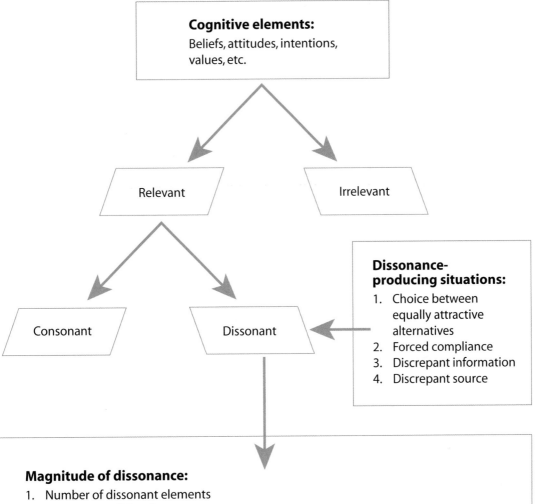

Figure 6.1

Cognitive dissonance.

information: "I won't listen to the American Cancer Society public service announcement warning about the health risks of smoking because the American Cancer Society is biased against cigarette smoking." Other methods of reducing dissonance are not as obvious. **Selective exposure** involves seeking information that supports your opinion but avoiding information that is unfavorable toward your opinion. The listener can also misinterpret the speaker's position so that the speaker seems to agree with the listener. One could also consider the dissonant elements unimportant so that the dissonance does not really matter. "The new car I just bought has little pickup, but I really don't need power and speed in a car anyway." Another alternative is to add consonant elements to "drown out" the dissonance. "Besides, my new car has great lines, a beautiful interior, an excellent stereo, and perfect handling."

A basic idea about persuasion from dissonance theory is that to persuade people, you must cause them to experience dissonance, then offer your proposal as a way to get rid of the dissonance. A persuader might try to make receivers feel dissonance about energy policies in the United States and then present a proposal for developing alternative and renewable energy sources such as hydrogen fuel cells or solar energy to free the United States from dependence on foreign oil. When a speaker arouses dissonance, the receiver will try to reduce it, using one of the methods just listed. However, dissonance can also be reduced by adopting or agreeing with the speaker's proposal. Although there is no guarantee that the audience will reduce dissonance by changing their minds, the speaker does have a chance to achieve persuasion.

According to the theory, if no dissonance is aroused, there will be no persuasion. People do not change an attitude unless they feel they need to change it. Feeling dissonance provides the motivation to change. The theory predicts that to persuade someone, you must first "upset" the person (make them feel dissonance) concerning the topic of your proposal. If you fail to persuade the audience, perhaps the dissonance they felt was not great enough to motivate action.

Ego-Involvement, or Social Judgment Theory

This approach to persuasion is distinctly different from cognitive consistency theories of persuasion. Ego-involvement or social judgment theory (Sherif, Sherif, & Nebergall, 1965) predicts successful persuasion by a message depending on how the message is related to the person's current beliefs. (The Sherifs were psychologists; Nebergall was a member of the communication discipline.) Research in physiological psychology indicates that if a person is given an "anchor" in making judgments, objects close to the anchor are seen as more similar to the anchor than they really are (they are assimilated). Objects far from the anchor are perceived as even more dissimilar than they really are

selective exposure
Exposing oneself only to agreeable messages; avoiding situations, such as public speeches by a political opponent, requiring us to listen to those with whom we disagree.

(they are contrasted). If you were handed a bar and told it weighs 10 pounds, you would probably judge too low when asked to guess what a 12-pound bar weighs. You probably would judge the 12-pound bar as just about the same as the 10-pound anchor; you would assimilate it. Next, if asked to guess the weight of a 40-pound bar, you probably would judge it heavier than it really is. It would seem more distant from the anchor; the contrast effect would occur.

What does this have to do with persuasion? **Ego-involvement** or **social judgment theory** indicates that assimilation and contrast effects also occur in persuasion. **Assimilation** constitutes persuasion; a **contrast effect** represents a failure to persuade. In the case of persuasion, the receiver's position on the topic of the persuasive message serves as the **anchor**. If a speaker slightly opposes gun control and you moderately oppose it, you tend to interpret the speaker's position as basically the same as yours. On the other hand, the more you favor gun control and the more the speaker opposes it, the greater the likelihood that you will view the speaker's position as more extreme than it really is (that is, a contrast effect). Basically, we accept assimilated messages but reject contrasted messages.

Although interesting, the assimilation–contrast notion leaves several questions unanswered. Under what conditions are messages assimilated or contrasted? Why do two individuals with the same position on an issue react differently to the same message about the issue, one person assimilating the message while the other person contrasts it? The concepts of latitude of acceptance, rejection, and noncommitment are needed to answer these questions.

The **latitude of acceptance** consists of all statements the person finds acceptable, including the favorite position, the anchor. Figure 6.2 illustrates the latitudes of acceptance for two individuals on an issue with 11 positions. Notice that Chris and Pat have the same most acceptable position (A) or anchor belief: "Final exams should be optional for graduating seniors." Chris rejects statements 6 and 7, while Pat agrees with them. The **latitude of rejection** (r) consists of all of the positions on the issue the person rejects (finds objectionable). Pat and Chris have latitudes of rejection that vary in width. Pat rejects only statement 1, the position that final exams should be required of all students, whereas Chris rejects statements 1–7. The **latitude of noncommitment** (nc) consists of all positions the person neither accepts nor rejects. The person is noncommittal or neutral on these issues. Chris is neutral about statement 8; Pat is neutral about statements 2–5.

The latitudes of acceptance, rejection, and noncommitment determine whether a given person will assimilate or contrast a message. Messages falling in the latitudes of acceptance or noncommitment will be judged closer to the favorite position (anchor belief) than they really are (assimilated). Messages falling in the latitude of rejection will be judged farther away (contrasted). According to ego-involvement theory, a basic principle of persuasion is that to change a person's most acceptable position on a topic, the message must

ego-involvement
Characterized by a wide latitude of rejection and narrow latitudes of acceptance and noncommitment.

assimilation The degree to which a person accepts the influence of the new culture or environment.

latitude of acceptance
Consists of all statements the person finds acceptable. This can include the favorite position or the anchor.

latitude of rejection
Consists of all of the positions on an issue the person rejects.

latitude of noncommitment
Consists of all of the positions a person neither accepts nor rejects.

Chris												
Topic Positions	1	2	3	4	5	6	7	8	9	10	11
	r	r	r	r	r	r	r	nc	a	A	a
Pat												
Topic Positions	1	2	3	4	5	6	7	8	9	10	11
	r	nc	nc	nc	nc	a	a	a	a	A	a

A = most acceptable position
a = other acceptable positions

r = positions which are rejected
nc = positions on that the person is neutral

POSITION STATEMENTS

11. Final exams should be optional for all students.
10. Final exams should be optional for graduating seniors.
9. Final exams should be optional in elective courses.
8. Final exams should be optional for students with an A average.
7. Final exams should be optional for students with an A or B average.
6. Final exams should be optional for students with an A, B, or C average.
5. Final exams should be optional for students with a passing average.
4. Final exams should be optional at the professor's discretion.
3. Final exams should be required only of freshmen.
2. Final exams should be required only of freshmen and sophomores.
1. Final exams should be required of all students.

Figure 6.2

Ego-involvement or social judgment theory.

fall within the person's latitude of acceptance. A persuader can also attempt to widen the latitude of acceptance by advocating a position in the person's latitude of noncommitment. If successful, the persuader will widen the receiver's latitude of acceptance, thus creating a larger "target" for a second persuasion attempt.

The latitudes also indicate whether the person is ego-involved. According to the theory, high ego-involvement is characterized by a narrow latitude of acceptance (the person's own favorite position is about the only position accepted), a wide latitude of rejection (almost everything other than one's own position is rejected), and a narrow latitude of noncommitment (nearly all positions are either accepted or rejected; the person is neutral about very few positions). Low ego-involvement is the opposite. The latitude of acceptance is wide (people are able to accept several other positions on the issue besides their anchor position), the latitude of noncommitment is wide (there are many positions on the topic that the person is neutral about), and the latitude of rejection is narrow (there is not much left to reject if one accepts most positions and does not care about most of the remaining ones).

Chris is highly ego-involved, and Pat is not ego-involved with final exam regulations. According to the theory, even though they both hold the same most acceptable position (statement 10), they would react differently to a message that advocated position 6. Chris would contrast the message because it falls in the latitude of rejection; it would be "heard" as a more extreme message than it actually is. On the other hand, Pat would assimilate the message, perceive it closer to the anchor (position 10) than it really is because it is one of the acceptable positions. Thus, Pat would be persuaded by the message; Chris would not.

This theory permits us to conceptualize how persuasion can be achieved with a highly ego-involved individual. In our example, to persuade Chris to change from position 10 to position 2 would take many messages. One message would not be enough—it would be contrasted. Persuasion would require many messages over a long period of time, each gradually expanding the latitude of acceptance and slowly moving the favorite position (anchor belief). This probably is a realistic view of persuasion. It is very difficult to persuade someone who is very ego-involved in a topic. The theory represents this idea clearly. When a person is highly ego-involved, a "one-shot" attempt to persuade the individual is surely doomed to failure. A "persuasive campaign" composed of many messages over a period of time is a more realistic way to try to change someone who is ego-involved.

The Theory of Reasoned Action

The **theory of reasoned action** by psychologists Martin Fishbein and Icek Ajzen is included here because it has been used a good deal by communication researchers (e.g., see recent research by Edwards, 1998; Stewart & Roach, 1998; Park, 1998). It is also a good example of theory building. The theory was introduced in the 1960s and enhanced through the next two decades (for instance, see Ajzen, 1985; Ajzen & Fishbein, 1980; Fishbein & Ajzen, 1975).

theory of reasoned action A theory of persuasion that is based on attitudes, belief strength, and the evaluation of the meaning of the belief.

The theory of reasoned action began with Fishbein's theory of attitude toward an object (an object could be a person, a physical thing, an idea, a social program, etc.); he conceptualized attitude as a sum of the beliefs that we have learned to associate with the object. Suppose we consider your attitude toward physical fitness. You might have learned to associate seven beliefs with physical fitness. The extent to which each belief contributes to your attitude depends on (a) belief strength and (b) evaluation of the meaning of the belief. You might have a belief that it is extremely likely (belief strength) that a physical fitness lifestyle results in a very favorable (evaluation) consequence, an attractive body shape. This belief would favorably affect your attitude toward physical fitness; you have a strong belief that the object produces something good. A second belief might be that you think it is slightly unlikely (belief strength) that you will get frequent colds if you are in good physical condition. This belief also is positive because it asserts that you will be less likely to experience something bad, but because it is not a very strong belief, it will have less impact on your attitude. If your remaining five beliefs followed the pattern of these two examples, you would have a moderately favorable attitude toward physical fitness. That is, if we add the degree of favorable feelings in your seven beliefs, the total would be much closer to the favorable end than to the unfavorable end of the attitude object continuum.

In the 1960s, psychology and sociology researchers found that attitude theories such as this one were poor predictors of a given behavior. For example, we could design a study to measure your attitude toward physical fitness. If your attitude was very favorable and we gave you a coupon for a free workout at a local gym, the prediction would be that you would use the coupon. Typically, that prediction would not be very accurate. In fact, flipping a coin might be just as accurate in predicting behavior as measuring attitude.

Fishbein, who was later joined by Ajzen, expanded the theory to deal with this problem of why attitude toward an object does not accurately predict a specific behavior relevant to the object. Fishbein declared that attitude does predict behavior, but not in the way that previous researchers had assumed that it should. The problem was the measure of behavior. A single act, observed once, was what most studies used as the criterion. This was a mistake because there is no theoretical reason why attitude toward an object should be closely related to a single behavior, unless there is only one behavior that is relevant to the object, which is seldom the case. Typically, many behaviors are relevant to an attitude object. When that is the case, attitude toward the object should be related to the total set of behaviors. Thus, one act, observed once, does not measure the entire set of relevant behaviors. The correct behavioral measure was what Fishbein called the **multiple-act**, repeated observations criterion. This means all the relevant behaviors should be counted; ideally, they should be observed more than once over a period of time.

multiple-act   A behavioral prediction in research based on a set of relevant behaviors ideally more than once over a period of time.

In terms of our example, then, your attitude toward physical fitness probably would not predict whether you will show up at the gym. We would be a bit more accurate if we could observe you showing up next week, the week after, and the next week, and so on (this would be a single-act, repeated measures criterion). An even better predictor would be observations of all other relevant behaviors, observed more than once. Two possibilities would be observing you eating a healthy diet each day for a month, or noting that you watched physical fitness shows on TV for a month. If we designated ten behaviors and observed them for a month, the total number of occurrences of the ten would constitute a multiple-act, repeated observations criterion. Research by Fishbein and others found an improved behavioral measure such as this is strongly related to attitude toward the object.

What this means in terms of persuasion, then, is if you succeeded in persuading someone who had an unfavorable attitude toward physical fitness to have a favorable attitude (probably by arguing successfully that several good things would likely follow), you should expect the total pattern of the person's fitness-related behaviors to change. However, any single behavior might not change. For instance, the person might go to the gym often, watch exercise shows on TV, attend fitness lectures, etc., but continue eating high-fat fast food. We might wonder at this point whether it is possible to target a single behavior not only for prediction but also for change in persuasion situations.

The theory of reasoned action was developed to deal specifically with the problem of predicting a single behavior, even if it is only observed once. Fishbein and Ajzen built on their earlier research. A core idea of the theory of reasoned action is that behavior is intentional; very little behavior is accidental. When people engage in a given behavior, it is because they formed intentions to do so, and they had reasons for their decisions to actualize their intentions. Thus, much of our behavior can be characterized as "reasoned action."

Attitude toward the specific act is one of two major components of a behavioral intention. The second is what has been called the *normative component.* Keep in mind that the Fishbein and Ajzen model works backward from a specific behavior. That is, a specific behavior is predicted or controlled by an intention to behave; that intention is predicted and controlled by two factors, attitude toward the act and the normative component. Each of these two components is controlled by particular factors.

Attitude toward the specific act is controlled by the beliefs that the person has about the consequences of performing the act. As with Fishbein's earlier theory of attitude toward an object, two aspects of each belief are important: belief strength and evaluation. Continuing with our gym visit example, suppose you have five moderately strong beliefs about five somewhat desirable consequences of accepting the offer for a free workout at a gym: the gym has superior equipment; it is easy to get to the gym because of its location; membership rates could be cheaper after a trial visit; a gym membership would increase motivation to exercise; you could meet interesting people there. At this point it might be tempting to predict that you probably will go to the gym. The five beliefs are reasons for action or inaction. In this case the reasons tilt somewhat toward action. However, there is more to the theory. The second determinant of an intention is the normative component, and we need to consider it before making a prediction about behavior.

The normative component is composed of our beliefs about what valued others expect us to do regarding the behavior. Each belief is weighted by our motivation to comply with the wishes of other people. In terms of our example, suppose one normative belief is that your good friend would not want you to join that gym, because he is planning on having a gym in the basement of his home and wants you to work out there so the two of you can motivate one another. Perhaps another normative belief is that your significant other does not like the manager of the gym and therefore is less than enthusiastic about the prospect of you being a member there. Suppose further that you have fairly strong motivation to comply with these normative expectations.

On the basis of these two components, attitude toward the act and the normative component, can we now offer a prediction of whether or not you will go to the gym for the trial workout? Often information about these two components is enough to make an accurate prediction, However, in a case like this where you are being pulled one way by one component and another way by the second component, more information is needed. The *subjective weights* of each component help evaluate conflicting influences. For some behaviors we feel that we can do whatever we feel like doing (i.e., we let our attitude toward the act guide us and feel no constraint from other people). For other behaviors we decide what we do must be compatible with the preferences of valued others (i.e., we look to the normative component for guidance).

In our example, suppose on a 1–10 scale your weight for attitude toward the act is 3 and your weight for the normative component is 8. In view of this data the theory would predict that you will not go to the gym for the trial workout. Suppose that the theory is accurate (as it has been most of the time), and you do not go to the gym. However, what would have happened if we had made a prediction based only on the first attitude that we considered, attitude toward physical fitness? Because the attitude in the example was moderately favorable, the prediction would have been that you would go to the gym. The prediction would have been wrong. If the prediction had been based only on attitude toward the act, once again it would have been wrong. An accurate prediction was achieved only when both components were considered and weighted. The theory became more accurate as it developed—an excellent illustration of the advantages of theory building. The theory of reasoned action has been a popular one in communication research because of its accuracy.

In addition to prediction strengths, the theory provides implications for persuasion. For example, if you want to influence a person to perform a specific behavior, do not devote much time to trying to change attitude toward the object. Instead, try to determine what the person's current attitude is toward that act and also the normative component. Importantly, how is each component weighted? Such analysis directs your focus for the persuasive attempt. The fundamental persuasion tactics would involve arguing the consequences of performing the act. For a favorable attitude toward the behavior you would claim good consequences would be likely and bad consequences would be unlikely. For an unfavorable attitude, the opposite would be argued (i.e., that good things would not happen, but bad things would occur). Influencing the normative component involves maintaining that persons valued by the individual either expect certain behaviors or do not want certain things to happen. Sometimes it could be necessary to convince people that they should have high motivation to fulfill the expectations of valued others. In other circumstances persuading people to perform a given behavior necessitates moving them to ignore the wishes of others and to act mainly on the basis of self-interest. This tactic could be especially difficult to accomplish because it is not unusual in persuasion situations for need for approval to be a major factor.

The Theory of Planned Behavior

As explained in the previous section, the core of Fishbein and Ajzen's theory of reasoned action is the notion of the **behavioral intention**; a person's intention of performing a given behavior is the best predictor of whether or not the person will actually perform the behavior. It may have occurred to you, however, that several factors can work against this behavioral intention → behavior sequence. Think about some examples where you, to use a cliché, "had the best intentions" to perform a behavior (e.g., taking your sibling to the mall to go shopping next Saturday morning) but certain personal limitations (e.g., you were too tired and overslept) and/or external obstacles (e.g., you didn't have a car available to you that day) prevented you from actually performing that behavior. The successful performance of a behavior also depends on one's ability to control factors that either allow or prevent performance of that behavior (Ajzen, 1988).

To resolve some of the difficulties in predicting behavior precisely, Ajzen (1985, 1988, 1991) proposed the theory of planned behavior (TPB), an extension of the theory of reasoned action (TORA). TPB is also based on the premise that the best predictor of an actual behavior is a person's behavioral intention. However, unlike its predecessor theory, TPB suggests that there are three, rather than two factors associated with a person's behavioral intention (see Figure 6.3).

In TPB, the first two factors associated with a behavioral intention are the same as in TORA: (1) attitude toward the specific act (or behavior), and (2) the normative component, our beliefs about what valued others expect us to do regarding the behavior in question. Ajzen (1985, 1988, 1991) added a third factor, **perceived behavioral control**, to TPB. Perceived behavioral control refers to "the degree to which a person believes they can control the behavior in question" (Roberto, Meyer, & Boster, 2001, p. 316)—how easy or difficult the person believes it will be to perform a given behavior.

TPB suggests that, in general, more favorable attitudes toward the specific act (or behavior), more favorable subjective norms (normative component), and greater perceived behavioral control (the ease of performing the behavior in question) strengthen the intention to perform the behavior. According to TPB, perceived behavioral control is directly related to behavioral intentions and to actual behavior.

behavioral intention A person's intention of performing a given behavior is the best predictor of whether or not the person will actually perform the behavior.

perceived behavioral control The degree to which a person believes that they control any given behavior.

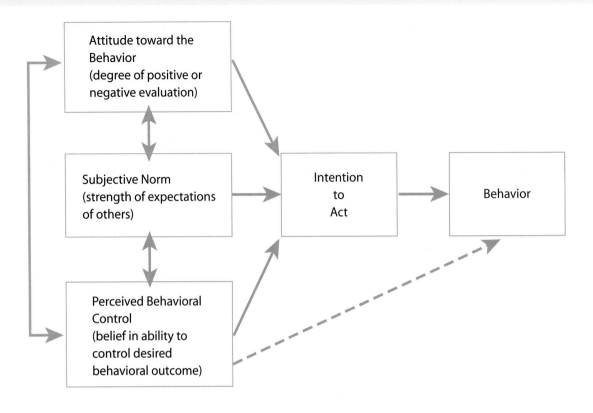

Figure 6.3

Theory of planned behavior.

self-efficacy The degree
of ease or difficulty in
performing the behavior or
likelihood that a person can
actually perform a behavior.

controllability People's
belief that they have control
over the behavior, that the
performance of the behavior
is-or-is not up to them.

Ajzen (2001) suggests that perceived behavioral control influences a person's confidence that they are capable of performing the behavior in question. Perceived behavioral control is, in essence, a combination of two dimensions, **self-efficacy** (ease or difficulty in performing the behavior or likelihood that the person can actually do it) and **controllability** (people's beliefs that they have control over the behavior, that the performance of the behavior is—or is not—up to them).

Returning to the physical fitness lifestyle example, let's say you want to predict whether a person will walk on a treadmill in a physical fitness center for at least 30 minutes each day in the next month (Ajzen, 2001). To assess the self-efficacy dimension of perceived behavioral control, you might ask the person to respond to an item such as, "For me to walk on a treadmill for at least 30 minutes each day in the forthcoming month would be" [impossible—possible]. To assess the controllability dimension of perceived control, you could ask, "How much control do you believe you have over walking on a treadmill for at least 30 minutes each day in the forthcoming month" [no control—complete control].

Thus, if you want to assess more accurately whether a person will actually perform a given behavior, you will need to measure perceived control, along with an assessment of the person's *behavioral intention*, "I plan to walk on a treadmill for at least 30 minutes each day in the forthcoming month" [strongly disagree—strongly agree], their *attitude toward the behavior*, "I believe walking on a treadmill for at least 30 minutes each day in the next month is [harmful— beneficial, worthless—valuable], and their subjective norm, "Most people who are important to me think that [I should—I should not] walk on a treadmill for at least 30 minutes each day in the next month" (Ajzen, 2001, pp. 4–7).

When put to the test, TPB has been able to predict a number of health-related behaviors such as weight loss (Schifter & Ajzen, 1985), adolescent use of alcohol (Marcoux & Schope, 1997), and adolescent abstinence from sex and/or use of condoms during sexual relations (Basen-Engquist & Parcel, 1992). Communication researchers have recently adopted TPB to predict actual behavior. For example, Roberto, Meyer, and Boster (2001) used TPB to predict adolescent decisions about fighting. In their study, several hundred seventh-grade boys and girls were questioned about their participation in physical fights "where two or more people hit, punch, slap, push, or kick each other in anger" (p. 317). They completed a survey instrument that measured their actual behavior (e.g., "During the last month how many times did you get into a fight?), their behavioral intentions (e.g., "How many times do you think you will get into a fight in the next month?"), the perceptions of subjective norms (e.g., "Do most of the kids you know think you should get into fights?"), their attitudes toward fighting (e.g., very cool—very uncool), and their *perceived behavioral control* (e.g., "How easy or hard is it for you to stay out of fights," and "When someone tries to start a fight with you, how easy or hard is it for you to avoid the fight?").

The results supported several of the assumptions of TPB in that attitudes toward fighting and perceived behavioral control were both related to an individual's behavioral intentions. That is, those adolescents who felt they were more "in control" of their fighting behaviors and who expressed unfavorable attitudes toward fighting were less likely to get into fights. Both behavioral intentions and perceived behavioral control emerged as predictors of actual behavior (Roberto et al., 2001).

TPB has also been used to predict smokers' interests in participating in a smoking-cessation program (Babrow, Black, & Tiffany, 1990). TPB suggests that measuring a person's attitudes toward participating in a particular smoking-cessation program allow better prediction of participation in the program than attitudes toward smoking in general or attitudes toward quitting smoking in general. Intentions to participate (behavioral intentions), attitude toward participation, beliefs about the consequences of participating, perceptions of the subjective norm, and perceived behavioral control were measured ("how frequently would the following factors: flexibility of program hours,

perceived control The degree to which people believe that they have control over a situation or behavior.

subjective norm The pressure a person feels to conform to the will of others to perform or not perform a behavior.

participation with other friends, convenience of location, etc. affect your ability to participate in this particular smoking-cessation program" [never—constantly]). Babrow et al.'s (1990) findings generally supported TPB. Beliefs about the consequences of participating in the program were related to attitude toward participation. Most important, attitude, subjective norm, and perceived behavioral control beliefs were strongly related to individuals' intentions to participate in the smoking cessation program.

The development of TPB in response to an earlier theory, TORA, allows us to see how theories are built by extension (see Chapter 2), where new theories emerge from expansion of existing theories. By adding new information, factors, and knowledge to existing theories, we can better explain, predict, and thus, control behavior.

Elaboration Likelihood Theory

We will now examine a theory that has been described as "the most promising recent theoretical development in persuasion research" (O'Keefe, 1990, p. 109). Social psychologists Petty and Cacioppo (1986) developed the **elaboration likelihood model** (ELM). They recognized that persuasion results primarily from characteristics of the persuasive message or from characteristics of the persuasion situation. ELM analyzes the likelihood that receivers will cognitively elaborate—engage in issue-related thinking—on the information presented in a persuasive message. Because of its focus on the conditions of certain types of thinking in persuasion, ELM fits the laws tradition of theories.

At times persuasion occurs because the receiver of a message considers the content of the persuasive message carefully and has favorable thoughts about the content. The favorable thinking about the message content causes a favorable attitude to form toward the object of the message. This represents one type of persuasion—the **central route** to persuasion, characterized by a good deal of persuasive, issue-related thinking. At other times persuasion occurs because the receiver is guided not by his or her assessment of the message but because the receiver decides to follow a principle or a decision-rule derived from the persuasion situation. The rule might be: "When everyone else goes along with the speaker's recommendation, I should too unless I have a very good reason to deviate from the group." This is an example of persuasion through a **peripheral route**.

According to Petty and Cacioppo, when persuasion takes a peripheral route, there is little or no elaboration of message content; that is, there is a lack of issue-related thinking. When a decision on a persuasive message is not based on the message itself, the receiver looks to other things to guide the decision, as in the preceding example. The persuasive situation provides many principles for evaluating a message if one does not want to engage in a critical assessment of the message content. We sometimes base message acceptance on the

elaboration likelihood model A model of persuasion that assumes persuasion results primarily from characteristics of the persuasive message or from characteristics of the situation.

central route The favorable thinking about the message content causes a favorable attitude to form toward the object of the message.

peripheral route When there is little or no elaboration of a message. Situational cues persuade people instead of the message.

trustworthiness of the source, the expertise of the source, or even the physical attractiveness of the source. Also, a decision-rule can be based on rewards or punishments. "I will accept the source's position if I can realize a financial gain from it or if I can avoid a punishment such as higher taxes." Sometimes we are guided by our relationship with the persuader, as in "I need to return a favor."

The ELM is based on the idea that people realize their attitudes are important because attitudes guide decisions and other behaviors. This importance motivates people to form attitudes that are useful in their lives. Although attitudes can result from a number of things, persuasion is a primary source. When a persuasive message attempts to influence an attitude the receiver realizes is significant to his or her life, the likelihood increases that the receiver will cognitively elaborate on the content of the message. This process takes a good deal of effort, so it is avoided whenever possible. That is, people generally prefer not to have to work hard mentally and will follow the "easy way" whenever possible. This probably is due not so much to people being lazy as to the reality of our cognitive limits. Our physical limits are pretty obvious. For instance, we cannot run a marathon as a sprint. The central route to persuasion is probably more like a "mental sprint." You can only do it for a limited period of time.

A peripheral route to persuasion is "easy" because not much thinking is necessary. All one has to do is realize an appropriate guiding principle and make a decision on the persuasive message based on the principle. "The source is a real expert so I can trust what she is saying." Little, if any, elaboration takes place when a simple principle, like this example, is used to guide assessment of a persuasive message.

It is important to note that persuasion, or lack of it, can take place with either route. What matters is the *cognitive product* of the process. When one takes the central route, thinking about the content of the message might result in unfavorable assessments of the source's arguments. This negative reaction would inhibit persuasion. Similarly, persuasion could fail to occur through a peripheral route when a receiver utilizes the negative side of a principle. "The source has no real credentials to speak on this topic, so I would not even consider changing my opinion."

Because elaboration or issue-related thinking is central to this theory, a good deal of research has explored the factors that influence how much we elaborate when we receive a persuasive message. Basically, two types of factors have been identified: (a) factors that influence our *motivation* to elaborate, and (b) factors that influence our *ability* to elaborate.

Motivation to elaborate has been investigated in terms of the receiver's involvement in the persuasive issue; the more the person is personally involved in the topic, the more likely he or she will elaborate on the message. Also, motivation to elaborate is increased when several sources present arguments on the topic. The variety of arguments presents a sense of conflict, and conflict tends to attract attention. The research also has discovered that some people are

need for cognition   A stable individual difference in people's tendency to engage in and enjoy effortful cognitive activity.

more likely than others to elaborate. Specifically, people who have a strong **need for cognition** (they enjoy thinking a lot) are more likely to elaborate on the content of a message.

The need for cognition trait is defined as "a stable individual difference in people's tendency to engage in and enjoy effortful cognitive activity" (Cacioppo, Petty, Feinstein, & Jarvis, 1996, p. 198). Cognitive activity refers to the degree of critical thinking a person engages in. People range from being high to being low in need for cognition. Individuals high in need for cognition enjoy thinking about abstract issues and often engage in contemplative thought, whereas people low in need for cognition tend to rely more on simple social cues that provide a shortcut to effortful thought. These cues can be things such as attractiveness and source credibility, as illustrated in the Elaboration Likelihood Model of Persuasion. That is, people who are high in need for cognition have a tendency to process information through the central route, whereas people low in need for cognition have a tendency to process information through the peripheral route.

Although it may appear that people high in need for cognition are somehow smarter than people low in need for cognition, this is not the case. Of course people high in need for cognition have to have a degree of critical thinking capacity. Sanders, Gass, Wiseman, and Bruschke (1992) compared Asian Americans, Hispanic Americans, and European Americans in need for cognition, argumentativeness, and verbal aggressiveness. The results of this study reveal that need for cognition was positively related to argumentativeness and negatively related to verbal aggressiveness. Further, Asian Americans reported being lower in need for cognition than both Hispanic Americans and European Americans. A similar link between need for cognition and argumentativeness was also observed by Mongeau (1989).

It is important to note that need for cognition is a motivational trait, not a behavior skill-related trait. Similar to the competing motivational tendencies that comprise the trait of argumentativeness, need for cognition simply suggests that we either enjoy abstract thinking or we do not.

You may be thinking, "Why is need for cognition in the Persuasion Approaches chapter and not in the Trait Approaches chapter?" The answer is that unlike other traits, need for cognition is an important motivational factor in the Elaboration Likelihood Model of persuasion. The need for cognition is a very important trait for researchers and theorists interested in a source-based factor that influences how people are persuaded.

The ability to elaborate is also influenced by several factors. Distractions are a key element. If people are distracted during the presentation of a message, they are less likely to elaborate on the content. They are more likely to take a peripheral route. For instance, distracting a friend by dining in a good restaurant while trying to persuade him or her makes it less likely that your friend will exert the cognitive effort to elaborate on the message (attention to the food subtracts from the attention available for message elaboration). In this example, it is again more likely that a peripheral route to persuasion will be taken. "Coming from so generous a friend, the message is probably valid." Knowledge of the topic also is a factor that influences ability to elaborate. Knowing little about the topic makes elaboration very difficult, and peripheral routes are welcomed when we find ourselves in such a circumstance. Similarly, the comprehensibility of a message influences elaboration. A very vague message or one that relies heavily on very difficult material reduces the ability to elaborate. However, this might not reduce persuasion if, instead of elaborating on the message content, the receiver relies on a principle such as "the speaker is such an expert that the message position surely is correct." Diverting receivers to a particular peripheral route at times could be a successful strategy of persuasion.

It should be noted that the two routes to persuasion are not mutually exclusive. Probably only one route is taken under circumstances of extremely high or extremely low elaboration. Thus, when elaboration of the message content is very extensive, no consideration might be given to a peripheral route. On the other hand, when there is no elaboration of the message, a peripheral route is taken exclusively. Between those extremes, however, probably both characteristics of the message and characteristics of the persuasion situation matter. For instance, after receiving a persuasive message, a person might say: "After thinking extensively about what was said, I must conclude that I am persuaded a bit, but not as much as I would have been if the speaker had been motivated less by self-interest." Research by James Stiff (1986) suggests people are influenced in persuasion not only by cues associated with the central route but also by cues pertaining to peripheral routes. Stiff demonstrated that, when they want to, people can "stretch" their capacity for processing information and process both message and situation information. Therefore, it is overly simplistic to view persuasion in an "either/or" (as in either a central or a peripheral route) sense. Allowing for both provides a richer explanation of persuasion.

We can avoid being overly simplistic also by saying that characteristics of sources (such as expertise or attractiveness) do not always pertain to peripheral routes. For instance, an actor's beautiful tan could be considered part of the persuasive message when trying to sell suntan lotion; the tan would constitute data (an example) for the claim that having a tan enhances physical attractiveness. In other circumstances, such as the actor talking about aiding the homeless, the tan would function as a component of attractiveness that, for some receivers, might be a peripheral route to persuasion.

O'Keefe's (1990) assessment of the ELM being most promising as a theoretical development is probably quite accurate. The theory is generating a good deal of research and is attracting the attention of a sizeable body of researchers. Although cognitive dissonance theory was the dominant theory of persuasion in earlier periods of persuasion research, the ELM might very well play a similar role in the future.

Compliance-Gaining Message Selection

A good deal of social influence research in the communication discipline through the 1980s focused on **compliance gaining**. Recall our earlier distinction that compliance gaining and persuasion are two different types of social influence (persuasion involves attitude change). The main emphasis of compliance-gaining research was on the various strategies that people use under different circumstances to influence another person to behave in a particular manner (see Dillard, 1990, for an analysis of this literature). This line of research had its beginning in the field of sociology, where Gerald Marwell and David Schmitt (1967) derived sixteen different compliance-gaining strategies from previous research and theory, which were later introduced to the communication field (Miller, Boster, Roloff, & Seibold, 1977). Figure 6.4 presents a definition of each strategy with an example from the Marwell and Schmitt study. Generally, research was conducted by presenting a hypothetical situation (for example, your roommate is playing the stereo too loudly). The set of compliance-gaining strategies was then presented, and participants were asked to rate the likelihood that they would use each strategy in the hypothetical situation. Another method was to ask participants to write what they would say in such a situation. Researchers then analyzed the written content to determine preferred strategies.

We will examine John Hunter and Franklin Boster's (1987) model of compliance-gaining message selection because it is a good example of the new direction taken in social influence theory building. The model posits that the source's selection of compliance-gaining messages is influenced greatly by the way the source thinks the receiver will react emotionally to the message. Emotional reactions to a message can range from extremely positive to extremely negative. Persuaders generally select messages that create a favorable emotional reaction in their receivers, and they would rather avoid messages that produce negative emotional states. However, this is a general pattern, and it does not apply to everyone. Some people are more willing than others to select messages that stimulate very unfavorable reactions in receivers. Some people only select messages that arouse positive emotions.

Willingness to select negative affect-producing messages is an individual difference, a variable from person to person. The persuader's willingness to stir negative emotional reactions in receivers serves as a "go, no-go" trigger for message selection. Sources are willing to use messages that stimulate negative reactions up to a certain degree. A given message is a candidate for use if it does not exceed the degree of negative arousal persuaders are willing to cause in receivers; it triggers a "go" response. If a persuader believes a particular message will exceed the amount of negativity the persuader is willing to stir, the message selection process triggers a "no-go." This means the source finds the message "unacceptable" as a means of persuasion.

The situation analyzed here involved a father attempting to persuade his son, Dick, to study.

1. Promise
If you comply, you will be rewarded.
Offer to increase Dick's allowance if he increases his studying.

2. Threat
If you do not comply, you will be punished.
Threaten to forbid Dick the use of the car if he does not increase his studying.

3. Expertise (Positive)
If you comply, you will be rewarded because of "the nature of things."
Point out to Dick that if he gets good grades he will be able to get into a good college and get a good job.

4. Expertise (Negative)
If you do not comply, you will be punished because of "the nature of things."
Point out to Dick that if he does not get good grades he will not be able to get into a good college or get a good job.

5. Liking
Actor is friendly and helpful to get target in "good frame of mind" so that he will comply with request.
Try to be as friendly and pleasant as possible to get Dick in the right "frame of mind" before asking him to study.

6. Pre-Giving
Actor rewards target before requesting compliance.
Raise Dick's allowance and tell him you now expect him to study.

7. Aversive Stimulation
Actor continuously punishes target, making cessation contingent on compliance.
Forbid Dick the use of the car and tell him he will not be allowed to drive until he studies more.

8. Debt
Compliance is owed because of past favors.
Point out that you have sacrificed and saved to pay for Dick's education and that he owes it to you to get good enough grades to get into a good college.

9. Moral Appeal
You are immoral if you do not comply.
Tell Dick that it is morally wrong for anyone not to achieve good grades and that he should study more.

10. Self-Feeling (Positive)
You will feel better about yourself if you comply.
Tell Dick he will feel proud if he studies more.

11. Self-Feeling (Negative)
You will feel worse about yourself if you do not comply.
Tell Dick he will feel ashamed of himself if he gets bad grades.

12. Altercasting (Positive)
A person with "good" qualities would comply.
Tell Dick that since he is mature and intelligent, he naturally will want to study more and get good grades.

13. Altercasting (Negative)
Only a person with "bad" qualities would not comply.
Tell Dick that only someone very childish does not study.

14. Altruism
Your compliance is very badly needed, so do it as a favor.
Tell Dick that you fervently want him to get into a good college and that you wish he would study more as a personal favor to you.

15. Esteem (Positive)
People you value will think better of you if you comply.
Tell Dick that the whole family will be very proud of him if he gets good grades.

16. Esteem (Negative)
People you value will think worse of you if you do not comply.
Tell Dick that the whole family will be very disappointed in him if he gets poor grades.

From Marwell & Schmitt, Dimensions of Compliance-gaining Behavior, *1967, pp. 357–58.*

Figure 6.4

Compliance-gaining strategies: Family situation examples.

Hunter and Boster reanalyzed the data from several earlier compliance-gaining studies and found considerable support for the idea that sources' anticipations about the emotional reactions of receivers to messages provide a foundation for the message selection process. According to this idea, a fundamental concern in persuasion theory involves understanding the persuader's willingness to use messages that cause negative affect. Hunter and Boster suggested that variability in willingness to create negativity might be explained by certain traits such as argumentativeness and verbal aggressiveness (these two traits were discussed in Chapter 5).

Hunter and Boster derived several speculations about how these traits might pertain to one's willingness to create negativity. For instance, high verbal aggressives may have a higher willingness because they like inflicting psychological pain on others. Thus, they should be more likely than other people to use compliance-gaining messages that threaten the receiver with some form of punishment. Low verbal aggressives, on the other hand, probably have a very low threshold for creating negative impact because they are very sensitive to others' self-concepts and try not to cause psychological pain. In terms of argumentativeness, it could be predicted that high argumentatives use a diverse group of messages (positive and negative) because they like arguing and will try numerous arguments to succeed. Low argumentatives, however, probably use few negative compliance-gaining messages to avoid an argument being instigated by such messages. Other research has supported these ideas (Boster & Levine, 1988; Boster, Levine, & Kazoleas, 1989; Infante, Anderson, Martin, Herington, & Kim, 1993).

Although a person's traits probably exert considerable influence on his or her willingness to create a negative emotional impact on receivers, a possibility is that factors in the particular persuasion situation also may have an impact. That is, situational influences may cause the willingness to create negativity to be a little higher or lower in some situations than in others. Although Hunter and Boster's model did not deal much with this idea, expanding the model to include situational influences seems like a natural development. Thus, we might speculate that there are several important situational factors. The nature of the receiver might influence the source's willingness to stimulate negativity. For instance, if the receiver is extremely stubborn, the source might become more negative than usual. The persuasive topic could be another factor. Persuaders might be willing to stir more negative reactions on some topics than on others. For example, willingness to cause negative emotional impact may be lower when the topic is a delicate, sensitive one. For some receivers, this might pertain to their religion, their physical appearance, or their sexual orientation. The emotional climate in the situation could alter the source's willingness to be negative. For instance, if the mood in a crowd of people turns very aggressive, the source's willingness might increase; the source might find negative messages more acceptable than at other times.

Although only a few studies have been based on Hunter and Boster's model, the focus on compliance-gaining message selection is of obvious relevance to communication theory. Moreover, the ideas that make up the model are intuitively valid and lead to interesting implications. Thus, it deserves continued attention from researchers.

Cialdini's Persuasive Heuristics

Robert Cialdini (1988) developed six principles of compliance gaining based on his experience in a variety of occupations, including advertising, public relations, and fund-raising. He defines compliance as "action that is taken only because it has been requested" (Cialdini, 1987, p. 165). He noted that there are consistencies across all occupations in terms of getting people to comply with a request, which he labeled "persuasive heuristics." The six heuristics consist of reciprocity, commitment and consistency, social proof, liking, authority, and scarcity.

The reciprocity principle assumes that when someone gives you something, you should give them something in return. The sense of owing someone something is believed to be a powerful compliance-gaining strategy. People are constantly being given things in an effort to enhance compliance. Whether it is free food samples in a supermarket, free mailing labels from a charity, or free Avon products, the feeling of obligation is powerful and transcends cultures. In a study of charitable solicitations, Cialdini and Ascani (1976) used the reciprocity principle to increase blood donation. A request was made for people to join a long-term blood donor program. When this initial request was rejected, the researchers then made a second smaller request of a one-time blood donation. This smaller request resulted in a 50% compliance rate as opposed to a 32% compliance rate for simply asking for the one-time donation. This compliance technique is also known as the door in the face technique.

The commitment and consistency principle assumes that when people take a stand on an issue, there is internal pressure to be consistent with what you committed to. For example, it is common practice in the toy industry to purposely understock the more popular toys around the holiday season. Parents promise their children the most popular toys for the holidays. When the parent goes to the toy store and finds that the promised toy is out of stock, other toys are purchased to make up for the promised toy. Conveniently, after the holidays there is an ample amount of the most popular toys. The parent, more often then not, will return to get the promised toy, thus increasing the toy stores' overall sales.

The social proof principle states that "we determine what is correct by finding out what other people think is correct" (Cialdini, 1988, p. 110). This is especially powerful when we are uncertain about what is correct behavior. To determine what is correct behavior, we look around us to see how other people

---

reciprocity heuristic A compliance gaining strategy that assumes when someone gives you something, you should give them something in return.

commitment and consistency heuristic A compliance gaining strategy that assumes when people take a stand on an issue, there is internal pressure to be consistent with what you committed to.

social proof heuristic A compliance gaining strategy that assumes that we determine what is correct by finding out what other people think is correct.

liking heuristic A compliance gaining strategy that assumes we comply with requests because we like the person.

authority heuristic A compliance gaining strategy that assumes people should be more willing to follow the suggestions of an individual who is a legitimate authority.

scarcity heuristic A compliance gaining strategy that assumes people want to try to secure those opportunities that are scarce.

door in the face technique A compliance gaining strategy that utilizes a large request followed by a smaller request. People are more likely to agree to the smaller request after rejecting the larger request.

are behaving. This serves as a guide as to what is correct. Consider your favorite television comedy. The producers will purposely include "laugh tracks" to cue the viewer when to laugh. It is common practice in churches to "salt" the collection plate (i.e., put a one or five dollar bill in the plate before it is passed to the parishioners). By doing this, it sets a standard amount for the donation. This also works in bars, where the bartender will "salt" the tip jar to indicate the standard rate of tipping.

The liking principle assumes that we comply with requests because we like the person. The police use this principle when interrogating suspects. If you have ever seen an episode of *CSI* or *Law and Order,* you most certainly are familiar with the "good cop/bad cop" interrogation technique. The principle behind this technique is that one interrogator will threaten and be aggressive to the suspect, and the other will be more understanding and calm. When the aggressive interrogator leaves the room, the suspect will have a greater tendency to give information to interrogator that he or she "likes" more. It is a common practice in sales to build a relationship with your clients and then work toward the sale. It is well documented that **homophily**, or similarities of attitudes and backgrounds, increases liking (Byrne, 1971; Stotland & Patchen, 1961). In a study of peace marchers, Suedfeld, Bochner, and Matas (1971) found that people were more likely to sign a petition if the person requesting the signature was similarly dressed.

The authority heuristic holds that "one should be more willing to follow the suggestions of an individual who is a legitimate authority" (Cialdini, 1987, p. 175). Our culture is filled with authority figures that tell us what to think, who to vote for, and what to buy. One study revealed that people were three and a half times more likely to follow a jaywalker into traffic when he wore a suit as opposed to just a shirt and pants (Lefkowitz, Blake, & Mouton, 1955). The authority heuristic, similar to that of social proof, is particularly effective in times of uncertainty. When we are uncertain, we look to authority figures to help us determine what is appropriate.

The final persuasive heuristic is scarcity. Ciladini (1987) defined this principle as "one should want to try to secure those opportunities that are scarce" (p. 177). The fact that something is offered for a limited time or in limited quantity makes the item that much more valuable. This concept is illustrated in television infomercials. It is a common tactic for vendors to put a counter in the corner of the television screen informing the viewer of how many units are left. This strategy gives the viewer the perception that once they are sold out of product, there will be no more available.

The persuasive heuristics developed by Robert Cialdini continue to represent one of the most comprehensive efforts in explaining the complex process of compliance gaining. Recall in the Elaboration Likelihood Model (ELM) of persuasion that people process messages either through the central route (critical thinking) or the peripheral route (cues in the environment).

The persuasive heuristics presented here would be processed through the peripheral route of the ELM.

Preventing Persuasion

We turn now to theories that explain how to prevent persuasion. In emphasizing how to persuade people, it is easy to forget that the reverse is often our goal. It is not unusual for us to want another person to resist being influenced by a third party. We might want a wavering Democrat to resist appeals to vote Republican. In a sense, we try to "persuade" a person not to be persuaded. There have been five approaches in persuasion research to the problem of how to prevent persuasion.

The *behavioral commitment* approach advises public statements about positions. If you know that someone supports your proposal, you would want him or her to express that opinion publicly. When other people learn someone holds a given position, it is more difficult for that person to change the position. Because the position has been associated with the individual, "losing face" might result from changing what was previously declared.

The *anchoring approach* is based on the idea that someone will be less likely to change a position if the position is anchored or "tied" to things that are significant for that person. With this approach you would try to convince an individual who valued others (friends, family, etc.) to agree with a position by pointing out that other people and/or reference groups (religious, political groups, etc.) also agree. You might add that important values (freedom, for instance) are upheld by the position. Changing an opinion would involve disagreeing with family and friends, would violate group norms, and would undermine values.

A third approach is creating *resistant cognitive states.* People are more difficult to persuade when they are in certain frames of mind. The major research finding in this area is that when persons experience an increase in self-esteem, they are particularly resistant to persuasion because people who feel high self-esteem believe they are valuable; they are confident and therefore less likely to say they were wrong in holding a position that a persuader tries to change. It is relatively easy to raise or lower self-esteem in a research laboratory. The main technique for raising self-esteem is to lead individuals to believe they have succeeded at an important task. Conversely, believing they have failed lowers self-esteem. Because a person with low self-esteem is particularly easy to persuade, an ethical issue arises. Is it acceptable to try to persuade someone who has just experienced failure? The person may be especially vulnerable at that time, and attempting persuasion may be taking advantage of him or her (Infante, 1976).

Training in critical methods is an approach that has met with mixed results. The idea appears sound. Train people to think critically when listening to a speech, to recognize fallacies in reasoning, and to detect propaganda techniques;

they will then not be so easily persuaded. In one study, students were trained in methods for critically evaluating speeches. Later they listened to a tape-recorded speech. Women in the study were persuaded less than the control group of women who had not been taught the evaluation methods. However, male participants were persuaded more than the control group of untrained men. American culture may have influenced men to be more dogmatic in their positions than women; therefore, men may pay less attention to opposing positions in the message. The training might have neutralized this cultural effect and made men more sensitive to the content of the message (Infante & Grimmett, 1971), thus yielding the variable results.

inoculation theory
Approach to preventing persuasion based on the biological analogy of preventing disease.

Inoculation theory from social psychology is the fifth approach (McGuire, 1964). This theory assumes that preventing persuasion is like preventing a disease. To keep a dangerous virus from causing a disease, the body can be inoculated with a weakened form of the disease-producing virus. The body's immune system will then create antibodies to destroy that type of virus. If the actual virus does invade the body at a later date, the defense will be in place and will prevent the disease. To prevent persuasion, according to this biological analogy, the person's cognitive system needs to be inoculated so a defense is in place when a strong persuasive message "invades the mind." How does *cognitive inoculation* work? The counterpart of the weakened virus would be weak arguments in support of an opponent's position. In theory, when an audience hears the weak arguments, they think of refutations for them. These refutations, like antibodies against a disease, form the foundation for attacking stronger arguments heard later. Thus, preventing persuasion from this approach involves "strengthening" the mind's defense systems so it will be able to destroy strong, attacking arguments.

SUMMARY

Persuasion is an integral topic for communication study because the skill of the persuader in using verbal and nonverbal symbols affects the interaction. In this chapter, we defined persuasion as attitude change toward a source's proposal. Persuasion differs from coercion because audience members can choose to agree or disagree. In this framework, belief change leads to attitude change, which can then produce behavior change. Adapting to the audience and the situation makes persuasion more effective.

As we said at the beginning of this chapter, persuasion research has changed greatly in recent years. We think it is important for persuasion research to continue with the enthusiasm it has enjoyed in the past. Current researchers are especially interested in how people influence one another in interpersonal relationships. The advertising and public relations professions provide another important persuasive context for the application of communication theory.

Research that enhances our understanding of the persuasion process is inherently valuable. Of course, there are other ways of influencing another person's behavior. Two particularly distasteful methods are physical aggression and coercion. Persuasion is infinitely more desirable than these alternatives because the process of persuasion respects the dignity of others and their right to choose among alternatives based on their beliefs. Persuasion offers hope for people to resolve differences in a satisfying and constructive manner.

KEY TERMS

assimilation
attitude
authority heuristic
behavioral intention
belief
central route
coercion
cognitive complexity
cognitive dissonance theory
commitment and consistency
    heuristic
compliance
constructivistic model of
    credibility
controllability

dogmatism
door in the face technique
ego-involvement
elaboration likelihood model
factor model of credibility
functional model of credibility
inoculation theory
latitude of acceptance
latitude of noncommitment
latitude of rejection
liking heuristic
Machiavellianism
multiple-act
need for cognition
need for social approval

opinionated acceptance
opinionated rejection
perceived behavioral control
perceived control
peripheral route
persuasibility
persuasion
reciprocity heuristic
scarcity heuristic
selective exposure
self-efficacy
self-esteem
social proof heuristic
subjective norm
theory of reasoned action

Verbal Behavior Approaches

H uman beings are the only creatures on earth that can talk themselves into trouble. Perhaps you told someone that they were "interesting," only to discover that rumors had spread across campus about your new intimate relationship! You might have made what you thought was a witty remark in class and suddenly found yourself in disfavor with the professor because of your "wisecrack." If you promised your mother that you would vacuum the house "soon," she might have been upset because you did not do it that *morning*.

If these examples sound familiar, you are aware of the difficulties that can arise when people communicate. Some students assume that the formal study of human communication will be an "easy" subject to master, remarking, "After all, I've been communicating since I was born and talking since I was twelve months old." The problem is when we've been doing something for so long, we repeat our behaviors automatically. We are often not particularly aware of what is actually happening. For example, we may not like being perceived as being unsure of ourselves, and we might not know that certain language choices (such as using verbal qualifiers) are contributing to this impression. Understanding our language choices can enable us to change.

SIGNS, SYMBOLS, AND SIGNALS

Some of the difficulty in understanding and practicing effective communication can be traced to the core symbol system of verbal communication. Language can be thought of as a collection of signs, symbols, codes, and rules used to construct and convey messages. These elements form the medium through which we communicate our ideas, desires, and feelings.

signs Something that stands for another thing.

symbols Type of sign that is created to stand for something else.

symptom Type of sign that bears a natural relation to an object.

rituals Type of sign that is a combination of being naturally produced, as in the case of a symptom, and being arbitrary or created, as would be a symbol.

As we discussed in Chapter 1, the concepts *sign, symbol,* and *signal* are related and often confused with each other. Signs stand for or represent something else. The object or concept the sign represents is called a referent. There are two types of signs: natural signs are called signals; artificial or conventional signs are called symbols. **Signals** stand in a direct one-to-one relationship with what they represent. They are not ambiguous or arbitrary but are linked with specific responses. Cronkhite (1986) defined a signal as, "That type of sign that stands for its significate by virtue of a natural relationship, usually by some relationship of causality, contingency, or resemblance" (p. 232). Signals technically cannot be arranged because they occur naturally; they are discovered, not created. This definition of signal differs significantly from common usage of the term "traffic signal." In order to avoid confusion, Cronkhite has substituted the word symptom for signal. A "symptom is a sign that bears a natural relationship to that for which it stands" (p. 232). For example, thunder, lightning, and dark clouds are symptoms of an approaching rainstorm. Calloused hands are symptoms of physical labor. High temperature, sneezing, and congestion are symptoms of a head cold or flu.

Signs also exist as conventional, human-made, artificial phenomena called *symbols.* Artificially created or conventional symbols provide meaning when a particular society has agreed on what they will look like and what they will represent. Increase in foreign travel has necessitated the creation of international traffic signs. These signs are now found on major freeways and highways across the United States and Western Europe. For example, a sign with a hand facing you, palm exposed, means stop. The meaning of that sign is becoming universally accepted.

One important characteristic of symbols is that they are *arbitrary* and *ambiguous;* they do **not** have a direct relationship with their referents. The word *elephant,* for example, does not possess any of the physical characteristics of a large animal. Unlike a physical sign or signal, a symbol can have many referents. A picture of an elephant in a children's book is another possible referent for the word-symbol *elephant.* The picture of the elephant is also a nonverbal symbol of the animal. Just like the word, the picture stands for, or represents, something other than itself.

A third category of sign behaviors, which are neither totally arbitrary nor symptomatic, are rituals. The fidgeting and foot-shuffling that occur just before the end of a class are examples of rituals (Cronkhite, 1986).

The communication discipline has focused largely on the study of human *symbolic activity.* Although research has been conducted into forms of nonsymbolic behavior and some communication scholars still argue that "all behavior is communication" (see Chapter 1), other scholars, including Cronkhite (1986), have suggested that the focus of our field needs to be more narrowly and realistically defined. They argue that primary attention should be focused on the effects of symbol systems and those who use them. The study of language and verbal behavior is inherently connected to the study of human symbolic activity.

LANGUAGE AND MEANING

The symbols used to create language are arbitrary and ambiguous. Yet communication is a process of exchanging mutually understood symbols to stimulate meaning in another (Steinfatt, 1977). Indeed, human language exists to allow us to share meanings. If symbols themselves do not contain meaning, how then is meaning created out of symbols? Meaning is accomplished when human beings *interpret* symbols. Meaning is a human creation: "Words don't mean; people mean." That is, the meaning of symbols is supplied by people and their culture. Symbols themselves carry no innate meaning; they may mean one thing to one person and something different to someone else. For example, the word-symbol *rock* can mean a hard substance found in quarries, a type of contemporary music, or a valuable stone set in a ring.

An eleven-year-old boy noticed that his mother was unusually quiet and did not appear to be "herself." When he asked his mother what was wrong, she replied that she was feeling depressed and did not know why. The son suggested that his mother see a psychiatrist to find out what was wrong. Before he could finish his sentence, he noticed that both of his parents became quite angry. They admonished him for being rude and impolite to his mother and punished him by sending him to his room! The boy honestly did not understand why he was being punished or why his parents had reacted so strongly. The parents soon forgot the incident, but it continued to haunt the boy. Several years later, while studying language and communication at college, he finally understood what had happened. To the mother and father, the word *psychiatrist* meant "doctor who treats crazy people." To the son, *psychiatrist* meant "counselor, advisor, and mental health professional who helps people understand their problems." The two generations had very different meanings for the symbol *psychiatrist*.

We learn meanings from our past experiences, from the mass media, and from interactions with friends, family, and authority figures. Even though the meaning of a given symbol can appear quite similar, no two people have the *exact* same meaning for the symbol. If people do not share the same meaning for symbols, how is communication possible? To answer this, we must distinguish between two types of meaning, denotative and connotative.

Denotative refers to the "actual" or "agreed-upon" meaning or meanings of a word. **Denotative meaning** is frequently referred to as the literal or "dictionary" meaning of a word. **Connotative meaning** refers to subjective associations— the personal and emotional attachments that people associate with a word or symbol. Connotative meaning contains all the judgments and evaluations that

denotative meaning The objective, descriptive, or agreed-upon meaning of a word. A dictionary definition.

connotative meaning Subjective associations, personal, or emotional attachments people associate with symbols.

individuals have for a word or symbol. The word *college,* for example, has both denotative and connotative meaning. Its denotative meaning is, "An institution of higher learning furnishing courses of instruction usually leading to a bachelor's degree." Its connotative meaning can differ considerably. One connotative meaning might be, "A place to party for four or more years." Another connotative meaning for college is, "An institution that will prepare me to get a job." Yet another connotative meaning could be, "The place where I became an adult and learned responsibility." Communication could not occur if people did not operate with some denotative meanings. Dictionaries are created to provide us with the "correct" or "accepted" definitions of words. We still run into difficulty, however, when the dictionary provides us with multiple definitions of symbols. For example, there are twelve different definitions of "college" in a large dictionary.

LANGUAGE AND PERCEPTION

Culture strongly influences the way a linguistic system develops and is transmitted. All languages have their own unique organization patterns. Language, as a set of signs, symbols and signals, has a grammar associated with it. Communication becomes possible when individuals share a system of order or grammar. Linguists and semanticists Benjamin Lee Whorf (1956) and Edward Sapir (1958) suggested that the language system we learn from our culture has a profound influence on how we interpret the world: "Language shapes perceptions of reality."

Theory of Linguistic Relativity

theory of linguistic relativity Assumes that all higher level of thought depend on language and the structure of language and the structure of the language we use influences the way we understand our environment.

The **theory of linguistic relativity** (also referred to as the Sapir-Whorf hypothesis) contains two fundamental principles: (1) all higher levels of thought depend on language; and (2) the structure of the language we use influences the way we understand our environment (Chase, 1956). The theory of linguistic relativity has never been tested through scientific experiments. Little if any research has explored the relationship between linguistic structure and actual behavior. Cronkhite (1976) stated that the theory "would be impossible to 'prove' even if it were true" (p. 271). We have no way of interpreting reality without thinking thoughts expressed in some language. Suppose we met a being from outer space who could perceive but had no means to communicate. Without language we could not share this creature's understanding of the world.

One study, although it was not a controlled experiment, did lend support to the theory of linguistic relativity. This study indicated that people with differences in words for colors perceive colors differently. The researchers discovered that differences in the ability to recognize and recall colors is associated with the availability of names for those colors (Brown & Lenneberg, 1954). More recent research appears to support the finding that linguistic differences affect thoughts and perceptions, including the categorization of color (Nisbett & Norenzayan, 2002; Roberson, Davies, & Davidoff, 2000). Researchers studied members of the Berinmo culture in Papua, New Guinea, and contrasted their perceptions of color with British participants. With both sets of participants, the experimenters pointed to color chips and asked participants in their respective native language to "Tell me what it is called." Each participant was also asked to give their best example of all the names they had given. It was discovered that the Berinmo have five basic color terms: white (including all pale colors); black; red; the color range of yellow/orange/brown; and a range of colors constituting green/yellow-green/blue, and purple, which correspond to words in their language system. The British participants had a significantly larger color categorization system based on the English language. This finding suggests that the possession of color terms in a language affects the way colors are perceived and organized into categories, the greater the number of words for color, the greater the color differentiation. The researchers concluded that color categories are formed primarily by language and that the results "in a substantial way . . . present evidence in favor of linguistic relativity" (p. 394).

Because languages develop in part in response to environmental conditions, a language is likely to have many words for classifying phenomena important to its physical and cultural environment. For example, the Eskimo language has many different words for snow. Eskimos are more likely to notice and think about differences in snowfalls than are native speakers of English, who have only a single term for snow. English leads us to "lump" all types of snow together and to ignore differences that the Eskimo notices (Cronkhite, 1976).

Much of the data that Whorf reported compares standard American English vocabulary to the language structure of Hopi, a Native American language. The Hopi and standard American English linguistic systems have very different rules for the discussion of time. Time in the Hopi system is a psychological time rather than a quantitative measure. Standard English makes a distinction between nouns and verbs. Objects or things are separated from action. Hopi language emphasizes differences in duration. Ellis (1992) clarified this distinction between the two linguistic systems. He stated that in the Hopi language, "the day or the year 'moves along' or 'gets later' but it cannot be broken into units" (p. 27).

The Sapir-Whorf hypothesis is important because it suggests that there is a connection between one's language and one's behavior. If language shapes perception and perception shapes behavior, then language can strongly influence one's actual behavior. Standard American English contains a great many polarized words—pairs of opposites. Think of the bipolar adjectives thick and thin, smart and stupid, tall and short, ugly and beautiful. Now try to think of a word that will fit exactly in the middle between those bipolar adjectives. The English language provides us with a ready store of opposites but does not provide us with many "moderate" words. We have difficulty finding them and using them (DeVito, 2001).

How does this linguistic situation influence our behavior? Let us suppose that your friend shows you a new outfit he or she has just purchased and asks your opinion of it. Suppose your attitude is somewhere right in the middle between love and hate. You don't want to say, "It's okay," as that answer sounds somewhat vague. What other alternatives quickly come to mind? "Nice" and "fair" do not accurately reflect your feelings. Thus, you are almost "forced" to say that you "love" or "hate" it. The constraints imposed on you by the linguistic system influence what you say. Indeed, you may then come to like the outfit more or less (another pair of opposites!) based on the word you chose.

Question Phrasing

A further illustration that language influences verbal responses is the finding that how questions are phrased affects perception and the responses given to the questions. Research has demonstrated that the way eyewitnesses are questioned in court alters the witnesses' memories and biases their testimony (Loftus, 1979, 1980). In one experiment participants were shown a film of an automobile accident and were then asked one of two questions: (1) "Did you see *the* broken headlight?" or (2) "Did you see *a* broken headlight?" In reality there was no broken headlight in the film. Participants asked about "*the* headlight" were more likely to report that they saw one. Including the term *the* biased perception because it implied a broken headlight existed. Participants then interpreted the question to mean, "Did you see it?" rather than, "Was a headlight broken?" In a second study, participants were asked what speed the vehicles in a film of a traffic accident had been traveling. Half the participants were asked, "About how fast were the cars going when they *smashed* into each other?" The others were asked, "About how fast were the cars going when they *hit* each other?" The group who heard "*smashed*" estimated the speed as much faster than the "*hit*" group. Even though both groups saw the same film of the accident, the word *smashed* created an expectation that the accident was more serious and that the cars must have been travelling very fast. The effects caused by the phrasing of the questions appear long-lasting and influence other perceptions. One week after seeing the film, participants in both groups were asked, "Did you see broken glass?" Although no broken glass appeared in the film, the *smashed* group were much more likely to say they had seen it. Thus, the original question biased what was perceived and remembered; people subsequently answered a new question in terms of their altered memories of the accident.

Research has also demonstrated that limiting the range of responses to a question affects a person's memory. The researcher questioned people about headache remedies, then asked one of two questions: (1) "In terms of a number, how many other products have you tried: 1, 2, 3?" or (2) "In terms of a number, how many other products have you tried: 1, 5, 10?" The group who heard the first question reported numbers much closer to those suggested (an average of 3.3), whereas the second group (who heard a much wider range) remembered trying an average of 5.2 products. The restrictive wording of the first question discouraged thorough memory searching (Loftus, 1979, 1980). This research indicates that it is very easy to structure a question to manipulate a particular answer, a fact well known to trial attorneys who cross-examine witnesses! Although the differences in how questions are phrased may be subtle and might not be noticed except by language experts, questions strongly affect the answers people give. Even though we use language almost every waking minute to communicate or think, we may be unaware of its power. Researchers are continuing to probe the subtle nuances of language to understand how it affects communication.

LANGUAGE AND POWER

Power, control, and status are at the core of many social relationships (Giles & Wiemann, 1987). More powerful speakers can exercise greater control over a communication interaction and even the entire relationship. Can you recall a situation where language made you feel powerless or low in status? Perhaps you remember a time when you felt inadequate because of your conversational partner's vocabulary level. Some individuals, for example, report feeling "left out," "ignorant," and "passive" when they communicate with their physicians. Doctors who lack effective communication skills often appear to "talk down" to their patients. They do this by using professional jargon and by interrupting when patients ask questions.

Communicating Power and Status

People commonly use several forms of verbal behavior that communicate powerful or powerless positions. These forms of language can influence how much power people believe that you have, and also your level of status in society.

VERBAL INTENSIFIERS

Verbal intensifiers include adverbs such as *so, such,* and *quite* and expressions such as "It was *really* nice." By increasing the intensity of the emotion being conveyed, intensifiers actually can reduce the strength of an utterance. Instead of saying, "The concert was delightful," including a verbal intensifier would modify the utterance to "The concert was really delightful." The extra adverb swings the audience's focus to the emotions of the speaker and away from the message, thus creating a more powerless position.

VERBAL QUALIFIERS

Verbal qualifiers also reduce the strength and impact of an utterance. Examples frequently cited are "you know," "possibly," "perhaps," "I guess," and "in my opinion." Instead of saying, "A communication degree will prepare me well for many careers," a lower-status or less powerful speaker might add a verbal qualifier to the statement: "In my opinion, a communication degree will prepare me well for many careers." The new statement sounds as if the speaker doubts that hearers will agree.

TAG QUESTIONS

In this form of verbal behavior, the speaker adds ("tags on") a question to the end of a statement. Tag questions often weaken the assertions of the speaker. Note, for example, the difference in the strength of the following statements: "Usher is a great singer," and "Usher is a great singer, isn't he?" The second speaker appears to be insecure and seeking reassurance. Some scholars argue that tag questions are used to draw a response from reluctant communicators (Pearson, 1995). However, tag questions appear to weaken the verbal behavior of the speaker by making assertions appear less certain.

LENGTHENING OF REQUESTS

The power and status of a speaker is often related to lengthening of requests. For example, if you want someone to open the window, you may say, "Open the window." If you want to appear more polite you might add, "Please open the window." People who add additional words to their requests are making "compound requests." Lengthening a request softens it and suggests that the speaker is less powerful, less assertive, and of lower status. For example, some speakers may add the additional phrase, "If it is not too much trouble" to the sentence. Although lengthening a request appears to signal politeness, it also makes the speaker appear to be more tentative, hesitant, and weak.

The interaction of context and linguistic indicators of power poses interesting questions for communication theorists to investigate (Bradac, 1988). For example, is it sometimes possible to increase power by hedging or being indefinite in language? Will high-power persons such as corporate presidents be able to enhance their power if they use low-power forms of verbal behavior? How will people respond to a woman C.E.O. who uses "feminine speech?"

Sex, Gender, and Power: Differences in Verbal Behavior

Over the last two decades, scholars have studied sex differences in verbal behavior (Bate & Bowker, 1997). Much of the early research indicated that females tend to use more verbal intensifiers, qualifiers, tag questions, and lengthening of requests than males (Lakoff, 1975). Because of this, "female speech" was often characterized as less powerful and less assertive than "male speech."

During the last fifteen years, society has become more sensitive to verbal displays of power. The feminist, senior citizen, gay and lesbian, black, disabled, and Hispanic movements have also had a significant impact on the language choices we make (Bate & Bowker, 1997). The women's movement, in particular, has done much to alter the verbal behavior of males and females. It has sensitized us to expressions of power and status in speech. As a consequence of this heightened sensitivity, changes have occurred in people's language. We now avoid using the masculine pronoun to stand for both males and females, and we avoid sex-stereotyped job titles such as *policeman* in favor of the gender-neutral *police officer*. Like *Mr.,* the title *Ms.* does not require a speaker or writer to know someone's marital status to address her politely.

Anthony Mulac, James Bradac, and Pamela Gibbons (2001) tested their gender-as-culture hypothesis in three different studies. They found that although men and women speak the same language, they do so differently because they learn to use language in very different cultures. Much of this learning takes place in groups of same-sex peers between the ages of 5 to 15. Learning how to carry on friendly conversations in two very different social contexts results in males and females developing different language preferences. These learned differences can produce communication breakdowns when members of one sex try to use their language behaviors in talking with members of the other sex. For instance, males may not be as skilled as females in using language to identify particular emotional states. This limits understanding in the interaction. A woman might conclude, "I just don't know what he is referring to." If men and women disagree on the interpretation of a given communicative behavior due to their different language models, the interaction will be affected. Thus, a man might see a woman's tag question as a sign of uncertainty and less self-confidence while she views the tag question as a method for involving the other person in an observation. Because men and women learned to use language differently, cross-gender interactions can be affected by differences in verbal behavior.

Language Intensity and Opinionation

LANGUAGE INTENSITY

One of the verbal behavior variables most frequently studied during the last forty years is the intensity of a speaker's language in a persuasive message. Language intensity is "the quality of language which indicates the degree to which the speaker's attitude toward a concept deviates from neutrality" (Bowers, 1964, p. 345). Speakers who use intense language exhibit more emotion and utilize stronger expressions, opinionated language, vivid adjectives, and more metaphors than speakers using less-intense language. For example, during a period of strained relations, President Ronald Reagan made a public speech calling the former Soviet Union an "evil empire." This term is clearly stronger and more intense than if the president had referred to the Soviet government as a "difficult power."

Language intensity is related to a communicator's use of metaphors, modifiers, and obscure words. One study tested whether sex and death metaphors used in the conclusions of speeches would have greater persuasive impact than less-intense, more literal conclusions (Bowers & Osborn, 1966). The statement, "Too long, we ourselves have stood by and permitted the ruination of our western economies by those who have proclaimed the doctrine of protective tariff" was used to test a literal conclusion. In the metaphorical conclusion, the word "rape" was substituted for "ruination." Speeches with metaphorical conclusions were more persuasive than speeches with literal conclusions. This finding contrasts with a previous study (Bowers, 1963) in which highly intense language produced less attitude change than low-intensity language. However, metaphors were not used in the earlier study.

Carl Carmichael and Gary Cronkhite (1965) reasoned that the frustration level of a receiver interacts with the language intensity of the speaker to affect persuasion. They speculated that a very intense persuasive message would be less effective when listeners were frustrated. Because frustrated people are already aroused, they should reject an intense message because it would push their level of arousal into an "uncomfortable zone." Carmichael and Cronkhite tested this relationship and found that frustrated listeners reacted less favorably to a highly intense message. Language intensity, however, made no difference to listeners who were not frustrated,

Thirteen generalizations about the relationship between intense language and persuasion were isolated after an extensive review of over twenty studies (Bradac, Bowers, & Courtright, 1979). Language intensity interacted with several variables to influence attitude change. Receivers hearing intense language will be more likely to change their attitudes when: (a) they view the speaker as highly credible; (b) the speaker is male; (c) the speaker advocates a proposal the receivers already support; and (d) the receivers are low in arousal and stress. These findings are useful to political and organizational communicators. For example, a sales manager wishing to increase quotas for the coming quarter and speaking to a staff that has just experienced record sales should use highly intense language to motivate them. Following the same line of reasoning, a political advisor confidently urged former President George H. Bush to use intense metaphors when speaking to the Veterans of Foreign Wars about a constitutional amendment to outlaw burning the American flag.

OPINIONATED LANGUAGE

A form of highly intense language, opinionated language, has received much attention from communication theorists and researchers (see Chapter 6).

When speakers use opinionated language, they indicate both their attitudes toward the topic and their attitudes toward those who agree or disagree with them. For example, a speaker might proclaim, "Only a fool would oppose the construction of nuclear power plants across the country," or, "Any intelligent person recognizes the danger in building nuclear power plants." The first statement is considered an "opinionated-rejection" statement. This type of statement reflects an unfavorable attitude toward people who disagree with the speaker. The second statement is considered an "opinionated-acceptance" statement. This type of statement expresses a favorable attitude toward people who agree with the speaker about the topic.

Researchers have conducted several studies on the effects of opinionated language. One study examined the effects of opinionated language in persuading open- and closed-minded listeners (Miller & Lobe, 1967). For one audience, two opinionated-acceptance and two opinionated-rejection statements were inserted in a message that advocated outlawing the sale of cigarettes (a proposal with which the audience disagreed). For the other group, no opinionated statements were inserted. The messages were otherwise identical and were attributed to the same highly credible source. Opinionated language was more persuasive if the source was highly credible than nonopinionated language. Opinionated language strengthens the intensity of the bond between the message *source* and the message *proposal.* When a highly credible source uses opinionated language, receivers think the speaker feels very strongly about an issue. Receivers are likely to change their attitudes to agree with the speaker. Using opinionated language also helps speakers emphasize the rewards listeners can expect if they accept the speaker's recommendations. Another study found that a highly trustworthy male speaker was more persuasive when he used opinionated language, but an untrustworthy speaker was more persuasive when he used nonopinionated language (Miller & Baseheart, 1969).

Other researchers have investigated the relationship between opinionated language and intensity of initial attitude toward a topic (Mehrley & McCroskey, 1970). A message containing opinionated language may be more or less persuasive depending on listeners' *initial* attitudes toward the topic. When listeners initially hold strongly negative or positive attitudes toward a topic, messages containing nonopinionated language enhance persuasion. However, when listeners hold relatively neutral attitudes, opinionated language results in greater persuasion. These findings can be explained by dissonance theory (see Chapter 6). The more a speaker pressures receivers to change their attitudes, the less their attitudes will change. When listeners are initially neutral, nonopinionated language statements are not strong enough to change attitudes, and opinionated language can be more effective. When listeners hold intense attitudes toward proposals, the opposite is true. Opinionated language statements are considered too strong, so that speakers who use opinionated language with intense listeners may find less attitude change and lower credibility ratings. No simple generalizations can be made about the effects of opinionated language; rather, outcomes depend on the interaction among a number of source, message, and receiver variables.

forewarnings Messages that warn the audience by mentioning the type of arguments an opposing speaker will present.

Several years later, other researchers examined opinionated language used in a particular type of message. **Forewarnings** are messages that warn the audience by mentioning the type of arguments an opposing speaker will present. For example, parents often warn their children not to accept candy or rides from strangers. Politicians often warn voters about upcoming attacks by their opponents. In studies of forewarnings and opinionated language, participants read an excerpt from a "symposium TV program," then indicated their reactions to the program. On the first page of the booklet containing the synopsis, participants read a message from either an authoritative (professor) or less-authoritative (freshman student) source. These sources used either opinionated or nonopinionated language to warn the reader about another authoritative (a second professor) or less-authoritative (a second student) speaker. Examples of opinionated statements included: "Any intelligent person will come to this same conclusion after considering the matter," and, "Only the most uneducated individual will accept the arguments that he is going to present...." For less-authoritative speakers, using a nonopinionated warning yielded greater persuasion. However, the use of opinionated language by an authoritative warner was effective in reducing the impact of a persuasive message. Thus, opinionated language appears to be one way to motivate listeners to resist persuasion (Infante, 1973).

A follow-up study tested whether opinionated language strengthened the attitudes of those later exposed to a message with which they disagreed. Each participant received both a "pro" and a "con" speech. Two groups received the "pro" speech before the "con" speech, and two groups received the "pro" speech after the "con" speech. One group received six opinionated rejection statements in the "pro" speech, and one group received six nonopinionated statements in the "pro" speech. Participants read the speeches, then evaluated the proposal and the character and authoritativeness of the two speakers. The "pro" speaker was viewed as less authoritative and less moral when he used opinionated language. With a favorable audience, using nonopinionated language seems to make the audience resistant to prior or subsequent persuasive efforts (Infante, 1975b).

Studying opinionated language has helped theorists develop "guidelines" for persuaders. Salespeople, advertisers, politicians, and public relations practitioners can use these findings to make their messages more successful.

THEORETICAL APPROACHES TO VERBAL BEHAVIOR

Communication Accommodation Theory

Derived from social psychological principles, communication accommodation theory (CAT) examines underlying motivations and consequences of shifts in verbal behavior (Giles & Wiemann, 1987). Similarity-attraction is a principal contributor to CAT, the idea being that we are attracted more to people who are similar to us. Two premises are central to **communication accommodation theory**: (a) During communication, people try to accommodate or adjust their style of speech to one another. (b) They do this to gain approval, to increase communication efficiency, and to maintain positive social identity with the person to whom they are talking. A core assumption of CAT is that our *perceptions* of another's speech determine how we will evaluate and behave toward that person. Two speech strategies, convergence and divergence, are central to this theory. In both speech convergence and divergence, the movement toward or away from the speech style of the other is motivated by an assumption about the other's speech style (Giles, Mulac, Bradac, & Johnson, 1987). Using **convergence**, individuals adapt to each other by slowing down or speeding up speech rate, lengthening or shortening pauses and utterances, and using certain forms of politeness, tag questions, and verbal intensifiers in their speech. Basically, when individuals try to converge their speech with the speech of another person, they try to match such things as the person's speech rate, volume, pitch patterns, tone quality, vocal energy, phrasing, pronunciation, and enunciation. **Divergence** refers to the way speakers accentuate vocal and linguistic differences to underscore social differences between speakers. In some situations, communicators often deliberately wish to maintain a social distance between themselves and others. Speech divergence is likely to occur when individuals believe that others are members of undesirable groups, hold distasteful attitudes, or display unsavory appearances (Street & Giles, 1982). For instance, if Person A wants to diverge in speech from Person B, A might pronounce a word correctly that was mispronounced by B (see Figure 7.1).

communication accommodation theory A language theory of how we have our language converge or diverge with the language of others.

convergence A dimension of communication accommodation theory that is a strategy where individuals alter their speech to adapt to each other.

divergence A dimension of communication accommodation theory that reflects accentuating vocal and linguistic differences to underscore social differences between speakers.

USE OF CONVERGENT STRATEGIES

Researchers have explored situations in which people use convergent and divergent forms of speech. In the area of gender and communication, Virginia Wheeless (1984) found that individuals classified according to gender orientation (masculine, feminine, androgynous, undifferentiated) rather than biological sex differed in their language use. Feminine and undifferentiated individuals were more accommodating than masculine and androgynous individuals. This finding is consistent with research that shows that "feminine language" is viewed as more considerate, cooperative, helpful, submissive, and accommodating (Stewart, Stewart, Cooper, & Friedley, 1996).

Stereotypes or expectations of others' abilities often influence the speech convergence process. For example, some nurses use "baby talk" to the institutionalized elderly, regardless of the individual's actual capabilities. Blind persons report that people who communicate with them often shout or exhibit other exaggerated behaviors completely unrelated to their ability to see. Attempting to adjust one's style to others in circumstances with which one has

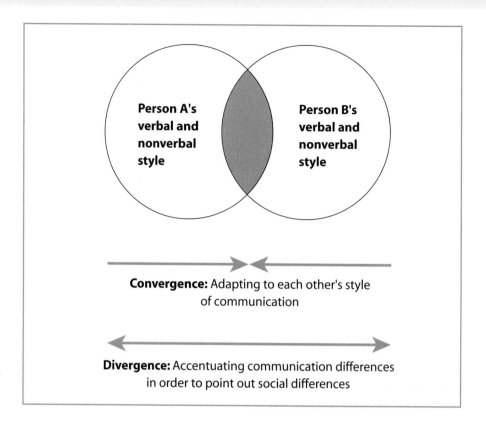

Figure 7.1

Communication
accommodation theory.

no experience can lead to "overconvergence." This conveys a sense of being talked down to and detracts from effective and satisfying communication.

Speech convergence suggests that people find approval from others satisfying. The greater the need for social approval, the greater the tendency for speech convergence. Power also plays a part in the degree to which convergence will be exhibited. Powerless individuals tend to adopt the verbal and vocal styles of those with power. This finding helps to explain some of the sex differences in verbal behavior. Females may use speech convergence in organizational communication contexts to "say the right thing" and to "fit in" with male organizational superiors. Communication theorists interested in gender and communication have identified the "double-bind" women face in organizations when they are asked to "speak like a man, but act like a lady."

In several instances, communication accommodation may be a scripted behavior. Individuals may "automatically" use a convergence script to make their speech appear more similar to another's (Giles et al., 1987). We may have a speech convergence verbal plan (see Chapter 1) ready to use when we need it.

USE OF DIVERGENT STRATEGIES

Groups with strong ethnic pride often use speech *divergence* or speech *maintenance* to underscore their identity and distinctiveness (Giles et al., 1987). In Chapter 5, we discussed the communication trait *rhetorical sensitivity. Noble selves* would be more likely to use speech divergence as a way of maintaining their identity than would rhetorical sensitives or rhetorical reflectors.

Occasionally, speech divergence is used as a power marker or to control the behavior of others. We may adopt a more formal, jargon-laden speech style when we wish to highlight educational differences. One professor uses speech divergence as a way to remind students gently and humorously that she has the power to determine when class will end. When students shuffle their feet and rearrange their books toward the end of a class period, the professor has been heard to say, "I see that you are engaging in significant leave-taking behaviors!" Giles and his colleagues report that we sometimes slow down our speech rate when we are talking with people who speak rapidly to slow them down. Parent–child interaction is another context in which speech divergence is frequently exhibited. As a child, you may have known you were "in trouble" when your parent called for you by using your first, middle, and surnames. This divergence was an attempt to increase the perceived (or real) status differences between parent and child.

Communication accommodation theory has also been used to investigate nonverbal communication. David Buller and Judee Burgoon (1986) found that changes in overall tone of voice and rate of speech (vocalics) altered listeners' interpretations of a speaker's level of intimacy and psychological closeness. Buller and James Aune (1988) tested the prediction that when a speaker seeks compliance with a request for help, the similarity of the speaker's speech rate to the listener's speech rate (a vocalic cue) improves compliance. It was thought that the similarity of speaker speech rate to listener speech rate would make the speaker appear more socially attractive. The study found that listeners who were better at decoding and interpreting vocalics (meaning stimulated by how we say something rather than what we say) were more likely to match the speech rate of the speaker and to comply with requests for help from a speaker with a fast rate than listeners who were poorer decoders. This finding suggests that perceived similarity in speech rate influences perceptions of a relationship and compliance with requests for help.

Although communication accommodation theory has generated considerable research, Howard Giles and his colleagues suggested that more questions need to be answered. For example, how do one's communication accommodation behaviors change during the course of a lifetime, and what is the relationship between communication accommodation and empathy? Communication scholars will explore these issues and continue to refine the theory.

Language Expectancy Theory

Language expectancy theory (LET) was developed by Michael Burgoon in 1995 and is based on an accumulation of research on how people are persuaded. Because language behavior is at the core of this theory, we have chosen to include in this chapter. LET focuses on language and how language affects both the

language expectancy theory A language theory persuasion that focuses on how cultural expectation of language use affect both the change and reinforcement of attitudes and beliefs.

change and reinforcement of attitudes and beliefs. It is considered a message-based theory of persuasion in that it seeks to explain why some linguistic forms of persuasive messages are more effective than others (Burgoon, 1995; Burgoon, Denning, & Roberts, 2002).

The concept of language expectation was adapted from the work of Brooks (1970), who believed that our stereotypes (later called expectancies) about what a source has to say, as well as the way they are expected to say it, influence the attitudes and beliefs of the receiver. For example, consider a person who has conservative views about financial investing and is about to hear a presentation from two different speakers. Both speakers share the same attitudes about investing (being fiscally conservative). One speaker is a male with a heavy Brooklyn, New York, accent and an animated presentation style, whereas the other speaker is a midwestern female with a more "standard American" accent and reserved presentation style. Based on our expectations concerning how we "think they should speak" and on their use of language, who will be more effective? Who will be less effective? LET is not concerned about each person's individual expectations (e.g., "This woman looks like my ex-girlfriend who was irresponsible with money, so therefore, this woman presenter has no credibility") as much as the expectations set forth by society and our culture at large (e.g., What language expectations do we have about financial advisors? Male financial advisors? Female financial advisors?).

The idea that the strategic linguistic choices made by persuaders can significantly predict success (Burgoon, Jones, & Stewart, 1975) served as the impetus for the development of Language Expectancy Theory. LET assumes that language is a rule-governed system and that people, through socialization of their home culture, come to expect and prefer particular message and language strategies over others. That is, when people engage in persuasion, they need to consider how the audience was culturally programmed to determine what is considered competent and appropriate persuasive communication as well as what is considered inappropriate and ineffective language use (Burgoon et al., 2002). Further, these culturally/socially developed expectations affect persuasibility based on whether the language conforms (i.e., is consistent with) or does not conform (i.e., is inconsistent with) with our expectancies. When we violate linguistic norms (either positively or negatively), these violations have effects on the perceived appropriateness and effectiveness of the persuasive message.

The formation of linguistic expectations can encompass entire social categories such as sex or ethnicity, and as such, these categories serve to define what is considered appropriate communication behavior. For example, people who are male have greater linguistic freedom (Burgoon et al., 2002). Having greater linguistic freedom is called having a **wide bandwidth** and results in a greater variety of persuasive linguistic strategies that will be seen as appropriate or falling within an expected range (Burgoon et al., 2002). Other social groups may be constrained to a **smaller bandwidth** regarding what is considered

wide bandwidth A term from language expectancy theory that reflects when people have a greater variety of persuasive linguistic strategies that will be seen as appropriate or within an expected range.

smaller bandwidth A term from language expectancy theory that reflects when people have a smaller variety of persuasive linguistic strategies that will be seen as appropriate or within an expected range.

"appropriate linguistic strategies." These linguistic strategies can include variations in language intensity (e.g., fear appeals, opinionated language, language intensity, and aggressive compliance-gaining strategies). Simply put, people with greater bandwidth are allowed to "get away with" utilizing more linguistic variation than others. An example of this would be an ex-convict addressing a group of at-risk youth about the benefits of staying in school. This speaker would be afforded a much greater bandwidth (e.g., be allowed to use profanity, intimidation, sympathy, support) than would a pastor addressing the same group. Societal expectations concerning a pastor's linguistic strategies are much more constricted when compared to those of an ex-convict.

Bandwidth variations have also been identified in the study of language use and gender. According to Burgoon et al. (2002), rigid norms have developed concerning what is and what is not acceptable use of language by men and women. The research suggests that males are allowed more linguistic variability. For example, men are afforded the cultural expectation that use of intense language can still be persuasive. On the other hand, women using intense language were not seen as persuasive because the use of intense language was perceived as a violation of expectations of what constitutes appropriate and effective persuasive messages for use by females.

Source credibility (i.e., people who are perceived as being trustworthy and having expertise) has also been interpreted using LET. People with high credibility are afforded greater bandwidth than people with low credibility (Hamilton, Hunter, & Burgoon, 1990). When we believe that a person has a degree of expertise or is highly trustworthy, we tend to afford them more latitude in the types of language they use when trying to influence us.

LET reflects how cultural and societal expectations about language use and how violations of norms, gender, and trustworthiness affect the persuasive process. However, LET also allows for the explanation of the contradictory research regarding the persuasiveness of fear appeals. More specifically, some research indicates that fear appeals are effective (e.g., getting a person to stop smoking by telling them they will die of lung cancer should they continue to smoke), whereas other research indicates that the use of fear appeals are not persuasive (see Chapter 6). When interpreted through the expectations of the culture at large, expectancies about fear-arousing appeals as well as other intense language types is dependent on the audience. For example, Burgoon (1989, 1990) reported that when a person is perceived as having low credibility or is a member of specific groups (i.e., females and minorities), the use of fear-arousing messages results in negative expectancy violation. On the other hand, males' use of fear appeals and other intense language was perceived as being more persuasive. This illustrates the different bandwidths that are created by cultural influence concerning language expectancy.

This research is further confounded by the particular state of mind of the receiver or audience. When the receiver is highly aroused (e.g., angry, anxious,

language intensity   Quality of speaker's language about objects or concepts that indicates a difference in attitude from neutral.

opinionated language Highly intense language that indicates a speaker's attitude toward topics and attitude toward others.

uncertain), then fear and intense language results in negative expectancy violation. When the receiver is calm or not aroused, fear and intense language results in positive expectancy violation. In other words, intense language use is more persuasive when it is delivered to an audience that is relatively calm. On the other hand, when the audience is uncertain or anxious, a smaller bandwidth is acceptable, and intense language results in negative expectancy violation.

LET was also applied to the research on the effects of preexposure to persuasive language. When a person is preexposed to persuasive language, it results in the creation of expectations. In turn, when the actual persuasive encounter occurs, the receiver has already developed an expectation that serves as a benchmark from which to compare the persuasive attempt (Burgoon, Cohen, Miller, & Montgomery, 1978; Miller & Burgoon, 1979). For example, parents often talk to their children about the types of language strategies that other people will use to get them to try illegal drugs or engage in underage drinking (e.g., "It is cool!" "Everyone is doing it!" "Don't you want to be part of the group?" "Only losers don't drink!"). This defines these language expectations for the child before they actually encounter the situation. When the child experiences the actual situation, the degree of persuasibility will be determined by whether there is no violation, positive violation, or a negative violation of language expectations. Given that the creation of language expectations is a factor in the degree to which a person is persuaded, the question then becomes: "Is it better to create highly intense language expectancies or low-intensity language expectancies?" There is no benefit or pitfall to the creation of high- or low-language-intensity expectations, but if there is a high-intensity language expectancy and the persuader uses low-intense language, then they are seen as more persuasive. On the other hand, if we are expecting low-intensity language and encounter a persuader using high-intense language, then there is minimal persuasive effect. Table 7.1 presents the propositions of language expectancy theory.

Language expectancy theory is focused on the prediction of behavior but is limited by the amount of research that presently exists. Burgoon et al. (2002) argued that "the empirical evidence supporting LET is the product of research conducted in but one culture, namely North American, western culture." However, it should be noted that if the theory is valid and generalizable, "the effects of *violations of expectations, whether positive or negative,* should be culturally invariant" (p. 128). In other words, although the studies supporting LET have relied primarily on experiments using college students in American universities, every culture has expectations about what constitutes the appropriate use of language and what constitutes competent communication. Therefore, language expectations transcend all cultures, but the definition of what constitutes appropriate language use is specific to each culture. In the end, LET is based on human expectations, which is believed to be an important factor in many theories of human communication (Burgoon & Burgoon, 2001).

Table 7.1	**PROPOSITIONS OF LANGUAGE EXPECTANCY THEORY**
PROPOSITION 1:	People develop cultural and sociological expectations about language behaviors that subsequently affect their acceptance or rejection of persuasive messages.
PROPOSITION 2:	Use of language that negatively violates societal expectations about appropriate persuasive communication behavior inhibits persuasive behavior and results either in no attitude change or in changes in position opposite to that advocated by the communicator.
PROPOSITION 3:	Use of language that positively violates societal expectations about appropriate persuasive communication behavior facilitates persuasive effectiveness.
PROPOSITION 4:	Highly credible communicators have the freedom (wide bandwidth) to select varied language strategies and compliance-gaining techniques in developing persuasive messages, whereas low-credible communicators must conform to more limited language options if they wish to be effective.
PROPOSITION 5:	Because of normative impact of source credibility, highly credible sources can be more successful using low-intensity appeals and more aggressive compliance-gaining messages than can low-credible communicators using either strong or mild language or more prosocial compliance-gaining strategies.
PROPOSITION 6:	Communicators perceived as low in credibility or those unsure of their perceived credibility will usually be more persuasive if they employ appeals low in instrumental verbal aggression or elect to use more prosocial compliance-gaining message strategies.
PROPOSITION 7:	People in society have normative expectations about appropriate persuasive communication behavior that are gender specific such that (a) males are usually more persuasive using highly intense persuasive appeals and compliance-gaining message attempts, whereas (b) females are usually more persuasive using low-intensity appeals and unaggressive compliance-gaining messages.
PROPOSITION 8:	People in society have normative expectations about the level of fear-arousing appeals, opinionated language, language intensity, sequential message techniques, and compliance-gaining attempts varying in instrumental verbal aggression appropriate to persuasive discourse.
PROPOSITION 9:	Fear arousal that is irrelevant to the content of the message as to the harmful consequences associated with the failure to comply with the advocated position will mediate receptivity to different levels of language intensity and compliance-gaining strategies varying in instrumental verbal aggression. Receivers aroused by the induction of irrelevant fear or suffering from specific anxiety are most receptive to persuasive messages using low-intensity and verbally aggressive compliance-gaining attempts but are unreceptive to intense appeals or verbally aggressive suasory strategies.

(continues)

Table 7.1   **PROPOSITIONS OF LANGUAGE EXPECTANCY THEORY** *(continued)*

PROPOSITION 10:	Communicators experiencing cognitive stress produce less-intense, more ambivalent messages and elect to use less-aggressive compliance-gaining message strategies.
PROPOSITION 11:	When forced to violate their own norms about appropriate communication behavior by encoding highly intense messages or using aggressive compliance-gaining message strategies, communicators experience increased cognitive stress, which facilitates attitude change toward the belief-discrepant position being advocated.
PROPOSITION 12:	There is a direct linear relationship between level of language intensity used in counterattitudinal advocacy and concomitant attitude change.
PROPOSITION 13:	When supportive pretreatment strategies are used, attitude change following a subsequent persuasive attack varies inversely with the linguistic intensity of the supportive pretreatment strategy.
PROPOSITION 14:	Refutational pretreatments create expectations by forewarning receivers about the nature of the forthcoming attacks such that (a) when persuasive attack messages do not violate the linguistic expectations created by refutational pretreatments, there is maximum resistance to persuasion, but (b) when the linguistic properties to attack messages violate the expectations created by refutational pretreatments either positively or negatively, receivers are less resistant to persuasion.
PROPOSITION 15:	Given passive message reception, low-intensity attack messages are generally more effective than highly intense messages in overcoming resistance to persuasion conferred by supportive, refutational, or combination pretreatments.
PROPOSITION 16:	When the persuasive attack relies on an active participation strategy, a direct relationship exists between language intensity in the actively created attack and overcoming resistance conferred by any kind of pretreatment message strategy (supportive, refutational, or combination) such that matching intensity in the pretreatment and attack messages confers the most resistance to persuasion.
PROPOSITION 17:	When receivers are exposed to more than one message arguing the same position, the confirmation or disconfirmation of linguistic expectancies in the first message systematically affects the acceptance of the second message such that (a) when linguistic expectations are positively violated in an initial message, the initial message is persuasive, but a reversal of attitudes to the original position occurs after exposure to a subsequent message advocating the same counterattitudinal position, and (b) when linguistic expectations are negatively violated in an initial message, the initial message is not persuasive, but receivers are more vulnerable to the arguments of a subsequent message advocating the same counterattitudinal position.

The Conversation and Discourse Analytic Perspectives

A third major verbal theory approach is concerned with patterns and forms of language activity. The analysis of conversational form and content has evolved into a body of knowledge referred to as discourse or conversational analysis. Scholars from several branches of social science including sociology, psychology, linguistics, anthropology, and communication are responsible for research and theory-building efforts in this area. Discourse analysis has been called one of the most promising methods for the study of interpersonal communication (Jacobs, 1988).

Although the terms are often used interchangeably, there are subtle differences between the discourse and conversational analysis perspectives; both investigate the properties, patterns, and forms of natural conversation. One of the major differences lies in the coding of natural conversation. When analyzing conversational data, **discourse analysis** favors a narrower coding procedure and greater statistical treatment of the data. For example, a discourse analysis might examine an exchange between individuals and count the number of times a person's credibility was attacked. That could then be compared to other forms of attack that occurred in the verbal exchange. **Conversational analysis** favors a broader descriptive method, choosing to include the subtleties of communication that would be lost with a narrower coding procedure (Hopper, Koch, & Mandelbaum, 1986). Regarding the previous example, a conversational analysis might identify the different types of credibility attacks and then try to determine which type produced the more negative outcomes in the situation.

Conversational analysis conceives of language as communicative action. That is, those who study language structure and flow believe that conversation is governed by rules that are implicitly known by speakers (Jacobs, 1980). Conversational analysts attempt to understand the rules of conversational action and how people use those rules to engage in natural discourse. For example, some of the research questions considered are (Knapp, 1984):

1. How do people in conversation signal the exchange of speaking turns?
2. How do speakers coordinate talk with eye gaze, body movement, and other action?
3. How do partners identify and "repair" problems that occur in conversations following "failures?"
4. How does conversation function in settings such as interviews, court hearings, or card games?
5. How do we label sections of talk?
6. What role do stories play in conversation?
7. How are disclaimers used to set the stage or offset potentially offensive or sensitive remarks?
8. How do people directly and indirectly respond to questions?

discourse analysis
The coding of natural conversation that has a narrower coding procedure and greater reliance on statistical analysis than conversational analysis.

conversational analysis
Coding of natural conversation that has broad description categories that allow researchers to get at the subtleties of communication.

communication competence Involves appropriateness and effectiveness; can be viewed as trait-like, context- or situationally bound.

Conversational analysts are concerned with the ability to use language appropriately in several communication contexts. Scholars suggest that this ability is one dimension of communication competence (see Chapter 5). Individuals are judged communicatively competent not simply because they follow the rules but also by how they use the rules. A competent rule user can skillfully manipulate the rules of conversation and can violate certain conversational rules to achieve a given purpose (Jacobs, 1980).

One of the most important aspects of conversational effectiveness is managing conversations. The ability of people to know when to start and when to stop talking is a fundamental concern of discourse analysts. A competent linguistic rule user is someone who can monitor the discourse of another and recognize the "points of possible completion." These points are moments during a conversation where the speaking turn can change. We are sure you can remember conversations that seemed to be "out of sync." You may have spoken while the other person was talking. At times, both of you may have talked "on top" of each other's utterances. More likely than not, this type of conversation did not seem satisfying to you. Discourse analysts refer to this as simultaneous talk or overlap in talk. Overlaps are distinguished from interruptions. Overlaps are talk that begins during a change of speaker turn but does not interfere with the current speaker's completion of her turn (McLaughlin, 1984). Overlaps are not always interpreted negatively. If the conversation is supportive and cooperative, the overlapping talk may not be viewed as a violation of turn-taking (Nofsinger, 1991). Overlaps most frequently occur within a syllable or two of a place in the conversation where speaking turns change. Interruptions do not occur near these places and are seen as more serious violations of conversational norms.

transition relevance places Those places in a conversation where a change of speaking turn is possible.

Those places in a conversation where a change of speaking turn is possible have been formally defined as transition relevance places (TRPs) (Hopper, Koch, & Mandelbaum, 1986). At each transitionally relevant place, a speaker may continue talking or may relinquish the turn and allow the other person to talk. The competent communicator recognizes TRPs by such conversational characteristics as falling intonation at the end of an utterance, drawing out the final syllable of a word, or by nonverbal cues such as changes in eye gaze.

recording A data gathering method of conversational analysis involving either audiotape or videotape.

transcribing A data gathering method of conversational analysis that involves using conventional symbols to indicate the verbal and vocal characteristics of the conversation.

METHODS OF CONVERSATIONAL ANALYSIS

One characteristic of conversational analysis research is the use of actual dialogue as primary data. When you read a study conducted from the conversation analytic perspective, you often see a transcription of naturally occurring dialogue. The analyst examines the details of the conversation and arrives at a characterization of the discourse. On the basis of this characterization, claims are made about the linguistic properties of the conversation (Jacobs, 1988). Researchers have identified four types of activities for conducting discourse analysis and recommendations for analysts to follow in each instance: recording, transcribing, **analyzing**, and **reporting** (Hopper, Koch, & Mandelbaum, 1986).

Recording.   These conversations would have occurred whether or not a researcher was present. Before recording a conversation, the researcher should obtain permission of all parties involved. If recording is not possible in natural situations, "role-playing" of conversations may be used. Although audiotape is often used, videotape provides a richer source of data. Two-party conversations are better subjects for analysis than multiparty conversations, which are more difficult to code and decipher. Reduce background noise as much as possible during the recording process.

Transcribing.   Transcribing involves repeated listening to the recordings. Start transcribing at the beginning of the tape. Use conventional symbols to indicate the verbal and vocal characteristics of the conversation. For example, underlining in transcripts indicates stress of the underlined sounds. Capital letters indicate loudness, and colons denote "stretched" sounds. Variable-speed playback devices are helpful in deciphering exact beginnings, endings, and overlaps in speech. Transcribe recordings until elements come into focus and patterns recur.

Analysis.   Listen to the recordings repeatedly and use the transcripts as you follow the recordings. Focus your attention on brief segments of dialogue. Listen to each segment at least twenty times while taking frequent notes. Number each line of the transcript for easy reference. Listen in groups to the transcribed recordings. Any claims you make about the characteristics of the conversation must be supported by details found in the recordings. Examine and describe the details of the conversation in order to sharpen your initial observations. Other analysts should be able to listen to the recordings, study the transcripts, read your written report, and reach the same conclusions you do.

Reporting.   State your conclusions clearly and provide evidence for them. Account for any exceptions you may observe or reservations you may have. The format of the report may vary. You can examine an entire single conversation or a conversational "fragment." You may choose to focus your report on a particular conversational characteristic, such as responses to compliments. Interaction sequences such as turn-taking or conversational openings and closings may be the focus of your report. Try to describe the events in detail rather than report only the numbers related to your observations. For example, do not limit the report to how many turn changes occurred with different speakers (Hopper et al., 1986, pp. 174-82).

CHARACTERISTICS OF CONVERSATION MANAGEMENT

Conversational analysts have investigated a broad range of factors associated with the development, maintenance, and management of natural discourse.

Researchers have investigated the production of self-serving utterances or "bragging" (McLaughlin et al., 1985), awkward silences (McLaughlin & Cody, 1982), compliance-gaining attempts (McLaughlin, Cody, & Robey, 1980), and failure events in conversations (McLaughlin, Cody, & O'Hair, 1983). Robert Nofsinger (1976) has also examined conversational rules used in answering questions indirectly.

The research on discourse analysis has identified several characteristics commonly found in natural conversation. **Turn-taking** is a fundamental conversational characteristic uncovered by discourse analysts. During turn-taking there is an exchange of speaker and listener roles. Turns are viewed as "opportunities at talk" into which utterances are slotted (McLaughlin, 1984). Turn-taking is managed through competent conversational interaction.

Nofsinger (1991) has written extensively about the turn-taking system. He suggested that the very essence of everyday conversation lies in taking turns in conversation and argued that many conversational variables that we attribute to individual personalities or specific interpersonal relationships actually derive from the turn-taking system.

People may listen to us not because they are interested in what we have to say but because they must as a consequence of turn-taking (Nofsinger, 1991). That is, individuals involved in conversation must monitor the current speaker's talk to determine who has been "selected" as the next speaker. People monitor turn-taking in everyday conversation very closely, as there is often a competition for speaking turns. When two listeners begin talking at the same time, one usually yields to the other. When one person starts talking before the current speaker is finished, he or she often apologizes for interrupting (p. 97).

Speech acts such as requests and compliments have also been studied. **Requests** have been found to vary in politeness and directness. **Compliments** are utterances in which the speaker bestows upon the listener some positively valued attribute or property. **Preventatives**, devices used by speakers to gain permission to violate conversational rules, have been noted. One frequent type of preventative is the disclaimer. For example, prior to telling an offensive ethnic joke, a person might say, "I'm Polish, so I can tell this one." Several types of preventatives (for example, **credentialling**, "Some of my best friends are, but . . . ," and **sin license**, "This really shouldn't be said here, but . . .") have been identified. **Repairs** are conversational devices used to smooth or reduce "troubles" after a conversational rule has been violated. One of the most frequently heard forms of repair is the utterance, "I was only kidding," used after a conversational remark has hurt or upset a listener.

The analysis of conversation provides the communication discipline with sound methodological techniques to examine verbal communication. One advantage of this method of analysis is that conversations are found everywhere in both formal and informal contexts. The conversational analyst needs

turn-taking   An exchange of speech and listener roles. Turns are viewed as "opportunities at talk" into which utterances are slotted.

preventatives   Devices used by speakers to gain permission to violate conversational rules.

credentialling   A type of preventative that uses membership or affiliation to violate conversational rules.

sin license   A type of preventative where a person overtly acknowledges the violation of conversational rules before violating the rules.

repairs   Conversational devices used to smooth or reduce "troubles" that arise in conversation.

only a good recording device to begin the data-gathering process. One disadvantage you have probably recognized is that this type of research requires much time and attention to detail. Secretarial and time costs associated with transcripts can be extremely high compared to the costs of other research methods. Discourse and conversational analysts believe that the rich data and detailed findings that emerge are worth the investment.

Conversation Analysis Theory

Conversation analysis theory (CA) views communication as "actions constructed by communicators out of talk and body behavior" (Mandelbaum, 2008, p. 182). Unlike other theories of communication that focus on message sending or receiving, CA is considered a constitutive process. That is, similar to any other resource such as air or water, CA views communication as a primary resource through which social life is constructed. Simply put, communication through this lens reflects how people construct and maintain relationships. Conversational analysis theory provides a framework through which the practice of talk can be analyzed in a way that reveals how communication patterns can constrain a relationship but also how changes in the action of talk can redefine relationships. For example, consider the relationship you have with your favorite professor. Perhaps you call her "Dr. A," and she refers to you by your first name. Using these specific words to address each other assumes a degree of power difference (Dr. A versus Tom). However, should you graduate and continue the friendship with your professor, you might stop calling her "Dr. A" and begin calling her by her first name. Thus, this change in communication pattern alters the relationship.

Mandelbaum (2008) argued that the primary goal of CA is to "lay out the basic sense-making practices and regularities of interaction that form the basis for everyday communication in both informal and professional settings" (p. 175). CA has its roots in the sociologist and symbolic interactionist Erving Goffman's assumption that communication or social interaction is a part of human behavior that is central to our social world. Further, CA is also influenced by ethnomethodology that "emphasizes the orderly procedures of everyday social conduct, and sees that orderliness as accomplished by its participants" (Mandelbaum, 2008, pp. 175–176).

MAIN COMPONENTS OF CONVERSATION ANALYSIS THEORY

CA has three main components for understanding talk. These components consist of **talk is action**, **action is structured**, and **action is locally organized**. The "talk is action" component assumes that to understand interpersonal interaction, we must have the understanding that talk is something people do. Similar to other behavior, talk is something that can be viewed as performance or

---

Conversation analysis theory A theory that views communication as a primary resource through which social life is constructed.

talk is action A component of conversational analysis theory that in order to understand interpersonal interaction, we must have the understanding that talk is something people do.

action is structured A component of conversation analysis theory that assumes that not only is talk an action, but that action is guided by a structure that allows the communicators to coordinate the interaction in a way that allows for things such as turn taking and establishes patterns of interaction.

action is locally organized A component of conversation analysis theory that reflects (a) what is relevant to the interactants within a specific or particular context, (b) local can refer to adjacency or sequence of action as a process for interactants to work interdependently and in predictable ways to construct a recognizable course of action.

something people do beyond merely describing something or transmitting information (Heritage, 1984). The "action as structure" component of CA holds that not only is talk an action, but that action is guided by a structure that allows the communicators to coordinate the interaction in a way that allows for things such as turn-taking and establishes patterns of interaction. For example, one common pattern or sequence of interaction would be when a high school student passes his friend on the way to class, he will most likely say something such as, "What's up?" Generally speaking, the structured sequence would have the friend reply, "Not much." This example is not to imply that the rules for interaction patterns, once established, are fixed. Instead, the various forms of turn-taking structures provide an organized framework to understand action (Mandelbaum, 2008).

Given that misunderstanding and confusion are inherent in human communication, people also develop patterns or practices of conversational repair (Schegloff, Jefferson, & Sacks, 1977). Conversational repair can be used not only to clarify problems of communication or meaning, but also to achieve other communication goals. That is, when someone says something that is not understood, the speaker has a set of practices for fixing the problem, and the recipients have a set of practices for prompting the speaker to fix it" (Mandelbaum, 2008, p. 180). For example, let's say that you are speaking to your significant other, and you are saying something that is soft in volume, that your significant other did not hear. They may say, "What?" tap their ear, or nonverbally look confused. These communication practices prompt you to repeat the message. According to Mandelbaum, the routinized practices of turn-taking, sequence organization, and conversational repair are viewed as universal to all communication and as such "constitutes an observation-based descriptive theory of fundamental features of interpersonal communication" (p. 180).

The third component of CA is that "action is locally organized." When using the term *local,* there are two ways that it is conceptualized. First, local can mean what is relevant to the interactants within a specific or particular context. The context is believed to be created and enacted by the particular behaviors of the interactants (Drew & Heritage, 1992). Simply put, conversation not only shapes the context, but also serves to renew the context, thus the context is constantly being created and recreated. Second, *local* can refer to adjacency or sequence of actions as "a process for communicators to work together in predictable ways to construct a recognizable course of action" (Mandelbaum, 2008, p. 180). Understanding adjacency is important in finding out what is relevantly local.

Raymond and Heritage (2006) proposed that there is an epistemics of social relations, which assumes there are "direct links between the identities of participants that are directly implicated in practices of speaking" (p. 681). What the epistemics of social relations reflects is that our various role identities (i.e.,

conversational repair Part of conversation analysis theory, that assumes both the speaker and the receiver both have sets of practices for clarifying miscommunication.

epistemics of social relations A perspective in conversation analysis theory that assumes that there are direct links between the communicators identity that is directly implicated in the practice of talk.

friend, brother, sister, parent) are identities that are enacted through communication when in relevant situations. Therefore, identities are something we do, not what we are. Sacks (1992) argued that to enact relevant identities, we must employ interactional rules or steps to invoke the relevant identity.

THE UTILITY OF CONVERSATION ANALYSIS THEORY

Researchers utilizing conversational analysis theory do so in an inductive way (see Chapter 2). That is, "in focusing on the structures, actions, and reasoning practices that constitute everyday and institutional talk-in-interaction, a body of CA work describes particulars of how communicators construct and manage their interpersonal relationships" (Mandelbaum, 2008, p. 182). Some studies applying CA theory have focused on analyzing telephone conversations between family members and friends (Drew & Chilton, 2000; Morrison, 1997).

Researchers utilizing conversation analysis will either audio or video record a conversation then decode the conversation for the various characteristics of the interaction. One of the best-known keys used to decode conversation was developed by Jefferson (2004). Following is a brief example of a conversation and the analysis of the conversation using a few of Jefferson's symbols.

Transcription Key:

//	Double obliques indicate the point at which a current speaker's talk is overlapped by the talk of another.

Example: PHIL: Where is the m//oney

SHARON: I gave it to you

(0.0) Numbers within the parentheses indicates elapsed time by the tenths of seconds.

Example: SARA: I think we should talk about this

MATT: Oh (0.2) no (0.6) wait

SARA: No

(●) Dot within parentheses indicates a brief interval (equal to or less than a tenth of a second) within or between utterances.

Example: BILL: Hi may I speak to Mary

BARBARA: Who (●) are you

As indicated in this example, transcribing and analyzing complete conversations can be, and is, quite time consuming and labor intensive. However, conversational analysts believe that the findings from such analyses are of central importance to understand how people "do" everyday talk.

STRENGTHS AND WEAKNESSES OF THE THEORY

Some critics of the theory suggest that a limitation of CA theory is that it seeks to describe particulars of specific conversations rather than focusing on generalization. A strength of CA is that it is a descriptive theory that aids in "breaking of new ground in our understanding of phenomena central to interpersonal communication that can be discovered in the seen but unnoticed interactional details that make up all relationships" (Mandelbaum, 2008, p. 186).

SUMMARY

Many theories of communication account for the verbal behavior of individuals. Language is at the core of verbal behavior, and human beings are distinct in their ability to use language-incorporating signs, symbols, and signals. Language helps shape our perceptions and influences our behavior. We presented three theoretical approaches to verbal behavior. Communication accommodation theory suggests that people accommodate or adjust their style of speech to gain approval, maintain social identity, and make communication more effective. Speakers use convergence to adapt to another's speech style and divergence to maintain social distance between themselves and others. Language expectancy theory focuses on how language affects both the change and reinforcement of attitudes and beliefs. The theory assumes that language is a rule-governed system and that people, through socialization of their "home" culture, come to expect and prefer certain message and language strategies over others. Conversational analysts attempt to understand the rules of conversational action. They identify conversational rules and ways people use those rules to manage conversation by following four steps: recording, transcribing, analyzing, and reporting when conducting discourse analysis. Important characteristics of conversational management are turn-taking, requests, compliments, preventatives, and repairs. Finally, we presented one theory, which comes from the conversational analysis perspective. Conversation analysis theory views communication as a central component in how people construct and maintain relationships. The theory provides a way through which the practice of talk can be analyzed to reveal how communication patterns can define, change, and redefine relationships.

KEY TERMS

action is locally organized

action is structured

communication accommodation theory

communication competence

connotative meaning

convergence

conversation analysis theory (CA)

conversational analysis

conversational repair

credentialling

denotative meaning

discourse analysis

divergence

epistemics of social relations

forewarnings

language expectancy theory (LET)

language intensity

opinionated language

preventatives

recording

repairs

rituals

signs

sin license

smaller bandwidth

symbols

symptom

talk is action

theory of linguistic relativity

transcribing

transition relevance places

turn-taking

wide bandwidth

Nonverbal Behavior Approaches

Communication often involves more than a verbal message. We typically send and receive several messages simultaneously. Messages sent without using words are called "nonverbal" messages. For instance, a person's verbal message concerning a new shirt you are wearing might be, "I really like your new shirt." If the person accompanied the verbal message with nonverbal behavior such as erratic eye contact, a downward twist of the lower lip, words spoken in a slightly higher than average pitch, shoulders turning away from you, eyes blinking, and feet shuffling, you might decide that the verbal message was inconsistent with the nonverbal cues. Which would you tend to believe? Probably you would conclude the person really does not like your new shirt and is simply trying not to offend you.

Our example suggests that nonverbal communication is important because it is highly believable. Understanding what people mean is central to how effective we are socially; determining what people mean is not always easy. Verbal statements are affected by a number of factors, including the desire not to offend, social pressure to agree when others are present, the desire to make a commitment when time and resources may not be available, worries about other issues that divert attention, and deceptive comments just to avoid questions asked. For example, individuals believe one thing but say they believe something else, claim to pay attention but are actually thinking about their next vacation, and say they will behave one way while intending to do just the opposite. The better we can "read" people, the more we know what to expect and can plan accordingly. Understanding nonverbal communication is a very valuable social tool.

There is widespread interest in nonverbal communication by both the general public and those in the communication field. *Body Language* (Fast, 1970) has enjoyed extensive popularity. In the communication discipline, nonverbal behavior is one of the major lines of research (for an overview of research see Burgoon, 1985). As with communication trait research (Chapter 5) and persuasion research (Chapter 6), nonverbal communication has been studied largely from a laws perspective.

Nonverbal behavior is thought to be at least as important as verbal behavior in understanding communication. Some researchers have argued that nonverbal behaviors typically stimulate much more meaning than the meaning created by the words used in a communication situation (Mehrabian, 1981). The nonverbal code may be viewed as a language, one that we begin learning just as early in life as we do the verbal code.

The popularity of nonverbal communication makes it necessary to emphasize that it is not a "cure-all" for social problems; studying nonverbal communication does not guarantee social effectiveness. Popular books sometimes characterize nonverbal codes as "secret weapons," requiring only that you learn the secrets to conquer any task. However, nonverbal communication is only one dimension of communication competence. Competence with the verbal code, constructing effective arguments, and good delivery are also very important.

AFFECTIVE-COGNITIVE DIMENSIONS OF COMMUNICATION

The potency of verbal and nonverbal communication varies according to what is being communicated. Understanding the **affective** and **cognitive dimensions** of communication will clarify the variation. The affective dimension includes the communication of emotion (such as anger, love, fear, or happiness), attitude (how much something is liked or disliked, for example), and predispositions (such as anxiousness, confidence, or depression). These feelings can be communicated by the verbal code, but the task is difficult. For instance, when you try to tell a friend how much you love another person, you may feel that you have not really been understood. Some ideas are difficult to put into words but can be expressed very clearly nonverbally. Simply observing how a person looks at you communicates a good deal about the degree of affection, for instance. Nonverbal behavior is particularly effective in communicating affect.

The verbal code, on the other hand, is more effective when the goal is to communicate thoughts or cognitions. The cognitive component of communication refers to *beliefs* about what is and/or is not related to the object of communication. You can have beliefs about attributes, characteristics, and consequences of an object. For instance you might believe that a candidate for the presidency is honest, sincere, friendly, and an expert in domestic issues, but a novice in foreign affairs. Beliefs have to do with how things are related. This might also be thought of as "an idea" or "thinking." Typically, abstract processes such as spatial reasoning are necessary to comprehend a belief. These processes are very difficult to express nonverbally. The verbal code seems to have been designed especially for communicating the cognitive aspects of our internal processes. In our example, expressing beliefs about a candidate's relationship to domestic issues and foreign affairs could be done verbally without much difficulty. However, to do this nonverbally would be a nearly hopeless task. Expressing affect for the candidate through the nonverbal code could be accomplished very easily. A negative opinion about the candidate could be expressed with a look of disapproval; positive feelings could be expressed with smiles, head nodding, or clapping.

CONTEXTUAL NATURE OF NONVERBAL COMMUNICATION

The idea that the meaning of a message depends on its context is important in understanding nonverbal communication. A context involves situations and variables in the situations that make it different from other contexts. These differences occur along the lines of who, what, how, why, where, and when. The characteristics of the context influence the meaning of a message. Take a symbol such as a handshake. In a situation where you are introduced to someone, the handshake might indicate "I'm very glad to meet you," whereas the very same behavior in greeting an old friend could mean "I'm so glad to see you again." A handshake with rivals before a contest can mean, "May the better person win"; after closing a business deal, "It was a pleasure to do business with you"; after a bitter quarrel, "Let's put this fight behind us." The behavior is essentially the same in all these examples. However, the meaning is considerably different. The reason is quite simple; we have learned that a given symbol (or set of symbols) means one thing in one situation but something different in another. Thus, the meaning of a message is influenced by context. We should note the context in which a message is presented when we decide on its meaning.

Despite the fact that the contextual nature of communication is discernible, some of the popular books on nonverbal communication overlook this concept. Instead, they suggest that certain nonverbal behaviors mean only one thing and ignore the other possible meanings that could be created by changes in the situation. For instance, a possible interpretation of a woman talking to a man with her arms folded in front of her is that she is signaling unavailability; he is "closed out." What if this behavior occurs in a chilly room or even in a warm room by a woman who has just come in from the cold? In such cases, the nonverbal arm behavior might say nothing about the woman's desire for a relationship. It is misleading to treat a set of nonverbal behaviors as a formula for social knowledge. In certain circumstances it might be true that "a woman is interested in you if she moves her shoulders back, is slightly flushed, and tilts her head to one side a bit." These behaviors might indicate interest in an intimate setting. If you are walking across campus to your next class, they might signal that she had a good workout at the gym, is stretching her deltoids, and is reacting to the muscle stimulation.

NONVERBAL BEHAVIOR AND INTENTIONALITY

In Chapter 1 we explained that all human behavior is not communicative behavior. *Communication occurs when humans manipulate symbols to stimulate meaning in other humans.* Symbols are only one of several things that can stimulate meaning. Nonsymbolic behavior can stimulate a response; however, intention is not involved. A woman may fold her arms for many reasons. If sending a message about unavailability is not one of her reasons, then communication about approachability does not occur when she folds her arms. Of course, others might "read meaning into" her behavior. She cannot stop people from thinking. Meaning can be stimulated by both symbolic and nonsymbolic elements. If a woman's arm folding is nonsymbolic regarding accessibility, imagine her confusion if a man said, "Why did you just send me a message that said you are unavailable?" Her response, in the terminology of this book might be, "I cannot stop you from seeing meaning in nonmessage behavior. If you do, do not act as though I am communicating with you. Realize that you are creating meaning for yourself that may have no relation to my ideas and feelings."

Perhaps one of the reasons the area of nonverbal communication has become so popular is that nonverbal behavior provides clues to detecting attitudes, traits, and deception. There are many examples. Pupil dilation shows interest. Frequent head nodding indicates a feeling of lower status. Deception is signified by less forward body lean. Nervousness is evidenced by fewer gestures. Such behaviors seem to reveal information that people themselves usually would not volunteer. As such, these nonverbal behaviors appear to be a valuable means for understanding people. Despite this appeal, the behaviors in question usually do not constitute communication because intentional manipulation of symbols to send messages is not apparent. Instead, the behaviors are more like symptoms as defined by Cronkhite (1986). For example, a drooping posture is a symptom of depression. Judee Burgoon (1985), probably the leading nonverbal communication researcher in the communication discipline, supports this interpretation.

emotional leakage A term used to describe when a person's feelings "leak out" through one or more nonverbal channels.

Similarly, **emotional leakage** is a consequence of the perception of symptoms. Emotional leakage is the term used to describe when a person's true feelings "leak out" through one or more nonverbal channels. Unknowingly, or at a very low level of awareness, individuals reveal their true emotions because of their nonverbal behavior. If you are bored with a conversation but pretend you are interested, emotional leakage might occur if your laughter were less relaxed and you used fewer vocal expressions and head nods. The idea that a person's boredom would leak out and foil the person's attempt to create a particular impression is intriguing. However, the "leaky" behaviors are not symbolic; most likely they are symptoms. As our conception of communication makes clear, all meaning does not result from communication. Although highly provocative, "emotional leakage" is not a communication concept because nothing is communicated. Instead, one-way meaning is formed in the mind of the observer. Communication is a "two-way" process involving social behavior and a deliberate message on the part of the sender. A person may create meaning because of naturally occurring symptoms or behaviors that cannot easily be controlled. Of course, even behaviors such as blinking in response to a threatening movement can be controlled. However, symptomatic behavior usually has nothing to do with symbols.

NONVERBAL COMMUNICATION ABILITIES

People vary widely in how well they encode and decode written and spoken messages. Because individuals range from very high to very low in verbal language abilities, we would expect to find differences in nonverbal communication as well. Research suggests that the ability to encode and decode nonverbal behavior may be an attribute of certain personality traits. People who are extroverted are more skilled at portraying emotions through vocal and facial codes. Introverts are less able to communicate emotions nonverbally, if for no other reason than they have not had as much practice due to their tendency to withdraw from people.

Self-monitoring of expressive behavior is another trait that appears related to nonverbal encoding ability (Snyder, 1974). High self-monitors are very aware of the impression they make on others. They are able to assess their behavior and reactions to it and make adjustments in their performance accordingly; high self-monitors are very adaptive. High self-monitors are also skilled at communicating emotions nonverbally when compared to low self-monitors. Having the motivation to monitor one's behavior with respect to the reactions of others appears necessary for the development of the ability to encode nonverbal messages skillfully.

Greater encoding skill by high self-monitors has been investigated in terms of deceptive communication (Miller, de Turk, & Kalbfleisch, 1983). Research participants were asked to tell the truth or to lie about the feelings that they had while viewing pleasant or unpleasant slides. Both high and low self-monitors took part in the experiment. Participants either spoke immediately or were given twenty minutes to rehearse what they would say. Observers viewed

self-monitoring of expressive behavior
A trait that involves monitoring one's nonverbal behavior and adapting it to situations in order to achieve communication goals.

videotapes of the participants' messages and judged whether the individual was telling the truth or not. When rehearsal was permitted, high self-monitors were more effective in deceiving observers. The more time they had to practice their behavior, the more successful they were. Low self-monitors who had not rehearsed displayed more pauses and had a higher rate of nonfluencies such as "um." This experiment confirmed the hypothesis that high self-monitors would be more effective in deceiving others.

There may be a sex difference in the ability to communicate emotions facially and vocally (Zaidel & Mehrabian, 1969). Females seem to be more skilled than males. One explanation for this is that culture has taught females to be more expressive and to reveal emotions. Males, on the other hand, have been conditioned to be more stoic and to inhibit expression of feelings. Because males engage less in emotionally expressive behavior, they are less skilled at encoding it. Nonverbal decoding ability is also related to sex. Psychologist Robert Rosenthal and his associates (1979) developed the PONS (Profile of Nonverbal Sensitivity) test to measure ability to decode nonverbal messages. One of the most consistent results in research using this test is that females tend to score higher in comparison to males. The finding that females are higher in both nonverbal encoding and decoding abilities further illustrates the point that the two abilities are related. That is, if you are high on one, you tend to be high on the other; if you are unskilled regarding one, you tend to be unskilled regarding the other.

Although females generally score higher on the PONS test, there are some males who score equally well. These tend to be males who are in very communication-oriented professions that require sensitivity to the needs of others. Teachers, clinical psychologists, and actors are examples. This finding further supports the social-influence explanation given earlier for male-female differences in nonverbal behavior.

High scorers on the PONS test differ from low scorers in several ways in addition to gender. Low scorers tend to be younger. Just as with verbal language, nonverbal ability seems to improve with age. High scorers tend to function better socially, to have closer same-sex relationships, and to predict future events with greater accuracy.

In developing the PONS, Rosenthal experimented with the amount of time a scene was shown to people. He found when exposure was reduced from five seconds to 1/24 of a second, some people were still able to identify the emotion portrayed. These individuals who appeared to be especially sensitive to the nonverbal code reported that they had less satisfactory relationships with other people. Perhaps it is possible to see "too much" in the behavior of others, and this creates dissatisfaction with people. That is, extreme accuracy in decoding may make one more aware of the "common deceptions" that are a regular component of social interaction. Common deceptions refer to "white lies," behaving one way but preferring something else, or concealing the truth because of a desire to protect someone's feelings.

FUNCTIONS OF NONVERBAL COMMUNICATION

Functional approaches have been used extensively to examine a number of areas in communication such as credibility, persuasion, and mass media. Viewing nonverbal communication in terms of the functions that it fulfills for the individual is similarly valuable. We will briefly examine six important functions.

Sending Uncomfortable Messages

Some messages are much easier to present nonverbally. Overt delivery of a verbal message could result in embarrassment, hurt feelings, discomfort, anxiety, and anger. One example of such a message involves initiating or preventing interaction. For instance, at a party Jamie might realize that Sean across the room wants to approach and talk. If Jamie does not want to meet Sean, a possible verbal message would be, "Don't bother coming here to talk with me; I don't want to get to know you." Of course, that is a difficult message to present in a social situation. An "easy way" to deliver the idea would be preferable. Nonverbal codes such as eye and facial behavior and the directness of body orientation can send the message without as much embarrassment. In fact, even in a crowded room, probably only Sean would be aware of Jamie's message of discouragement.

Once interaction has been initiated, another difficult message is to inform someone that you wish to terminate the interaction. Imagine that Sean in our previous example ignored the nonverbal message and approached Jamie anyway. The verbal message: "Why did you come across the room to talk with me? Couldn't you see I'm not interested? Please leave" would be a very difficult message to deliver. Nonverbally, the task would be easier. Jamie could avoid eye contact, turn so as not to face Sean directly, and talk in short phrases with little expression (sound bored).

These examples illustrate that negative messages are communicated with efficiency by the nonverbal code. However, some types of positive messages also are easier to say nonverbally. One example is communicating love. Some people find it difficult to say "I love you" and instead rely on **eye behavior**, **touch**, and close proximity. Another example is communicating favorable internal states such as feeling very good about oneself. Nonverbally, this can be done by sounding confident (vocally), reflecting this feeling in facial behavior, and walking with a confident gait.

eye behavior　Nonverbal behavior that communicates attitude, interest, dominance or submission.

Forming Impressions

Nonverbal communication is especially useful in the process of forming first impressions. Initial interaction and the early stages of a relationship are influenced a good deal by the first impressions that people form of each other. Gerald Miller's (1978) developmental approach to interpersonal communication provides a way to conceptualize this. Communication between people is viewed as ranging from impersonal to interpersonal. At the *impersonal* end of the continuum, people use sociological variables such as age, sex, and race to form an impression that guides what to say and how to say it. When communication is impersonal, you rely on stereotypes and other assumptions about what people are like to guide your communicative behavior. We typically place a good deal of importance on first impressions because we do not want to say something that the other will view as foolish. We are strongly motivated to reduce uncertainty about the other so that we can predict with confidence how to and how not to communicate. (You will read more about this process in the discussion of uncertainty reduction theory in Chapter 9.)

When communication is *interpersonal,* the impression of the other that guides interaction is based mainly on *psychological* data. In comparison to sociological data, psychological is more personal. The major types of psychological data are values (very strong, wide-ranging beliefs that guide behavior), attitudes (like or dislike for things), and personality (traits that define the person). Thus, when communication is interpersonal, it is less stereotypic and is individualized according to the psychological characteristics of the people involved.

The nonverbal messages we send contribute substantially to the first impression others form of us. This impression then guides how people talk with us in the early stage of interaction. Many of these messages pertain to physical appearance—fashion, grooming, body type, and attractiveness. For instance, the first impression that you make might be: a black male, late teens, highly fashion conscious, very neat and clean looking, a "physical fitness" type who values being attractive. These cues would provide a basis for others to guess how to communicate with you. For instance, clothes or physical fitness would be "excellent bets" for successful topics of communication.

Nonverbal cues provide data relevant to your psychological characteristics. If the cues are clear, communication moves from the impersonal to interpersonal levels more readily. The cues just discussed, fashion consciousness and physical fitness, are examples. Other cues derive from nonverbal codes such as the way we use our voices. For instance, a person might sound very self-confident or move very confidently. Another individual's movements might suggest nervousness or apprehension about some-thing. If the nonverbal cues are not clear, then there is the tendency for communication to remain at the impersonal level. For instance, if the messages from your eyes, face, and body movements make it unclear whether you are a very cautious or a carefree person, a person talking with you will exercise discretion, selecting only "safe" topics such as the weather, one's major, or hometown.

Making Relationships Clear

In addition to content, communication has a **relationship** dimension (Watzlawick, Beavin, & Jackson, 1967). Content refers to the topic of the message. For instance, a parent might say, "Did you have a nice time at the party last night?" The content is clear. It has to do with how favorable your experience was with the party. The relationship dimension refers to the interpersonal relationship between the individuals, and this influences how the message will be handled. For instance, you might respond, "Oh, I had a marvelous time!" If a friend had asked the same question, you might have said: "I had a marvelous time . . . until I reached the point where I had too much to drink." The relationships we have with people exert a powerful force on our communicative behavior.

Nonverbal communication functions to establish and clarify the relationship dimension of communication. It does this very well because at times the relationship message would be offensive if spoken verbally. For example, "I am your boss even though you do not like it." Communicating such a message without words serves to "soften" the message, making a destructive outcome of the situation less likely. If the relationship is not clarified, the danger of a misunderstanding increases. For instance, in the early stages of a new job you might be uncertain as to whether you must comply with what a certain person tells you to do. This uncertainty could result in your responding to the person with indifference when the other person's expectation was for you to be compliant. This would be a costly mistake if the person was your superior and not a peer.

There are many types of relationships that are important in communication. Some of these are parent–child, superior–subordinate, husband–wife, friends, and siblings. Others are based on competition, cooperation, liking, love, or disdain. Nonverbally, we tell one another what we believe the nature of our relationship to be. If there is correspondence between the parties, the relationship dimension of communication can recede to the background. For instance, if you want to be dominant in a relationship, you might communicate that by steady eye contact, holding the floor most of the time, interrupting and touching the other person more. If the other person accepts this relationship definition, there is no problem. Nonverbally, this acceptance might be communicated by eyes cast downward while looking "up" to you, frequent head nods, and passive smiles. On the other hand, if the nonverbal messages that people send one another about the nature of their relationship are not congruent, then the definition of the relationship becomes an issue and usually predominates until resolved. When a relationship issue emerges, it becomes more likely that the attempt to define the relationship will shift from the nonverbal to the verbal code. That is, it is easier, less disruptive, and less offensive if we tell one another nonverbally of the nature of our relationship. If this fails to produce an agreeable outcome, then more overt communication is necessary; there is a need to talk about the relationship.

Regarding our earlier example, suppose you are new on a job and respond with indifference to someone who says you should stop what you are doing for a while and work at a different task. Suppose further that this person's eye contact was not steady and the tone of voice was unsure—two behaviors that do not indicate a superior relationship. Because the command is incongruent with the nonverbal cues, it probably would be necessary to clarify the relationship verbally. This could be done by having your supervisor explain to you whom else in the organization you must obey.

Regulating Interaction

Regulating our interaction with others is a fourth major function of nonverbal communication. Imagine the following: two people recognize one another in a college library. They begin to talk in a pleasant tone with occasional laughter. They take turns talking with little silence between utterances. After about 15 minutes the conversation ends, and they return to separate places in the library. Imagine further that both individuals derived considerable satisfaction from the interaction. This is an example of successful communication. Although such episodes are extremely common, we could also view them with amazement—an example of complex human activity made to look easy. A major reason why communication events such as this go smoothly is they are carefully and skillfully regulated. The central regulating mechanism appears to be nonverbal communication. As a regulator, nonverbal behavior operates in terms of *initiating interaction, clarifying relationships, directing turn-taking, guiding emotional expression,* and *leave-taking.*

Greeting behaviors that suggest a desire to interact are largely nonverbal. In our example, each person could send such messages by raising eyebrows while widening the eyes, raising the chin with a smile, and perhaps waving the hand in greeting. When the individuals approached one another and positioned themselves about three feet apart, the conversation could begin.

During the conversation, several nonverbal behaviors regulate the interaction. We discussed the function of clarifying relationships in the previous section. Directing turn-taking involves communicating when you want the floor and when you are or are not willing to relinquish the floor. When we want the floor (our turn to speak), a number of nonverbal messages may be used: throat clearing, vocal sounds such as "uh, uh," opening the mouth as if beginning to speak, raising eyebrows and opening eyes wide. Willingness to give up the floor is indicated by pausing, looking to the other as if searching for a response, nodding approval to begin, or gesturing toward the person to begin. Wanting to hold the floor when someone desires to talk is expressed by increasing volume somewhat, employing an aggressive tone in the voice, breaking eye contact and adopting a determined facial expression.

Guiding emotional expression involves the tone of the conversation. Nonverbally we say whether the tone should be happy, sad, angry, hurried, or serious. As we explained earlier, nonverbal communication is especially effective at expressing the affective or emotional dimension of communication.

Regulating leave-taking is accomplished nonverbally in many ways (Knapp, Hart, Friedrich, & Shulman, 1973). Messages that indicate a desire to end the conversation include breaking eye contact and glancing around the area, looking at a watch, shuffling feet, and leaning in the direction of the exit. The actual leave-taking will either be positive or negative, depending on the desire for future communication. Some positive nonverbal messages are a handshake, a smile, and a wave. Negative messages include an abrupt ending, turning and leaving with no goodbye, an angry goodbye, and a gesture of disgust on exiting.

Influencing People

Nonverbal communication appears to be very important in the process of persuasion. Certainly the verbal message matters. However, there is increased awareness that people are influenced by nonverbal messages as well. Whether the verbal message is accepted seems to depend on how well the persuader communicates nonverbally. The adage, "It's not what you say but how you say it," is an overstatement, but "What you say cannot overrule how you say it" is accurate.

There are several types of nonverbal messages that can enhance a source's persuasiveness. Some involve physical appearance that appeals to the receiver, such as dress and grooming. Others include body movement or eye and facial behavior—creating a dynamic image, a sincere look, or appearing sociable. Vocal behavior, meaning the way the voice is used, is also important. This entails sounding dynamic and interesting. These nonverbal messages all contribute to the individual's *image* or total impression. In political communication especially, there is increased use of terms such as image building, image management, and image rebuilding or repairing. The use of these terms acknowledges the principle that one's nonverbal messages are not independent of the verbal message. Perhaps this causes you to think that the influence process, whether it occurs in the political, business, or personal arena, is extremely superficial because appearances matter so much. However, there is a very good reason for this. People pay close attention to persuaders' nonverbal behavior as a basis for deciding whether to *trust* the person. Trust is a necessary condition for persuasion in almost all cases.

A person's nonverbal behavior provides a major source of data in deciding on a person's character. Eye behavior is usually emphasized as a criterion for deciding whether to trust someone. Voice is also a focus. What qualities do we look for when deciding trust? The answer is rather well established in terms of research. We are more attracted to people and trust them when they are similar to us (Infante, 1978). Similarity tends to breed attraction, and the more our nonverbal behavior says to a person, "As you can see, I am a lot like you," the more the person probably will trust you. This is true mainly because they know what to expect from a similar other. They assume the person is guided by similar values.

nonverbal response matching Matching another's nonverbal behavior in order to create perceived similarity, which leads to trust.

This analysis has identified an approach to nonverbal communication in persuasion that has been termed **nonverbal response matching** (Infante, 1988) and may be considered an aspect of communication accommodation theory, which was discussed in Chapter 7. The idea is for the persuader to match the receiver's nonverbal behavior so that a bond of trust develops because the receiver perceives similarity between self and the persuader. For instance, if the receiver talks fast with short, quick gestures, the persuader would adopt this style to identify with the receiver. This is not mimicry, which is a form of insult. Instead, it is a message that says, "I understand how you are, and I like being that way myself." This behavior confirms the saying, "Imitation is the sincerest form of flattery." Studies that compared successful salespersons to mediocre ones revealed that the successful sellers used response matching, whereas the unsuccessful ones did not (Moine, 1982). Clearly, our nonverbal behavior provides important input in our decision about whether to trust others.

Reinforcing and Modifying Verbal Messages

Finally, one of the most basic functions of nonverbal communication is to affect the verbal message. The verbal and nonverbal messages are often produced together. As such, there is not one message but several, comprising a set of messages. The idea of a set emphasizes that things go together, influence one another, and the whole is more than simply a sum of the parts. Thus, a given configuration of nonverbal messages along with certain words will communicate one thing, whereas the very same words with a different set of nonverbal messages will communicate something else. Nonverbal communication may reinforce or modify the verbal message.

Nonverbal communication reinforces verbal messages in a variety of ways. Imagine gestures that would accompany the phrases in parentheses in the following sentence. Gestures are used to illustrate size ("the fish was this big"), position ("I was here; the fish jumped there"), effort ("I struggled to keep the rod tip high while he pulled really hard"), movement ("I reached into the water quickly and picked up the fish by the lower jaw"). Facial, eye, and vocal behavior are especially effective in emphasizing the emotional content of a message. For instance, if you are talking about hunger in America, your nonverbal messages should reflect concern and reinforce the seriousness of this social problem. While you discuss the issue, your face, eyes, and voice could express sympathy and gravity. If proposing a solution such as a guaranteed job program, your face, eyes, and voice could communicate hope, enthusiasm, and confidence.

At times, nonverbal messages are used to modify verbal messages. This is especially likely when we do not want our words to be taken literally. There are at least four ways this happens. One is when it is socially desirable to say one thing, but we want to express our displeasure with the contents of the verbal message. For example, imagine working for a company that invested much of its resources in a new but very unsuccessful product. In talking with coworkers your verbal message might be, "Oh, yes, our . . . is a wonderful innovation." Nonverbally, with eyes, face, and tone of voice, you might say that the product is not so wonderful and actually not much of an innovation either. Mock verbal aggression is a second means of altering literal meaning; it includes playfulness commonly termed "kidding" or "teasing." However, one must be careful to avoid miscalculation. Receiving a birthday present wrapped in paper that reads, "Happy birthday to a sweet old buzzard" may or may not be taken as a joke! Third, nonverbal messages are used to modify the verbal message in requests. Terry asks Dale for something, and Dale really would like to say "no" but uses a nonverbal message that says, "OK, I will if you *really* want me to." The verbal "yes" is expressed with little enthusiasm, looking away, and breathing out while drooping the shoulders (as if burdened by a great load). In the fourth situation, the individual's verbal messages create a certain image, but the person wants to modify that to say, "I am not exactly what you think" or "There is more to me than you realize." For instance, a person's verbal messages might leave no doubt that she is a lawyer, but her nonverbal messages might add, "I am opposed to this culture and seek to change it." These messages might come from very unconventional grooming (brightly colored, spiked hair) and dress (wearing beads and buckskin clothes) and from negative nonverbal messages when talking about mandatory sentencing.

EXPECTANCY VIOLATIONS THEORY

Judee Burgoon (1978, 1983, 1985) and Steven Jones (Burgoon & Jones, 1976) originally designed **expectancy violations theory** (EVT) to explain the consequences of changes in distance and personal space during interpersonal communication interactions. EVT was one of the first theories of nonverbal communication developed by communication scholars. EVT has been continually revised and expanded; today the theory is used to explain a wide range of communication outcomes associated with violations of expectations about nonverbal communication behavior.

expectancy violations theory Theory that explains a wide range of communication outcomes associated with violations of expectations about nonverbal communication behavior.

According to EVT, several factors interact to influence how we react to a violation of the type of nonverbal behavior we expect to encounter in a particular situation (Burgoon & Hale, 1988). EVT first considers our *expectancies.* Through social norms we form "expectations" about how others should behave nonverbally (and verbally) when we are interacting with them. If another person's behavior deviates from what we typically expect, then an expectancy violation has occurred. Anything "out of the ordinary" causes us to take special notice of that behavior. For example, we would notice (and probably be very uncomfortable) if a stranger asking for directions stood very close to us. Similarly, we would notice if our significant other stood very far away from us at a party. A violation of our nonverbal expectations is unsettling; it can cause emotional *arousal.*

We learn expectations from a number of sources (Floyd, Ramirez, & Burgoon, 1999). First, the culture in which we live shapes our expectations about different types of communication behavior, including nonverbal communication. As we will describe in our discussion of nonverbal immediacy behaviors, contact cultures have more eye contact, more frequent touch, and much smaller zones of personal distance than noncontact cultures. The context in which the interaction takes place also affects expectations of others' behavior. A great deal of eye contact from an attractive other may be seen as inviting if the context of the interaction is in a social club, whereas the same nonverbal behavior may be seen as threatening if that behavior is exhibited in a sparsely populated subway car late at night. Depending on the context, "a caress may convey sympathy, comfort, dominance, affection, attraction, or lust" (Burgoon, Coker, & Coker, 1986, p. 497). The meaning depends on the situation and the relationship between the individuals. Our personal experiences also affect expectancies. Repeated interactions condition us to expect certain behaviors. If our usually cheerful roommate suddenly stops smiling when we enter the room, we encounter a distinctly different situation than we expected. EVT suggests that expectancies "include judgments of what behaviors are possible, feasible, appropriate, and typical for a particular setting, purpose, and set of participants" (Burgoon & Hale, 1988, p. 60).

Our *interpretation and evaluation* of behavior is another important element of the theory. EVT assumes that nonverbal behaviors are meaningful and that we have attitudes about expected nonverbal behaviors. We approve of some and dislike others. *Valence* is the term used to describe the evaluation of the behavior. Certain behaviors are clearly negatively valenced, such as being subjected to a rude or insulting gesture (e.g., someone "flips you the bird" or rolls their eyes at you). Other behaviors are positively valenced (e.g., someone signals "v" for victory after a touchdown or "thumbs up" for your new sweater). Some behaviors are ambiguous. For example, imagine that you are at a party and a stranger to whom you are introduced unexpectedly touches your arm. Because you just met that person, that behavior could be confusing. You might interpret the behavior as affection, an invitation to become friends, or as a signal of dominance. EVT argues that if the given behavior is more positive than what was expected, a positive violation of expectations results. Conversely, if the given behavior is more negative than what was expected, a negative violation of expectations results. In ambiguous situations, the following element tips the balance.

Communicator reward valence is the third element that influences our reactions. The nature of the relationship between the communicators influences how they (especially the receiver) feel about the violation of expectations. If we "like" the source of the violation (or if the violator is a person of high status, high in credibility, or physically attractive), we may appreciate the unique treatment. However, if we "dislike" the source, we are less willing to tolerate nonverbal behavior that does not conform to social norms; we view the violation negatively.

EVT posits that it is not just a matter of the nonverbal behavior violations and the reactions to them. Instead, EVT argues that who is doing the violations matters greatly and must be accounted for to determine whether a violation will be seen as positive or negative. Unlike other nonverbal interaction models such as discrepancy arousal theory (see LePoire & Burgoon, 1994), EVT predicts that even an "extreme violation of an expectancy" might be viewed positively if it was committed by a highly rewarding communicator (Burgoon & Hale, 1988, p. 63).

Expectancy violations theory has generated much interest and research over the last twenty-five years. We will mention a few studies based on this theory. Burgoon and Jerold Hale (1988) conducted an experiment in which individuals participated in discussions with friends and with strangers who either increased, reduced, or acted normal regarding immediacy behaviors (especially **proxemics**, body orientation, forward lean, eye contact, and open posture). They found that low-immediacy behaviors (i.e., negative violations of expectations such as less eye contact than normal or indirect body/shoulder lean) resulted in lower credibility ratings than high or normal levels of immediacy in both the friends and the stranger conditions. Being less immediate than expected was perceived as communicating detachment, lower intimacy, dissimilarity, and higher dominance. However, being more immediate than normal (e.g., standing closer, leaning forward) was viewed as expressing more intimacy, similarity, and involvement.

Burgoon and Joseph Walther (1990) examined a variety of touch behaviors, proxemics, and postures to determine which are expected or unexpected in interpersonal communication and how expectations are influenced by the source's status, attractiveness, and gender. Some findings were that a handshake is most expected, whereas an arm around the shoulder is least expected. Erect posture is most expected, and tense posture is least expected.

proxemics How people use space to communicate.

Several studies have examined the role of expectancy violations in different kinds of interpersonal relationships. For example, EVT was used to study sexual expectations and sexual involvement in initial dating encounters. Previous research suggested that males enter female-initiated first dates with heightened sexual expectations (Mongeau, Hale, Johnson, & Hillis, 1993), and that less sexual intimacy is reported in female-initiated as compared to male-initiated first dates (Mongeau & Johnson, 1995).

Using an experimental design, Paul Mongeau and Colleen Carey (1996) varied the directness in initiating a date. Male and female participants read a scenario in which a female asks a male out on a date to a movie (*female asks*), a female indicates interest in seeing a movie followed immediately by male asking her on the date (*female hints*), or the male asks the female on the date without the preceding hint (*male asks*). The gender of the target varied; half the participants evaluated the male target and the other half the female target. The extent to which the target took an active role in making the date, measures of dating and sexual expectations, and the target's general level of sexual activity were measured. Mongeau and Carey report that results of this study were consistent as predicted by expectancy violations theory: "males enter female-initiated first dates with inflated sexual expectations. As a consequence, that less sex occurs on female-initiated first dates is certainly consistent with a negative violation of the males' expectancies" (p. 206).

Kory Floyd and Michael Voloudakis (1999) used EVT to explore the communication of affection in adult platonic friendships. Their study involved 40 mixed-sex dyads. The first encounter consisted of conversation between the participants. For the second encounter, the researchers asked some participants (confederates) to increase or to decrease their "affectionate involvement" with the naive subject. The researchers hypothesized that unexpected increases in affection would be considered positive expectancy violations, whereas unexpected decreases would be considered negative expectancy violations. The research supported their hypotheses. In addition, naive participants in the low-affection condition saw the confederates as less immediate, less similar to themselves, less composed, and less equal to themselves. Again, these findings support EVT's prediction that negative expectancy violations can produce negative outcomes.

One study manipulated the reward value of the communicator and the valence and extremity of the violation behavior to explore their effects on student-professor interactions (Lannutti, Laliker, & Hale, 2001). A scenario was created involving a student-professor conversation. An experimental study manipulated the location of a professor's touch (no touch, arm, or thigh), reward value for the professor (e.g., low—"one you dislike and disdain," or high—"one you like and admire"), and sex of the participant (male or female). The sex of the professor was also adjusted so that it was always the opposite sex of the participant. Evaluation of the professor, desire to interact with the professor, and perceptions of sexual harassment were measured.

Nonverbal expectancy violations theory was "partially supported" in this study in that female participants' evaluations of the professor became more negative as the intimacy of touch increased, regardless of the reward value of the professor. The more unexpected the touch, the less favorable the professor and the interaction were evaluated by the female participants (Lannutti, Laliker, & Hale, 2001).

Expectancy violations theory continues to generate research; modifications and revisions of the theory are still emerging. EVT makes us more aware of the influence of our nonverbal behavior (i.e., distance, touch, eye contact, smiling). It suggests that if we engage in nonverbal communication behavior that violates expectations, it might be wise to contemplate our "reward value." Unless our "reward value" is sufficiently high to offset a violation of expectations, it might be wise to rethink our behavior.

INTERACTION ADAPTATION THEORY

Interaction adaptation theory (IAT) was conceptualized to explain behavior that is "mindful, intentional, and symbolic" (Burgoon, LaPoire, & Rosenthal, 1995, p. 11). IAT assumes that adaptation is a systematic pattern of behavior that is in direct response to the interactive pattern of another communicator (Burgoon et al., 1995). Therefore, there are no random adaptations when people interact with each other. This suggests that all adaptation is considered intentional. IAT also assumes that our relationships with each other are based on both verbal and nonverbal messages that are adapted to the behavior of the interaction partner. Adaptation reflects the degree to which we alter our behavior in response to the behavior of another person. Further, adaptation during interaction serves as a signal to the interactants and observers of the interaction as to the nature or basis of the relationship between the two communicators (White, 2008). That is, the way people engage in adaptive behavior during an interaction relays important relational information that can include the type of relationship, degree of positive/negative affect between the interactants as well as power and status differences.

The two adaptation patterns that people utilize when in an interaction reflect patterns that either **reciprocate** or **compensate**. Adaptation that "reciprocates" reflects matching behavior or reciprocating the behavior of the other person. This is similar to the Communication Accommodation Theory concept of converging our speech patterns to the other person to show liking and affiliation (see Chapter 7). Convergence means we adapt our interaction patterns to match those of the other person. Matching, within the IAT framework,

interaction adaptation theory   A theory of how we alter our behavior in response to the behavior of another person.

refers to both verbal and nonverbal behavior and is not restricted to just verbal or paraverbal behavior as it is in Communication Accommodation Theory. To illustrate how IAT accommodations function, consider a scenario where a close friend is very upset and discloses to you that their mother is gravely ill. When communicating with this friend, you will probably use matching adaptation reflecting behavior that is somber, empathetic, and caring.

Adaptation that "compensates" reflects the "balancing out" of the other's behavior and seeks to represent the "whole spectrum" of the interaction. An example of this would be a friend who is very excited and calls us to say that they are putting their entire life savings into the buying and selling of real estate based on an investment product that they had purchased from an infomercial they just viewed on television. In this case, our interaction pattern may be one of a cautious, reserved, and skeptical tone, thus not matching the euphoric, excited, and determined patterns of our friend. This concept of compensation is also reflective of the yin and yang concept found in Chinese philosophy. The yin and yang concept reflects the intertwining of opposing forces. In the current example, your behavior is cautious, reserved, and skeptical and is exhibited to compensate for your friend's overly euphoric, excited, and determined behavior.

Although adaptation is considered nonrandom (i.e., intentional), IAT treats interaction adaptation as a primal survival need. That is, we choose our adaptation in a way that satisfies survival needs and seeks to establish important links to other people, thus ensuring or significantly increasing our survival (i.e., strength in numbers). There is more to adaptation than the simple idea that we engage in reciprocating or compensating patterns or we do not. The theory also speaks to the amount to which we engage in adaptation. The degree of adaptation is influenced by both the role we play in society (i.e., societal norms) and idiosyncratic personal preferences. For example, a person who is a mortician will probably have a much more restricted degree of adaptation than a professional athlete due to the fact that societal norms for a mortician's behavior are far more conservative than they are for the professional athlete.

IAT assumes that several main factors (both socially and personally derived) influence a person's needs, wants, and expectations of other people when engaged in interaction. More specifically, when we first encounter someone in conversation, we bring with us a host of **requirements**, **expectations**, and **desires** with regard to the person and the specific interaction conversation. These three components of the theory were originally conceptualized as being hierarchically organized so that "requirements" influence "expectations," which in turn influence "desires." The theory maintains conversational requirements are a person's basic psychological/physiological needs related to approach-avoidance behavior (a.k.a. the fight-or-flight biological activation of the brain; see Chapter 4). These requirements are believed to be primarily unconscious and are said to influence our conversational expectations. The expectations are formed by societal norms of appropriateness as well as the degree of knowledge that we have developed from past interactions with that specific person. These expectations, in turn, influence our desire, which are "highly personalized and reflect things such as one's personality and other individual differences" (White, 2008, p. 193). This hierarchical approach was later refuted by the research findings of Floyd and Burgoon (1999). However, the three components, although not hierarchically organized, are believed to be highly interdependent and that requirements, expectations, and desires can be weighted differently based on the specific interaction. In other words, in one interaction, expectations may play more of a role than desires or conversational requirements, whereas in another interaction, another factor may be weighted more heavily. For example, a person may have a great need to avoid a particular person (i.e., conversational requirement) that is so strong that this need for avoidance supersedes our expectations (i.e., what is socially appropriate behavior in that situation) and our desires (i.e., individual interests).

The three components—requirements, expectations, desires—combine to form a unique collection of individualized communication information known as a person's **interaction position**. According to Burgoon et al. (1995), an interaction position represents "a net assessment of what is needed, anticipated, and preferred as the dyadic interaction pattern in a situation" (p. 266). By understanding a person's interaction position, people have better predictability about how one interprets a communication situation and the likely communicative behaviors that they will enact.

Interpersonal adaptation theory offers two basic predictions about a person's response to behavior and is based on the dynamic relationship between the interaction position and the actual behavior that is enacted (Burgoon & Ebesu Hubbard, 2005).

- P1: When the interaction position is more positively valenced than the actual behavior, the interpersonal pattern is divergence, compensation, or maintenance.

- P2: When the actual behavior is more positively valenced than the interaction position, the anticipated interpersonal pattern is convergence, matching, or reciprocity.

In terms of how this would work in explaining communication, consider the example of a supervisor who is about to conduct a meeting with a subordinate concerning the quarterly performance review of the subordinate. The supervisor has, throughout their career, engaged in many conversations with subordinates concerning both positive and negative aspects of their performance. According to IAT, any given conversation is influenced by the supervisor's psychological and/or physiological needs at any given time. These may take the form of the need to mentor, need for affiliation, or need to control. This would constitute the supervisor's conversational "requirements." Second, the supervisor has an "expectation" about how employees generally respond to negative evaluations and even more specific expectations about how a particular employee will respond to such information (e.g., anger, sorrow, remorse, embarrassment). Finally, the supervisor has a "desire" for employees to be open, involved, and eager to make needed changes to improve performance. These three components constitute the supervisor's "interaction position."

Imagine that a subordinate who has had a history of poor performance and a generally negative attitude is about to come into the supervisor's office for the performance evaluation meeting. Based on the supervisor's interaction position described earlier, the supervisor would expect a hostile and generally emotionally charged interaction. Therefore, the supervisor would prepare herself to console the subordinate and try to give some comforting words. However, imagine further that when the subordinate arrives for the review, he is proactive in strategies to improve his performance and optimistic about his future contribution to the department and the organization as a whole. Interaction Adaptation Theory predicts that the supervisor will have an interaction style of convergence, matching, and reciprocity due to the fact that the subordinate was more positively valenced than the supervisor's interaction position. Thus, P2 is what would be predicted for such a communication situation.

According to White (2008), important research directions in the application of interaction adaptation theory include romantic and intimate relationships and the particular communicative exchanges that occur within these relationships (e.g., problematic interactions). For example, when studying deception in interpersonal interactions, White and Burgoon (2001) found support for IAT in that the interaction position of both the deceiver and truth-tellers influenced their initial behavior. That is, both the deceiver and truth-tellers were affected by the behavior of the interaction partner.

Strengths and Weaknesses of IAT

One of the many strengths of IAT is that it conceptualizes expectancies as being formed by personal and biological factors as well as the degree to which these factors are further influenced by actual communicative behavior. IAT can be considered a cousin of expectancy violations theory discussed earlier in this chapter as it accounts not only for the expectations of the communicators but also integrates actual communicative behavior in the prediction of interaction behavior. The primary weakness of IAT lies in the fact that it is a relatively new theory with modest empirical support. However, the evidence that does exist lends support for the assumptions of IAT and holds exciting implications for interpersonal scholars.

NONVERBAL IMMEDIACY AND COGNITIVE VALENCE THEORY

Imagine the following scenario. You have been waiting at the doctor's office for about half an hour and have finally been called into the examination room. Your level of anxiety is already high, as you wonder if your lower abdominal upset is serious. After waiting another ten minutes in the examination room, you hear a knock on the door and the doctor enters. The doctor looks at you very briefly and then turns away. He takes a seat at the other end of the examination room. He appears somewhat tense as he asks you to identify the nature of your medical concern. During his questioning, he speaks with a dull and monotonous voice, does not smile very much if at all, uses very few gestures, and avoids eye contact throughout the interview. He asks you to sit on the examination table but fails to mention what will happen next. As the medical interview progresses, you are more worried and concerned than you were before the doctor came in.

Perhaps you can relate to the scenario outlined. Many patients describe such experiences during initial interaction with their physician. Patients often describe such interactions as being uncomfortable at best and frightening at worst, even if their medical condition was easily diagnosed and treated. Quite often patients delay return visits to the doctor or seek alternative health-care options rather than subject themselves to a repeat of this scenario. The anxiety and frustration can happen in communication encounters in other contexts as well, from close interpersonal interactions (such as a first date) to relatively impersonal communication interactions (such as communication with a salesperson in an automobile dealership).

The degree of closeness between individuals is an important factor influencing the ease of communication. Researchers have identified and labeled a set of nonverbal behaviors that influence the degree of perceived closeness. **Immediacy behaviors** is the term used to describe a set of messages (both verbal and nonverbal) that signal feelings of warmth, closeness, and involvement with another person (Andersen, 1999, p. 187). Immediacy behaviors can result in positive or negative interpersonal communication outcomes, depending on how they are manifested (Richmond & McCroskey, 2000b).

Although originally conceived by the psychologist Albert Mehrabian (1971), research and theory-building efforts in identifying and understanding the impact of nonverbal immediacy has come largely from communication scholars such as Peter Andersen, Janis Andersen, Virginia Richmond, and James

immediacy behaviors
Messages that signal feelings of warmth, closeness, and involvement with another person.

McCroskey. Peter Andersen (1985, 1999) suggested the following four functions of immediacy behaviors:

- Immediacy behaviors signal to others that we are *available* for communication and make others feel included in the interaction.

- Immediacy behaviors signal *involvement*—that we are interested in those with whom we are communicating. It makes receiver(s) feel that we are closer to them. Immediacy behaviors that signal involvement can be something as benign as a wave or as intimate as a kiss or prolonged eye contact.

- Immediacy behaviors *stimulate our senses* both psychologically and physiologically. Andersen argued that blood pressure, heart rate, and brain activity are increased when we receive immediacy cues from another person.

- Immediacy behaviors communicate *closeness and warmth.* In positive relationships immediacy behaviors (such as looking another person in the eye or smiling) bring people closer. Lack of nonverbal immediacy can do just the opposite.

What are nonverbal immediacy behaviors? One powerful set of immediacy cues is associated with eye behavior, specifically *eye contact* and *gaze.* When someone locks eyes with you, they offer an invitation to engage in communication and to interact. Gaze functions as a primary immediacy cue in a number of contexts including relational and instructional communication.

Proxemics, the use of **personal space**, is the most frequently studied nonverbal immediacy cue; closer proxemic distances convey greater feelings of immediacy. Recall in our earlier example that the physician sat at the far end of the room, conveying a sense of avoidance rather than immediacy. Other proxemically oriented immediacy behaviors include interacting on the same physical plane (the same level) as your receiver and leaning forward when communicating with another.

personal space Zones of space that surround us: intimate, casual-personal, socioconsultative, public.

Touch has also been identified as a powerful nonverbal immediacy cue, especially in intimate relationships. Perceptions of touch, however, are modified by the nature of the interpersonal relationship (the level of intimacy), the culture a person conies from (some cultures use more touch than others), personal norms concerning touch, and the context in which the individuals are communicating (on the job or in a romantic setting, for example).

Kinesics, body motion and movements, comprise a fourth set of immediacy behaviors. Kinesic behaviors that communicate immediacy include facial expressions such as smiling, head nods (signaling agreement), gestures that show approval, open body positions (e.g., arms open, head up, legs not crossed), and speaking with someone while facing them directly (as opposed to turning away from them).

Paralinguistics (vocalics—not what we say, but *how* we use our voice to express feelings) is a fifth set of immediacy cues. Vocal synchrony (adjusting your paralinguistic style to fit or match the person with whom you are communicating) is another type of vocalic immediacy cue. Perhaps you can recall an instance when you spoke more softly to match the tones of the person with whom you were talking. One of the authors recalls that his father occasionally took on the accent of the person he was talking to in an effort to promote immediacy and to achieve vocal convergence (see our discussion of communication accommodation theory in Chapter 7). When discussing this cluster of nonverbal immediacy behaviors, it is important to point out that individuals do not receive these behaviors in a fragmented fashion.

What causes a person to communicate using this cluster of immediacy behaviors? Peter Andersen (1999, 1998, 1985) suggested several antecedents that either promote or dampen the exhibition of immediacy behaviors. A powerful antecedent (cause) of exhibiting nonverbal immediacy (or not) is a person's *culture.* Certain cultures have been called "contact cultures," and people from these cultures tend to use more nonverbal immediacy behaviors when they communicate. That is, they may use more gestures, touch each other more, and stand closer together. A second cause of immediacy behavior is the *valence of the interpersonal relationship,* which refers to whether the relationship is seen as positive or negative. We tend to exhibit of a lot of immediacy behaviors (e.g., closer distance, greater use of gestures, greater eye contact) with someone whom we like. A third cause of immediacy behavior is the *perception or the stage of the relationship;* as relationships develop, more immediacy cues are exhibited. *Individual differences and traits* constitute another cause of immediacy behaviors. Factors such as biological sex, orientation to touch, and communication and personality traits can influence the exhibition of nonverbal immediacy behaviors. *The nature of the situation* or environment can influence expressions of immediacy. Touching someone in public may be perceived as situationally inappropriate; however, the same type of touch might be seen as appropriate if you were in more private surroundings. Finally, the *temporary state* of the individual can influence the exhibition of immediacy behaviors. Feeling physically ill, in a "bad mood," or "stressed out" can dampen one's exhibition of nonverbal immediacy cues.

What are the consequences of engaging in nonverbal immediacy cues? A great deal of communication research during the last two decades supports the potency of employing nonverbal immediacy in a variety of contexts. One of the contexts in which the exhibition of nonverbal immediacy has a significant impact is instructional communication. In one of the first studies to introduce the immediacy construct in the communication discipline, Janis Andersen (1979) found that teacher immediacy favorably influenced students' attitudes toward the teacher and the course. Highly immediate teachers increased student liking for both high school and college courses (Flax, Kearney, McCroskey,

& Richmond, 1986). Teachers highly skilled in immediacy behaviors were perceived as higher in competence, trustworthiness, and caring (Thweatt & McCroskey, 1998). The influence of teacher immediacy does not appear to be bound by culture. Increases in teacher immediacy resulted in increased learning across four cultures including American (U.S.), Australian, Finnish, and Puerto Rican (McCroskey, Sallinen, Fayer, Richmond, & Barraclough, 1996).

Research in the health-care context has also pointed to the advantages of nonverbal immediacy behaviors. Patients' perceptions of their physicians' nonverbal immediacy behaviors influence their reported satisfaction with those physicians (Conlee, Olvera, & Vagim, 1993). In addition, physicians who were perceived as immediate had patients who reported lower levels of fear (Richmond, Smith, Heisel, & McCroskey, 2001). Doctor–patient relationships might yield very different outcomes if the physician uses more nonverbal immediacy behaviors.

Nonverbal immediacy also operates in the organizational context, especially in superior–subordinate communication. Immediacy stimulates a reciprocity of immediacy; subordinates report more satisfaction with supervisors who exhibit nonverbal immediacy and engage in more immediacy behaviors themselves (Richmond & McCroskey, 2000a). Supervisors who use immediacy cues make subordinates feel more valued, respected, and relationally attractive (Koermer, Goldstein, & Fortson, 1993).

Marital relationships also appear to be influenced by immediacy cues. Research has found that "individuals who engage in nonverbal immediacy behaviors tend to be more inclined to be liked by their marital partners than are those who are not nonverbally immediate" (Hinkle, 1999, p. 87). In addition, use of immediacy behaviors and liking for your spouse appear to persist throughout the duration of a marriage (Hinkle, 1999).

In Chapter 4, we introduced the communibiological paradigm for the study of human communication. One assumption of this new paradigm is that people are born with a set of biologically determined temperaments that are consistent across life. These temperaments (traits) are expressed as behavioral tendencies that differentiate people. Recent research has demonstrated that use of immediacy behaviors may indeed be related to aspects of an individual's temperament. The trait of extraversion (i.e., having more outgoing tendencies, higher levels of sociability) was found to be strongly related to the perceived use of nonverbal immediacy (Cole, 2000, p. 92).

An Extension of Nonverbal Immediacy— Cognitive Valence Theory

Working from an interactionist approach to studying communication and relationships, Peter Andersen (1999) considered the question, "When one person increases intimacy or immediacy, how can you explain the response of their partner?" (p. 454). **Cognitive valence theory** (CVT) maintains that when a person in an interaction perceives an increase in immediacy behaviors "cognitive schemata" are activated. Cognitive schemata are expectations about the consequences of behaving in a certain way that allow people to interpret, explain, and act upon information (Andersen, 1998, p. 47).

An important component in CVT is *arousal.* Arousal is "the degree to which a person is stimulated or activated" (Andersen, 1999, p. 161). When arousal is increased, there is a tendency to engage in more nonverbal immediacy behaviors, which builds even greater levels of arousal. Levels of arousal that are too low produce virtually no change in the relationship. However, too much arousal can lead to negative relational outcomes. CVT suggests that moderate levels of arousal (found in most interactions) are most likely to activate cognitive schemata.

CVT suggests that relationships usually develop when individuals communicate using immediacy; that is, one person sends messages using immediacy cues, and the other person reciprocates. Interactions such as these are called "positively valenced." Sometimes, however, immediacy behaviors exhibited by one person are not seen favorably by another; they are instead "negatively valenced." CVT also addresses the question, "What happens when efforts to increase relational closeness by using nonverbal immediacy are rejected?" If the cognitive schemata are positively valenced, the theory states positive relationship outcomes will result; if cognitive schemata are negatively valenced, negative relationship outcomes are more likely.

According to CVT, six cognitive schemata (similar to the factors that influence immediacy discussed earlier) form the basis of whether the relationship will become positively or negatively changed as a result of an increase in immediacy and intimacy (Andersen, 1999).

1. **Cultural Appropriateness.** Cultures vary in the degree to which they use immediacy behaviors. As we have mentioned, some cultures use touch more than others. Noncontact cultures (Japan, for instance) prefer little touch; contact cultures (such as Greece) prefer greater amounts of touch. When communicating with a person from Japan, using a great deal of touch would be culturally inappropriate and thus negatively valenced.

2. **Personal Predispositions.** Personality and communication traits (such as dogmatism, self-esteem, communication apprehension, and interaction involvement), as well as personal predispositions such as touch-avoidance, influence reactions to increases in immediacy behaviors. For example, an increase in eye contact might be seen as positive for an extrovert, while the same behavior may be negatively valenced for the person high in communication apprehension.

3. **Interpersonal Valence.** According to Andersen (1999), "interpersonal valence is the evaluation of another person's qualities, not one's

cognitive valence theory
A perceived increase in immediacy behaviors from one person in a relationship activates expectations.

relationship with that person" (p. 232). CVT suggests that an increase in immediacy by someone who has qualities we admire (for example, credibility or physical attractiveness) will be positively valenced, whereas the same behavior will be negatively valenced if it comes from someone whose qualities we evaluate less positively.

4. **Relational Appropriateness.** These schemata deal with expectancies about where one individual thinks a relationship should be heading, the "relational trajectory." According to CVT, nonverbal immediacy behaviors that correspond to the anticipation of greater relationship intimacy should be seen positively. According to Andersen (1999), "the key to relational success is to anticipate your partner's desired relational trajectory and to behave accordingly" (pp. 232–233). If your relational partner has expressed a desire for the relationship to become more intimate, then engaging in immediacy behaviors should result in positive outcomes. If you engage in more touch, greater eye gaze, and less proxemic distance, your partner will likely judge those immediacy behaviors positively because they fall along his or her perceived relational trajectory (i.e., the desire for increased intimacy). On the other hand, immediacy behaviors that do not correspond to another person's anticipated relational trajectory will likely be seen negatively.

5. **Situational Appropriateness.** Immediacy behaviors that are inappropriate to the situation or context are likely to be negatively valenced. For example, behavior that would be acceptable in a romantic restaurant could be considered inappropriate in a college classroom.

6. **Psychological or Physical State.** These schemata "represent intrapersonal, internal dispositions (Andersen, 1999, p. 235) and refer to our moods, our temporal physical conditions (e.g., having a bad cold or flu), and temporal emotional and psychological states such as feeling happy or sad, tired, or excited. Getting a costly traffic ticket, receiving an unexpected grade of "A" on a course paper, receiving a compliment on your appearance from a valued other, or having a fight with your roommate can influence how you will react to immediacy and intimacy behaviors. CVT suggests that, in general, positive psychological or physical states are related to positive reactions to immediacy and intimacy behaviors, whereas negative psychological or physical states are related to negative reactions to immediacy and intimacy behaviors.

If the immediacy behaviors exhibited by person A match person B's six cognitive schemata, those immediacy behaviors will be positively valenced and positive relationship outcomes will ensue. Relationships develop based on a number of factors, including the degree of preferred closeness. CVT suggests that for relationships to become closer and more satisfying, one must match the relationship partner's cultural, personal, interpersonal, situational, state, and relational schemata (Andersen, 1998, 1999).

INTERPERSONAL DECEPTION THEORY

Deception is a special form of communication that involves much more behavioral management than other forms of communication. What exactly is deception? According to Burgoon and Buller (2008), deception includes "not just bald-faced lies but also omissions, equivocations, hedges, and the like" (p. 227). Deception is so common in today's society that it is believed that over one third of conversations involve deception, with the average person telling two lies per day (DePaulo, Kashy, Kirkendol, Wyer, & Epstein, 1996). Deception in this case can have relatively little impact, such as telling a friend that you enjoy their artwork when indeed you do not, or more significant such as telling a romantic partner that you were faithful to them when you were not.

Interpersonal deception theory (IDT) assumes that both people in a communicative situation utilize a variety of strategies to achieve particular interpersonal goals. Burgoon and Buller (2008) argued that "it is cognitively demanding to engage in conversation, and the demands can escalate when one decides to deceive or suspects deceit" (p. 235). Given that interpersonal communication is shaped by the normative expectations of the interactants (e.g., honesty, reciprocity, goodwill), any deviation from normal patterns (i.e., engaging in deception), when recognized, will influence the interpretation of the receiver. That is, when a person believes they are being deceived, the perception of, and attention to, the sender's message changes considerably.

Deception, as conceptualized by IDT, is no different than any other form of communication in that all forms of communication are believed to satisfy particular goals and are adaptive in nature. Therefore, regardless of whether a person is being deceptive or truthful, the universal goals of effectiveness, appropriateness, and so forth are still being pursued. Burgoon and Buller (2008) argued that because deception is an interpersonal act, people will try to use a variety of communication tactics to achieve any given interaction goal. The variety and effectiveness of communication tactics will depend on the person's communication competence when using such tactics. Some people are simply more effective at strategic communication than others.

Another important concept of IDT is the idea that to be an effective deceiver, one must manage a large amount of information in an effective way to be successful. In a study investigating the role of information in deceptive communication, Burgoon, Buller, Guerrero, Afifi, and Feldman (1996) found that deceivers not only have to make strategic decisions as to what information to omit, avoid, or distort, but also make decisions as to the style with which the

> **interpersonal deception theory**   A theory of deception in interpersonal communication that bases its predictions about outcomes on the characteristics of the source, receiver, context, message, feedback, and channel.

information is relayed. This can include style components of message relaying, which include, among others, veracity (authenticity) and completeness of the message. This is further complicated by the myriad nonverbal elements that need to be manipulated successfully for the deceiver to be seen as credible and truthful.

The final key assumption of IDT, which is radically different from previous models of deception such as the leakage hypothesis (Ekman, 1985) and the four-factor theory (Zuckerman, DePaulo, & Rosenthal, 1981), assumes the receiver is active in, and coregulates, the deceptive encounter. Generally speaking, traditional research on deception has treated the receiver as passive in the process. In this tradition the deceptive messages are believed to "do things" to people whether they want them to or not. Buller and Burgoon (2008) argued

> Receivers are active information processors whose "antennae" are tuned into the actions of senders; who experience greater cognitive difficulty, unpleasantness, and vigilance when their suspicions are aroused; who provide various forms of feedback to senders that can range from acceptance to skepticism to outright disbelief; and who themselves can actively and strategically adapt their own styles as their suspicions wax and wane. (p. 229)

Buller and Burgoon over a fifteen-year research program have developed twenty-one propositions for the theory of interpersonal deception.* A proposition, as defined in Chapter 2, is a statement about the relationships between concepts of a theory (for examples of this longitudinal body of research, see Buller, Burgoon, White, and Ebesu, 1994; Buller, Strzyzewski, and Hunsacker, 1991; Burgoon, Buller, and Floyd, 2002).

- **PROPOSITION 1:** Context features of deceptive interchanges that systematically affect sender and receiver cognitions and behaviors are the demands of the conversational task.
- **PROPOSITION 2:** Relational features of deceptive interchanges that systematically influence sender and receiver cognitions and behaviors are familiarity and relationship valence (i.e., importance of the relationship).

Propositions 1 and 2 are ubiquitous (universal) statements that affect all deceptive encounters and are contextual and relational in nature. That is, context refers to both **interactivity demands** and **task demands**. Activity demands reflect the degree to which messages are connected to previous messages, occur in real time, and number of verbal and nonverbal channels available to interactants. Simply put, a context that is considered high in interactivity demands would be influenced by the previous messages sent by the communicators, occur instantaneously and simultaneously (e.g., face-to-face interaction), and utilize most if not all available verbal and nonverbal aspects of communication. Task

* Propositions used with permission of Sage Publications, Inc., from Engaging Theories in Interpersonal Communication *by Leslie Baxter & Dawn Braithwaite, 2008; permission conveyed through Copyright Clearance Center, Inc.*

demands reflect the degree to which the conversation is mentally and/or emotionally involved for the participant (Burgoon & Buller, 2008). As indicated earlier, truthful interactions are cognitively demanding only to be seen as even more demanding when deception is detected.

⬭ **PROPOSITION 3:** Interactive contexts and positively toned relationships are associated with higher expectations that a sender is truthful.

⬭ **PROPOSITION 4:** The more receivers expect truthfulness and the more they are familiar with the deceivers or deceptive behavior, the less the deceivers fear detection.

The third and fourth propositions concern how quality of the relationship, partner familiarity, and interpersonal trust all influence the deceptive encounter. These factors also affect the emotional and cognitive states of both the deceiver and the receiver. That is, the receiver may have positive feelings toward the deceiver and, as such, is more willing to be trusting that information is indeed true. On the other hand, the deceiver may have a high level of positive feeling toward the receiver and thus become anxious when communicating because the deceiver may believe that he/she is engaging in deception with someone whom they care greatly about (i.e., experience a level of cognitive dissonance). For example, if a husband confronts his wife about her drinking, she may engage in successful deception yet feel terrible at the reality that she lied to her husband.

⬭ **PROPOSITION 5:** Deceivers engage in both strategic and nonstrategic activities. Strategic activity includes managing information content of messages, associated nonverbal behavior, and overall image. Nonstrategic activity reveals arousal, negative or dampened affect, depressed involvement, and impaired speech.

⬭ **PROPOSITION 6:** Interactive contexts heighten strategic activity and lessen nonstrategic activity over time.

⬭ **PROPOSITION 7:** Deceiving for self-gain prompts more strategic activity and nonstrategic behavior than deceiving for the benefit of others.

⬭ **PROPOSITION 8:** The more receivers expect truthfulness, the less deceivers are motivated to behave strategically.

⬭ **PROPOSITION 9:** Greater familiarity prompts more strategic and nonstrategic activity by senders.

⬭ **PROPOSITION 10:** Skilled communicators display more strategic activity and less nonstrategic activity than less-skilled communicators.

Buller and Burgoon (1996) and Burgoon and Buller (2004) asserted that Propositions 5 and 6 concern behavioral displays that people utilize during a deceptive episode. The fifth proposition concretizes the belief that deceptive communication (and communication in general) is both intentional (i.e., strategic and controlled messages) and unintentional (i.e., nonstrategic and often unconsciously sent) in nature. Propositions 6 to 10 reflect how strategic and nonstrategic communication change outcomes. Changes in communication patterns are believed to be influenced by: (a) whether or not the communicative context is interactive in nature; (b) the degree to which the relationship is familiar and if the relationship is positively or negatively toned; and (c) the particular motivations that the deceiver had, the degree of communication skills (i.e., communication competence) possessed by the deceiver, as well as the degree of suspicion that the receiver has about being deceived.

> PROPOSITION 11: Receivers are more likely to judge senders as credible when the context is interactive, when receivers have high truth biases, and when senders are skilled communicators.

> PROPOSITION 12: Receivers are less likely to detect deception when the context is interactive, when receivers have truth biases, and when senders are skilled communicators.

> PROPOSITION 13: Receivers are less likely to judge senders as credible when sender communication deviates from expected patterns.

> PROPOSITION 14: Receivers are more likely to detect deception when sender communication deviates from expected patterns, when receivers are familiar with sender information and behavior, and when receivers have strong decoding skills.

Propositions 11 to 14 reflect the receiver's perception of the source's credibility and the degree of accuracy of detecting deception. Burgoon and Buller (2008) argued that the same factors that allow deceivers to act strategically (i.e., medium interactivity, receiver's truth bias, and the deceiver's communication competence) should result in the deceiver being perceived as more credible and more likely to evade detection. The degree to which a deceiver acts in normative ways or expected patterns of behavior, the more likely the deceiver evades detection and can be seen as credible and truthful. On the other hand, when an interactive medium is not used, there is a bias toward deception (i.e., the receiver expects the sender to be lying). For example, consider the act of calling in sick to work. It is much easier to "sound" sick over the phone or by e-mail (media of low interactivity) than it is to actually "look" sick in a face-to-face interaction with your boss (high interactivity). The idea is that the greater the interactivity, the more the deceiver is given the benefit of the doubt or the benefit that they are being truthful. Further, if the deceiver is not a skilled strategic communicator, which results in awkward and unexpected ways of behaving, the probability of deception detection by the receiver increases.

> PROPOSITION 15: Suspicion evokes changes in both strategic and non-strategic behavior by receiver.

- **PROPOSITION 16:** Senders perceive suspicion when it is present such that (a) deviations from expected receiver behavior and (b) receiver behavior signaling disbelief, uncertainty, or the need for additional information increase sender perceptions of suspicion.

- **PROPOSITION 17:** Suspicion (perceived or actual) evokes changes in both strategic and nonstrategic behavior by senders.

Propositions 15 to 17 concern the influence that receiver suspicion has on the deception process and resulting communication behavior. Any alteration in the receiver's behavior that is detected by the sender (e.g., altering verbal or nonverbal behavior as a prolonged stare or a clearing of throat that may be interpreted as a degree of deception suspicion) will result in the sender altering the deceptive message to reinstate the perception of believability. This alteration of sender behavior (in relation to the receiver) is also believed to include nondeceptive or truthful communication as well (Burgoon & Buller, 2008). Recall in Chapter 1 the systems perspective and concept of homeostasis, which reflects a dynamic balance of a system that, when upset, will bring about changes to reestablish itself. Applying this concept to IDT, the altered behavior of the receiver will bring about alterations in the deceiver in an effort to reestablish the perception of believability.

- **PROPOSITION 18:** Deception and suspicion displays change over time.

- **PROPOSITION 19:** Reciprocity is the dominant interaction adaptation pattern between senders and receivers during interpersonal deception.

Propositions 18 and 19 concern the ever-changing behavioral and cognitive patterns of both the sender and receiver during a deceptive communication encounter. Because both are engaged in a relationship, there is an evolution of strategies and tactics that takes place. In other words, each person in the encounter is in a constant state of adaptation, whether strategic or nonstrategic in direct response the other person. This reciprocity of behavioral alteration between sender and receiver has an evolutionary quality to it.

The final two propositions, 20 and 21, address outcomes of the deception process. More specifically, the perceptions of outcomes regarding the sender (perception of successfully deceiving) and receiver (perception of believability). Burgoon and Buller (2008) argued that the beliefs of the receiver, the receiver's competence level in decoding messages as well as the sender's most recent communication are very influential in the outcomes of the deceptive encounter.

- **PROPOSITION 20:** Final sender credibility and receiver detection accuracy are functions of (a) final receiver cognitions (suspicion, truth biases), (b) receiver decoding skill, and (c) final sender behavioral displays.

- **PROPOSITION 21:** Sender-perceived deception success is a function of perceived suspicion and final receiver behavioral displays.

THEMES	PROPOSITION(S)
Context and Relationship Influences	1 and 2
Relationship Quality, Partner Familiarity, and Interpersonal Trust	3, 4
Influence of Changes in Strategic and Nonstrategic Communication on Deception Outcomes	6, 7, 8, 9, 10
Source Credibility and Accuracy of Detecting Deception	11, 12, 13, 14
Receiver Suspicion and Influence on the Deceptive Communication Process	15, 16, 17
Longitudinal Changes in the Deception Communication Processes	18, 19
Possible Outcomes of the Deception Process	20, 21

Figure 8.1

Interpersonal deception theory propositional themes.

Interpersonal deception theory is one of the more comprehensive and developed theories available to communication theorists interested in deceptive communication. This is due to attention IDT affords to most components of the original SMCR model of communication developed by Berlo (see Chapter 3). More specifically, IDT considers characteristics of the source, receiver, context, message, feedback, and channel. Since its inception, the theory has continued to be expanded and elaborated as new influences in the deception process emerge. We expect that the influence of new technology such as text messaging and social networking sites will also serve to prompt IDT theorists to extend the existing propositions to account for the ever-increasing media choices for interacting and, thus, increasing our media choice with which to engage in deceptive communication.

SUMMARY

Nonverbal behavior functions best in communicating affect; it is highly believable. The meaning of nonverbal behaviors depends on the communication context. Similarly, our expectations of appropriate nonverbal behaviors depend on the situation and the relationship between individuals. The authors believe symbolic activity is a necessary condition for nonverbal behavior to be considered communicative. Without an intention to convey a message, the behavior is usually a symptom. We use nonverbal communication to perform a number of important functions: to express messages that are uncomfortable to present verbally, to form impressions, to clarify and establish the nature of the relationship between the people who are communicating, to regulate the interaction between people, to persuade people by conveying a basis for trust, and to reinforce and modify verbal messages. Research on nonverbal immediacy and expectancy violations helps us understand the effects of various nonverbal behaviors. Our responses to violations of expectations are determined by our expectancies our interpretation and evaluation of the behavior; the valence of the violation (positive or negative) and the reward level of the person with whom we are communicating. These ideas were explored in the theories covered: expectancy violations theory, interaction adaptation theory, nonverbal immediacy and cognitive valance theory, and interpersonal deception theory.

KEY TERMS

cognitive valence theory

emotional leakage

expectancy violations theory

eye behavior

functions of nonverbal
   communication

immediacy behaviors

interaction adaptation theory

interpersonal deception theory

nonverbal response matching

personal space

proxemics

self-monitoring of expressive
   behavior

vocalics/paralanguage

The idea that communication is highly contextual is widely accepted. A message that has one meaning in one context can take on a much different meaning in another context. Chapter 9 discusses theory building in interpersonal communication contexts. This is one of the most active research areas in the field. We discuss uncertainty reduction theory, which has had perhaps the most significant impact on interpersonal communication recently. Next we discuss predicted outcome value theory and its relationship to uncertainty reduction theory, attraction theories and relational development, the theory of interpersonal motives, a systems model of relational interaction, and a stage theory of relationship development.

Chapter 10 explains theory building in group contexts. Problem-solving discussion groups have been the major focus of study in the field of communication. The chapter first examines ideas about group size, the various types of groups, group roles, leadership, conflict, and pressure to conform in small groups. Then, three theories are discussed: functional theory of group decision quality, the theory of groupthink, and the multiple sequence model of group decisions.

Organizational communication is examined in Chapter 11. The evolution of organizational communication theory is traced through three major approaches in the field of management: scientific management, human relations management, and human resource management. Next, several theories of leadership are discussed: trait, situational, exchange, functional, and transformational. This is followed by the major theories of worker motivation: hierarchy of needs, hygiene, and acquired needs. Organizational socialization is viewed from several perspectives taken in the organizational assimilation research. Organizational culture is illustrated by the extensive line of research conducted on climate in organizations. Finally, theories of organizational ethics are examined. This has become an increasingly important area of the communication field in recent years. Major perspectives on ethics along with the prevalent theories are discussed.

Chapter 12 identifies basic questions explored by mass media researchers. After reviewing early theory-building efforts in mass communication, we discuss the functions of mass media in society. Next, we present agenda-setting theory, which addresses the powerful influence of the media. The theory of parasocial interaction, uses and gratifications, cultivation theory, spiral of silence, and media dependency theory probe the effects of the media on users.

Chapter 13 offers a review of seminal theory-building efforts in what we term the tributary contexts of family, health, intercultural, and political communication. The chapter begins with a conceptualization of family communication, followed by a discussion of characteristics of family communication. Systems and human action (rules) approaches to studying family communication are reviewed. Three theoretical developments in family communication are presented: a typology of couple types, communication privacy management theory, and the argumentative skill deficiency model of intrafamily violence. After a discussion of functions of communication in health, we discuss important research directions in provider-client communication, the health belief model, and uncertainty management theory. This section ends with a theory of organizational information applied to health communication. Next we present a discussion of intercultural communication along with three theories: anxiety/uncertainty management theory, face negotiation theory, and integrative theory of cross-cultural adaptation. In the final section, we see the application of important theories in the political context: symbolic convergence theory, agenda-setting theory, and constructivism.

Interpersonal Contexts

During the late 1950s and early 1960s, few communication scholars engaged in research and theory building about interpersonal relationships. Research in interpersonal interaction was conducted primarily by sociologists, social psychologists, and anthropologists. When the study of dyadic (one-on-one) communication began in earnest, researchers investigated how communication could be used to develop and improve interpersonal relationships with friends, lovers, and spouses. The first textbooks in interpersonal communication appeared in the early 1970s (Giffin & Patton, 1971; Keltner, 1970; McCroskey, Larson, & Knapp, 1971). Later in the decade, the communication discipline experienced a surge in researching and theorizing about interpersonal communication and relationship development.

This chapter will attempt to illustrate the variety of theory-building options available by showing the differences between laws, rules, and systems approaches to communication. Recall that advocates of the *law-governed* approach to communication theory emphasize the causes of interpersonal communication. *Rules and human action* researchers and theorists stress the influence of individual choice in following rules to accomplish a goal. *Systems* scholars accentuate the interaction, interdependence and coordination of behavior between individuals. They examine the entire "interpersonal system," which can range in size from the friend–lover, friend–friend, or husband–wife dyad to a larger extended family system or social network. As each theory is described, you will see how the underlying perspective shaped the development of the theory.

UNCERTAINTY REDUCTION THEORY

uncertainty reduction theory   A theory that explains and predicts interpersonal communication during the beginning of an interaction.

One example of a theory developed from the *law-governed* approach is **uncertainty reduction theory** (URT) (Berger, 1979; Berger & Calabrese, 1975). URT was initially presented as a series of axioms (universal truths that do not require proof) and theorems (propositions assumed to be true) that describe the relationships between uncertainty and several communication factors. Recall that one goal of theories is to help us control our environment. URT explains and predicts interpersonal communication during the *beginning* of an interaction. One core assumption of this theory is that when strangers meet, they seek to *reduce uncertainty* about each other. Simultaneously, people seek to increase their ability to predict their partner's and their own behavior in the situation. Interviews, first dates, and interactions with foreigners are situations in which we are highly uncertain. One of the concerns we face when we first meet people is the uncertainty of predicting their behavior. If we could predict others' behavior, we could choose more appropriate behaviors ourselves. According to URT, different types of communication occur during three stages of first meetings.

Three Stages of Initial Interactions

entry phase   Dimension of uncertainty reduction theory that reflects the initial phase of relationships where physical appearance, sex, age, socio-economic status, and other biographic and demographic information is most important.

personal phase   A dimension of uncertainty reduction theory that reflects communicating attitudes, beliefs, values, and more personal data.

exit phase   Dimension of uncertainty reduction theory that assumes that during this phase, the communicators decide on future interaction plans.

Some information about others is easily observed. Physical appearance cues indicate sex, age, and economic or social status. This information is then supplemented with additional biographic and demographic information obtained during the **entry phase** of relationship development. Much of the interaction in this entry phase is controlled by communication rules and norms. For example, it is considered improper to ask strangers for intimate details about their behavior. When communicators begin to share attitudes, beliefs, values, and more personal data, the **personal phase** begins (Berger & Calabrese, 1975). During this phase, the communicators feel less constrained by rules and norms and tend to communicate more freely with each other. The third phase of initial interaction is the **exit phase**. During this phase, the communicators decide on future interaction plans. They may discuss or negotiate ways to allow the relationship to grow and continue. However, any particular conversation may be terminated at the end of the entry phase.

Uncertainty Reduction Axioms

Uncertainty reduction theory was developed to describe the interrelationships between seven important factors in any dyadic exchange: verbal communication, nonverbal expressiveness, information-seeking behavior, intimacy, reciprocity, similarity, and liking. The seven axioms offered in uncertainty reduction theory follow the "If . . . , then . . ." statements typical of the law-governed approach. For example, the first axiom of the theory can be phrased "if uncertainty levels are high, the amount of verbal communication between strangers will decrease." The more we learn about someone, the less uncertain we are, and the amount of verbal communication increases.

Two other factors that reduce uncertainty between communicators are information-seeking behavior and the degree of similarity individuals perceive in each other. When strangers first meet and interact, the amount of information they seek from each other is quite high. As a relationship progresses, the amount of overt information-seeking behavior decreases. The degree of perceived similarity (in background, attitudes, and appearance) among communicators reduces uncertainty. (Perceived similarity is one of the components of interpersonal attraction theory and will be discussed in more detail later.) Individuals use cues about similarity and dissimilarity (especially background and attitude cues) to help them understand why other people communicate as they do. For example, if I am talking with Dana, who comes from a large city similar to mine, then I would have some basis to explain why Dana uses an assertive or aggressive communication style. Similarity in background (real or imagined) may help us explain and predict attitudes and beliefs. Indeed, Berger (1979) found that perceived background similarity led to predictions of attitude similarity.

If communicators are very uncertain, URT suggests they will exchange information and will self-disclose at about the same rate. High levels of uncertainty will produce high and about equal rates of information exchange between communicators. Under conditions of high uncertainty, such as when strangers meet, an imbalance in the exchange of information may create tension. One person may be accused of dominating the conversation, and the relationship may be terminated.

Nonverbal expressions of interest and attention increase as uncertainty decreases. Communicators may exhibit more direct eye contact, touch more, and sit closer to each other. As uncertainty decreases further, intimate messages may be exchanged. Self-disclosing statements reveal more intimate information and may rapidly move the relationship from the entry phase. The final result of less uncertainty is that communicators will like each other more because they feel they know and understand each other better.

Uncertainty Reduction Theorems

Charles Berger and Richard Calabrese also developed twenty-one theorems about how the seven factors in the axioms are related and interact to reduce uncertainty. Six of the theorems suggest that when the *amount of communication* between strangers in initial interaction increases, nonverbal expressions of interest (such as direct eye contact, head nods, pleasantness of voice), intimate communication content, liking, and similarity also increase. More communication lessens the need for immediate and equal exchanges of information.

Five other theorems deal with nonverbal cues associated with affiliation or liking (factors of *nonverbal expressiveness*). These theorems suggest the greater the nonverbal expressiveness, the more intimate content, perceived similarity, and liking there will be. Nonverbal expressiveness also reduces the need for information-seeking behavior and for equal, immediate exchanges of communication.

Four theorems are related to the *intimacy level of communication content*. As communication content becomes more personal, perceived similarity and liking between communicators increase. In addition, as self-disclosing messages become more intimate, the tendency to seek information and the need for immediate and equal exchanges of information also decrease.

Three theorems address the concept of *information seeking*. One suggests that strangers use less information-seeking communication as they begin to like each other more. As a relationship develops, there is less need to ask questions and "interrogate" people; they are more willing to volunteer information about themselves.

Two theorems deal with *reciprocity,* or *rates of information exchange.* As two individuals perceive greater similarity and are more attracted to each other, they feel less need to exchange information with equal frequency. However, the theory also suggests that when uncertainty is high, communicators tend to echo behaviors; as one person increases information seeking, so does the other.

The final theorem suggests that the greater the real and perceived similarity between communicators in a developing relationship, the more likely attraction or liking will exist. During the last thirty years, social psychological and communication researchers have conducted much research into the relationship between similarity and liking. For uncertainty reduction theory (URT), the key to this relationship is our need to reduce uncertainty. Berger and Calabrese suggested that the concept of uncertainty reduction explains many of the research findings concerning the similarity-attraction relationship.

In the years since the initial presentation of URT, many communication scholars have examined its assumptions through quantitative and empirical research. For example, URT has been used to study the development and maintenance of romantic relationships (Parks & Adelman, 1983) and relationships between people of different cultures (Gudykunst & Nishida, 1984). Berger and Calabrese (1975) suggested that, in our increasingly mobile society, we may all need to decrease uncertainty in new relationships several times during our lives. As we move from job to job, from city to city, and perhaps from one intimate relationship to another, we may spend a great deal of time developing new relationships by communicating to reduce uncertainty. These applications of URT will be discussed in more detail in the sections that follow.

Moving Beyond Initial Interaction Stages

In an effort to explain how uncertainty reduction works *beyond* the initial stages of relational development, Berger (1979, 1986) has extended the boundaries of the original theory by including new concepts and refining the original ones. **Cognitive uncertainty** (the type of uncertainty presented in the original formulation of the theory) refers to a generalized state of uncertainty between individuals, whereas **linguistic or behavioral uncertainty** refers to the level of uncertainty felt in a *particular* conversation.

> **cognitive uncertainty** A generalized state of uncertainty between individuals.

> **linguistic or behavioral uncertainty** The level of uncertainty felt in a particular conversation.

Under several conditions, the desire to gain knowledge about others is quite strong. The first condition concerns **incentive**. We want to know more about people who control rewards or who can satisfy our needs. The more we learn, the better our strategies to obtain the rewards. For example, we may develop relationships with fraternity or sorority members so that our new friends can help us earn an invitation to join their group. When they can help us, these people possess *high incentive value*. We monitor their behavior, as well as our own communication with them, more closely. For example, we may look at how they respond to praise. If we discover that they enjoy being complimented and are more gracious and giving after being praised, we may then compliment them frequently to speed the relationship development.

> **incentive** A motivation associated with uncertainty reduction theory where we want to know more about people who control rewards or who can satisfy our needs.

A second motive that stimulates information seeking is the **unpredictable behavior** of others. When a communication behavior deviates from our expectations, we monitor the communication of others more closely to get additional information. We often respond less favorably to the unusual or unpredictable behavior of others than to behavior consistent with our expectations. Berger (1979) found that if a stranger in an initial interaction gave more compliments, he or she was rated as friendlier. However, he or she was also judged more dishonest and less sincere. Interactants probably imputed *ulterior motives* to the stranger to explain the increase in compliments. Thus, when a person's communication follows conventional norms and rules, we may pay less attention to it. However, when a person's communication deviates from conventions, rules, and norms, we pay closer attention to that behavior (increase our monitoring) to generate more reliable information about the person.

> **unpredictable behavior** A motivation associated with uncertainty reduction theory that assumes when communication behavior deviates from our expectations, we monitor the communication of others more closely to get additional information.

A third and final motive for acquiring information about others is the **likelihood of interacting with them in the future.** Generally, desire for future contact causes people to pay closer attention to their own and others' communication. Expecting future interaction strongly influences our evaluation of another's behavior. People who believe that they will be communicating with another person in the future may change their communication behavior to be viewed more favorably. People generally do not disclose intimate information to strangers. However, spontaneous and intimate self-disclosure to strangers does occur in two contexts. The "stranger-on-the-plane" situation is

> **likelihood of interacting with them in the future** A motivation is associated with uncertainty reduction theory that assumes a person's desire for future contact causes people to pay close attention to their own and other's communication.

one context in which we suspend normal communication rules because we never expect to meet the other person again. You may recall a long airplane ride during which your seatmate revealed intimate personal details after meeting you only a few hours earlier. An out-of-town pub or bar is the other context in which we may ignore the rules we typically follow for self-disclosure (Berger, 1979).

Strategies to Reduce Uncertainty

passive strategies
An uncertainty reduction strategy that involves watching someone without being observed.

There are three general strategies to reduce uncertainty about others. Passive strategies involve watching someone without being observed. You may have engaged in a passive strategy to reduce uncertainty about someone to whom you were attracted. You may have unobtrusively observed this person talking with other students in class, in the cafeteria, or in the dormitory. Note that while you were gaining information, no *direct* communication occurred between you. We often observe others in informal social situations where norms and rules are frequently relaxed and more revealing information may emerge (Berger, 1979). Active strategies of uncertainty reduction require more effort to discover information, but there is still no direct contact between the two parties. An active strategy may include finding out about another person by asking third parties for information. You may have discovered someone's "availability" for a relationship by asking friends whether the person was involved with someone. Interactive strategies include obtaining information *directly* through asking questions (interrogation) and offering personal information about yourself (self-disclosure). The self-disclosure strategy relies on the fact that self-disclosure by one person stimulates self-disclosure in another. If I reveal something important about myself to others, they feel "obliged" to reveal something equally important about themselves to me. A party is a good place to observe people using interactive strategies.

active strategies
An uncertainty reduction strategy that requires effort to discover information, but there is still no direct contact between the two parties.

interactive strategies
An uncertainty reduction strategy that consists of obtaining information directly through asking questions (interrogation) and offering personal information about yourself.

When individuals give information about themselves, they may exaggerate or lie. Thus, it is important to be able to detect deception. One useful type of interactive strategy is deception detection, which includes the careful scrutiny of nonverbal behavior (see Chapter 8). A good deal of research has focused on people's ability to detect deception in others (see Knapp & Comadena, 1979).

deception detection
An uncertainty reduction strategy which includes the careful scrutiny of nonverbal behavior.

A Test of Uncertainty Reduction Theory

Parks and Adelman (1983) tested uncertainty reduction theory as it applies to *premarital romantic relationships.* All relationships are embedded within a larger social framework composed of each partner's separate communication networks and relationships. Parks and Adelman suggested that these individual networks help reduce uncertainty by providing "third-party" information about one's romantic partner. For example, observing your partner's family interactions may be quite telling. You may discover patterns of communication you have never observed before. The mere act of meeting a partner's larger social network or family may also reduce uncertainty. Indeed, failing to introduce a partner to one's friends and family may make the partner uncertain and provoke such questions as, "If I'm so important to you, how come I've never met your friends?" (p. 58). Using interviews and questionnaires, Parks and Adelman found that people who received support for their romantic involvement from family and friends expressed less uncertainty about their relationships and were less likely to terminate the relationship than people who received less support.

PREDICTED OUTCOME VALUE THEORY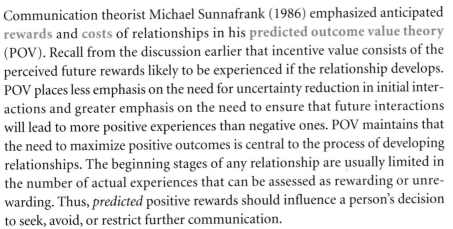

Communication theorist Michael Sunnafrank (1986) emphasized anticipated **rewards** and **costs** of relationships in his **predicted outcome value theory** (POV). Recall from the discussion earlier that incentive value consists of the perceived future rewards likely to be experienced if the relationship develops. POV places less emphasis on the need for uncertainty reduction in initial interactions and greater emphasis on the need to ensure that future interactions will lead to more positive experiences than negative ones. POV maintains that the need to maximize positive outcomes is central to the process of developing relationships. The beginning stages of any relationship are usually limited in the number of actual experiences that can be assessed as rewarding or unrewarding. Thus, *predicted* positive rewards should influence a person's decision to seek, avoid, or restrict further communication.

POV offers several key explanations for how people predict outcomes in developing relationships. Individuals who predict positive outcomes will be more attracted to relationships; they will try to extend their relationships more often than will people who predict less-positive outcomes. Individuals who predict negative outcomes will probably communicate in a way that blocks relational development. Individuals generally guide conversations toward topics that they expect will generate more positive results. According to predicted outcome value theory, reducing uncertainty allows people to control their communication to achieve positive results and to become better predictors of future outcomes.

POV modifies all seven axioms of the original uncertainty reduction theory by suggesting that *predicted outcome value* acts as a mediating variable. Advocates of POV believe research shows these modifications strengthen uncertainty reduction theory. Berger (1986) suggested that predicting an outcome value is itself one type of uncertainty-reducing activity. He views POV as an expansion of, not an alternative to, his theory. More research is needed to determine which theory best explains the role of communication

rewards   Anything that we see as a benefit from a relationship.

costs   Anything that we see as a punishment or detriment from a relationship.

predicted outcome value theory   Theory that places less emphasis on the need for uncertainty reduction in initial interactions and greater emphasis on the need to ensure that future interactions will lead to more positive experiences than negative experiences.

in developing relationships. Additional research is also necessary to test whether these two theories accurately describe communication in the later stages of relationship development.

ATTRACTION THEORIES AND RELATIONAL DEVELOPMENT

The questions "Why do people like each other?" and "What attracts people to each other?" have stimulated research by theorists in communication and social psychology for years. Clearly, attraction is important to a variety of social outcomes and relationships of varying levels of intimacy. We choose to spend "the rest of our lives" with someone to whom we are attracted. We may hire someone or be hired because of attraction. We may temporarily feel "crushed" because someone to whom we are attracted does not share those feelings.

The Interpersonal Goal-Oriented Theory of Attraction

Sunnafrank and his associates have studied the similarity-attraction relationship from a goal-oriented perspective. They looked at attitude information during early stages of relationships. Remember that uncertainty reduction theory predicts that more personal information is exchanged as relationships become more intimate (Berger & Calabrese, 1975). Predicted outcome value theory states that people seek information about others to enhance the *quality* of their interactions. Thus, both uncertainty reduction theory and perceived outcome value theory predict that people will seek information *prior* to an initial encounter when they anticipate meeting someone new. People may believe that simply knowing the attitudes of a stranger will help them better predict and control the situation. Such information as age, sex, or social status can be obtained from mutual acquaintances or from the context in which the people meet. Attending the same house of worship, political rally, class, party, or professional meeting reveals certain shared characteristics.

Sunnafrank and Miller (1981) designed an experiment to discover how a "normal" first conversation between strangers affected the relationship between similar attitudes and attraction. Participants were told that they would be working on a project with a stranger who had attitudes either like or unlike their own. Half the participants engaged in a five-minute interaction with their partner; the other half did not. The participants then completed a questionnaire that measured how much they were attracted to their partner. Participants from the half that did not interact preferred the "similar" stranger. Those who did communicate were more attracted to a stranger unlike themselves. Initial, nonthreatening communication appears to facilitate attraction to dissimilar others. To explain this finding, Sunnafrank and Miller suggest that when people engage in brief encounters with strangers, they feel better able to predict the stranger's behavior in future interactions. This feeling of stability and control, in turn, influences attraction; in fact, Sunnafrank (1983) believes that it is the most important factor in determining attraction. To underscore this point, the researchers reported that participants who met dissimilar strangers but had no opportunity to communicate with them were least attracted to the strangers. This study appears to support the basic assumption of uncertainty reduction theory that individuals try to predict and control their environments. Stable and predictable environments are reinforcing to individuals; unstable ones are not.

Sunnafrank (1985) extended this research by studying later stages of conversations about attitudes. He discovered that both first conversations and first conversations followed by discussions of attitudes made people more attracted to dissimilar—but not to similar—strangers. If you already believed that a stranger shared your attitudes, confirmation would simply support your expectations. It would not necessarily increase your attraction to the stranger. However, if you believed that you would meet someone very different from you (e.g., an anti-gun supporter meeting a pro-gun supporter), a normal first conversation should reduce the threat associated with the different attitudes. You could then be more attracted to that person than before. Sunnafrank's goal-oriented theory of attraction helps explain the *later* stages of the process of developing relationships; the similarity-attraction theories best explain attitudes of individuals *before* communication takes place. When we communicate with others who are different from us at work, at school, or at parties, the communication may reduce our tendency to be attracted only to those we think are like ourselves. Sunnafrank's work also extended the previous findings to include interactions between opposite-sex partners.

Reinforcement Theory and Attraction

Psychologist Donn Byrne, a pioneer in the study of interpersonal attraction, has devoted much of his career to studying why we like some people and dislike others. Byrne and other theorists first identified many of the factors of interpersonal attraction and then studied each one separately. They later looked at the experimental findings to determine the relative contribution of each component to understanding the whole. This technique, *inductive theory building,* involves collecting findings from specific and narrowly focused studies and then drawing more general conclusions from the specific results.

Byrne (1971) felt that the principle of **reinforcement** explains most of interpersonal attraction; we like and are attracted to those people who reward us. Rewards can range from verbal compliments or praise to actual gifts. Similarly, we dislike and are repelled by individuals who punish us. Again, punishment can take many forms from unfavorable comments to uncomfortable or

reinforcement We like and are attracted to those people who reward us.

damaging experiences. Byrne believed that similarity in attitudes is particularly rewarding and therefore a reliable indicator of whether people will like each other (see Figure 9.1).

Similarity and Interpersonal Attraction

People find similarity in a number of areas. If the behavior, attitudes, beliefs, values, abilities, and personality of another individual are similar to our own, we generally find that positively rewarding. If we believe people are similar to us, we are more attracted to them. This factor, which is called *homophily* in communication and *similarity* in social psychology, is important when we evaluate people with whom we intend to develop relationships. **Perceived similarity**—the degree to which we *believe* another's characteristics are similar to ours—is often sufficient to attract us to others. Communicators frequently make judgments about the attractiveness of others based on inferred, rather than actual, characteristics. Cappella (1984) suggested that, "We are as much studying who people think they are attracted to as who they are attracted to" (p. 241).

Several consistent findings have emerged in the research on similarity. We are more likely to be persuaded by communicators if we believe they are similar to us (Berscheid, 1966). Similar individuals communicate more with each other (Rogers & Bhowmik, 1970). The more someone else seems similar to us, the more comfortable we are (Byrne, Griffitt, & Stefaniak, 1967). Berscheid and Walster (1978) suggested that similarity consists of six dimensions: attitude,

perceived similarity   The degree to which we believe another's characteristics are similar to ours – is often sufficient to attract us to others.

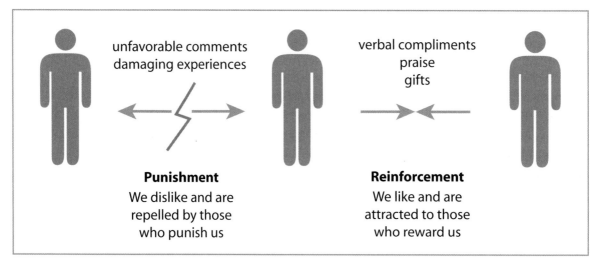

Figure 9.1

Byrne's reinforcement theory.

personality, physical characteristics, social characteristics, intelligence, and education. McCroskey, Richmond, and Daly (1975) offered four dimensions of similarity: attitude similarity, value similarity (morality), background similarity, and appearance similarity. They developed a questionnaire to measure perceived similarity between communicators and tested it with high school, college, and adult participants. For all groups, attitude similarity was the most important factor in perceived similarity.

In conducting much of his research on attraction and attitude similarity, Byrne employed the "bogus stranger" technique. In this method, participants completed an attitude questionnaire (scale). They were then given another scale supposedly completed by a stranger; the researcher actually chose the answers on "the stranger's" questionnaire. The researcher divided people into two groups to create two experimental conditions: the "similar" and "dissimilar" attitude conditions. In the "similar" condition, the stranger's scale almost duplicated the responses of the research participant. In the "dissimilar" condition, the questionnaire had almost opposite responses from those of the participant. Participants were attracted to the "stranger" who had responded with similar attitudes. We are usually more comfortable when we think others are similar to us. Whatever our goals for a situation, we can feel more confident when confronting familiar attitudes and values. Similarity provides reassurance and reinforcement that the person is functioning in a logical and meaningful way because the interaction seems more understandable and predictable.

Evaluating the Attraction-Reinforcement Research

Byrne's research and that of many interpersonal attraction researchers is conducted under the law-governed method of inquiry. The research methods used to test hypotheses and research questions about interpersonal attraction and attitude similarity are designed to establish *causes* of attraction. Some critics (Eiser, 1980; Gergen, 1980) challenged Byrne's experimental methods as too contrived and artificial to predict how people are actually attracted to each other. For example, we rarely read questionnaires completed by those we have just met and might be considering as friends. These critics feel that because the studies were so artificial, the findings cannot be generalized to actual attraction situations and thus are not very useful.

Other critics have described more fundamental limitations of the early work. Steven Duck (1985) suggested that the studies investigating the relationship between attitude similarity and attraction did not describe *how* people recognize reinforcing attitudes in normal, everyday encounters with strangers. Early researchers did not study the *communication* of attitudes, beliefs, and values between individuals. Skill and knowledge of interpersonal communication are critical elements in assessing the relationship between attitude similarity and attraction. As Duck stated, "Relationship development requires different sorts of knowledge and communicative skill at different points" (p. 661). Perhaps some people fail to communicate the right messages about their attitudes, inadequately self-disclose to others, or have difficulty with expressions of warmth, concern, and interest. Some people even consciously hide or disguise their real attitudes to be more attractive to others (Snyder, 1974, 1979). It may be very difficult for people to interpret messages about others' attitudes. Perhaps only very competent communicators can accurately discern others' true attitudes.

Early research on the relationship between attraction and similar attitudes failed to recognize the importance of these factors. Byrne's research also failed to acknowledge that an individual's attitudes may change as a relationship develops. This change in attitudes may affect a person's ability or desire to reward the partner. Arguing from a communication perspective, Duck and Barnes (1992) stated, "Similarity and recognition of similarity are both important ways in which people convey meaning" (p. 207). That is, the *process* by which we decide that similarities exist aids in relationship development. Elaine Hatfield and Richard Rapson (1992) listed several factors that affect the connection between attitude similarity and interpersonal attraction: (1) the kind of relationship, (2) the stage of the relationship, and (3) the kind of similarity/dissimilarity involved. They suggest that people must be aware of their own attitudes if they are to be affected by the perceived or actual attitude similarity/dissimilarity of another. In addition, people must also be aware of others' attitudes if they are to be affected by them. Attitude, temperament, and behavioral similarity increase the chances that a given encounter will be rewarding. The longer a relationship continues, the more important similarities/dissimilarities will be. Hatfield and Rapson argued that when people must spend considerable time together in close proximity, dissimilarities begin to cause tension. "At first such differences are merely slightly irritating, then they become teeth-clenchingly annoying. Eventually they may become unbearable" (p. 211).

The controversy regarding attitude similarity and interpersonal attraction continues. Sunnafrank (1992) attacked the premise that attitude similarity *causes* interpersonal attraction. He stated, "There is absolutely no justification for the strong belief that attitude similarity creates attraction" (p. 177). Sunnafrank does acknowledge that perceived attitude similarity and conversational expressions of agreement are "associated" with attraction. He maintains, however, that the cause-and-effect relationship believed to exist between those variables is a myth. Sunnafrank contends that normal "beginning conversations" among individuals can overcome any effect of attitude similarity on interpersonal attraction. He suggests that the relationship between attitude similarity and attraction should remain an open question until more research is conducted and data accumulated.

Relationship Interaction Stages Model

A common feature of any model of interpersonal relationships is to describe or explain the basic assumption that relationships and relational partners change over time. Most models describing relational progression tend to focus on the two processes of relationship development and relationship deterioration. One of the more popular model is that of Mark Knapp's (1978) **Relationship Interaction Stages Model**. This model seeks to explain the entire spectrum of relationship development and decline. There are ten stages in the model, five of which describe how relational partners "come together," and five stages describe how relational partners "come apart" (see Figure 9.2). The stages of coming together consist of the **initiation stage**, the **experimenting stage**, the **intensifying stage**, the **integrating stage**, and the **bonding stage**. The stages of coming apart consist of the **differentiation stage**, the **circumscribing stage**, the **stagnation stage**, the **avoiding stage**, and the **terminating stage**.

As indicated in Figure 9.2, Knapp (1978) presented his model using a dual staircase metaphor on which all relationships have characteristics of ascending (i.e., coming together), descending (i.e., coming apart), and stabilizing (i.e., periods of balance and consistency). Knapp believed that Social Exchange Theory best determines the direction of movement and the relational partners motivations for being in a particular stage. Social Exchange Theory assumes that people evaluate relationships based on the ratio of rewards received from the relationship to the costs received from the relationship. When the rewards outweigh the costs, the relationship has a greater chance of survival "evaluations or relational rewards and costs result in decisions about where the relationship will go and how fast it will get there" (Avtgis, West, & Anderson, 1998, p. 281). The relationship interaction stages model makes several assumptions concerning how relationships progress through each stage. That is, movement through the staircase model is systematic and sequential and may move in an ascending, descending, or stabilizing fashion. As with any theoretical explanatory model, empirical support is an important factor when assessing a model's worth.

Avtgis et al. (1998) conducted an inductive study (see Chapter 2), which sought to identify cognitive (i.e., what people think), affective (i.e., what people feel), and behaviors associated with each relationship stage. The results of the study revealed that in the initiation stage, people talk about relaxing things and commonalities, feel nervous and cautious, smile, and use flirting nonverbal behaviors. In the experimenting stage people talk about past relationships and try to create a good impression, feel connected and comfortable, call on the telephone, and freely violate each other's personal space. In the intensifying stage people probe about the partner's morals and values, feel loving and happy, display affectionate behaviors, and buy gifts. In the integrating stage

relationship interaction stages model A model that describes how relationships and relational partners change over time.

initiation stage A stage of the relationship interaction stages model that reflects the first interactions of relational partners.

experimenting stage A stage in the relationship interaction stages model that reflects relational partners focusing on finding similarities between them.

intensifying stage A stage in the relationship interaction stages model that reflects relational partners seek to find similarities in terms of morals and values.

integrating stage A stage in the relationship interaction stages model that reflects when relational partners begin to talk about the future together and share a sense of being committed.

bonding stage A stage in the relationship interaction stages model that reflects a strong emotional and psychological link between relational partners.

differentiation stage A stage in the relationship interaction stages model that reflects highlighting how different you are from your relational partner.

Bonding	Stabilizing	Bonding
Integrating	Stabilizing	Differentiating
Intensifying	Stabilizing	Circumscribing
Experimenting	Stabilizing	Stagnating
Initiating	Stabilizing	Avoiding
	Terminating	

Figure 9.2

Relationship interaction
stages model.

From Knapp, M. L. (1978) Social intercourse: From greeting to goodbye. *Boston: Allyn and Bacon.*

circumscribing stage
A stage in the relationship
interaction stages model
that reflects relational
partners focus
communication on
everyday matters in order
to avoid conflict.

stagnation stage   A stage
in the relationship
interaction stages model
and reflects the boredom
experienced in a relationship

avoiding stage   A stage in
the relationship interaction
stages model that reflects
the physical or
communication avoidance
of a relational partner.

termination stage   A
stage in the relationship
interaction stages model
reflecting the ending of a
relationship.

people share intimate feelings and talk about the future, feel unhappy when apart and feel one with their partner, go on vacations, and meet each other's family. In the bonding stage people pledge love for the other person and make arrangements about the future, feel a sense of unity and overwhelming joy, have joint possessions, and make sacrifices.

In terms of the stages of coming apart, within the differentiation stage people argue and talk about incompatibility, feel lonely and inadequate, and attempt to make compromises. In the circumscribing stage people talk about simple everyday matters, feel frustrated and distant, and pursue different activities. In the stagnation stage people give short answers to questions, feel unwanted and bored, and stop physical contact. In the avoiding stage people only discuss general matters and avoid talking about the relationship, feel nervous and helpless, and spend a lot of time away from each other. In the terminating stage, people talk about discussing where the relationship failed, feel unhappy but relieved, and spend time dividing up belongings. Other research indicates that the relational stages model can also be applied to nonromantic relationships such as coworker relationships (Welch & Rubin, 2002).

The relationship interaction stages model is a comprehensive description of how relationships develop, decline, and change. It is important to remember that this model is not linear in nature as much as it is a dynamic model where people can move into and out of any given stage at any given time. For example, consider a romantic relationship that you have been a part of. There were probably times when you felt extremely close to your partner, then in a short time were ready to terminate the relationship. This relational scenario is reflective of moving from the intensifying stage to the terminating stage.

THE THEORY OF INTERPERSONAL COMMUNICATION MOTIVES

Research into why people communicate with one another led Rebecca Rubin, Elizabeth Perse, and Carole Barbato to develop of a **theory of interpersonal communication motives** (Barbato & Perse, 1992; Rubin, Perse, & Barbato, 1988). In developing this theory, the researchers incorporated existing theories and "theoretical frameworks," including the functional approach to communication (Chapter 1), the theory of interpersonal needs, and the uses and gratifications theory of mass media (Chapter 12). The goal of the theory is to identify reasons (or motives) for *why* people initiate and engage in interpersonal communication. Those motives influence how people communicate and how they are likely to respond to others. For example, a need for affiliation may produce a motive to use communication to seek companionship. Interpersonal communication motives affect our choices of people with whom we talk, about what we talk, and how we talk.

In Chapter 1 we discussed three "automatic" (working below the conscious level) functions of communication: linking, mentation, and regulation. Although functional analysis describes and categorizes communication, there are limitations with this approach for interpersonal communication. Rubin, Perse, and Barbato (1988) thought that the uses and gratifications theory of mass communication would help in studying motives for interpersonal communication. Some aspects of media appear to satisfy interpersonal needs. Looking at the choices people make regarding the media as well as the choices they make in interpersonal interactions gave the researchers a broader base from which to uncover interpersonal communication motives.

Individuals have certain goals or endpoints for interpersonal communication. A motive is an internal state of readiness to act to achieve that goal. For example, an individual's goal might be to feel less lonely. According to the theory of interpersonal communication motives, one might choose to activate the *inclusion* motive to achieve that goal and to feel less lonely. Another core assumption of this theory is that people recognize and acknowledge their choices, that these choices are "purposeful and goal-directed," and "that people are mindful of their communication choices" (Graham, Barbato, & Perse, 1993, p. 173). Because of its emphasis on choice, the theory of interpersonal communication motives fits the rules paradigm. Rubin, Perse, and Barbato (1988) believe that there are regularities in the relationship among motives, individuals' traits, communication choices, and outcomes of communicating interpersonally. Much of the early work in the development of

theory of interpersonal communication motives A theory that identifies the motives people have for interpersonal communication.

this theory investigated whether people are consistent in the types of persons with whom they choose to communicate, based on the motives that they have for communicating. Six motives for engaging in interpersonal communication were identified:

1. **Affection**—interpersonal communication used to express concern, caring, and appreciation for others
2. **Control**—interpersonal communication used to gain compliance from others, to get others to do what you want them to do
3. **Escape**—interpersonal communication used to avoid engaging in other activities and to "fill the time"
4. **Inclusion**—interpersonal communication used to share feelings, avoid loneliness, to be with others (i.e., companionship)
5. **Pleasure**—interpersonal communication used for social benefits, for fun, stimulation, and entertainment
6. **Relaxation**—interpersonal communication used to help relax and unwind

Affection, pleasure, and inclusion are seen as the more "relationally oriented" motives. The Interpersonal Communication Motives Scale (Figure 9.3) helps assess why people engage in conversations with others.

Several factors appear to influence individuals' choice of motives for interpersonal communication. Locus of control (the amount and type of control individuals believe they have over their behavior) is one factor that is thought to influence interpersonal communication motivation. Specifically, Rebecca Rubin and Alan Rubin (1992) suggested that locus of control exists or occurs before interpersonal communication motivation. For example, individuals with an *external* locus-of-control orientation (those who believe that chance and powerful others control their lives) seem to be motivated by the inclusion motive to communicate with others. People with an *internal* locus-of-control orientation (those who feel that they exert control over their environment and lives) tend to be motivated to communicate by the control motive. Individuals satisfied with the quality of their lives, those who are active socially, and those who are physically healthy appear to communicate more for pleasure, affection, and relaxation motives.

It appears that gender and culture affect the choice of interpersonal communication motives. Women appear to be motivated to communicate to show affection, whereas men are more likely than women to communicate for control (Barbato & Perse, 1992). A cross-cultural study on interpersonal communication motives found that American students were more motivated than Mexican students to communicate for affection, pleasure, and inclusion. There were no differences observed between the two cultures on the interpersonal motives of control, relaxation, and escape (Rubin, Fernandez-Collado, & Hernandez-Sampieri, 1992).

INSTRUCTIONS: Here are several reasons people give for why they talk to other people. For each statement, provide a number that best expresses your own reasons for talking to others. Use the following scale:

Put a "5" if the reason is **exactly** like your own reason.
Put a "4" if the reason is **a lot** like your own reason.
Put a "3" if the reason is **somewhat** like your own reason.
Put a "2" if the reason is **not much** like your own reason
Put a "1" if the reason is **not at all** like your own reason.

"I talk to people . . ."

_____ 1. Because it's fun.
_____ 2. To help others.
_____ 3. Because I need someone to talk to or be with.
_____ 4. To put off something I should be doing.
_____ 5. Because it relaxes me.
_____ 6. Because it's a pleasant rest.
_____ 7. Because I want someone to do something for me.
_____ 8. Because it's exciting.
_____ 9. To let others know I care about their feelings.
_____ 10. Because I just need to talk about my problems sometimes.
_____ 11. To get away from what I am doing.
_____ 12. Because it allows me to unwind.
_____ 13. To thank them.
_____ 14. Because it makes me feel less lonely.
_____ 15. Because I have nothing better to do.
_____ 16. To get something I don't have.
_____ 17. To have a good time.
_____ 18. To tell others what to do.

Scoring: Total your scores for each subscore below. The range for each subscore is 3–15.

Your score:

Pleasure:	(Items 1, 8, 17)
Affection:	(Items 2, 9, 13)
Inclusion:	(Items 3, 10, 14)
Escape:	(Items 4, 11, 15)
Relaxation:	(Items 5, 12, 6)
Control:	(Items 7, 18, 16)

From: Rubin, R. B., Perse, E. M., & Barbato, C. A. (1988). *Conceptualization and measurement of interpersonal communication motives.* Human Communication Research, *14, 602–28. Copyright 1988 by Wiley-Blackwell. Reprinted by permission.*

Figure 9.3

The interpersonal communication motives scale.

Studies have examined interpersonal communication motives in a variety of situations, including family interaction, dating, and organizational and small-group contexts. The results suggest that we tend to communicate with family members, spouses and lovers, and close friends for affection, pleasure, and inclusion. Parents report communicating with their children primarily for affection and pleasure motives, and secondarily for relaxation and inclusion (Barbato, Perse, & Graham, 1995). This is not surprising because these motives produce more personal and intimate communication. One study discovered that inclusion, affection, and pleasure accounted for a great deal of communication between fathers and young adult children (Martin & Anderson, 1995). Another study found that escape, control, inclusion, and pleasure motives accounted for much communication between mothers and adult children (Anderson & Martin, 1995a). Interpersonal communication motives theory has identified a number of motives for communication among family members. It is possible that this research can help us identify sources of potential conflict in families. For example, it may be helpful in identifying whether members of "functional" families choose different interpersonal motives for family communication than members of families that have experienced relational distress.

In the organizational context, employees seem to communicate with coworkers for relaxation (Graham et al., 1993) and communicate with superiors for pleasure (Anderson & Martin, 1995d). In the context of small-group communication, the interpersonal motives of escape, control, inclusion, pleasure, and affection, along with providing appropriate feedback, are factors that influence members' satisfaction with a group (Anderson & Martin, 1995c).

A number of interpersonal communication motives are influential in attempts to resolve conflict between romantic partners. A motive labeled "concern for relationship" (for example, "I don't want him/her to get upset") was cited most frequently by individuals when they were asked for reasons why they resolved a conflict with a romantic partner (Myers, Zhong, & Mitchell, 1995). "Avoidance" (for example, "I don't like to fight") was also cited as an important motive for resolving conflict among romantic partners. Affection, control, and inclusion were also mentioned as significant motives for resolving interpersonal conflict.

Finally, researchers have explored differences in interpersonal communication motives between "competent communicators" and those who are less competent. Competent communicators are those people who are assertive (dominant, competitive, aggressive) *and* responsive (gentle, friendly, empathic). Competent communicators seem to communicate more for affection and pleasure, whereas less competent individuals seem to communicate more for control and escape (Anderson & Martin, 1995b).

The theory of interpersonal communication motives can help us understand multiple aspects of interpersonal communication: why people become attracted to each other, why some teams are more productive than others, and even why some people appear more "competent" in interpersonal communication. The development of this theory has produced a number of studies, but more research is needed to test and extend the theory further. Like other theories mentioned in this textbook, the paradigm with which it is most closely associated differs from the most frequent method of investigation. Because of its emphasis on choice, this theory fits the rules paradigm. However, much of the research testing the theory has been quantitative. As scholars who embrace different perspectives conduct more research, the scope and direction of the theory of interpersonal communication motives will expand.

TWO RULES-BASED/HUMAN ACTION GENERAL THEORIES OF COMMUNICATION

Most of the theories discussed in this chapter were developed under the law-governed approach to communication. We would like to briefly introduce you to two theories that emerged largely from the rules or human action perspective. These theories generated a great deal of research over the last thirty years and have also been used in applied communication situations.

Constructivism

The theory of **constructivism** was developed and introduced to the communication discipline by Jessie Delia during the mid 1970s. Several other communication scholars, most notably Professors James Applegate, Brant Burleson, Ruth Anne Clark, Barbara O'Keefe, Daniel O'Keefe, and Wendy Samter, have contributed to the testing, extension, and application of this theory.

Advocates of constructivism are interested in how individuals perceive the world and how they use a system known as personal constructs to view others and to make sense of their perceptions and experiences. Constructivists place great emphasis on human beings as active interpreters of their social world. As such, they reject many of the assumptions of the law-governed, positivist perspective on human communication. For constructivists, reality is socially constructed and individually interpreted and cannot be separated from the perceiver (Nicotera, 1995).

According to constructivists, people create their own social reality because we are constantly processing and interpreting the information we receive. That is, constructivists believe that reality does not exist separate from our perceptions and thoughts. A key tenet of constructivist theory is that "much of your own communicative conduct toward others, as well as your understanding of others' communicative efforts, is grounded in your perceptions of these others"

constructivism Cognitive theory of communication that explains how people use personal constructs (bi-polar opposites) to classify, interpret, and produce messages.

personal constructs   The elements (i.e., bi-polar opposites) which individuals use to interpret, anticipate, evaluate, and make sense of the world.

(Burleson, 2007, p. 109). This perspective differs quite a bit from the view of reality held by the logical positivists (see Chapter 4 for the treatment of logical positivism). The positivist perspective maintains that there is a "true" reality separate from the reality interpreted by the perceiver.

Central to the theory of constructivism is the concept of **personal constructs**. Personal constructs are the elements that individuals use to help them perceive and make sense of the world. Personal constructs are "the basic cognitive structures through which persons interpret, anticipate, evaluate, and understand aspects of the world" (Burleson & Caplan, 1998, p. 236). Personal constructs might be likened to a set of prescription glasses that influence the way in which we view the world. They provide us with a way of grouping events on the basis of similarities and differences (Nicotera, 1995) and influence the way people interact with others, form impressions, and produce messages.

In constructivist theory, personal constructs take the form of bipolar adjectives (e.g., rich–poor). Some personal constructs are very concrete, such as those dealing with the physical attributes of others (e.g., tall–short), whereas others are more abstract and deal with the personality orientations of others (e.g., kind–cruel). Let's take the example of a personal construct that some use in perceiving others: spiritual–secular (or religious–nonreligious). To some this is a very salient construct used to form impressions and make predictions about others' behavior. Under the "spiritual/religious" pole of this construct, a person might list attributes such as kind, helpful, giving, honest, and older. Under the "secular/nonreligious" pole, the same person might list attributes such as unsympathetic, reserved, selfish, dishonest, and younger. The "spiritual/religious–secular/nonreligious" construct might constitute the most overriding and prominent construct in a person's interpretive schema. An *interpretive scheme* is a general classification system used to interpret the world. "Interpretive schemes allow coordination of actions by providing general rules for social interaction and specific guidelines for particular situations" (Nicotera, 1995, p. 51). As such, this construct will likely be used to help a person understand, predict, and control their world. For example, if they are soliciting donations for charity, they would likely seek out someone who they consider "spiritual/religious" for in their perception of the world, spiritual/religious people would be more likely to contribute than would people who they identify as secular/nonreligious.

differentiation   From the communication theory Constructivism, it is a measure of the number of constructs a person has in their cognitive system.

abstractness   In the theory of Constructivism, it refers to how abstract (i.e., intangible) or concrete a construct is.

integration   From the communication theory of Constructivism, refers to the organization of the constructs in a person's interpretive scheme, or how the constructs are ordered and interconnected.

Personal constructs are said to differ along three dimensions (Burleson, 2007): **differentiation**, **abstractness**, and **integration**. Differentiation is a measure of the number of constructs a person has in their cognitive system. Abstractness refers to how abstract or concrete a construct is. As mentioned earlier, some constructs are quite concrete (e.g, taller–short), whereas others are more abstract (kind–cruel). Integration refers to the organization of the constructs in a person's interpretive scheme, or how the person's constructs are ordered and interconnected.

COGNITIVE COMPLEXITY

Individuals vary in the number of constructs they have (i.e., differentiation). According to Burleson (2007), individuals who possess a large number of constructs, whose constructs are well organized and more abstract are said to be higher in **cognitive complexity**. Being cognitively complex has several advantages in communication situations as those higher in cognitive complexity have been found to be better able to generate and process information about others and the environment and are better at taking the perspective of others (Burleson & Caplan, 1998).

Cognitive complexity is measured using an instrument called the Role Category Questionnaire (RCQ; Crockett, 1965). When using this measure, participants are asked to provide written descriptions of two peers who they know quite well, one they like and one they dislike. Participants are instructed to describe each peer in as much detail as possible and to focus on the peer's traits, personality characteristics, habits, beliefs, mannerisms, and the way they treat others. The written impressions generated by the Role Category Questionnaire are scored for the number of different interpersonal constructs they contain. The resulting score is seen as a measure of construct differentiation and, hence, a measure of cognitive complexity.

Burleson provides an example of how two individuals would differ in the way they describe their partners. One person might offer something like, "My partner, Chris, is a generally happy person, who has a great smile. Chris works hard in school, is concerned about physical appearance, and is really good-looking. Chris is a caring and good friend. Chris likes to be the center of attention, but also has a good sense of humor. I think Chris's jokes are really funny. Chris treats people with respect. We are a lot alike in many ways." Another person might offer something like, "My partner, Jamie, is self-confident, outgoing, friendly, and curious about the world in general. Jamie is open-minded and is always willing to learn new things. Jamie is open to constructive criticism and new ways of thinking. Jamie sometimes gets frustrated and shows some temper, but channels that negative energy into a positive form of expression. Jamie has a caring and supportive nature. Overall, Jamie is an independent and compassionate individual." Although each of these written impressions contains the exact same number of words (70), "the first one appears more superficial, fragmented and disorganized, while most people would suggest that the second one is more revealing and insightful" (Burleson, 2007, p. 110). In addition, because the second written impression contains a larger number of interpersonal constructs mentioned, it would receive a higher score on the RCQ for cognitive complexity.

Cognitively complex people are higher in perspective-taking than those lower in cognitive complexity. As such, they are better able to infer and represent the perspectives (i.e., thoughts and feelings) of others. Consequently, they

cognitive complexity
Highly developed system of personal constructs capable of sophisticated distinctions and abtractions.

are seen as more competent communicators (Burleson, 1984, 2007). Because perspective-taking ability has been positively related to the strategic adaptation of persuasive messages, individuals higher in cognitive complexity are said to be more effective at persuasion (Clark & Delia, 1977; O'Keefe & Delia, 1979).

It has been suggested that construct differentiation and abstractness tend to increase with age and experience, and for the most part, we tend to become more cognitively complex with age. An early study tested this speculation. Clark and Delia (1976) tested whether the use of persuasive strategies associated with higher levels of perspective-taking ability increased with age. Children in grades 2 through 9 were asked to perform three persuasive tasks: (a) reveal something she or he would like to have a parent buy for him or her, and then persuade the parent to buy it; (b) persuade his or her mother to host a large overnight birthday party for friends; and (c) ask a stranger to keep a lost puppy they found. The children were told to construct messages for each task and to share these messages with an interviewer. The messages produced were audiotaped and coded in terms of the perspective-taking skill required. Using the "lost puppy task" as the example, the children's messages were coded as "0" if they failed to offer any support, "1" if they demonstrated a need for the request (e.g., "The puppy looks skinny"), "2" if they dealt with counterarguments either in the statement or request (e.g., "I'll bring you food to feed the dog if you'll keep it"), and "3" if they supplied an advantage to the other, or attempted to adapt to the interests and values of the other (e.g., "This dog would be a good watchdog. A dog makes a good companion," or "If I were you and I lived alone, I'd like a good watchdog like this one"). The results indicated that older children used more higher-order strategies and fewer lower-order strategies as well as more diversified messages than did younger children. This findings supports the contention that cognitive complexity and, hence, perspective-taking increases with age.

The communication theory of constructivism generated a great deal of research throughout the 1970s, 1980s and 1990s. As it progressed, the lines of inquiry broadened to include not just persuasion, but also number of other communication skills, most notably the production and use of comforting messages (Burleson, 2003). Like most theories, however, constructivism has received it share of criticism as well. For example, Nicotera (1995) suggested that individuals do not consistently act based on their individual meanings, hence, constructivists cannot always link individual interpretations to behavior. Another common criticism leveled at this theory is that the existence of cognitive structures is "neither verifiable nor falsifiable" (Nicotera, 1995, p. 60).

Coordinated Management of Meaning

coordinated management of meaning
Communication theory which is concerned with how people interpret messages during interaction and act upon those interpretations using constitutive and regulative rules.

Coordinated Management of Meaning (CMM) is one of the earliest and most influential of the rules-based or human action theories of communication. It was developed during the mid 1970s by Professors W. Barnett Pearce and Vernon Cronen and emerged during the period when ferment in the communication discipline existed over which paradigm (e.g., laws, rules, and systems, see Chapter 4) was most productive in building communication theory. Over its development and history, CMM has undergone several revisions and has generated much research. Although lacking in simplicity and parsimony (see Chapter 2), CMM is a rich theory with many elements and is one that clearly satisfies the criterion of usefulness. To its credit, the theory has been applied to many communication problems encountered in intercultural, family, organizational, relational, and political contexts, among others.

As with the theory of constructivism described earlier, CMM falls under the domain of interpretive theories of communication. That is, CMM is concerned with how reality is constructed by individuals in social interaction. Its very name, *coordinated* management of *meaning,* suggests several key concepts that comprise the theory, including coordination, meaning, and action. A major tenet of this theory is that people use rules to coordinate their meanings and actions as they communicate with each other. The theory suggests that communicators interpret each other's messages during interaction and act on that interpretation. Thus, in CMM terms, meaning leads to action (Pearce & Cronen, 1980). Using a unique and somewhat unconventional perspective on meaning, CMM theory suggests that how one person interprets another's messages and acts on that interpretation is more relevant and, hence, more important, than whether the "persons in conversation" understand each other. According to CMM, even though individuals do not fully understand each other, they can indeed coordinate their interaction to achieve goals. As such, because individuals have the ability to interpret and act on that interpretation, they can "construct" meaning and order during communication, which can, and often does, lead to very satisfying and productive relationships, even though partial or complete understanding is never achieved.

As a rule-governed/human action-based theory, CMM is a reaction against the more law-governed theories of communication. Unlike law-governed theories of communication, CMM does not seek to discover universal propositions or cause-and-effect relationships that govern communication behavior. Philipsen (1995) provided an example of how CMM would take a different approach from the more positivist-oriented theories of interpersonal violence. Researchers who investigate the role of verbal aggression in interpersonal violence working from a law-governed approach, seek to uncover and discover universal propositions about the relationship between verbal aggression and interpersonal violence. For example, one proposition that emerges from this corpus of research suggests that destructive forms of communication such as hostility and verbal aggression are catalysts to physical aggression and interpersonal violence, whereas constructive forms of communication such as argumentativeness and problem-focused speech decrease the likelihood of physical

coordination How individuals organize their meanings and actions to communicate. The rules they use to act on meanings can allow the actions of individuals to be compatible or consistent with one another without complete understanding being present between the persons.

meaning From the communication theory Coordinated Management of Meaning, it refers to the process by which individuals in conversation interpret and decode the messages of others.

action Concept inherent in the Coordination Management of Meaning Theory. Behaviors individuals engage in as a result of interpreting another person's messages.

aggression (see, for example, Infante, Chandler & Rudd, 1989; Straus, 1974). This proposition takes the form of *if x, then y* (see Chapter 4). Research on this topic derived from CMM (i.e., operating from a rules-oriented and human action perspective) would take a very different approach to investigating communication and interpersonal violence. It would investigate, for example, why a husband and wife act violently toward each other or why they do not. Thus, for a CMM theorist, "a fundamental concern with theory is the formulation of a general scheme that facilitates the apprehension of communicative particulars in a particular case" (Philipsen, 1995, p. 17), rather than attempt to develop propositions about the causes of human aggression.

As a rules-oriented theory, CMM is concerned with how meaning and action are accomplished via rules. Recall from Chapter 4 that, in general terms, rules are prescriptions for behavior. In the parlance of CMM, rules are guidelines that people use to assign meaning and take action. In a CMM study, as in other studies under the rules perspective, rules are discovered by asking the communicators what they believe the rules are for the particular interaction. CMM researchers, in particular, seek to uncover two particular types of rules: **constitutive rules** and **regulative rules**. Constitutive rules are rules of meaning that are used to interpret or understand events or messages; they tell what something should mean in a given event. For example, a stare may mean that someone is very interested in you, but might also mean that someone is trying to dominate you. "A constitutive rule is like an individual's definition of some social object, for example if, for an individual, to utter the statement "you are beautiful" counts as the speech act of compliment, then that is, for that individual, a constitutive rule" (Philipsen, 1995, p. 20). Regulative rules, on the other hand, are rules of action; they help individuals determine how to respond or behave. For example, one person's regulative rule may be that if someone pays you a compliment, then you are obligated to respond with, " Thank you." According to CMM theorists, it is the context, or those features of a situation, that help determine how to apply the constitutive and regulative rules. People construct meanings of behavior by applying aspects of the context that determine what a given behavior counts as.

Of course, one of the most important principles of CMM is the notion of coordination. Coordination is conceptualized as the way individuals organize their meanings and actions in an attempt to have them "fit together" in a way that permits and, hopefully, optimizes communication. When coordination takes place, one communicator acts while the other attempts to interpret or provide meaning to that action. The receiver will then respond based on their interpretation of the other's action. Hopefully, there will be sufficient coordination so that some degree of mutual understanding and "effective" communication takes place between the parties. As we know, however, that is not always the case, and CMM theorists recognize that, on many occasions, coordination is achieved, but without complete understanding. "Coordination is

constitutive rules Defines or creates speech acts by specifying what counts as a command or request.

regulative rules Rules of action which help individuals determine how to respond or behave.

not necessarily the meshing of perfectly shared meanings. It is the perceived meshing of actions. Although the producers of those actions, and outside observers of them as well, might perceive them to mesh smoothly, his does not necessarily mean that producers of those actions agree as to the meaning of the actions" (Philipsen, 1995, p. 19). Two individuals can engage in a communication event in which coordination was achieved, although the two individuals had very different meanings from the messages and actions presented. A husband and wife can go through an entire forty-plus-years marriage, including raising children, all the while engaging in a sufficient amount of coordination, yet never fully understanding each other.

Intercultural communication is a particular context in which some degree of coordination is often achieved, without the accompanying degree of understanding, unless acknowledgment of differences and adjustments are made. Pearce (2005) described meeting between a group of North Americans (from the United States) and Central American (from El Salvador) academics. Acknowledging that Central Americans have a different sense of time than North Americans, the North American academics agreed to alter the agenda for the first meeting and to make it more of a relational, friendship-building event and to abstain from substantive discussions. However, the El Salvadorians, ahead of time, decided to accommodate the North Americans' cultural predisposition to "get to work immediately." In this case, both groups took into account each others' cultural differences and adjusted their orientations to first meeting behaviors. This resulted in confusion and tension between the two groups, who were functioning exactly opposite of what each expected from the other! However, "with a lot of laughter and goodwill, each group confessed their strategy to each other" (Pearce, 2005, p. 38), and the rest of the meetings progressed with respect and accomplishment.

CMM, like other theories, has been met with some criticism. For example, Brenders (1987) has suggested that CMM distorts or obscures "the distinction between constitutive and regulative rules" (p. 330). Philipsen suggested that other psychological, sociological, or cultural variables "could produce just as strong a result independent of prefigurative force or other CMM variables . . . if they were incorporated into the measurement model," and that "the 'communication' part (of CMM) is not well developed. In short, no theory or framework of discourse informs and guides the program" (1995, p. 39).

More recently, CMM has been cast as a "practical theory" designed to make life better, to inform communication practices in a wide variety of communication contexts, and to address the question of, "How can we make better social worlds?" (Pearce, 2005, p. 45). To that end, CMM principles have been applied to research on organizational communication and management to explore and identify attributes of effective leadership conversation (Barge, Downs, & Johnson, 1989). In family therapy contexts, CMM has been used to reconceptualize important rules in a distressed family with a history of constant fighting

(Cronen, Pearce, & Tomm, 1985) and in mediation sessions to redesign the order of disputant speaking in an effort to give both disputants equal voice in mediation efforts (Cobb & Rifkin, 1991).

A SYSTEMS MODEL OF RELATIONAL INTERACTION

A systems-oriented view suggests that communication scholars studying interpersonal dynamics should focus on *patterns of exchange during interaction.* Frank Millar and Edna Rogers (1987) developed the **interpersonal dynamics model**, which suggests that relationships emerge from patterns of interaction made up of "redundant, interlocked cycles of messages, continually negotiated and co-defined rather than unilaterally caused by personal qualities and/or social role prescriptions" (p. 118). According to this systems theory, interpersonal relationships are much less influenced by causes (law-governed) or social rules (rule-governed) than by patterns of message exchange. The Millar and Rogers model is consistent with the principles of the systems approach: a relationship is viewed as a joint product of behavior and is more than the sum of the individual parts.

Millar and Rogers (1987) identified three types of message exchange patterns: control, trust, and intimacy. The ***control*** dimension reveals which partner currently defines and directs the actions of the pair (dyad). Control is exhibited in messages such as, "I'm in charge here," "You can't talk to me like that," and "You don't have the right to tell me what to do" (p. 120). The partner who creates the most relational definitions or defines the system's actions is the partner who has the most control. According to Millar and Rogers, relational control can be measured by redundancy (how much change there is in partners' negotiation over rights), dominance (how much one partner dominates the interaction), and power (the potential to influence or restrict a partner's behaviors). ***Trust*** requires both members of a relationship to be trusting and trustworthy. By trusting, people admit that they are dependent on another and that they believe the partner will not exploit them or take advantage of their trust. ***Intimacy*** measures how often partners use the other to confirm their feelings of "separateness or connectedness" in the relationship (p. 123). Very intimate relationships involve a great deal of mutual self-confirmation, behavior in which partners use each other primarily to fulfill their needs. Intimacy is communicated in such comments as, "No one understands me the way you do," and "I couldn't live without him" (p. 124).

interpersonal dynamics model A model that assumes relationships emerge from patterns of interaction made up of redundant and interlocking cycles of messages continually negotiated.

SUMMARY

This chapter explored several theories that explain and predict communication during the process of developing relationships. Some of the theories reviewed reflect the law-governed approach to interpersonal communication: uncertainty reduction theory, predicted outcome value theory, attraction theories, and Knapp's relationship interaction stages model. Next we considered rule-governed approaches to interpersonal communication: the theory of interpersonal communication motives, constructivism, and coordinated management of meaning. We concluded with a systems model of interpersonal dynamics by Millar and Rogers.

KEY TERMS

abstractness

action

active strategies

avoiding stage

behavioral uncertainty

bonding stage

circumscribing stage

cognitive complexity

cognitive uncertainty

coordinated management of
    meaning

coordination

constitutive rules

constructivism

costs

deception detection

differentiation

differentiation stage

entry phase

exit phase

experimenting stage

homophily

incentive

integration

interactive strategies

interpersonal communication
    motives

interpersonal dynamics model

interpretive scheme

initiation stage

integrating stage

intensifying stage

intimacy

likelihood of interacting with
    them in the future linguistic
meaning

passive strategies

perceived similarity

personal construct

personal phase

predicted outcome value theory

regulative rules

reinforcement

relationship interaction stages
    model

rewards

stagnation stage

terminating stage

theory of interpersonal
    communication

trust

uncertainty reduction theory

unpredictable behavior

Group Contexts

Important aspects of relationships (affection, trust, and attraction, for example) differ when they occur between two individuals and when they occur in a small group. The feeling of trusting one other person is not the same feeling as trusting a given group of people. Differences in communication between two individuals and the communication among several people necessitate identifying interpersonal and small group as two distinct contexts of communication. After clarifying certain aspects of groups, we will discuss several concepts that set communication in groups apart from communication in other contexts. Then we will examine some recent and significant developments in the communication field in terms of building group communication theories.

NATURE OF GROUPS

Group Size

Small-group communication refers to communication in gatherings that vary in size from three to about fifteen persons. A group is considered small if members are able to switch roles from receiver to source with relative ease (DeVito, 2002). When groups are composed of fifteen people or more, it becomes difficult to switch from receiver to source. In such a situation, the order of speaking is often assigned, and more formal rules of parliamentary procedure may be followed.

The size of a small group influences the likelihood that everyone will get along with one another. A group of four people involves six dyadic relationships, whereas a group of twelve has sixty-six. The greater the number of possible relationships, the more potential for individual dyads within the group to be incompatible. Group size affects satisfaction. The larger the group, the

small-group communication Communication in gatherings that vary in size from three to about fifteen persons.

greater the probability that some members will not be able to talk as much as they would like. Size can also impair group performance, as implied in the adage "too many chefs spoil the broth." There may be an optimal number of people for solving a given problem; additional people may cause confusion and impede, rather than help, group progress.

Types of Groups

When you think of "groups," what comes to mind? You can probably identify quite a few reasons for people to gather together. A group's *purpose* provides perhaps the clearest way of distinguishing one type of group from another.

Task-oriented groups are those that have a job to do. Within this designation, we can make additional divisions. A **problem-solving group** attempts to discover a solution to a problem by analyzing it thoroughly. Typically, problem-solving groups use discussion to investigate a problem and examine possible solutions in terms of which solution best solves the problem. Problem-solving groups have received the most attention from researchers, and problem- solving discussion is also the most common assignment in group communication courses in communication departments. **Decision-making groups** are also concerned with problem solving. However, they have the added function of actually deciding which solution will be implemented, when and how it will be put into effect, how progress will be monitored, how changes in the solution will be handled, and how the program involving the solution will be evaluated. The **idea-generation group** is a third kind of task group. The purpose of idea-generation groups is to discover a variety of solutions, approaches, perspectives, or consequences for a topic. The ideas generated are not evaluated because value judgments tend to inhibit members. For example, a member might hesitate to express an idea if he or she fears a negative reaction. The idea-generation group is often called a "brainstorming" group.

A second type of group is the **therapy group**. The purpose of therapy groups is to help the individual solve personal problems. These groups are conducted by professionals such as clinical psychologists. There are many different kinds of therapy groups. Some of the most common are encounter groups, T-groups, and sensitivity groups, all of which hope to promote personal growth. Tactics to stimulate personal insights often include challenges, criticism, personal attacks, displays of strong emotions, and demonstrations of support. Assertiveness training involves the use of groups to help individuals learn to protect their rights, to resist group pressure, to assume leadership roles, and to approach social situations confidently. Other examples include groups to help people exercise regularly, lose weight, quit smoking, and stop drinking alcoholic beverages. The communication discipline has conducted little research and has had little experience with therapy groups because few communication scholars are trained therapists.

task-oriented groups Groups that have a particular job to do.

problem-solving group A type of task oriented group that attempts to develop a solution to a problem by analyzing it thoroughly.

decision-making groups A type of task-oriented group that problem solves plus decides what solution will be implemented, when and how the solution will be implemented, how progress will be monitored and how changes in the solution will be handled.

idea-generation group A type of task-oriented groups that seeks to discover a variety of solutions, approaches, perspectives, consequences, etc., for a topic.

therapy groups Groups that have the purpose of helping individuals solve personal problems.

Consciousness-raising groups exist to increase members' awareness of shared characteristics or concerns. These commonalities can be a characteristic such as gender, nationality, or religion; a value such as respect for animal rights; an experience such as serving in the military; an ability such as intercollegiate athletics; or a profession. The purpose of consciousness-raising groups is to have members realize more vividly who they are, to be proud of what makes them unique, and to have members change their behavior so it is more in line with this new consciousness. For instance, consciousness-raising group might help members realize various ways that women today are victims of discrimination and offer methods for dealing with each form of discrimination.

consciousness-raising groups Groups designed to increase persons' awareness of characteristics and concerns in order to stimulate action.

Learning groups constitute a fourth type of group. The purpose is for individuals and the group to acquire more information and understanding of a topic. This type of group is sometimes used in educational settings such as high schools and colleges. There are some advantages to group versus individual effort in learning. For example, group members can divide the work; each member adds his or her unique perspective to enrich what the group learns; members gain insight from discussing information that might not have been gained in the absence of such discussion; and motivation to continue learning can be enhanced.

learning groups Groups whose major purpose is to acquire more information and understanding of a topic.

Therapy, learning, and consciousness-raising groups have been studied generally by the fields of psychology, sociology, education, and counseling. As mentioned earlier, group communication theory and research in the communication field has focused primarily on problem-solving and decision-making groups. We will now examine several important elements in such groups.

Roles

The concept of roles is a very basic one in the study of group communication. Certain communicative behaviors in groups (such as using humor to get members to relax) are intended to accomplish certain goals (releasing group tension, for example). Someone enacting those behaviors can be described as playing or taking a given role. In 1948 Benne and Sheats provided an analysis of roles that has remained influential over the years. They said there are three main categories of roles enacted by group members. *Group task roles* pertain to group discussions aimed at selecting, defining, and solving problems. The specific task roles identified by Benne and Sheats are

1. **Initiator–Contributor**—proposes new ideas, changes, procedures.
2. **Information Seeker**—asks questions about information and others' suggestions.
3. **Opinion Seeker**—asks questions about the values guiding the group.
4. **Information Giver**—presents evidence relevant to the group problem.
5. **Opinion Giver**—states his or her position on issues.

6. **Elaborator**—clarifies what is being considered, extends the analysis of an issue.
7. **Coordinator**—gets people to function together, puts information together
8. **Orienter**—keeps group focused on goals, points out departures from goals.
9. **Evaluator–Critic**—argues the evidence and reasoning pertaining to issues.
10. **Energizer**—motivates group toward a quality decision.
11. **Procedural Technician**—performs routine tasks, busywork.
12. **Recorder**—writes group proceedings so a record exists.

These roles are often performed by more than one person in a group. One person might perform several of the twelve task roles during the course of a discussion. In fact, a single incident of communication might involve several roles: a member offers an opinion, follows that with a question, and then tries to energize the group so it will not "drag its heels."

The second category of roles is termed *group building and maintenance.* These roles are concerned with the socioemotional climate in the group. That is, the feelings that group members have for one another and the task are recognized as very important in terms of the group achieving its task goals. These roles are

1. **Encourager**—provides positive feedback to members, shows warmth.
2. **Harmonizer**—reduces tension between members and mediates conflict.
3. **Compromiser**—attempts to have each party in a conflict gain something.
4. **Gatekeeper**—promotes open channels of communication and participation by everyone.
5. **Standard Setter**—suggests and uses standards to evaluate the group.
6. **Group Commentator**—describes the processes operating in the group to change or reinforce the group climate.
7. **Follower**—conforms to group ideas, acts as a good listener.

These seven roles and the first twelve roles are all concerned with the group achieving its purpose. Thus, each of these nineteen roles is very group centered. However, not all behavior in a group conforms to this selfless behavior. Sometimes a person tries to satisfy individual needs, which may be totally irrelevant to the group's task. Such behavior can be counterproductive to the group achieving its goals. These behaviors are termed *individual roles.*

1. **Aggressor**—attacks self-concepts of others to assert dominance.
2. **Blocker**—is hostile by being negative and opposing things unreasonably.

3. Recognition-Seeker—offends members by calling too much attention to self.
4. Self-Confessor—works personal problems into the discussion in hope of gaining insight.
5. Playboy—indicates a desire to be somewhere else, preferably having fun.
6. Dominator—interrupts, manipulates, and tries to control others.
7. Help-Seeker—wants sympathy, acts insecure, confused, and helpless.
8. Special Interest Pleader—argues for a "pet" idea, often based on prejudice.

Leadership

It is not difficult to imagine how chaotic our institutions, corporations, organizations, clubs, and political parties would be if they had little leadership. However, such speculation is a moot point. Without leadership, the groups would never have formed in the first place! The many fields studying leadership have produced an enormous body of literature. In his classic analysis of leadership, Ralph Stogdill (1974; Stogdill & Bass, 1981; see also Bass & Stogdill, 1990) identified forty major topics and examined over 3,000 books and articles. He found that most topics were organized around seven main categories: leadership theory, leader personality and behavior, leadership stability and change, leadership emergence, leadership and social power, leader–follower interactions, and leadership and group performance.

The communication field has taken four approaches to leadership: trait, functional, style, and situational. A **trait approach to leadership** is based on the idea that leaders have traits that distinguish them from followers. You will recall from Chapter 5 that a trait is a characteristic of an individual that is generally consistent from one situation to the next. Trait research suggests leaders are more likely than followers to be high on traits such as self-esteem, extroversion, open-mindedness, aggression, achievement motivation, analytical thought, sociability, and argumentativeness.

trait approach to leadership Assumes that leaders have traits that distinguish them from followers.

A **functional approach to leadership** focuses on the leadership behaviors needed by a group to accomplish its goals (Barnlund & Haiman, 1960), not on the individual as in the trait approach. The leadership behaviors that are essential to the success of a group do not have to be performed by a single person. Instead, leadership can be enacted by any number of group members. Two types of leadership behaviors are task and group maintenance. One person in a problem-solving group might provide leadership for the task, another person for group maintenance, while a third person might provide some help in both areas. Task leadership behaviors include initiating ideas and procedures, coordinating members' contributions, summarizing to let the group know its progress, and elaborating on ideas; group maintenance behaviors involve

functional approach to leadership Focuses on the leadership behaviors needed by a group to accomplish its goals, not on specific individuals.

releasing tension that builds to an unproductive level, regulating the amount of talk by each member, improving group morale, and mediating group conflict (Beebe & Masterson, 2003).

John Cragan and David Wright (1999) provided a useful analysis of the leadership behaviors needed in a problem-solving or decision-making small group. Leadership communication behaviors in the *task area* are contributing ideas, seeking ideas, evaluating ideas, asking others to evaluate ideas, and fostering understanding of ideas. The leadership behaviors in the *procedural area* are setting goals for the group, preparing an agenda or outline for the group to follow, clarifying ideas, summarizing at various points in the discussion, and verbalizing when the group is in complete agreement on something. There also are several leadership communication behaviors in the *interpersonal relations area*: regulating participation so no one feels "left out," creating a positive emotional climate, promoting group self-analysis, resolving conflict in the discussion, and instigating conflict to stimulate a more thorough examination of issues.

The **style approach** has identified three major types of leadership: authoritarian, democratic, and laissez-faire (White & Lippett, 1968). Each style represents a unique set of leadership behaviors. In contrast to individual traits or functions any group members can perform, the emphasis is on different ways of leading.

The **authoritarian style** involves the leader being very directive in terms of the group goals and procedures, the division of work, and deciding the outcome of conflict. Group members do not feel free to argue with the leader on these matters. Research suggests that groups can be quite productive with an authoritarian leader; however, members' satisfaction with their experience in the group tends to be lower than with other leadership styles. The authoritarian style is said to be most appropriate in situations that are highly stressful or dangerous (emergencies, for instance) or highly competitive (such as an athletic contest). The belief is that argument in such situations can be counterproductive; what works best is a strong, competent central figure who guides the group forcefully down an efficient and productive path.

In contrast, the **democratic style** views all issues (including goals, procedures, and work assignments) as matters to be discussed by the group. The actual decision on the issues can be made in one of three ways. A *majority decision* is produced when members vote. The agreed-upon percentage (for example, 51 percent, 67 percent) of votes must be obtained for an idea to pass. *Consensus* occurs when the group tries to find a resolution to the given issue that everyone in the group can support. This can be difficult to achieve. If such a solution can be found, it will enjoy significant group support. A *participative decision* involves members contributing ideas and the leader then being guided by the expressed preferences in making the decision. On a more macro level, of course, this is a central feature of our representative form of government. The democratic style of leadership tends to produce the most member satisfaction,

style approach to leadership A leadership approach that focuses on the different ways or styles people use to lead others.

authoritarian style A style of leadership that involves the leader being very directive in terms of the group goals and procedures, the division of work, and deciding the outcome of conflict.

democratic style A style of leadership that involves viewing all issues (including goals, procedures, and work assignments) as matters to be discussed by the group.

even if the group is not as productive as those operating under another leadership style.

The **laissez-faire style** of leadership involves a minimum of involvement by the leader in group activity. Basically, the leader provides as much information as needed, and then the group members are left to make decisions as a group, to act as individuals, or as subgroups. This lack of direction from a leader can be counterproductive, especially in groups with low motivation for a task. However, this style can work very well with people who are highly motivated, experienced self-starters who work well together. The leader says in essence, "You don't need me to tell you what to do."

laissez-faire style A style of leadership that involves a minimum of involvement by the leader in group activity.

Conflict

The term *conflict* has unfavorable connotations for some people. Certainly, there are types of conflict that are destructive. However, not all forms of conflict are necessarily bad. In fact, certain kinds of conflict are essential to the success of a problem-solving or decision-making group. The theory of groupthink discussed later in this chapter illustrates rather vividly what happens when there is too little conflict in important decision-making groups.

Conflict exists in a small group when proponents of differing positions on an issue are motivated to defend their positions. Overt disagreement in a group is another way to think of conflict. According to B. Aubrey Fisher (1970), problem-solving and decision-making groups typically go through four stages: orientation to the task, conflict over what the group should do, the emergence of a group position, and group reinforcement of the decision. The conflict stage is especially important in determining what will be the final group product.

The influence of conflict on the group product was clearly illustrated in research by Charlan Nemeth (1986). She discovered that conflict in a small, problem-solving group improved the quality of the group's process in making decisions. The conflict she studied took the form of an argumentative minority that opposed the majority opinion. Nemeth found that having a vocal minority view did not necessarily persuade the majority away from their initial position. Instead, an argumentative minority tended to stimulate the majority toward a more careful, thoughtful, and thorough decision. This illustrates an important function of conflict in small groups. The conflict does not have to result in the proponents of one position "converting" the believers of another position. Instead, conflict can lead to a more carefully considered decision—one that looks at a number of advantages and disadvantages before reaching a conclusion.

Conflict in small groups can be viewed in terms of argument. That is, the interaction in problem-solving groups can be analyzed according to the issues over which there was disagreement, the positions taken and defended by the various group members, the attempts to refute the positions, and whether these aspects of argument help explain the group outcome, especially the quality of the group decision. An argumentative approach to studying small group communication holds considerable promise. Randy Hirokawa's functional theory (discussed later in this chapter) reveals that certain kinds of communication in small groups, including argument, distinguish effective from ineffective problem-solving groups.

Following the principles of argumentation theory (careful analysis of issues, emphasis on evidence, use of rigorous forms of reasoning, avoiding fallacies in reasoning, etc.) can produce constructive conflict; other forms of disagreement or competition can be very destructive. For instance, conflict over scarce resources with individuals who are concerned only with "getting their share" can result in long-lasting bitter feelings. Another destructive type of conflict involves personal disagreements between people that result in the use of verbal aggression. Recall from Chapter 5 that a verbally aggressive message attacks the self-concept of the receiver to deliver psychological pain. This tactic used in conflicts between people makes it very difficult for them to work together on a problem-solving task.

A central premise in the belief that conflict can be constructive is the idea that argumentation is a tool for discovering which ideas are valid and which are not. Whenever there is concern over whether something is right or wrong, valuable or worthless, exists or not, and especially whenever there is a solution to be selected, conflict is an asset rather than something to be avoided. The solution that survives the rigors of argumentation is the one that is most likely to be effective. This is "trial by fire" or a "survival of the fittest" test as applied to ideas.

Conformity

conformity A type of group influence, a change in the individual brought about by pressure (real or imagined) for the person to behave in a manner advocated by the group.

Conformity is sometimes a product of group communication. Conformity can be defined as: *"A change in behavior or belief toward a group as a result of real or imagined group pressure"* (Kiesler & Kiesler, 1969, p. 2). Conformity is a type of group influence, a change in the individual brought about by pressure (real or imagined) for the person to behave in a manner advocated by the group. For example, some students in a study group might say, "Let's take a break and finish this job tomorrow." One member might dissent and say he or she wants to continue and to finish the job today. After all the other members of the group express dissatisfaction with continuing, the lone dissenter says, "Well, OK, let's call it quits for now." The person was not able to resist the pressure to conform to the wishes of other members. This experience is generally a universal one. All of us at times decide to conform to what the group wants to do rather than to resist. Often we conclude that to resist would be too costly. It would create many more problems than it would solve, so we decide resistance is not worth it, and we "go along to get along."

One type of conformity is *public compliance;* the individual behaves in the way desired by the group only when being observed by group members, because the person does not really believe in the behavior. Thus, a person might speak favorably about a given political candidate because of pressure from a group. However, in the privacy of the voting booth the person might vote for someone else. This type of conformity recognizes that our behavior is not always consistent with our beliefs and attitudes. Sometimes we believe one way but behave in another manner because of group pressure. *Private acceptance* is a second kind of conformity. Here the person behaves as suggested by the group because the group produces a change in the person's beliefs and attitudes. Thus, the person is not "pretending" when behaving in a particular manner (Kiesler & Kiesler, 1969).

In our study group example, one of the members in the majority might say to the lone dissenter, "You are suggesting that we make this a marathon session. However, I recently read some research that showed the quality of performance for a group with a task such as ours falls off sharply right about where we are now in the number of nonstop hours worked." Our lone dissenter might then say, "I didn't realize that, but it certainly is plausible given other things that I've read about achievement. OK, let's finish tomorrow." Conformity in this instance is different because it is based not only on group pressure but also on an internal change in the individual.

There also is the possibility that one does not have to change a behavior to conform. A group can essentially reinforce the individual's ideas by pressuring him or her to remain a certain way, to continue a certain behavior and not to change. For instance, a physical fitness club might take a strong stance against the use of anabolic steroid drugs as performance enhancers. One of the members might be tempted to try steroids. However, the group pressure might keep the person from experimenting with the drug. In this case, the group influenced the person by strengthening or reinforcing previous beliefs (for example, the knowledge that steroids cause liver damage) and patterns of behavior (following a routine to build muscles gradually and safely, for instance). This reinforcement can be viewed as a type of conformity—one that has received little attention from researchers, but one that could have some useful applications, especially in preventing destructive influences on children and adolescents.

There are several reasons for our compliance with group pressure. Being a member of a given group partially satisfies our *need to belong,* to be included. Thus, if the group threatens to exclude us because we do not want to go along, our feelings of belonging are endangered. The group is also influential because it serves a valuable *reference function* by informing members on what is and what is not acceptable behavior. The group provides a basis for comparison so that individuals can evaluate their behavior. "I must be dressing OK; everyone in the group dresses just like me." *Group attractiveness* is a third reason for being influenced by group pressure. Generally, the more attractive a group is to us, the more we are likely to be influenced by it. If we are attracted to a group, we have strong feelings of liking, and it is difficult to go against those feelings unless the issue is very important. Moreover, because we usually evaluate a group as attractive because its members express liking for us, we find it difficult to resist pressure from the group because we fear members will stop liking us. This is a powerful incentive to yield to group pressure because we have a need for affection and generally deplore losing the respect of others. Such a loss could threaten our need to belong (the first reason). Finally, *group maintenance* sometimes is a reason for conforming. We realize that the group needs to put on a united front. If one member behaves differently, it will weaken the image of the group. Thus, we may conform for the good of the group.

FUNCTIONAL THEORY OF GROUP DECISION QUALITY

Groups—and researchers who study them—want to know whether decisions reached were good or bad. In a problem-solving discussion, can you distinguish high- from low-quality decisions by what is said? Do certain types of communication lead to an effective decision, whereas others predict that the decision will be defective? This issue of group decision quality is the focus of Hirokawa's functional theory. The principles of the theory involve the communication characteristics of group interaction that lead to quality decisions. Stating such principles in probability terms constitutes a law: if a group does A, B, and C, it is highly likely that they will make a quality decision.

One study analyzed videotaped discussions of various groups who were judged to have reached an effective or an ineffective decision (Hirokawa & Pace, 1983). Four communication characteristics distinguished effective from ineffective groups. The first was that effective groups rigorously evaluated the validity of opinions and assumptions made by the individuals in the group. Ineffective groups, however, glossed over the evaluation procedure and accepted opinions and assumptions as facts without critical analysis. A second difference in communication pertained to how groups evaluated alternatives. Effective groups analyzed possible solutions thoroughly with very critical attention paid to consequences—what would happen if the solution were adopted. Ineffective groups were superficial. Usually they simply said a given solution did or did not meet the criteria for a good solution; they did not argue why. Third, effective groups based their decisions on reasonable premises (assumptions); ineffective groups based their decisions on inaccurate, highly questionable premises. No member of the ineffective groups made an effort to correct these mistakes. The fourth communication characteristic was the quality of leadership. In effective groups, the leaders encouraged *constructive argumentation* by introducing issues, challenging other positions, and identifying fallacies in reasoning. The leaders of ineffective groups exerted a negative effect on the quality of the group's decision by influencing the group to accept faulty ideas, introducing ridiculous ideas, or leading the group on a tangent.

Interestingly, this study also identified communication characteristics that did *not* distinguish effective from ineffective groups: participating equally, trying to identify important information, attempting to generate a number of possible solutions to a problem, and using a set of criteria in evaluating the various possible solutions. These characteristics were found in both effective and ineffective groups.

Hirokawa's functional theory maintains that a group needs to fulfill four critical functions to reach an effective, high-quality decision:

1. Achieving a thorough understanding of the problem that requires a decision
2. Discovering a range of realistic and acceptable possible solutions
3. Identifying the criteria for an effective, high-quality solution
4. Assessing the positive and negative consequences of possible solutions to select the solution with the most desirable consequences

Hirokawa (1985) conducted a study that examined the communication behavior of groups and found that the more the four functions were satisfied, the higher the quality of the group's decision. Statistical analysis revealed that understanding the problem and recognizing the possible negative consequences of each potential solution best differentiated the groups that reached effective decisions from those which were ineffective. In a later study Hirokawa (1988) found the amount of time spent talking about the four functions did not predict decision quality. Instead, it was the quality of talk that mattered.

Hirokawa and Scheerhorn (1986) identified factors that contribute to a group making a faulty decision. Their basic idea is "that group members influence the quality of a group's decision by facilitating or inhibiting the occurrence of errors (for example, faulty interpretations and conclusions) during various stages of the decision-making process" (p. 63). The five factors are:

1. Inadequate assessment of the problem (failing to recognize signs of the problem, its full extent, seriousness; not identifying the causes of the problem)
2. Inappropriate goals and objectives for dealing with the problem (not identifying objectives that will correct the problem; selecting unnecessary objectives that burden the group)
3. Improper assessment of consequences (ignoring or underestimating the positive and/or negative consequences of a possible solution; overestimating the positive and/or negative consequences)
4. Establishment of an inadequate information base (flawed information, group rejecting valid information, group collecting too little or too much information)
5. Invalid reasoning from the information base (making mistakes in reasoning; using only the information that supports a preferred but flawed choice)

These five sources of faulty decisions result from the communication of the group members. A group member facilitates the errors through social influence by convincing members to accept an invalid inference. Group members can also prevent these five factors from contributing to a bad decision. This too is accomplished through communication, as when a member corrects a fallacious conclusion by another group member.

Dennis Gouran and Randy Hirokawa (1986) termed this kind of corrective communicative behavior **counteractive influence**. It counteracts by neutralizing or negating faulty communication. In doing so, the group is then able to make progress toward an effective decision. This type of influence is very important in getting a group back on track. Both effective and ineffective groups make mistakes. However, a characteristic of effective groups is that counteractive influence is prevalent, and uncorrected mistakes are rare in comparison to ineffective groups. Counteractive influence is another illustration of the positive role of argument in group decision making.

Hirokawa's theory, and the one by Janis discussed next, represent the laws perspective for theory building. The emphasis is on discovering conditions that lead to certain outcomes; this probabilistic reasoning takes an "if this, then that" form. There is a direct interest in what happens to groups and the antecedent conditions that lead to an outcome, such as decision quality. Hirokawa's theory represents an important step in understanding the communicative conditions that need to exist for a group to reach a quality decision. Future research will build on that foundation and further our understanding of the type of communication necessary for effective decision making in groups.

counteractive influence A behavior in functional group decision making where a member corrects a fallacious conclusion by another group member.

THEORY OF GROUPTHINK

Social psychologist Irving Janis's (1982) theory of groupthink is also concerned with the quality of decisions reached in groups. However, whereas functional theory centered on explaining superior group decisions, the theory of groupthink is about group failures—decisions that in hindsight seem incredibly poor, ill advised, and generally incompetent. The basic problem Janis tried to solve is how a group of persons, who individually are quite competent, can make a collective decision that is utterly incompetent. The theory was based on historical analyses of national fiascoes such as the Bay of Pigs invasion, inactivated defenses at Pearl Harbor, and escalation of the Vietnam War. The theory of groupthink was offered as an explanation of such failures.

Groupthink is a communication process that sometimes develops when members of a group begin thinking similarly, greatly reducing the probability that the group will reach an effective decision. To explain groupthink, we will first say what it is *not*. Groupthink is not critical thinking, where decisions are based on thorough discussions of the problem and the possible good and bad

groupthink
A communication process that sometimes develops when members of a group begin thinking similarly, greatly reducing the probability that the group will reach an effective decision.

consequences of potential solutions. Groupthink does not involve group argumentation where ideas are tested for validity; remember, superior ideas are those that survive the argumentation process. Groupthink is not an attitude that says, "I am going to present this objection to what the group favors even if it means some people will be a little upset with me for not going along."

The definition by negation, then, suggests several features of groupthink. When groupthink develops, there is a high level of cohesiveness among members and a great deal of reluctance to deviate from the group position. Cohesiveness is the feeling of "oneness" in a group, being "close-knit," bound to one another, and united, as members of a team. Cohesiveness is normally a desirable condition in groups. It is undesirable when members place such a priority on solidarity that they do not analyze problems thoroughly and reach decisions without adequately considering the consequences of proposed solutions. As a result, groups reach consensus on a course of action prematurely. This can cause a group of superior individuals to make a very inferior decision and to select the wrong solution. The communication in a group that is operating under groupthink lacks argumentation and has little rigorous clash of positions on issues. Figure 10.1 presents a summary of the theory of groupthink.

cohesiveness The feeling of "oneness" in a group, being "close-knit," bound to one another, and united as members of a team.

Facilitating Conditions	Symptoms of Groupthink	Defective Decision Making	
Cohesive group	Overestimation of power and importance a. illusion of invulnerability b. belief in the inherent morality of the group	Inadequate analysis of problem Limited range of solutions No rigorous assessment of consequences of preferred solution Failure to reconsider initially rejected solutions	
Group structure a. too isolated b. biased leadership c. lack of procedure	Closed-mindedness a. collective rationalizations b. stereotypes of out-groups	Inadequate research Biased processing	Successful Solution Unlikely
Environment a. external pressure b. lack of alternatives c. low self-esteem	Great pressure toward consensus a. self-censorship b. illusion of unanimity c. direct pressure on dissenters d. self-appointed mindguards	Lack of contingency plans	

Adapted from Janis (1982), p. 244.

Figure 10.1

The theory of groupthink.

According to the theory, groupthink is more likely when three conditions are present in decision-making groups. The first is a necessary condition but not a sufficient one. For groupthink to develop, *the group must be cohesive* with a strong desire for the group to remain that way. However, just because a decision-making group is cohesive is not sufficient for groupthink to develop. At least two other conditions are necessary: group structure that promotes groupthink and an environment where groupthink flourishes.

The *structure of a decision-making group* can lead to groupthink. For example, if a group is isolated from information and from other persons in a larger organization, the structure can preclude exposure to differing opinions. A biased leader, one who clearly establishes very early the solution he or she prefers, creates a group structure conducive to groupthink. Group members may not advance other possible solutions and may be reluctant to question critically the leader's preferred solution. Another structural factor occurs when the group does not have established procedures for making decisions. Having a set of rigorous procedures (such as bringing in outside experts before the final decision is reached) can reduce the chance of a disastrous decision. Without a tradition of rigorous decision-making procedures, a group can more easily succumb to pressure toward uniformity and thus agree to a very flawed course of action.

The *nature of the situation* represents another facilitating condition for groupthink. Stress nurtures groupthink, especially when the group feels pressure from outside sources to solve a particular problem. A group can make a very bad decision because they feel pressure to present a united front and not to "rock the boat." If the group fails to consider and evaluate a number of solutions, perhaps because they don't have sufficient resources or time, they may agree to one solution without considering other possibilities. If a group feels low in esteem because of recent failures, they will also be more susceptible to pressure toward consensus.

Three major symptoms indicate the groupthink syndrome. First, the *group tends to overestimate its power and importance*—believing strongly that "right" is on its side and that opposing forces are "evil." This creates a false sense of confidence that entices groups to take greater risks than they otherwise would. A second symptom is that the *group becomes very closed-minded.* In selecting a risky course of action, they discount clear warnings and avoid considering information that refutes their choice. In the case of foreign policy decisions, enemy leaders are viewed as too weak or too stupid to find any flaws in the group's selected course of action, so success seems assured. The third symptom of groupthink is *great pressure in the group to reach consensus.* Individuals minimize the importance of their doubts to preserve unanimity. Pressure is exerted against any group member who expresses a strong argument against the group's positions. When these symptoms occur, the process of groupthink is probably operating.

Groupthink impairs decision making, greatly increasing the probability of a blunder. Of course, pure luck can "save" a group in such circumstances; the solution selected by a flawed procedure could serendipitously turn out to be the best of all possible solutions. However, the likelihood of that happening is low because the process by which a decision is reached through groupthink will have several major defects. First, the pressure of cohesiveness results in faulty analysis. The problem is not understood thoroughly; thus, its causes are not well known. Because a solution should deal with a problem's cause, this defect is indeed serious. There are also other deficiencies. Other possible solutions are ignored or dismissed because there is an early preference for a particular solution. The consequences of the preferred solution are not examined rigorously. This is perhaps the most fatal flaw in the process. Also, there is not enough reanalysis of solutions that were initially rejected. When groupthink operates, there is typically a lack of research and thus a shortage of necessary information. Because there is an early preference for a particular solution, information is processed in a biased fashion. For instance, information that suggests the preferred solution will cause economic hardship may be viewed as outdated despite its accuracy in the past. A final defect is that groups tend not to make contingency plans when they fall into the trap of groupthink because of the unjustified confidence they have in their solution. For example, if a decision was made by a company to save labor costs by moving its manufacturing plant to a developing country, a necessary contingency plan would deal with possible political instability in that country.

Although groupthink can be a serious problem in decision-making groups, Janis pointed out that several strategies can avoid groupthink. All the procedures are designed to prevent a group from reaching premature consensus and to keep feelings of cohesiveness from turning into group pressure for uniformity.

- The leader of a decision-making group should encourage group members to voice doubts, concerns, or objections.

- The leader should be impartial in presenting the task to the group by using unbiased language and being careful not to show a preference for a particular solution.

- The organization or larger group should set up more than one group with different leaders to work on the same problem.

- The decision-making group should at times divide into two or more subgroups that work separately and then meet together to debate differences.

- Each member should get the reactions of someone outside the group and report concerns back to the group.

- Trusted members of the organization who are not members of the actual decision-making group should be brought into some meetings to challenge the positions of the group.

- To stimulate debate, one member of the group should be assigned the role of devil's advocate when solutions are being evaluated.

- When the decision involves rivals, such as a competing organization, scenarios of the rival's possible reactions should be created. Emphasis should be placed on the potential risks of the various solutions.

- Once preliminary agreement is reached on a solution, a "last chance" meeting should be held for members to present lingering doubts and to rethink the issue before making the final decision.

It is apparent that the groupthink remedies involve communication that is argumentative in nature. The prevention of groupthink involves encouraging group members to engage in vigorous debate. The idea is that confidence in a solution is warranted if it survives in a competition of intense debate with other possible solutions.

Although the theory of groupthink has been used mainly to study historical accounts of bad decisions, one study demonstrated that groupthink can be examined in a laboratory setting (Courtright, 1978). The results supported the theory of groupthink. This support is important for a laws theory. Remember that a basic goal of laws theories is to identify the antecedent conditions that lead to the prediction.

MULTIPLE SEQUENCE MODEL OF GROUP DECISIONS

unitary sequence model
Model of group decision making that identifies stages that groups go through as they move toward a decision.

multiple sequence model
A model of group decision making that suggests groups can have different patterns of sequences because they can take various paths to a decision.

There have been two distinctive approaches to how groups reach decisions in discussions concerned with problem solving. The **unitary sequence model** suggests groups pass through certain stages as they move toward a decision. For instance, a problem-solving group first determines the nature of the problem to be solved, the standards that a solution should meet, which of the available solutions best meet the standards, and how the solution selected should be implemented and evaluated. According to Marshall Scott Poole (1981) the unitary sequence model represents a logical ideal of how groups should move toward a decision. Groups do not often follow this ideal.

One study looked at forty-seven group decisions to determine the paths taken in reaching decisions (Poole & Roth, 1989). Only eleven of the forty-seven decisions followed the unitary sequence. Fourteen of the decisions followed a solution-oriented path because almost none of the communication pertained to the problem. Twenty-two of the decisions involved complex paths in which the group followed from two to seven problem-solution cycles.

Research such as this suggests a second approach to how groups reach decisions. The **multiple sequence model** (Poole 1981, 1983a, 1983b) contends groups can have different patterns of sequences because they can take various paths to a decision, depending on the contingencies in the situation. This model uses a systems perspective; the emphasis is on patterns of interaction and situational contingencies. The multiple sequence model identifies three separate tracks of group communication activity: *task, relational,* and *topical.* The three **activity tracks**, in a given decision-making group, develop simultaneously but usually at uneven rates. The development of the tracks is influenced by breakpoints that tend to interrupt the development of the activity tracks. There are three kinds of **breakpoints**: *pacers, delays,* and *disruptions.*

The **task activity track** includes the processes in which the group engages to accomplish its task. Some of these are deciding how to proceed, gathering information, analyzing the problem, establishing standards for solutions, and selecting a solution. Imagine a group responsible for acquiring football players for a professional football team. They begin meeting well before the National Football League collegiate player draft in April. Their task is to decide which eligible collegiate players they should draft to strengthen their team. One of the tasks the director of player personnel would introduce early is a problem analysis. Specifically, what positions were weakest this past season; where is the need for new talent greatest? If it is decided the need is most apparent at defensive tackle, another task process will be to establish the standards for a solution. For instance, what should the player's time be in the 40-yard dash, what height and weight are ideal, does he have to be a proven pass-rusher, etc.? The process of selecting a solution would involve strategies such as: in the first round of the player draft, if our first choice for defensive tackle has been selected, we will go to our second; if the second has also been selected, we will switch to our first, second, and third choices for free safety (our second greatest need).

The **relational activity track** involves the activities that emphasize the relationships among the group members that pertain to how the group works together. These include how ideas are introduced and criticized, how conflict is managed, and how roles are defined and reinforced. In our pro football example, the director of player personnel might specify how scouts will work together to evaluate players. At meetings where prospective players are evaluated, one person in the group might be asked to give an overview of a player's strengths and weaknesses, and then the other members are invited to argue for or against drafting the player. When traveling to evaluate players, hotel room assignments might be made so that good friends room together.

The **topical activity track** is made up of the content of the issues and arguments of concern to the group at various times in the discussion. The distinction between the first two tracks and the topical track is process versus content. The first two tracks concern the paths the group follows in discussing content. An example of the topical process track in our pro football example might be: player A has the size and speed that we are looking for but he only had three quarterback sacks last season; player B managed fifteen sacks, but he is not quite big enough for us. This topic could be considered while a group is selecting a solution (task track) or while managing a conflict (relational track).

activity tracks Component of the multiple sequence model that entails task, relational, and topical tracks.

breakpoints Component of the multiple sequence model that are interruptions in an activity track.

task activity track A decision-making track in which the group engages to accomplish its task.

relational activity track A decision-making track in which the group activities emphasize the relationships among the group members that pertain to how the group works.

topical activity track A decision-making track made up of the content of the issues and arguments of concern to the group at various times in the discussion.

pacers A type of breakpoint in the small group decision-making process that determines how a discussion moves along.

delays A type of breakpoint in the small group decision-making process that occurs when the group cycles back to rework an issue.

disruptions A type of breakpoint in the small group decision-making process that occurs when there is a major disagreement or when the decision-making process agreed upon by the group fails.

Breakpoints influence how decisions develop. There are three types. Pacers, or normal breakpoints, determine how a discussion moves along. A topic shift is the most common breakpoint influencing pacing. Other normal or expected breakpoints are adjournments, planning periods, or getting away to reflect on topics. Delays occurs when the group cycles back to rework an issue. The group might go back through the very same analysis several times to solve a problem. For instance, an argument might be repeated several times. This may be a difficult period for the group, but it can also stimulate great creativity if the group rises to meet the challenge. Disruptions are a type of breakpoint that occurs in at least two different forms. The first is a major disagreement. When this happens, all three activity tracks could be disrupted. Even after the disagreement is settled, it may take the group a while to get back on track. For example, relational difficulties might be created by conflict that hinders task and topical activities. In our example, two scouts who dislike each other (a relational difficulty) may argue about a particular player, slowing down the decision-making procedure (a task activity). Further, they might distort the player's strengths and weaknesses (topic track), which makes it difficult for the group to get back to a productive discussion. A second type of disruption occurs when a process adopted by the group fails. This could occur when the work is divided among group members, but one assignment turns out to be many times more difficult than the others. Another example is a group selecting the wrong criteria for a solution. In our pro football example, this could involve emphasizing the size of a player when, instead, the number of quarterback sacks should have been the major consideration.

The activity tracks and the breakpoints in Poole's model identify what goes on when a group meets to solve a problem. The objective of all the activities is to accumulate what is needed to complete the task. What is needed to solve a problem might be thought of as *prerequisites* for decision making. Sometimes a group will begin a problem-solving discussion with some of the prerequisites already satisfied. For a decision-making group, the prerequisites include recognition of the need to make a good decision, analysis of the problem to be solved, determining the criteria for a good solution, discovering the possible solutions, adapting the solutions to the needs of the group, selecting a solution, planning to implement and also to evaluate the solution.

Groups can vary greatly on how ready they are to satisfy each of these prerequisites for a decision. If a group has completed most of the prerequisites, the path to a decision could be relatively simple. On the other hand, if a group has satisfied none of the prerequisites, the path to a decision could be very complex; there could be several problem-solutions cycles.

The decisions resulting from a given path or cycle are governed by several contingencies. Poole's model emphasizes two. The first is the nature of the task. Two dimensions are important. *Difficulty* refers to the amount of effort necessary to complete the task. *Coordination requirements* pertain to the degree that members must integrate their actions and work together. The likelihood of a group accomplishing its task is influenced by these factors. That is, the likelihood of task accomplishment is lower when task difficulty and coordination requirements are higher.

A second contingency of decision development is *group history*. What happened earlier in a group creates expectations about what will happen in the future. Such expectations influence current progress toward an effective decision. Poole (1983b) identified three aspects of a group's history that affect how decisions develop. One aspect pertains to how *involved* members are in the group. Low levels of involvement indicate an individualistic, competitive climate. Higher levels of involvement indicate that members are more dependent on one another. This is typified by a more cooperative climate of decision making. A second factor of a group's history relates to their beliefs about *leadership*. Who the leader is, whether leadership changes over time, and the functions of the leader are relevant concerns. The third factor involves *procedural norms*. A group develops rules, procedures, and roles for guiding its work.

Poole's multiple sequence model of group decisions has emerged as an elaborate and sophisticated explanation of communication and group decision making. The idea that there are three interlocking tracks of activity involved in group decision making is a powerful concept, especially when combined with the concepts of breakpoints and prerequisites.

SUMMARY

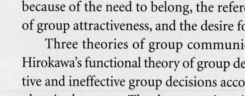

This chapter examined communication in the small-group context—discussions involving three to approximately fifteen members. The problem-solving group is the one studied most by communication scholars. The kinds of roles that people take in groups are task roles, group building/maintenance roles, and individual roles. Leadership behaviors needed in problem-solving groups include task behaviors, procedural behaviors, and interpersonal relationship behaviors. Conflict in group communication can be either constructive or destructive; argumentation is essential for constructive conflict. Conformity is a frequent outcome of group communication; two types of conformity are public compliance and private acceptance. Group pressure creates conformity because of the need to belong, the reference function of groups, the influence of group attractiveness, and the desire for group maintenance.

Three theories of group communication were discussed in some detail. Hirokawa's functional theory of group decision quality attempts to explain effective and ineffective group decisions according to the communication that takes place in the group. The theory posits critical functions groups need to fulfill to reach a quality decision. Janis's theory of groupthink also addresses decision quality. The theory identifies the conditions that encourage groupthink, its symptoms, and consequences; it also suggests methods for controlling groupthink. Poole's multiple sequence model of group decisions explores the paths groups take in reaching decisions. Activity tracks are identified along with breakpoints and discussed in terms of how they develop in problem-solving discussions.

KEY TERMS

activity tracks
authoritarian leadership style
breakpoints
cohesiveness
conflict
conformity
consciousness-raising groups
counteractive influence
decision-making group
delays
democratic leadership style

disruptions
functional approach to leadership
groupthink
group size
idea-generating group
laissez-faire leadership style
learning groups
multiple sequence model
pacers
problem-solving group

relational activity track
roles
small-group communication
style approach
task activity track
task-oriented groups
therapy groups
topical activity track
trait approach to leadership
unitary sequence model

Organizational Contexts

Communication theory within the organization requires that any useful scientific-based theory have bottom-line effects for both organization members as well as organization productivity. Recall in Chapter 2 that the predictive function of theory is paramount for social scientific theory. To that end, many organization theories have been forwarded, discredited, and/or ignored because they either lack predictive power (e.g., critical cultural theories) or are simply bad/flawed theories (see the human relations approach presented later in this chapter). In contemporary organizations, we live in a world in which organizations sometimes operate in unethical and immoral ways in efforts to maximize profits for the few, from the labor of many. Whether it be the collapse of the Enron Corporation or the overbilling of the government by Halliburton Energy Services, communication and communication theory serve as the matrix through which organizations operate. Given this, some organizations utilize theory for prosocial and noble causes, whereas others use theory for the systematic manipulation of the markets with which they serve.

This chapter will present some of the most popular theories that have guided organizations and organizational researchers since the early twentieth century. As will be evidenced in this chapter, communication, although not explicitly termed in early organizational theory building, serves as the main factor for organization productivity and worker satisfaction.

CLASSICAL MANAGEMENT PERSPECTIVES

The first theories addressing how organizations function primarily focused on how to get workers to be efficient producers. With the development of the Industrial Revolution, people moved from the agricultural and rural areas throughout the United States and into industrialized centers. To organize human beings, managers had to become more effective communicators in an effort to coordinate work shifts, give job instruction, and make sure the organization ran as smoothly as possible. It should be noted that these early efforts at organizing workers were fraught with worker exploitation and manipulation. The lack of concern for worker needs permeates early organizational theories, which are known as the **classical management perspective**.

Scientific Management Theory

The **scientific management** theory was developed by Frederick Taylor in 1911. He tested his management approach at the Bethlehem Steel Mill in Cleveland, Ohio. In observing workers in the steel mill, Taylor concluded that workers intentionally work below their full capacity. This intentional underachieving behavior is known as **soldiering**. Soldiering is believed to occur because (a) workers believe that increased productivity will result in a reduction in the number of workers needed to perform a specific task, (b) a wage system does not compensate more productive workers and actually encourages lower productivity from employees, and (c) most worker training has been conducted through unstandardized on-the-job training, which leads to inefficient job performance.

The scientific management approach has three basic assumptions. First, any worker can perform at a high level if given a task that is **scientifically efficient**. A task is considered scientifically efficient when all elements of the task are analyzed, scrutinized, and made optimally efficient. Consider the task of shovel coal into a furnace necessary for the production of steel. To be made scientifically efficient, we would need to consider the distance between the pile of coal and the furnace, the size and type of shovel, and the technique used to pick up, carry, and deposit the coal into the furnace. Once all these elements are analyzed and made optimal, the result is the scientifically efficient way to shovel coal. This process is known as a **time-motion study**. Second, workers are motivated by money and will only perform if paid. This principle "cheapens" human beings in that workers see no other value in high levels of performance other than a means of achieving money. This is what is known as the **dangling carrot approach** to performance. Unfortunately, millions of people get up every morning and go to jobs simply because it pays well, not because they are proud of what they do. Once the job stops paying well, the worker simply finds another well-paying job. Scientific management is not concerned with how you feel as much as how you perform. The third assumption holds that any tasks assigned to workers should be simple and unambiguous. The types of message exchange associated with scientific management theory consist of **upward communication** (i.e., messages that flow from workers to supervisors) and **downward communication** (i.e., messages that are handed down from management to workers).

---

classical management perspective A management perspective that seeks to maximize productivity and has little concern for the worker.

scientific management A management perspective that assumes any worker can be productive if given a scientifically efficient task.

soldiering The assumption that workers purposely work below their capacity.

scientifically efficient A term used to reflect a task that has been analyzed for efficiency so that any worker can optimally perform it.

time-motion study A process used in scientific management theory that reflects the analysis of any given task in an effort to make that task optimally efficient.

dangling carrot approach An approach to performance that assumes people only work for tangible rewards.

upward communication Messages that flow from the worker up to the supervisor.

downward communication Messages that flow from the supervisor down to the worker.

The overall principles of scientific management are logical and relatively simple to institute. However, this perspective tends to treat workers like cogs in a wheel or parts of a machine. In today's society, scientific management is still used in many industries. For example, the fast-food industry utilizes scientific management theory. All employees are trained in performing simple tasks in the same way. Because the training of new employees is so standardized, or scientifically efficient, the high employment turnover rates associated with the fast-food industry do not adversely affect the earnings of these restaurant chains.

Bureaucracy Management Theory

Max Weber (1947) developed a management theory that emphasized tight structure and control over employees. His **bureaucratic management theory** makes a distinction between **power** and **authority**. Power is the ability to force people to do what you want, regardless of their willingness to do so, whereas authority is the ability to get people to voluntarily obey orders. Perhaps the most notable contribution of this theory was the **rational-legal authority system**. The term *rational* refers to designing the organization to achieve certain goals with maximum efficiency, and the term *legal* refers to the use of authority through rules and regulations set forth by the organization.

A main assumption of the bureaucratic structure is that it is believed to be the optimal means for organizing people. This structure has many levels set in a hierarchy. Each hierarchical level regulates the level beneath it. There is also a strong emphasis on **depersonalization**, which refers to a clear separation between personal matters and business matters. It is assumed that this large hierarchical structure and tight organizational rules and regulations allows for control and coordination of worker behavior. One of the drawbacks of this approach is that there is little personal accountability for the quality of production. This lack of accountability has been linked to the emphasis on the depersonalization of the worker from the organization (see Jablin & Putnam, 2001).

Effective Management Theory

The **effective management theory** forwarded by Henri Fayol (1949) assumes that management action should be comprised of planning for the future, organizing, commanding, coordinating, and controlling. Fayol is best known for his militarylike principles of management, which are highlighted in Table 11.1. As you can see from the table, many of Fayol's tenets involve communication and are relationally based. Although Fayol's tenets do indicate some concern for the worker, his approach to management is considered a classic management theory because it overwhelmingly is designed for maximizing organization function and productivity.

bureaucratic management A management perspective that advocates a tight structure with many levels in the hierarchy as well as control over employees.

power The potential to influence or restrict another person's behaviors.

authority The ability to get people to voluntarily obey order.

rational-legal authority system A system of bureaucratic management that advocates organizations should be designed to achieve certain goals through the use of rules and regulations developed by the organization.

depersonalization The process of focusing all interaction in the workplace on task completion and discouraging interactions that are relational in nature.

effective management theory A theory that assumes management action should be comprised of planning for the future, organizing, commanding, coordinating, and controlling.

Table 11.1   **FAYOL'S FOURTEEN FUNDAMENTAL TENETS TO EFFECTIVE MANAGEMENT**

Tenets	Description
Division of Work	Workers who are trained in one task become experts and, thus, most productive.
Authority	The ability to issue orders as well as use power in an appropriate way.
Discipline	Employees will only follow orders to the degree to which management provides effective leadership.
Unity of Command	Employees should only have one manager, thus keeping information clear and consistent.
Unity of Direction	Employees who do similar tasks should all be given the same plan of action.
Subordination of Individual Interest to General Interest	Management must put the needs of the organization above those of any single employee.
Remuneration	Compensation is an important motivating tool.
Centralization or Decentralization	Whichever management chooses to do should be based on current personnel as well as the current health of the organization.
Scalar Chair	Clear hierarchy of information is necessary, and lateral communication is encouraged.
Order	Order is needed at both the production level as well as the personnel level.
Equity	There must be a degree of respect for employees as well as equal justice throughout the organization.
Stability of Tenure	Keeping quality management is crucial, given the cost and time involved in training new management.
Initiative	Employees at all levels of the organization should be allowed to be innovative.
Esprit de Corps	Management is responsible for maintaining high morale levels for all employees.

scalar chain Type of information transfer that reflects the clear lines of upward and downward communication.

By far, the most significant contribution of this approach lies in the **scalar chain** concept of information transfer. The scalar chain is the clear hierarchical information exchange between different levels of the organization. Similar to the communication structure used in the U.S. Armed Services, Fayol believed that there should be clear lines of both upward and downward communication. Further, organizational members at the same level should be able to share

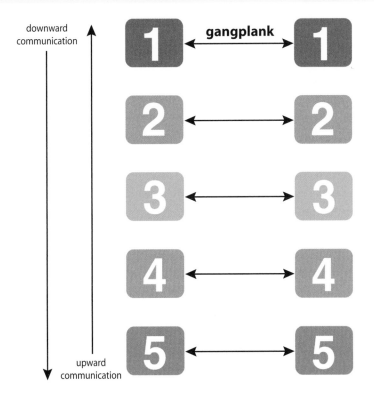

downward communication

gangplank

upward communication

Figure 11.1

Fayol's bridge.

information with one another as long as the organization is aware of this exchange. This lateral exchange of information is known as a gangplank, or **Fayol's bridge** (see Figure 11.1). Reflecting back on the U.S. Armed Services analogy and the scalar principle, the military uses the term GI when referring to a soldier. GI is an acronym for *government issue,* indicating that the soldier is the property of the military (as are tanks, jeeps, and boots). As this indicates, there is concern for the soldier, but in the end, it is about the optimal function of a military force.

The classic management approaches, which advocated productivity over concern for the worker, were a reflection of early industrialization, where organizations had a large uneducated workforce that was easily exploited. In the next section, we see the repercussions of this type of worker treatment.

gangplank   Also known as Fayol's bridge and is the lateral exchange of information between members at the same level in the organization.

HUMAN RELATIONS MANAGEMENT PERSPECTIVES

Unlike the classical management approaches that focus on maximizing productivity with little regard for the worker, the human relations perspective emerged as a direct result of the poor treatment of workers. The researchers most noted for their pioneering work in this area are Elton Mayo, Fritz Roethlisberger, and William Dickson. These researchers served as consultants for what has become

human relations perspective A management approach that advocates management should satisfy the interpersonal and emotional needs of workers.

Hawthorne studies A series of studies between 1927–1932 which gave rise to the human relations approach to management.

known as the Hawthorne studies. Between the years of 1927 and 1932, a series of experiments were conducted to determine the effects of illumination on productivity at the Western Electric Company's Hawthorne Plant located in Chicago, Illinois.

The employees at this plant assembled induction coils needed for telephone systems produced by Western Electric. Because assembling induction coils was considered a "specialized" job, a new management team was assembled to oversee production. The workers were assigned to either the experimental group, consisting of workers who assembled the coils in varied lighting conditions, or a control group, consisting of workers who assembled the coils under normal lighting conditions. Other manipulations during the experiment included additional work breaks, performance-based compensation, and altering lunch and work schedules.

The initial results indicated that there was an increase in productivity. Mayo and his colleagues concluded that the reason for the increased productivity was not the lighting conditions, but the attention given to the workers by the experimenters and the management team. Further, it was also concluded that the strong interpersonal relationships that developed among coworkers made for a cohesive and supportive work group, resulting in increased productivity.

Mayo strongly believed that the workers' need for supportive and high-quality relationships within the workplace was a result of a breakdown in society (Roethlisberger & Dickson, 1949). As a result of industrialization, people who moved away from family and friends to find employment developed unfulfilled relational needs that must be fulfilled by the organization. In this light, Mayo (1933) argued that one of the major functions of management was to foster spontaneous cooperation, which refers to the fostering of teamwork and quality relationships. With regard to conflict, the human relations management perspective strongly advocates that competition and conflict be avoided at all costs, as it has a negative effect on spontaneous cooperation.

spontaneous cooperation The fostering of relationships and teamwork among workgroup members.

These conclusions from the Hawthorne studies marked a paradigmatic change in management approaches from the classic management assumption of maximizing efficiency and productivity to the focus on quality interpersonal relationships and satisfying the psychological needs of the worker.

In more recent years, researchers have reinterpreted the findings of the Hawthorne studies and offer alternative conclusions to those of Mayo, Roethlisberger, and Dickson. Augustine Brannigan and William Zwerman (2001) argued that the major findings of the study came about when one particular group, known as the mica splitting test group, were moved into isolation from the other groups in the experiment, resulting in a 15% increase in productivity. The increased productivity of the mica splitting test group led to the experimental effect known as the Hawthorne effect. The Hawthorne effect is defined as a threat to the internal validity of the experiment where a change in experimental conditions (e.g., moving the mica splitting test group

Hawthorne effect A threat to the internal validity of an experiment where a change in experimental conditions bring about a change in the behavior of the participants in which the experiment was originally intended to identify.

into isolation) brings about a change in the behavior of the participants that the experiment was originally intended to identify.

In a study using the original data from the Hawthorne studies, it was found that managerial discipline, financial incentives, the economic hardship of the Great Depression, and increased rest periods significantly predicted worker productivity. Although Mayo's conclusions that quality interpersonal relationships were responsible for increased productivity, it appears that Mayo, Roethlisberger, and Dickson ignored other factors that influenced performance and only focused on the human relationships in an effort to forward the human relations ideology (Franke & Kaul, 1978). In summary, the human relations approach to management resulted in lower productivity because it was based on faulty information and faulty interpretation of the data obtained from the Hawthorne studies. However, as a result of the human relations approach, management theorists began to consider the psychological well-being of the worker, which brought about needed change in working conditions and theorizing about communicating in the organization.

HUMAN RESOURCE MANAGEMENT PERSPECTIVE

The most contemporary approach to management is the **human resource management perspective**. The underlying assumption of this approach is that the employee is viewed as a valuable asset of the organization who needs to be developed to meet the needs of both the employee and the organization. Unlike the previous two approaches to management, theorists from this perspective have developed several theories that are used in contemporary organizations.

human resource management perspective A management approach that assumes employees are a valuable asset who should be developed for the benefit of both the organization as well as the worker.

System 4 Management Theory

The **system 4 management theory** of Rensis Likert (1961, 1967) contains management styles that range from low concern for workers to high concern for workers. **system 1** is the **exploitive-authoritative type management**, which regularly uses threats and fear to motivate workers. Decision making within this management style is conducted at the top levels of the organization then handed down to workers. Downward communication is most valued in these organizations. The content of the communication is primarily task focused. Upward communication is discouraged and kept to a minimum, as this discouragement serves to keep supervisors and subordinates psychologically distant from one another.

The second system is known as **system 2**, or **benevolent-authoritative type management**, which uses punishment similar to that of system 1, but also incorporates some level of reward. However, system 2 still devalues employee input and only considers management input in decision making. Although communication is generally downward, the amount of upward communication is

system 4 management theory A human resource approach to management that ranges from depersonalization of employees to the full integration of employee input and potential.

exploitive-authoritative type management Type of management that uses fear and threats to motivates employees.

benevolent-authoritative type management Type of management that uses rewards for employee motivation.

consultative type management   Type of management that uses reward and punishment to motivate employees.

greater than that found in system 1 and consists of only messages that are deemed important by management.

The third system is **system 3**, or consultative type management, which uses both reward and punishment along with considering some employee input. Although employee input is considered, major decisions are still made at the higher levels of the organization, whereas smaller decisions (i.e., those that have relatively little impact on the organization) are left to lower-level employees to solve. Both downward and upward communication are utilized. System 3 contains some relational messages, with the majority of messages being those that serve the benefit of the organization.

participative type management   Type of management that emphasizes quality interpersonal relationships to maximize individual potential and organizational productivity.

The most employee centered system is **system 4**, or participative type management, and reflects management's valuing and encouraging input from subordinates. There is a strong psychological connection between the superior and subordinate, with quality communication flowing in both upward and downward directions. It is believed that system 4 management results in high productivity and quality interpersonal relationships at all levels of the organization. This also results in employees who are more committed to the organization.

X,Y Management Theory

X,Y management theory   A theory of management that contains bipolar assumptions about employee behavior.

The approach to management developed by Douglas McGregor (1960, 1966) focused on the manager's assumptions about the work ethic of employees. The X, Y management theory represents bipolar assumptions about employee behavior. Theory X assumes three basic assumptions about employees. First, employees are lazy, have a tendency to do the minimum, and actively seek to avoid work. Second, because of this dislike for work, management must use threats, coercion, control, and direction as motivational tools to achieve organizational goals. Third, employees have little ambition and strive for a world free of uncertainty. This need for certainty is what employees desire to be controlled (Pugh & Hickson, 1997).

Theory X   A management approach that assumes workers are lazy, have little ambition, and are motivated by coercion and threats.

Theory Y   A management approach that assumes workers are motivated by an internal need to excel and actively pursue responsibility.

On the other hand, Theory Y contains six basic assumptions about workers. First, within every worker there is an internal motivation to be productive and excel. Second, managerial control is only one of many devices that can be used to increase productivity. Third, the pursuit of satisfaction and maximized potential is the most valued reward for employees. Fourth, employees cannot only be taught to accept responsibility, but also can be taught to actively seek opportunities for responsibility. Fifth, employees are much more capable of contributing to creative problem solving than they are given credit for. Sixth, the employees' full potential as an attribute of the organization is sorely underutilized by the organization (Pugh & Hickson, 1997). As McGregor's theory indicates, Theory X assumes a much more classic management approach when contrasted to Theory Y. These dichotomous approaches are developed from a manager's past employment experiences as well as the manager's assumption about human nature.

Theory Z of Management

One of the first management approaches focusing on culture and management was William Ouchi's (1981) **Theory Z** approach to management. In the late 1970s and 1980s, due to the incredible growth and success experienced by Japanese organizations within the United States and in international markets, it became common practice for theorists to compare and contrast American organizations (**type A organizations**) with Japanese organizations (**type J organizations**). Type A organizations encourage individual decision making, performance appraisals based on short-term behavior, and specialized career paths. In contrast, type J organizations encourage collective decision making, long-term performance appraisals, and nonspecialized career paths. Table 11.2 indicates differences between type A and type J organizations.

There was a prevailing assumption that due to the success of Japanese management techniques, simply importing these techniques into American organizations would result in similar success. However, most of these attempts at integrating management approaches failed to be effective when applied outside the culture of origin. That is, the Japanese management models were interwoven with Japanese culture, not that of the United States.

Ouchi (1981) believed that the most effective management theory should be based on the specific culture within which it is going to be applied. A major assumption of Theory Z is that workers are actively involved in the process and success of the organization. Further, this active involvement represents the key to optimal productivity. The theory is grounded in four components consisting of: (a) trust between superior and subordinate in that all interactions between workers and management are conducted in an open and honest fashion; (b) management should have implicit personal knowledge of each employee and use this knowledge to match people who are compatible with one another; this compatibility should be based on personality and job specialty to maximize efficiency; (c) productivity is based on a certain standard of performance that is expected of all employees at all levels of the organization; and (d) a level of intimacy that reflects the belief in caring, support, and selflessness through quality relationships among all members of the organization.

Unlike McGregor's theory, which focused on employees' work ethic, Theory Z is focused on the attitudes and individual responsibilities of each employee. Ouchi (1981) believed that collective beliefs and attitudes of employees should be based on mutual respect for each other as well as for the organization. The Theory J cultural assumption of lifetime employment speaks to the concept of collective beliefs and attitudes. Approximately 20% of the Japanese workforce is under lifetime employment in government and large corporations

Theory Z An approach to management that advocates matching the organization's culture to that of the larger society and assumes that involved workers are the key to increased productivity.

type A organizations An organization that uses typical American management style of individuality, short-term employment, and rapid advancement.

type J organizations An organization that uses typical Japanese management style of collectivism, long-time employment, and nonspecialized career paths.

Table 11.2

OUCHI'S COMPARISON OF TYPE A VERSUS TYPE J ORGANIZATIONS

Type A Organization (American)	Type J Organization (Japanese)
Employment is short term.	Employment is long term and often for a lifetime.
Evaluation and promotion occur frequently and at a rapid rate.	Evaluation and promotion are slow and usually are within the same organization.
Specialized career paths that may lead them to switch employment to competing organizations.	Nonspecialized career paths that are malleable to the needs of the organization.
Explicit control mechanisms that leave no ambiguity as to what rules and regulations the organizations wants followed by employees.	Implicit control mechanisms that reflect the more subtle organizational/societal expectations of worker performance and productivity.
Individual decision making is encouraged, whereas innovation and creativity are seen as individual pursuits that are the primary influence in decision making.	Collective decision making is encouraged, and individuality is discouraged while group rule and group harmony are primary influences in decision-making behavior.
Individual responsibility as a cultural assumption reflects accountability for themselves and not our coworkers. Employees are rewarded and punished based on individual performance.	Collective responsibility as a cultural assumption reflects that everyone has a stake in the whole organization, and a failure or success at any one level or by any one employee is a failure or success for the entire organization.
Segmented concern as cultural assumptions dictate localized problems and localized solutions without regard to implications on the greater good or the organization as a whole.	Wholistic concern as cultural assumptions dictate the subordination of local concerns if those concerns are harmful to the whole. Individual sacrifices are expected if the organization as a whole will prosper.

Adapted from Ouchi, W. G. Theory Z: How American business can met the Japanese challenge. *Reading, MA: Addison-Wesley.*

(Kato, 2001). Theory Z holds that workers are loyal to their employer, are not looking to leave the organization at the first sight of an opportunity for advancement at another company, and will typically wait 5, 10, or even 20 years for a promotion, which generally occurs within the same organization. The Theory Z approach advocates that organizations spend a large amount of time and money in the development of interpersonal skills of every employee within the organization. Given the organization's stress on competent employee communication, processes such as decision making and information exchange are greatly improved.

Model I and Model II Theory

Chris Argyris (1965) believed that the personal and professional growth of a person is directly related to, and affected by, their work situation. Previous management approaches (i.e., classical management) were so focused on bottom-line productivity/profit goals that they became communicatively incompetent with regard to growing employees and utilizing employee creativity and potential. This myopic focus results in employees developing a preventative or reactive posture as opposed to a proactive posture. This development of a preventative or reactive posture is known as **defensive routines** (Argyris, 1985). Simply put, workers are so resistant to change, even when change can enhance their careers, that they develop a "work to not get fired" perspective, as opposed to a "work toward excellence perspective." When workers internalize this "work to not get fired" philosophy, it results in a form of **learned helplessness** (Seligman, 1992). An example of this can be seen in an employee who shows initiative on the job, yet continually receives negative feedback for this initiative. The employee will eventually cease to show initiative. This learned helplessness is not self-induced, but induced by the organization in that most organizations tell employees to be focused on long-term personal and organizational goals, yet proceed to evaluate employees in short-term cycles (e.g., quarterly job performance reviews).

Chris Argyris and Donald Schon (1978) argued that workers are constantly caught in a paradoxical situation. For example, employees are constantly being encouraged to "think outside the box." But to do so requires breaking existing organizational rules. Any deviation from organizational rules and norms, more often than not, results in reprimand, demotion, or termination. This paradox is perpetuated in two different theories employed by management. The first is known as **Espoused Theory** and concerns what the manager tells an employee about the manager's behaviors, ethics, and management philosophy. The second is known as **Theory in Use** and reflects the actual behaviors, ethics, and management philosophy enacted by the manager. For example, a manager may tell the employees that he or she is employee centered, values feedback, and has an open door policy (i.e., espoused theory). However, when this manager is approached by an employee, the manager dismisses the feedback as trivial, seems impatient, and is nonverbally confrontational toward the employee (i.e., theory in use; Argyris & Schon, 1978).

Model I and **model II approaches** to management are believed to bring about distinctively different outcomes for employees and the organization. Model I assumes four types of managerial behavior. First, the manager sets unilateral goals that are then pursued by employees. Second, the manager is self-reliant to the point where the manager seeks to maximize success and minimize failure. Third, the manager rarely, if ever, expresses negative affect or behavior in public and keeps opinions and attitudes private. Fourth, the manager treats

defensive routines When workers develop preventative or reactive routines instead of being proactive in the workplace.

learned helplessness Helplessness that occurs from repeated negative consequences resulting in the worker showing little initiative if any.

Espoused Theory What a manager tells employees about the manager's ethics, management style, and management philosophy.

Theory in Use The actual behaviors that a manager engages in with employees that exposes the manager's ethics, management style, and management philosophy.

Model I approach Management approach that assumes unilateral goals, self-reliance, failure to disclose negative opinions, and reliance on objectivity and logic.

Model II approach Management approach that assumes pro-action, consultative decision making, solution implementation, and the ability to adapt should the solution need adjustment.

all issues objectively and rationally to the point where any emotional expression will be minimized if not absent. These behaviors are believed to bring about **single-loop learning** in workers. Argyris (1985) argued that this type of learning is self-oppressive. Single-loop learning is the understanding of *how* a process is conducted, not *why* the process is conducted. For example, in the fast-food industry there is a large amount of single-loop learning. Employee training is so scripted and standardized that employees are taught how to assemble a particular hamburger, reset the fryer, make coffee, and so forth. What these employees are not shown is why the tasks are performed in a particular order and how the appropriate execution of these tasks results in the employee contributing to the overall success of the organization.

The model II approach to management allows for organizational learning and growth. Model II managers routinely engage in the following three behaviors: (a) the manager takes action on information they see as valid, regardless of who the information comes from or whether it is based on logic or emotion; (b) the manager consults all the people who are both relevant to and competent to make decisions; the manager then acts on that decision; and (c) the manager is committed to the decision and is active in the implementation yet flexible enough to adjust the course of action if needed. By utilizing these behaviors, managers are open to feedback and trusting of others. This results in **double-loop learning**, also known as **generative learning**. Generative learning reflects learning the process, understanding the rationale for the process, and knowing how this process contributes to the function of the entire organization. This model of management allows for employee feedback and employee identification with the task, the manager, and the organization.

In an effort to train managers to utilize model II behaviors, Argyris (1993) conducted a 5-year study of managers, which resulted in the development of a seminar directed at improving model II communication and management skills. It is believed that this type of training aids in overcoming the defensiveness and mistrust that results from model I management behaviors. This training approach to model II management indicates that effective management behaviors can be learned and that these skills can be acquired and utilized by any manager.

Managerial Grid Theory

Instead of conceptualizing concern for task and concern for a worker as a single continuum, Robert Blake and Jane Mouton (1964, 1978) proposed the **Managerial Grid Theory**. The grid contains two continua comprised of concern for worker and concern for task that results in a managerial style profile. Managers are assessed on a scale from 1 (very low) to 9 (very high) on the degree to which they have concern for their workers and an identical scale assessing concern for the task.

single loop learning A learning of how a process is executed, not why it is executed. This type of learning is believed to be self-oppressive.

double-loop learning Type of learning that entails learning the process, and how this process contributes to the function of the entire organization.

generative learning *See* double-loop learning.

Managerial Grid Theory A theory that contains two continua resulting in five managerial profiles ranging in concern for task and concern for relationship.

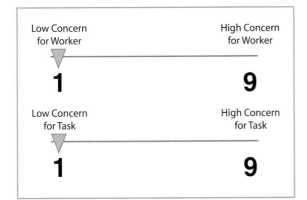

Figure 11.2

Impoverished manager.

Figure 11.3

Country club manager.

The **impoverished manager** is a person who scores low in concern for worker and low in concern for task (i.e., scoring at or near 1 on both scales). Impoverished managers are ineffective, are costly to the organization, and have less tenure in management positions (see Figure 11.2).

The **country club manager** is a person who scores high in concern for worker and low in concern for task (i.e., at or near 9 on concern for worker and at or near 1 on concern for task). Country club managers are valued by subordinates due to a high level of communication and relational competency that fosters positive affect (feelings) from subordinates. Given that this type of manager is reflective of human relations, the country club manager is not valued by upper-level management because of the lack of focus on the task (see Figure 11.3).

The **task manager** is a person who scores low in concern for worker and high in concern for task (i.e., scoring at or near 1 on concern for worker and at or near 9 on concern for task). The task manager is not well liked by subordinates but is highly valued by the organization because of the bottom-line productivity that is associated with a high focus on task. This style of management is most representative of the scientific management approach (see Figure 11.4).

The **moderate manager** is a person who scores moderate in both concern for worker and task (i.e., scoring at or near 5 on both scales). This management style results in average success with regard to productivity and average levels of relational quality with subordinates. More people report using a moderate management style than any other style because people tend to score in the middle of both scales, with less people scoring on the extremes of the measures (e.g., country club and task managers; see Figure 11.5).

impoverished manager
A management style that indicates a low concern for worker and a low concern for task.

country club manager
A management style that indicates a high concern for worker and a low concern for task.

task manager A management style that indicates a low concern for worker and a high concern for task.

moderate manager A management style that indicates a moderate concern for worker and a moderate concern for task.

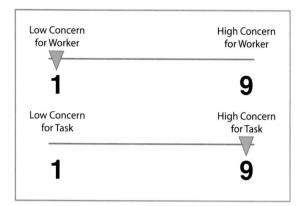

Figure 11.4

Task manager.

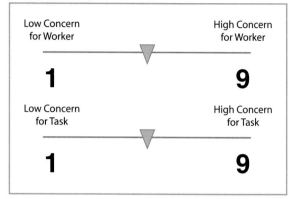

Figure 11.5

Moderate manager.

team manager A management style that indicates a high concern for worker and a high concern for task.

The **team manager** is considered the optimal management style because the manager has a high concern for worker and a high concern for task (i.e., scoring at or near 9 on concern worker and on concern for task). The team manager enjoys both high levels of productivity and quality interpersonal relationships with workers (Blake & Mouton, 1982). Dean Tjosvold (1984) found that employees reported working hardest when the manager was high in both concern for worker and task (i.e., team manager). Further, people reported working the least for managers who were high in concern for worker and low in concern for task (i.e., country club manager). The team manager style is most reflective of the human resource approach (see Figure 11.6). The value of the Blake and Mouton (1964, 1978) managerial grid can be found in the way different combinations of management styles can be derived from treating concern for task and concern for the worker as two separate independent dimensions that range from low to high concern.

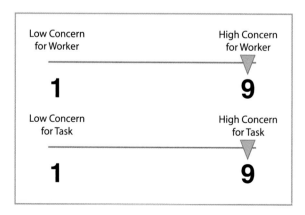

Figure 11.6

Team manager.

Theory of Independent Mindedness

The **Theory of Independent Mindedness** (TIM) (Infante, 1987a, 1987b) is a uniquely communication-based theory as opposed to being economic, business, or psychologically based. The TIM seeks congruity or similarity between the culture created within the specific organization (i.e., microculture) with that of the larger culture (i.e., macroculture) within which it operates (see Figure 11.7). The cultural coordination advocated by the TIM also serves as the foundation of Ouchi's (1981) Theory Z. American culture values freedom of expression and individual rights. Both of these values are made explicit in the Constitution of the United States. The TIM assumes that these values should be reflected and fostered within the organization.

Theory of Independent Mindedness A communication based organizational theory that advocates cultural congruity between the organization and the larger culture within which it operates.

> Organizational Cultural Values A (microculture)
>
> Overall Cultural Values B (macroculture)
>
> *If a ≠ b then cultural mismatching is present and thus detrimental to organizational success and productivity.*
>
> Overall Cultural Values B (macroculture)
>
> Organizational Cultural Values A (microculture)
>
> *If a = b then cultural matching is present and thus optimal for organizational success.*

Figure 11.7

The TIM and culture congruity.

argumentativeness
Personality trait in which individuals present and defend positions on controversial issues while attempting to refute the positions others take.

verbal aggressiveness
Tendency to attack the self-concept of people instead of, or in addition to, their positions on issues in order to inflict psychological pain.

communicator style The way a person verbally and paraverbally interacts to signal how literal meaning should be taken, interpreted, filtered, or understood.

dominant style A dimension of communicator style that reflects coming on strong , speaking frequently, taking leadership roles, and wanting to control social situations.

dramatic style A dimension of communicator style that involves telling jokes and stories to illustrate points, exaggerating for emphasis, and generally creating the impression of "acting" when talking with people.

contentious style A dimension of communicator style that is a disposition to challenge other when disagreements occur, to argue with others.

impression-leaving style
A dimension of communicator style that is a disposition to create a lasting image in the minds of the receivers.

As a corporatist theory, the TIM is believed to bring about employee motivation, satisfaction, and productivity. Employees should be active in decision-making processes, which includes the robust exchange of ideas and perspectives. However, unlike most Eastern management approaches that advocate the downplaying of power and status, the TIM, conceptualized from a Western perspective, advocates that power and status differences should not be downplayed, but acknowledged and emphasized as they are in the larger American culture (Avtgis & Rancer, 2007).

This theory is a radical departure from classical management-based theories that emphasize the use of unilateral control and power (Ewing, 1982; Infante & Gorden, 1987). In fact, the TIM assumes that power and control are fluid ideas that move both downward from superior to subordinate as well as upward from subordinate to supervisor. In an effort to exert control and power in an appropriate fashion, competent communication skills must be developed. More specifically, three communication traits are believed to influence the degree of independent mindedness in an organization: **argumentativeness** (Infante & Rancer, 1982), **verbal aggressiveness** (Infante & Wigley, 1986), and **communicator style** (Norton, 1978).

As discussed in Chapter 5, trait argumentativeness is believed to be a constructive trait that has been found to bring about many organizational benefits, such as the appropriate expression of organizational dissent (Kassing & Avtgis, 1999), greater job satisfaction (Infante & Gorden, 1985), and solution-oriented conflict resolution strategies (Martin, Anderson, & Sirimangkala, 1997). Trait verbal aggressiveness is a destructive trait that has been found to be linked to employee inattentiveness and unfriendliness, lower levels of job satisfaction (Infante & Gorden, 1989), and the use of ineffective and inappropriate organizational dissent strategies (Kassing & Avtgis, 1999). The trait of communicator style represents the ten distinct styles of communication, including **dominant style**, **dramatic style**, **contentious style**, **impression leaving style**, **animated style**, **relaxed style**, **open style**, **attentive style**, **precise style**, and **friendly style**. Of these ten dimensions, certain combinations of these styles create either an **affirming communicator style** (i.e., communicating in a way that validates another person's self-concept) or a **nonaffirming style** (i.e., communicating in a way that negates or threatens another person's self-concept). Combining the ten communicator style dimensions along with argumentativeness and verbal aggressiveness represent particular trait profiles that range from complete independent mindedness (i.e., Profile 1) to the absence of independent mindedness (i.e., Profile 4). Table 11.3 indicates the various profiles.

Table 11.3	COMMUNICATION TRAIT PROFILES OF THE THEORY OF INDEPENDENCE MINDEDNESS	
Profile	**Trait Level**	**Outcome**
ONE	High Argumentativeness Low Verbal Aggressiveness Affirming Communicator Style	High Employee Commitment High Employee Satisfaction High Employee Productivity
TWO	High Argumentativeness Low Verbal Aggressiveness Nonaffirming Communicator Style	Moderate Employee Commitment Moderate Employee Satisfaction Moderate Employee Productivity
THREE	Low Argumentativeness Low Verbal Aggressiveness Affirming Communicator Style	Lower Employee Commitment Lower Employee Satisfaction Lower Employee Productivity
FOUR	Low Argumentativeness High Verbal Aggressiveness Nonaffirming Communicator Style	Lowest Employee Commitment Lowest Employee Satisfaction Lowest Employee Productivity

THEORIES OF ORGANIZATIONAL LEADERSHIP

A common assumption in our culture is that everyone should "shoot for the stars" and strive to achieve great things. Leaders have always been part of history and folklore. Consider great leaders such as Robert E. Lee, Margaret Thatcher, Franklin Delano Roosevelt, Martin Luther King, and General George C. Patton. Most people ascribed great personality characteristics and sense of mission to their pursuits. This section will review several theories of leadership that seek to explain how and why people are either put into, or emerge into, positions of leadership.

Trait Approach to Leadership

The **trait approach to leadership** assumes that people possess the characteristics to be effective leaders based on predispositions or traits that are either biologically derived or developed through the environment. The study of leaders and leadership is not a recent development. For centuries people have studied the qualities of effective leaders in an effort to determine what traits and behavior make an effective leader. These efforts have been called the **Great Man Theories of Leadership**. In one of the first major social scientific approaches to trait leadership, Ralph Stogdill (1948, 1974) believed that any leadership research should take the perspective that leadership qualities are part of a person's personality, and therefore, personality traits should always be accounted for.

animated style Tendency to expend considerable energy when communicating.

animated style A dimension of communicator style which is a trait that signifies extensive use of eyes, face, and gestures to express meaning.

relaxed style Tendency to show no signs of stress when communicating.

open style A dimension of communicator style that is a predisposition to reveal feelings, thoughts, and personal information.

attentive style A dimension of communicator style and is the tendency to listen carefully to people, to be able to repeat back what others say.

precise style A dimension of communicator style that includes insisting that people document what they are saying and that they give definitions.

friendly style A dimension of communicator style that reflects communicating in a more intimate way.

affirming communicator style A communicator style that reflects the validation of another person's self-concept.

nonaffirming style A communicator style that reflect communicating in a way that negates or threatens another person's self-concept.

trait approach to leadership Assumes that leaders have traits that distinguish them from followers.

Great Man Theories of Leadership An approach to leadership where great leaders were studied in an effort to determine what traits and behaviors make an effective leader.

narcissism A personality trait that assumes that a person is more gifted than another. This is a characteristic of a leader.

charisma A trait that reflects the leader's ability to display a high degree of communication competence, the ability to inspire subordinates, as well as have the subordinates buy into the leader's vision.

Several traits have been associated with leadership. First, leaders possess the trait of **narcissism**, which is the belief that they, as opposed to someone else, are qualified to lead. This trait assumes a higher level of self-confidence and self-love than those levels found in followers. Second, the trait of **charisma** reflects the leader's ability to display a high degree of communication competence, the ability to inspire subordinates, as well as have the subordinates buy into the leader's vision (Conger, Kanungo, & Associates, 1988). The term **communication competence** refers to the ability to be effective (i.e., achieve a desired goal) and appropriate (i.e., achieve goals in a way that respects other people and is deemed socially appropriate). The study of organizational leadership can be seen in the work of Max Weber (1947), who distinguished between charisma based on behavior (i.e., **pure charisma**) and charisma based on the position of power the person holds within the organization (i.e., **routinized charisma**). Charisma is a trait that has been possessed by effective leaders such as John F. Kennedy, Oprah Winfrey, David Koresh, and Charles Manson. As this list illustrates, charisma can be used to lead people to perform either constructive or destructive behaviors.

How people interpret events has also been found to distinguish effective leaders from ineffective leaders. The trait of **locus of control** is a trait that concerns how people attribute causes to outcomes in life (Rotter, 1966). Carl Anderson and Craig Schneier (1978) found that people who exhibit an *internal locus of control* (i.e., see outcomes as being a function of their own behavior) were more likely to be leaders than people who exhibited an *external locus of control* (i.e., see outcomes as being a function of luck, chance, fate, other people). Internally oriented people also reported having greater amounts of previous leadership experience (Hiers & Heckel, 1977) and emerge as group leaders more frequently than people who reported being externally oriented (Lord, Philips, & Rush, 1980).

Perhaps the most well known trait that affects so many behaviors is that of biological sex. Much debate and research has centered on whether men or women make more effective leaders. Sex and gender are considered biological and psychological traits, respectively. Research indicates that men and women do, in fact, have different approaches to leadership and that each approach includes both effective and ineffective behaviors. Rosabeth Moss Kanter (1977) found that women in organizations tend to be more nurturing and socially sensitive whereas men tend to be more assertive and use more overt power. Recent research indicates that the most effective leaders are those who display a more gender neutral or **androgynous style** that is comprised of both masculine and feminine behaviors (Hackman & Johnson, 2000). Although trait leadership studies have declined in recent years, the predispositions and traits (whether physical or psychological) that effective leaders possess have provided important insight into what makes some people more effective than others.

Situational Approach to Leadership

The **situational leadership approach** assumes that there is no such thing as a born leader as much as people acting as leaders, depending on the specific situation. Consider the following list of people and whether they would be considered leaders without the particular situations in which they were involved: Rosa Parks (without segregation), Abraham Lincoln (without the Civil War), Winston Churchill (without the Battle of Britain), Martin Luther King (without the civil rights struggles of the 1960s), Rudy Giuliani (without the terrorist attacks on the World Trade Center), and Mother Teresa (without Third World oppression). The Situational Leadership Theory of Paul Hersey and Kenneth Blanchard (1977) assumes that any leadership style should be based on both the employees' *psychological maturity* (i.e., degree of self-efficacy and willingness to accept responsibility) and *job maturity* (i.e., degree of skills and knowledge of the task). As employees' maturity increases, the most appropriate leadership style would be more relationally focused than task focused. More specifically, a hierarchy of maturity levels requires a degree of both task and relational leadership styles.

At the most basic maturity level, a leader would use the **tell style**, which is high task focus and low relationship focus. The tell style is advocated because employees have low self-efficacy and are unmotivated. Therefore, the leader must simply instruct or train employees in skills to accomplish the task. Second on the continuum would be the **sell style**, and it assumes that employees have some maturity and are resistant to being told what to do, yet are not fully motivated to show initiative. Therefore, the leader should be high in both task and employee focus. This type of leadership style includes explaining decisions and advising employees in an effort to motivate them for task accomplishment. At the third level is the **participate style**. This style assumes that employees have high levels of job maturity and low levels of psychological maturity. Therefore, a low task focus and high relational focused style is required, as employees are capable of performing the task but are unwilling or resistant to perform the task. The final approach is the **delegating style** and reflects high levels of employee psychological and job maturity. With these types of employees, a low task focus and a low employee focus is required. In this case, employees are capable of performing the task and are motivated to do so. Therefore, the leader should simply allow employees to perform (Hersey, 1984).

Exchange Approaches to Leadership

The **exchange approaches to leadership** focus on the quality of the relationship between leaders and their followers. The quality of the relationship is

communication competence Involves appropriateness and effectiveness; can be viewed as trait-like, context- or situationally bound.

pure charisma Charisma based on the behaviors that a leader exhibits.

routinized charisma Charisma based on the position of power a person holds within the organization.

locus of control A personality trait that concerns how people interpret outcomes in their life.

androgynous style Style of leadership that contains both masculine and feminine communication behaviors.

situational leadership approach Assumes that there is no such thing as a born leader as much as people acting as leaders depending on the specific situation.

tell style Reflects that workers have a high task focus and a low relationship focus.

sell style Reflects that workers have a certain degree of maturity, are reluctant to be told what to do, and are not fully motivated to show initiative.

participative style Reflects workers have high levels of job maturity and low levels of psychological maturity.

delegating style A management style that assumes workers have high levels of psychological and job maturity.

exchange approaches to leadership   A leadership approach that assumes the quality of the relationship is believed to be the determining factor for effective leadership.

Leader-Member Exchange Theory   A leadership theory that focuses on the quality linkages between both the leader and the follower.

Transformational Leadership Theory   A theory of leadership that focuses on the empowerment of individual workers and aiding the organization in adapting to change in both internal and external environments.

contingency theory   A theory of leadership that assumes the degree of success of any leader is contingent on the situational demands as to whether the leader should have a task or employee focus and the amount of influence and control the leader has over the situation.

believed to be the determining factor for effective leadership. **Leader-Member Exchange Theory** (LMX) is one such theory that focuses on the quality of relational linkages between both the leader and followers (a.k.a. members). It is assumed that relational linkages are the main influence on effective leadership (Dansereau, Cashman, & Graen, 1973). How the leader and followers negotiate their specific roles directly affect how the leader and followers will interpret work and the work experience. LMX theory assumes that leaders behave differently to individual members of the organization based on the nature of the dyadic relationship. The nature of the linkage can be either high or low in quality. High-quality linkages between the follower and leader are termed *in-group relationships,* whereas low-quality linkages are termed *out-group relationships* (Dansereau, Graen, & Haga, 1975). The development of high-quality linkages is the key to effective leadership. Research findings indicate that subordinates with high-quality linkages report more rapid promotion and were more team oriented than out-group members (Erdogan, Liden, & Kraimer, 2006; Scandura, Graen, & Novak, 1986).

Another exchange approach to leadership is that of **Transformational Leadership Theory.** Given that American culture is one that values equal rights, justice, competition, and commitment, transformational leadership is focused on the empowerment of individual workers and aiding the organization in adapting to change in both internal and external environments. Among all the leadership theories discussed thus far, transformational leadership is believed to be the most paradigmatic, as it is based on a worldview rather than just another approach to explaining leadership behavior. The three basic premises are (a) the leader is an agent of change, (b) the leader emphasizes the self-actualization of subordinates, and (c) leaders pursue the goals of the organization as well as satisfying the higher-level needs of the followers. Noel Tichy and Mary Anne Devanna (1986) highlighted the seven characteristics that separate transformational leaders from other types of leaders. Table 11.4 describes these characteristics.

Another variation in situational leadership-based theories is that of Fred Fiedler's (1972) **contingency theory.** This theory assumes that the degree of success of any leader is contingent on the situational demands as to whether the leader should have a task or employee focus and the amount of influence and control the leader has over the situation. When situations are extreme in nature (i.e., there is a possibility of a high degree of success or a high degree of failure), it is best to adopt a task-focused approach. If the situation is moderate in gravity (i.e., the possibility of moderate success or moderate failure), it is best to adopt an employee-focused approach. Contingency leadership theory assumes that you cannot change the internal qualities of the leader and that we should find situations (i.e., task focused or employee focused) that match the leader's specific style as well as situations that offer a degree of control and influence over subordinates. For example, in professional sports you will find

Table 11.4	CHARACTERISTICS OF TRANSFORMATIONAL LEADERS
Transformational Characteristics	**Thoughts, Feelings, and Behaviors**
Is identified as a change agent	Understands that the only thing that remains stable in organizations is instability. Welcomes the challenge of being innovating and changing as the environment demands.
Show courage	Will risk being ridiculed for the success of the organization and followers
Have a clear vision	Has the ability to constantly envision the future and possibilities that accompany change and innovation.
Are driven by values	Demonstrates impeccable moral fiber and integrates this moral code into the day-to-day function of the organization and organizational members.
Never stop learning new information	Are lifelong learners who are always interested in better ways of doing things. Rarely satisfied with the status quo and are always looking for the next innovation.
Uncertainty and ambiguity are welcomed	Thrive on chaos and welcome complex challenges. Uncertainty and ambiguity are motivating and represent an opportunity for growth.
Believe in workers	Has an undying commitment to bettering organizational members through opportunities for learning and growth.

coaches who have accomplished incredible things in terms of turning around a losing franchise or getting the most from a particular player. However, when this same coach goes to a different team with a different culture and different players (i.e., the situation changes), they may only experience average success.

WORKER MOTIVATIONAL THEORIES

Many researchers have hypothesized why some people are more motivated to work than others. We all know people who, when given a task, will put all their effort into making sure the job is completed to the best of their ability. On the other hand, we also know people who, when given a task, will put out only enough effort to meet the minimum standards. The difference between these two people can be explained by analyzing the factors that motivate them. This section presents some of the most popular theories of motivation that researchers use to explain human behavior in the organization.

primary needs   A dimension of Maslow's theory of motivation concerning the satisfying the needs, of air, water, and food.

safety needs   One of Maslow's hierarchy of needs reflecting the need for a life free of turmoil, relative stability, and preference for predictability.

love needs   One of Maslow's hierarchy of needs reflecting the need for affection and belonging.

esteem needs   One of Maslow's hierarchy of needs reflecting the need for recognition, appreciation, and respect from others.

self-actualization   Highest level of Maslow's needs reflecting achieving one's potential.

Hierarchy of Needs Theory

Abraham Maslow (1943) proposed a theory of motivation that was based on the pursuit to fulfill human needs. This hierarchical approach to motivation holds that **primary needs** have to be satisfied before a person can pursue higher-level needs. The lower or more primary needs concern those that sustain physiological survival. These are reflected in the need for air, water, food, and so on. Once the physiological needs are met, we then are motivated to satisfy our **safety needs**. Safety needs reflect a life free of turmoil, relative stability, and a preference for predictability. After meeting the safety needs, we are then motivated to satisfy our **love needs**, which are reflected in the pursuit of affection and belonging. Once the love needs are met, people are then motivated to satisfy their **esteem needs**, which are reflected in pursuing recognition, appreciation, and respect from other people. This leads to the highest level of needs and satisfaction known as **self-actualization**. To be self-actualized is to achieve the pinnacle of human potential and achievement. Figure 11.8 reflects the Maslow hierarchy of needs.

Motivator Hygiene Theory

This theory of motivation was developed by Fredrick Herzberg (1968) and is based on the degree of satisfaction and dissatisfaction that workers experience

Figure 11.8

Maslow's hierarchy of needs.

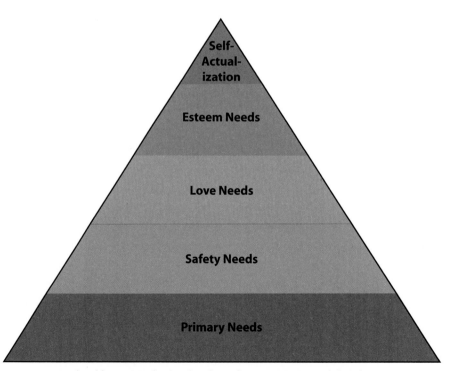

Adapted from A. H. Maslow (1943). A Theory of Human Motivation, Psychological Review, 50, *370–396.*

in the workplace. Motivator Hygiene Theory is a departure from the more traditional theories of motivation that work on a single continuum ranging from satisfied to dissatisfied. Instead, Herzberg proposed a two-continua model in which the first continuum reflects a range from being satisfied to not being satisfied, whereas the second continuum reflects a range from being dissatisfied to not being dissatisfied. Figure 11.9 illustrates these continua. The rationale for creating two continua is based in the logic positing the opposite of something is not something different. This is best illustrated when verdicts are handed down in our legal system. When a person is found to have not committed a crime of which they were accused, they are found to be not guilty, as opposed to innocent. The absence of something (e.g., guilt) cannot be something else (e.g., innocent). Instead, it is not guilty. Simply put, the opposite of apple, is not apple as opposed to orange.

Similar to Maslow's lower-level needs (i.e., physiological and safety needs), the factors related to job dissatisfaction concern the person's need to avoid being deprived of physical and social rewards. Herzberg (1968) illustrated the pursuit of these needs using an analogy of the biblical characters Adam and Abraham. The **Adam personality** concept reflects behavior that occurred after Adam was sent out of the Garden of Eden. That is, he was faced with the need to satisfy the primal needs of food, security, and safety. The motivation to satisfy these needs become Adam's sole focus. This is similar to the **hedonic philosophy of life**, or the idea that life is about the pursuit of pleasure and happiness for the individual.

The factors associated with being satisfied in a job are similar to Maslow's concept of self-actualization and reflect the need to achieve the maximum of human potential and perfection (Pugh & Hickson, 1997). This type of motivation is reflected in the biblical character Abraham and is known as the **Abraham personality**. According to the Bible, God summoned Abraham because he believed that Abraham was capable of accomplishments that were far beyond primal needs. The pursuit of self-realization and great achievement for an entire people was his primary focus, as opposed to just Abraham's own immediate needs. The Abraham personality is reflective of the **eudaimonic philosophy of life** in that people seek deeper meaning in life and move beyond the simple pursuit of pleasure and happiness.

Although both the Adam and Abraham type personalities seek to be satisfied at work, they seek satisfaction in different places. The Adam personality seeks to avoid pain or, in this case, avoid being dissatisfied. This motivational force results in seeking out things within the immediate environment to avoid pain. These can be things such as pay, good coworker relationships, and working environment. Therefore, this person is motivated to avoid being dissatisfied as opposed to being motivated to be satisfied. The Abraham personality seeks achievement, recognition, and opportunity for growth.

Adam personality A motivational tendency to focus on immediate satisfaction and pleasure.

hedonic philosophy of life A philosophy of life that reflects the pursuit of pleasure and happiness for the individual.

Abraham personality A motivational tendency to focus on the need to achieve the maximum of human potential and perfection.

eudaimonic philosophy of life A philosophy of life that reflects the pursuit of deeper meanings in life beyond those of the pursuit of pleasure and happiness.

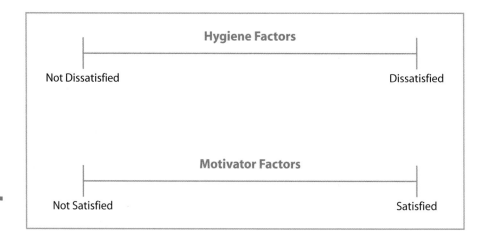

Figure 11.9

Herzberg's motivator-hygiene continua.

hygiene factors Factor of motivation based on factors associated with being dissatisfied such as working conditions and interpersonal relationships, etc.

motivator factors Factors of motivation that reflect the need for growth, accomplishment, and self-realization.

growth factors *See* motivator factors.

Herzberg (1968) termed the things that make us dissatisfied hygiene factors (e.g., pay, working conditions). Using a biological analogy, poor hygiene can lead to disease, but good hygiene does not necessarily stop disease. In other words, just providing a worker with good pay and good working conditions does not mean that they will be motivated. On the other hand, the things that make us satisfied are known as motivator factors or growth factors and concern the need for great accomplishment, human growth, and self-realization. The lack of motivator factors will not cause a worker to be dissatisfied (assuming good hygiene is present) but will cause a worker to not be satisfied.

To test this theory, Herzberg (1982) assessed over 1,600 employees and found that 81% of motivator factors reflected human growth and development, whereas 69% of hygiene factors contributed to dissatisfaction. The overall principle of motivator-hygiene theory is that workers should be given all the appropriate tools to perform well. Although providing these tools will not motivate someone, it will simply keep them from becoming dissatisfied. Further, this theory encompasses the complexity of human nature and the innate need for human growth. Figure 11.9 illustrates this concept.

Acquired Needs Theory Theory of motivation that holds people are motivated to behave in order to acquire things that the culture at large deems important.

need for achievement Factor of acquired needs theory that reflects striving to acquire positions of responsibility and strive to achieve moderate goals.

Acquired Needs Theory

The influence of culture on the individual is the underlying assumption of the Acquired Needs Theory of motivation. This theory assumes that people are motivated to work to acquire the things that the culture at large deems important (McClelland, 1962). All the needs that are dictated by the culture can be broken down into three main or overarching needs that, according to Western culture, are pursued by people through work.

The first is the need for achievement. People who are high in this need are motivated to acquire positions of responsibility and strive to achieve moderate goals. The reason people pursue moderate goals is that goals that are seen as too easy will be reached by everyone and thus not viewed as a significant success. On the other hand, goals that are seen as too difficult will be reached by very few and thus viewed as a failure. Research indicates that workers who are high in the need for achievement are also open, are sensitive, and report higher levels of job satisfaction (Mitchell, 1984). The second need is the need for power. People who are high in this need are motivated to aspire to greatness and positions of respect (Kotter, 1988). This motivation also includes the pursuit for control, influence, and being responsible for other people. Although it may seem that people who pursue the need for power have selfish intent, people who are high in the motivation for power use this power to help others around them (McClelland, 1975). The final need is the need for affiliation, and it reflects the need to develop and enjoy quality relationships with others, avoid conflict, and be less dogmatic and assertive in an effort to maintain these relationships. Overall, Acquired Needs Theory highlights the different motivating factors that people possess and utilizes these factors to explain why people are motivated to perform certain jobs at certain productivity levels. For example, a productive social worker who makes an annual salary of $22,000 per year is motivated by different needs than a productive stockbroker who makes $220,000 per year.

> **need for power** Factor of acquired needs theory and reflects aspiring to greatness and seek control over others.

> **need for affiliation** Factor of acquired needs theory and reflects the need for relationships, conflict avoidance, and the need to be nonassertive.

Theories of worker motivation seek to predict, explain, and understand the things that motivate people to work as well as how to tap into these motivating factors to achieve maximum employee performance. Motivation will continue to be an intriguing part of productive organizational function. Beyond the theories reviewed here, there are many different perspectives concerning how or why workers are motivated. Most, however, differentiate the more primal needs (i.e., physiological needs) from those higher-level needs (i.e., psychological needs). Regardless of how you view motivation, the fact remains that people are complex beings that have a wide range of needs that they strive to satisfy. The role of communication and relationship building and maintaining are central in these theories of worker motivation. The ability to satisfy workers' physiological, psychological, and interpersonal needs, by most accounts, results in motivated, committed, and long-term employees.

ORGANIZATIONAL SOCIALIZATION

Model of Organizational Assimilation

Organizational assimilation is defined as "the process by which individuals become integrated into the culture of an organization" (Jablin, 2001, p. 755). Frederic Jablin's model proposes that people move through three distinct stages of assimilation. These stages consist of anticipatory socialization, organizational entry and assimilation, and disengagement and exit.

anticipatory socialization stage Reflects how people develop expectations about work starting at childhood and include parents, peers, and the media.

The **anticipatory socialization stage** reflects how people develop expectations about work. These expectations begin to develop at a very young age through sources such as our parents and the media. Listening to our parents discuss their jobs is our first exposure of what we should expect from our work life. Our educational system is another powerful influence on the creation of our organizational expectations as it exposes children to hierarchical order and information about specific vocations. How to communicate in the workplace is another important facet of anticipatory socialization. We learn appropriate behaviors from watching television shows based on certain occupations (e.g., *CSI, Gray's Anatomy, The Office*). Some of these communication skills that we develop include emotional control, conflict management, and role taking. People engage in information gathering in developing expectations about work. Information can be gathered from organizational newsletters, Web sites, current employees, and other people with knowledge of the organization. According to Katherine Miller and Frederic Jablin (1991), newcomers utilize surveillance (observation of past behaviors), testing limits (breaks organizational rules and norms then observe the reaction of others), indirect questions (hinting at a topic without directly asking about the topic), third party (solicits information from coworkers when the newcomer should really be asking the supervisor), disguising conversations (disguise information seeking within everyday conversation), and observing (information seeking by observing the behavior of others).

organizational entry and assimilation stage A dynamic interrelated process between planned as well as unintentional efforts to socialize employees and attempts of organizational members to individualize or change their role.

The second stage in the assimilation model is the **organizational entry and assimilation stage**. According to Jablin (2001), assimilation "is generally considered to be composed of two dynamic interrelated processes: (1) planned as well as unintentional efforts by the organization to socialize employees, and (2) the attempts of organizational members to individualize or change their roles and work environments to better satisfy their values, attitudes, and needs" (p. 755). People entering the organization are called *newcomers* and are given more latitude with regard to making mistakes. This latitude is based on the fact that the newcomer has to adapt to a new environment, new procedures, new policies, and new relationships.

organizational disengagement/exit stage When people decide to leave the organization, they engage in behaviors to end interpersonal relationships.

The final stage of organizational assimilation is the **organizational disengagement/exit stage**. When people decide to leave the organization, they begin a slow withdrawal process that includes deidentifying with the organization and other organizational members. For example, a person found a new job and gave a four-week notice to their supervisor. During that four-week period, the employee will slowly decrease communication with others as well as increase relational distance. Organizational exit can take the form of being terminated, transferring to another department within the same organization, retiring, or quitting.

ORGANIZATIONAL INFORMATION PROCESSING

Information Systems Theory

Karl Weick (1979) proposed a theory of how people make sense of information in an environment. The main goal of the Information Systems Theory is to explain how information and sense-making is a perceptual process that varies from person to person. This general systems-based theory seeks to identify how ambiguity and equivocal information lead people to different realities. Thus, the organization should seek to ensure a "most single" reality that is shared by all members of the organization. Simply put, organizations should seek to reduce uncertainty or equivocation (i.e., requisite variety).

Weick (1995) argued that organizations operate or exist within an environment that is both physical and informational. People within the organization are in a constant state of organizing. Weick believes that we should use verbs such as *managing* and *organizing* as opposed to nouns such as management and organization. The use of verbs are advocated to reflect the fluidity of the sense-making process as opposed to using nouns that reflect stationary or fixed entities. People create their environment through enactment, which is the action of making sense. Any one person will attribute different realities to information. Given that people have different perceptual schemas and selective perception, people create different information environments. When there is a low equivocal environment, people use assembly rules, which are standard processes that aid people in standard routines for making sense of information. Sense-making does not only involve interpreting information but also includes generating what was interpreted. As Weick argued, "People know what they think when they see what they say" (Weick, 1979, p. 175). For example, your college or university has a student handbook, which explicitly provides all students standardized procedures for everything from academic standards of conduct to applying for graduation. These standards help increase the probability that each student will enact in a similar way. On the other hand, when there is high equivocation, people engage in communication cycles. Communication cycles are sense-making actions where people create and react to ideas. For example, a professor assigns her students an assignment with only the following instructions: "I want you to develop a term paper on the Civil War. The length of the paper should be long enough to be complete." The information provided by the professor is full of uncertainty and equivocal information. In this case, the students will probably engage in communication cycles to make

Informational Systems Theory An information processing theory that seeks to explain how information and sense-making is a perceptual process that varies from person to person.

requisite variety When the organization seeks to ensure a single reality that is shared by all members of the organization.

enactment The act of making sense of equivocal information.

perceptual schemas The perceptual "wiring" of each person. All of us have a different perceptual schema resulting in different information environments.

selective perception When people perceive things differently resulting in different information environments.

assembly rules Standard processes that aids people in standard routines for making sense of information.

sense-making Consists of both the interpretation of information and generating what is interpreted.

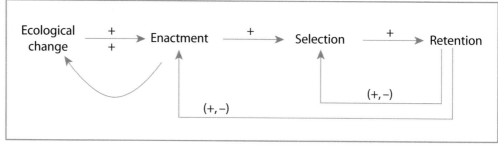

Adapted from Karl Weick. (1973). The Social Psychology of Organizing. *Reading, MA: Addison-Wesley.*

Figure 11.10

Structure of the organizing process.

communication cycles
Sense-making actions where people create and react to ideas. Most prevalent when there is high equivocation.

selection stage of organizing   The stage of selecting meanings and interpretations directly while indirectly selecting individuals, departments, groups, or goals indirectly.

retention stage of organizing   Stage of organizing involving deciding whether or not assembly rules and communication cycles should be retained or discarded in future sense-making.

organizational intelligence
The variety of rules that an organization has developed and engages in.

sense of the equivocal directions. Weick (1979) believes that both assembly rules and communication cycles are utilized most during the **selection stage of organizing**. "The selection process selects meanings and interpretation directly and it selects individuals, departments, groups, or goals indirectly" (Weick, 1979, p. 175). On the other hand, when sense-making is effective, people are sharing the same information environment, and people should use the **retention stage of organizing** as the organization should save both the assembly rules and the communication cycles as a rubric for future sense-making processes. The retention stage of organizing involves deciding whether or not assembly rules and communication cycles should be retained or discarded in future sense-making. It is argued that the more information that is retained from past information processing, the more difficult it will be to process more complex information in the future. However, some retention of past sense-making is valuable. Simply put, Weick believes we should "treat memory as a pest." The variety of rules that an organization has developed and engages is known as **organizational intelligence** (Kreps, 1979) (see Figure 11.10). Information Systems Theory serves as a rubric from which shared sense-making can be accomplished in the process of organizing.

ORGANIZATIONAL ETHICAL PERSPECTIVES AND THEORIES

Throughout the history of industrialized society, employees have taken unfair advantage of workers, customers, and competitors. What does it mean to be ethical? What is right? Appropriate? Good? The answers to these questions are difficult to derive due to their subjective nature. This section will introduce you to several ethical traditions that seek to explain the various ways that people interpret ethical behavior.

The foundational ethical perspective assumes that ethics and ethical behavior are absolute and universal across all people and cultures. A standard code of ethics is to be adhered to by all people. Foundational ethics can be found in classic religious documents such as the Bible, Torah, or Koran. Many professions also have universal codes of ethics. Some of these codes are legally binding, and some are used to serve as general guidelines for behavior. For example, Table 11.5 reflects the modern version of the Hippocratic Oath (Lasagna, 1964) that is recited by newly appointed medical doctors entering the field of medicine and the oath of enlistment that is required of all new recruits enlisting in the U.S. Armed Services.

foundational ethical perspective Assumes that ethical behavior is absolute and universal to all human beings.

The situational ethical perspective assumes that people make ethical decisions based on the situation and not a universal truth. Situation-based ethics holds that ethical standards change based on the specific circumstances in which the behavior occurs. For example, consider the following question: "Is stealing wrong?" To answer this question from the situational ethics perspective would be, "It depends on the circumstances." Another term used to describe ethics in this tradition would be *contingency ethics*. Recall when Hurricane Katrina ravaged the city of New Orleans. The media made a distinction between people who were stealing diapers, food, and clothing from those who were stealing jewelry and electronics. The former were referred to as foragers (and thus behaving ethically), and the later were referred to as looters (and thus behaving unethically).

situational ethical perspective Assumes that ethical decisions are unique to any given situation and are not universal in nature.

The Deontological ethical perspective is also known as virtue ethics. Deontological ethics extend back to Aristotle and his writings on Nichomachean ethics. This perspective is based on the intentions of the person. If a person's intent is based on sound and ethical reasoning, then the resulting behavior is seen as ethical. For example, if a pharmaceutical company markets a drug that will increase the quality of life for millions of people, but the development and testing of the drug resulted in the deaths of dozens of animals and human test subjects, the intention to help millions of people would make any resulting loss of life seen as unavoidable, resulting in the pharmaceutical company's pursuits seen as ethical.

Deontological ethical perspective Assumes that if a person's intentions are based on sound ethical reasoning, the action is ethical.

The utilitarian ethical perspective is considered the opposite of the Deontological perspective in that ethical behavior is based on outcomes, not intentions. This perspective can be associated with philosophers such as Jeremy Bentham, John Stuart Mill, and Henry Sidgewick and makes a distinction between a person's moral commitments (e.g., a person's personal sense of duty) and the actual behavior of the person. The assumption is that a person's moral commitments and behaviors should be in a dialogue. That is, both the intention and the behavior are considered when deciding if a specific action is ethical. Although considered together, intent and behavior may not necessarily be related to each other (i.e., the behavior may or may not be reflective of a person's moral comittments). The underlying assumption of utilitarianism should

utilitarian ethical perspective Assumes that ethical behavior is based on outcome as opposed to intention.

Table 11.5   ## THE MODERN HIPPOCRATIC OATH AND THE OATH OF ENLISTMENT

MODERN HIPPOCRATIC OATH

I swear to fulfill, to the best of my ability and judgment, this covenant. I will respect the hard won scientific gains of those physicians in whose steps I walk, and gladly share such knowledge as is mine with those who are to follow.

I will apply, for the benefit of the sick, all measures that are required, avoiding those twin traps of over-treatment and therapeutic nihilism.

I will remember that there is art to medicine as well as science, and that warmth, sympathy, and understanding may outweigh the surgeon's knife or the chemist's drug.

I will not be ashamed to say "I know not," nor will I fail to call in my colleagues when the skills of another are needed for a patient's recovery.

I will respect the privacy of my patients, for their problems are not disclosed to me that the world may know. Most especially must I tread with care in matters of life and death. But it may also be within my power to take a life; This awesome responsibility must be faced with great humbleness and awareness of my own frailty. Above all, I must not play as God.

I will remember that I do not treat a fever chart, cancerous growth, but a sick human being, whose illness may affect the person's family and economic stability. My responsibility includes those related problems, if I am to care adequately for the sick.

I will prevent disease whenever I can, for prevention is preferable to cure.

I will remember that I remain a member of society, with special obligations to all my fellow human beings, those sound of mind and body as well as the infirm.

If I do not violate this oath, may I enjoy life and art, respected while I live and remembered with affection thereafter. May I always act so as to preserve the finest traditions of my calling and may I long experience the joy of healing those who seek my help.

OATH OF ENLISTMENT

I, (name), do solemnly swear (or affirm) that I will support and defend the Constitution of the United States against all enemies, foreign and domestic; that I will bear true faith and allegiance to the same; and that I will obey the orders of the President of the United States and the orders of the officers appointed over me, according to regulations and the Uniform Code of Military Justice. So help me God.

rights/justice-based ethical perspective Assumes that ethical behavior is based on a certain level of dignity and justice afforded and provides a level of fairness for all.

be aimed at increasing utility or happiness. That is, the best ethical decision is the one that guarantees the most happiness. If the overall result is positive, then the action is ethical.

The **rights/justice-based ethical perspective** assumes ethical behavior is derived from natural law. An ethical person or organization is one in which a certain level of dignity, justice, and fairness is afforded to all people. An example of rights/justice-based ethics can be seen in Wal-mart's decision to provide a variety of generic prescription medications for three dollars each. This decision resulted in making medications affordable to a much wider segment of the population. The two general types of rights/justice are **distributive justice** and **procedural justice**. Distributive justice reflects normative or societal definitions of what is just or right with regard to the allocation of goods within an organization. Procedural justice reflects decision making and implementing those decisions based on fair and sound principles.

The **relationship-based ethical perspective** assumes that ethical behavior is a creation of, and maintained through, communication. All relationships within the organization as well as between organizations and their various external publics are based on quality and honest communication. Honest communication involves spontaneous interaction that is void of ulterior motives. Another assumption of the relational ethical perspective is that dialogue is the foundation for which all relationships are developed, maintained, or terminated. Any person communicating should be mindful of the effect that dialogue (i.e., communication) has on the other person and that dialogue should be focused on the development of the other person. Richard Johannesen (1996) argued that the relationship-based ethical perspective "allows free expression, seeks understanding, and avoids value judgments that stifle. One shows desire and capacity to listen without anticipating, interfering, competing, refuting, or warping meanings into preconceived interpretations (p. 68).

The final ethical perspective is known as **Stakeholder Theory**. The term *stakeholder* refers to parties whose interests are directly affected by business activity. Stakeholder Theory emerged as a reaction to the writings of Milton Friedman (1970) in his article entitled, "The Social Responsibility of Business Is to Increase Its Profits." Friedman believed that the social world is organized into separate zones of activity. Simply put, people are trained in different disciplines in different ways. For example, a businessperson is trained differently from a doctor, who is trained differently from a philosopher. Each of these professions, as well as many others, have different ways of looking at the world and thus interpreting what is and what is not ethical. This separation of spheres is also true to political, economic, and social activity, and social activity should not be commingled with the others.

Friedman (1970) argued that the sole responsibility of the organization is to those people who own the instruments of production (i.e., stakeholders). Therefore, according to Stakeholder Theory, the organization and its members are behaving ethically if they generate profits for the stakeholders. Ethical behavior, within the corporate world, is solely based on maximizing shareholder profit within the limits of the law. For example, when people argue that "big oil" companies are posting enormous quarterly profits and should be investigated, people are basing their ethical judgment from the right/justices-based perspective, as opposed to Stakeholder Theory, which argues that if

distributive justice Normative principles that concern what is just or right regarding the allocation of goods in the organization.

procedural justice Reflects decision making and implementing those decisions based on fair and sound principles.

relationship-based ethical perspective Assumes that ethical behavior is a creation of, and maintained through, communication.

Stakeholder Theory A theory that assumes the sole responsibility of an organization is to those people who own the instruments of production.

alignment An ethical practice that matches the organization's formal practices and informal practices to the needs of its members.

dialogic communication An ethical practice that emphasizes open channels of communication that constitutes the cornerstone of teamwork.

participation An ethical practice of valuing feedback and recognizing contributions of organizational members.

transparent structure An ethical perspective that assumes every practice the organization engages in should be up front and open.

accountability An ethical practice of going above and beyond the minimal standards set by the industry and government regulations.

courage An ethical practice where the organization values employee dissent, listening to employee dissent, as well as admitting when the organization has made a mistake.

profits are not as high as they could be within the limits of the law, then the organization and organizational members are not behaving ethically.

Stakeholder Theory was developed over thirty-five years ago. Since then, the concept of stakeholder has been expanded to include members of the board of directors, managers, and production workers, as well as shareholders. Outside the organization, stakeholders include customers, suppliers, competitors, local committees, and government regulating bodies. In the end, stakeholders fall into the five categories of shareholders, customers, employees, suppliers, and communication.

Practices of Ethical Organizations

Steve May (2006) believed that for an organization to be considered ethical, it should follow six practices. First, **alignment** refers to the ethical practice that matches the organization's formal practices (e.g., performance appraisal policies, employee pay and benefits) with the informal practices of the organization (e.g., norms, rituals) that serve the needs of the organizational members. Alignment requires effort on the part of both the organization and organizational members. Second is the practice of **dialogic communication**, which refers to having open channels of communication that constitute the cornerstone of teamwork. Dialogic communication should be decentralized and lack a hierarchical structure. Regardless of a person's position or status, all employees are encouraged to interact. Third, the practice of **participation** reflecting the value of feedback and the recognition of contributions from members. **Transparent structure** is the fourth practice and reflects that every practice that the organization and its members engage in should be up front and open (i.e., aboveboard) to both internal and external members (e.g., customers, community). This transparency should be in all organizational practices, including hiring policies and employee appraisals. The fifth practice is that of **accountability** and reflects exceeding the minimal standards set by the industry in which the organization operates as well as governmental standards. **Courage** is the sixth practice and concerns the degree to which the organization values employee dissent, listening to dissent, admitting when the organization is wrong, and promises to rectify any injustice. These six practices are the hallmarks of ethical organizations.

SUMMARY

This chapter began with the development of management theories that have evolved over the nineteenth and twentieth centuries. These efforts included scientific management, human relations, and human resource perspectives. In all these perspectives, the importance of communication, whether it be controlled (i.e., scientific management) or encouraged (i.e., human relations and human resource), is central to explaining human production. We then discussed leadership theories that highlight the various perspectives on how effective leadership is conceptualized and implemented. These varying perspectives include leadership that is believed to be a feature of personality (e.g., trait approaches), a feature of the circumstances (e.g., situational leadership), or a function of the relationship between the leader and the members (e.g., leader–member exchange). The theories of worker motivation discussed included the need for becoming self-actualized (e.g., hierarchy of needs theory), the need for recognition (e.g., motivator-hygiene theory), and the need to satisfy various inner needs (e.g., acquired needs theory). All these theories hold that there is indeed a drive within workers that moves them in varying degrees to accomplish organizational goals. The model of assimilation presented in the chapter maps how a person becomes a member of the organization. As discussed, this process begins in childhood and follows us through retirement. Each of us has a different experience in the organization, and that is why so much effort is expended in the creation of a socialization process that provides a similar experience for all new employees. This sense-making function was also highlighted in information systems theory that utilizes assembly rules and communication cycles in an effort to organize information. Finally, we presented various theories of ethics and how these theories effect how we view something as right or wrong. These perspectives ranged from ethical behavior as being universal to all people (i.e., foundational ethics) to those that are dependent on the situation (i.e., situational ethical perspectives).

KEY TERMS

Abraham personality

accountability

Acquired Needs Theory

Adam personality

affirming style

alignment

androgynous style

animated style

anticipatory socialization

argumentativeness

assembly rules

assimilation stage

attentive style

authority

benevolent-authoritative type

Bureaucratic Management Theory

charisma

classical management perspective

communication cycles

communication competence

communicator style

consultative type

contentious style

Contingency Theory

country club manager

courage

dangling carrot approach

defensive routines

delegating style

deontological ethical perspective

depersonalization

dialogic communication

distributive justice

dominant style

double-loop learning

downward communication

dramatic style

Effective Management Theory

enactment

Espoused Theory

esteem needs

Eudiamonic Philosophy of Life

exchange approaches to leadership

exploitive-authoritative type

Fayol's bridge

foundational ethical perspective

friendly style

gangplank

generative learning

Great Man Theory of Leadership

growth factors

Hawthorne effect

Hawthorne studies

hedonic philosophy of life

Hierarchy of Needs Theory

human relations perspective

human resource management perspective

hygiene factors

in-group relationships

Information Systems Theory

impoverished manager

impression leaving style

job maturity

Leader-Member Exchange Theory

learned helplessness

locus of control

love needs

Managerial Grid Theory

Model I aapproach

Model II approach

model of organizational assimilation

moderate manager

motivator factors

Motivator-Hygiene Theory

narcissism

need for achievement

need for affiliation

need for power

newcomers

nonaffirming style

open style

organizational disengagement/exit stage

organizational entry

organizational intelligence

organizing

out-group relationships

participate style

participation

participative style

perceptual schemas

power

precise style

primary needs

procedural justice

psychological maturity

pure charisma

rational-legal authority system

relational-based ethical perspective

relaxed style

requisite variety

retention stage of organizing

rights/justice-based ethical perspective

routinized charisma

safety needs

scalar chain

Scientific Management Theory

scientifically efficient

KEY TERMS (continued)

selective perception
selection stage of organizing
self-actualization
sell style
sense-making
single-loop learning
situational ethical perspective
situational leadership approach
soldiering
spontaneous cooperation

Stakeholder Theory
System 4 Management Theory
task manager
team manager
tell style
Theory in Use
Theory of Independent
 Mindedness (TEM)
Theory X
Theory Y

Theory Z
time-motion study
trait approach to leadership
transformational leadership
transparent structure
type A organizations
type J organizations
upward communication
utilitarian ethical perspective
verbal aggressiveness

Mass Media Contexts

MASS COMMUNICATION IN CONTEMPORARY SOCIETY

C ontemporary society maintains a reciprocal, interdependent relationship with the mass media. Society influences the media and is itself influenced by mass or mediated communication. Rarely a day goes by without some mention of how the media and mass communication affect our lives. Newspaper and radio reports scream headlines such as, "Studies link teen suicides with TV news and movies," "Kids, TV Don't Mix," and "Music videos found to be less violent than prime-time TV." Through mass media, people learn almost immediately about major happenings across town or across the globe. As viewers, we are frequently eyewitnesses to global events both joyous and tragic.

Definitions and conceptualizations of mass media and mass communication have changed considerably over the last decade. At one time, not too long ago, mass media was defined primarily as radio, television, newspapers, and magazines. Today, the term *media* is likely to conjure terms such as *cable* and *satellite television, satellite radio, HD radio,* and *interactive media,* also referred to as computer-mediated communication (CMC). Some even include the cell phone as a form of mediated communication (Noll, 2007, p. 1). Indeed, "the idea of 'new media' captures both the development of unique forms of digital media, and the remaking of more traditional media forms to adopt and adapt to the new media technologies" (Flew, 2002, p. 11). That is, new media combines computing and information technology, communications networks, and digitized media and information content. There are a few fundamental differences between what has been termed "new media" and traditional media. The new mediated technologies allow the user to communicate in a two-way fashion with others. In the past, after reading a story in a print newspaper, you had an opportunity to write a letter to the editor and send that via conventional (or snail) mail. Today, after reading the same story on the Internet-based version of the news source, you can send immediate feedback to the source via e-mail. This immediacy factor represents another major difference. Putting a print newspaper or magazine together takes an enormous amount of time. Adding a story to a news Internet site, often complete with video, reduces that time frame considerably.

One consequence of these innovations and of the changing nature of media use has been the development of new theories of mass communication. These theories attempt to explain how individuals respond to media, to predict how rapidly a society will adopt these innovations, and to determine what effect mass communication has on individuals, society, other forms of human communication, and culture. Current research looks at the role of society, culture, and the individual in the *production* of mass communication content. The distinction between mass communication and interpersonal communication has stimulated a considerable amount of investigation by communication researchers. Some theories address how mass communication and interpersonal communication *jointly* influence an individual's decision-making processes. Other theories attempt to offer a new synthesis of interpersonal and mass communication, which has been labeled *mediated interpersonal communication.* Three broad questions have stimulated much of the research and theory building in mass communication:

1. What is the impact of a society on its mass media?
2. How does mass communication function?
3. What effect does exposure to mass communication have on people?

The bulk of mass communication theory and research has concentrated on the third question. Many theorists have investigated how mass media messages affect people's perceptions and behaviors. Examples of those theories will be detailed in this chapter. Some of the theories explore audience involvement in mass communication. Other theories try to explain how mediated messages shape our perceptions of reality. Yet another body of research examines how communication rules are used to guide audience members' collective interaction with mass media.

reflective projective theory of mass communication
A theory that asserts the mass media acts like a mirror for society.

The **reflective-projective theory of mass communication** asserts that the mass media act like mirrors for society. The media reflect society's attitudes and values as they simultaneously project idealized visions of a society. Individuals interpret these reflections, seeing both their own images and alternative realities. Interpretations are affected by the intellectual, emotional, and sensory responsiveness of each individual. Lee Loevinger (1979) argued that nations or communities are not necessarily formed by maps or geographical boundaries. Rather, nations or communities are formed by common images and visions, along with common interests, ideas, and culture.

EARLY THEORY-BUILDING EFFORTS IN MASS COMMUNICATION

During World War I, the new mass media were used to help activate the population. The mass media presented messages designed to stimulate support for the war effort. The newly developed media effectively promoted the beliefs of the warring nations. Mass communication became an important tool used by individuals engaged in large-scale persuasive efforts. The term *propaganda* first emerged during this time. After World War I, U.S. society witnessed an increasing growth in diversity; the society became less homogeneous. Individuals were no longer so closely dependent on one another. The term "mass society" was created by sociologists to describe not merely a large number of people in a given culture but the *relationship* between the individuals and the social order around them (DeFleur & Ball-Rokeach, 1982).

The "Magic Bullet" Theory

Sometimes referred to as the "hypodermic needle theory," the **magic bullet theory** was one of the first developed to explain the influence of the new forms of communication on society. The bullet theory and the many variations of it were derived from the stimulus-response perspective of several early mass communication theorists and researchers (e.g., Lasswell, 1927). This view asserts that any powerful stimulus such as a mass media message can provoke a uniform response from a given organism, such as an audience. Recall that the mass media at this time were thought to exert powerful, direct influence over the audience. The magic bullet or hypodermic needle theory suggested that the mass media could influence a very large group of people *directly* and *uniformly* by "shooting" or "injecting" them with appropriate messages designed to trigger a desired response.

magic bullet theory
A theory of mass communication that suggests media influences people directly and uniformly.

The popularity of these early stimulus-response theories of mass communication was consistent with that of the existing psychological and sociological theories of mass society. In addition, "evidence" of the power of the media existed in its ability to mobilize support for the country's war effort. The newly emerging mass media did have a profound effect on the audience, but several intervening factors also exerted considerable influence on audiences during that time. After years of additional research, mass communication theorists concluded that the early stimulus-response theories lacked explanatory and predictive power. They developed alternative theories that address both the power of the media to influence attitudes and behavior and also the influence of different message sources and different audience reactions. Examples of these alternative theories will be presented later in this chapter.

The Two-Step Flow Theory

Several researchers had designed a study to examine how individuals from different social groups select and use mass communication messages to influence votes (see Lazarsfeld, Berelson, & Gaudet, 1944). The researchers expected to find empirical support for the direct influence of media messages on voting intentions. They were surprised to discover, however, that *informal, personal contacts* were mentioned far more frequently than exposure to radio or newspaper as sources of influence on voting behavior. When questioned further, several participants revealed that they had received their information about the campaign *first* from *others* (who had received information directly from the mass media).

Armed with this data, Elihu Katz and Paul Lazarsfeld (1955) developed the **two-step flow theory** of mass communication. This theory asserts that information from the media moves in two distinct stages. First, individuals who pay close attention (are frequent "attenders") to the mass media and its messages receive the information. These individuals, called **opinion leaders**, are generally well-informed people who pass information along to others through informal, interpersonal communication. Opinion leaders also pass on their own interpretations in addition to the actual media content. The term "personal influence" was coined to refer to the process intervening between the media's direct message and the audience's ultimate reaction to that message. Over the last fifty years, a substantial amount of research has contributed to our knowledge about opinion leadership.

Several characteristics of opinion leaders have been identified. Opinion leaders are quite influential in getting people to change their attitudes and behaviors and are quite similar to those they influence. Think of an individual whom you consult before making a major purchase. Perhaps you have a friend who knows a great deal about cars. You may hear a number of messages on television about the favorable qualities of the Ford Fusion and the Toyota Camry. The mass media have clearly provided you with information about each car, but do you rely solely on this information to decide which car to buy? If you are like most people, probably not. You may check *Consumer Reports* to determine what it says about those two cars. Will this information be enough to persuade you to prefer one car to the other? Possibly, but chances are you will also seek out the advice of someone you consider an opinion leader on the topic of automobiles.

two-step flow   Theory that asserts information from media is processed first by opinion leaders who then pass it along via interpersonal channels.

opinion leader   A component of the two-step flow theory that reflects a person who pays close attention to the mass media then exerts their influence on others concerning the messages received from the media.

The two-step flow theory has improved our understanding of how the mass media influence decision making. The theory refined our ability to predict the influence of media messages on audience behavior, and it helped explain why certain media campaigns may have failed to alter audience attitudes and behavior. Despite this contribution, the two-step flow theory has also received its share of criticism. First, some major news stories seem to be spread directly by the media with only modest intervention by personal contact. Acts of terrorism or natural disasters are often heard first from the media, then discussed interpersonally. Second, definitions of opinion leadership are often vague. Werner Severin and James Tankard (2001) suggested that some opinion leaders are self-nominated and are not reported to be opinion leaders by their supposed followers. Another difficulty is that opinion leaders have been found to be both active and passive. The two-step flow theory argues that opinion leaders are primarily active media seekers, whereas their followers are primarily passive information "sponges." This distinction between media behavior of leaders and followers does not necessarily hold true. Finally, although Katz and Lazarsfeld argued the need for a *two-step* model, the process of media dissemination and audience behavior can involve more steps. Thus, the two-step flow theory gave way to the concept of multistep flow, often used to describe the *diffusion of innovations.*

Diffusion Theory

Diffusion theory examines how new ideas spread among groups of people. The two-step flow theory of mass communication was primarily concerned with the exchange of information between the media and others. Diffusion research goes one step further. It centers around the conditions that increase or decrease the likelihood that a new idea, product, or practice will be adopted by members of a given culture. Diffusion research has focused on five elements: (1) the *characteristics of an innovation* that may influence its adoption; (2) the *decision-making process* that occurs when individuals consider adopting a new idea, product or practice; (3) the *characteristics of individuals* that make them likely to adopt an innovation; (4) the *consequences* for individuals and society of adopting an innovation; and (5) *communication channels* used in the adoption process (see Rogers, 1995).

Communication channels include both the mass media and interpersonal contacts. The multistep flow and diffusion theories expand the number and type of intermediaries between the media and the audience's decision making. In multistep diffusion research, opinion leaders still exert influence on audience behavior via their personal contact, but additional intermediaries called change agents and gatekeepers are also included in the process of diffusion. **Change agents** are those professionals who encourage opinion leaders to adopt

diffusion theory   The study of how new ideas spread among groups of people.

change agents
Professional who encourage opinion leaders to adopt or reject an innovation.

gatekeepers People
who control the flow of
information to a given
group of people.

or reject an innovation. Gatekeepers are individuals who control the flow of
information to a given group of people. Whereas opinion leaders are usually
quite similar to their followers, change agents are usually more educated and
of higher status than either the opinion leaders or their followers. A change
agent might be a representative from a national cable television company who
tries to persuade local opinion leaders in a community (town officials, for
example) to offer cable television or a computer company representative who
convinces local school officials to introduce a particular personal computer
into the school system. This representative is probably more knowledgeable
about the computer system than the opinion leaders (school officials). However, the task of influencing the school board to budget money still rests with
the local opinion leaders. Recall that opinion leaders are similar to those they
represent. Previous research (see Chapter 9) suggests that similarity or
homophily enhances attraction, liking, and influence. A gatekeeper might be
the editor of a local news show or newspaper. This person decides what stories
will be printed or broadcast. Gatekeepers represent yet another intermediate
step in the flow of information between the media and audience. Thus, a number of intermediaries and channels are involved in the process of information
dissemination and influence.

Early theory-building efforts in mass communication relied heavily on
psychological and sociological theories. The field of mass communication now
has produced theory that can "stand on its own." Several contemporary theories developed by communication scholars will be presented next. The first
theory, the functional approach, was based on the early research and continues
to be refined today.

THE FUNCTIONAL APPROACH TO MASS COMMUNICATION THEORY

The mass media and mass communication serve many functions for our society. Clearly, one of the main attractions is escapism and entertainment value.
We come home after a hard day at school or the office and turn on our favorite
television comedy, game show, or dramatic program. Another major use of the
media is to provide information. Driving to school or work, we turn on the
radio and catch the latest news, weather, and sports scores. We may listen to
our favorite talk program to hear what others think about relations between
the United States and China. Harold Lasswell (1948) articulated three functions of mass communication: *surveillance, correlation,* and *cultural transmission.* Charles Wright (1960) added a fourth function, *entertainment.* In 1984,
Denis McQuail added a fifth function: *mobilization.*

surveillance A dimension
of the functional theory of
mass communication and is
the information and news
providing function of mass
communication.

Surveillance refers to the information and news-providing function of
mass communication. When we turn on the radio to obtain the latest weather,

traffic, or stock market reports, we are using the media primarily for its surveillance function. When the stock market dropped 508 points on October 19, 1987, millions of Americans turned on their radio and television sets to obtain information about the plunge. In every major office in the country that day, workers were "glued" to their radios to discover how much their companies' stocks had fallen. Individuals who did not own stock read in-depth reports in local newspapers concerning the potential influence of the stock market crash on the national and global economies.

The second function, **correlation**, deals with how the mass media select, interpret, and criticize the information they present to the public. The editorials on radio and television and the persuasive campaigns waged using the media are primary examples of the correlation function. "USA for Africa," "Live Aid," "Farm Aid," and "Hands Across America" were campaigns whose origins and major fund-raising drives were stimulated by and developed in connection with the media. The outpouring of funds to help the starving people of Ethiopia was largely stimulated by the poignant images that came into our homes via television. Many political critics suggest that the media, and not the American people, select our political leaders. They point to the tremendous media coverage and scrutiny given to the private lives of politicians and media celebrities as an example of the correlation function of the media. Along with criticism and selection of events, the correlation function of the media also *confers status* on selected individuals. The mass media choose to highlight a number of individuals who then become "legitimized" to audiences.

correlation A dimension of the functional theory of mass communication that concerns how the mass media select, interpret, and criticize the information they present to the public.

The third function, **cultural transmission**, refers to the media's ability to communicate norms, rules, and values of a society. These values may be transmitted from one generation to another or from the society to its newcomers. Cultural transmission is a teaching function of the media, which brings many social role models into the home. Those role models frequently engage in behaviors considered appropriate in a given society (prosocial behaviors). Johnston and Ettema (1986) cited shows such as *Mister Rogers' Neighborhood*, *Sesame Street*, and the *ABC After School Specials* as examples of children's programs that attempt to teach or to promote such prosocial behaviors as being polite, dealing with anger or fear, handling new situations, coping with death, persisting at tasks, caring, and cooperating. Prime-time television shows such as *Brothers and Sisters* and *Friday Night Lights* have been mentioned as programs that promote values such as respect for authority, family harmony, and a solid work ethic. As the number of television hours watched increases, regional and subcultural differences appear to be decreasing. The media's powerful cultural transmission of "common" messages has caused us to speak, think, and dress more alike. These common or unifying messages may have further "homogenized" U.S. culture by dictating the "proper" way to act.

cultural transmission A dimension of the functional theory of mass communication that concerns the media's ability to communicate norms, rules, and values of a society.

The fourth function of mass communication, **entertainment**, may be the most potent one. Mass communication helps fill our leisure time by presenting

entertainment A dimension of the functional theory of mass communication that reflects how mass communication helps fill our leisure time by presenting messages filled with comedy, tragedy, play, and performance.

messages filled with comedy, drama, tragedy, play, and performance. The entertainment function of mass communication offers an escape from daily problems and concerns. The media introduce us to aspects of culture, art, music, and dance that otherwise might not be available to us. The mass media can stimulate excitement in viewers (as with sporting events) or calm us (as with classical music broadcasts). Mass communication as entertainment provides relief from boredom, stimulates our emotions, fills our leisure time, keeps us company, and exposes us to images, experiences, and events that we could not attend in person. Numerous critics, however, assert that the media and its messages lower expectations and reduce fine art to pop art.

mobilization A dimension of the functional theory of mass communication that reflects the ability of the media to promote national interests.

McQuail's fifth function of mass communication, mobilization, refers to the ability of the media to promote national interests (as we saw in the discussion about World War I), especially during times of national crisis. Although this mobilization function may be especially important in developing nations and societies, it can occur anywhere. We may have seen evidence of it in the United States during the days after the assassination of President John F. Kennedy and during the coverage of the terrorist attacks of 9/11. The media's central function was not only to inform us but also to counsel, strengthen, and pull us together.

AGENDA-SETTING THEORY AND MASS COMMUNICATION

agenda setting A theory that holds intense media attention increases the importance of certain topics, issues, and individuals.

Agenda setting describes a very powerful influence of the media—the ability to tell us what issues are important. For example, if the media choose to highlight declining wages and lower standards of living for the current generation of adults, then concern over the economy becomes an important issue, regardless of the level of importance we placed on it before the media attention. Books addressing the issue start to sell across the country. Suddenly, people are concerned about loss of leisure time compared to previous generations. Entertainers joke about children in their thirties moving home to live with their parents.

Agenda setting has been the subject of attention from media analysts and critics for years. As far back as 1922, the newspaper columnist Walter Lippman was concerned that the media had the power to present images to the public. Because firsthand experiences are limited, we depend on the media to describe important events we have not personally witnessed. The media provide information about "the world outside"; we use that information to form "pictures in our heads" (Lippman, 1922). Political scientist Bernard Cohen (1963) warned that "the press may not be successful much of the time in telling people what to think, but it is stunningly successful in telling its readers what to think about." Prior to the early 1970s, the prevailing beliefs of mass communication research were that the media had only limited effects. Most research assumed the following sequence: the media generate awareness of issues through presentation of information; that information provides a basis for attitude change; the change in attitude includes behavior change. Most research looked for attitude and behavior change and found very limited influence. A study by Max McCombs and Donald Shaw (1972) in Chapel Hill, North Carolina, changed the emphasis of research efforts and stimulated a flurry of empirical investigations into the agenda-setting function of the mass media.

McCombs and Shaw focused on awareness and information. Investigating the agenda-setting function of the mass media in the 1968 presidential campaign, they attempted to assess the relationship between what voters in one community *said* were important issues and the *actual* content of media messages used during the campaign. They first analyzed the content presented by four local papers, the *New York Times,* two national newsmagazines, and two national network television broadcasts. They ranked importance by looking at the prominence given a story (lead, frontpage, headline, editorial, etc.) and the length. The researchers then interviewed 100 undecided voters (the assumption being that voters committed to a candidate would be less susceptible to media influence). McCombs and Shaw concluded that the mass media exerted a significant influence on what voters considered to be the major issues of the campaign. In addition to pioneering an entire line of research, McCombs and Shaw provided an excellent example of the thinking on which this textbook is premised. They believe that effective scientific research builds on previous studies. As a result, their study of the next presidential election (Shaw & McCombs, 1977) extended the scope of the original study, the objectives, and the research strategies. The study took place in Charlotte, North Carolina, and extended the analysis over time using a panel design. One of the interesting objectives added to this study was the investigation of what types of voters would be more likely to depend on the media. The researchers looked at two factors—the relevance of information to an individual and the degree of uncertainty—in determining **need for orientation**. Voters with a high need for orientation would be more likely to be influenced by the media in determining the importance of issues when issues were relevant and uncertainty was high. Just as McCombs and Shaw expanded their focus, other researchers have extended investigations of agenda setting to issues including history, advertising, foreign, and medical news.

need for orientation Part of the agenda-setting theory of mass communication concerning the relevance of information to an individual and the degree of uncertainty.

Despite the extensive outgrowth from the original hypothesis, critics charge that there is insufficient evidence to show a causal connection between the order of importance placed on issues by the media and the significance attached to those issues by the public. McQuail (1984, p. 276) argued that, at least for the time being, agenda-setting theory remains "within the status of a plausible but unproven idea." The direction of influence still needs to be resolved. Do the media influence the opinions of the audience or reflect public concerns? Are both dictated by actual events? Do external or internal forces have more influence on media content? What roles do the elite media play? That is, if the *New York Times* runs a story, can the *Washington Post* afford to ignore it? How much power do special interest groups, the president, senators, or chief executive officers of large corporations have to pressure the media to present their views? Is credibility a balancing factor? The media are in business; does profit and loss play a larger role than a culture that prides itself on presenting unbiased reports? Other research could look at internal processes. What effects do deadlines, space restrictions, and the use of official sources have? The number of variables offer new opportunities for research on this topic for years to come.

MASS COMMUNICATION AND PARASOCIAL INTERACTION

parasocial interaction
A relationship that exists between television viewers and remote media communicators.

The influence of mass communication and the media extends into the domain of relationship development. The concept of **parasocial interaction** has received considerable attention from both mass communication and interpersonal communication theorists. The concept was introduced forty years ago by Horton and Wohl (1956) to describe a new type of "relationship" that exists between television viewers and remote media communicators. In a parasocial relationship, members of the audience view performers or the characters they portray as belonging to the audience's peer group. Media performers with whom audiences develop parasocial relationships include entertainers, talk show hosts, journalists, sport personalities, and a number of other national and local media personalities.

We often develop a sense of involvement with media performers. We follow their careers just as we follow the careers of actual friends and colleagues. We may look forward to reading Internet, newspaper, and magazine accounts of their lives. We may even go to great lengths to meet them. One of your authors, for example, is a fan of "talk radio" programs. For years, he listened to TalkNet radio celebrity Bruce Williams give advice to listeners on a variety of topics. When visiting other cities, the author would scan the dial to locate the nationally syndicated program. This gave the feeling of having the performer "travel with him" and made it seem that he had a "friend," even in the most distant city. Bruce Williams scheduled a local appearance at a very large ballroom; the author immediately purchased tickets. Convinced that he would be among only a small audience on a wintry evening, the author arrived only fifteen minutes before the event was to begin. He was amazed to discover a capacity crowd, with only a few seats left in the very back of the ballroom! Clearly, he had underestimated the number of people who had also developed a parasocial interactional relationship with this particular radio celebrity.

In parasocial interaction, viewers believe that they know and understand the media personality in the same way as they know and understand their "real" friends (Perse & Rubin, 1989). The parasocial relationship is based on the belief that the media performer is similar to other people in their circle of friends (Rubin, Perse, & Powell, 1985). For most audience members, these parasocial interactions augment their actual face-to-face relationships.

In another study, researchers hypothesized that viewers would regard their favorite media performer as "closer" to them than actual "acquaintances" but more distant than "friends." Because most of our interpersonal relationships can be classified as "acquaintanceships," this hypothesis projected that we place our favorite media personality as "closer" to us than many people with whom we interact. Results showed that television personalities hold an intermediate position in "closeness" between friends and acquaintances. Koenig and Lessan (1985) suggested that the term *quasi-friend* may be most appropriate in describing the relationship between viewer and television personality.

Levy (1979) reported that news viewers occasionally reply to a newscaster's opening greeting with a greeting of their own. Almost 70 percent of network news viewers said they noticed when their anchorperson was on vacation, and 25 percent of viewers indicated that the anchorperson's absence "upset" them (p. 72). Levy also portrayed parasocial interactions as an alternative to face-to-face relationships for some people who have few or weak social ties with other people. A report by the American Psychological Association's Task Force on Television and Society reported that the elderly watch television more than any other age group. For this group in particular, as well as for other isolated individuals, television viewing becomes a parasocial activity that helps create the illusion of living in a world surrounded by people. Parasocial relationships with media personalities often fill the "gaps" caused by the death of a spouse or by children leaving home. Alan Rubin and Rebecca Rubin (1985) argued that "it is possible and beneficial to see media in certain contexts as being functional alternatives to interpersonal communication" (p. 38).

Influences of Interpersonal Communication Theory

In Chapter 9 we discussed the major assumptions of uncertainty reduction theory, which suggests that individuals seek to reduce uncertainty about those with whom they wish to develop relationships. We communicate more to reduce the uncertainty we feel about how to behave. We are more comfortable when we have more information. Rubin and McHugh (1987) applied these principles to understand parasocial interaction relationships. They examined whether increased television exposure leads to increased liking and whether parasocial interaction results from both exposure and attraction. The researchers found that television exposure was not influential in either parasocial interaction or attraction to a media personality. This finding contrasts with the assumptions of uncertainty reduction theory. They did discover, however, that parasocial relationships develop only when we are attracted to the media persona.

A study by Turner (1993) attempted to unite another theory of interpersonal communication with the research on parasocial interaction. Interpersonal attraction and attitude similarity, examined in Chapter 9, argues that similarity (in attitudes, background, value/morality, appearance) between individuals leads to interpersonal attraction or "liking." Turner found that attitude similarity emerged as the factor most closely related to parasocial interaction. Background and appearance similarity were also related to parasocial interaction, but the relationship was not as strong. Turner contributed additional insight into what leads to the development of a parasocial interaction and reinforced the mutual influence of interpersonal communication theory and media research.

Measuring Parasocial Interaction

Rubin, Perse, and Powell (1985) developed a reliable and valid questionnaire to measure relationship importance and affinity with media personalities. The Parasocial Interaction Scale (PSI) is a 20-item measure designed to assess an individual's feelings of friendship, involvement, and personal concern for a television newscaster and news team. By modifying the target (from newscaster to another type of persona), you can obtain a measure of parasocial interaction with any media personality.

The PSI (see Figure 12.1) includes such items as: "When I'm watching the newscast, I feel as if I am part of their group"; "My favorite newscaster keeps me company when the news is on television"; and "I think my favorite newscaster is like an old friend." Individuals respond to each of the 20 items by choosing one of five response options ranging from "strongly agree" (5) to "strongly disagree" (1). The PSI addresses the concepts of empathy, perceived similarity, and physical attraction. The researchers suggested that a fondness for television news would make a viewer feel more attracted and similar to the newscaster, thus contributing to the likelihood of a parasocial interaction.

The PSI was used in a study (Auter, 1992) conducted to determine if parasocial interaction can be increased by certain camera techniques and behavior by mediated personalities "in order to help 'blur' the line between audience and characters" (p. 174). To conduct the study, Auter used a 1950s episode from the *George Burns and Gracie Allen Show.* This show was unique at the time because George Burns frequently stepped out of character to address the audience, thus "breaking the fourth wall." Two versions of the program were created, one in which George Burns addressed the audience in asides and one in which those segments were edited out to create a "standard" situation comedy. Students were randomly divided into two groups and shown one version of the show. After watching the tape, the students completed a version of the PSI scale. The results of the study found that parasocial interaction scores were higher for those students who saw the "out of character" version of the

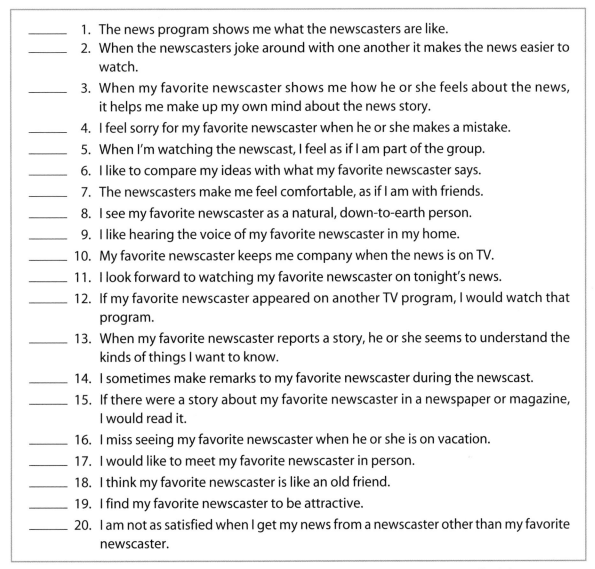

_____ 1. The news program shows me what the newscasters are like.

_____ 2. When the newscasters joke around with one another it makes the news easier to watch.

_____ 3. When my favorite newscaster shows me how he or she feels about the news, it helps me make up my own mind about the news story.

_____ 4. I feel sorry for my favorite newscaster when he or she makes a mistake.

_____ 5. When I'm watching the newscast, I feel as if I am part of the group.

_____ 6. I like to compare my ideas with what my favorite newscaster says.

_____ 7. The newscasters make me feel comfortable, as if I am with friends.

_____ 8. I see my favorite newscaster as a natural, down-to-earth person.

_____ 9. I like hearing the voice of my favorite newscaster in my home.

_____ 10. My favorite newscaster keeps me company when the news is on TV.

_____ 11. I look forward to watching my favorite newscaster on tonight's news.

_____ 12. If my favorite newscaster appeared on another TV program, I would watch that program.

_____ 13. When my favorite newscaster reports a story, he or she seems to understand the kinds of things I want to know.

_____ 14. I sometimes make remarks to my favorite newscaster during the newscast.

_____ 15. If there were a story about my favorite newscaster in a newspaper or magazine, I would read it.

_____ 16. I miss seeing my favorite newscaster when he or she is on vacation.

_____ 17. I would like to meet my favorite newscaster in person.

_____ 18. I think my favorite newscaster is like an old friend.

_____ 19. I find my favorite newscaster to be attractive.

_____ 20. I am not as satisfied when I get my news from a newscaster other than my favorite newscaster.

From Rubin, A. M., Perse, E. M., & Powell, R. A. (1985). Loneliness, parasocial interaction, and local television news viewing. Human Communication Research, 12, 155–180. Copyright 1985 by Wiley-Blackwell. Reprinted with permission.

Figure 12.1

Parasocial interaction scale.

program. In addition, the highest parasocial interaction scores came from those who saw that version and those who chose George Burns as their favorite character. The results suggest that not only does the PSI Scale measure what it says it does but that the development of parasocial interaction is "affected by message attributes and audiences' predisposition to interact with television characters" (p. 180).

Parasocial interaction is an important concept in assessing the relationship between the media and audience members. It offers many avenues for future research.

USES AND GRATIFICATIONS THEORY

As director of the Office of Radio Research at Columbia University, Paul Lazarsfeld published the first work on uses and gratifications (Lazarsfeld & Stanton, 1944). One of his former students, Herta Herzog, worked extensively on a program of research on daytime radio serials. She investigated the characteristics of women who listened to serials, the uses they made of the information they listened to, and the gratifications they received from their choice of programming (Lowery & De Fleur, 1995). The perspective that resulted from this early research presented a direct challenge to the powerful effects conceptualization of the magic bullet theory.

The next major study from this perspective was by Schramm, Lyle and Parker (1961). They conducted eleven studies from 1958 through 1960 on how children used television. The emphasis was on the choices of programming children made to satisfy their needs and interests. After these pioneering efforts, numerous studies have mined this vein of research. **Uses and gratifications theory** attempts to explain the *uses* and *functions* of the media for individuals, groups, and society in general; it represents a *systems approach* that uses covering laws methods of investigation.

uses and gratifications theory   A theory of mass communication that attempts to explain the uses and functions of the media for individuals, groups, and society in general.

One tenet of the systems approach is that a change in one part of the system will, of necessity, cause a change in another part of the system. Many claim that DVRs, DVDs, and TiVo have altered television viewing patterns. For example, recording television programs allows people to fast forward through the commercials. As a consequence, advertisers and advertising agencies have reexamined the placement and the format of commercials shown during network programming. Earlier we looked at the five functions of mass communication in terms of the *content* of mass media. The emphasis on content implies a passive audience absorbing what is offered. Uses and gratifications research changed the emphasis to audience members as active participants selecting particular forms of media.

Objectives of the Theory

Communication theorists had three objectives in developing uses and gratifications research. First, they hoped to explain *how* individuals use mass communication to gratify their needs. They attempted to answer the question: *What* do people do with the media (A. Rubin, 1985)? A second objective was to discover the *underlying motives* for individuals' media use. *Why* does one person rush home (or stay up late at night) to watch the local news on television while another person prefers reading the newspaper during breakfast or after dinner, while another prefers to get news only from the Internet? Why do some people only watch HBO movies? These are some questions that uses and gratifications theorists attempt to answer in their research. A third objective of this line of theory building was to identify the positive and negative *consequences* of individual media use. Here the systems aspect of uses and gratifications theory emerges. Relationships between the individual and the mass media, media content, the social system, alternative channels of communication (such as friends), and the consequences of media choice are all avenues of inquiry for systems researchers.

Examples of Uses and Gratifications Research

At the core of uses and gratifications theory lies the assumption that audience members actively seek out the mass media to satisfy individual needs. For example, Rubin (1979) uncovered six reasons why children and adolescents use television: learning, passing time, companionship, to forget or escape, excitement or arousal, and relaxation. Television viewing for passing time, for arousal, and for relaxation emerged as the most important uses of television for this age group. Rubin also designed a questionnaire called the Television Viewing Motives Instrument to discover reasons why people watch television. Complete the survey in Figure 12.2 to get a sense of your primary motives for watching TV.

Rubin (1983) designed another study to explore adult viewers' motivations, behaviors, attitudes, and patterns of interaction. The study looked at whether TV user motivations could predict behavioral and attitudinal consequences of television use. Five primary television viewing motivations were examined: pass time/habit, information, entertainment, companionship, and escape. The strongest viewing motivation relationships were found between pass time/habit and both companionship and escape viewing. The two categories of viewers identified in this study were predecessors to the *ritualized* and *instrumental* users of television discussed next. The first group of viewers used television to pass time and out of habit. The second group used television to seek information or as a learning tool.

Rubin (1984) identified two types of television viewers. The first type (habitual) consists of people who watch television for **ritualized use**. This type has a high regard for television in general, is a frequent user, and uses television primarily as a diversion. The second type (nonhabitual) consists of people who attend to television for **instrumental use**. This type exhibits a natural liking for a particular television program or programs and uses media content primarily for information. This person is more selective and goal oriented when watching television and does not necessarily feel that television is important. Rubin

ritualized use Using television viewing primarily as a diversion.

instrumental use Using television viewing primarily for information acquisition.

INSTRUCTIONS: Here are some reasons that other people gave us for watching TV. Please tell us how each reason is like your own reason for watching television. (Put one check in the correct column for each reason.)

I watch television . . .	A Lot	A Little	Not Much	Not At All
1. Because it relaxes me	_____	_____	_____	_____
2. So I won't be alone	_____	_____	_____	_____
3. So I can learn about things happening in the world	_____	_____	_____	_____
4. Because it's a habit	_____	_____	_____	_____
5. When I have nothing better to do	_____	_____	_____	_____
6. Because it helps me learn things about myself	_____	_____	_____	_____
7. Because it's thrilling	_____	_____	_____	_____
8. So I can forget about school and homework	_____	_____	_____	_____
9. Because it calms me down when I'm angry	_____	_____	_____	_____
10. When there's no one to talk to	_____	_____	_____	_____
11. So I can learn how to do things I haven't done before	_____	_____	_____	_____
12. Because I just like to watch	_____	_____	_____	_____
13. Because it passes the time away	_____	_____	_____	_____
14. So I could learn about what could happen to me	_____	_____	_____	_____
15. Because it excites me	_____	_____	_____	_____
16. So I can get away from the rest of the family	_____	_____	_____	_____
17. Because it's a pleasant rest	_____	_____	_____	_____
18. Because it makes me feel less lonely	_____	_____	_____	_____
19. Because it teaches me things I don't learn in school	_____	_____	_____	_____
20. Because I just enjoy watching	_____	_____	_____	_____
21. Because it gives me something to do	_____	_____	_____	_____
22. Because it shows how other people deal with the same problems I have	_____	_____	_____	_____
23. Because it stirs me up	_____	_____	_____	_____
24. So I can get away from what I'm doing	_____	_____	_____	_____

SCORING INSTRUCTIONS FOR TELEVISION VIEWING MOTIVES INSTRUMENT:

Give a numerical value for each statement in each column. Use the following scale:

A Lot = 4
A Little = 3
Not Much = 2
Not At All = 1

Add your score for each of the following viewing motive factors:

Viewing Motive	Statement Numbers	Mean Score
Relaxation	1, 9, 17	2.41
Companionship	2, 10, 18	1.68
Habit	4, 12, 20	1.97
Pass Time	5, 13, 21	2.13
Learning About Things	3, 11, 19	1.84
Learning About Myself	6, 14, 22	1.84
Arousal	7, 15, 23	1.67
Forget/Escape	8, 16, 24	1.67

After you have added up the scores for each factor, divide that score by 3 to obtain a mean or average score for each television viewing motive factor. Compare your average score on each dimension with the norms obtained from a nonrandom sample of 464 adults (Rubin, 1983).

From Rubin, A. (1979). Television use by children and adolescents. Human Communication Research, 5, 109–120. Copyright © 1979 by Wiley-Blackwell. Reprinted with permission.

Figure 12.2

Television viewing motives instrument.

argued that ritualized television use represents a more important viewing experience for the audience member, whereas instrumental television use represents a more involving experience for the viewer.

In a study of Swedish television users, Levy and Windahl (1984) identified three types of audience activity. The first, called *preactivity,* is practiced by individuals who deliberately seek certain media to gratify intellectual needs. For example, some viewers deliberately select newscasts to be informed about current events. The second type, *duractivity,* deals with the degree of psychological attentiveness or involvement audience members exhibit during a television viewing experience. The focus is on how individuals interpret and decipher mediated messages. The comprehension, organization, and structuring of media messages leads to certain intellectual and emotional gratifications for viewers. For example, trying to figure out the plot or ending of a dramatic program on television is one example of the duractivity use of the media. The third type of audience activity, *postactivity,* deals with audience behavior and message use after exposure to mediated messages. People involved in postactivity attend to a mediated message because they feel the information may have some personal or interpersonal value. Individuals who actively seek out television news to provide content for interpersonal communication such as "small talk" exhibit postactivity audience behavior.

Another assumption of uses and gratifications theory is that audiences use the media to fulfill expectations. For example, you may watch a science fiction program such as *Star Trek* to fantasize about the future.

A third assumption of uses and gratifications theory is that audience members are aware of and can state their motives for using mass communication. In Levy and Windahl's study, participants were able to describe how particular media gratified certain needs. The researchers found that the primary motivation for watching TV news was to gain information about the world, rather than for diversion. Studies that investigate how individuals use the media for gratification primarily employ *self-report measures*, questionnaires that ask participants about their motives for using the mass media. The television viewing motives instrument is one such questionnaire.

One study addressed several social and psychological factors associated with patterns of audience media use. Donohew, Palmgreen, and Rayburn (1987) tested a random sample of subscribers to cable television. Through telephone and mailed questionnaires, they collected demographic (age, sex, income, education, marital status) and lifestyle information. Participants also provided information on their social, political, economic, cultural, and communication-related behaviors. The researchers asked questions about the need for stimulation, gratifications sought from cable TV, satisfaction with cable TV offerings, number of hours of cable TV viewing per day, and number of newspapers and magazines subscribed to by the respondents. Four lifestyle types emerged. Type I was labeled the **disengaged homemaker**. This individual was primarily female, middle-aged, lower in education and income and used the media for companionship and to pass the time rather than for information or arousal. According to Rubin's classifications, the disengaged homemaker appears to represent the *ritualized* media user. The second type of individual, the **outgoing activist**, was also frequently female, somewhat younger, well-educated, had a good income, and was less likely to be married. Outgoing activists were highest in need for stimulation among the four types. They enjoyed staying informed and were primarily print media users. They did not watch a great amount of television and were least gratified by cable TV. Donohew, Palmgreen, and Rayburn speculated that type II's active lifestyle leaves them little time for television viewing. The third type of individual was labeled the **restrained activist**. These individuals were older and had the highest educational levels. More than half were female, and they were likely to be married and to have relatively high incomes. They had low need for sensation but high need for intellectual stimulation. They exhibited strong informational needs and viewed

disengaged homemaker A lifestyle type indicating primarily female, middle-aged, lower in education and income, and use the media for companionship and to pass time.

outgoing activist A lifestyle type primarily consisting of female, younger, well educated, with a high need for stimulation, good income, and less likely to marry.

restrained activist A lifestyle type primarily male and female who are older, highly educated, opinion leaders likely to marry, and have high incomes.

themselves as opinion leaders. They were heavy users of both print media and television, especially for informational purposes. Their media use patterns follow those of Rubin's *instrumental* user. The final type of user identified was called the **working class climber**. This person was primarily male, lower in education and income, and middle-aged; most were married. Working class climbers were ambitious and self-confident. They did not engage in an activist lifestyle and ranked low in need for intellectual stimulation. They were highest among the four types on television exposure and satisfaction with cable TV. They were quite low on print media usage. According to Rubin's taxonomy, they would be classified more as ritualized than as instrumental media users. The results of this study helped clarify our understanding of the many lifestyle variables that influence mass media use.

working class climber A lifestyle type primarily consisting of males, lower in education and income, middle-aged, and married.

Criticisms of the Theory

Since its inception, uses and gratifications theory has enjoyed widespread popularity among mass communication theorists, researchers, and practitioners. The theory has also received its share of criticism. Much of the criticism points to an insufficient theoretical basis, particularly in defining key concepts. Alan Rubin (1985) argued that there are too many different meanings associated with the terms "audience motives," "uses," and "gratifications," which has slowed unified theoretical development in this area.

The research has been criticized on methodological grounds. Self-report questionnaires have typically been used in uses and gratifications studies; the *reliability* and *validity* of self-report data have been questioned. Some critics believe that individuals cannot respond accurately to questions about their own feelings and behavior. For example, researchers often identify the "needs" of participants through questions asked about why they use the media (Severin & Tankard, 2001). The self-reported answers about motive may be suspect or the categories assigned by the researcher may be questioned as to whether they are scientifically verifiable. If respondents cannot supply reasons when asked open-ended questions but quickly select answers from a list provided by the researcher, are those answers reliable and valid?

Even contributors to this body of research find problems with its scope. Blumler (1979) and Windahl (1981) suggested that uses and gratifications does not represent a single theory. They call uses and gratifications an umbrella concept in which several theories reside. McQuail (1984) argued that scholars have tried to do too much—trying to link the identity and attributes of audiences with the behavior traits of individuals and the role of the media in society plus the cultural origins of the patterns and meanings sought by users and producers. He suggests that the research should be more limited in scope and should take a cultural-empirical approach to how people choose from the abundance of cultural products available.

Other critics find that the theory pays too much attention to the individual without looking at the social context and the role of media in that social structure. This lack of a unified theory has led to misuse of the empirical method of inquiry. Alan Rubin (1985) suggested that audience motive research based on this theory has been too compartmentalized within particular cultures or demographic groups. This has thwarted synthesis and integration of research results, activities critical to theory building.

CULTIVATION THEORY

cultivation theory of mass communication This theory asserts that television influences our view of reality.

The **cultivation theory of mass communication** effects was developed by George Gerbner and his associates at the Annenberg School of Communication at the University of Pennsylvania. The theory has been tested by numerous empirical studies. Cultivation theory asserts that television influences our view of reality. A causal relationship is suggested between television viewing and perceptions of reality—thus situating the theory in the law-governed approach to mass communication. Cultivation theory (Gerbner, Gross, Morgan, & Signorielli, 1980, 1986) asserts that television is primarily responsible for our perceptions of day-to-day norms and reality. Establishing a culture's norms and values was once the role of formal religion and other social initiations. Previously the family, schools, and churches communicated standardized roles and behaviors, serving the function of **enculturation**. Television now serves that function. It has become the major cultural transmitter for today's society (Gerbner & Gross, 1976a, 1976b). "Living" in the world of television cultivates a particular view of reality. Some argue that television provides an experience that is more alive, more real, and more vivid than anything we can expect to experience in real life!

enculturation A type of cultural adaptation reflecting when we learn to speak, listen, read, interpret, and understand verbal and nonverbal messages in such a fashion that the messages will be recognized and responded to by the individuals with whom we communicate.

The Interaction of Media and Reality

One of the authors read an article in a local newspaper that illustrates the tendency to confuse a real event with images absorbed from television. A reporter had stopped his car at the intersection of a rural road and a larger highway. He noticed a car speeding on the highway at approximately 100 miles per hour. As the car reached the point where the reporter was stopped, it suddenly tried to make a left turn without slowing down. It clipped a light pole and flipped over on its back, wheels still spinning. No one else was in sight. The reporter described staring forward, not believing what he had just seen. He recalled his mind saying to him very clearly, "What you are seeing isn't real, You are just watching a movie." For almost ten seconds he just sat there, waiting to see what would happen next. Of course, nothing happened, and he realized that it was up to him to help. He fell prey to two fears as he approached the car—one artificial (induced by previous television images) and one very real (which contradicted other images received). Television portrayals of over-turned cars invariably end with fires and explosions. With televised accidents, no "real man" thinks twice about rushing to a scene where someone may be dead or horribly mutilated. The reporter was very afraid on both counts. Television is so pervasive that the line between illusion and reality is blurred. We sometimes mistake a real event for a televised one; we probably make the opposite mistake more frequently. This phenomenon provided the basis of the research into cultivation theory.

Heavy versus Light Television Viewers

George Gerbner's participation in two national studies provided the foundation for cultivation theory. He contributed a content analysis of television programming to the National Commission on the Causes and Prevention of Violence in 1967 and 1968 and for the Surgeon General's Scientific Advisory Committee on Television and Social Behavior in 1972. Gerbner and his colleagues tracked the incidents of violence portrayed during a randomly selected week of fall prime-time programming plus children's weekend programming. They compiled the percentage of programs marked by violence, the number of violent acts, and the number of characters involved in those acts. They found violent acts portrayed in 80% of prime-time programming; children's shows were the most violent of all. Older people, children, women and minorities were the most frequent victims—despite the fact that three quarters of characters portrayed on television were white middle-class males.

Building on this work, the researchers surveyed viewers to determine the number of hours spent watching television daily, the programs selected and why, attitudes about the probability of being a victim of crime, perceptions about the numbers of law enforcement officials, and general attitudes about trusting other people. Gerbner and his associates classified people as heavy viewers (four or more hours daily) and light viewers (two hours daily or less).

Cultivation theory predicted that heavy viewers would perceive the world as more dangerous because of repeated exposure to violent television portrayals. Persistent images of danger and violence color views of reality and create the perception of a mean world. Heavy viewers overestimated their chances of being involved in a violent crime. They also overestimated the number of law enforcement workers in society.

Individuals frequently confuse media-constructed reality with actual reality. Gerbner and Gross (1976b) reported that in the first 5 years of its broadcast life, the television show *Marcus Welby, M.D.* (a fictional doctor portrayed by Robert Young), received over a quarter of a million letters from viewers. Most of the letters contained requests for medical advice! Television is highly effective in the cultivation process because many of us never personally experience some aspects of reality but the pervasive presence of television—constantly available for relatively little expense—provides a steady stream of mediated reality. We may have limited opportunities to observe the internal workings of a real police station, hospital operating room, or municipal courtroom. Thus, the media images become our standards for reality. Have you noticed that the New Year's Eve parties we actually attend *never* seem quite as exciting as the New Year's Eve parties we see on television?

The theory predicted uniform effects for all heavy viewers—regardless of factors such as gender, education, socioeconomic group, or media preferences (for example, reading newspapers versus viewing televised newscasts). As the primary source of socialization, television's messages provide a symbolic environment that transcends demographic differences. The only factor that seemed to have an independent effect on perceptions was age. Respondents under thirty consistently reported that their responses were more influenced by television than those of people over thirty (Gerbner & Gross, 1976b). Because people thirty and under have been "weaned" on television, the influence of media messages may be especially potent.

Refinement of Cultivation Theory

mainstreaming   The power of television to present uniformed images acceptable to a majority of viewers.

In response to criticisms that cultivation theory ignored the contributions of other variables (see next section), Gerbner and his associates introduced the factors of mainstreaming and resonance (Gerbner, Gross, Morgan, & Signorielli, 1980). **Mainstreaming** refers to the power of television to present uniform images. Commercial sponsors want to appeal to the broadest possible range of consumers, so television presents mainstream images. Differences are edited out to present a blended, homogenous image acceptable to a majority of viewers. Differences in perceptions of reality due to demographic and social factors are diminished or negated by the images projected on television. Ritualistic patterns reinforce sameness and uniformity. **Resonance** describes the intensified effect on the audience when what people see on television is what they have experienced in life. This double dose of the televised message amplifies the cultivation effect.

resonance   Argues that media's influence on perceptions are intensified when media depict "real life."

Criticisms of the Theory

Despite the large data set supporting the theory, the cultivation effect has encountered several challenges. Hughes (1980) reanalyzed data used in the original research and failed to support the core assumptions of cultivation theory. He suggested that the measures of heavy viewing only relate to total exposure to television, not specifically to what is watched. Certain personality characteristics related to the selection of television programs were not controlled in the earlier studies. He also reported that television may actually cultivate realistic and functional perceptions of the world. Hirsch (1980) found that if other variables are controlled simultaneously, very little effect remains that can be attributed to television. In his review of the original data, he found that even people who did not watch television perceived the world as violent and dangerous.

Conversely, it has been argued that major assumptions of cultivation theory may be correct, but the procedures used to study it may be incapable of uncovering the effect. Hawkins and Pingree (1982) reviewed 48 research studies conducted on the cultivation effect. They concluded that modest evidence supports the influence of television viewing on perceptions of reality. In fact, covering laws researchers find fault with the admission by Gerbner and his associates that the measurable effects of television are relatively small. Although the creators of the theory point to the cumulative effect of repeated exposure to limited influence (something like the steady drip of a faucet that eventually overflows the pail), scientific research relies on observable effects in laboratory settings that control for other influences. Cultivation researchers used self-reports of viewing habits; they did not observe respondents in a carefully controlled setting.

Potter (1986) concluded that the cultivation effect may be more complex than is currently stated; the amount of exposure to television may be less important than the attitudes and perceptions of individuals exposed. His conclusions match the criticisms from the rules perspective that fault cultivation theory with treating all viewers as helpless to withstand the manipulated images of reality projected by television. The interactions of audiences, television, and society are complex and cannot be reduced to simple cause and effect.

Cultivation theory links heavy television viewing with a distrustful view of a violent world. The final criticism questions the meaning of that link. The research has demonstrated a correlation between certain behaviors and certain attitudes, but has it proven the direction of influence? Do people who are distrustful watch more television because they have few friends? Cause and effect have not been established. There is no doubt that the controversy surrounding the media's influence on our perceptions and behavior will continue to rage. We can expect more research from scholars of mass communication in this area. New findings will refine and advance our efforts to theorize about the effects associated with the mass media.

spiral of silence theory   A theory about how minority viewpoints disappear from public awareness. People remain silent because of the fear of being different and isolated. The media play a major role in informing people what is normative.

THE SPIRAL OF SILENCE THEORY

The **spiral of silence theory** was developed by Elisabeth Noelle-Neumann, a German researcher, in 1974. The theory has implications in three areas: (a) mass media and communication, (b) the individual and interpersonal communication, and (c) public opinion (Salmon & Glynn, 1996). It is considered one of the "most highly developed and one of the most researched theories in the field of public opinion" (McDonald, Glynn, Kim, & Ostman, 2001, p. 139). The theory has generated a considerable amount of research, as well as controversy, since its debut.

Contemplating the question: "Are you more or less willing to express your beliefs on an issue depending on whether you think those beliefs are widely shared by those individuals around you?" guides us to an appreciation of the theory. Noelle-Neumann's spiral of silence theory argues that individuals who think that their opinions and beliefs are not widely shared by others (in a given reference group, or in society in general) will feel pressure to express another opinion (the majority opinion) or will choose to remain silent.

According to the theory, people assess whether their opinions match those of the majority from several cues in their environment (Glynn, Hayes, & Shanahan, 1997). The media are important sources for these cues. The mass media often "serve as the representation of the dominant views in society" (Perse, 2001, p. 110) and help shape public opinion. People depend on the media as a primary source of information about social norms, customs, acceptable styles of dress and fashion, and even what to think.

Spiral of silence theory suggests that people have a fear of social isolation; that is, they do not want to be seen as different from the majority. Adolescents are especially sensitive to "fitting in" with the majority regarding the clothes they wear and the expressions they use to communicate. Noelle-Neumann believes that most people also strive to avoid social isolation by refusing to express beliefs and opinions that they feel do not enjoy majority support. To express a belief that is either "old-fashioned" or "socially unacceptable" is more than most people are willing to do (Salmon & Moh, 1992). Indeed, isolating yourself from others by expressing your true belief, when it goes against the majority view, is seen as a far worse outcome than remaining silent (Glynn, Hayes, & Shanahan, 1997). Noelle-Neumann suggested that this "spiral of silence" leads one viewpoint or one position to dominate public opinion, while others (perceived minority viewpoints) often disappear from public awareness because the people who hold less accepted views or positions remain silent. However, if people find that their opinions are widely shared by the majority or are gaining acceptance, they will be more likely to express their positions.

Some people do not succumb to the spiral of silence. Labeled "hardcores," these people do not feel the same constraints of social pressure or fear the social isolation attached to expressing minority viewpoints. Hardcores have an unusually high amount of interest in the issue; their positions remain relatively unchanged (McDonald, Glynn, Kim, & Ostman, 2001). Hardcores represent only about 15 percent of the population (Salmon & Moh, 1992).

The issue of cigarette smoking in public offers an excellent example of the effects of majority opinion on verbal (and nonverbal) behavior. For many years nonsmokers were apprehensive about speaking out against smoking in public, and the nonsmoker almost certainly did not approach smokers and request that they put out their cigarettes. In the last two decades, however, this situation appears to have changed dramatically. The nonsmoker now represents the majority opinion—that smoking has no place in public contexts (Salmon & Glynn, 1996). The reticence about criticizing smoking behavior disappeared when public opinion changed.

How did this change occur? How did the former "minority view" become the current "majority view"? The spiral of silence theory suggests that the changing messages projected by the mass media contributed greatly to the change of public opinion. According to the theory, individuals scan the environment for information about which opinions are gaining support and which are losing (Gonzenbach, King, & Jablonski, 1999). Clearly, over the last two decades the media's predominant message has been one of "antismoking." The removal of ads for cigarettes on broadcast television, the increased frequency of "public service" spots describing the dangers of smoking, and the reports in the media that fewer Americans are smoking today compared to two decades ago have helped create change. Today, the smoker is caught in the "spiral of silence" regarding expressing opinions about smoking in public. This reversal of positions is a prime illustration of a tenet of the theory: willingness to speak out changes the climate of opinion so that the dominant opinion becomes stronger. In turn, the dominant view as presented in the media yields a greater likelihood that individuals will speak up (Gonzenbach et al., 1999).

People who hold the less-dominant position will become increasingly reluctant to express their position. Their silence erodes the less-supported position even more. When the media report that adherents to a given position are criticized frequently or even physically attacked (Gonzenbach et al., 1999), they reduce the probability that individuals will voice the unfavored position. For example, when the antifur message of groups such as P.E.T.A (People for the Ethical Treatment of Animals) received more attention from the media, including reports of individuals wearing natural fur being physically attacked, individuals who previously expressed support grew more silent.

Communication studies have examined the role of the spiral of silence theory regarding a number of different issues and from several methodological perspectives to help refine and extend the theory. One study tested the spiral of silence theory that judgments about majority opinion are made through direct observation and, in particular, from television. The researchers measured both the exposure to media by individuals in the national sample and their perceptions of what position was most supported on the issue of whether homosexuals should be allowed to serve in the U.S. military. The study found that respondents with higher levels of media exposure believed that more of the public agreed with them, whereas those with low levels of media exposure perceived lack of support for their position on that issue (Gonzenbach et al., 1999, p. 290).

Spiral of silence theory was also used to test public opinion on another controversial issue: whether the United States should declare English as the official language (Lin & Salwen, 1997). The study hypothesized that an individual's willingness to speak out about this issue would be related to his or her perceived national and local public opinion. Participants in two diverse cities (Miami, FL, and Carbondale, IL) were randomly surveyed by telephone. They were asked whether they were "willing" or "unwilling" to express their opinion about this issue in public with another person who held a different opinion about the issue of making English the official language of the United States. The findings generally supported the assumptions of the spiral of silence theory. Respondents in both cities indicated greater willingness to discuss the issue in public when the media coverage of this issue was seen as generally positive or supportive (Lin & Salwen, 1997). As the national and local media coverage of this issue became more positive, younger and better-educated respondents indicated even more willingness to express their opinion on this issue (Lin & Salwen, 1997).

Some researchers have explored how the realism of the setting for the expression of public opinion might affect an individual's willingness to speak out (Scheufele, Shanahan, & Lee, 2001). Would people in a more realistic setting be less willing to present their position than those who were asked to speak out in a hypothetical situation? College students responded to questions concerning their levels of media use, their knowledge about genetically altered foods, and their attitudes toward that topic. Half of the respondents were asked if they would be willing to discuss their opinion about the topic at a hypothetical "social gathering." The other half were told that there would be a second part of the study in which they could express their opinions about genetically altered food in greater detail with other students in a focus-group interview context. The study supported a major tenet of the spiral of silence theory: fear of isolation was negatively related to people's willingness to express an opinion on genetically altered food. The data also suggested that the situation influences willingness to speak out on an issue. Respondents who were told that they would be presenting their opinions in a focus group interview context were less willing to present their opinions than those in the hypothetical "social gathering" context.

Researchers have questioned whether the "spiral of silence" effects can be observed or even studied in cultures other than Germany (Salmon & Glynn, 1996). Several researchers have challenged the methodology used in studies attempting to test the theory (Scheufele & Moy, 2000). In particular, they questioned whether the "fear of isolation" adequately explains willingness to speak out in experimental studies (Glynn & McLeod, 1985) and whether the hypothetical versus actual nature of this willingness to speak out in experimental studies may be sufficient to produce "spiral of silence" effects (Glynn, Hayes, & Shanahan, 1997). Some researchers have proposed alternative methods to measure willingness to speak out, a critical variable in spiral of silence research. Jeffres, Neuendorf, and Atkin (1999) suggested that the results of studies using the "hypothetical situation" method (where participants are asked to place themselves in a hypothetical situations and then asked how they would respond) "either have been mixed or have not supported the theory" (p. 121). Instead, these researchers obtained actual opinions and quotations both orally and in writing during interviews in shopping centers, waiting rooms, on the street, and in coffee shops, thus securing behavioral measures of willingness to express an opinion to a stranger. Another study employed a unique method to obtain the measure of "willingness to speak out." The researcher studied letters to the editor published in *Time, Newsweek,* and *U.S. News and World Report* before and after the shootings at Columbine High School to determine attitudes toward gun control (Lane, 2002).

MEDIA DEPENDENCY THEORY

Media dependency theory was developed by Sandra Ball-Rokeach and Melvin DeFleur (1976). Although Ball-Rokeach is a professor of sociology and communication, this research emerged from the communication discipline. Media dependency theory's debut was in a communication journal, and many of the articles that present extensions of this theory also appear in communication journals.

media dependency theory
A theory of mass communication that assumes the more dependent an individual is on the media for having his or her needs filled, the more important the media will be to the person.

Media dependency theory argues that the more dependent an individual is on the media for having his or her needs fulfilled, the more important the media will be to that person. Although some communication scholars consider media dependency theory to be an offshoot of the uses and gratifications theory of mass media, there are some differences. A major issue in uses and gratifications theory is, "*Where* do I go to gratify my needs?" whereas media dependency theory focuses on the issue, "*Why* do I go to *this* medium to fulfill *this* goal?" (Ball-Rokeach, Power, Guthrie, & Waring, 1990). Dependency theory suggests that media use is primarily influenced by societal relationships, whereas uses and gratifications theory places greater emphasis on individual media selection. Uses and gratifications theory focuses more on a person's active participation with mass media, whereas dependency theory tends to focus more on the social context in which media activity occurs. Because it emphasizes the interaction of the individual, media, and society, dependency theory uses a systems approach to studying mediated communication.

Dependency theory emphasizes the *relationship between society and the media.* There are a number of mutual dependencies. The media rely on government for legislation to protect media assets and for access to political information. The political systems of a society rely on the media to reinforce political values and norms, to help mobilize citizens to vote, and to inspire active involvement in political campaigns. Society depends on the media for the creation of information, advertising, and technology that it uses (Rubin & Windahl, 1986).

The commercial broadcasting system of the United States, for example, is built on dependency between the media, advertisers, and audiences. Television programs are produced to attract large audiences so that advertisers can sell their products and services to those audiences. The media then depend on this advertising revenue to stay in business. Each system depends on the other.

The *relationship between the media and the audience* is crucial as well, for it influences how people use mass media. Audiences may depend on the media for information, for escape, and for "information" on what is considered appropriate or normative behavior. Television programs that emphasize prosocial messages such as honesty and morality are designed to teach acceptable behavior in our society.

The *relationship between society and the audience* examines how society influences the audience and vice versa. Society depends on audiences because individuals who comprise a society are seen as potential voters, potential consumers, and as members of different social and cultural groups who contribute in numerous ways to the development of a society and its culture.

The theory's authors define dependency as a relationship in which the attainment of goals by one party is contingent on the resources of another party. People develop dependency relationships with the mass media as a way of attaining their goals of understanding, orientation, and play (Grant, Guthrie, & Ball-Rokeach, 1991). According to the theory, people develop expectations that the media can help them satisfy their needs. Thus, people develop "dependency relations" with the media (or a particular medium) that they believe will be most helpful in attaining a particular goal (Loges & Ball-Rokeach, 1993).

The theory identifies dependency relations on media information sources. Ball-Rokeach and DeFleur suggested that individuals depend on media for information in situations ranging from the need to identify the best buys at the supermarket to more general informational needs such as how to maintain a sense of "connection" with the world outside your neighborhood. The theory suggests that an individual's reliance on mass media develops when the person's informational needs on certain issues cannot be met by direct experience.

Media dependency is also linked to media *influence*. That is, the more important the media are to an individual, the more influence the media exert on that individual. Our society relies heavily on the mass media for information, entertainment, and the communication of societal norms and values. In our society, information is considered a prized commodity; we regard information as power. Today, most people use their personal computers to access information sources on the Internet. The theory recognizes, however, that dependency on the media varies greatly from one individual to another, from one group to another, and even from one culture to another.

A number of key assumptions about the media, the audience, and audience dependency have been identified: (a) if the media influence society it is because the media meet the audience's needs and wants, not because the media exert any "control" over individuals; (b) the uses people have for media in large part determine how much the media will influence them. For example, the more the audience depends on information from the media, the greater the likelihood the media will influence the audience's attitudes, beliefs, and even behavior; (c) because of the increasing complexity of modern society, we depend a great deal on the media to help us make sense of our world, to help us make decisions that allow us to cope better with life. The theory suggests further that we come to understand and even experience our world largely through the media. What a person learns about the world beyond their direct experience is influenced by the media. Our understanding of international politics, the global economy, and music, for example, are in part shaped by the content offered by the media (Baukus, 1996); (d) Individuals who have greater needs for information, escape, or fantasy will be more influenced by the media and have greater media dependency.

Ball-Rokeach and DeFleur suggested that media dependency ranges on a continuum from individuals who are totally dependent on the media to satisfy their needs to individuals who satisfy their needs independently from the media. (Remember that Shaw and McCombs addressed a similar concept with their *need for orientation.*) In addition, each individual displays variations within each category of media dependence. For example, you may depend heavily on news and newsmagazine shows for information yet have very little interest in escape and fantasy programs such as soap operas or situation comedies. Others may depend totally on the media for business news—monitoring sources such as CNN Business News, the Financial News Network, and CNBC, but ignoring the Weather Channel.

Most individuals are media dependent when conditions demand quick and accurate information. If you live in a climate that is prone to many tornadoes or hurricanes during the summer months or blizzards during the winter months, you may need an almost constant source of information about the weather. Your dependency on the media for weather-related information may even have stimulated you to purchase a "weather radio," which broadcasts bulletins and information from the local office of the National Weather Service. During times of weather-related crises, individuals become very dependent on the media.

Constant attention to and dependence on the media also emerged during the explosion of the space shuttle *Challenger* in 1986, the stock market crash of 1987, the war in the Persian Gulf in 1991, the bombing of the federal building in Oklahoma City in 1995, and the destruction of the World Trade Center by terrorists on September 11, 2001. Other crises, both local and national, also cause individuals to become more dependent on the media. For example, in the days following an airplane crash individuals tend to become more media dependent on the medium they believe will best satisfy their informational needs. For some this may mean purchasing national newspapers, such as *USA Today,* which will devote additional coverage to this type of story. For others, this may mean monitoring CNN throughout the day. Still others may turn to one of the many news-related websites to learn more details as they become available. Given the complex interactions of the individual, the media, and society, the social context often dictates the level of dependency. In times of conflict and uncertainty, the need for information increases, and dependency on the media also rises. During relatively calm periods of stability the audience relies less heavily on the media for guidance.

Media dependency is related to the complexity of the society in which a person lives. In a society as complex as ours, the media provide a number of essential functions: they provide information useful for the elections that are the centerpiece of democracy, they serve as whistle-blowers if the government oversteps its authority, they announce important economic or technological developments, they provide a window to the rest of the world, and they are a primary source of entertainment. The more functions served by the media, the more important they become.

Depending on the type of information goal a person has, he or she may choose one particular medium over another. Different media require different degrees of effort in satisfying one's informational goal. Preferences for particular media (for example, television, newspapers, Internet, or radio), differ according to information needs, the sources of media available, and the effort expended by the information seeker. For example, an individual may prefer to get information from television due to its immediacy, but because that medium may not be available in an office or an automobile, they must use radio instead. Some individuals choose newspapers over television because newspapers are perceived to cover stories in greater depth than television.

Media dependency theory asserts that the media have powerful effects on individuals and society. During the last decade several studies have investigated the assumptions of media dependency theory. One study investigated the union of media dependency theory and the theory of parasocial interaction discussed earlier. Grant, Guthrie, and Ball-Rokeach (1991) wondered if the development of parasocial interaction with a television personality increases the intensity of one's dependency on that medium or the reverse. Did an intense media dependency relationship stimulate the development of a parasocial interaction? They used the medium of television shopping (such as QVC and the Home Shopping Network) to investigate this relationship. One of the most important findings was that individuals who developed strong media dependency relationships with television shopping tended to develop parasocial relationships with television shopping personalities. In addition, they found that purchasing a product from a television shopping channel reinforced media dependency on that channel because it gave viewers a greater sense of connection to the show. The researchers also suggested that people tune in to television shopping not only to purchase products but to satisfy their entertainment goals and to learn about new products. The more the viewers had these goals, the more they watched, and the more parasocial interactions they developed with television shopping hosts.

Alan Rubin and Sven Windahl (1986) proposed a combination of uses and gratifications theory. They offered a "uses and dependency model," which incorporates elements of both theories. The uses and dependency model recognizes that the audience is somewhat active in their media-related behavior, and that individuals seek media that will fulfill personal needs. The model also represents the society-media-audience interaction and the mutual influences working to create interests and to influence the selection of particular media to satisfy goals. Needs are not always the sole product of the social and psychological characteristics of individuals; they are influenced by culture and society. This union of two theories also bridges the gap between the limited effects model of uses and gratifications and the powerful effects posited by dependency theory.

One test of the uses and dependency model found that "television dependents" contrasted with "newspaper dependents" (Baukus, 1996). Television dependents tend to see media coverage of conflict as "entertainment." This may account for why heavy television users may have been more likely to watch a great deal of coverage of the trial of O.J. Simpson or watch cable channels such as truTV. The study also found that television dependents believed the media are a source of information that helps us better understand the impact of social conflict on a community, country, or culture. Highly involved television-dependent groups differed from the other groups in their information belief. People who are highly involved *and* television dependent seem to want information as quickly as possible, and the ability of television to cover an event instantly with accompanying video is very important to this type of individual. Another study observed that dependency needs for understanding oneself and society were related to newspaper readership. Individuals who had greater need for understanding how society and its institutions function were more dependent on the newspaper than those without that need (Loges & Ball-Rokeach, 1993). Thus, media dependency theory helps us understand the relationships between the media and society, dependency relations with particular media, and the choice of particular media to satisfy information goals.

Media scholars have challenged media dependency theory on the grounds that it has "not yet been conclusively demonstrated that the experience of media dependency by average people is strongly related to a broad range of effects. Is there some ideal level of media dependency? Will new media increase our dependency or make us more independent?" (Baran & Davis, 1995, p. 229).

THEORIES OF MEDIATED INTERPERSONAL COMMUNICATION

The impact of mediated communication on interpersonal communication is more dramatic today than ever before. The computer has emerged as the primary medium in which individuals interact with each other for both personal and professional communication. According to the Pew Internet and American

Life report (Fallows, 2004) about 30 billion e-mails are sent every day, and 93% of Americans adult Internet users report using e-mail. This statistic supports the notion that much "interpersonal communication" is being conducted via that medium. One indication of this is that the number of phone messages professors receive from students has decreased dramatically, whereas the number of e-mail messages they receive has increased dramatically.

We are confident that many readers of this text have their own pages on "social networking" sites such as MySpace and Facebook, suggesting that people are using computer-mediated communication to fulfill social and interpersonal needs. Stefanone and Jang (2007) reported that even blogs are being widely adopted by individuals to engage in a form of mediated interpersonal communication.

The communication discipline has developed a number of scholars who identify their specialty as "CMC, or computer-mediated communication." The *Journal of Computer-Mediated Communication* (JCMC) is a Web-based, peer-reviewed scholarly journal whose focus is on social science research on computer-mediated communication via the Internet, the World Wide Web, and wireless technologies.

A Theory of Mediated Interpersonal Communication

The union of mass, or mediated, and interpersonal communication is not a new phenomena. As noted in the two-step flow theory, the individual plays a significant role in the mass communication process. Almost a quarter century ago, Gumpert and Cathcart (1986) examined the social and personal uses people have for mass communication. With the diffusion of computer-mediated communication, their theory is even more relevant today. Cathcart and Gumpert (1983) argued that media is not synonymous with mass communication (meaning communication over time and space to large numbers of people). They argued that the term *media* should not be excluded from other forms of human communication such as intrapersonal, interpersonal, group, or public. When we talk or text-message a friend or family member on the cell phone, we are using a medium to make our interaction possible. When using instant messaging or participating in an Internet chat group, we are engaged in mediated interpersonal and small-group communication.

Cathcart and Gumpert claimed (a) some interpersonal communication situations require media, (b) the media influence attitudes and behavior, (c) media content both reflects interpersonal behaviors and contains projections of them, and (d) the development of an individual's self-concept depends on the media. They offer the term "mediated interpersonal communication" to refer to any situation in which a mediated technology is used to replace face-to-face interaction. Cell phone conversations, text messaging, e-mail, the use of videoclips on YouTube, and even T-shirts are "media" that are used to facilitate interpersonal interaction. Another form of communication that bridges mediated and interpersonal forms are the teleparticipatory media, such as the terrestrial and satellite forms of two-way talk radio in which callers and the host(s) communicate with each other on the radio.

Gumpert and Cathcart's theory of mediated interpersonal communication emphasizes the pervasiveness of media and its importance as an element in interpersonal communication. It is gratifying to note that their call to theorists to incorporate the notion of media in their efforts to build theories of interpersonal and group communication has been heeded. One such theory, Social Information Processing Theory, is presented next.

SOCIAL INFORMATION PROCESSING THEORY

In this chapter, we described an early theory of mediated interpersonal communication developed by Cathcart & Gumpert (1983). **Social information processing theory** (SIPT) represents a more contemporary theory that also addresses this phenomenon of mediated interpersonal communication. SIPT "explains how people get to know one another online, without nonverbal cues, and how they develop and manage relationships in the computer-mediated environment" (Walther, 2008, p. 391). The computer-mediated environment lacks the traditional nonverbal information that is exchanged in face-to-face (FTF) interaction. This nonverbal exchange provides invaluable sense-making feedback for the participants. In its absence, people interacting in the computer-mediated environment tend to group others as being either part of their in-group (i.e., people who share similar demographics, values, interests) or their out-group (i.e., people who do not share similar demographics, values, interests) (Reicher, Spears, & Postmes, 1995). According to Walther, SIPT predicts that "people may indeed get to know one another online, albeit more slowly and through different mechanisms than face to face interaction" (p. 392).

SIPT is based on two principle arguments. The first concerns impression-bearing (i.e., there is something in the information [misspellings, word choices, etc.] that makes an impression on the receiver) and the emotional, and relational management of information (Walther, 2003). In other words, we generally gather relational information, as opposed to task information, through nonverbal cues. When online, the nonverbal aspects are absent, so we must seek other ways of gathering such relational information. Therefore, it is also important to understand how nonverbal cues are translated into verbal and textual information. The second argument of SIPT reflects the rate of information that flows through computer-mediated communication (CMC) as compared to face-to-face communication. The main assumption about the rate of information is that when enough time has passed, and there are many communication exchanges between people, personal and relational information builds

social information. processing theory A theory that explains how people get to know one another online, without nonverbal cues, and how they develop and manage relationships in the computer mediated environment.

up and eventually renders CMC as equal to face-to-face communication in relational development and relational maintenance. For example, it is common for people to join computer dating services and make initial contact via computer-mediated communication. Consider Web sites such as Eharmony.com and Match.com, which serve as testaments to the effectiveness of romantic relationship development via CMC.

Another unique feature of SIPT concerns "the functions of impression-bearing and relational cues, and the degree to which nonverbal and verbal or textual cues may perform them" (Walther, 2008, p. 393). Previous theories of computer-mediated communication assume that due to the absence of nonverbal cues, people lose relational interest in each other as real people as well as lose the ability to relay information regarding descriptive, emotional, and personal information. Instead, SIPT assumes that people have an innate need to form impressions of other people, regardless of the medium being used. With nonverbal cues unavailable, people use surrogate communication systems to the point where the written word (via e-mail or text messaging) is considered the same as nonverbal cues. According to Walther (2008), SIPT considers time and rate differently from other theories of computer mediated communication in that "SIPT recognizes that verbal and textual cues are those that convey social and affective information in CMC, and that these written cues are the only cues to convey that information within text-based online communication" (p. 395). Unlike in face-to-face communication where there is a simultaneous exchange of verbal and nonverbal information (which can serve to accentuate, duplicate, or compliment messages), when verbal and nonverbal are restricted to one code as it is in CMC, the one code becomes responsible for the functions of other meaning transmission systems (e.g., occulesics [eye behavior], haptics, proxemics). As such, SIPT assumes that the rate of both social and task information are slower than FTF because people transmit less information per exchange. Thus, it takes more exchanges in computer-mediated communication to reach the same level of relational development that it does for FTF. Walther (1993) believes that this information exchange process is further hampered by the level of typing skills people possess as well as whether or not the mediated communication is synchronous (i.e., real-time exchange such as chat rooms and instant messaging) or asynchronous (i.e., time-delayed exchange such as e-mail).

SIPT treats communication symbols as interchangeable. In other words, besides nonverbal information, there are many other ways to express attitudes and emotions. As human beings are resourceful creatures, and in light of the absence of nonverbal information, people interacting via CMC cleverly utilize word content, word style, and message length, among other devices to fill the nonverbal void. This is not to suggest that CMC is deficient in the transfer of meaning as much as it takes more time to achieve the same goal when compared to the more rapid transfer of information that occurs during the multichanneled face-to-face communication.

The SIPT takes a developmental perspective on relationship development. That is, relationships develop as a process based on time and move from relational infancy to relational maturity. Given one of the main assumptions (i.e., a longer rate and time associated with the exchange of information in CMC compared to FTF), Walther (2008) made the logical connection that close relationships via CMC are going to take longer to develop than those of FTF. Walther argued that SIPT has a broad scope and is applicable to a host of CMC settings that include, among others, virtual work groups (Walther & Bunz, 2005), chat rooms (Henderson & Gilding, 2004), and online dating (Gibbs, Ellison, & Heino, 2006). Walther (2008) argued that "SIPT appears to be a popular theory of CMC for two contrasting reasons: (a) its intuitive application, on the one hand, and (b) its formal articulation of assumptions and propositions, on the other" (p. 399).

The future of SIPT, in terms of it refinement and extension, is based on technological advancement. For example, synchronous Webcams allow people to utilize nonverbal channels in real time. Thus, the future of SIPT is only constrained by what future technological developments may evolve. Another phenomenon is the popularity of social networking sites such as Facebook and MySpace. According to Walther (2008), these forums hold unique challenges for SIPT regarding whether or not the theoretical assumptions of the theory hold true in these CMC venues. Interpersonal factors such as interpersonal deception is also a potential fruitful avenue for the test of social information processing theory. According to deception scholars such as Buller and Burgoon (1996, interpersonal deception theory) and Ekman (1985, leakage hypothesis), much of deception takes place via nonverbal channels. Given that SIPT compensates for nonverbal communicating through other avenues, investigating deception over a variety of CMC venues should prove fruitful in the extension and further development of social information processing theory.

SUMMARY

Mass communication and other forms of mediated communication exert a profound influence on the world. Mass communication is said to serve five functions for a society: surveillance, correlation, cultural transmission, entertainment, and mobilization. The mass media also serves an agenda-setting function as they influence our attitudes and perceptions of events by selectively focusing attention on certain issues. The media influence extends into the domain of relationship development. Parasocial interaction theory suggests that we often develop a sense of personal involvement and a type of "relationship" with media performers such as news and weather forecasters, talk show hosts, and other media celebrities and personalities. Uses and gratifications theory explains the underlying motives for individual use of mass communication. A core assumption of this theory is that an audience is an active group that seeks out and uses certain media to satisfy their needs. Cultivation theory suggests that television is largely responsible for the development of perceptions of day-to-day norms and reality. The theory argues that cumulative exposure to television's ritualistic patterns of images manipulates how we see ourselves, others, and society in general. Spiral of silence theory argues that because people are reluctant to express beliefs contrary to widely accepted opinions and because the media are often the source for conveying accepted opinions, the media contribute to a spiral of silence in which minority views are suppressed, which creates a climate that reinforces majority views. Media dependency theory is derived from the systems approach and examines the multiple interactions of audience, media, and society in determining why a medium is selected, for what goal, and the dependencies created by the intricate relationships. As the computer has emerged as a primary medium in which people interact with each other for personal and professional communication, theories of computer-mediated communication have emerged. Gumpert and Cathcart's theory of mediated interpersonal communication examines the interaction of media and interpersonal communication. This theory recognizes the impact of mediated technology such as the computer and the cell phone on interpersonal communication. Social information processing theory represents one such theory. This theory explains how people develop relationships using computer-mediated technology. It takes into account the absence of nonverbal cues in forming mediated interpersonal relationships.

KEY TERMS

agenda setting

change agents

correlation

cultivation theory of mass communication

cultural transmission

diffusion theory

disengaged homemaker

duractivity

enculturation

entertainment

gatekeepers

instrumental use

magic bullet theory

mainstreaming

media dependency theory

mobilization

need for orientation

opinion leaders

outgoing activist

parasocial interaction

postactivity

preactivity

reflective-projective theory of mass communication

resonance

restrained activist

ritualized use

social information processing theory

spiral of silence theory

surveillance

two-step flow theory

uses and gratifications theory

working class climber

Tributary Contexts

I nterest in building and using communication theories to address specific problems is growing and will undoubtedly continue to flourish in the communication discipline. Applied communication research serves three valuable functions: (a) it can help people solve problems relevant to their lives; (b) it can provide evidence of how well certain theories function in "real-world" settings; and (c) it can help enhance the public's perceptions of the importance of communication theory and research (Kreps, Frey, & O'Hair, 1991).

The communication theorist's primary mission is to conduct research and to build theory. Communication practitioners and researchers often test the applicability and viability of those theories in more "natural" settings. An exciting union of communication theorists and practitioners has emerged. William Eadie (1990) stated that communication researchers have evolved from an awareness of problems in the "real world" to the desire to attack those problems employing theory and research as useful guides. Eadie cited many examples of this, including how health-care communication can be improved and how conflict in families can be managed more productively.

Throughout Part III, we have presented a synthesis of theory-building activity in specific contexts. We have seen how theory building in one context has been extended to address particular concerns in another. Organizational communication, for example, incorporates research from other areas and has, in turn, generated research with applications to other contexts. Four additional communication contexts have seen steady increases in the research-theory-application process in the last several years: *family, health, intercultural,* and *political.* We have chosen to call this chapter communication theory in "Tributary Contexts" for a specific reason. The term *tributary* suggests a "branch of," or an "offshoot of." Each of the four communication contexts that are covered in this chapter we consider to be a branch of one, or more, of the areas that we covered in this text. For example, *family* communication is an area of research that has branched off interpersonal communication. *Health* communication is a branch of research on interpersonal, organizational, persuasion, and mass communication. *Political* communication is a branch of research on persuasion and mass media. And, *intercultural* communication is a branch of mass and interpersonal communication. Each of the four contexts (family, health, political, intercultural) has generated a considerable amount of research, albeit, not the same amount as the major contexts we covered in Part III of the text. This condition may change, however, in the next few years. Consequently, in the next edition of this text, the reader may find that a few, or all, of these contexts will warrant their own separate chapters. In this chapter, we will explore research, theory-building, and application efforts in these significant contexts. As stated in the preface, we have selected representative theories and encourage you to explore other theory-building efforts using the principles taught in this text as a foundation for analysis.

FAMILY COMMUNICATION

Communication scholars suggest that family communication shapes how we communicate in many other contexts and influences how we communicate with work colleagues and romantic partners. It is "where most of us learn how to think about communication" (Vangelisti, 1993, p. 42).

One of the most fundamental units of human interaction is the family. We are in large part socialized within the framework of a "family." Satir (1972), a recognized family therapist, noted the impact of family communication on the relationships we make with others during the course of our lives, as well as the central role it plays in the development of our self-concepts.

Although communication scholars have recently adopted the family as a context in which to conduct research and build theory, studies of family interaction have been conducted for some time. A variety of academic disciplines including psychology, social work, and sociology have explored behavior in families. Scholarly attention to marital and family communication by communication theorists adds much to our understanding of family interaction by focusing on symbolic interaction and the exchange of verbal and nonverbal messages between family members.

Conceptualizations of the Family

Arthur Bochner (1976) defined a family as "an organized, naturally occurring relational interaction system, usually occupying a common living space over an extended time period, and possessing a confluence of interpersonal images which evolve through the exchange of messages over time" (p. 382). He noted that systems scholar Gregory Bateson is considered a pioneer in the study of families as "holistic communication systems." Janet Yerby, Nancy Buerkel-Rothfuss, and Bochner (1990) suggested that a family is a "multigenerational social system consisting of at least two interdependent people bound together by a common living space (at one time or another) and a common history, and who share some degree of emotional attachment to or involvement with one another" (p. 9). A broader definition of family has been offered by Kathleen Galvin and Bernard Brommel (2000), who suggested that a family constitutes "networks of people who share their lives over long periods of time; who are bound by ties of marriage, blood or commitment, legal or otherwise, who consider themselves as family, and who share future expectations of connected relationship" (p. 3). This definition encompasses numerous interpersonal associations and diverse interaction patterns.

Jan Trost (1990) conducted both quantitative and qualitative research to discover how individuals conceptualize "the family." One conclusion reached was that there is a great deal of variability in conceptualizations of what a family is and what it is not. It appears that there is little consensus regarding how to define a family. Trost's research revealed that conceptualizations of family range from the nuclear family (parents and children) to kinships of various sorts, which includes friends and even pets! Understanding the differences in these conceptualizations of family is important. It gives us insight into who should be included as objects of study in family communication and also what kinds of questions the researcher should ask (Fitzpatrick & Wamboldt, 1990).

Characteristics of the Family Communication Context

Several characteristics distinguish family from interpersonal communication (Yerby, Buerkel-Rothfuss, & Bochner, 1990):

- **Nonvolition**—while you can choose your friends, you do not choose to be born into a specific family. The history, sets of relationships, and network of relatives are already established when we are born.

- **Commitment and Intimacy**—higher levels of commitment and intimacy are shared by family members. Family members see each other under all circumstances. In order for a family to stay intact, active participation and commitment are necessary, even at minimal levels.

- **Development of Self-Concept**—our self-concepts are formed through interactions with family members. These interactions are probably the most potent sources of information and influence.

- **Longevity of Influence**—the influence of one's family endures for a lifetime; its traditions are passed on from generation to generation. This is true whether the family is considered functional or dysfunctional.

nonvolition A characteristic of the family that assumes that we do not choose to be born to a specific family.

commitment and intimacy A characteristic of the family where higher levels of commitment and intimacy are shared by family members.

development of self-concept A characteristic of the family that assumes our self concepts are formed through interactions with family members.

longevity of influence The influence of one's family endures for a lifetime; its traditions are passed on from generation to generation.

dialectical tensions   A characteristic of the family that assumes there are polarities, paradoxes, contradictions and/or competing demands all operating within families as members interact with each other.

interaction complexity   A characteristic of the family that assumes there is a complex set of rules (especially communication rules) exists within families.

- **Dialectical Tensions**—polarities, paradoxes, contradictions and/or competing demands all operate within families as members interact with each other.

- **Interaction Complexity**—a complex set of rules (especially communication rules) exists within families. These rules are often understood only by the members of the family.

Because of these unique characteristics, the study of family interaction and communication is highly complex, with large numbers of variables influencing each other. These characteristics make family communication especially well suited to analysis from a systems perspective, as the definitions presented earlier suggested (see Figure 13.1).

Families as Systems

Although a great deal of research on relational communication has used the individual as the unit of analysis, this focus is too narrow for understanding how communication functions in a family. Bavelas and Segal (1982) advocated

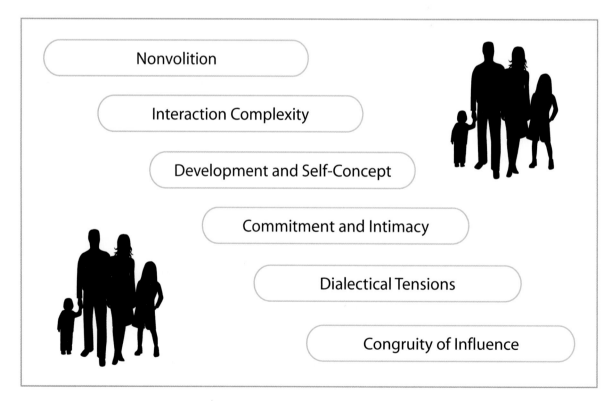

Figure 13.1

Characteristics of family communication.

focusing on the whole (people *and* relationships) because studying isolated individuals will never reveal the relationships among them. The systems perspective puts people in the background while "bringing their relationships to the foreground" (p. 102). These relationships are the elements that make a family system *nonsummative* (the system is greater than the sum of its individual components). For example, studying a single family member will probably not be sufficient to discover why a family has problems. The *relationships* among family members expose more clues to the source of the conflict. The systems approach to family communication allows us to investigate the reactions that other family members have to each other's communication and helps us understand how family members coordinate their communication during conflict or decision making (Petronio & Braithwaite, 1993). A systems approach can help us uncover the interrelationships among the members of the family.

A systems approach to family communication examines the relationships among family members as they work toward *equifinality* (the concept that there are many different ways by which a system may reach the same end state or goal). Communication scholars study the relationships between family members by examining the verbal and nonverbal messages sent—as well as the communication that is conspicuously absent in the family. *Content* (cognitive information being communicated) and *relationship* (information about the nature of the relationship such as status, power, or dependency) dimensions of communication behavior are also studied. Recall that all communication contains both dimensions. "We are not going to watch football," conveys specific content about what will or will not occur, as well as probable status differences between the communicators.

Another principle highlighted by the systems perspective is *interdependence*. This principle suggests that all members of a system influence all other members of a system. For example, let us suppose that one spouse in a dual-career family is suddenly unemployed. This change will permeate all parts of the family system. One effect may be increased opportunities for communication. This increased interaction could lead to both functional and dysfunctional consequences. Possible functional consequences might be: greater frequency and quality of interaction between family members, more time for the children to spend with the parent, and potential realignment of family roles and responsibilities. One dysfunctional consequence could be the highlighting of status differences within the family. One member is now the "breadwinner" in the family. With decreased family income, greater conflict between the family members regarding individual and family spending may also result.

If the family as a whole is the system, members of the family (for example, spouses or siblings) can be considered *subsystems*. An individual family member contributes his or her own unique set of characteristics that influence family communication. One member may be excitable and assertive; another member may be more relaxed and nonassertive. If the nuclear family is the system, the extended family (including grandparents, cousins, aunts, and uncles) can be considered the *suprasystem.* By studying the family as a whole, we move away from the more narrow models of family inter-action and recognize the "interactional complexity" of the family and of family communication (Bochner & Eisenberg, 1987, p. 540).

Several models of family processes, all within the domain of the systems perspective, have been developed (Bochner & Eisenberg, 1987; Yerby, Buerkel-Rothfuss, & Bochner, 1990). The **interactional model** focuses on messages. Assumptions from this approach are that communication episodes within families repeat, that messages within family communication are highly complex in both content and relationship dimensions, and that family communication is a process with no distinct beginning or end.

The **structural model** examines the social organization of the family. The *spouse subsystem* has the goal of achieving complementarity and mutual support among the spouses. The *parenting subsystem* involves the relationship between parents and children and includes nurturing and discipline. The *sibling subsystem* examines the relationships among children in the same family. It explores cooperation and competition inside and outside of the family (Bochner & Eisenberg, 1987).

Fitzpatrick's Typology of Couple Types

A typology is a classification scheme. Typologies help scholars make sense of the phenomena they are studying by suggesting what should be included and "what goes with what." Mary Anne Fitzpatrick (1977, 1983, 1984, 1988) developed a typology that allows family communication researchers to classify "enduring relationships." This theoretical model is useful because it represents an organized way of examining the nature of marital communication and conflict.

Using the Relational Dimensions Inventory (RDI), a researcher can characterize couples as traditional, independent, separate, or mixed. Spouses complete the RDI independently; if they both choose the same relationship type, they are considered pure types (for instance, independents, traditionals, or separates). Spouses who differ on the type of relationship are considered a mixed type (for example, separate husband/ independent wife).

Fitzpatrick and her colleagues reported that the various combinations of "mixed type" couples have family systems with different patterns of communication than marriages with two traditionals or two separates (Fitzpatrick & Ritchie, 1994). **Traditional couple types** hold more conventional values about marriage (for example, women use husbands' surnames), demonstrate interdependence, and describe their communication as nonassertive. Traditionals are less likely than the other couple types to experience conflict in their marital relationships. **Independents** value individual freedom and subscribe

interaction model   A model that assumes communication episodes within families repeat, that messages within family communication are highly complex in both content and relationship dimensions, and that family communication is a process with no distinct beginning or end.

structural model   A model tht examines the social organization of the family.

traditional couple types   A couple who have traditional views about marriage (for example, women use husbands' surname), demonstrate interdependence, and describe their communication as non-assertive.

independents   A couple that values freedom and subscribe less to conventional male/female roles than do traditional couple types.

less to conventional male/female roles than do traditionals. They maintain separate physical space (for example, bathrooms or offices). Although they try to spend time together, they do not keep regular schedules for dinner or weekend activities. Independents tend to express anger openly toward each other during conflict (Burrell & Fitzpatrick, 1990). Separates are more conventional on marital and family issues than independents, yet they maintain individual freedom, have less companionship and sharing, and describe their communication as assertive. Separates tend to withdraw emotionally from one another during discussions of marital problems. When one separate displays anger, the other tends to withdraw from the conflict by remaining silent or leaving the scene. Research indicates that approximately 60% of the couples are classified as pure. Of the 40% of mixed couples, no single mixed-type predominates.

The Fitzpatrick (1988) typology of couple types has reliably predicted a variety of communication behaviors: sequences of communication between spouses (including interpretation, attentiveness, and responses to the verbal and nonverbal behavior of each spouse); emotional outcomes for individuals in the marriage, and especially conflict behaviors. Understanding what stimulates marital conflict is an important prerequisite to the development of treatment programs designed to help couples manage conflict more productively.

Communication Privacy Management Theory

Communication privacy management theory (CPM) is based on explaining how people reveal private information as well as how people conceal private information. According to Petronio and Durham (2008) "CPM views 'disclosure' as the process of revealing information, yet always in relationship to concealing private information" (p. 310). CPM is organized around six major principles (Petronio, 2002). CPM is being included in the family section of this chapter due to the fact that existing research and tests of the theory have primarily been conducted within the family context. The first three principles are called assumption maxims and concern the management of private disclosures. The last three principles are called interaction maxims, as they concern how we regulate interactions with others when revealing or concealing private information (Petronio & Durham, 2008).

PUBLIC-PRIVATE DIALECTICAL TENSION

Dialectical tension can be considered two opposing forces that are in constant struggle with one another. In the case of CPM, the tension is between the revealing or the concealing of private information. For example, when we start to date someone, we are hypervigilant about how and what we disclose to the other person. We have a need to disclose private information as sharing information serves as an indicator of intimacy. Yet, simultaneously we are careful to

separates   A couple type that are more conventional on marital and family issues than independents, yet they maintain individual freedom, have less companionship and sharing, and describe their communication as assertive.

communication privacy management theory   A theory that is based on explaining how people reveal private information as well as how people conceal private information.

assumption maxims Principles of Communication Privacy Management Theory that concern how people regulate interactions with others when revealing or concealing private information.

interaction maxims Principles of Communication Privacy Management Theory that concerns how people regulate interactions with others when revealing or concealing private information.

control certain information that we believe is exclusively ours and is nobody else's business.

PRIVACY MANAGEMENT CONCEPTUALIZATION

CPM assumes private information is something that people believe they own (just as you own any other possession such as a car or a house). It is a commodity we control regarding who has the right to know such information. Our choice to disclose, or not to disclose, is determined by our perception of what is in our own best interest. For example, when on a first date, one would not readily disclose a felony conviction. In fact, a person may wait a considerable amount of time before disclosing that information or may choose to never disclose it. The disclosure issue goes well beyond just developing relationships. Take an example of family addiction issues (e.g., drugs, alcohol, gambling). We may have very close friends that will never reveal "family secrets" because people simply choose to keep that information between the nuclear family members.

Petronio (2002) argued "CPM uses the metaphor of boundaries to illustrate that, although there may be a flow of private information to others, borders mark ownership lines so control issues are easily understood" (p. 3). Our privacy boundaries vary from one person to another. Simply put, some people readily reveal information that others would never reveal. What is private information to one individual may not necessarily be private to another.

PRIVACY RULES

privacy rules The way in which people make choices about how and when to disclose private information based on the criteria of culture, gender, motivation, context, and risk-benefit ratio.

Privacy rules reflect the way in which people make choices about how and when to disclose private information. Petronio (2002) believes that privacy rules are developed on the five criteria of culture criteria (societal values, ethnicity, etc.), gendered criteria (women and men have differing rules for disclosure), motivational criteria (reasons that people have for disclosure), contextual criteria (relational aspects that either encourage or discourage disclosure), and risk-benefit ratio criteria (what are the benefits and pitfalls for revealing private information).

Privacy rules are believed to be socially learned. Consider the process of a child growing up, parents tell children what is appropriate disclosure and what should not be discussed with outsiders (e.g., "Don't tell anyone outside of our immediate family how much money we make"). Children basically learn what are appropriate privacy boundaries from both overt and covert messages sent from their parents. The acquisition of privacy rules are not limited to children. When a person changes careers or joins a new organization, that person learns what the desired privacy boundaries of the new group are. For example, if you belong to a fraternity or sorority, you probably have strong privacy boundaries regarding the initiation process, secret handshake, and other rituals. Sometimes, privacy rules are overtly stated so that newcomers will understand what exactly is expected of them (e.g., signing a nondisclosure clause).

We establish our rules for privacy through enactment. That is, we use certain privacy rules and alter them based on the outcome. If you disclose something private to someone and that person turns around and tells someone else, chances are that you will not disclose anything private to that person again. Thus, this event will alter your privacy rules.

The final three maxims are considered interaction maxims and fully ground CPM as a true communication theory. That is, "fundamentals of the theory and the tests of the principles are predicated on seeking an understanding about the domain of a communication phenomenon, using the knowledge about communication that largely comes from communication literature" (Petronio & Durham, 2008, p. 313).

SHARED BOUNDARIES

According to Petronio (2002), once a person discloses personal information, the nature of that information is forever changed. That is, we are no longer the exclusive owner of the information, we have now shared that information with another person, who is now considered a co-owner of the private information. The *shared boundaries* can be at the dyadic level, group level, family level, organizational level, and societal level (Petronio & Durham, 2008).

BOUNDARY COORDINATION

CPM assumes disclosure of personal information affects both the sender and the receiver of the information. Petronio (2002) argued that **boundary coordination** involves the three processes of regulation of **boundary linkages**, **boundary ownership rights**, and **boundary permeability**. Boundary linkage reflects the relationship that is formed between the discloser and the recipient(s) of the information. Boundary linkages can be either intentional and unintentional in nature. For example, you may reveal to your best friend that you are having relational problems, yet your friend's spouse overhears you from another room. In this example, your friend is the intended link of the private disclosure whereas the spouse would be the unintended link for the private disclosure.

BOUNDARY OWNERSHIP

Boundary ownership rights refers to the responsibility, privileges, and rights that go along with ownership of private disclosures. The ownership of private information may also result in the creation of new dilemmas (Petronio, Jones, & Morr, 2003). For example, when a child is finally told that they were adopted, this disclosure may create great conflict or dissonance for the child in terms of

boundary coordination Part of Communication Privacy Management Theory that involves the regulation of boundary linkages, boundary ownership rights, and boundary permeability.

boundary linkages Part of Communication Privacy Management Theory reflecting the relationship that is formed between the disclosure and the recipient(s) of the information.

boundary ownership rights Part of Communication Privacy Management theory and is the responsibility, privileges, and rights that go along with ownership of private disclosures.

boundary permeability Part of Communication Privacy Management Theory and is the degree of access or openness of a privacy boundary.

coping with the revelation of such private information. In terms of expectations, when expectations are negotiated clearly, the co-owners are less likely to betray the trust of the discloser. When rules for managing the information are made implicit, then there is a greater chance for the mismanagement of the private information.

BOUNDARY PERMEABILITY

According to Petronio (2002) boundary permeability reflects the degree of access or openness of a privacy boundary. The greater the access to private information, the more permeable the boundary. For example, a friend tells you that they contracted a sexually transmitted disease and then tells you that if you share that information with anyone, your friendship would end. This example is reflective of a low access to private information (i.e., just you and your friend) with a thick privacy boundary or low permeability. On the other hand, if you disclose the same information to your friend and he or she does not seem bothered by sharing the private information, your friend may interpret that information as a high access to private information and would reflect a thin privacy boundary with high permeability (see Figure 13.2).

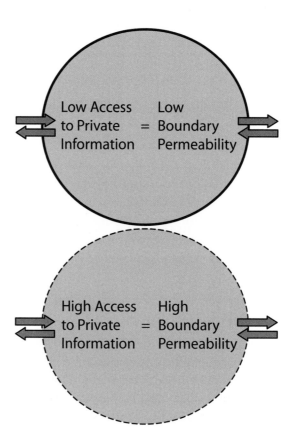

Figure 13.2

Communication privacy management theory.

CPM theory assumes that boundaries are managed in three ways. First, collective boundaries can be disproportionate. This occurs when a person shares more private information at a greater or lesser rate than the receiver of the information. This lack of reciprocity can lead to the perception that the person who receives the greater amount of information is more powerful or has a degree of control over the discloser. Second, collective boundaries can share information in an equitable way, which is also known as managing in an intersected fashion. Third, managing boundaries can also take the form of a unified way where the private information affects the entire group (Petronio, 2002). For example, a mother's history of mental illness affects all family members and also influences if/how the family members will share that information with outsiders.

BOUNDARY TURBULENCE

According to Petronio and Durham (2008), a conflicted state known as boundary turbulence occurs due to "incongruent expectations, misunderstandings of privacy parameters, or access rules, and the handling of private information" (p. 316). The contributing factors to boundary turbulence include violations of privacy, dilemmas, and misconception about ownership.

Empirical support for CPM abounds. The theory has been shown to be a valid explanation in several different contexts, including family and health communication contexts. For example, Caughlin (2002) found that demand/withdraw patterns in marriage or "a pattern in which one spouse avoids discussion while the other nags or complains" (p. 49) were found to be negatively correlated with marital satisfaction. This suggests that as the level of demand/withdraw patterns in a marriage increases, marital satisfaction tends to decrease. However, in terms of CPM, demand/withdraw patterns may have a link to boundary turbulence "such as privacy dilemmas and disclosures represent important areas of research in interpersonal communication because of the intrinsically complex nature of privacy management within relational systems" (Petronio & Durham, p. 317). In a follow-up study specifically looking at demand/withdrawal patterns through CPM theory, Caughlin and Afifi (2004) investigated 114 parent/child dyads as well as 100 heterosexual dyads and found that a person's motivation for avoiding topics may indeed moderate levels of relational dissatisfaction. In sum, when a person has a motivation to avoid discussing a topic in an effort to protect a relationship, the link between avoidance and dissatisfaction is less than when it is compared to people citing a lack of closeness for topic avoidance.

Communication privacy management theory is truly a communication theory that is based firmly in the field of communication studies. The theory seeks to redefine the traditional conceptualization of disclosure to indicate that private information, once revealed, is a commodity that needs to be managed through relational boundaries. The strength of the theory lies in the many empirical studies indicating support for the validity of the theory. Given that the theory was first developed in 2002, it still is in its "theoretical infancy," and we expect that it will continue to contribute to the field of communication in a variety of ways. According to Petronio and Durham (2008), "future research needs to continue testing the variability of application. In addition, it is necessary to develop a diagnostic tool to help us understand the reasons turbulence occurs and a repair mechanism to teach us how to mend privacy breakdowns" (p. 320).

The Argumentative Skill Deficiency Model of Intrafamily Violence

Conditions often exist in which marital conflict escalates into aggression. Infante and his colleagues (Infante, Chandler, & Rudd, 1989; Infante, Sabourin, Rudd, & Shannon, 1990) developed a model to explain and predict how certain conditions stimulate and encourage intrafamily violence.

The model, based on the communication traits of *argumentativeness* and *verbal aggressiveness* (see Chapter 5), describes how the interaction of personality traits, factors related to a particular situation, and characteristics of the general environment may lead to physically aggressive behavior between family members. Personal qualities that stimulate family violence include a hostile personality, low self-esteem, and poor verbal ability. Revenge or alcohol consumption are two specifics that could cause a particular situation to escalate into violence. Environmental conditions such as poverty or prejudice sometimes promote violence. According to the model, verbal aggression becomes a *catalyst* to violence when other conditions for violence are present; it serves as a trigger.

Individuals who lack skill in argument may be at greater risk of family violence. Although verbal aggression may be caused by several other factors (psychopathology, disdain, social learning), an argumentative skill deficiency is a major and important contributing factor. Several types of verbally aggressive behaviors have been identified: character attacks, competence attacks, teasing, ridicule, maledictions, profanity, and physical appearance attacks (Infante & Wigley, 1986). The model suggests that individuals who suffer from an "argumentative skill deficiency" may be more prone to engage in these verbally aggressive behaviors.

The theorists argued that family and spousal abuse results in physical aggression, which is often preceded by verbal aggression as a catalyst to violence. Infante and his colleagues tested the hypothesis that husbands and wives in violent marriages will be less argumentative (a constructive trait) and more verbally aggressive (a destructive trait) than husbands and wives in nonviolent marriages. The data strongly supported this hypothesis. The researchers also compared the self-reports from a sample of nonabused wives to the self-reports from a sample of abused wives about verbal aggression by the husband and wife in a recent dispute. Of the ten types of verbally aggressive messages examined, character attacks (such as "You are a liar!") most clearly differentiated violent from nonviolent marital disputes. Swearing, competence attacks (for example, "You never do anything right!"), and threats also differentiated violent from nonviolent disagreements between husbands and wives. A communication approach to the problem of intrafamily violence is uniquely valuable; it provides a framework for understanding the problem as well as the means to design intervention treatments, such as training couples on how to argue constructively.

Stephen (1990) argued that progress in the development of theories of family and marital communication has been hampered because theoretically based research studies have been rare. More theoretical research is needed along with alternative methodologies for gathering data for the family context to maximize its potential in the communication field.

HEALTH COMMUNICATION

Over the last several years, numerous articles have appeared in newspapers and magazines decrying the lack of effective and satisfying health-care communication. Charges of insensitivity, lack of empathy, lack of respect, poor listening behavior, and lack of trust have been leveled by the media against physicians, dentists, and other health-care providers. Krupat (1986) related an example of a distressing encounter. A middle-aged man noticed a dark mole on his shoulder. Concerned that it might be serious, he made an appointment with a physician. He and the doctor engaged in some casual conversation, during which the man mentioned his arthritis. The doctor picked up on this complaint, prescribed medication to relieve the arthritis pain, and began to usher the man out the door. The patient had been shut out of the conversation. He left the office flustered, upset, and still worried about the mole.

Some researchers in health communication (Kreps & Thornton, 1992) have advocated a change in vocabulary. If you study this topic, you may find the word *patient* replaced by *consumer* or *client*. The last two terms project an image of actively seeking health-care services; patient implies a dependent/subordinate role. Consumer or client is a proactive designation incorporating participation and responsibility. The fact that physician/client probably sounds foreign to you highlights the problem illustrated in our example. The man—in a physician/patient role—did not control the outcome of his appointment. Rather than correcting the physician when medication for arthritis was prescribed, the man was intimidated by the situation and perceived his role as subordinate to the physician.

You may recall examples in which the communication between yourself and your health-care provider was unsatisfactory. To be sure, many health-care providers are quite sensitive to client needs and exhibit competent communication behaviors. The image of the empathic, sensitive, friendly, and open health-care provider, however, has sufficiently deteriorated in the public's mind to stimulate the health community to explore ways to alter these perceptions. Fortunately, many health-care organizations and health-care providers are beginning to understand that human communication is the singularly most important tool health professionals have in providing health care to their clients.

Over the last three decades, health communication has emerged as an important context in which to examine the influence of human communication (Kreps & Atkin, 1991). Two communication journals are dedicated to the study of communication and health, *Health Communication* and the *Journal of Health Communication*. Health communication has a strong orientation toward applied communication. Health communication theorists and researchers often focus their efforts on identifying, examining, and offering insights into how to improve health care and to promote taking responsibility for one's health. Like the family context, the health context is an extremely broad area in which to conduct research and attempt theory building. Communication has been associated with numerous health-related factors including well-being, patient satisfaction, confidence in the doctor, and even malpractice (Arntson & Droge, 1988). Researchers have investigated such diverse topics as physician–client nonverbal communication (Street & Buller, 1988) and the development of an AIDS prevention campaign (Brown, 1991). Research in the area of health communication has "tended to focus around three main themes: physician-client communication, health information dissemination, and social support" (Sharf, 1993, p. 35).

The following definition of health communication is consistent with the symbolic exchange and message-centered focus of this text: "Health communication is the dissemination and interpretation of health-related messages" (Donohew & Ray, 1990, p.4). The disseminator (the sender of information) can be an individual, an organization, or a mass medium. The interpreter (decoder/translator) can be an individual, a group, an organization, or a public. Scott Ratzan (1994) offered this definition of health communication, "Health communication . . . is the art and technique of informing, influencing, and motivating individual, institutional, and public audiences about important health issues. Its scope includes disease prevention, health promotion, health-care policy, business, as well as enhancement of the quality of life and health of individuals within the community" (p. 362).

Functions of Communication in the Health Context

Four functions of communication have been identified regarding health provider/consumer communication (Costello, 1977). To a large degree, most of the functions involve interpersonal communication (see Figure 13.3).

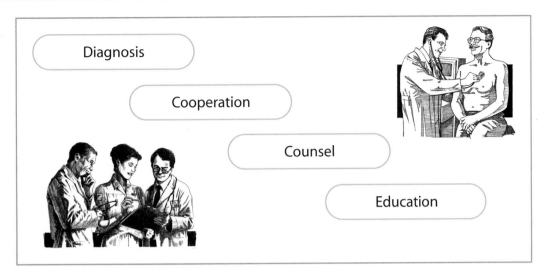

Figure 13.3

Four functions of health communication.

- Diagnosis—the data-gathering, data-interpretation, and problem-solving skills used by the health-care provider.

- Cooperation—communication concerning the nature of one's illness and the implication of measures prescribed for care.

- Counsel—involves the role of the provider as "therapist." DeVito (2002) included therapeutic communication as one of the major purposes of interpersonal communication. The health-care provider engaged in the therapeutic function deals with the client's "symbolic" symptoms.

- Education—health education is the process of disseminating information to individuals to attempt to reduce health risks and to increase the effectiveness of health care. Health education proceeds through channels ranging from informal provider/consumer interaction to more formal mass-mediated campaigns designed to achieve clear and planned objectives (the "AIDS Awareness" campaign is one such effort).

diagnosis A function of health communication that involves data-gathering, data-interpretation, and problem-solving skills used by the health-care provider.

cooperation A function of health communication that involves communication concerning the nature of one's illness and the implication of measures prescribed for care.

counsel A function of health communication that involves the role of the provider as "therapist."

education A function of health communication that assumes health education is the process of disseminating information to individuals in order to attempt to reduce health risks and to increase the effectiveness of health care.

Communication Contexts within Health Communication

Researchers have attempted to provide some structure for studying health communication. Some believe it is helpful to categorize and define the study of health communication according to communication contexts (Ratzan, Payne, & Bishop, 1996). Most of the research in health communication has examined the interpersonal communication relationship between the client and the health-care provider. The other most frequent context of analysis of health communication is mass communication, which "focuses on effective message dissemination for health promotion, disease prevention, and health-related messages transmitted through mediated channels, including health marketing and policy-making" (p. 28).

For most individuals, the term "health communication" refers to the interpersonal context. Despite the importance of competent interpersonal communication, few providers or clients receive training in one-on-one communication. Effective message exchange requires that clients communicate their symptoms and physical problems accurately to the provider. Similarly, the provider must be able to communicate instructions accurately and competently on how to relieve, eliminate, or manage health-care problems. The "costs" of ineffective or unsatisfying provider/client interpersonal communication are many. Even if instructions are delivered clearly, if the interaction between the health-care provider and the consumer is abrupt, hurried, and impersonal, the client may not be satisfied, and compliance with provider recommendations may not result. At a minimum, effective interpersonal communication between providers and clients is a necessary prerequisite for the development of openness and trust—factors so critical in the health-care context. Diagnosis and treatment are far more likely to be accurate and to result in a speedy recovery if both parties are skilled communicators. Fewer malpractice suits will result if provider/client interpersonal communication is enhanced.

A number of researchers have concentrated their theory-building efforts on the interpersonal interactions between health-care providers and consumers. Several important issues have been highlighted.

RELATIONAL CONTROL

Many people feel that physicians dominate most interactions. Physicians can engage in control tactics before they even see clients by making them wait for appointments and treatment. Health-care providers control the interaction and conversation when they engage in one-way communication: asking questions but not encouraging others to do the same; interrupting; changing topics abruptly; or ignoring clients completely (Cline & Cardosi, 1983).

In Chapter 9, we looked at a model of relational interaction by Millar and Rogers. Recall that the model includes the message exchange patterns of control, trust, and intimacy. The control dimension refers to the process by which individuals establish the defining and directing actions of the relationship. Relational control is measured by **redundancy**, **dominance**, and **power**. Redundancy refers to the amount of change in interactants' negotiations over rights. Dominance describes how much one individual commands the interaction. Power is the potential to influence or restrict another person's behaviors.

redundancy Refers to the amount of change in interactant's negotiations over rights.

dominance Degree to which one partner is said to dominate a dyad's interaction.

power The potential to influence or restrict another person's behaviors.

Although the model was conceptualized and developed as a way to examine marital dyads, O'Hair (1989) has applied the relational control component of the model to study provider/consumer relationships in the health-care context. He argued that the model is especially appropriate to study physician/client communication in general and control in particular. Clients are no longer passive participants in the medical relationship; they are beginning to challenge the authority and control of physicians. The relational control model allows us to observe and examine the control strategies attempted by consumers. Clients dissatisfied with the control exercised by physicians generally engage in fewer compliance behaviors. Thus, identifying relational control patterns of *both* physician and client has direct bearing on client health.

To examine the issue of relational control in physician/client communication, O'Hair taped actual interactions and looked for indications of redundancy, dominance, and power. His findings indicated that clients attempted control almost as often as physicians. O'Hair calls this *competitive symmetry*. The following conversation illustrates this:

DOCTOR: "I would continue on the antibiotics until your throat clears."

CLIENT: "They haven't helped. I would prefer a new medication."

Complementarity emerged as the second most frequently used control sequence. Messages are complementary if one speaker attempts control of the exchange, while the other yields, or if one speaker yields control while the other assumes control. O'Hair found that clients were twice as willing to yield control of the interaction after the physician sought control. For example:

DOCTOR: "If you are going to travel long distances, be sure to stop periodically to empty your bladder."

CLIENT: "I'll schedule stops to make sure I do that."

The results of this application of interpersonal theory in the health-care context show the benefit of extending an existing theory of communication. O'Hair suggested that relational control analyses could be used to examine the incidence of client noncompliance. For example, relational control analyses could help us determine which clients are willing to challenge the authority and competence of physicians—two factors that may predict noncompliance with physician recommendations.

LOCUS OF CONTROL

Another construct, locus of control, has been profitably applied to the health communication context. Brenders (1989) stated that perceptions of personal control have been linked to such health-related factors as life stress, coping with illness, and the success of preventative practices. Individuals with internal locus

locus of control A personality trait that concerns how people interpret outcomes in their life.

internal locus of control
A perception that the person has direct control over their lives and behaviors.

external locus of control
A perception that the person perceives that their lives and behavior are controlled by others.

of control expectancies perceive that they have direct control over their lives and behavior. Individuals with external locus of control expectancies perceive that their lives and behavior are controlled by other people. The major assumption of this body of work is that "persons are likely to evaluate information and advice from within the context of their preferred control orientation" (p. 119). Brenders reported that individuals with internal expectancies for control are more assertive, proactive, and autonomous in interpersonal situations. For example, internals seek and acquire more information about their health condition than do externals. Brenders argued that internals, anticipating control over the health communication event, see the value of this information in helping them facilitate control.

After reviewing the array of research on locus of control in the health communication context, Brenders concluded: (a) internals are more receptive to health-care information and advice; (b) internals may respond poorly to treatment unless provided with specific information about procedures and a rationale; (c) congruent control messages (similar control style of providers and consumers) facilitate actual treatment success; and (d) the interaction between control beliefs, communication, and health care are likely to yield promising theory building and practical results in health communication.

COMPLIANCE

In Chapter 6 we examined the research on compliance gaining in communication. Compliance is a critical dimension in provider/client interactions. In the health-care context, compliance is defined as following the provider's suggestions for lifestyle changes or treatment procedures, such as taking medicine in a specific dose at a specific time. Providers supply numerous messages to clients regarding aspects of their treatment program. These messages include what drugs to take and when to take them, how to administer proper treatment, what to eat, and what not to eat. Kreps (1988) argued that from a relational perspective the responsibility for "getting well" is a product of the interaction of both provider and consumer; compliance is influenced by specific strategies used by both the client and the provider.

Research on compliance in the health-care context has taken two distinct directions: (a) efforts to determine what kinds of compliance gaining strategies health-care professionals use, and (b) the relationship between the use of specific strategies and outcomes such as client satisfaction with health-care quality and individual health status. Michael and Judee Burgoon (1990) explored the use of verbal and nonverbal compliance gaining strategies by physicians; they offered twenty-two propositions. After testing these propositions, the researchers concluded that physicians use nonthreatening verbal strategies when attempting to convince their clients to follow the suggested treatment. Physicians emphasize their expertise as an incentive to comply (for example, "If you comply with my recommendations to lose weight and take the prescribed medication, your high blood pressure should go down"). If patients resist, physicians adopt more aggressive strategies, especially threats ("If you don't adhere to my recommendations, you will likely get another, more severe, heart attack!"). Physicians seldom report using positive or reinforcing compliance gaining strategies in their communication with clients ("You will feel better about yourself if you lose weight" or "An intelligent person like you would naturally want to lower your blood pressure").

Providers employ a range of nonverbal communication behaviors, which can either enhance or undermine compliance. Certain nonverbal behaviors signal approval: closer physical proximity, increased touch, leaning forward, head nods, smiles, pleasant facial expressions, or vocal reinforcers such as "uh huh." These nonverbal behaviors fall under the broad category of **immediacy behaviors** (Chapter 8). Immediacy behaviors indicate liking and create high sensory involvement between provider and client. **Nonimmediacy behaviors** signal avoidance and dislike. Some nonimmediacy behaviors include excessive distances between communicators, frowns, use of prolonged silence, and "cold" or harsh voices. Such behaviors by health-care providers make clients less willing to follow a provider's instructions.

immediacy behaviors Behaviors that indicate liking and create high sensory involvement.

nonimmediacy behaviors Behaviors that signal avoidance and dislike.

Research has identified several communication behaviors physicians can use to enhance compliance. Judee Burgoon and her colleagues found compliance was enhanced and clients were more satisfied when physicians exhibited greater similarity to patients, communicated greater receptivity, composure, immediacy/affection, and were moderately formal (Burgoon et al., 1987). Client satisfaction was also found to be related to the use of an affiliative nonverbal style and less-dominant behaviors by physicians (Street & Buller, 1987).

Implications of this research are that physicians should be encouraged to smile more, employ more eye contact while listening, engage in fewer interruptions, and speak with softer and higher pitched tones. An indirect route to enhanced compliance is through increased provider credibility. Physicians can use the character, sociability, composure, and dynamism factors of credibility to enhance compliance (Burgoon & Burgoon, 1990). Clients prefer providers who appear caring, friendly, moderately composed, and expressive. The enhanced relationship and increased credibility should stimulate clients to follow the advice and recommendations of their providers more closely.

COMMUNICATOR STYLE

Recall that communicator style (Chapter 5) may be viewed as an overall impression of a number of traits: contentious, open, dramatic, dominant, precise, relaxed, friendly, attentive, and animated. The traits can be combined to form a particular style. For example, an "affirming communicator style" consists of relaxed, friendly, and attentive traits.

Communicator style has been used to study how patients' perceptions of their health-care provider's style was related to patient satisfaction. Research has identified communicator styles such as affiliation (friendly, open, attentive, and relaxed styles) and control (dominant and contentious styles). One study found that the more a physician used an affiliative communicator style and the less they used a control style, the greater the patient satisfaction with that physician (Buller & Buller, 1987). In another study on communicator style in the health-care context, physicians who were seen as attentive, very animated, not too dominant, and not contentious were perceived as more empathic. Physicians seen as very relaxed and very animated were more likely to be seen as having the ability to enhance patient understanding (Cardello, Ray, & Pettey, 1995). Clearly then, the communicator style of a physician can have an impact on the satisfaction a patient has with that physician.

UNCERTAINTY REDUCTION

Understandably, people are frequently apprehensive when they seek medical treatment. People feel uncertain about their illness, about the interpersonal dynamics (relational uncertainty) between their health-care provider and themselves, and about the medical setting (Sheer & Cline, 1995). Illness uncertainty refers to the degree an individual feels uncertain about her or his illness before they see the physician. Relational uncertainty refers to the degree to which individuals feel uncertain about their relationships with their physicians. Medical setting uncertainty refers to patients' uncertainty and lack of familiarity with the physical setting of the health-care environment, the medical/technical procedures they may have to undergo, and the different roles and jobs that various health-care providers perform. Reducing a patient's illness uncertainty by providing information about the illness, providing adequate information about medical treatments, and creating a more relaxing atmosphere increased the ability to cope with illness and to accept solutions offered by health-care providers. Simple gestures such as maps of the hospital or information about appointment procedures before arrival at a health-care facility reassure consumers. In addition, doctors should ask more open-ended questions, avoid using technical terms, and be more empathic. Patient satisfaction and commitment increased, and the overall outcome of the medical treatment was enhanced when uncertainty was reduced.

The Systems Perspective

The study of health communication has profited significantly from the use of the systems paradigm. At the interpersonal level we have the dyadic relationship of health-care provider/consumer communication. Expanding the boundaries, we have the health-care team and other small groups involved in health communication (for example, the surgical team or a hospital ethics committee). If we expand this further, we can examine the dynamics of health communication in the organizational context. This context focuses on how structural aspects of the organization influence health care. For example, if ineffective or minimal communication exists between the physician and the pharmacy regarding dosage of medicine, the client's health may be adversely affected. Further expansion incorporates how the mass media disseminate health information to the public.

The principle of *nonsummativity* argues that we must explore the relationships between the parts of the health-care system, not just the components. The dynamics of the health-care provider/consumer interaction are an integral part of the health-care process. The interactive nature of provider/client encounters is often overlooked by researchers. Arntson (1985) suggested, "The real unit of analysis is not what the doctor does or what the patient does, but what they are doing together. They are influencing each other mutually in the encounter" (p. 119). The concept of *equifinality* argues that goals of systems may be reached in many different ways. Treatable diseases can often be approached from a number of venues. The client may consult a specialist for treatment or may seek advice and counsel from family members, the media, and other individuals who have been successfully treated for the disease.

Eileen Berlin Ray and Katherine Miller (1990) suggested that health-care organizations differ from other types of organizations. They noted that the major task performed—the establishment, maintenance, and enhancement of medical and psychological well-being—is quite different from that of most organizations. Teresa Thompson (1986) cited the intensely hierarchical structure of health organizations and increased specialization as two additional characteristics that differentiate health-care organizations. Ineffective communication at the organizational level can work against client care by distorting information, blocking the exchange of important messages, and alienating health-care workers from one another (Kreps & Thornton, 1992).

An important component in Weick's theory of organizational information (Chapter 11) is *equivocality*—how understandable, complex, ambiguous, or obscure messages are. If you visit a health-care practitioner for relief from a head cold, the health-care provider can suggest a number of basic rules (offer prescriptions for behavior) such as get plenty of rest, drink fluids, take aspirin. These messages are direct and unequivocal. If you visit with more vague complaints—general weakness or lack of energy, for example, the number of immediately applicable rules are reduced, and the provider's messages become more equivocal until more information is available.

In the health-care context, the provider will search his or her repertoire of rules to respond to the health-care problem. The provider must perform communication behavior cycles (for example, ask a series of questions and then analyze the responses) to make a diagnosis and to reduce equivocality. The doctor selects a rule or prescription for behavior from his or her repertoire that should alleviate the problem. If the provider has past experience with symptoms congruent with the current problem, the prescriptions for behavior are reinforced by the positive feedback loop. If rules in the repertoire are incongruent with the current problem, they are rejected by the negative feedback loop.

Health-care diagnosis depends on the effective coordination of the enactment and retention phases of organizing. Enactment involves paying attention to the information environment, whereas retention involves the storage of information (Kreps & Thornton, 1992). In the health-care context, a provider frequently relies on information from other members of the organization to make an effective diagnosis and to prescribe appropriate treatment. In situations that are highly uncertain (equivocal), information needs to be processed quickly and efficiently, and equivocal messages need to be made more understandable.

The Health Belief Model

Developed in the early 1950s, the health belief model (HBM) is considered one of the first systematic, theory-based research efforts in health communication and one of the most accepted models of behavioral change dealing with health and safety issues. The first research effort on the HBM attempted to identify factors that underlie decisions to get a chest x-ray for the early detection of tuberculosis. The health belief model permits researchers to explain and predict (and thereby allows people to control their behavior). One of the originators of the theory stated: "The early researchers concerned with the health belief model would work cooperatively, build on each other's work, develop a theory that would include a heavy component of motivation and the perceptional world of the behaving individual . . . toward developing a theory not only useful in explaining a particular program problem, but also adaptable to other problems" (Rosenstock, 1974, p. 329).

The HBM is composed of five components that may influence a person to take some type of action, for example to lessen the chances of getting a disease or suffering a health-related malady.

Perceived susceptibility refers to the perceived subjective risks of contracting a disease or health-related condition (Rosenstock, 1974). Some people (low perceptibles) believe it very unlikely that they would contract a particular disease or health-related condition. Other people (high susceptibles) perceive that it is very likely or inevitable that they will experience a disease or health condition. Still others, moderate in their perceptions of susceptibility, operate on statistical probabilities (e.g., "My mother and grandmother had diabetes, therefore it is quite probable that I, too, will develop this condition").

Perceived seriousness or severity refers to an evaluation of the types of difficulties potential health and safety conditions would have on lives, emotional states, and the lives of families. Individuals make physical, emotional, and even financial assessments. They might ask, "How much pain, suffering, and discomfort would I experience if this condition emerged?" "How will I cope with potential loss of income?" and, "What emotional effects will the condition have on the rest of my family?"

Perceived benefits of taking action involves an assessment of the possible benefits of performing the recommended behaviors to lessen the chances of being affected by the health or safety threat. If the susceptibility of getting the condition is perceived to be high, the individual assesses the benefits of taking some type of action to prevent the disease. In essence, the individual performs a cost-benefit analysis. Decisions are often influenced by norms and group pressure, as well as recommendations by health professionals and physicians (Rosenstock, 1974). If the perceived benefits of taking action outweigh the perceived barriers, the likelihood of adopting the recommended preventative actions increases.

Perceived barriers to taking action are also part of the assessment process. Individuals assess whether the suggested recommendation or preventative action will be expensive, painful, upsetting, time consuming, or simply inconvenient. If the individual perceives a high probability of encountering these conditions, then he or she may not adopt the recommended behaviors that could lead to better health and safety outcomes. If the perceived barriers of taking action outweigh the perceived benefits, the likelihood of adopting the recommended preventative actions decreases.

Cues to action motivate people to adopt or incorporate behaviors that could lead to a desired goal, such as better health and increased safety. The assumption is that in addition to the individual's beliefs, certain health-related actions might need to be prompted or triggered. These cues to action are "the specific stimuli necessary to trigger appropriate health behavior" (Mattson, 1999, p. 243). In the area of health communication, cues to action can be internal or external. Internal cues are more intrapersonal; that is, they are messages one sends to oneself about a health-related concern (e.g., "My cough is getting much worse, so I should get a chest x-ray to determine what is causing this"). External cues to action are communicated by someone or something outside the person, such as a conversation with a physician or a friend, a warning from your mother to see a doctor, an advertisement in a newspaper or magazine, getting a postcard from the dentist reminding you to make an appointment for a examination, or a television program that presents quite graphically the dangers associated with smoking cigarettes (Chew, Palmer, & Kim, 1998; Rosenstock, 1974; Witte, Stokols, Ituarte, & Schneider, 1993).

The HBM has been one of the most utilized frameworks in health communication research. For example, researchers have used it in a study designed to promote the use of bicycle safety helmets. The goal of the study was to investigate how the HBM's perceived threat factor and cues to action influenced bicycle safety helmet practices (Witte et al., 1993). In interviews with parents, researchers asked, "How often do you worry about your child being involved in a bicycle accident?" and "Do you believe that most head injuries resulting from bicycle accidents are (serious/not serious)?" to measure perceived susceptibility and perceived severity. In addition, the researchers used several external cues to action, including a community event that demonstrated bicycle safety, public service announcements on the radio about bicycle safety, direct mail brochures designed to increase perceptions of susceptibility and severity of head injury when not wearing a helmet, phone messages that presented similar information, and bicycle helmet coupons redeemable for $10 off the price of a helmet distributed through the mail.

The results of the study generally supported the HBM. Those individuals receiving the external cues to action (e.g., the community event, mass media announcements, the telephone message) perceived bicycling injuries to be more serious and more likely to occur to their children than those not receiving the cues to action (Witte et al., 1993). Parents who perceived greater threat of bicycle injury had more favorable attitudes toward using bicycle helmets, were more likely to buy helmets for their children, and were more likely to insist that their children wear the bicycle helmet. In addition, the more cues to action received, the greater the perception of threat.

The HBM has also been used to guide research efforts designed to develop interpersonal communication strategies to prevent drug abuse by health-care professionals and the elderly. The problems of impaired health-care professionals are quite significant, with the incidence of health-care professionals suffering from addiction to drugs and alcohol greatly exceeding that of the general population (Beisecker, 1991). The elderly are considered another at-risk group particularly susceptible to abuses of prescription and nonprescription medications. Analee Beisecker recommended using the HBM to develop appropriate prevention strategies for both groups because the model focuses on two major needs of those groups, "education regarding the seriousness of substance abuse and a feeling of vulnerability or susceptibility to addiction" (p. 247). In particular, it is recommended that the HBM's cues to action in the form of interpersonal communication be considered, with mentors or peer counselors used to provide the interpersonal contact cues for health-care professionals at risk and health-care counselors used to provide the interpersonal contact cues for the elderly.

The impact of another important HBM cue to action, a television program, was tested to determine its influence on healthy eating practices. A one-hour television program, *Eat Smart,* was used in a naturalistic setting to determine its impact on healthy eating habits (Chew, Palmer, & Kim, 1998). The results of the study suggested that those individuals who watched the program perceived increased health benefits and reduced health barriers to healthy eating habits. In addition, participants who viewed the program became more concerned about food and fitness, had more confidence in the recommendations about healthy eating, and reduced their consumption of unhealthy foods after exposure to the program.

Marifran Mattson (1999) focused on interpersonal communication itself as a critical cue to action. The study explored the influence of a counseling session during HIV testing. It was thought that this interpersonal interaction would be especially useful in influencing individuals to change risky sexual behaviors and to comply with the recommendations for safer sex. Participants received an interpersonal counseling session designed to increase their awareness of the severity and their susceptibility to HIV/AIDS. Mattson measured several HBM factors, including risk appraisal (perceived severity of HIV/AIDS and perceived susceptibility to the disease), perceived benefits and barriers to taking action (employing safer sex practices such as using condoms), and perceived self-efficacy (perceptions of their ability to perform the safer sex recommendations). The results produced qualified support for the HBM. Clients' perceptions of their susceptibility to HIV/AIDS after participation in the interpersonal counseling session were moderately related to their decisions to comply with the safer sex recommendations (primarily using condoms). In addition, after the counseling session, clients also perceived that safer sex benefits outweighed the barriers to safer sex behavior. This research suggests that we move toward "reconceptualizing the HBM in favor of centralizing the role of communication cues to action" (p. 258). Thus, it is recommended that the cues to action, originally located on the periphery of the HBM, be moved to a more central position in the model.

UNCERTAINTY MANAGEMENT THEORY

Uncertainty management theory (UMT) was developed by Dale Brashers (2001a) as a reaction to the simplistic way that the term *uncertainty* has been conceptualized in communication theory. He believed that uncertainty is a multifaceted concept that can be more valuable and serve many more functions if not treated as an aversive state that needs to be reduced (see uncertainty reduction theory). Instead, Brashers believes that although UMT was developed to predict people's experience with uncertainty (i.e., postpositivist perspective), he readily acknowledged that the experience of uncertainty is also a situation-based phenomenon (Brashers, Goldsmith, & Hsieh, 2002).

UMT was originally conceptualized to explain how people react to health-related uncertainty (Brashers, 2001b; Brashers et al., 2006). According to Afifi and Matsunaga (2008), the three features of UMT consist of: (a) the meaning and the experience of uncertainty, (b) the role of an individual's response to uncertainty, and (c) the psychological and communicative strategies used to manage uncertainty. Unlike other theories that conceptualize uncertainty, a key term with UMT is "management of uncertainty" as opposed to "reduction

uncertainty management theory Explains how people react to health-related uncertainty.

of uncertainty." In fact, Brashers (2001a) argued that the equation of more "information = less uncertainty" is false. He argued that information and uncertainty are not unidimensional constructs, but that both are separate constructs. The key question is, "How much information is enough?" The concept of "enough" varies from person to person. Therefore, Brashers believes that when people feel insecure about the amount of knowledge they possess or the amount of knowledge available, uncertainty is present. Simply put, "abandon the assumption that uncertainty will produce anxiety" (Brashers, 2001a, p. 477). A person, when experiencing uncertainty, can experience a plethora of other emotions. For example, consider a student who is on the border between receiving a course grade of C– or D+. After the final exam the student's lack of effort in contacting the instructor about the course grade (i.e., little information about the final grade) may in fact serve as a comforting feeling, and that the uncertainty may give the student "hope" of a better grade. This can also be seen in a person who sends out a resume for a position, then after one or two weeks does not follow up with a phone call to the employer to determine if they are still being considered for the position.

Uncertainty is evident in health-related issues. In a study investigating the effects of illness on uncertainty, Brashers (2001b) investigated how HIV patients experience and manage uncertainty. Today, due to modern medicine and the destigmatization of the disease, the diagnosis of HIV is not to be thought of as the death sentence that it once was in the 1980s and 1990s. In terms of UMT, patients may actively seek out medical practitioners who provide them with uncertainty in an effort to give patients a sense of hope and a chance of some other outcome (i.e., controlling disease progression or cure). This provides an alternative to the certainty that the disease will eventually progress. Thus, uncertainty, in this case, can provide a sense of control and optimism (see Seligman, 1990). It has been revealed in a variety of medical studies that hope can prolong life and slow down the progression of the disease (Frank & Frank, 1991).

Another key component of UMT is that our reaction to uncertainty directly affects the influence of uncertainty on our psychological well-being. For instance, if a person affects uncertainty in a negative fashion (i.e., negative emotional response), then uncertainty is a dangerous state that is avoided whenever possible. On the other hand, when uncertainty is perceived as a positive experience (i.e., positive emotional response), uncertainty becomes beneficial to our physiological and psychological well-being. Figure 13.4 illustrates this process.

Research on information seeking has provided scholars with an abundance of findings that primarily focus on the premise that the more information we seek, the more control it provides us. This process has been described from a skill development perspective as a way to gain control over a particular situation

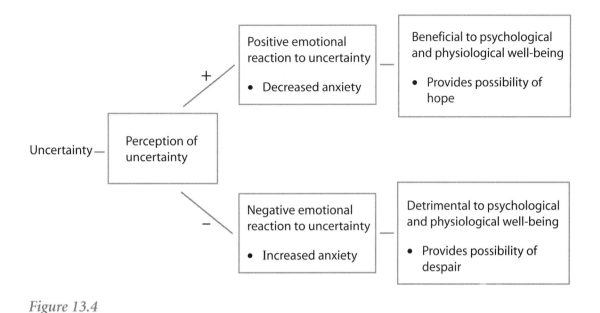

Figure 13.4

A model of uncertainty management theory (UMT).

(Cegala & Lenzmeir Broz, 2003) as well as a personality characteristic that predisposes people to seek information (Lefcourt, 1981). However, UMT holds that our perceptions of uncertainty (positive versus negative) directly affect the strategies and types of communication that we engage in and expose ourselves to. The following experiment will illustrate this point: Ask ten people you know, if they had a choice, would they want to know the types of diseases that they will develop in the future? Chances are that some people will respond "yes." In this case, uncertainty is a negative state that needs to be reduced to be effectively maintained. By *maintained,* we mean that every person has a level of uncertainty that they feel comfortable managing. Some people can only effectively manage uncertainty if it is totally reduced, whereas others can effectively manage some uncertainty. Still others feel comfortable in managing high levels of uncertainty. People who respond "no" to the question reflect a different perception about the function of uncertainty. For these people, uncertainty is seen as a positive state that needs to be maintained, as it generates less anxiety to the person rather than knowing about the specific disease they might develop.

In the health-care context, people do not simply either seek information or not, and Brashers (2001a) provided three additional ways in which people can interpret information regarding illness. First, some people who live with chronic disease or chronic states of uncertainty adapt to the state of chronic uncertainty (e.g., It is something that I have to deal with, so I must get use to it). Second, social networks consisting of family and friends as well as social role models, such as people acting in prosocial ways may serve to aid in the management of high uncertainty. For example, a person with a spinal cord injury can rely on family and friends but may also rely on other people who have suffered a spinal cord injury. This experience is reflected by the late actor Christopher Reeve, who dedicated his life to helping people with spinal cord injuries, as well as by Michael J. Fox, who helps people cope with Parkinson's disease, and the late Princess Diana, who worked for land mine extraction. Third, we engage in uncertainty management at a metalevel. That is, we manage our uncertainty management. We can metamanage uncertainty in two ways: First, we can manage our uncertainty management by distributing our needs for certainty in one area of our lives and uncertainty in other areas. This is not to suggest that there is only so much management that we have to spread around (i.e., zero-sum game approach). Rather, our psychological efforts, in a protective way, naturally determine where our uncertainty management efforts are needed (i.e., vital for effective management) and which are discretionary (i.e., desired but not vital). Second, through time and experience, people develop the flexibility to discern what information is trustworthy and relevant and what information is not in the management of uncertainty.

As noted earlier, research using UMT has been conducted primarily in the health context (see, for example, Brashers, Hsieh, Neidig, & Reynolds, 2006). As such, UMT is in its early stages and as such has great potential for further testing and theoretical extension to other contexts. For example, within the family context, how does UMT explain issues in at-risk marriages, in sibling relationships? Stepfamilies? The theory has been questioned as to whether UMT can be rooted in both postpositivistic and interpretive paradigms (Afifi & Matsunaga, 2008). However, as discussed in Chapter 2 (see Craig, 1999), the constitutive metamodel of communication theory suggests that the blending of theoretical perspectives is something that is necessary for future communication theory-building efforts.

Theory building in the health communication context has seen modest progress. Health communication research has had no all-encompassing theory from which to proceed and few, if any, models or standards of research. Three conditions may be responsible: the "peculiar" nature of the health-care context (for example, difficulty in distinguishing and defining "medical" versus "health"); the vast scope of communication phenomena to study; and the multidisciplinary approach to studying communication (Pettegrew & Logan, 1987). Duplication of research efforts has also been a problem, and much of the research in the health communication context has involved observational/descriptive methods (Thompson, 1990). The experimental paradigm has been underused. Despite these limitations, communication scholars approach the study of health communication with vigor; a number of promising research directions have emerged. Because of the importance of communication in the diagnosis, treatment, and prevention of illness, research and theory building should intensify.

INTERCULTURAL COMMUNICATION

The study of cultural influence on how people relate is perhaps one of the most important areas of study for communication theorists. Partly due to technological advancements and economic pursuits, the world has become much more pluralistic in nature. Whether it's our study of distant cultures for explaining behavior, describing behavior, or predicting behavior, our ability to relate to different people from different places can make the difference between war and peace. Cultural differences have been attributed as the cause of many military and political conflicts throughout time. It is the responsibility of any civilized society to investigate what makes any one culture different from another as well as how to account for such differences to find common ground from which relationships can be maintained and fostered. In many ways, the intercultural theorist serves as an ambassador in that the theories that are developed help people from different cultures work through issues that in earlier times, may have resulted in conflict or distrust. The theories presented here represent some of the most developed and comprehensive intercultural theories in the field of communication studies and have been applied in many cultures throughout the world.

Anxiety/Uncertainty Management Theory

Anxiety/uncertainty management theory (AUM) is a theory that has been evolving since 1985. AUM addresses the ambiguity of new situations that involve a pattern of information seeking (i.e., managing uncertainty) as well as tension reduction (i.e., managing anxiety, see Ball-Rokeach, 1973). William Gudykunst (1985) began the construction of AUM based on Uncertainty Reduction Theory (Berger & Calabrese, 1975; see Chapter 9), and it was designed to model the process of intergroup communication. This was followed by an extension of the theory that used the reduction of uncertainty and anxiety to explain how people adapt to other cultures (see Gudykunst & Hammer, 1988).

uncertainty When you are unsure about something. In information theory, when you do not know exactly what will happen in a situation.

As with many of the theories presented in this text, AUM makes explicit metatheoretical assumptions. Some of these assumptions include (a) the basic processes of communication are the same across cultures but culture provides rules for how the content of communication should be interpreted; (b) data that is considered useful for testing a theory is comprised of both a person's interpretation of communication and objective observation of communication; and (c) when we are not conscious of our communication behavior, communication is influenced by cultural and group membership as well as structural, situational, and environmental factors.

anxiety A key component of AUM theory that is believed to be the affective equivalent of uncertainty.

strangers Concept in AUM theory representing people whom we do not know and who are themselves in an unfamiliar environment.

AUM theory focuses on the underlying processes of communication with people we do not know and who are themselves in an unfamiliar environment. Such people are considered strangers in an interaction. The term *stranger* represents both the idea of nearness in that the person is physically close, yet also has the concept of being remote in that they have different values and utilize these values when making decisions about communicating. Thus, interaction with strangers is characterized by *anxiety* and *uncertainty*. For example, imagine yourself sitting in an airplane seat next to someone from another culture. Although the person is sitting next to you (i.e., physically close), their value system influencing communication behavior is different from yours and thus may cause you to become anxious and uncertain. Uncertainty can be defined as a cognitive phenomenon that affects how we think about strangers. Uncertainty is ubiquitous throughout all aspects of life and believed to be a "fundamental condition of human life" (Marris, 1996, p. 1). Further, uncertainty is a function of our own expectations about a situation and how that situation should be ordered or interpreted. Given that we tend to have more accurate expectations about people with whom we are familiar, or are of the same social/cultural groups as us, we tend experience less uncertainty. On the other hand, we would experience more uncertainty when communicating with people who belong to out-groups or groups that we do not belong to or have membership with.

maximum threshold for uncertainty A maximum level of uncertainty that when not exceeded, allows people to remain comfortable when interacting with other people.

minimum threshold for uncertainty The minimal level of uncertainty that when not exceeded, allows people to remain comfortable when interacting with other people.

general level of uncertainty acceptance A level of uncertainty that exists between a person's maximum and minimum thresholds for uncertainty.

People react differently to uncertainty, and this reaction is heavily influenced by culture and ethnicity. Therefore, each person has a degree of certainty that, when experienced, allows them to remain comfortable when interacting with other people. For example, consider how your closest friends react to an upcoming house party; one friend probably has to know all the details about the party such as exactly where the house is located, what time you will arrive, who will be there, when you will be leaving, what you will be wearing, and who is driving. Another friend may only need to know when you are going to pick them up and is not too concerned about the details of who, what, where, or when. These two friends demonstrate how each person has a different level of uncertainty with which they are comfortable. "The highest amount of uncertainty we can have and think we can predict strangers' behavior sufficiently to feel comfortable interacting with them" is known as our **maximum threshold for uncertainty** (Gudykunst, 2005, p. 286). At the other end of the continuum, our **minimum threshold for uncertainty** is the "lowest amount of uncertainty we can have and not feel bored or overconfident about our predictions of strangers' behavior" (p. 286). If uncertainty levels exceed our maximum or minimum threshold levels, then we lose our ability to communicate effectively. However, if we remain within our maximum and minimum thresholds for uncertainty, we are within our **general level of uncertainty acceptance**, and thus, we have our greatest predictability about another person's behavior.

Anxiety, similar to uncertainty, is believed to be experienced when we encounter new intercultural situations. According to AUM, anxiety is the "affective equivalent of uncertainty" (Gudykunst, 2005, p. 287). In other words, uncertainty is more reflective of our cognitions, whereas anxiety reflects our emotional reaction to experiencing uncertainty. This can take the form of feeling uneasy, tense, worried, or apprehensive about communicative outcomes. The **maximum threshold for anxiety** is the highest amount of anxiety we can have and still feel comfortable interacting with strangers. If we exceed this maximum threshold, people tend to display communication avoidance behavior. Our lowest amount of anxiety that we can have and still feel comfortable interacting with strangers is our **minimum threshold for anxiety**. Should we fall below our minimum threshold for anxiety, we generally become lazy or blasé about communicating with other people. If our level of anxiety falls within our **general level of anxiety acceptance**, we can use this anxiety to our advantage as a motivating factor that "keeps us on our toes" and can result in a very competent interaction.

AUM theory is based on effective communication, which is a process of exchanging messages and creating meaning (Barnlund, 1962). **Effective communication** reflects the degree to which the other person assigns or attaches a similar meaning to the meanings that were intended by the sender. When communication is ineffective, communication can be misinterpreted. Some misinterpretations can be readily identified, but many misinterpretations may never be recognized. Misinterpretation is assumed to be a symptom of not being mindful of the messages we are creating and sending, as well as not ensuring that those messages are received in the ways in which we intended. The term "not being mindful when communicating" reflects a tendency for people, both the sender and receiver, to interpret messages based on their own frame of reference, not the frame of reference of the other person. The way to reduce these misinterpretations is to become aware of our own frame of reference as well as the frame of reference of the receiver(s). This process of awareness is known as **mindfulness**. Where mindlessness reflects an automatic process involving attention, intention, and control (Bargh, 1989), mindfulness assumes that there is a "(1) creation of new categories; (2) openness to new information; and (3) awareness of more than one perspective" (Langer, 1989, p. 62). Mindlessness assumes that people share our interpretive schema, whereas mindfulness assumes that different people interpret information differently than we do, and we need to account for these differences when communicating.

The basic idea of this theory is that to be effective in intercultural communication we must experience levels of uncertainty and anxiety that fall between our minimum and maximum thresholds for uncertainty and anxiety. Also, we must be mindful of the perspectives and customs of strangers and their cultures. The theory posits 47 axioms which deal with these ideas, resulting in a

maximum threshold for anxiety A maximum level of anxiety that when not exceeded, allows people to remain comfortable when interacting with other people.

minimum threshold for anxiety The minimum level of anxiety that when not exceeded, allows people to remain comfortable when interacting with other people.

general level of anxiety acceptance A level of anxiety that exists between a person's maximum and minimum thresholds for anxiety.

effective communication The degree to which the other person assigns or attaches a similar meaning to the meanings that were intended by the sender.

mindfulness A process of awareness where we become aware of our own frame of reference as well as the frame of reference of the receiver.

very complex conceptualization of intercultural communication. Figure 13.5 presents an overview of the theory and illustrates the factors involved in effective intercultural communication. It also reveals the difficulties of avoiding communication breakdowns when talking with people from other cultures.

FACE NEGOTIATION THEORY

face negotiation theory A theory that explains intercultural conflict and how people from different cultures work through the various cultural and communicative obstacles to get a resolution based on mutual respect and communication competence.

Face negotiation theory (FNT) was developed by Stella Ting-Toomey (1988). The theory attempts to explain intercultural conflict and how people from different cultures work through the various cultural and communicative obstacles to get to a resolution based on mutual respect and communication competence. Face negotiation theory is a conflict-based theory in that conflict situations pose a multidimensional threat to our self-identities as well as the self-identities of the other people with which we are engaged. Further, FNT accounts for the unique and idiosyncratic influences of culture on our communication behavior. For example, when we engage in conflict with another person, we are not only concerned about the issue surrounding the conflict but also about being treated with respect. When people do not treat us with the respect we deserve, we may feel unintelligent, gullible, guilty, or angry. All these feelings are representative of our reaction to perceived attacks on our self-identity. These feelings are further complicated by personal characteristics such as self-esteem, social role, and socioeconomic status.

face   Our self-image and the image we want others in society to have of us.

One of the fundamental concepts of FNT is **face** and how face is enacted and protected (i.e., **facework**). Face can be defined as our self-image and the image we want others in society to have of us. Facework reflects the "specific verbal and nonverbal behaviors that we engage in to maintain or restore face loss and to uphold and honor face gain" (Ting-Toomey, 2005, p. 73). That is, face is our self-identity, whereas facework is the communication behaviors we engage in to protect any threats to that identity (also known as **face threats**). For example, a person who believes that they are intelligent and humorous will engage in verbal and nonverbal behaviors in an attempt to present that image to other people. As you can probably conclude, culture plays a central role in the formation of identities as well as the behaviors we enact to protect any threats to our face. **Face loss** occurs when people treat us in ways that are inconsistent with our self-image. **Face gain** occurs when people treat us in ways that enhance our existing self-image.

facework   Specific verbal and nonverbal behaviors that we engage in to maintain or restore face loss and to uphold and honor face.

face threats   Any threats to our self-image or face.

face loss   Reflects when people treat us in ways that are inconsistent with our self-image.

face gain   Reflects when people treat us in ways that enhances our existing self-image.

Face is considered an important concept in communication because it can be threatened or enhanced in every interaction that we have with others. The gain or loss of face has both affective (emotional) and cognitive effects. For example, consider a situation in which you have a professional relationship with another person that is based on mutual respect and equal power. One day

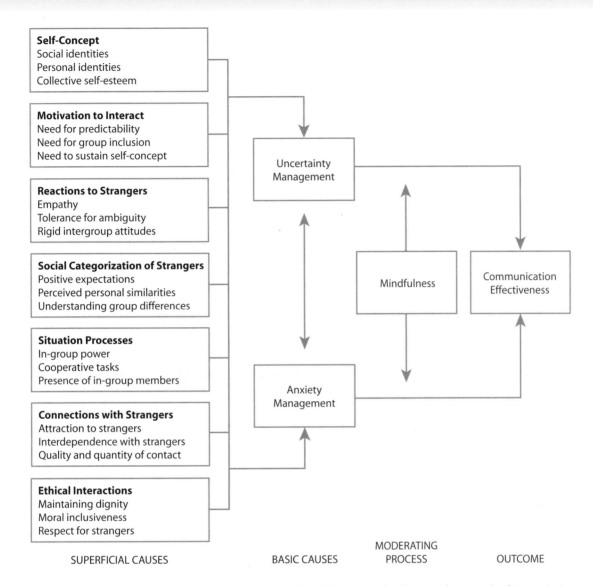

SUPERFICIAL CAUSES   BASIC CAUSES   MODERATING PROCESS   OUTCOME

Used with permission of Sage Publications, Inc., from Theorizing About Intercultural Communication *by W. B. Gudykunst, 2005; permission conveyed through Copyright Clearance Center, Inc.*

Figure 13.5

Anxiety/uncertainty management theory.

self-face The degree to which we are concerned with our own face needs during a conflict episode.

other-face The degree to which we are concerned with the face of the other party in a conflict episode.

mutual face protection moves Reflects when we have high concern for self-face and high concern for other-face movements.

mutual face obliteration moves Reflects when we have a low concern for self-face and low concern for other-face movements.

self-face defensive moves Reflects when we have high concern for self-face and low concern for other-face movements.

other-face upgrading moves Reflects when we have low concern for self-face and high concern for other-face movements.

dominating facework Facework strategy where conflict is seen as a competition where the most important goal is to win the conflict and maximize reward.

avoiding facework Facework strategy where during conflict, the focus is on maintaining interpersonal harmony between the parties by not overtly addressing the conflict .

integrating facework Facework strategy where during conflict, the focus is on the resolution of conflict issues as well as making sure the relationship remains positive and both parties maintain face.

this person begins to condescend to you (a face threat). This threat will affect you both emotionally (e.g., "How dare this person treat me like a child!") as well as your thought process (e.g., "Perhaps he knows more than I do about the subject") regarding the relationship. Given that FNT is an interpersonal conflict theory based on people from different cultures, the basic face elements involved are self-face versus other-face. Self-face concerns the degree to which we are concerned with our own face needs during a conflict episode. Other-face concerns the degree to which we are concerned with the face of the other party involved in the conflict situation.

Ting-Toomey (2005) presented a variety of different face moves that people may utilize when deciding whether to maintain, defend, and/or enhance self-face when engaged in a conflict situation. These are mutual face protection moves (i.e., high concern for self-face and high concern for other-face movements), mutual face obliteration moves (i.e., low concern for self-face and low concern for other-face movements), self-face defensive moves (i.e., high concern for self-face and low concern for other face movements), and other-face upgrading moves (i.e., low concern for self-face and high concern for other-face movements). Our choice of face moves is but one facet of FNT. Different types of facework strategies can be employed regardless of the face move a person chooses to employ. The first type of facework strategy assumes the conflict is a competition, and the most important goal is to win the conflict and maximize reward (i.e., dominating facework). Avoiding facework focuses on maintaining interpersonal harmony between the parties by not overtly addressing the conflict. Integrating facework focuses on the resolution of conflict issues as well as making sure the relationship remains positive and both parties maintain face. Given these different facework strategies, facework can be used to "(a) defuse a conflict via avoidance and compromise tactics, (b) aggravate a conflict via direct and passive-aggressive tactics, (c) repair damaged images via excuses and justifications, and (d) mend broken relationships via apologies and third-party help" (Ting-Toomey, 2005, p. 78).

Model of Face Negotiation

The model of face negotiation represents how culture influences our sense of self and our self-image, the type of facework we engage in, and the resulting face strategies that we use when involved in a conflict situation. Figure 13.6 shows how our culture plays a central role in our perceptions and communication when engaged in conflict situations. Each of the components of the model is described next.

Cultural Factors

As indicated in the model, our communication behavior is guided by the traditions and values that have been instilled within us from birth. Because culture is a central component of FNT, it is important to understand how the theory

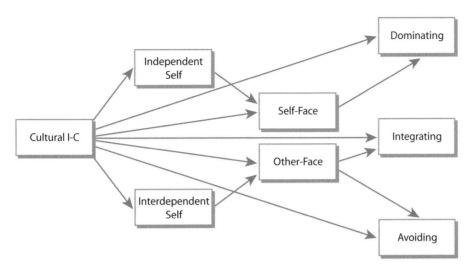

Figure 13.6

Model of face negotiation.

conceptualizes culture. Culture can be defined as "a learned system of meanings that fosters a particular sense of shared identity and community among its group members. It is a complex frame of reference that consists of patterns of traditions, beliefs, values, norms, symbols, and meanings that are shared by varying degrees by interacting" (Ting-Toomey, 2005, pp. 71–72). As this definition indicates, the culture in which a person is a part shapes their conceptions not only in terms of their self-identity, but also the identity of the people from other cultures. Further, culture has a unique influence on how we communicate and on our expectations about how people from other cultures communicate. The first basic cultural distinction is between **individualistic cultures** and **collectivist cultures**. People from individualistic cultures (e.g., United States) tend to emphasize the importance of the individual interest over the group interest and focus on their own feelings as opposed to the collective feelings of the group. People from collectivist cultures (e.g., Japan) tend to emphasize the importance of the group and group goals over the individual and group goals over the individual and individual goals. Other cultural factors include **power distance**, which reflects the way a culture treats status differences and social hierarchy. Cultures with **low power distance** value the equal distribution of power, equal power relationships, and equal reward (e.g., Sweden). **High power distance** cultures value unequal power, unequal relationships, and unequal rewards that are based on status, role, gender, age, and so on (e.g., China). These cultural dimensions are believed to have great influence on the way people perceive face and engage in facework. These cultural factors are represented in propositions 1 to 12 of FNT and are displayed in Table 13.1

individualistic cultures
Culture that emphasizes the importance of the individual's interest over the group interest and focus on their own feelings.

collectivist cultures
Cultures that emphasize the importance of the group and group goals over the individual and individual goals.

power distance A characteristic of culture that concerns how a culture treats status differences and social hierarchy.

low power distance A culture that values the equal distribution of power, equal power relationships, and equal reward (e.g., Sweden).

high power distance A culture that values unequal power, unequal relationships, and unequal rewards that are based on status, role, gender, age, etc. (e.g., China).

Table 13.1	**CULTURAL FACTOR PROPOSITIONS OF FNT**
PROPOSITION 1:	Members of individualistic cultures tend to express a greater degree of self-face maintenance concerns than members of collectivist cultures.
PROPOSITION 2:	Members of collectivistic cultures tend to express a greater degree of other-face concerns than members of individualistic cultures.
PROPOSITION 3:	Members of collectivistic cultures tend to express a greater degree of mutual-face maintenance concerns than members of individualistic cultures.
PROPOSITION 4:	Members of individualistic cultures tend to use a greater degree of direct, dominating facework strategies in a conflict situation than members of collectivistic cultures.
PROPOSITION 5:	Members of collectivistic cultures tend to use a greater degree of avoidance facework strategies than members of individualistic cultures.
PROPOSITION 6:	Members of collectivistic cultures tend to use a degree of integrative facework strategies than members of individualistic cultures.
PROPOSITION 7:	Members of individualistic cultures tend to use more dominating/competing conflict styles than members of collectivistic cultures.
PROPOSITION 8:	Members of individualistic cultures tend to use more emotionally expressive conflict styles than members of collectivistic cultures.
PROPOSITION 9:	Members of individualistic cultures tend to use more assertive to aggressive conflict styles than members of collectivistic cultures.
PROPOSITION 10:	Members of collectivistic cultures tend to use more avoiding conflict styles than members of individualistic cultures.
PROPOSITION 11:	Members of collectivistic cultures tend to use more obliging conflict styles than members of individualistic cultures.
PROPOSITION 12:	Members of collectivistic cultures tend to use more compromising to integrating conflict styles than members of individualistic cultures.

Used with permission of Sage Publications, Inc., from Theorizing About Intercultural Communication *by W. B. Gudykunst, 2005; permission conveyed through Copyright Clearance Center, Inc.*

self-construal A person's self-image that is comprised of both independent and interdependent self.

independent self-construal A person's self-image that assumes we are unique with our own repertoire of feelings, cognitions, and motivations that are separate from other people.

Individual Factors

The individual factors explained by FNT include a person's self-image. **Self-construal** is a person's self-image that is composed of both independent and interdependent self (Markus & Kitayama, 1991, 1998). The **independent self-construal** is a self-image that we are unique with our own repertoire of feelings, cognitions, and motivations that are separate from other people. The **interdependent self-construal** is a self-image reflecting that our identity is tightly linked to the relationships we have with other people of our culture. For example, independent self-construals are more common in individualistic cultures such as the United States, where people from collectivist cultures such as Japan have a greater tendency to display interdependent self-construals. For example, in the United States, we generally strive to become "something" when we grow up, such as "president," "CEO," "doctor," or "lawyer," which are pursuits that are more individual in nature. In collectivist cultures, people tend to become "something" through pursuing vocations and careers that are mandated by the needs of society as a whole, not individual pursuits of money, fame, or prestige. These two types of self-construals are not independent of one another. In fact, they exist at varying levels within each person. Different combinations of self-construals consist of biconstrual orientation (i.e., person high on both independent and interdependent self-construals), independent orientation (i.e., person high on independent and low on interdependent self-construals), interdependent orientation (i.e., person low on independent and high on interdependent self-construals), and the ambivalent orientation (i.e., person low on independent and interdependent self-construals). These individual orientations directly affect how people use facework strategies when in a conflict situation and are articulated in propositions 13 to 22 of FNT presented in Table 13.2.

Relational/Situational Factors

Many factors in any given situation or relationship can influence how people employ different types of facework strategies. Relational factors can include length of relationship, intimacy, and familiarity with the other party in the conflict. Situational factors can include importance of the conflict, intensity, and whether or not the conflict is in a public or private setting. When people form relationships, they tend to make a general distinction between relationships in which they share a great deal of background and similarity with the other person and those with whom they do not share as much connection. When we share a great deal of important characteristics with other people, they are considered part of our in-group, whereas when we feel relatively unconnected to other people, they are considered part of the out-group. Research has indicated that people from collectivist cultures tend to make a greater distinction from in-group relationships versus out-group relationships than people from individualistic cultures (Triandis, 1995). The relational/situational factors are articulated in propositions 23 and 24 of FNT presented in Table 13.3.

Conflict Styles

The way in which people engage in conflict is a direct derivative of our assumptions about right and wrong, perceptions of equity and fairness, as well as a host of other idiosyncratic differences that each person possesses. In other

interdependent self-construal A person's self-image that assumes our identity is tightly linked to the relationships we have with other people in our culture.

biconstrual orientation An orientation that is based on high independent and high interdependent self-construals.

independent orientation An orientation that is based on high independent and low interdependent self-construal.

ambivalent orientation An orientation that is based on low independent and low interdependent self-construal.

out-group When we feel relatively unconnected to other people or group.

Table 13.2   **INDIVIDUAL FACTOR PROPOSITIONS OF FNT**

PROPOSITION 13:	Independent self is associated positively with self-face concern.
PROPOSITION 14:	Interdependent self is associated with other and is associated positively with other-face/mutual-face concern.
PROPOSITION 15:	Self-face maintenance is associated with dominating/competing conflict style.
PROPOSITION 16:	Other-face maintenance is associated positively with avoiding/obliging conflict style.
PROPOSITION 17:	Other-face maintenance is associated positively with compromising/integrating conflict style.
PROPOSITION 18:	Independent self-construal type is associated positively with dominating/competing conflict style.
PROPOSITION 19:	Interdependent self-construal type is associated positively with obliging/avoiding conflict style.
PROPOSITION 20:	Interdependent self-construal type is associated positively with compromising/integrating conflict style.
PROPOSITION 21:	Biconstrual type is associated positively with compromising/integrating conflict style.
PROPOSITION 22:	Ambivalent type is associated positively with neglect/third-party conflict style.

Used with permission of Sage Publications, Inc., from Theorizing About Intercultural Communication *by W. B. Gudykunst, 2005; permission conveyed through Copyright Clearance Center, Inc.*

Table 13.3   **SITUATIONAL/RELATIONAL FACTOR PROPOSITIONS OF FNT**

PROPOSITION 23:	Individualists or independent self-personalities tend to express a greater degree of self-face maintenance concerns in dealing with both in-group and out-group conflict situations.
PROPOSITION 24:	Collectivists or interdependent self-personalities tend to express a greater degree of other-face concerns with in-group members and a greater degree of self-face maintenance concerns with out-group members in intergroup conflict situations.

words, our cultural upbringing, which is responsible for the formation of all these expectations, are central influences on how we behave in conflict situations. Within the theoretical framework of FNT, the way people engage in conflict behavior is considered an outcome or result of the way we interpret conflict. As Figure 13.6 illustrates, conflict styles are located at the far right side of the model, which indicates that they are to be considered the result of cultural influence (e.g., individualistic vs. collectivistic), our self-identity (e.g., independent self vs. interdependent self), and face concerns during conflict (e.g., self-face vs. other-face). Researchers have identified several different conflict styles that people may take when engaging in conflict communication (see, for example, Blake & Mouton, 1964; Putnam & Wilson, 1982).

The first conflict style is that of the dominating style (a.k.a. competitive style), where the most important thing is to achieve personal goals without regard to the interests of the other party. Avoiding style reflects eluding any discussion of the conflict with the other party. This may even take the form of avoiding the person or situation involved in the conflict. The obliging style (a.k.a. accommodating style) reflects great concern for the other party's position and interests above and beyond our own interests and goals. The compromising style is the give-and-take style that seeks a midpoint where both parties concede some of their interests in an effort to reach an equitable settlement. The final conflict style is the integrating style (a.k.a. collaborating style), which reflects a need for conflict resolution with a high degree of concern for the individual interests of all parties involved.

Given the preceding discussion of cultural, individual, and relational/situations influences accounted for by face negotiation theory, the twenty-four propositions of FNT represent the most up-to-date conceptualization of the theory. As we discussed in Chapter 2, it is expected that FNT will be extended to include more factors that influence how people engage in conflict resulting in more theoretical propositions (Ting-Toomey, 2005; Ting-Toomey & Kurogi, 1998).

The concept of face and facework, since introduced by Erving Goffman (1959), has contributed a great deal of insight and understanding to human communication. Face negotiating theory is the most advanced conceptualization of face and facework. This is evidenced in the popularity of FNT in contemporary intercultural and communication theory texts and research programs. Given the evidence supporting the propositions and utility of FNT in explaining how cultural influences determine our conflict behavior, this theory will continue to provide intercultural communication researchers a valuable tool for understanding conflict.

Cross-Cultural Adaptation Theory

Young Kim (1988) developed Cross-cultural adaptation theory to explain the process of how people adjust to a new environment. In this theory, environment refers to any cultural experience that is different from that person's home experience (i.e., the culture within which the person was raised). Previous attempts to explain the intersection of person and culture have focused on how the new culture influences the person and that person's behavior. In other words, this process has been traditionally viewed as linear in nature, with the

dominating style   A conflict style where the most important thing is to achieve personal goals without regard to the interests of the other party.

avoiding style   A conflict style where we elude to any discussion of the conflict issues with the other party. This may even take the form of avoiding the person or situation involved in the conflict.

obliging style   A conflict style where there is great concern for the other party's position and interests above and beyond our own interests and goals.

compromising style   A conflict style where we seek a midpoint where both parties concede some of their interests in an effort to reach an equitable settlement.

integrating style   A conflict style where there is a need for conflict resolution with a high degree of concern for the individual interests of all parties involved.

cross-cultural adaptation theory   An intercultural theory that explains the process of how people adjust to a new environment.

culture exerting influence on the person who is considered passive in the process. Cross-cultural adaptation theory (CCAT) seeks to account for both the influence of the new cultural as well as the influence of the person's previous cultural experience. For example, consider the culture of the university you are presently attending. This university has a culture that students, to one degree or another, identify with. If we were only to consider how the university influences the student and the student's adaptation without accounting for the student's prior culture (e.g., educational experiences before they came to college or other college experiences) and ways of doing things (i.e., cultural practices), this would be an incomplete explanation of the adaptation process.

CCAT was designed to account for the following voids in present intercultural theories. First, it accounts for both macrolevel (cultural patterns) and microlevel factors (a person's background and personality) when explaining the adaptation process. Second, Kim's (1988) theory accounts for both a person's long-term and short-term adaptation, as they are both important in explaining the adaptation process. Third, any adaptation must be explained in the context of the new learning that a person experiences when encountering a new culture. Explaining adaptation within the new learning context, we are provided with a complete explanation of what people psychologically experience when adapting to a new culture. Fourth, given that many factors are involved in the cross-cultural adaptation process, many of these factors need to be distilled into a few all-encompassing factors to make explaining and describing the adaptation process possible. Finally, CCAT seeks to recognize and merge the mutual influence of the new culture on the person and the influence of individual factors in the adaptation process.

CCAT is organized under a set of principles that frame the theory to reflect both universal assumptions about human behavior as well as culture-specific influences. First, adaptation is a universal phenomenon. Adaptation is believed to be a natural instinct that is experienced by all human beings when adapting to another culture. Thus, cross-cultural adaptation is considered "a common process of environmental adaptation" (Anderson, 1994, p. 293). Therefore, adaptation can be defined as "a basic human tendency that accompanies the internal struggle of individuals to regain control over their life changes in the face of environmental challenges" (Kim, 2005, p. 378).

Second, adaptation is an evolutionary process. A person is believed to experience this process whenever attempting to make sense of a new environment. The evolution process takes the form of changes occurring within the person based on influences from both the environment and the individual, as well as the interplay between the two. For example, consider meeting a dating partner's parents for the first time. Once we encounter the parents, our adaptation to the "new experience" changes our behavior, and our behavioral change alters the way we think about ourselves. Third, adaptation is a communication-based phenomenon. Given that adaptation is based on information from the new environment, the vehicle through which information travels is that of verbal and nonverbal communication. As such, adaptation is truly a communication process. This information is transmitted as long as the person and the environment continue to interact. Once a person is no longer interacting with the new environment, new information ceases to be exchanged. In our dating example, as long as we are in the new environment of our dating partner's parents, we will be constantly receiving and sending verbal and nonverbal messages that will affect the adaptation process. Fourth, CCAT is not concerned as much with prediction as it is with the description and explanation of how people adapt to new environments. The theory does not address the issue of *if* people adapt, as it is assumed that all people adapt to one degree or another. Rather, the theory seeks to address the *how* and *why* of adaptation.

One of the unique features of CCAT is that it utilizes both deductive and inductive theory-building approaches. Recall from Chapter 2 that deductive theory building consists of moving from general observations to more specific observations, whereas inductive theory building involves moving from specific observations to more general observations. This is achieved through the assumptions that all people experience the adaptation process (deductive approach), yet we must also account for a person's "lived story" to fully explain intercultural adaptation (inductive approach). That is, this theory accounts for general human tendencies while also accounting for the specific experiences of the person.

The term *cross-cultural adaptation* is an umbrella term that consists of several smaller processes that a person experiences when encountering a new environment. The entire CCAT process includes the subprocesses of assimilation (i.e., the degree to which a person accepts the influence of the new culture or environment), acculturation (i.e., the degree to which a person acquires the beliefs and practices of the new culture or environment), coping/adjustment (i.e., the response of the individual to encountering new or changing cultures or environments), and integration (i.e., the degree to which the person participates in the new culture or environment). All these subprocesses are involved under the larger process of cross-cultural adaptation.

The factors related to adaptation are represented in Figure 13.7. As indicated, the term enculturation is regarded as a type of cultural adaptation as this reflects our home culture. More specifically, in our home culture, "we learn to speak, listen, read, interpret, and understand verbal and nonverbal messages in such a fashion that the messages will be recognized and responded to by the individuals with whom we interact" (Kim, 2005, p. 382). Enculturation is not considered cross-cultural because it is our primary way of adjusting to the world. All new experiences are compared and contrasted with our home culture.

assimilation The degree to which a person accepts the influence of the new culture or environment.

acculturation The degree to which a person acquires the beliefs and practices of the new culture or environment.

coping/adjustment The response of the individual to encountering new or changing cultures or environments.

integration The degree to which the person participates in the new culture.

enculturation A type of cultural adaptation reflecting when we learn to speak, listen, read, interpret, and understand verbal and nonverbal messages in such a fashion that the messages will be recognized and responded to by the individuals with whom we communicate.

deculturation   The degree
to which a person unlearns
the beliefs and practices of
a culture or environment.

acculturation   The activity
of learning a new cultural
system.

Deculturation and acculturation processes are considered part of cross-cultural adaptation because they both involve the new learning that occurs when the person and the new culture interact. Acculturation is the activity of learning a new cultural system (Shibutani & Kwan, 1965). On the other hand, deculturation is the activity of unlearning some old cultural elements. For example, take a person who is born and raised in on the East Coast of the United States (e.g., New York or Boston). Given the practices of the home culture, this person comes to learn ways of behaving from that urban environment that may include being confrontational, direct, and to the point when communicating; use a great deal of sarcasm in humor production; and being opinionated, aggressive, and sometimes overtly disagreeable. This person learned these behaviors as a result of the enculturation process from his/her home culture. If this person should relocate to Iowa and have a desire to become an accepted member in the Midwest culture, he/she may have to learn new or different ways of behaving in that new culture (i.e., acculturation), which may consist of being less confrontational, less direct, use more subtlety when making a point, and reducing the level of sarcasm in humor production so as not to seen so "abrasive" or "aggressive." To learn these new ways of behaving, the person must simultaneously unlearn their old ways of behaving. Thus, to one degree or another, our East Coast person will take on Midwestern cultural characteristics and, thus, become more "Midwestern" and "less East Coast."

As indicated in Figure 13.7, the ultimate goal of cross-cultural adaptation is assimilation, which is the "maximum possible convergence of strangers' internal and external conditions to those of the native" (Kim, 2005, p. 383). In our earlier example, this would be reflected in the East Coast person having taken on all the cultural values and practices of Midwesterners (external conditions), as well as share the thoughts and feelings of Midwesterners (internal conditions). It is important that we not consider cross-cultural adaptation as something that is either achieved or not achieved. Instead, consider adaptation as a degree to which some people experience, or are willing to experience, a cross-cultural adaptation that is more reflective of the new culture than others experience. Assimilation, in this case, should not be considered an attainable end result of cross-cultural adaptation as much as an ideal toward which people move via the cross-cultural adaptation process. Some people may realize assimilation during a lifetime of adapting, but more often than not, assimilation is a product of generations of cultural adaptation (Kim, 2001).

Cross-cultural adaptation theory provides a holistic approach to cultural adaptation in that influences of both the culture and the individual are taken into the consideration. Further, CCAT makes explicit that it's designed to explain and describe the adaptation process, not predict how a person will adapt when faced with a new culture or experience. As such, this theory is of great utility for researchers interested in understanding the dynamic process of newcomer–new experience interaction and how these processes unfold.

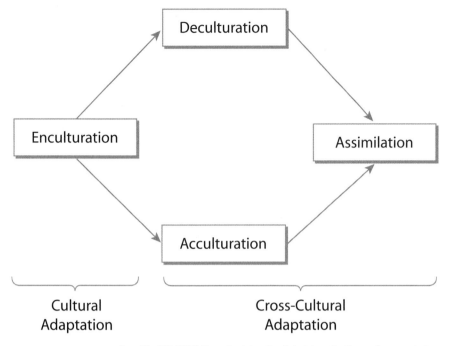

From Kim, Y. Y. (2001). Becoming intercultural: An integrative theory of communication and cross-cultural adaption *(p. 53). Thousand Oaks, CA: Sage.*

Figure 13.7

Relationship among cross-cultural adaptation concepts.

POLITICAL COMMUNICATION

Rhetorical scholars trace the study of political rhetoric to its roots in ancient Greece and Rome. Rhetorical theorists such as Plato, Aristotle, Cicero, and Quintilian taught principles that improved effective speaking and persuasive skills, which were often used to enhance political oratory. In the *Rhetoric,* the *Politics,* and the *Nicomachean Ethics,* Aristotle linked politics, persuasion, and communication. Although the roots of political communication can be found in antiquity, the political communication context began with behavioral science inquiries that emerged during the 1950s. The mid-1950s to the early 1970s saw an increase in the amount of research classified as "political communication," or "political campaign communication." Research and theory building in this context have increased exponentially since then. Several journals, including *Political Communication and Persuasion* and *Presidential Studies Quarterly,* now specialize in research pertaining to political communication.

Under the broad heading of political communication, a number of subspecialties have emerged: political advertising and propaganda, political symbolism, election campaigns, and political imagery and the media. Scholars in political communication have broadened the scope of their research to include the total communication environment of an election campaign (Johnson, 1990). Political communication thus encompasses a broad territory with many different definitions and conceptualizations.

Robert Denton and Gary Woodward (1998) define political communication as public discussion about the allocation of *public resources* (money), *official authority* (who decides), and *official sanctions* (what is to be rewarded or punished). They suggest that political communication may inspire, alienate, divide, counsel, or inform, depending on who uses it and for what purposes.

Symbolic Convergence Theory and Political Communication

Recall from Chapter 3 that convergence refers to the way people achieve a "meeting of the minds" by trying to unite their private symbols. Symbolic convergence occurs when individuals share group fantasies. Symbolic convergence theory and its methodology (fantasy theme analysis) have been used to explain several dimensions of political communication. Political communication theorists recognize that political rhetors must "tap into" (recognize and appeal to) the fantasies of several groups (for example, supporters, uncommitted voters, and/or the opposition) to help create a political message. Rather than limiting the study of political rhetoric to the delivery of public speeches, symbolic convergence theory stimulated the investigation of political fantasy links that "chain out" (become established, develop, and grow) in small groups.

The mass media offer fertile ground for both the identification and the development of fantasy themes. When key words, images, or phrases are reported and repeated in the media, that process helps identify and/or create certain political fantasy themes among the electorate. Some fantasies and rhetorical visions become *national* fantasies, such as the outpouring of patriotism after the September 11, 2001, terrorist assault. Suppliers could not keep up with the demand for the American flag.

Dan Nimmo and James Combs (1982) contended that different news media can offer different rhetorical visions of the same event. They cite, for example, the coverage of the Three Mile Island nuclear plant accident of 1979. For one network (CBS), a rhetorical vision of trustworthy experts, beneficial technology, and an orderly society emerged. Another network (NBC) offered the rhetorical vision of "life will continue," regardless of what the experts and the public do. The third network (ABC) offered a rhetorical "nightmare," in which a monster (radioactivity) was released into the atmosphere. The rhetorical vision included the sense that public lives were endangered because "rulers" and "technocrats" made it so.

Studies of political persuasion and voting behavior using fantasy theme analysis have established a link between campaign messages and audience effects (Bormann, Kroll, Watters, & McFarland, 1984). Using symbolic convergence theory, these studies attempt to identify shared fantasy themes and rhetorical visions among groups of voters. When similar figures of speech and analogies emerge in several political communication messages and in different contexts, evidence of symbolic convergence is said to occur. Political slogans often emerge from these shared fantasies. Bormann and his colleagues cite "voodoo economics"—a slogan that referred to the fantasy theme that (former) President Ronald Reagan's economic program was unrealistic. This slogan was adopted by the media and incorporated into the political communication jargon. It was used frequently by political candidates to demean an opponent's economic program. A central fantasy of the campaign of (former) President Jimmy Carter was the following: "The idea of Reagan sitting in the Oval Office by the nuclear button is scary, but Carter has proven to be calm and careful in a crisis" (pp. 293–294).

One study used symbolic convergence theory and fantasy theme analysis to investigate how Oliver North became a hero to many Americans. North was suspected of committing criminal activity during the Iran-Contra incident and testified before the congressional committee investigating military assistance to Iran and Nicaragua. The study suggests that some of North's appeal was the result of his unified rhetorical vision, which extended familiar cold war rhetoric (the United States vs. the Soviet Union) to include Middle Eastern terrorism. In addition, he used another rhetorical vision of the United States as the defender of the weak (the Contras) and the champion of democracy. The analysis suggests that North's persona as a "clean-cut all-American Marine," the "individualist who stood for his beliefs," and a type of modern "James Bond" were attractive to many Americans. These fantasies were created and "chained-out" among a number of Americans who even suggested that Oliver North run for president (Nelson, 1988). As Donald Shields (1981) suggested, fantasy themes "may depict heroes, villains, and supporting players, graphically describe their characteristics, assign motives to their actions, portray them doing certain things or manifesting certain behaviors, and place them in a given setting or scene" (p. 6). Using qualitative, quantitative, and rhetorical techniques plus assumptions from the rules perspective, symbolic convergence theory has helped bridge the gap between the humanistic and scientific approaches to the study of political communication.

Agenda-Setting Theory in Political Communication

Agenda setting (see Chapter 12) argues that intense media attention increases the importance of certain topics, issues, and individuals. Early applications of the theory to political communication dealt primarily with the influence of the mass media on political campaigns, but research has revealed that agenda setting extends to *candidate image* characteristics as well.

Two basic assumptions underlie most research on agenda setting: (a) the press and the media do not *reflect* reality; they filter and shape it; (b) media concentration on a few issues and subjects leads the public to perceive those issues as more important than other issues. For example, Weaver and his colleagues (1981) found a strong relationship between how much media coverage is given to candidates before the primaries and the familiarity of the voters with those candidates. This research reveals that "independent" voters, in particular, place a great deal of emphasis on information gleaned from the media and vote on the basis of that information. Indeed, information broadcast by the media was a better predictor of voting behavior than actual political party affiliation.

Shanto Iyengar and Donald Kinder (1985) tested three psychological explanations of agenda setting: affect, source credibility, and counterarguing. According to the affect hypothesis, television news is a powerful agenda setter because its vivid pictures and dramatic stories evoke strong emotions in viewers, especially in the area of political communication. When individuals feel fear, anger, sadness, or guilt, they may change their political judgments. An adjunct explanation of the affect hypothesis maintains that news coverage focused on a particular problem causes viewers to attribute more importance to that particular problem. The credibility hypothesis views television news as a powerful agenda setter because people perceive the news to be credible and authoritative. Viewers who perceive television news to be objective and accurate should thus be the most persuaded by its coverage. The counterarguing hypothesis projects that viewers who are critical consumers of television news stories about national issues (that is, they argue against what they see and hear on television news) are less likely to change their political views than individuals who do not engage in counterarguing.

These three hypotheses were subjected to experimental research to determine which offered the best explanation of the agenda-setting effects of televised news. Results indicated the strongest support for the source credibility hypothesis and only modest support for the counterarguing hypothesis. The study also suggested that television news is somewhat effective as an agenda setter because it evokes strong emotions in viewers (the affect hypothesis). The researchers argue that the *credibility* explanation works best because it separates those viewers who pay attention to television news from those who do not.

Agenda-setting theory has proved profitable in exploring the influence of the media on political issues, candidate images, and voter preferences. This line of research is moving beyond the influence of the media on elections and has begun to explore the influence of the media on the behavior of politicians themselves (Weaver, 1987). Agenda-setting theory seems quite appropriate to help us understand the pervasive role of the media on political communication systems.

affect hypothesis
Assumes that television news is a powerful agenda setter because its vivid pictures and dramatic stories evoke strong emotions in viewers, especially in the area of political communication.

credibility hypothesis
Assumes television news is a powerful agenda setter because people perceive the news to be credible and authoritative.

counterarguing hypothesis
Assumes that viewers who are critical consumers of television new stories about national issues (that is, they argue against what they see and hear on television news) are less likely to change their political views than individuals who do not engage in counterarguing.

A Constructivist View of Political Communication

Whereas early research on political communication grew largely out of the "effects model," research in this context has employed alternative methodological perspectives, including constructivism. In Chapter 9 we identified the major assumptions of constructivism—a human action approach to studying communication behavior that argues that reality is subjectively experienced. According to constructivism, an individual's view of the world is influenced by his or her personal constructs (categories used to interpret experiences). Constructivists approach voting behavior as action based on voters' beliefs about the political world. Beliefs emerge as a result of voters' interpretation of political messages.

Personal constructs influence perceptions of political candidates and political messages. A voter, for example, might use the constructs honest/ dishonest, Democrat/Republican, and liberal/conservative as the most important constructs from which to form impressions of a political candidate. Indeed, individuals develop *political construct subsystems* to judge political candidates and political messages.

David Swanson (1981) developed a framework of categories for a political construct subsystem to help us understand how individuals interpret political communication messages.

1. **Personal qualities** (friendliness, honesty, etc.)
2. **Personal background** (Southerner, religious upbringing, etc.)
3. **Political background** (former Senator, little experience in government, etc.)
4. **Political ideology** (conservative, Democrat, favors big government, etc.)
5. **Specific issue stands** (opposes national health care, advocates strong national defense, etc.)
6. **Campaign style** (enjoys talking to voters, fuzzy on the issues, etc.)
7. **Other** (personal constructs pertaining to political communication, which do not fit into any of the other categories)

Constructivists argue that this coding system represents a major enhancement over less-defined categories such as "issue" and "image" frequently used to assess candidates. Using the seven categories listed earlier, constructivists identify two subgroups on the basis of how they assess the viability and attractiveness of a candidate. *Political specialists* use constructs that are specifically *political* in content; they focus on categories three through six. In contrast, *political nonspecialists* concentrate on the first two categories, which relate to a candidate's *personal qualities*. Nonspecialists use the same constructs to judge political candidates as the ones they use to judge potential friends and acquaintances.

According to the constructivist perspective, political construct subsystems greatly influence orientations toward political campaigns. From the primary season to election day, newspapers, radio talk shows, television news, and Internet sites turn most of their attention to issues surrounding the campaign. Hundreds of political ads blanket the airwaves. For some, campaigns are annoying intrusions into daily lives; for others, the election season is an exciting "play." The campaign and its coverage provide "tickets" to the drama (Swanson, 1981). The two subgroups of voters thus operate with a highly salient political/nonpolitical interpretative category or construct.

Recall from Chapter 6 that the number of personal constructs individuals use to interpret the world is one measure of their *cognitive complexity*. People with highly differentiated construct systems and larger numbers of political constructs have been identified as *politically complex perceivers*. Individuals who are politically noncomplex perceivers rely on fewer and less differentiated political constructs to interpret candidates' messages and images (Swanson, 1981). This distinction is important in helping researchers understand political attitudes and voting behavior. Cognitively complex and cognitively noncomplex perceivers give very different information when asked to respond to standard political attitude scales. Politically noncomplex perceivers appear to be more strongly influenced by their general attitudes toward candidates or their general political party affiliation. Political complexity has been found to relate to such behaviors as registering to vote and the frequency with which individuals discuss political issues with colleagues.

The constructivist approach has generated a respectable amount of research on political communication. It has enhanced our knowledge about why people respond to candidates and their messages, form beliefs about them, and engage in political communication behaviors.

SUMMARY

Family communication is a context that has witnessed tremendous growth during the last decade. Several communication scholars argue that family communication is best understood by applying the tenets of the systems paradigm concentrating on the family "as a whole." The rules perspective argues that rules are developed or emerge within families and that these rules establish a family's identity. Fitzpatrick's typology of couple types is useful in classifying married couples and understanding marital conflict. The argumentative skill deficiency model of intrafamily violence suggests how marital conflict can escalate into patterns of verbal and physical aggression.

Communication has been associated with numerous health-related factors, including well-being, consumer satisfaction, client compliance, and confidence in a health-care provider. Application of theories from various communication contexts has increased knowledge about each of these factors. Relational communication models have been used to examine preferred control orientations; a number of verbal and nonverbal strategies have been advanced to enhance client compliance. The systems perspective offers insights into provider/consumer communication by focusing on the interaction at all levels in health organizations. The health belief model helps explain and predict whether individuals will act on suggestions to improve their health.

Anthropological studies sparked interest in intercultural communication. Changes in the fields of government, politics, communication, and business, to name only a few, have created a need for a deeper understanding of intercultural communication processes and skills. The field of communication has responded to these needs with a rapid growth of research and theory building in the area. We presented three applications of theory building to intercultural communication: anxiety/uncertainty management theory, face-negotiation theory, and cross-cultural adaptation theory.

Several theoretical approaches have been applied to the study of political communication. Symbolic convergence theory has been used to explain several dimensions of political communication, including how voters become actively involved in the process of political persuasion, how politicians invent and deliver messages, and the role of the media in political campaigns. Agenda-setting theory has been used to study candidate image characteristics and voter preference behavior. Finally, the constructivist perspective recognizes the importance of individual interpretation and evaluation of political messages.

KEY TERMS

acculturation
affect hypothesis
ambivalent orientation
anxiety
anxiety/uncertainty management theory (AUM)
assimilation
assumption maxims
avoiding facework
avoiding style
biconstrual orientation
boundary coordination
boundary ownership
boundary ownership rights
boundary permeability
boundary requirements
candidate image
collectivist cultures
commitment and intimacy
communication privacy management theory (CPM)
compromising style
cooperation
coping/adjustment
counsel
counterarguing hypothesis
credibility hypothesis
cross-cultural adaptation theory
cues to action
deculturation
development of self-concept
diagnosis
dialectical tensions
dominance
dominating facework
dominating style

ecological fallacy
education
effective communication
enculturation
external locus of control
face
face gain
face loss
face negotiation theory (FNT)
face-threats
facework
general level of anxiety acceptance
general level of uncertainty acceptance
high power distance
immediacy behaviors
independents
independent orientation
independent self-construal
individualistic cultures
in-group
interaction complexity
interaction maxims
interactional model
internal locus of control
interdependent orientation
interdependent self-construal
integrating facework
integrating style
integration
locus of control
longevity of influence
low power distance
maximum threshold for anxiety
maximum threshold for uncertainty

mindfulness
minimum threshold for anxiety
minimum threshold for uncertainty
mutual face obliteration moves
mutual face protection moves
nonimmediacy behaviors
nonvolition
obliging style
other-face
other-face upgrading moves
out-group
perceived barriers to taking action
perceived benefits of taking action
perceived seriousness or severity
perceived susceptibility
political construct subsystems
politically complex perceivers
power
power distance
privacy rules
redundancy
regulation of boundary linkages
self-construal
self-face
self-face defensive moves
separates
shared boundaries
strangers
structural model
traditional
uncertainty
uncertainty management theory (UMT)

Communication Research Methods

A

W e would now like to introduce you to the methods used in communication research. It is important to understand how scholars conduct research to obtain knowledge about communication. Although we have already explored a good deal of information about human communication, we believe it will be more meaningful if you have a sense of how that information was discovered. We cannot present all possible methods of research, but we would like to highlight the framework behind many of the theories we have discussed. Thus, this appendix will describe in some detail what is involved in doing behavioral science research.

Many methods are used to investigate the nature and origin of knowledge. In fact, one of the major areas of study in philosophy—epistemology—is devoted solely to that purpose. Almost all the knowledge in this book was learned through the practice of behavioral science. The exclusion of other methods of studying communication in no way reflects the superiority of one way of knowing over another. We have attempted to provide a solid foundation for one method of investigation, the behavioral science approach.

The underlying foundation of this line of research is that behavioral science research in communication involves controlled observation of humans to understand their communicative behavior. The two key words in this definition are *controlled* and *observation*. Control is achieved by design. That is, procedures are followed so that a social scientist's confidence in what is observed about humans approaches the confidence that physical scientists have in fields such as biology. Thus, research design is a major type of method that we will examine. The second key word, observation, pertains to what is of interest and how it is observed. Specifically, the concern is with measurement. Numerous ways of measuring various aspects of communication will be surveyed.

THE SCIENTIFIC METHOD

Before examining research design and measurement, we will discuss some basic ideas about scientific research. Let us consider a research problem to illustrate the ideas. Imagine you are interested in the impact music videos have on television viewers. At this point you do not know exactly what effects to look for or what aspects of music videos are the most important. Raymond Cattell's (1966) outline of the scientific method offers guidelines for how your thinking on this problem could develop:

> **Induction** leads to **hypothesis**,
> **which leads to** deduction
> and finally to **experimentation**.
> Then, experiments lead to **new induction**.

The induction phase involves understanding the research problem. In our example, you could watch a number of videos and/or think, read, or talk about them. Suppose you decide that your primary interest is to determine whether music videos have an impact on how the audience likes the song. Your thinking is that a music video provides the viewer with a fantasy and that fantasy, will have a favorable effect on how the song is evaluated. When you begin speculating like this, you are entering the second phase—hypothesis.

In the hypothesis phase, you make a prediction based on your thinking. Thus, you might hypothesize that a person's fantasy ability will influence (mediate) the effects of music videos. Specifically, when viewers are low in fantasy ability, music videos will make songs more likeable, but videos will have no effect when viewers are high in fantasy ability because they do not need others to provide fantasies for them.

When you specify the outcomes that should occur if your thinking is correct, you are in the third phase—deduction. In our example your deduction is, "How much a song is liked, in terms of ratings on a scale, will be affected positively by music videos only when people are low in fantasy ability."

Experiment is the fourth phase; an experimental design begins to emerge when the deduction phase is complete. The experiment must provide a test of the hypothesis. What design would allow us to see whether the deduced effects will occur? The design is straightforward. Select a group of viewers. Determine whether they are high or low in fantasy ability. Have half of the high fantasizers

	Music Video	*Audio Only*
High Fantasy Ability		
Low Fantasy Ability		

Figure A.1

A research design.

and half of the low fantasizers view a music video and then rate the song on a set of attitude scales. Have the other research participants (again, divided into high and low fantasizers) listen to the song (no video) and then rate the song. This design can be depicted as a 2 × 2 design (two levels of fantasy ability [high and low] by two types of music stimuli [music video and audio only]). This design is represented in Figure A.1.

Let us suppose you conducted this study. Would that be the end of it? According to the model, no. Even if you pursued this area no further, the investigative process has the potential to continue. What this means is that the set of results from your experiment is now added to the set of particulars that inspired your original hypothesis. This combination of new and old information creates a new configuration that has the potential for stimulating new hypotheses to be tested. The process continues on and on (it is recursive). We never learn everything about an area of research.

Suppose we extend our example. If your hypothesis was supported, you might reflect on the results (the inductive phase). Perhaps it is not fantasy ability so much as another trait (the need for stimulation, for example) that best explains the effect of music videos. Or you may decide that the impact of music videos on how much people like the song may not be as important as how music videos influence political and social attitudes. Are the women in music videos treated as "sex objects" so that music videos influence viewers to have sexist attitudes toward women? These are just two examples of new inductions with numerous implications for hypotheses, deductions, and experiments. Even if your original hypothesis was not supported, the feedback would be sufficient to energize the induction process. For instance, you might decide your hypothesis did not receive a good test because your measure of fantasy ability might have measured IQ rather than the ability to fantasize. Thus, a new study with a different measure of fantasy ability would be in order. If the process is recursive, then theories should not be accepted as fact. There is always the possibility that a new theory will provide better explanations than the original theory and also explain events not addressed by the existing theory.

FUNDAMENTAL CONCEPTS

Several concepts are fundamental to research design and measurement and to understanding research.

Variable

The most obvious attribute of a variable is that it varies. Aside from that, the notion of a variable is not a simplistic concept in communication research. The words *concept, construct,* and *variable* are used interchangeably. They represent an abstraction or a way of referring to a class of things. For instance, fantasy ability refers to the ways in which people use their imagination. Whether one word or the other is used depends on the level of discourse. When discussing something at the theoretical level, scientists usually use *concept* or *construct,* as in "a person's fantasy ability is a construct, which is necessary to explain the effects of music videos." On the other hand, when discussing the level of measurement and analysis, scientists commonly use *variable,* as in "fantasy ability is a difficult variable to measure with a scale."

CONTINUOUS AND DICHOTOMOUS VARIABLES

dichotomous variable
Variable with two discrete values.

Some variables can have only two values. Whether someone has seen the video for a song on TV may be viewed as a **dichotomous variable**: there are only two values. You have or you have not seen the video. In communication research, the most common variable treated as a dichotomy is biological sex; you are either male or female. However, some variables are continuous in that there is a meaningful high and low value for the variable with increments between the extremes so that you could say a variable applies to a person to a certain degree. Fantasy ability is an example. We can conceive of what it is like to be very high or very low in the ability to fantasize; people can also be located at any one of numerous positions between the two extremes.

continuous variables
When there are meaningful degrees of a variable between the highest and lowest values.

Scientists may convert **continuous variables**—those with a range of values—into a dichotomy to make them more convenient to study and easier to observe through an experiment. They usually do this by splitting a group of scores at the middle score (the median). Thus, if we wanted to study how the fantasy ability of 200 students affected their liking of a song, we could (a) administer a measure of fantasy ability such as the Richness of Fantasy Scale (Hovland & Janis, 1959), which measures fantasy ability as a continuous variable, (b) find the median score for the group, then (c) classify all students who scored above the median as "highs" and all those who scored below the median as "lows." Although this procedure loses distinctions (for example, do people who are very high differ from those who are moderately high?), it does provide a way to address the basic issue of whether fantasy ability matters in judging songs.

independent variables
Variables that cause and/or predict dependent variables.

INDEPENDENT AND DEPENDENT VARIABLES

dependent variables
Presumed effect in cause-effect relationship with independent variables.

In experimental research, independent and dependent variables have a cause–effect relationship to each other. **Independent variables** (causes) are studied to determine their effects on **dependent variables** (results). Variables not of interest to the study (such as snacking while viewing the video, viewing alone, or viewing with friends) are kept constant. When variables are studied as independent variables, they are either manipulated or they are not. Manipulating a variable means the experimenter changes something to create at least two conditions for the variable: present and absent. The condition in which the variable is absent is called the control condition. The minimum conditions for manipulating exposure to music videos to determine effects on liking the song would be to have one group of participants watch and listen to a video and a second group listen only to the soundtrack. This second group would serve as a control group because they are exposed to the control condition; they do not see the music video, our independent variable. A more complex design could involve more degrees of exposure. An experiment with four conditions for the variable would have groups exposed to the video three times, two times, or once, plus exposure to the soundtrack only.

When variables are not manipulated, it is often because they cannot be manipulated feasibly or ethically. **Attribute variables** are characteristics of research participants; they are probably the most common nonmanipulated variables. Usual attribute variables in communication research pertain to: physical characteristics such as biological sex; demographic characteristics such as age; and personal characteristics such as communication apprehension. Instead of sending people to Denmark to undergo sex change operations or conditioning them to have stage fright habitually when they previously had none, researchers select groups of people who reflect the attribute variable they wish to study. If we wish to contrast the levels of fantasy ability in males with those of females, we select a group of research participants that is evenly divided between men and women. For example, we might test our participants until we found two groups of 50 males and 50 females each. One male and female group would be high in fantasy ability and the other would be low in fantasy ability. However, when a variable is not manipulated, we lose confidence that it is the cause of effects in an experiment. If a variable is not under the direct control of the experimenter, there is always the possibility that it is not the true cause of the effect but is only related to the actual cause. For example, male–female biological differences may have no effect on fantasy ability but how children are raised in our society might. So, if we found that females who viewed the video rated the songs much more favorably than their high-fantasy-ability male counterparts, we could not be sure whether the difference was due to biological sex or to cultural influences.

Dependent variables are the effects in the cause–effect model. A variable is dependent if you are interested in explaining it in terms of other variables that influence it (independent variables). In our example, liking for the song in a music video is the dependent variable because liking is assumed to be affected by the images in a video and the fantasy ability of the viewer (the independent variables). The idea of measurement is very important when considering

attribute variables
Characteristics of research participants that are studied as independent variables.

dependent variables and nonmanipulated variables and will be covered in the final section of this appendix.

Definitions

constitutive definitions
Definition of a concept that
utilizes other concepts.

operational definitions
Definition of a concept in
terms of the operations
utilized in order to observe
the concept.

Two types of definitions provide crucial foundations for scientific research: **constitutive** and **operational definitions**. A constitutive definition defines a concept by using other concepts. Thus, liking for a song could be defined as "a learned predisposition to evaluate a song in a consistently favorable or unfavorable manner." We can divide the constitutive definition into several concepts: a learned predisposition, to evaluate, in a consistent . . . manner. Utilizing other concepts is an indication that the given concept can be made theoretically meaningful (Kerlinger, 1986, p. 28). Operational definitions define something in terms of the operations or procedures that were followed to experience the object of definition. This is very important in terms of *replication* in scientific research. That is, one scientist, working independently, should be able to duplicate the results of another researcher. Operational definitions provide a mechanism for this.

There are two types of operational definitions: measured and experimental. A *measured operational definition* presents essential information about how a variable was measured. For instance, an operational definition of how liking for a song was measured might be: "Liking for the song was measured by a set of six, seven-space semantic differential scales [to be explained later] representing the evaluative dimension of meaning: beautiful–ugly, nice–awful, pleasant–unpleasant, exciting–dull, interesting–boring, valuable–worthless. These scales were pretested with 50 students who were from the same population as the 200 students used in the actual experiment." (A description of the statistical procedures for assessing reliability and validity would follow.) If the operational definition is accurate, you could re-create the results by following the same procedures specified by the researchers. Sometimes, as in the case of published scales, a measured operational definition can be quite brief. For instance: "Fantasy ability was measured by the Richness of Fantasy Scale (Hovland & Janis, 1959)." If the procedures used in measurement have been published, you generally do not need to repeat them because the duplication is considered unnecessary. That is, the procedures used for published scales are considered common knowledge in the research community. (Of course, persons should read the published source if they are unfamiliar with the scale.)

An *experimental operational definition* outlines the procedures followed in manipulating a variable. Thus, if other researchers want to study that independent variable, they would know how to replicate what the original researchers studied. Regarding the earlier example, a researcher might be interested in whether sexist music videos affect viewers' attitudes toward women. An experimental operational definition of sexist music videos might be: "Thirty individuals, who were similar to the people used in the actual experiment, were shown the twenty top music videos for 2009 and asked to rate each on a ten-point scale in terms of how much women were derogated in the video. The three rated highest and the three rated lowest were selected for the experiment. Participants in the experiment viewed either the three derogatory or the three nonderogatory videos (the independent variable) and then completed a scale for measuring attitudes toward women (the dependent variable)."

Hypothesis

Three kinds of hypotheses are important in scientific research. A **research hypothesis** is the prediction of the results of an experiment. That is, if the thinking that is the basis for a study is correct, then certain results ought to be obtained. If the hypothesized results are observed, this supports the thinking or theory. Theories are tested by testing hypotheses. For our music video example, a research hypothesis might be: "Music videos will have a favorable effect on how much a song is liked when people are low in fantasy ability but will have no effect when people are high in fantasy ability." Research hypotheses are verbalizations of predicted outcomes; they need to be tested by being compared to something else. The most obvious test is a statistical one. The **statistical hypothesis** in our example is: "The mean (average) score for liking of the song by participants who are low in fantasy ability and who view the music video will be greater than the mean for participants who are low in fantasy ability and who hear only the soundtrack, whereas the means will not differ for participants who are high in fantasy ability." A problem is that the statistical hypothesis cannot be tested directly because of error. Because of measurement and sampling error, we cannot be certain that the means we obtain for the four groups are exactly what we would have obtained if we had measured everyone in the population to which we wish to generalize our results. That is, we cannot be sure that testing 200 people in Boston or Cleveland will allow us to predict what would be true for the entire populations of those cities. If the results contained no error, we would simply look at the four means and see whether they corresponded to our predicted pattern.

Because of error, we need a standard for testing the statistical hypothesis. The standard is the **null hypothesis**: "There is no real difference between means." Probability theory and inferential statistics provide the full explanation, but we will simplify the concept to say that the logic of testing the null hypothesis is to determine whether it is likely that the difference among means is due to error. If you measure some variable (height, weight, or communication apprehension, for example) for four groups of people, the four means almost always will differ. However, the issue is whether the differences are real or whether the observed differences could be due to error. Error might be caused, for example, by using a faulty measuring stick to calculate height or by

research hypothesis Predictions of the results of a study based on a theoretical framework.

statistical hypothesis Statement of a research hypothesis in mathematical terms.

null hypothesis Statement that relations observed in a study were due to chance.

chance, as in unwittingly forming groups consisting of only very confident or very apprehensive people.

Using the methods of probability theory and inferential statistics, we can calculate the amount of error probably present in a given mean or average. Then we can examine the difference between two means. Taking into account the error in each mean, we can make a claim about how likely it is that the difference could be caused simply by error. Suppose we did this for two means and concluded that there was a .62 probability of obtaining by chance or error a difference between means as larger or larger than the difference we measured. We would not be very confident that our difference was real. If 62 times out of 100 a difference is a chance occurrence, there really is no difference at all. It would be too "chancy" to reject the null hypothesis. If something is different from something else, there should be a very low probability that the difference could be explained by error. The probability standard in the behavioral sciences for rejecting the null hypothesis is .05. The chance has to be less than five times out of a hundred that a difference could have occurred due to error or chance. When the probability is low that a difference is simply due to chance fluctuations, the researcher concludes the difference observed probably is real—a nonchance occurrence.

The logic of hypothesis testing follows this pattern: if the null hypothesis for a predicted difference is rejected, the statistical hypothesis is supported, which in turn supports the research hypothesis. Further, if the null hypothesis is not rejected, the statistical hypothesis is not supported, and this provides no support for the research hypothesis. This may seem a bit "roundabout" to you, but the null–statistical–research sequence is particularly valuable because probability statistics allow us to state our results with a specific degree of confidence. For instance, you would regard the following situations differently: (a) calculations show the difference between groups A and B could occur by chance 20 times out of 100; (b) the probability is one out of 1,000 that the difference between groups A and C is due to chance. In this example it is apparent that you would have more confidence that A is different from C than that A differs from B. If you were to bet on which difference is real based on probability theory, you should bet on the A–C difference.

Research Questions

At times it is not possible to state a hypothesis for a study because theory does not provide a basis for predicting what will happen. Also, there are times when one framework suggests a particular result, and a second theory predicts another outcome. When this happens, a **research question** is stated instead of a hypothesis. Suppose we are interested in whether male or female viewers are influenced more to make derogatory remarks about women after watching sexist music videos. On the one hand, we might predict male viewers would

research question
Question guiding investigation; usually used when hypothesis is not warranted.

derogate women more because sexist music videos reinforce the notion of male dominance and thus encourage males to "put down" women. On the other hand, some older research claims that women can be more derogatory about other women than men (e.g., Miller & McReynolds, 1973). On the basis of that research, we might predict that female viewers would be more derogatory. Because of this uncertainty of outcome, the research would center on the research question: Do male and female viewers differ in how they evaluate women after watching sexist music videos? This difference would have theoretical importance, and answering the research question would provide a basis for the next study instead of a hypothesis, which might then be able to state a hypothesis. If a research question is presented in a study, the researcher should explain why it was not possible to offer a hypothesis. Unfortunately, this is not always done in research articles, and consequently the theoretical significance of such studies is blurred.

Sampling

Seldom, if ever, is an entire population of interest studied. Instead, a part of the population is examined in hopes that what is found will be valid for the whole. For example, if we are interested in the communication characteristics of superiors in organizations that relate most to their subordinates' commitment to the organization, the population would be superior–subordinate pairs in corporations in the United States. Because of the influence of culture, we would not try to generalize to all the superior–subordinate pairs in the world. Sampling is necessary because it is seldom practical or even possible to study an entire population. At times, populations can be relatively small, for example, POWs in the Vietnam War. However, sampling is usually necessary even with small populations because of the difficulty of avoiding exclusions.

sampling A method of studying part of a population in order to draw conclusions about the entire population.

RANDOM

Random sampling involves selecting individuals from a population in such a manner that each member of the population has an equal chance of being selected. If this ideal of an "equal chance of being selected" is achieved, we would be rather confident that our sample is not biased—that the selection process has created a "population in miniature." Suppose we wanted to study the communication traits of state governors in the United States. The number in the population is 50. If we decided to take a random sample of 20 governors, each governor would have a 1 in 50 chance of being selected. Imagine we have the names of the 50 governors on folded slips of paper in a box. We draw the first name and put the slip of paper on a table. Then we draw a second name and put it with the first. We do this 20 times. Have we drawn a random sample according to the ideal? No, we have not. The first name drawn had a

random sampling Selecting individuals from a population so that each member of the population has an equal chance of being selected to represent the population.

1 in 50 chance of being drawn but the second had a 1 in 49 chance, and the third a 1 in 48 chance. This procedure is called sampling without replacement. Sampling with replacement means once a name is selected it is returned to the original pool so that the chance for successive draws remains constant. We seldom can determine if a random sample is representative of the population. A common way to assess the representativeness of a sample is to compare it to the population on a number of demographic variables such as age, education, or income. To find no differences regarding these variables is reassuring. However, that does not guarantee that the sample is typical of the population with reference to the variable of interest in a study. In our music video example, we could not be certain that our group is typical of the population in their liking for a song on a music video.

STRATIFIED RANDOM

stratified sample Partitioning a population and then drawing a random sample at each level of stratification.

A **stratified sample** is one that is partitioned according to some meaningful criteria. Often the most recent census data are used to determine the proportions of each type selected. For instance, census data on religious affiliation could be used to determine the number of Catholics that should be included for a sample to represent the population proportionately. A sample of governors could be stratified so that five are selected from each of the major geographic regions of the United States. A stratified random sample can be more representative, in practice, than a regular random sample. The reason is that unless the random sample is very large, the extreme cases tend to be underrepresented. For example, if there are 2,000 rich people in a state with a population of 5 million people, a random sample of 200 could miss the rich because it takes a while for extremes to show up in a random sample. A sample of only 200 does not give the random process much time. Thus, if the characteristics of a population that matter for a particular study can be determined, a stratified random sample can produce a sample that we can be confident is truly representative.

AVAILABLE

available sample Group of research participants selected based on convenience, and lack of evidence that the group is biased.

An **available sample** is not a random or a stratified sample. Instead the sample is selected because it is convenient. For instance, in studying the communication characteristics of superiors that predict their subordinates' organizational commitment, we might select 200 superior–subordinate pairs from a wide variety of companies in our geographic area. If we live in New York, the greater New York City area would be an available or convenient sample. However, our interest in studying this problem is not to specify the communication characteristics of New York managers that inspire corporate commitment in New York subordinates. Rather, we want to be able to say something that is valid with reference to all managers in the United States. Thus, available samples are taken with the assumption that they are representative of the population. Researchers with available samples do not say their results apply only to this group of research participants, at this point in time. Instead, results are discussed as if they pertain to the entire population. Over the years, this practice has stirred debate among behavioral scientists who are concerned that the widespread use of available samples may be producing knowledge that is not generalizable. The most frequently mentioned concern is the widespread use of college students as research participants. The issue raised is: if college students are not typical of the population, then the knowledge claimed in so many behavioral studies may say little about other people. The other school of thought on this issue maintains that available samples, as long as they are within normal ranges in terms of intellect, emotional health, and so on, produce results in studies that are equivalent to what would be found in the population. Although it is possible to take a variable such as education and create a scenario where it really matters in terms of how people respond in a study, in reality such variables seldom explain much variability in response. Thus, it is said, sampling "purists" have inflated the amount of error in a typical available sample. This position says, in essence, that "people are people." Going to the lengths necessary for a true random sample does not return results worth the time, effort, and expense.

RESEARCH DESIGN

We will examine two types of research designs. **Experimental designs** involve manipulation of at least one variable. A manipulated or independent variable, as we explained earlier, is under the direct control of the experimenter. In our example, the number of times research participants are shown a music video in a communication laboratory would be the independent variable. A manipulated variable is viewed as the cause of the dependent variable. **Nonexperimental designs** do not involve manipulation of variables. Instead, variables are measured, and the relationships between variables are studied. Because other causes generally cannot be ruled out, claims about causality based on nonexperimental designs do not inspire much confidence. This type of result is usually termed *correlational data* and is discussed in terms of one variable being related to or associated with another instead of one variable causing or being responsible for another.

A nonexperimental design for the effects of music videos would be to ask people whether or not they have watched a particular music video and to have them rate the song in terms of liking. This method will permit a conclusion as to whether liking for a song is related to seeing a video based on the song. However, we cannot conclude that the video caused more liking for the song. It might be that people who most like contemporary rock simply watch TV more.

experimental designs
Involve manipulation of at least one variable with control of other variables that could influence results.

nonexperimental designs
Involve no manipulation of variables.

Thus, their liking a song might have nothing to do with watching music videos. Other variables such as watching the video with friends and being influenced by their opinions might also have affected the song ratings.

General Purpose of Research Design

The general purpose of research design is to isolate the variables of interest in a study. This means being able to distinguish one variable from another. At first, this does not appear to be a very complicated task. However, it is quite a feat, one that is responsible for much of what has been achieved by science. Research design is an important part of the scientific method. Many procedures have been developed for isolating variables so that they can be studied and understood. The scientific method in general (and research design in particular) provides a way of knowing—one that is regulated by confidence. When established procedures have been followed for isolating the effects of a variable, confidence is strong that the knowledge gained is valid. On the other hand, if the design of a study is faulty because a necessary procedure was not used, confidence is weak, and there is serious doubt whether knowledge about the variable was gained.

How does research design permit confidence? This is primarily achieved by controlling any variables that can influence results. Research design, then, represents a set of procedures for isolating how variables relate to one another by accounting for and controlling variables that could influence results. As you might suspect, we can never have total confidence in the results of a study because it is always possible that the results were due to a variable we did not anticipate because our theory was not sophisticated enough. Also, results could simply be due to chance. Random occurrences—such as people liking everything because they are in an unusually good mood—cannot be predicted.

In our example of the effects of music videos, the research design attempted to isolate the variable exposure to music videos in terms of one effect, liking the song. Let us suppose that in actually running the study, we conducted the two conditions (music video and audio-only) in an un-air-conditioned room during a hot and humid period of August. Further, suppose all the sessions with the music videos were in the morning and all the audio-only sessions were in the later afternoon. If our results showed that people in the music video condition liked the song more than those in the audio-only condition, could we have much confidence in the results? As you may have concluded, the answer is no. When people are distracted by an uncomfortable environment, they tend to make less-favorable judgments. Thus, the results may not have been due to the music video at all. Rather, results could have varied according to comfort. Of course, the temperature may not have made any difference. The music video may have been totally responsible for the difference in liking of the song. However, we can never know for certain when the design of a study is faulty. If a variable could have mattered and is not controlled, the study is invalid. We may have gained some information about how to study the problem of interest, but no actual knowledge was gained regarding the original research question or hypothesis.

Achieving Control by Random Assignment

Research design attempts to rule out other possible causes of the relationship observed in a study. In experimental research, the most powerful procedure for accomplishing this is random assignment of participants to the experimental conditions. If some people happen to possess an expected quality that could affect the results, they will be equally distributed across the various experimental conditions when randomly assigned to experimental groups. Thus, variables that might matter in a study "cancel out" in terms of their impact and therefore do not affect the results.

random assignment
Method of achieving control in an experiment by utilizing probability theory to cancel the effects of potentially biasing conditions.

Here is how the principle operates. Suppose we select 50 people to view a music video and a second group of 50 to listen to the sound track only; we then measure liking of the song on a 10-point scale, with 10 representing the most liking. Suppose the first group consists of 50 students enrolled in an introduction to mass communication theory course. Unknown to us, they are very representative of the population of young adults to which we wish to generalize our results. Suppose the second group is a class of 50 students enrolled in an organizational communication course. This group is typical of the population except they are more conservative and like the rock-and-roll of the 1950s and 1960s better than contemporary rock. In fact, on a 10-point scale, they tend to like today's songs about 3 points less than the population's rating. You can see the problem in using these two groups. Because the groups differ initially and in all likelihood we would not know this, the results of the experiment could show a difference between means. However, this result would be an illusion because the difference could have been due to their preference for rock-and-roll, not because of music videos. To illustrate, suppose all people in the music video condition rated the song 8 and all people in the audio-only condition rated it 5. Because of the possibility that some initial difference between the two groups of participants could be responsible for this rating difference, we can have little confidence that the 3-point difference says anything about the effects of music videos.

With random assignment of participants to experimental conditions, this would not be the case. If chance is allowed to operate, about 25 people with a conservative rock-and-roll predisposition would be assigned to the music video condition and about 25 to the audio-only. This would also be the case for the other 50 people. Thus, in each condition, 25 people will reduce a song's "normal" rating by 3 points. This could be termed "error," but because it is equally present in both conditions, it is canceled as a factor in the study. We will give two examples to show how this works.

Suppose, in reality, music videos do not matter in terms of liking for the song. Using the data from the previous example, suppose we observe 25 scores of 8 and 25 ratings of 5 on the 10-point scale in the music video condition and also in the audio-only condition. Each group would have a mean (average) of 6.5, reflecting exactly the fact of no difference; in other words, the error canceled. However, let us suppose there actually is a 2-point difference in liking caused by music videos. If the 25 representative participants in the music video condition rate the song 8 and the 25 conservative people rate it 5, the mean would be 6.5. If the 25 representative people in the audio-only condition rate the song 6 (2 points lower than in the video condition because of the 2-point effect) and the 25 conservatives rate it 3 (also a 2-point effect), the mean would be 4.5. The difference between the 6.5 and 4.5 means is 2.0, which is exactly what we said the "real" difference is between the two conditions.

In the second example, having 50 "biased" research participants had no effect on the outcome of the study because they were evenly distributed in the groups. The "3 points" of bias possessed by each of the 50 persons was canceled out because of random assignment. If we allow chance to operate, such differences in a sample will almost always balance out. Of course, as mentioned earlier, there is always the very small possibility that chance will result in a biased distribution. That is why we said we can never have complete confidence in our results. We must always be aware that there is some level of probability that the results of a study could be due to error or chance.

Validity of Designs

When designing research, it is necessary to be aware of the various ways the internal and external validity of a study can be threatened (Campbell, 1957; Campbell & Stanley, 1963). **Internal validity** pertains to whether the actual procedures followed in a study rather than the variables of interest could be responsible for the results. The four major threats to internal validity are *history, maturation, measurement,* and *selection*. **External validity** relates mainly to the generalizability of results: To whom do the results of a study apply? Four influences on external validity are *pretests, experimental arrangements, sampling,* and *multiple treatments*.

History is concerned with things that take place during the time of the study. If people are exposed to a music video once a day for five consecutive days and then liking for the song is measured, a concern would be whether anything happened during the exposure before the measurement of liking that could have influenced the results. For instance, if the recording artist for the song is accused of a serious crime during the exposure, liking for the song

internal validity Check to determine whether something other than the independent variables such as history, maturation, measurement, or selection, could be responsible for results.

external validity Concerned with the generalizability of a study; major threats are pretesting, experimental arrangements, sampling, and multiple treatment effects.

could be affected. Even if a little time passes between exposure and measurement, an event could occur that will affect validity. For instance, suppose an audience is exposed to a music video, and their liking is measured afterward. If the experimenter shows liking of the song by his or her nonverbal behavior (for example, facial expression), the research participants' ratings might be influenced because the experimenter's response could serve as a "model" for how the participants should respond.

Maturation refers to changes in the research participant that could affect results. This is a problem in studies that are conducted over a period of time. A study of the long-term effects of music videos, for instance, would be complicated by the possibility that the research participants' taste in music might have changed, perhaps in the direction of classical music. However, there are also changes that can take place during a relatively short laboratory session. For example, if people watch a fairly large number of new music videos and are then asked which one they like best, the results could be subject to error because of "confusion" caused by too much exposure. The participants' cognitive systems could be overloaded with "too much of a good thing."

Measurement is a threat to the validity of a study when the measurement procedure affects how the person reacts. This is especially troubling when a study measures something before an experimental treatment (a *pretest*) and again afterward (a *posttest*) to see how much change was caused by the treatment. People realize they are expected to change when they are tested before an event and again after the event. Thus, they might change to be seen as "cooperative." A common misperception is that a pretest is necessary if you want to see whether a treatment affected someone. Because random assignment of participants to treatments equalizes the groups, the effects of a treatment can be seen by looking only at a posttest. Thus, a posttest-only design is superior to a pretest–posttest design because the former increases internal validity.

Selection ruins the internal validity of a study because of a bias in assigning research participants. Suppose an independent variable of interest in studying music videos is how familiarity with the musical group enhances liking for the song. Perhaps the hypothesis is, "Liking for a song is enhanced more when the group is familiar because with a new group we give more attention to the group than to the song." To study this, we select music videos of new songs by five well-known groups and new songs by five unfamiliar groups. We would not use only one group for each condition because any difference could be due to something unique about the two groups (such as a difference in their clothing); therefore, our results would not be valid for all familiar and unfamiliar groups. Suppose when each participant arrives at our research laboratory, we greet him or her and then make a decision to have the person watch one of the five familiar-group videos or one of the five unfamiliar-group videos. This procedure would invalidate the study because a bias of which we may have been unaware might have led us to assign people to view particular videos to increase the chance that our hypothesis would be supported. For instance, we might assign older people to the unfamiliar-group videos because they are more established in their likes and therefore would be less likely to be attracted immediately to a new group and its song. The correct procedure, as described earlier, would be random assignment of participants to the groups (we could use a table of random numbers or draw lots).

Now, let us examine external validity. A *pretest* may affect external validity by increasing or decreasing how a research participant will react to an experimental treatment. As noted earlier, the pretest sensitizes the person to the idea of change as the focus of the study.

The *experimental arrangements* can affect external validity because a response to an independent variable in the relatively "artificial" environment of a laboratory may be different from how people respond to the variable in more naturalistic settings. For instance, music videos might have little impact on liking for the song in a laboratory because people cannot relax as well as they do when watching music videos in the comfort of their living rooms. Thus, results of an experiment may be misleading. A solution that greatly increases the confidence we have about our conclusions is to gather more than one type of data. In addition to experimental data, evidence could be gathered from a survey or an interview. If several different types of data all point to the same conclusion, we can be more confident that the conclusion is valid.

Sampling is a major threat to the external validity in most social science research because of the predominant tendency to use an available, convenient sample rather than a true random sample. Thus, if a convenient sample differs from the population we want to measure, the results will not be generalizable. For example, in studying how familiarity with a rock group affects liking for a song in a music video, suppose we select by chance a group of participants who are so knowledgeable about rock groups that they are equally aware of our "well-known groups" and our "new, unfamiliar groups." Our results would not be generalizable. We might find no difference in liking because, unknown to us, we actually compared reactions to other familiar groups. However, in the general population there may be an actual difference in liking for songs of familiar and unfamiliar groups.

Multiple treatment effects result when research participants are exposed to more than one experimental treatment; how they respond in one treatment affects how they respond in another. In our example so far, each participant experienced one condition. Later we will see that under certain circumstances, a very valuable research design involves having a person exposed to more than one condition. Suppose we are interested in how familiarity with a rock group in a video affects remembering the song. Research participants view a video of a familiar and an unfamiliar rock group (random order for each person). At the conclusion of each, the experimenter asks the participant to recite the lyrics.

The problem here is that participants will do better for the second video. Because they know they will be expected to recite the lyrics, they will pay closer attention to them and probably practice subvocally during the second video.

Experimenter Effects

Even if all of the preceding seems like enough problems to have to contend with in conducting research, another major source of potential error are experimenter effects (Brooks, 1970). In a valid experiment, participants' responses should be due to the independent variables, not to the person running the experiment. If a characteristic, trait, or behavior of an experimenter is equally present in all of the conditions in an experiment and if it has an equal impact in all conditions, then there is no real problem in terms of the outcome of the study because this is comparable to adding or subtracting a constant from each participant's dependent variable score.

A real problem occurs when something about the experimenter distorts how people respond in one condition, thus affecting the statistical comparison of that condition with all of the other conditions. This can occur in several ways. *Biological characteristics* of the experimenter such as sex, age, race, and physical attractiveness can affect participants' responses. For instance, male participants may be more cooperative when the experimenter is female. This could manifest itself by the participants' displaying a good deal of change. The *experimenter's personality traits* are one of the most potent sources of bias. Some of the more obvious ones are dominance, hostility, sociability, communication apprehension, and self-esteem. This becomes a serious problem if a trait is expressed more when the experimenter conducts one condition as compared to another. For example, if the experimenter is more sociable in an experimental treatment than in a control condition, results might be biased because the friendly behavior might motivate participants to give the experimenter what he or she seems to want. Thus, there might seem to be a difference between experimental and control conditions when in fact there is no difference caused by the independent variable.

Experimenter modeling occurs when the experimenter shows the participant how to respond. As we mentioned earlier, if an experimenter seems to be reacting favorably to the song (for instance, by tapping a finger to the music's beat) during a video presentation, the experimenter's behavior provides the participant with a model of how to react to the song and biases the experiment—particularly if the experimenter's behavior is neutral during the audio-only presentation. A somewhat different problem is *experimenter expectancy.* This occurs when the experimenter communicates the research hypothesis to the research participants by reinforcing "correct" behavior. That is, behavior that supports the researcher's hypothesis is conditioned. Subtle cues of approval

experimenter effects
Error in a study caused by the experimenter's characteristics and/or behavior.

(like a nod and a slight smile) could be given when a participant begins to show liking for a song in the music video condition and cues of disapproval (such as a slight frown or a blank stare) when a person in the audio-only condition begins to reveal liking. The experimenter might be completely unaware of this expectancy behavior, making the problem particularly troublesome.

Controlling Experimenter Influence

Several established procedures can be used for neutralizing the impact of the person conducting a study (Brooks, 1970). *Using several experimenters* and rotating them throughout the various conditions serves to lessen the impact of a particular experimenter; he or she does not have contact with all of the participants. *Training the experimenters* to standardize their behaviors is a very important technique for solving this problem. Often a script for an experiment is written. Just as in a theatrical performance, the players practice their lines with the director, who in this case is the director of the research project. The idea is to standardize the experimental experience for all participants.

Blind contact with participants means the experimenter does not know in which condition the person is participating. This procedure is easily used in pharmaceutical studies, for example. The basic idea is that the experimenter who has contact with the participants does not know which person is receiving the experimental drug treatment and which person receives a placebo. The same procedure could be used with a music video and an audio-only condition. The experimenter would greet participants when they arrive, give them a sealed envelope containing instructions unknown to the experimenter for either viewing a video or listening only to the sound, take them to a place for the stimulus to be presented, leave and have either a second experimenter or a computer present the video or audio-only condition. Later, the first experimenter could return to administer the liking scale and debrief participants about the purpose of the study.

Using written or recorded instructions as much as possible is another way to reduce the impact of the experimenter by standardizing instructions. Often it is possible for the experimenter to say very little and to have minimal contact with participants. When this is achieved through the use of written or recorded instructions, confidence increases that the experimenter did not bias the study.

Finally, procedures can be developed for *masking the research hypothesis.* Often this involves the use of deception; participants are led to believe the study is about one thing but it is actually about something else. There have been debates in the fields of psychology and communication on the ethics of misleading people in this manner. A reasonable position appears to be that deception should be used only when it is necessary, and the participants must then be debriefed about the study's real purpose.

Experimental Research Designs

There are numerous ways to design an experiment (for example, see Edwards, 1972). We will describe three of the most common designs used in communication experiments: the completely randomized factorial design, the randomized blocks design, and the repeated measures design. Other designs such as incomplete factorials, Latin squares, and nested designs are rarely, if ever, used in communication research, so they will not be covered.

In the **completely randomized factorial design**, all independent variables are manipulated, and research participants are randomly assigned to the various conditions. A manipulated variable, you will recall, is created by and therefore under the direct control of the experimenter. The number of manipulated variables in communication studies typically varies from one to three for practical reasons. A study can become virtually unmanageable with a large number of manipulated independent variables. In our music video example, the following is a completely randomized factorial design for studying three manipulated variables: (a) each research participant would be randomly assigned to view a music video or to listen to the audio portion only for a new song; (b) the musical group would be either a well-known group or a new one; and (c) the participant would be exposed to the treatment on one, two, or three occasions (consecutive days). This design is illustrated in Figure A.2.

> **completely randomized factorial design** An experimental design in which all independent variables are manipulated and research participants are randomly assigned to treatment conditions.

Because each independent variable is present at every level of every other independent variable, there are a total of 12 conditions. Multiplying the number of levels of each variable produces this total ($2 \times 2 \times 3$). Adding just one more independent variable, with three levels, to the design (for example, whether the group is all male, all female, or male and female) would increase the number of conditions to 36 (in other words, $2 \times 2 \times 3 \times 3$). If you can imagine using groups of about 20 people in each of the 36 conditions, you can appreciate the point made earlier that as the number of manipulated variables in a study increases, difficulty in conducting the study also increases. The experimenter would need a minimum of about 720 participants for 36 conditions.

		FAMILIARITY OF GROUP					
		Well Known			New		
	Days of Exposure	1	2	3	1	2	3
Music	Music Video Condition	___	___	___	___	___	___
	Audio-Only Condition	___	___	___	___	___	___

Figure A.2

Completely randomized factorial design.

randomized blocks design
Mixed research design involving a combination of manipulated and nonmanipulated independent variables.

A **randomized blocks design** (also termed a "mixed design") involves a combination of manipulated and nonmanipulated independent variables. This is a favorite design in communication experiments because of the interest in personality and gender differences. Personality traits and sex variables are studied as they are found in people. That is, the experimenter does not change or manipulate anything, and therefore personality and gender are nonmanipulated independent variables. The idea of "randomized blocks" means blocks of people are identified. People who are high or low in self-esteem would be an example. Then the individuals within each block are randomly assigned to the levels of the manipulated variables. For instance, (a) people who are either high or low in fantasy ability, (b) would be shown a music video or listen to the audio-only, (c) on one, two, or three consecutive days. This design is presented in Figure A.3. This design "looks like" the previous one. However, when a variable is not manipulated, what can be said about its influence is limited. That is, our confidence in discovering a cause of something is highest when we have manipulated the believed cause.

repeated measures design
Research design where research participants are exposed to all levels of one or more manipulated variables.

In the **repeated measures design**, participants are exposed to all levels of one or more manipulated variables. The previous two designs were different because each participant experienced only one of the conditions. In the example for the first design (Figure A.2) twelve different groups of participants would be needed. However, if participants are exposed to more than one level of an independent variable, the number of participants needed in a study can be substantially reduced. Thus, a repeated measures design can be very economical. Another benefit is that the participant serves as his or her own control group. It is nearly impossible to match people for a valid comparison in an experiment. As a result a "matched samples" design is seldom used in research. Comparing a person to him- or herself surpasses even a sample of matched identical twins.

Here is an example to illustrate how this would work. Let us turn the example for the first design (see Figure A.2) into a repeated measures design. Instead

		MUSIC CONDITION					
		Music Video			*Audio-Only*		
	Days of Exposure	1	2	3	1	2	3
Fantasy Ability	High	——	——	——	——	——	——
	Low	——	——	——	——	——	——

Figure A.3

Randomized blocks design.

of twelve groups of research participants, we will only need two groups because we will have repeated measures over two independent variables: (1) familiarity with group and (2) one, two, or three exposures. Record several new songs by a well-known group; do the same for a new group. Program the songs so that they appear equally in the various conditions and so each participant would be exposed to two new songs. Participants would be told the study is investigating how we get to know a new song. The researchers would say: (1) that they were able to acquire the music videos for two new songs or that they were able to acquire audio recordings of two new songs and (2) that each participant would hear two songs on three consecutive days. One group would participate in the music video condition. They would watch a music video of a song by a well-known group and also one by a new group. They would rate each song on a set of scales. The order in which songs by the well-known and by the new group appeared would be varied for each participant. This procedure would be repeated on the second and third days. The second group of participants would be exposed to the audio-only. The same procedures would be followed here as with the previous participants. You can see how economical this design is. Instead of 12 groups of participants, we need only two—or about 40 people rather than 240.

In light of this difference, you might wonder why repeated measures designs are not used for all experiments. The answer is that the repeated measures design is only appropriate when exposure to one condition does not influence how the person responds to another condition. Unfortunately, for many independent variables of interest in communication research, if a person is exposed to one level of an independent variable, the first exposure would have an effect on how he or she reacted to another level of the variable. For example, learning might take place between the first and second exposures as in the preceding example about recalling lyrics from the songs. However, there are instances, and our music video example may be one, where a repeated measures design is appropriate.

Nonexperimental Research Designs

The value of experimental research designs is fairly obvious. When a variable is manipulated and other variables controlled, resulting effects can be viewed as caused by the manipulated variable. Confidence in a supposed causal relationship is greatest when this degree of control is achieved by the researcher. That is why Kerlinger (1986) claimed the ideal of science is the controlled experiment. The researcher should deviate from this ideal only when it is necessary. Although the standards of experiments are highly desirable, the reality of communication research is that many of the areas of interest do not lend themselves readily to experimental research. Some variables are difficult or not feasible to manipulate. It is easier to study such variables naturally, as they already exist. However, when this is done, the researcher does not have control over the independent variables. These designs are not less valuable than experimental designs, but they are different in that statements about which variable causes which result are not warranted. Thus, the researchers using nonexperimental designs are concerned about what is related to what, and how things vary together. We will examine three nonexperimental designs. There is no manipulation of variables in these designs. However, the concern with controlling variables that can influence results is just as strong as it is with experiments. Nonexperimental research can and should be rigorous.

investigational design
A design where no independent variable is manipulated.

When diagrammed, an **investigational design** has the appearance of an experiment. However, the critical difference is that no variable is manipulated. This is illustrated by the design in Figure A.4. The design involves males who are either high, moderate, or low in fantasy ability and who are either younger or older. They are shown a music video with a number of attractive female actors and then asked to complete a scale that measures liking of the video. The hypothesis could be that the video will be liked most by younger males who are lower in fantasy ability. The reasoning might be that music videos satisfy fantasy needs, and inexperienced young males who are low in fantasy ability might need the fantasies more than others and hence be more receptive to sources that provide satisfaction. Nothing is manipulated in this study. That is, the need for fantasy is measured by a personality scale. Males are classified as high, moderate, or low according to norms for that scale. The second independent variable is created by the person's age. For instance, teenage males could be classified as "younger," whereas males beyond their teens could be termed "older." Because there is no manipulation, an important procedure of experiments for controlling other variables cannot be followed. Research participants cannot be randomly assigned to the various parts of the design. Rather, participants in effect assign themselves according to their level of need for fantasy and their age.

field research   Research conducted in a naturalistic setting.

Field research is conducted in natural settings as contrasted to investigational designs, which are conducted in a laboratory. Experiments can be conducted in the field, but communication researchers have seldom done so. Organizational communication research probably is the most common form of field research in the communication discipline. Researchers go to the participants in their natural setting (their workplace) instead of having the participant come to the researcher (the laboratory or college campus). As with the

Figure A.4

Investigational design.

Age	FANTASY ABILITY		
	High	*Moderate*	*Low*
Younger			
Older			

investigational design, no variable is manipulated. All the variables of interest are measured, and the associations among the variables are studied. Hypotheses about predicted relationships are tested. Alternatively, a field study can be exploratory in that no hypothesis is tested. Instead, the purpose is to determine what should be studied in future investigations.

The basic design of **survey research** is to select a sample from a population to infer how frequently certain variables occur and how they are related in the population. Interviews and mail surveys are two major types of surveys. Each is capable of yielding a good deal of information. Personal interviews of participants are expensive in terms of time and effort. However, the span and depth of information gained can make the cost worthwhile. Mail surveys are easier to conduct. However, a major disadvantage is a typical low return rate, often below 50%. The results from a study with a low return rate can be very misleading because if everyone had returned the survey, the results could have been significantly different. The "missing data" could matter greatly, but there is no way to determine the difference other than the exhausting and sometimes impossible task of studying those who did not return the survey. An alternative to the mail survey of a random sample of people is visiting group meetings. Your community probably offers a number of group gatherings such as students in classes, church and social groups, or professional meetings. A major advantage is that participation is usually near 100%. However, an important disadvantage is that the sample is not random; it is a convenient sample. The group could have peculiarities that could account for results. For instance, all members of the social group might have a high ability to fantasize. A good procedure to test for this possibility is to gather demographic data on the sample and compare it to the characteristics of the population of interest. If there are no differences, the researchers can have some confidence that the sample is not biased.

The music video topic could be investigated using survey methodology. A mail survey would involve selecting a random sample and sending participants a scale that contains a list of music videos. People could be asked how often they have seen each in the past week. Next, a scale could be used to measure liking of the song in each video. Demographic questions could be included. Also, a personality scale measuring the need for fantasy, for example, could be a part of the questionnaire. You can see how this survey could address some of the same concerns as the experiments designed earlier in the chapter, such as whether frequency of exposure to a video enhances liking of the song. The major difference between this study and earlier experiments would be in terms of what is claimed. An experiment that manipulates exposure may be justified in contending that causal relationships are present—as in "more exposure produces greater liking." However, a survey that measures rather than manipulates exposure would be on firmer ground if it stated an association such as "more exposure is related to greater liking."

survey research
Interviews and mail surveys.

You might think the difference between these two claims is minute, hair-splitting, or "picky." However, A being the cause of B is different from A and B both being the effects of cause C. Without the control of an experiment, the second claim is a possibility, so it is not prudent to claim the first. For instance, in a survey of music videos, exposure might be related to liking for the song in a video; however, both of these effects could be produced by socioeconomic status. That is, teenagers from wealthier households might have had more exposure to the video tested because they have more leisure time to watch TV, and they might like the particular song more because it appeals to people who are wealthy but is repugnant to others. An experiment would control for this potentially biasing factor because random assignment of participants to the experimental conditions probably would equalize family income across the manipulated levels of exposure, hence canceling its influence.

MEASUREMENT

nominal level of measurement Level of measurement that results in assigning an object to a category.

Most of the results of studies cited in this book were derived from questionnaires where people rated themselves, another person's behavior, messages, ideas, or aspects of a communication situation. Measurement ratings can be at any of four different levels: nominal, ordinal, interval, and ratio. The **nominal level of measurement** involves assigning an object of judgment to a category. A nominal level variable in communication is biological sex. A person is classified as either male or female. In terms of data, male could be coded "1" and female "2." However, the numbers are meaningless as data other than to identify a person's category. That is, a 2 is not greater than a 1.

ordinal level of measurement Level of measurement where objects are rank ordered according to some standard.

In the **ordinal level of measurement**, the levels of a variable are ordered and meaningful. This is commonly termed *rank order data.* If five speeches were rank ordered from 1 to 5 with 1 meaning "best," the speech ranked first would be better than the speech ranked second, and so forth. What you cannot tell from this rank order data is "how much better" each speech is than the next. It is not necessarily true that a speech rated 2 is twice as good as a speech rated 4. There are many possible patterns. The best speech might be much better than the other four, which are clustered together. Or all five might be extremely close or clustered. These two very different patterns could not be distinguished by the ordinal data because the rank order would be exactly the same in both cases.

interval data Represents a level of measurement where the points on the scale are assumed to increase or decrease by a constant degree.

Interval data are different in that the intervals between data points are equal, or at least approximately equal. Thus, if we had a 10-point interval scale for measuring speech quality, quality would increase an equal amount from 1 to 2, from 2 to 3, and so forth on the scale. A speech rated 8 would be considered 4 points higher in quality than a speech rated 4; we could state that there is a 4-point difference. If one speech was rated 8 and other speeches were rated

4 or lower, this scale would clearly reflect that one speech was far superior to the others.

Ratio data are similar to interval data because the assumption of equal intervals between data points also applies. The major difference is that a meaningful zero point exists for a ratio measure but not for an interval measure. Weight is an example of a ratio scale. Zero is a clear starting point. Moreover, it registers on a scale. Speech quality is not a ratio scale. It is not clear what it means for a speech to have zero quality. In fact, there have been few, if any, ratio scales in communication research. Because ratio scales have a zero point, it is meaningful to multiply and divide scores. For instance, you can say one score is twice another. Thus, a 200-pound person is twice as heavy as a 100-pound person. Or, one person is half as heavy as another. We could not do that with the speeches rated 8 and 4 in the earlier example. Because we do not know where zero quality is for a speech (it is somewhere below 1), we cannot say that the speech rated 4 was only half as good as the speech rated 8. If there is a "true" zero that we are not aware of, and if, for example, it is considerably below 1, 4 might really be only three fourths as good as 8. Thus, if zero is unknown for a scale, it does not make sense to use multiplication or division in interpreting the data.

Measurement in communication research has utilized four primary methods: rating scales, behavioral observation, content analysis, and physiological measures. We will explain each briefly and develop an illustration based on our music video example.

Rating Scales

Most communication research data has come from *rating scales.* Three types have been employed almost exclusively: semantic differential, Likert scales, and simple linear scales. Semantic differential scales were developed by Osgood, Suci, and Tannenbaum (1957) in conjunction with their theory of meaning. They believed that the meaning of something can be located in "semantic space," which has three major dimensions: evaluation, potency, and activity. These dimensions are measured by scales composed of *bipolar terms,* which allow an object of judgment to be placed somewhere on the continuum between the polar opposites. For instance, good–bad is a pair of bipolar adjectives that measure the evaluative (or attitude) dimension of meaning. Typically, the continuum between the poles is represented by seven spaces. For each pair of bipolar adjectives, a check in the space next to the favorable end is given a score of "7"; the second space is given a score of "6," etc. A total score is then computed by summing across all pairs of the bipolar adjectives for a given object of judgment.

Figure A.5 contains an example of a semantic differential scale used to measure how much a song in a music video is liked. (A rating of liking is considered

ratio data Represents a level of measurement that entails a natural zero point, and a constant and equal difference between points of the scale.

semantic differential scales Rating scales that utilize a seven-point continuum bound by bipolar terms in order to locate an object in semantic space.

Rate the song to which you just listened on the following set of six scales. For each pair of adjectives, a check in the space next to the word means "extremely," the second space from the word means "moderately," the third space means "slightly," and the middle space means "neutral." Remember, use only one check for each pair of words (six checks total on this page). Please make your checkmark on one of the blanks, not the spaces.

I personally feel the song was:

beautiful _____ : _____ : _____ : _____ : _____ : _____ : _____ ugly

awful _____ : _____ : _____ : _____ : _____ : _____ : _____ nice

unpleasant _____ : _____ : _____ : _____ : _____ : _____ : _____ pleasant

exciting _____ : _____ : _____ : _____ : _____ : _____ : _____ dull

interesting _____ : _____ : _____ : _____ : _____ : _____ : _____ boring

worthless _____ : _____ : _____ : _____ : _____ : _____ : _____ valuable

Figure A.5

Semantic differential scale.

a measure of attitude toward the object of judgment.) Notice the instructions and also the scale format. The order of the bipolar adjectives, in terms of whether the favorable or unfavorable adjective appears on the left, is varied to discourage people from checking straight down a column without thinking of the given pair of adjectives as it applies to the concept being rated. Having to determine the location of the favorable and unfavorable ends of the continuum results in the person's considering the pair of bipolar adjectives at least briefly.

Likert scales Rating scales that utilize a five or seven point agree-disagree format to rate value statements about an object.

Likert scales (1932) are based on the idea of determining belief statements that are relevant to the object of judgment, assessing the extent to which the research participant accepts each statement, and then summing the person's acceptance across the total set of beliefs to derive a score for the person's attitude toward the object. Acceptance of a belief statement is usually measured by a five-point scale that spans from "strongly agree" to "strongly disagree." To discourage an automatic pattern of responses, half of the statements are worded positively and half negatively. This pattern is illustrated in Figure A.6: an example of a Likert-type scale for measuring attitude toward a song in a music video. The mix of positively and negatively worded items also guards against "yea-saying" and "nay-saying" response tendencies. That is, some people tend to agree with statements that are positive, whereas other people tend to disagree with anything worded negatively. Having a mix of items somewhat controls the degree to which these tendencies influence scores.

linear scales Rating scales that specify placing an object along a continuum, often dealing with degree or quantity.

Simple **linear scales** are usually five- or seven-point scales, which rate something along a dimension specified by the endpoints. For instance, a scale item might ask you to rate the organization of a speech on a five-point scale,

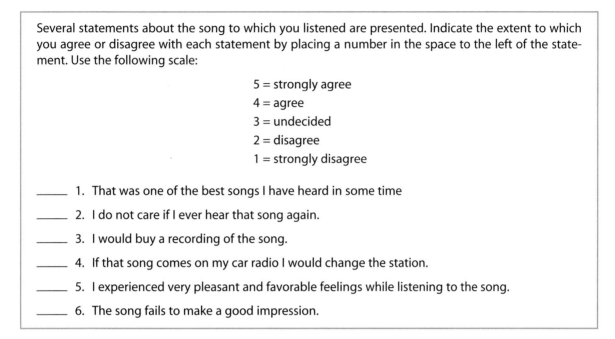

Several statements about the song to which you listened are presented. Indicate the extent to which you agree or disagree with each statement by placing a number in the space to the left of the statement. Use the following scale:

> 5 = strongly agree
> 4 = agree
> 3 = undecided
> 2 = disagree
> 1 = strongly disagree

_____ 1. That was one of the best songs I have heard in some time

_____ 2. I do not care if I ever hear that song again.

_____ 3. I would buy a recording of the song.

_____ 4. If that song comes on my car radio I would change the station.

_____ 5. I experienced very pleasant and favorable feelings while listening to the song.

_____ 6. The song fails to make a good impression.

Figure A.6

A Likert scale.

which spans from "poor" to "excellent." Another item could ask the degree of something (for example, how much you liked something) on a seven-point scale using "not at all" to "greatly" as endpoints. One of the most frequently used formats to measure personality and communication traits presents a statement and asks how often the statement is true for you; for example, "I get a great deal of pleasure from watching music videos." The rating scale usually consists of five points: "almost never true, occasionally true, sometimes true, often true, almost always true." Notice, the endpoints specify "almost" rather than never or always. People are reluctant to say never or always because confidence is seldom high for such absolute judgments. "Almost never" provides a margin for error in judgment and thus is preferred. Because of this tendency, a five-point scale that does not include "almost" with the endpoints becomes in effect a three-point scale because people tend not to use the endpoints in the rating.

Behavioral Observation

In addition to studying what people verbally report on questionnaires, communication researchers sometimes use **behavioral observation**. The behavior might be studied "live" or videotape-recorded. The researcher usually does not rate or categorize the participant's behavior because the purpose of the study

behavioral observation
Involves observing behavior, classifying it according to a framework, and determining the reliability of the classification.

could cause the researcher to distort what is seen—that is, to see support for a hypothesis when there is no support. Instead, researchers usually train research assistants who do not know the purpose of the study to observe the subjects' behavior. Sometimes researchers ask participants to report whether they engaged in certain behavior. In our music video study, we could observe behavior instead of or in addition to gathering questionnaire data. For instance, participants could be videotaped while watching a music video. Then a research assistant could look for behavior that was specified before the experiment as relevant. Some of the behaviors might be: amount of time smiling during the video; how often the person marked time with hand, head, or foot; or moving lips in synch with the lyrics. A week later, the participants might be asked whether they had purchased a recording of the song.

Reliability of measurement is just as important with behavioral observations as it is with questionnaire data. Reliability of behavioral observations is assessed by having a second research assistant observe the behavior of the participant. The research assistants should not do this together because they could influence one another, thus giving the illusion of agreement and hence reliability. In fact, the only reliable behavior might be one assistant's ability to influence the other. The observations of both assistants are compared, and a reliability coefficient is computed. If the coefficient is too low, the categories of behavior and instructions may have to be revised extensively, new assistants trained, and the process repeated. A weakness in behavioral data obtained as self-reports from research participants is that reliability and validity are seldom checked. In the preceding example, if we asked participants a week after viewing the video whether they had purchased a recording of the song, we probably would accept their answers as fact because it would be impractical to check to determine that they actually had such a recording.

reliability Accuracy, stability or consistency of a scale, test or measure across time.

Content Analysis

content analysis Method of measurement for studying the content of messages, which utilizes a category system and checks the reliability of categorizing message units.

A limited amount of communication research has employed content analysis. In this very useful method of measurement, messages are examined for the occurrence of certain themes, types of language, organizational structures, language intensity, types of evidence, and reasoning. The procedures are similar to those used for behavioral observation. Categories of things to look for in the message are formed ahead of time or after a preliminary reading of the messages if theory does not provide guidance for the categories. Coders are trained to use the category system. If satisfactory reliability is not achieved, the category system and instructions are revised and the process is repeated. Content analysis can be used in a number of ways. For example, a single speech by a political leader could be analyzed for types of reasoning, or a number of speeches by the person could be analyzed to look for trends. A number of individuals' messages on a topic could be analyzed. In our example, research participants could be asked to write an assessment of the video just seen. Content analysis also can be used to analyze the interaction between people. For instance, the dialogue between husbands and wives in happy or troubled marriages could be analyzed to determine the occurrence of certain types of verbally aggressive messages, supportive messages, and instances of intense language.

Physiological Measures

A relatively small number of communication studies have used measures of involuntary responses such as heart rate and, to a lesser extent, blood pressure and skin conductivity. These physiological measures have been used in studying communication apprehension—probably a good place to begin because an increase in heart rate, for instance, is often associated with presenting a speech. It probably would be beneficial if more research examined how changes in our central nervous system relate to and influence communication. As Bostrom (1980) pointed out, there are a large number of causes of physiological change: alcohol, tobacco, caffeine, tranquilizers, various other drugs, controlled substances such as marijuana, and physical states such as fatigue, pain, hunger, and stress. Given this range of factors, it may be somewhat uncommon to talk with someone who is in a completely unaltered physiological state. These factors tend to be one of two types: stimulants or depressants. For example, stimulants can result in greater persuasion, whereas depressants can reduce persuasion. Using physiological measures to study how altered physiological states function in other areas of communication besides communication apprehension and persuasion may yield some interesting knowledge. For instance, do stimulants or depressants influence how attracted we are to new acquaintances? Perhaps future research will take that direction.

physiological measures Method of measurement that quantifies involuntary responses such as heart rate and blood pressure.

SUMMARY

A model of scientific research that involved induction, hypothesis, deduction, experiment, and feedback to the induction phase was discussed. Several concepts fundamental to behavioral research in communication were explained: variables (continuous–dichotomous, independent–dependent, manipulated–attribute), constitutive definitions, operational definitions (measured–experimental), hypotheses (research–statistical–null), research questions, and sampling (random–stratified–available). Types of research designs were introduced in terms of whether manipulation of variables was involved. The purpose of research designs is to isolate the variables of interest in a study. Random assignment in experiments is a primary means for achieving control of extraneous variables that could influence results. Four threats to the internal validity of a study are history, maturation, measurement, and selection. External validity can be threatened by pretesting, experimental arrangements, sampling, and multiple treatment effects. Biological and personality characteristics of the experimenter, experimenter modeling, and expectancy can bias results. Experimenter bias can be controlled by using several experimenters, standardizing behavior, having blind contact with participants, using written or recorded instructions, and masking hypotheses. Three experimental research designs were explained: the completely randomized factorial design, the randomized blocks design and the repeated measures design. Three types of nonexperimental research discussed were investigational, field, and survey. Four levels of measurement were specified: nominal, ordinal, interval, and ratio. Measurement in communication research has generally utilized four methods: rating scales, behavioral observation, content analysis, and physiological measures. The most frequently used rating scales are the semantic differential, Likert scales, and linear scales.

KEY TERMS

activity, evaluation, potency

attribute variables

available or convenient sample

behavioral observation

behavioral science

bipolar terms

completely randomized factorial design

constitutive definition

construct

content analysis

continuous variable

controlled observation

deduction

dependent variable

dichotomous variable

epistemology

experimental design

experimenter effects

external validity

field research

hypothesis

independent variable

internal validity

interval data

interview

investigation design

Likert scales

linear scales

manipulation

measurement

nominal level of measurement

nonexperimental design

null hypothesis

operational definition

ordinal level of measurement

physiological measures

pretest

random assignment

random sampling

randomized blocks design

rating scales

ratio data

reliability

repeated measures design

replication

research design

research hypothesis

research question

sampling

scientific method

semantic differential scales

statistical hypothesis

stratified sample

survey research

Conclusion

After completing this book, we hope you have gained an appreciation for the process and extent of theory building in the communication field. You may be amazed at the number of theories included in the text, but there are many more theories and theoretical approaches that were omitted because of limited space. In this last section, we want to mention other approaches and present some trends in communication theory building.

In Chapter 3 we contrasted general communication theories (designed to explain all types of communication with one theoretical framework) with specific theories that describe and explain how communication functions in specific contexts. Recent communication theories have been context bound, and we believe the trend will continue. The growth in theory building in specific communication contexts may be the result of two factors: frustration among scholars attempting to develop a single, general theory of communication and greater emphasis on the union of theory and application among communication researchers and theorists. Although progress toward the development of a "grand" theory of human communication continues, general theories have not as yet been universally accepted across the discipline. There has been a pronounced trend for scholars to develop, test, and apply their theories in "field" and "naturalistic" settings. Naturalistic research occurs when the researcher studies the behavior of individuals in natural surroundings, rather than in controlled laboratory conditions set up by the researcher. The increased interest in the application of theory is marked by the rise of *The Journal of Applied Communication Research* to national status.

We expect more studies about legal communication and communication conflict and negotiation, two areas not addressed in Part III. Another area of theory building only briefly indicated in this text is the rich body of theory and research developed from rhetorical-critical and interpretive methodologies.

Work done by European scholars in this area will continue to influence rhetoric and communication theory building. Consistent with the resurgence of rhetorical theories, many of the new communication theories will be developed from the rules approach. The diversity of approaches taken by communication scholars will continue to be a feature of our field. We believe that this approach is healthy. No one perspective is most appropriate for answering the varied questions posed by communication scholars. A variety of philosophical and methodological strains reflects the healthiest and most productive environment for building communication theories of the future.

The field of communication encompasses all discourses—spoken, written, and mediated. Although oral communication will continue to be the chief focus, scholars concerned with messages will study them in whatever form they occur. The challenge is for communication scholars to combine theory and research to make recommendations for effective communication practice. To enhance the heuristic function of theory, it is important that we not neglect the communication skills that are so essential in everyday life.

No matter how inclusive the text or how astute the authors, no book can ever truly capture the state of communication theory building at a particular time. You have learned specifics of many different theories in studying this book. No matter what your field of future employment, communication will continue to be a vital part of your life. Learning to communicate effectively is a lifelong process, and communication is a skill that can affect your job performance and how quickly and to what level you are promoted. Effective communication can also sustain and enrich your personal and family life. We hope some of the theories you have studies in this text will help you to communicate more effectively in your social and work life.

Ten years from now, many of the theories you have studied in your communication classes will have been revised, expanded, replaced, or faded from popularity. There will always be new theories and even new theoretical perspectives. The most important skill a course in communication theory building can provide is the ability to be a critic of theories. We hope that you are now able to recognize the perspectives and theoretical assumptions that lie beneath the surface of communication theories. We hope that you have learned to judge a theory's strengths and weaknesses and that you have developed your own criteria for a good theory. We hope that you have come to understand that theory and research are "two sides of the same coin."

In a communication theory course, many students are uncomfortable; they feel they have been unable to grasp the "big picture." We have tried to emphasize the "big picture" in a course in communication theory is not related to any one theory or group of theories but to the critical framework of theory building on which all theories depend. By presenting this frame-work, we hope the book has helped you to integrate all the communication classes you have taken into a larger framework. We hope that the book has broadened your knowledge of the many different areas studied by communication scholars and has stimulated your interest, perhaps in an area of which you were previously unaware. Sometimes we encounter the misconception that "research" means sitting in the library. Certainly, academic research involves reading about what others have discovered, but it involves much more. Communication research is an exciting activity for each of us, and we hope through reading this book you now share some of that excitement.

Glossary

Abraham personality. A motivational tendency to focus on the need to achieve the maximum of human potential and perfection.

Absolute information. Total amount of knowledge present in a system.

Abstractness. In the theory of Constructivism, it refers to how abstract (i.e., intangible) or concrete a construct is.

Accommodative style. An approach to resolving conflict concerned primarily with not hurting interpersonal relations.

Account analysis. A research method used by investigators who ask organization members to provide reasons for their actions.

Accountability. An ethical practice of going above and beyond the minimal standards set by the industry and government regulations.

Acculturation. The activity of learning a new cultural system.

Acquired needs theory. Theory of motivation that holds people are motivated to behave in order to acquire things that the culture at large deems important.

Action is locally organized. A component of conversation analysis theory that reflects (a) what is relevant to the interactants within a specific or particular context, (b) local can refer to adjacency or sequence of action as a process for interactants to work interdependently and in predictable ways to construct a recognizable course of action.

Action is structured. A component of conversation analysis theory that assumes that not only is talk an action, but that action is guided by a structure that allows the communicators to coordinate the interaction in a way that allows for things such as turn taking and establishes patterns of interaction.

Action. Concept inherent in the Coordination Management of Meaning Theory. Behaviors individuals engage in as a result of interpreting another person's messages.

Active strategies. An uncertainty reduction strategy that requires effort to discover information, but there is still no direct contact between the two parties.

Activity tracks. Component of the multiple sequence model that entails task, relational, and topical tracks.

Adam personality. A motivational tendency to focus on immediate satisfaction and pleasure.

Adaptors. Bodily movements that serve a physical need and express personality and individuality.

Affect displays. Bodily movements which express emotion.

Affect hypothesis. Assumes that television news is a powerful agenda setter because its vivid pictures and dramatic stories evoke strong emotions in viewers, especially in the area of political communication.

Affection. Interpersonal communication motive used to express concern, caring, and appreciation for others.

Affective dimension of communication. Involves the communication of emotion, attitude, and predispositions and is more effectively conveyed through the non-verbal than the verbal code.

Affirming communicator style. A communicator style that reflects the validation of another person's self-concept.

Agenda-setting theory. A theory that holds intense media attention increases the importance of certain topics, issues, and individuals. Assumes that the press and the media do not reflect reality; they filter and shape it as well as media concentration on a few issues and subjects leads the public to perceive those issues as more important than other issues.

Aggression. Applying physical and/or symbolic force to dominate and even destroy the locus of attack.

Alignment. An ethical practice that matches the organization's formal practices and informal practices to the needs of its members.

Ambiguity. Uncertainty, having more than one meaning.

Ambivalent orientation. An orientation that is based on low independent and low interdependent self-construal.

Amount. A dimension of disclosiveness that pertains to the frequency of disclosure relative to other people.

Analysis (conversational analysis). The analysis phase of conversational analysis involves the extracting of meaning from the transcribes dialogue.

Anchoring approach. Advocates that people are less likely to change a position if the position is anchored or tied to things that are significant for that person.

Androgynous style. Style of leadership that contains both masculine and feminine communication behaviors.

Animated style. Tendency to expend considerable energy when communicating.

Animated style. A dimension of communicator style which is a trait that signifies extensive use of eyes, face, and gestures to express meaning.

Anomaly. Unexplained event or finding often resulting from research under an old paradigm during a period of scientific change.

Antecedent conditions. Events occurring earlier in time that relate to subsequent conditions or effects.

Anticipatory function of theory. A function of communication theory that reflects the theory's ability to develop expectations about events that we have yet to encounter or experience.

Anticipatory socialization stage. Reflects how people develop expectations about work starting at childhood and include parents, peers, and the media.

Anxiety. A key component of AUM theory that is believed to be the affective equivalent of uncertainty.

Anxiety/uncertainty management theory. AUM is a theory that seeks to explain interpersonal and intergroup communication effectiveness. Explains how people reduce uncertainty and anxiety to explain how people adapt to other cultures.

Apathetic. Experienced by a moderately argumentative person who is low on both approach and avoidance.

Appropriate disclosure. A dimension of communicative adaptability that reflects the degree to which a person reveals personal information in the appropriate amount as dictated by any given situation.

Appropriateness. Dimension of communication competence that is verbal and nonverbal communication that results in no loss of face for the parties involved.

Argumentative skill deficiency. Cause of verbal aggression due to inability to argue skillfully; attack and defend needs are not satisfied.

Argumentativeness. A person's tendency to present and defend positions on controversial issues while attempting to refute the positions others take.

Articulation. A dimension of communicative adaptability that reflects the degree to which a person is proficient or skilled in the expression of ideas.

Assembly rules. Standard processes that aids people in standard routines for making sense of information.

Assertion/questions of fact. Statements or questions that concern whether something is or isn't, occurred or didn't occur, will or will not occur. These statements are considered scientific in nature.

Assertion/questions of policy. Statement or questions that concern whether something should or shouldn't be done. These questions are subjective and thus, not considered scientific.

Assertion/questions of value. Statements or questions that concern whether something is good or bad, favorable or unfavorable. These are not considered scientific questions.

Assertiveness. A person's general tendency to be interpersonally dominant, ascendant, and forceful. Involves four dimensions: directiveness, social, defense, independence.

Assimilation. The degree to which a person accepts the influence of the new culture or environment.

Assumption Maxims. Principles of Communication Privacy Management Theory that concern how people regulate interactions with others when revealing or concealing private information.

Asymmetrical link. Communication link used unequally by two organization members; i.e., only one member initiates communication with the other while the other merely responds when contacted.

Atheoretical. Lacking a theoretical framework to draw upon.

Attentive style. A dimension of communicator style and is the tendency to listen carefully to people, to be able to repeat back what others say.

Attentiveness. A dimension of interaction involvement that is the extent to which one tends to heed cues in the immediate environment.

Attitude similarity. One of the factors associated with interpersonal attraction; degree of perceived or actual similarity in attitudes between people.

Attitude. How favorably we evaluate something.

Attribute variables. Characteristics of research participants that are studied as independent variables.

Audience adaptation. Making a message compatible with receivers' attitudes and values and the nature of the situation.

Authoritarian style. A style of leadership that involves the leader being very directive in terms of the group goals and procedures, the division of work, and deciding the outcome of conflict.

Authority heuristic. A compliance gaining strategy that assumes people should be more willing to follow the suggestions of an individual who is a legitimate authority.

Authority. The ability to get people to voluntarily obey order.

Available sample. Group of research participants selected based on convenience, and lack of evidence that the group is biased.

Avoiding facework. Facework strategy where during conflict, the focus is on maintaining interpersonal harmony between the parties by not overtly addressing the conflict .

Avoiding stage. A stage in the relationship interaction stages model that reflects the physical or communication avoidance of a relational partner.

Avoiding style. A conflict style where we elude to any discussion of the conflict issues with the other party. This may even take the form of avoiding the person or situation involved in the conflict.

Axiology. The study of what is valuable, important, and worthy of study and how theory contributes to the overall body of knowledge and practice.

Axiom. A proposition that is not proven or demonstrated but simply considered true in nature, also known as a postulate.

Background structure. The rules and resources that allow people in an organization to interact and that give meaning to an activity (for example, rules about how one interviews for a job).

Because-motive. Term used by Alfred Schutz to label the reason for taking some action based on an event that happened in the past.

Behavior rules. In the coordinated management of meaning theory, rules that individuals use to decide how to behave.

Behavioral activation system. System used in the communibiological perspective to explain communication by identifying the brain circuitry that results in anxiety about behavior.

Behavioral commitment approach. Advocates that people make public statements about their position and thus less inclined to change their position.

Behavioral inhibition system. System used in the communibiological perspective to explain communication by identifying the brain circuitry that results in anxiety about behavior.

Behavioral intention. A person's intention of performing a given behavior is the best predictor of whether or not the person will actually perform the behavior.

Behavioral observation. Method of measurement that involves observing behavior, classifying it according to a framework, and determining the reliability of the classification.

Belief. A perception of how two or more things are related.

Benefit of presumption. Assumption that the status quo is adequate.

Benevolent-authoritative type. Also known as System 2. Type of management that uses rewards for employee motivation. Employee input is sought only to the extent that management deems appropriate.

Biconstrual orientation. An orientation that is based on high independent and high interdependent self-construals.

Biological time. Cycles or rhythms that our bodies follow: ultradian (hour and a half), circadian (daily).

Bit. Binary digit, such as 0 and 1; components of the binary number system representing a two-choice situation. A measure of the amount of information in a message.

Body orientation. Degree to which a person's shoulders and hips are turned toward another person.

Bogus stranger technique. Method used to manipulate degree of similarity to an unknown other in attraction research. Technique where "information" about the stranger is created by the researcher.

Bonding stage. A stage in the relationship interaction stages model that reflects a strong emotional and psychological link between relational partners.

Boundary coordination. Part of Communication Privacy Management Theory that involves the regulation of boundary linkages, boundary ownership rights, and boundary permeability.

Boundary linkages. Part of Communication Privacy Management Theory reflecting the relationship that is formed between the disclosure and the recipient(s) of the information.

Boundary ownership rights. Part of Communication Privacy Management theory and is the responsibility, privileges, and rights that go along with ownership of private disclosures.

Boundary permeability. Part of Communication Privacy Management Theory and is the degree of access or openness of a privacy boundary.

Boundary requirements. Component of Anxiety/Uncertainty Management theory that assumes certain criteria must be present for any axiom to be true.

Boundary spanning. Activity of going beyond the boundary of a system to link it with its environment.

Boundary turbulence. A conflicted state due to incongruent expectations, misunderstandings of privacy parameters, or access rules, and the handling of private information.

Breakpoints. Component of the multiple sequence model that are interruptions in an activity track. The three breakpoints are pacers, delays, and disrupts.

Bridge. Group member who links two groups and actually belongs to one of them (see gangplank, liaison).

Burden of proof. Obligation to show status quo should be changed.

Bureaucracy. Organization characterized by hierarchical chains of command and power, each with its own separate function and rules for efficient mass administration.

Bureaucratic management. A management perspective that advocates a tight structure with many levels in the hierarchy as well as control over employees.

Causality. A concept of the covering laws approach that assumes if an antecedent condition exists then some consequent effect will occur.

Causation. Relationship in which previous (antecedent) events produce later (consequent) effects.

Central route. The favorable thinking about the message content causes a favorable attitude to form toward the object of the message.

Centrality. Numerous direct contacts in a communication network.

Change agents. Professional who encourage opinion leaders to adopt or reject an innovation.

Channel. Means by which a message is conveyed from source to receiver (radio, television, telephone, face-to-face, for example).

Charisma. A trait that reflects the leader's ability to display a high degree of communication competence, the ability to inspire subordinates, as well as have the subordinates buy into the leader's vision.

Chronemics. Study of how time is used in communication.

Circumscribing stage. A stage in the relationship interaction stages model that reflects relational partners focus communication on everyday matters in order to avoid conflict.

Classical management perspective. A management perspective that seeks to maximize productivity and has little concern for the worker.

Classical theory of organizations. The earliest theory of organizations; classical theory emphasizes the study of structures and power relationships. The organization is compared to a machine, and workers are considered to be one of several means of production, like capital and raw materials.

Closed system. System that has little or no interaction with its environment. System that is not open to new information and tends toward entropy, chaos, or total disorganization.

Code switching. Process of moving from one linguistic code or dialect to another.

Code. Set of rules or symbols used to translate a message from one form into another.

Coercion. Source applies force or pressure as a substitute for the motivation provided by attitudes.

Cognitive complexity. The complexity of one's construct system affects their persuasive ability.

Cognitive dimension of communication. Beliefs about what is and/or is not related to the object of communication.

Cognitive dissonance theory. Assumes that two beliefs are related either in a state of consonance or dissonance.

Cognitive dissonance. Exists when two related beliefs are incompatible with one another or when one belief does not logically follow the other.

Cognitive flexibility. The degree to which a communicator considers options for behaving in different situations.

Cognitive uncertainty. A generalized state of uncertainty between individuals.

Cognitive valence theory. A perceived increase in immediacy behaviors from one person in a relationship activates expectations. If the immediacy behaviors are perceived favorably (positively valanced), positive relationship outcomes will result. If they are not seen favorably (negatively valenced), negative relationship outcomes can result.

Cohesiveness. The feeling of "oneness" in a group, being "closeknit," bound to one another, and united as members of a team.

Collaborative style. A problem-solving approach to conflict situations where consulting with affected parties is considered important.

Collaterality. Cultural value that focuses on the extended group, such as a tribe or racial or religious group.

Collective attitudes. The ideas and impressions that members generally share about an organization.

Collective rationalization. A symptom of groupthink where members dismiss or rationalize any information or warnings that are counter to the groups thinking.

Collectivist cultures. Cultures that emphasize the importance of the group and group goals over the individual and individual goals.

Commitment and consistency heuristic. A compliance gaining strategy that assumes when people take a stand on an issue, there is internal pressure to be consistent with what you committed to.

Commitment and intimacy. A characteristic of the family where higher levels of commitment and intimacy are shared by family members. Family members see each other under all circumstances. In order for a family to stay intact, active participation and commitment are necessary, even at minimum levels.

Communibiological perspective. Approach to explaining communication that claims there is a genetic basis for most communicative behavior based on temperaments.

Communication accommodation theory. Assumes that during communication people try to accommodate or adjust their style of speech to one another and people do this in order to gain approval, increase communication efficiency, and to maintain positive social identity with the other person.

Communication and international relations. The study of communication between nations and their political leaders.

Communication apprehension. Fear or anxiety associated with real or anticipated communication with others. Can take four forms: trait-like, context-based, audience-based, situational.

Communication competence. Involves appropriateness and effectiveness; can be viewed as trait-like, context- or situationally bound.

Communication cycles. Sense-making actions where people create and react to ideas. Most prevalent when there is high equivocation.

Communication isolates. Members who have few communication links or contacts with others in the organization.

Communication plan. Set of behaviors that a person believes will accomplish a purpose.

Communication privacy management privacy (CPM). A theory that is based on explaining how people reveal private information as well as how people conceal private information.

Communication trait. An abstraction constructed to account for enduring consistencies and differences in message-sending and message-receiving behaviors among individuals.

Communication-behavior cycles. Communication interacts (such as questions and answers) that an organization uses to process complex information received from the environment.

Communication. Human manipulation of symbols to stimulate meaning in other humans.

Communicative adaptability scale. The measure of communicative adaptability that assesses social composure, social confirmation, social experience, appropriate disclosure, articulation, and wit.

Communicative adaptability. A trait that is the ability to perceive socio-interpersonal relationships and adapt interaction goals and interpersonal behaviors appropriately.

Communicator image. An overall impression of a communicator that is composed of at least ten traits.

Communicator reward valence. The reward level of the other person in a communication interaction determines the outcome when expectancies are violated; if the reward level is high, we accept violations, if it is low we view the violation negatively.

Communicator style. The way a person verbally and paraverbally interacts to signal how literal meaning should be taken, interpreted, filtered, or understood.

Comparative mass communication. Study of theories comparing media systems from different cultures.

Compensate. Part of Interaction Adaption Theory and reflects the balancing out of the others behavior and seeks to represent the whole spectrum of the interaction.

Competitive style. A win/lose approach to conflict situations that typically involves a good deal of argumentation.

Completely randomized factorial design. An experimental design in which all independent variables are manipulated and research participants are randomly assigned to treatment conditions.

Compliance. Social influence where the source implies that the desired behavior will make the receiver more socially accepted.

Compliments. Utterances in which a speaker bestows positively valued attributes upon a listener.

Compromising style. A conflict style where we seek a midpoint where both parties concede some of their interests in an effort to reach an equitable settlement.

Concept. Abstraction referring to a class of things; a term used at the theoretical level.

Concertive control. Subtle influence of organizations on members to identify with the organization and therefore to make decisions for the benefit of the organization.

Confirmation. Arguments which confirm and support the speaker's case.

Conflict phase. An interact phase that is characterized by members introduced proposals more directly than before. They debate alternative proposals, form coalitions, and struggle for dominance and leadership.

Conflict styles. Distinctive ways of dealing with conflict in interpersonal and group situations.

Conflict. Part of the tolerance for disagreement communication trait and reflects competition, suspicion, distrust, dislike, hostility, and self-perpetuation.

Conflicted feelings. Experienced by a moderate argumentative person who is high in both approach and avoidance.

Conformity. A type of group influence, a change in the individual brought about by pressure (real or imagined) for the person to behave in a manner advocated by the group.

Connotative meaning. Subjective associations, personal, or emotional attachments people associate with symbols.

Consciousness-raising groups. A group that seeks to increase members' awareness of shared characteristics or concerns.

Consensus. A type of decision making from a democratic style of leadership that reflects a group trying to find a resolution of the given issue that everyone in the group can support.

Constitutive definitions. Definition of a concept that utilizes other concepts.

Constitutive metamodel of communication theory. An approach to communication theory building that assumes any theory, regardless of perspective, should be conceptualized as a means to fixing practical problems.

Constitutive rules. Defines or creates speech acts by specifying what counts as a command or request. Also known as definition rules. Rules of meaning which are used to interpret or understand events or messages, from the communication theory called CMM (Coordinated management of meaning).

Construct. Abstraction referring to a class of things, a term used at the theoretical level.

Constructivism. Cognitive theory of communication that explains how people use personal constructs (bi-polar opposites) to classify, interpret, and produce messages.

Constructivist model of credibility. How individuals use their personal construct systems to form, reinforce, and change impressions of sources.

Consultative type. Also known as System 3. Type of management that uses reward and punishment to motivate employees. Smaller decisions are left to the employees while bigger decisions are made by upper management.

Content analysis. Method of measurement for studying the content of messages, which utilizes a category system and checks the reliability of categorizing message units.

Content dimension of communication. Reflects the content of the message.

Contentious style. A dimension of communicator style that is a disposition to challenge other when disagreements occur, to argue with others.

Context. Type of situation in which communication others.

Contextual view. Behavior is consistent within contexts but varies across contexts.

Contingency theory of leadership. A theory of leadership that assumes the degree of success of any leader is contingent on the situational demands as to whether the leader should have a task or employee focus and the amount of influence and control the leader has over the situation.

Continuous variables. When there are meaningful degrees of a variable between the highest and lowest values.

Control. Interpersonal communication motive used to gain compliance from others, to get others to do what you want then to do. Also a dimension of the interpersonal dynamics model that reveals which partner currently defines and directs the actions of the pair.

Controllability. People's belief that they have control over the behavior, that the performance of the behavior is-or-is not up to them.

Conventional message design logics. Conversation follows a particular set of rules in a particular way in order to accomplish goals.

Convergence. A dimension of communication accommodation theory that is a strategy where individuals alter their speech to adapt to each other.

Conversation analysis theory (CA). A theory that views communication as a primary resource through which social life is constructed. Also provides a framework through which the practice of talk can be analyzed in a way as to reveal how communication patterns can constrain a relationship but also how changes in the action of talk can also redefine the relationship.

Conversational analysis. Coding of natural conversation that has broad description categories that allow researchers to get at the subtleties of communication.

Conversational repair. Part of conversation analysis theory, that assumes both the speaker and the receiver both have sets of practices for clarifying miscommunication.

Cooperation. A function of health communication that involves communication concerning the nature of one's illness and the implication of measures prescribed for care.

Coordinated management of meaning. Communication theory which is concerned with how people interpret messages during interaction and act upon those interpretations using constitutive and regulative rules.

Coordination. How individuals organize their meanings and actions to communicate. The rules they use to act on meanings can allow the actions of individuals to be compatible or consistent with one another without complete understanding being present between the persons.

Coping/adjustment. The response of the individual to encountering new or changing cultures or environments.

Correlation. A dimension of the functional theory of mass communication that concerns how the mass media select, interpret, and criticize the information they present to the public.

Costs. Anything that we see as a punishment or detriment from a relationship.

Counsel. A function of health communication that involves the role of the provider as "therapist." Also includes therapeutic communication as one of the major purposes of interpersonal communication. The health-care provider engaged in the therapeutic function deals with the client's "symbolic" symptoms.

Counteractive influence. A behavior in functional group decision making where a member corrects a fallacious conclusion by another group member.

Counterarguing hypothesis. Assumes that viewers who are critical consumers of television new stories about national issues (that is, they argue against what they see and hear on television news) are less likely to change their political views than individuals who do not engage in counterarguing.

Country club manager. A management style that indicates a high concern for worker and a low concern for task.

Courage. An ethical practice where the organization values employee dissent, listening to employee dissent, as well as admitting when the organization has made a mistake.

Covering laws perspective. Developed from logical positivism, a theoretical paradigm that asserts the true nature of reality is contained in regular, observable, natural patterns.

Covering laws. Law-like regularities in nature that operate according to cause-and-effect principles.

Credentialing. A type of preventative that uses membership or affiliation to violate conversational rules.

Credibility hypothesis. Assumes television news is a powerful agenda setter because people perceive the news to be credible and authoritative.

Critical theories. This perspective examines power, control, and liberating the oppressed from those who oppress them. Critical theorist work to reveal who has power over whom, to empower disadvantaged groups, and to effect change through critique and education.

Critical tradition. A tradition of theory building that views communication as a discourse that freely reflects on assumptions that can be related to ideology, power, and un-scrutinized rituals.

Cross cultural adaptation theory. An intercultural theory that explains the process of how people adjust to a new environment. Environment refers to any cultural experience that is different from the person's home experience.

Cross cultural communication. Subset of intercultural communication that refers to communication between people from different cultures.

Cross-situational consistency. Consistency of behavior across situations; involves validity of trait approaches to behavior.

Cues to action. A dimension of the health belief model that are stimuli necessary to trigger appropriate or desired health behavior.

Cultivation theory. This theory asserts that television influences our view of reality.

Cultural transmission. A dimension of the functional theory of mass communication that concerns the media's ability to communicate norms, rules, and values of a society.

Culture-bound. Appropriate only for a particular culture or group of people; not true for all cultures.

Culture. The traditions, customs, norms, beliefs, values, and thought patterning which are passed down from generation to generation.

Cybernetic learning. A type of learning that reflects adjusting thoughts and behaviors based on feedback from the environment (e.g., management).

Cybernetic systems. A system that tries to maintain a balance with their environment through a process called homeostasis or self-regulating. After a change in the environment, the system adapts to maintain equilibrium.

Cybernetic tradition. A tradition of theory building as information processing and concerns analyzing communication problems.

Cycles. A dimension of the interaction system model that entails the analysis of group phases.

Dangling carrot approach. An approach to performance that assumes people only work for tangible rewards.

Deception detection. An uncertainty reduction strategy which includes the careful scrutiny of nonverbal behavior.

Deception. A special form of communication that involves much more behavioral management than other forms of communication.

Decision-making groups. A type of task-oriented group that problem solves plus decides what solution will be implemented, when and how the solution will be implemented, how progress will be monitored and how changes in the solution will be handled.

Decoding. The process of taking the stimuli that has been received and giving those stimuli meaning through individual interpretation and perception.

Deculturation. The degree to which a person unlearns the beliefs and practices of a culture or environment.

Defense of rights and interests. A willingness to confront others to protect rights and interests.

Defensive routines. When workers develop preventative or reactive routines instead of being proactive in the workplace.

Definition rules. In the coordinated management of meaning theory, rules that individuals use to interpret another's words and actions.

Delays. A type of breakpoint in the small group decision making process that occurs when the group cycles back to rework an issue.

Delegating style. A management style that assumes workers have high levels of psychological and job maturity.

Deliberative speaking. Oratory which pertains to political topics.

Democratic leadership style. The leader seeks group member participation in determining group goals and procedures.

Democratic style. A style of leadership that involves viewing all issues (including goals, procedures, and work assignments) as matters to be discussed by the group.

Denotative meaning. The objective, descriptive, or agreed-upon meaning of a word. A dictionary definition.

Deontological ethical perspective. Assumes that if a person's intentions are based on sound ethical reasoning, the action is ethical.

Dependent variables. Presumed effect in cause-effect relationship with independent variables.

Depersonalization. The process of focusing all interaction in the workplace on task completion and discouraging interactions that are relational in nature.

Depth. A dimension of disclosiveness that refers to how superficial or intimate the information is.

Description. Goal of theory that serves to focus attention or particular parts of an event or phenomenon as well as provide a blue-print with which the theory can be applied.

Desires. Part of Interaction Adaptation Theory and are "highly personalized and reflect things such as one's personality and other individual differences.

Development of self-concept. A characteristic of the family that assumes our self concepts are formed through interactions with family members. These interactions are probably the most potent sources of information and influence.

Developmental communication. Communication related to social change, often in developing countries. Spans the boarder between mass communication and interpersonal communication.

Diagnosis. A function of health communication that involves data-gathering, data interpretation, and problem-solving skills used by the health-care provider.

Dialectic. Ongoing tension or struggle between two forces.

Dialectical tensions. A characteristic of the family that assumes there are polarities, paradoxes, contradictions and/or competing demands all operating within families as members interact with each other.

Dialogic communication. An ethical practice that emphasizes open channels of communication that constitutes the cornerstone of teamwork.

Dichotomous variable. Variable with two discrete values.

Differentiation stage. A stage in the relationship interaction stages model that reflects highlighting how different you are from your relational partner.

Differentiation. From the communication theory Constructivism, it is a measure of the number of constructs a person has in their cognitive system.

Diffusion of innovation. The study of how new ideas spread among groups of people.

Direct personalization. A dimension of taking conflict personally reflecting the hurt a person experiences during a conflict episode.

Directiveness. A dimension of assertiveness that involves leadership: taking charge in group situations and seeking positions where one can influence others.

Disagreement. Part of the tolerance for disagreement communication trait and reflects the difference of opinion on issues.

Disclosiveness. Personality trait that reflects a person's predilection to disclose to other people in general. It contains five dimensions of; intent, amount, positive/negative, depth, honesty.

Discourse analysis. The coding of natural conversation that has a narrower coding procedure and greater reliance on statistical analysis than conversational analysis.

Discourse. Expression of thought through extended speech.

Disdain. Cause of verbal aggression that involves the desire to communicate dislike for a person through verbally aggressive messages.

Disengaged homemaker. A lifestyle type indicating primarily female, middle-aged, lower in education and income, and use the media for companionship and to pass time.

Displacement. Moving mentally from the present to either a past or future time framework. In language study, the ability to communicate about things that cut across time, space, reality and fantasy.

Disposition. The arrangement and organization of arguments to for a case to be presented to listeners.

Disruption. A type of breakpoint in the small group decision making process that occurs when there is a major disagreement or when the decision-making process agreed upon by the group fails.

Distributed information. Information that has been communicated throughout an organization.

Distributive justice. Normative principles that concern what is just or right regarding the allocation of goods in the organization.

Divergence. A dimension of communication accommodation theory that reflects accentuating vocal and linguistic differences to underscore social differences between speakers.

Dogmatism. Individual's willingness to consider belief systems other than the ones they hold.

Dominance. Degree to which one partner is said to dominate a dyad's interaction.

Dominant style. A dimension of communicator style that reflects coming on strong, speaking frequently, taking leadership roles, and wanting to control social situations.

Dominating framework. Facework strategy where conflict is seen as a competition where the most important goal is to win the conflict and maximize reward.

Dominating style. A conflict style where the most important thing is to achieve personal goals without regard to the interests of the other party.

Domination. A concept referring to how much one individual commands the interaction.

Door in the face technique. A compliance gaining strategy that utilizes a large request followed by a smaller request. People are more likely to agree to the smaller request after rejecting the larger request.

Double loop learning. Also known as generative learning. Type of learning that entails learning the process, and how this process contributes to the function of the entire organization.

Double-interact. A dimension of the interaction system model that consists of a pattern of behavior-response adjustment.

Downward communication. Communication from higher members of the organization (i.e., managers, vice-presidents) to members lower in the organizational hierarchy (subordinates).

Dramatic style. A dimension of communicator style that involves telling jokes and stories to illustrate points, exaggerating for emphasis, and generally creating the impression of "acting" when talking with people.

Dramatism. Rhetorical theory of Kenneth Burke; dramatism emphasizes the drama as a metaphor for understanding human communication.

Duractivity. A dimension of uses and gratification theory that consists of the degree of psychological attentiveness or involvement audience members exhibit during a television viewing experience.

Education. A function of health communication that assumes health education is the process of disseminating information to individuals in order to attempt to reduce health risks and to increase the effectiveness of health care. Health education proceeds through channels ranging from informal provider/consumer interaction to more formal mass-media campaigns designed to achieve clear and planned objectives.

Effective communication. The degree to which the other person assigns or attaches a similar meaning to the meanings that were intended by the sender.

Effective management theory. A theory that assumes management action should be comprised of planning for the future, organizing, commanding, coordinating, and controlling.

Effectiveness. A dimension of communication competence that refers to the speaker achieving communicative goals.

Ego-involvement theory. Predicts persuasion is most likely when a message falls within the person's latitude of acceptance.

Ego-involvement. Characterized by a wide latitude of rejection and narrow latitudes of acceptance and noncommitment.

Eide topoi. Beliefs, values, and attitudes held by listeners that may be states in propositional for and use for major premises in an argument.

Elaboration likelihood model. A model of persuasion that assumes persuasion results primarily from characteristics of the persuasive message or from characteristics of the situation.

Elocution. Rhetorical canon of oratory concerned with language style.

Emblems. Bodily movements that are functionally equivalent to words.

Emergence phase. An interact phase that is characterized by conflicts and arguments being reduced; coalitions formed earlier tend to dissolve. Consensus if formed.

Emotional leakage. A term used to describe when a persons feelings "leak out" through one or more nonverbal channels.

Empathy. Ability to share another person's feelings, to feel as the other does.

Empirical. Information or data that is gathered by systematic observation.

Empiricists. People who develop theory based on observation such as that found in social science.

Enactment. The act of making sense of equivocal information.

Encoding. Process of taking an already conceived idea and getting it ready for transmission.

Enculturation. A type of cultural adaptation reflecting when we learn to speak, listen, read, interpret, and understand verbal and nonverbal messages in such a fashion that the messages will be recognized and responded to by the individuals with whom we communicate.

Energia. The use of energy in language which creates vivid, thrilling, exciting, and lively images.

Entertainment function of media. Use of the media to delight, stimulate, enchant, escape.

Entertainment. A dimension of the functional theory of mass communication that reflects how mass communication helps fill our leisure time by presenting messages filled with comedy, tragedy, play, and performance.

Enthymeme. A form of argument which relies upon the listener supplying part of the argument.

Entropy. Chaos, randomness, and disorder in a system. Entropy is the final state of a closed system.

Entry phase. Dimension of uncertainty reduction theory that reflects the initial phase of relationships where physical appearance, sex, age, socio-economic status, and other biographic and demographic information is most important.

Epideictic oratory. Ceremonial speaking, including funeral orations and holiday speeches.

Epistemics of social relations. A perspective in conversation analysis theory that assumes that there are direct links between the communicators identity that is directly implicated in the practice of talk. Our identity is something we do, not something we are.

Epistemology. The study of how people come to know knowledge as well as how theory is investigated.

Equifinality. Concept from systems theory that assumes there are many different ways by which a system may reach the same end state.

Equilibrium. Point of balance.

Escape. Interpersonal communication motive used to avoid engaging in other activities and to "fill the time."

Espoused theory. What a manager tells employees about the manager's ethics, management style, and management philosophy.

Esteem needs. One of Maslow's hierarchy of needs reflecting the need for recognition, appreciation, and respect from others.

Ethos. A form of proof that refers to the way listeners perceive the speakers.

Eudaimonic philosophy of life. A philosophy of life that reflects the pursuit of deeper meanings in life beyond those of the pursuit of pleasure and happiness.

Evidence. Information or data used to support the truth or probability of a proposition or a speaker's claims.

Excessive stereotyping. A symptom of groupthink where the group creates negative stereotypes of rivals and others outside of the group.

Exchange approach to leadership. A leadership approach that assumes the quality of the relationship is believed to be the determining factor for effective leadership.

Exit phase. Dimension of uncertainty reduction theory that assumes that during this phase, the communicators decide on future interaction plans.

Exordium. Part of the introduction of a speech which stimulates attention for the speech topic by using a device such as a story.

Expectancy violation theory. Theory that explains a wide range of communication outcomes associated with violations of expectations about nonverbal communication behavior.

Expectations. Part of Interaction Adaptation Theory and are formed by societal norms of appropriateness as well as the degree of knowledge that we have developed from past interactions with that specific person.

Experimental designs. Involves manipulation of at least one variable with control of other variables that could influence results.

Experimental paradigm. Tool of the law-governed approach used by researchers to create controlled situations in order to test the effects of antecedent conditions on subsequent outcomes.

Experimenter effects. Error in a study caused by the experimenter's characteristics and/or behavior.

Experimenting stage. A stage in the relationship interaction stages model that reflects relational partners focusing on finding similarities between them.

Explanation. Goal of theory that concerns understanding how a phenomenon or event occurs.

Exploitive orientation. Tendency to take, by cunning or force, what is valuable to other people.

Exploitive-authoritative type. Also known as System 1. Type of management that uses fear and threats to motivates employees. Decisions are made at top levels of the organization and handed down to the workers. Employee input is devalued.

Expression-privacy dialectic. This tension takes the form of openness/closedness within a relationship; the public form is revelation/concealment.

Expressive message design logics. Message created by focusing on expressing individual opinions and feelings.

Extension. Type of theory building that reflects a theory's ability further, describe, explain, predict, and control an ever growing number of concepts and situations.

External locus of control. A perception that the person perceives that their lives and behavior are controlled by others.

External validity. Concerned with the generalizability of a study; major threats are pretesting, experimental arrangements, sampling and multiple treatment effects.

Eye behavior. Nonverbal behavior that communicates attitude, interest, dominance or submission.

Face gain. Reflects when people treat us in ways that enhances our existing self-image.

Face loss. Reflects when people treat us in ways that are inconsistent with our self-image.

Face threats. Any threats to our self-image or face.

Face-negotiation theory. A theory that explains intercultural conflict and how people from different cultures work through the various cultural and communicative obstacles to get a resolution based on mutual respect and communication competence.

Face. Our self-image and the image we want others in society to have of us.

Facework theory. Process people use to communicate their face and to support or challenge another person's face; addresses relationship and identity concerns as well as substantive issues.

Facework. Specific verbal and nonverbal behaviors that we engage in to maintain or restore face loss and to uphold and honor face.

Factor model of credibility. Aspects of credibility are a source's expertise, character, and goodwill.

Falsification. The ability for a theory to be falsified. If a theory cannot be disproven, it is of no utility to science.

Family communication. Communication between family members.

Family system. A set of people (objects) in a family and the relationships between them.

Fantasy theme analysis. Method of rhetorical criticism used by Bormann to analyze the symbolic communication of a group in order to discover the group's shared culture and values.

Fantasy type. In symbolic convergence theory, a recurring story or script in a group's culture.

Fear appeal. Argument or persuasive appeal designed to scare or frighten receivers into compliance.

Feedback. Verbal and/or nonverbal reactions to a message received by the source.

Feeling understood. Emotional state associated with feelings of satisfaction, acceptance, pleasure, importance.

Field of approachables. Subset of field of availables. Those individuals who possess desirable attributes and with whom we would consider relational development.

Field of availables. All individuals with whom we can expect contact in order to develop a relationship.

Field of reciprocals. Subset of field of approachables. Those with whom we will begin the relational development process.

Field research. Research conducted in a naturalistic setting.

Fight or flight system. System used in the communibiological perspective to explain communication by identifying the brain circuitry involved in response to a threat.

Flow. Stream of communication messages.

Forensic Speaking. Courtroom oratory, speaking in courts of law.

Forewarning. Messages that warn the audience by mentioning the type of arguments an opposing speaker will present.

Formal communication systems. Communication links and networks determined and sanctioned by the organization (see also bridge and liaison).

Foundational ethical perspective. Assumes that ethical behavior is absolute and universal to all human beings.

Friendly style. A dimension of communicator style that reflects communicating in a more intimate way.

Functional approach to leadership. Focuses on the leadership behaviors needed by a group to accomplish its goals, not on specific individuals.

Functional model of credibility. Analysis of source credibility in terms of the degree to which the source satisfies the receiver's needs.

Functional theory of group decision making. The principles of the theory involve the communication characteristics of group interaction that lead to quality decisions. Four critical functions are achieving a thorough understanding of the problem that requires a decision, discovering a range of realistic and acceptable possible solutions, identifying the criteria for an effective, high-quality solution, and assessing the positive and negative consequences of possible solutions.

Fundamental ethical perspective. Assumes that ethical behavior is true in nature and universal.

Gangplank. Also known as Fayol's bridge and is the lateral exchange of information between members at the same level in the organization.

Gatekeepers. People who control the flow of information to a given group of people.

General level of anxiety acceptance. A level of anxiety that exists between a person's maximum and minimum thresholds for anxiety.

General level of uncertainty acceptance. A level of uncertainty that exists between a person's maximum and minimum thresholds for uncertainty.

General theories. Universal explanations which account for broad classes of events. Such theories are neither time or culture-bound.

Generalizability. Characteristic of the covering laws approach that assumed conclusions are true across situations and many different time periods.

Generative learning. See double loop learning.

Great man theories of leadership. An approach to leadership where great leaders were studied in an effort to determine what traits and behaviors make an effective leader.

Group attractiveness. A function served by the group that leads to compliance in that the more attractive a group is to us, the more we are likely to be influenced by the group.

Group history. A contingency dimension in the multiple sequence model that governs the decision making process. Reflects events that happen earlier in the group process will create expectations about what will happen in the future. This dimension contains how involved group members are, their beliefs about the leadership of the group, as well as the procedural norms of the group.

Group maintenance. A function served by the group that leads to compliance where we realize that the group needs to put on a united front. If a member behaves differently, it will weaken the image of the group.

Group roles. Individual, task, group-building and maintenance behaviors enacted in groups to accomplish group and individual goals.

Groupthink. A communication process that sometimes develops when members of a group begin thinking similarly, greatly reducing the probability that the group will reach an effective decision.

Growth factors. See motivator factors.

Habitual rituals. Rule behavior that is typically non negotiable, usually imposed by those in positions of authority, and yielded negative consequences if they are violated.

Haptics. The use of touch in communication. Can be a powerful nonverbal immediacy cue.

Hawthorne effect. A threat to the internal validity of an experiment where a change in experimental conditions bring about a change in the behavior of the participants in which the experiment was originally intended to identify.

Hawthorne studies. A series of studies between 1927–1932 which gave rise to the human relations approach to management

Health belief model (HBM). Model of behavioral change developed to help explain and predict preventative health behaviors—methods of educating people to adopt or incorporate behaviors that could lead to better health and safety outcomes.

Health communication. Communication involving healthcare providers and healthcare recipients.

Hedonic philosophy of life. A philosophy of life that reflects the pursuit of pleasure and happiness for the individual.

Heuristic function of a theory. Role a theory plays in leading to new discoveries by stimulating future research.

Heuristic value. The assumption that the value of a theory lie within the theory's capacity to solve problems or provide solutions that are closest to the "best solution."

Hierarchy of needs theory. A motivational theory indicating that people seek to become self-actualized only after satisfying more primary needs such as food/water, safety, love, and esteem needs.

Hierarchy. Ordering in which parts are related to each other in subordinate or superordinate fashion. For example, they may be more or less important, large, or complex.

High power distance. A culture that values unequal power, unequal relationships, and unequal rewards that are based on status, role, gender, age, etc. (e.g., China).

High-context culture. Culture in which most of the information in a message is encoded in the physical context or in the person's mental catalog of rules, roles, and values.

Holistic. Cannot be divided into parts without destroying its nature; systems are holistic (sometimes spelled wholistic).

Homeostasis. Process of self-regulation by which a cybernetic system maintains an equilibrium with the environment.

Honesty. A dimension of disclosiveness that involves the sincerity of disclosure.

Horizontal chain of communication. Communication between organizational members on the same hierarchical level (between two managers or between two subordinates, for example).

Hostility. Personality trait where symbols are used to express irritability, negativism, resentment, and suspicion.

Human relations approach. A management approach that advocates management should satisfy the interpersonal and emotional needs of workers.

Human resource approach. A management approach that assumes employees are a valuable asset who should be developed for the benefit of both the organization as well as the worker.

Hygiene factors. Factor of motivation based on factors associated with being dissatisfied such as working conditions and interpersonal relationships, etc.

Hypothesis. An educated guess as to the probable results made before a measurement of the concepts under study.

Idea-generation groups. A type of task-oriented groups that seeks to discover a variety of solutions, approaches, perspectives, consequences, etc. for a topic.

Identification. Applied by Tompkins and Cheney to work groups or organizations, Burke's idea that individuals identify with others by accepting their values, goals, and decision rules.

Identity objective. Desired image the individual wants to communicate.

Identity objectives. The image the communicator wants others to have of him or her.

Illocutionary acts. Speech acts designed to communicate the speakers intention to the receiver.

Illusion of invulnerability. A symptom of groupthink where members ignore apparent danger, take unsafe risks and are unrealistically optimistic.

Illusion of morality. A symptom of groupthink where members believe their actions are inherently noble, right, and moral without considering the consequences.

Illusion of unanimity. A symptom of groupthink where members of the group falsely interprets everyone in the group as agreeing even when members are silent.

Illustrators. Gestures that accompany words for emphasis.

Immediacy behaviors. Behaviors that indicate liking and create high sensory involvement.

Impersonal impression formation. Communication that relies on stereotypes and other assumptions about what people are like to guide your communicative behavior. Based on sociological data.

Impoverished manager. A management style that indicates a low concern for worker and a low concern for task.

Impression leaving style. A dimension of communicator style that is a disposition to create a lasting image in the minds of the receivers.

In-group relationships. This type of relationship between leader and follower indicates a high quality linkage or relationship.

In-group. When we share a great deal of important characteristics with other people.

In-order-to motive. Term used by Alfred Schutz to refer to the mental picture of a goal that someone wants to attain. We think about such goals as though they had already been completed in the future.

Incentive. A motivation associated with uncertainty reduction theory where we want to know more about people who control rewards or who can satisfy our needs.

Inclusion. Interpersonal communication motive use to share feelings, avoid loneliness, to be with others (i.e., companionship).

Independence. A dimension of assertiveness and involves maintaining personal convictions even when in the minority and receiving pressure from the majority to conform.

Independent couple type. A couple that values freedom and subscribe less to conventional male/female roles than do traditional couple type.

Independent orientation. An orientation that is based on high independent and low interdependent self-construal.

Independent self-construal. A person's self-image that assumes we are unique with our own repertoire of feelings, cognitions, and motivations that are separate from other people.

Independent-mindedness. Characteristic values of individuality and constructive argument.

Independent variables. Variables that cause and/or predict dependent variables.

Individualistic culture. Culture that emphasizes the importance of the individual's interest over the group interest and focus on their own feelings.

Informal communication systems. Communication links and networks (not determined by the organizational chart) that arise through natural human interaction. For example, two workers who might have no formal communication links may be connected in the informal communication system because they both play on the company golf team or eat lunch together.

Informal norms. Standards for behavior that are shared, often implicitly, by work group members. These norms may contradict formal, management-directed norms.

Information theory. Theory first developed by Shannon and Weaver in 1949 which sought to identify the most efficient way to get a message from one point to another.

Information. In information theory, refers to the degree of uncertainty present in a situation.

Informational reception apprehension. A pattern of anxiety and antipathy that filters informational reception, perception, and processing, and/or adjustment (psychologically, verbally, physically) associated with complexity, abstractness, and flexibility.

Informational systems theory. An information processing theory that seeks to explain how information and sense-making is a perceptual process that varies from person to person.

Initiation stage. A stage of the relationship interaction stages model that reflects the first interactions of relational partners.

Innovation. Function of a communication system to change itself and to generate new ideas.

Inoculation theory. Approach to preventing persuasion based on the biological analogy of preventing disease.

Inputs. Raw materials an open system receives from its environment.

Instrumental objectives. A speaker's intention to entertain, inform, stimulate, and/or persuade people on the topic of the message.

Instrumental use. Using television viewing primarily for information acquisition.

Integrating facework. Facework strategy where during conflict, the focus is on the resolution of conflict issues as well as making sure the relationship remains positive and both parties maintain face.

Integrating stage (relationship development). A stage in the relationship interaction stages model that reflects when relational partners begin to talk about the future together and share a sense of being committed.

Integrating style (conflict). A conflict style where there is a need for conflict resolution with a high degree of concern for the individual interests of all parties involved.

Integration-separation dialectic. This tension takes the form of connection-autonomy within a relationship; the public form is inclusion-seclusion.

Integration. The degree to which the person participates in the new culture.

Integrative strategy. Melds of conflicting goals of conversational clarity and relationship/face maintenance by truly resolving the conflict goals.

Intellectual inflexibility. The degree to which people are unwilling to consider different points of view.

Intensifying stage. A stage in the relationship interaction stages model that reflects relational partners seek to find similarities in terms of morals and values.

Intent. A dimension of self-disclosure that involves the degree of awareness that one is revealing information about self.

Intention. Type of theory building that reflects the theories ability to further understand the concepts already explained by the theory.

Intentionality. Criteria for determining whether communication occurred.

Interact phases. A dimension of the interaction system model that consists of four phases through which decisions emerge in task groups.

Interact. A dimension of the interaction system model that is a behavior followed by an answer.

Interaction adaptation theory (IAT). A theory that seeks to explain behavior that is mindful, intentional, and symbolic and assumes that adaptation is a systematic patterns of behavior that is in direct response to the interactive pattern of another communicator.

Interaction complexity. A characteristic of the family that assumes there is a complex set of rules (especially communication rules) existing within families. These rules are often understood only by the members of the family.

Interaction deception theory. A theory that assumes that both people in a communicative situation utilize a variety of strategies to achieve particular interpersonal goals.

Interaction involvement. The extent to which an individual participates with another in conversation.

Interaction maxims. Principles of Communication Privacy Management Theory that concerns how people regulate interactions with others when revealing or concealing private information.

Interaction model. A model that assumes communication episodes within families repeat, that messages within family communication are highly complex in both content and relationship dimensions, and that family communication is a process with no distinct beginning or end.

Interaction position. A unique collection of individualized communication information reflective of what is needed, anticipated, and preferred in interaction situations.

Interaction system model. A systems approach to small group interaction that focuses on group member interactions instead of focusing on individual human behavior.

Interactional perspective. An approach to studying families that explores how family members' communication meshes and interlocks.

Interactionist position. Assumes that behavior in a particular situation is a joint product of a person's traits and of variables in the situation.

Interactionist. Approach to communication that emphasizes traits and situational variables in explanations of communication.

Interactive strategies. An uncertainty reduction strategy that consists of obtaining information directly through asking questions (interrogation) and offering personal information about yourself.

Interactivity demands. The degree to which messages are connected to previous messages, occur in real time, and number of verbal and nonverbal channels available to interactants.

Intercultural communication. Communication between people from different cultures.

Intercultural. Communication between people from different cultures or between people from different subcultures of the same sociocultural system.

Interdependent orientation. An orientation that is based on low independent and high interdependent self-construal.

Interdependent self-construal. A person's self-image that assumes our identity is tightly linked to the relationships we have with other people in our culture.

Internal locus of control. A perception that the person has direct control over their lives and behaviors.

Internal validity. Check to determine whether something other than the independent variables such as history, maturation, measurement, or selection, could be responsible for results.

Interpersonal attraction. Perceived liking for another individual based primarily on: similarity, proximity, attractiveness (physical, task and social), and reinforcement.

Interpersonal communication. Communication between two people.

Interpersonal deception theory. A theory of deception in interpersonal communication that bases its predictions about outcomes on the characteristics of the source, receiver, content, message, feedback, and channel.

Interpersonal dynamics model. A model that assumes relationships emerge from patterns of interaction made up of redundant and interlocking cycles of messages continually negotiated.

Interpersonal impression formation. Impression of other that guides interaction is based mainly on psychological data such as values, attitudes, and personality.

Interpersonal objectives. The relationship that the speaker desires with the message receiver.

Interpersonal relations area of group communication. Communication behaviors that regulate participation so no one feels "left out," creating a positive emotional climate, promoting group self-analysis, resolving conflict in the discussion, and investigating conflict in order to stimulate a more thorough examination of the issues.

Interpretation and evolution of behavior. An element of expectancy violation theory that assumes behaviors are meaningful and that we have attitudes about expected nonverbal behaviors.

Interpretive perspective. Theoretical paradigm whose followers believe that the true nature of reality can best be discovered by under-standing individuals' subjective interpretations of reality.

Interval data. Represents a level of measurement where the points on the scale are assumed to increase or decrease by a constant degree.

Intimacy. A dimension of the interpersonal dynamics model that concerns how often partners use the other to confirm their feelings of being separate or connected in a relationship.

Invention. The discovery of arguments that pertain to the particular object of persuasion in the situation.

Investigational design. A design where no independent variable is manipulated.

Irritability. A dimension of hostility and is reflected in a quick temper in response to the slightest provocation, being generally moody and grouchy, showing little patience, being exasperated when there is a delay or something goes wrong, and being rude and inconsiderate of others' feelings.

Job maturity. The degree of knowledge that workers have of their task.

Kinesics. The use of body motion when communicating. Can be used as a nonverbal immediacy cue.

Knowledge extension function. The function of communication theory that entails the further investigation or understanding of an event or phenomenon that is already explained by the theory.

Koinoi topoi. A unique paradigm of rhetorical invention.

Laissez-faire style. A style of leadership that involves a minimum of involvement by the leader in group activity.

Language expectancy theory (LET). A language theory of persuasion that focuses on how cultural expectation of language use affect both the change and reinforcement of attitudes and beliefs.

Language intensity. Quality of speaker's language about objects or concepts that indicates a difference in attitude from neutral.

Latitude of acceptance. Consists of all statements the person finds acceptable. This can include the favorite position or the anchor.

Latitude of noncommitment. Consists of all of the positions a person neither accepts nor rejects.

Latitude of rejection. Consists of all of the positions on an issue the person rejects.

Laws. Regularities in nature which can be observed and/or discovered.

Leader member exchange theory. A leadership theory that focuses on the quality linkages between both the leader and the follower. The relational linkage is the main influence on effective leadership.

Learned helplessness. Helplessness that occurs from repeated negative consequences resulting in the worker showing little initiative if any.

Learning groups. A group that seeks to acquire information and understanding of a topic.

Learning. Approach to persuasion that emphasizes how feelings are conditioned to an object of persuasion.

Length of requests. The longer the request the less powerful and less status the person is perceived to have.

Liaison. Person who links two groups but is not a member of either group (see bridge).

Like/dislike valence. A dimension of taking conflict personally that reflects the degree to which people enjoy engaging in conflict.

Likelihood of interaction with them in the future. A motivation is associated with uncertainty reduction theory that assumes a person's desire for future contact causes people to pay close attention to their own and other's communication.

Likert scales. Rating scales that utilize a five or seven point agree-disagree format to rate value statements about an object.

Linear process. Viewing communication in terms of one thing leading to another, which leads to something else in sequence.

Linear scales. Rating scales that specify placing an object along a continuum, often dealing with degree or quantity.

Linguistic or behavioral uncertainty. The level of uncertainty felt in a particular conversation.

Linking function. Inherent function of communication that involves the person establishing relationships with the environment.

Linking heuristic. A compliance gaining strategy that assumes we comply with requests because we like the person.

Listening apprehension. The fear associated with either anticipated or real listening situations.

Locus of control. A personality trait that concerns how people interpret outcomes in their life.

Logical force. In the coordinated management of meaning theory, the strength of the influence that meanings and rules have on behavior.

Logical positivism. A particular way of knowing that asserts we can only know something in two ways, through our senses, or discover it through some type of logical derivation or mathematical modeling.

Logically consistent. Theory that does not contain contradictory propositions. Opposite predictions should not be possible.

Logos. A form of proof from the speaker building arguments, especially enthymemes, within the predispositional fields of the listeners.

Longevity of influence. The influence of one's family endures for a lifetime; its traditions are passed on from generation to generation. This is true whether the family is considered functional or dysfunctional.

Love needs. One of Maslow's hierarchy of needs reflecting the need for affection and belonging.

Low power distance. A culture that values the equal distribution of power, equal power relationships, and equal reward (e.g., Sweden).

Low-context culture. Culture in which most information in a message is contained in the explicit or verbal message.

Machiavellianism. Personality trait in which people believe that manipulating others is a basic strategy of social influence.

Macronetwork. Network along which messages are transmitted between groups in the organization.

Magic bullet theory. A theory of mass communication that suggests media influences people directly and uniformly.

Mainstreaming. The power of television to present uniformed images acceptable to a majority of viewers.

Maintenance. Function of a communication system to maintain interpersonal relations among organizational members.

Majority decision. A type of decision making from a democratic style of leadership that assumes an agreed upon percentage of votes must be obtained for an idea to pass.

Managerial grid theory. A theory that contains two continua resulting in five managerial profiles ranging in concern for task and concern for relationship.

Marketplace of ideas. A way of viewing a free society.

Maslow's hierarchy of needs. Theory of motivation that holds people are motivated to satisfy essential human needs starting with physiological needs and moving to higher psychological needs.

Mass communication. Communication to large audiences that is mediated by electronic or print media.

Maximum threshold for anxiety. A maximum level of anxiety that when not exceeded, allows people to remain comfortable when interacting with other people.

Maximum threshold for uncertainty. A maximum level of uncertainty that when not exceeded, allows people to remain comfortable when interacting with other people.

Meaning. From the communication theory Coordinated Management of Meaning (CMM), it refers to the process by which individuals in conversation interpret and decode the messages of others.

Mechanistic approach. Theoretical perspective that compares human behavior to that of machines. Actions are thought to occur because of prior events without the necessity of individual purposes or goals.

Media dependency theory. A theory of mass communication that assumes the more dependent an individual is on the media for having his or her needs filled, the more important the media will be to the person.

Mediated interpersonal communication. Any situation where mediated technology (for example, telephone, computer) is used to advance face-to-face interaction.

Mediator. Neutral third party who helps settle a conflict.

Memoria. Memory devices taught to enable the memorizing of an oration.

Mentation function. Inherent function of communication that stimulates the development of higher mental processes.

Message design logic. Differences in persuaders' cognitive processes are reflected in the persuasive message strategies they use; persuaders with more sophisticated cognitive systems create more sophisticated messages that accomplish multiple goals and overcome multiple obstacles.

Message. The stimulus that the source transmits to the receiver. A message may be verbal, nonverbal, or both.

Meta-perspective. What you think others think you think about an object, person, or concept.

Meta-theory. A theory that seeks to explain another theory. It is commonly referred to as a theory of theories or theorizing about theories.

Micronetwork. Network that links individuals within a group.

Mindfulness. A process of awareness where we become aware of our own frame of reference as well as the frame of reference of the receiver.

Mindguards. A symptom of groupthink where members insulate the group from outside information that can hurt the group or disrupt the trajectory of the group.

Mindlessness. Tendency to avoid cognitive effort and to behave automatically.

Minimum threshold for anxiety. The minimum level of anxiety that when not exceeded, allows people to remain comfortable when interacting with other people.

Minimum threshold for uncertainty. The minimal level of uncertainty that when not exceeded, allows people to remain comfortable when interacting with other people.

Mobilization. A dimension of the functional theory of mass communication that reflects the ability of the media to promote national interests.

Model I approach. Management approach that assumes unilateral goals, self-reliance, failure to disclose negative opinions, and reliance on objectivity and logic.

Model II approach. Management approach that assumes pro-action, consultative decision making, solution implementation, and the ability to adapt should the solution need adjustment.

Model of politeness. Brown and Levinson's model of how people use polite phrasing in conversations as a way of balancing the goal of protecting the other person's face with the goal of communicating a particular message.

Moderate manager. A management style that indicates a moderate concern for worker and a moderate concern for task.

Motivator factors. Factors of motivation that reflect the need for growth, accomplishment, and self-realization.

Motivator hygiene theory. Theory of motivation that holds people are motivated to action based on the degree of satisfaction and dissatisfaction workers experience on the job.

Multiple identities. The different identities (including values, goals, and decision rules) people have as members of different groups (see identification).

Multiple sequence model. A model of group decision making that suggests groups can have different patterns of sequences because they can take various paths to a decision.

Multiple-act. A behavioral prediction in research based on a set of relevant behaviors ideally more than once over a period of time.

Mutual face obliteration moves. Reflects when we have a low concern for self-face and low concern for other-face movements.

Mutual face protection moves. Reflects when we have high concern for self-face and high concern for other-face movements.

Narcissism. A personality trait that assumes that a person is more gifted than another. This is a characteristic of a leader.

Narratio. Presents a general overview of one's case to be developed in a speech.

Nature of the task. A contingency dimension in the multiple sequence model that governs the decision making process. Reflects the difficulty of the tasks and the coordination requirements required by the group members.

Need for achievement. Factor of acquired needs theory that reflects striving to acquire positions of responsibility and strive to achieve moderate goals.

Need for affiliation. Factor of acquired needs theory and reflects the need for relationships, conflict avoidance, and the need to be nonassertive.

Need for cognition. A stable individual difference in people's tendency to engage in and enjoy effortful cognitive activity.

Need for orientation. Part of the agenda-setting theory of mass communication concerning the relevance of information to an individual and the degree of uncertainty.

Need for power. Factor of acquired needs theory and reflects aspiring to greatness and seek control over others.

Need for social approval. The extent to which people fear social disapproval.

Need to belong. A function served by the group that leads to compliance in the group setting.

Negative face. The desire for others not to impose upon us; it is the desire to remain autonomous.

Negative relational effects. A dimension of taking conflict personally that reflects the extent to which people feel that conflict communication can have negative outcomes for both social and task relationships.

Negativism. A dimension of hostility that is expressed by refusing to cooperate, expressing unwarranted pessimism about the outcome of something when other people are very hopeful, and voicing antagonism concerning authority, rules, and social conventions.

Networks. Patterns through which messages flow between individuals or groups in an organization.

Newcomers. People who are new to an organization.

Noble self. A person who believes in expressing exactly what they think or feel. Noble selves do not value flexibility in adapting to different audiences.

Noise. Any physical or psychological stimulus that inhibits the receiver from accurate message reception. Any distortion in a communication channel.

Nominal group technique. Procedure for small group decision making in which members form a group in name only without personal contact. Members of nominal groups individually generate written ideas that are compiled into a round-robin list and commented on using very strict turn-taking, evaluation, and decision-making rules and procedures.

nominal level of measurement. Level of measurement that results in assigning an object to a category.

Non-affirming style. A communicator style that reflect communicating in a way that negates or threatens another person's self-concept.

Nonexperimental designs. Involves no manipulation of variables.

Nonimmediacy behaviors. Behaviors that signal avoidance and dislike.

Nonsummativity. Characteristic of a system that states the system is more than the contributions of each individual part. The interactions of the parts also contribute to the system; changing one part causes changes in the entire system.

Nonverbal codes. Process of manipulating nonverbal symbols to stimulate meaning in other humans.

Nonverbal expressiveness. Nonverbal cues associated with affiliation or liking.

Nonverbal response matching. Matching another's nonverbal behavior in order to create perceived similarity, which leads to trust.

Nonvolition. A characteristic of the family that assumes that we do not choose to be born to a specific family. The history, sets of relationships, and network of relatives are already established when we are born.

Normal science. Period of time during which most scientists accept a particular theoretical paradigm to guide their research; i.e., not during a scientific revolution.

Normative component. The component used in predicting behavior based on the beliefs that valued others have about the behavior expected of the individual.

Null hypothesis. Statement that relations observed in a study were due to chance.

Object adaptors. Using objects to express individuality.

Obliging style. A conflict style where there is great concern for the other party's position and interests above and beyond our own interests and goals.

Occam's razor. Concept named after the 14th century logician William of Ockham and assumes that no theory should be made more complicated than necessary.

Occulesics. The use of eyes in communication. Can be a very influential nonverbal immediacy cue.

Ontology. The study of the exact nature of reality as well as the most basic measuring units of reality.

Open style. A dimension of communicator style that is a predisposition to reveal feelings, thoughts, and personal information.

Open system. System that interacts with its environment, interchanging inputs and outputs.

Operational definitions. Definition of a concept in terms of the operations utilized in order to serve the concept.

Opinion leader. A component of the two-step flow theory that reflects a person who pays close attention to the mass media then exerts their influence on others concerning the messages received from the media.

Opinionated acceptance. Language that expresses a favorable attitude toward people who agree with the speaker.

Opinionated language. Highly intense language that indicates a speaker's attitude toward topics and attitude toward others.

Opinionated rejection. Language that expresses an unfavorable attitude toward people who disagree with the speaker.

Ordinal level of measurement. Level of measurement where objects are rank ordered according to some standard.

Organization. Hierarchically organized group of people so large that personal relationships with every member of the group are impossible. Organizations tend to outlive individual members and to be regulated by formal structures and rules.

Organizational assimilation. Jablin's theory that explains how workers both influence and are influenced by their organizations. Assimilation occurs in four stages: (1) vocational socialization, (2) anticipatory socialization, (3) encounter, and (4) metamorphosis.

Organizational communication. Communication within and between organizations.

Organizational disengagement/exit stage. When people decide to leave the organization, they engage in behaviors to end interpersonal relationships.

Organizational entry and assimilation stage. A dynamic interrelated process between planned as well as unintentional efforts to socialize employees and attempts of organizational members to individualize or change their role.

Organizational Function. The function of communication theory that entails a sense-making process that aids in interpreting the event that allows for processing information effectively.

Organizational intelligence. The variety of rules that an organization has developed and engages in.

Organizing. A constant state of sense-making reflected in the verb "organizing" as opposed to the noun "organization."

Orientation phase. An interact phase that is characterized by tentative and ambiguously phrased statements.

Other-face upgrading moves. Reflects when we have low concern for self-face and high concern for other-face movements.

Other-face. The degree to which we are concerned with the face of the other party involved in the conflict situation.

Out-group. When we feel relatively unconnected to other people or group.

Outgoing activist. A lifestyle type primarily consisting of female, younger, well educated, good income, and less likely to marry. These people have a high need for stimulation, use the media to stay informed and prefer print media.

Outputs. Finished products an open system sends to its environment.

Overload. Occurs when the flow of messages is too great for a person to manage.

Pacers. A type of breakpoint in the small group decision making process that determines how a discussion moves along. Also known as a normal breakpoint.

Paradigm shift. When one paradigm eclipses another in adoption and support.

Paradigm. "Grand model" or sets of theoretical assumptions shared by many theories.

Paralanguage. Vocal (but nonverbal) dimension of speech; the manner in which something is said rather than what is said.

Paralinguistics. The use of our voice when communicating. Can be used as a nonverbal immediacy cue and also directs the receiver on how to interpret the message (tone, pitch, volume, inflection etc.).

Parametric rules. Patterns of action considered appropriate within certain mutually understood boundaries.

Parasocial interaction. A relationship that exists between television viewers and remote media communicators.

Parenting subsystem. Involves the relationship between the parents and children and includes nurturing and discipline.

Parsimony. The degree to which a theory can be reduced into the most simple form possible.

Participation. An ethical practice of valuing feedback and recognizing contributions of organizational members.

Participative decision. A type of discussion making from a democratic style of leadership that reflects members contributing ideas and the leader then being guided by the expressed preferences in making the decision.

Participative style. Reflects workers have high levels of job maturity and low levels of psychological maturity.

Participative type management. Also known as System 4. Type of management that emphasizes quality interpersonal relationships to maximize individual potential and organizational productivity.

Partitio. An announcement of the main points of the main points or headings to be covered in a speech.

Passive strategies. An uncertainty reduction strategy that involves watching someone without being observed. No direct communication occurs between the two parties.

Pathos. A form that involves causing listeners to experience emotions that reinforce the object of persuasion.

Perceived barriers to taking action. A dimension of the health belief model that refers to an individual's assessment whether the suggested recommendation or preventive action will be expensive, painful, upsetting, time consuming, or simply inconvenient.

Perceived behavioral control. The degree to which a person believes that they control any given behavior.

Perceived benefits of taking action. A dimension of the health beliefs model that involves an assessment of the possible benefits of performing the recommended behaviors to lessen the chances of being affected by the health or safety threat.

Perceived control. The degree to which people believe that they have control over a situation or behavior.

Perceived outcome value theory. Modification of uncertainty reduction theory that focuses on perceived future rewards and costs in the process of relationship development.

Perceived seriousness or severity. A dimension of the health belief model that refers to an evaluation of the type of difficulties potential health and safety conditions would have on lives.

Perceived similarity. The degree to which we believe another's characteristics are similar to ours—is often sufficient to attract us to others.

Perceived susceptibility. A dimension of the health belief model that refers to the perceived subjective risks of contracting a disease or health-related condition.

Perception. Process through which individuals interpret sensory information.

Perceptiveness. A dimension of interaction involvement and is an individual's general sensitivity to: (1) what meaning ought to be applied to others' behavior; and (2) what meanings others have applied to one's own behavior.

Perceptual schemas. The perceptual "wiring" of each person. All of us have a different perceptual schema resulting in different information environments.

Peripheral route. When there is little or no elaboration of a message. Situational cues persuade people instead of the message.

Perlocutionary acts. A speech act used to illicit a response in the receiver.

Peroratio. The conclusion of a speech, including a summary of the case and a final appeal.

Persecution feelings. A dimension of taking conflict personally and reflects the perception that other people are just seeking to pick a fight with you and purposely seek to engage in conflict.

Personal construct theory. Developed by psychologist George Kelly to explain how individuals use bipolar concepts of judgment to classify information in explaining, predicting, and controlling their environments.

Personal constructs. The elements (i.e., bi-polar opposites) which individuals use to interpret, anticipate, evaluate, and make sense of the world.

Personal knowledge. As used by Polanyi, this term refers to a scientist's feeling that a particular theory is "correct" and will prove profitable for future research.

Personal phase. A dimension of uncertainty reduction theory that reflects communicating attitudes, beliefs, values, and more personal data. During this phase communicators feel less constrained by rules and norms.

Personal space. Zones of space that surround us: intimate, casual-personal, socioconsultative, public.

Persuasibility. The trait of being influenced easily regardless of the topic, source, or situation.

Persuasion situations. Differences in intimacy, dominance, resistance, rights, personal benefits, and consequences affect each persuasive interaction.

Persuasion. Attitude change toward a source's proposal resulting from a message designed to alter a receiver's beliefs about the proposal.

Phenomenological tradition. A tradition of theory building that views communication as dialogue or experience to otherness and believes that objectivity and subjectivity are both necessary in order to understand the human experience.

Philosophical Normative Approach. An approach to theory-building from which rational and abstract principles are tested, with results providing methods for the evaluation and practice of communication.

Physiological needs. One of Maslow's hierarchy of needs reflecting the need for air, food, water, etc.

Physiological measures. Method of measurement that quantifies involuntary responses such as heart rate and blood pressure.

Pleasing to the Mind. Attribute to good theory building stating that the theory should have intuitive appeal and be eloquently simply.

Pleasure. Interpersonal communication motive used for social benefits, for fun, stimulation, and entertainment.

Political communication. Communication involving the governing part of our society.

PONS test. Profile of nonverbal sensitivity test used to measure ability to decode nonverbal messages.

Positive face. The desire for others to appreciate and approve the self-image we present.

Positive relational effect. A dimension of taking conflict personally that reflects the extent to which people feel conflict communication can be positive for both social and task relationships.

Positiveness. A dimension of disclosiveness that measures the extent to which the information revealed about self is positive or negative.

Postactivity. A dimension of uses and gratification theory that consists of audience behavior and message use after exposure to mediated messages.

Postulate. A proposition that is not proven or demonstrated but simply considered true in nature, also known as an axiom.

Posture. Position of the body that communicates a particular orientation, for example, approach or withdrawal.

Power distance. A characteristic of culture that concerns how a culture treats status differences and social hierarchy.

Power. The potential to influence or restrict another person's behaviors.

Preactivity. A dimension of uses and gratification that is a behavior when people deliberately seek certain media to gratify intellectual needs.

Precise style. A dimension of communicator style that includes insisting that people document what they are saying and that they give definitions.

Predicted outcome value theory. Theory that places less emphasis on the need for uncertainty reduction in initial interactions and greater emphasis on the need to ensure that future interactions will lead to more positive experiences than negative experiences.

Prediction. Characteristics of the law-governed approach that uses antecedent conditions to predict how people will respond or behave in communication situations.

Prerequisites for decision making. The groups understanding of what it needs to solve a problem.

Pressure for conformity. A symptom of groupthink where the group applies psychological pressure to conform on any member who argues against the groups beliefs or decision making direction for fear it will threaten the group.

Preventatives. Devices used by speakers to gain permission to violate conversational rules.

Primary needs. A dimension of Maslow's theory of motivation concerning the satisfying the needs, of air, water, and food.

Principle of requisite variety. In Weick's theory, the principle that organizations can most effectively process information by using the same level of equivocality as the messages themselves. Very complex or equivocal messages require equivocal organization processes, communication-behavior cycles, while simple messages only require the application of rules.

Privacy rules. The way in which people make choices about how and when to disclose private information based on the criteria of culture, gender, motivation, context, and risk-benefit ratio.

Private acceptance. The individual behaves as suggested by the group because the group produces a change in the person's beliefs and attitudes.

Probabilistic. Occurring with a particular probability (usually less than 100%) rather than always. The statement, "There is a 60% chance of rain today" reflects a probabilistic relationship.

Probabilists. Communication theorists who advocate a probabilistic view of covering laws and causality; this view recognizes the presence of human choice.

Problem-solving groups. A type of task oriented group that attempts to develop a solution to a problem by analyzing it thoroughly.

Procedural area of group communication. Communication behaviors that include setting goals for the group, preparing an agenda or outline for the group to follow, clarifying ideas, summarizing at various points in the discussion, and verbalizing when the group is in complete agreement on something.

Procedural justice. Reflects decision making and implementing those decisions based on fair and sound principles.

Process. View that communication is unique, continual, and not identically repeatable.

Production. Throughputs and outputs of a communication system.

Pronuntiatio. Dealing with the vocal and nonverbal delivery of a persuasive speech.

Proposition. Statement about the relationships between concepts of a theory.

Propositional acts. A speech act that makes a reference or acts that use words to represent something else.

Proxemics. How people use space to communicate.

Psychological equity restoration. Distortion of reality to make one believe that an inequitable relationship is, in fact, equitable.

Public communication. Involves a speaker addressing a large audience.

Public compliance. The individual behaves in the way desired by the group only when being observed by group members, because the person does not really believe in the behavior.

Pupil dilation. Indicates interest and perhaps cognitive effort.

Pure charisma. Charisma based on the behaviors that a leader exhibits.

Random assignment. Method of achieving control in an experiment by utilizing probability theory to cancel the effects of potentially biasing conditions.

Random sampling. Selecting individuals from a population so that each member of the population has an equal chance of being selected to represent the population.

Randomized blocks design. Mixed research design involving a combination of manipulated and nonmanipulated independent variables.

Rapid fading. Fleeting, nonpermanent nature of verbal messages.

Rate. Speed with which communication messages flow.

Ratio data. Represents a level of measurement that entails a natural zero point, and a constant and equal difference between points of the scale.

Rational-legal authority system. A system of bureaucratic management that advocates organizations should be designed to achieve certain goals through the use of rules and regulations developed by the organization.

Reading anxiety. Refers to the degree of anxiety a person experiences when reading information.

Reasoned action theory. A theory for predicting behavior that deals with the ways in which learned beliefs control behavior.

Receiver apprehension. Fear of misinterpreting, inadequately processing, and/or not being able to adjust psychologically to messages sent by others.

Receiver. Destination of a message.

Reciprocal self-concept support. Agreement on created identities thereby confirming each other's conception of self.

Reciprocate. Part of Interaction Adaptation Theory and reflects matching behavior or reciprocating the behavior of the other person.

Reciprocated link. Communication link that both organization members report using.

Reciprocity heuristic. A compliance gaining strategy that assumes when someone gives you something, you should give them something in return.

Recording. A data gathering method of conversational analysis involving either audiotape or videotape.

Redundancy. Refers to the amount of change in interactant's negotiations over rights.

Reference function. A function served by the group that leads to compliance by informing members on what is and what is not acceptable.

Referent. Person, object, or event to which a word or symbol can refer.

Reflective projective theory of mass communication. A theory that asserts the mass media acts like a mirror for society. The media reflects society's attitudes and values as they simultaneously project idealized visions of society.

Reflective thinking. Procedure for small group decision making based on John Dewey's *How We Think* (1910). The reflective thinking procedure leads group members to identify a problem and its causes and to identify criteria for an effective solution before solutions are discussed and one eventually selected.

Refutation. Arguments which refute the oppositions arguments against your case.

Regulating interaction. Involves greetings, turn-taking, and leave-taking; these regulators are communicated efficiently by the nonverbal code.

Regulative rules. Rules of action which help individuals determine how to respond or behave. From the communication theory of Coordinated management of Meaning.

Regulators. Bodily movements used to guide how interaction takes place, especially in terms of greetings, turn-taking, and leave-taking.

Regulatory function. Inherent function of communication where the individual is influenced by people and thereby learns to influence.

Reinforcement principle. Suggests that we like, and are attracted to, those people who reward us.

Reinforcement. Characteristic of reinforcement theory of attraction that assumes we like and we attracted to those people who reward us.

Relational activity track. A decision making track in which the group activities emphasize the relationships among the group members that pertain to how the group works.

Relational based ethical perspective. Assumes that all relationships within the organization as well as between the organization and its various publics are based on quality and honest communication.

Relational dialectics. A dialectic consists of two opposites in tension with one another; the point of equilibrium that balances tensions in relationships changes constantly. Baxter's theory identifies three unresolvable internal and external tensions present in all interpersonal relationships: integration–separation, stability–change, and expression–privacy.

Relational dimension of communication. Refers to the interpersonal relationship between individuals and this influences how the message will be handled.

Relationship based ethical perspective. Assumes that ethical behavior is a creation of, and maintained through, communication.

Relationship interaction stages model. A model that describes how relationships and relational partners change over time.

Relaxation. Interpersonal communication motive used to help relax and unwind.

Relaxed style. A dimension of communicator style that reflects not having nervous mannerisms in speech or bodily communication; pride is taken in appearing relaxed in stressful situations.

Reliability. Accuracy, stability or consistency of a scale, test or measure across time.

Repairs. Conversational devices used to smooth or reduce "troubles" that arise in conversation.

Repeated measures design. Research design where research participants are exposed to all levels of one or more manipulated variables.

Repeated observations criterion. See multiple act.

Replicable. The ability of a research design to be replicated in order to determine if the results of the original study are similar to those results.

Requirements. A person's basic psychological/physiological needs related to approach avoidance behavior and are primarily unconscious and said to influence our conversational expectations.

Requisite variety. When the organization seeks to ensure a single reality that is shared by all members of the organization.

Research hypothesis. Prediction of the results of a study based on a theoretical framework.

Research question. Statement that inquires as to whether or not variables under study are related.

Resentment. A dimension of hostility that involves expressing jealousy and hatred, brooding about real or imagined mistreatment so that feelings of anger develop, and indicating that others do not really deserve success.

Resistant cognitive states. Advocates that people are either more easily or more difficult to persuade based on their state of mind.

Resonance. Argues that media's influence on perceptions are intensified when media depict "real life."

Responsiveness. A dimension of interaction involvement that is a tendency to react mentally to one's social circumstance and adapt by knowing what to say and when to say it.

Restrained activist. A lifestyle type primarily male and female who are older, highly educated, opinion leaders likely to marry, and have high incomes. These people have a high need for intellectual stimulation and use the mass media for informational needs.

Retention stage of organizing. Stage of organizing involving deciding whether or not assembly rules and communication cycles should be retained or discarded in future sense-making.

Retention. Part of the evolution of ideas and pertains to institutionalizing what is adopted.

Rewards. Anything that we see as a benefit from a relationship.

Rhetoric. Use of symbols to prompt a particular response from other humans.

Rhetorical communities. Groups of people who share a rhetorical vision and style.

Rhetorical message design logics. Communicators using this design strategy view messages and meanings as negotiated between the sender and receiver, who co-create the conversation.

Rhetorical pedagogy. A set of utilitarian procedures for teaching oratory, eloquence, or simply public speaking.

Rhetorical reflector. People who have the tendency to conceive their "selves" not as fixed entities, but as social "characteristics" who take on whatever role is necessary for the particular situation.

Rhetorical sensitivity. A person who believes there is no single self but a complex network of selves. The rhetorical sensitive person is in between the noble self and the rhetorical reflector.

Rhetorical tradition. A tradition of theory building as the art of discourse and focuses on communication in direct relation to problems encountered within the socio-historical context in which they occur.

Rhetorical vision. In Bormann's theory, group members' shared view of their identity in relation to each other and to nongroup members.

Rhetoricians. Those who study the principles of rhetoric.

Rights/justice based ethical perspective. Assumes that ethical behavior is based on a certain level of dignity and justice afforded and provides a level of fairness for all.

Ritual. Type of sign that is a combination of being naturally produced, as in the case of a symptom, and being arbitrary or created, as would be a symbol.

Ritualized use. Using television viewing primarily as a diversion.

Role category questionnaire. From the communication theory of Constructivism. It is the instrument used to measure construct differentiation, or the degree of cognitive complexity.

Role shock. In Jablin's organizational assimilation theory, the stress that occurs when an employee's expectations about his/her role in the organization do not match the work environment. Role shock is mostly likely to occur during the encounter stage of organizational assimilation (see role surprise).

Role surprise. The condition that occurs when a new employee's expectations about his/her role in the organization match the work environment (see role shock).

Routinized charisma. Charisma based on the position of power a person holds within the organization.

Rule-following approach. An approach to communication behavior that views individuals as acting with some degree of regularity.

Rule-governed approach. An approach to communication behavior that views rules as an "individual's belief about what should be done or what probably will occur as a consequence of his or her action."

Rules approach to persuasion. Replaces the central concept of the laws approach (cause and effect sequences) with the idea of contingency rules.

Rules perspective. Theoretical paradigm whose followers believe that the true nature of reality can best be discovered by understanding the subjective experience of people acting in the situation. Behavior is assumed to be governed by socially agreed-upon norms or individual guidelines for behavior, both of which may be called rules.

Rules. Rules may refer either to socially agreed-upon norms or to individual guidelines for behavior. In Weick's theory, standard procedures an organization has developed to process simple information received from the environment.

Safety needs. One of Maslow's hierarchy of needs reflecting the need for a life free of turmoil, relative stability, and preference for predictability.

Sampling. A method of studying part of a population in order to draw conclusions about the entire population.

Sapir-Whorf hypothesis. Suggests that the language we speak influences or shapes our perceptions, thoughts, and behavior. Also referred to as "linguistic relativity."

Scalar chain. Type of information transfer that reflects the clear hierarchical exchange of information.

Scarcity heuristic. A compliance gaining strategy that assumes people want to try to secure those opportunities that are scarce.

Scientific management. A management perspective that assumes any worker can be productive if given a scientifically efficient task. This perspective does not concern the well-being of the worker and is focused on efficient task completion.

Scientific method. Consists of four interdependent phases: induction, hypothesis, deduction, experiment.

Scientific revolution. Scientific revolutions constitute major scientific change in which long-accepted theories are rejected in favor of theories that indicate new metaphors, new concepts, or other new ways of knowing. A scientific revolution often comes about when some problem in a field cannot be solved by current theories or paradigms.

Scientifically efficient. A term used to reflect a task that has been analyzed for efficiency so that any worker can optimally perform it.

Script. Sequence of events a person expects in a situation.

Selection stage of organizing. The stage of selecting meanings and interpretations directly while indirectly selecting individuals, departments, groups, or goals indirectly.

Selection strategy. Makes one goal primary and ignores others.

Selection. Part of the evolution of ideas that requires vigorous debate.

Selective exposure. Exposing oneself only to agreeable messages; avoiding situations, such as public speeches by a political opponent, requiring us to listen to those with whom we disagree.

Selective perception. When people perceive things differently resulting in different information environments.

Self-actualization. One of Maslow's hierarchy of needs reflecting the pinnacle of human potential and achievement.

Self-adaptors. Involve touching or doing something to one's body to express individuality.

Self-censorship. A symptom of groupthink where members withhold dissent or any view that deviates from the group.

Self-concept. Image people have of their attributes, which influences their communicative behavior.

Self-construal. A person's self-image that is comprised of both independent and interdependent self.

Self-disclosure. Communication in which information about self normally hidden is revealed honestly and accurately to another.

Self-efficacy. The degree of ease or difficulty in performing the behavior or likelihood that a person can actually perform a behavior.

Self-esteem. How favorably the individual evaluates self.

Self-face defensive moves. Reflects when we have high concern for self-face and low concern for other-face movements.

Self-gain. The degree to which we are concerned with our own face needs during a conflict episode.

Self-monitoring of expressive behavior. A trait that involves monitoring one's nonverbal behavior and adapting it to situations to achieve communication goals.

Sell style. Reflects that workers have a certain degree of maturity, are reluctant to be told what to do, and are not fully motivated to show initiative.

Semantic differential scales. Rating scales that utilize a seven-point continuum bound by bipolar terms in order to locate an object in semantic space.

Semiotic tradition. A tradition of theory building that views communication as a process in which shared meaning between languages or sign systems become a place of common understanding between people.

Sender. A person who transmits a message. The sender may or may not be the originator of the message.

Sense-making. Consists of both the interpretation of information and generating what is interpreted.

Sensitized perception. Type of perception that results when a person is exposed frequently over time to messages perceived in a hostile setting, for example, racial epithets.

Separate couple type. A couple type that are more conventional on marital and family issues than independents, yet they maintain individual freedom, have less companionship and sharing, and describe their communication as assertive.

Separation strategy. Manages different goals in turn rather than at the same time.

Sibling subsystem. Involves the relationships among children in the same family.

Sign. Something that stands for another thing.

Signal. Type of sign that stands for something by virtue of a natural relationship of causality, contingency, or resemblance.

Sin license. A type of preventative where a person overtly acknowledges the violation of conversational rules before violating the rules.

Single loop learning. A learning of how a process is executed, not why it is executed. This type of learning is believed to be self-oppressive.

Situational ethical perspective. Assumes that ethical decisions are unique to any given situation and are not universal in nature.

Situational leadership approach. Assumes that there is no such thing as a born leader as much as people acting as leaders depending on the specific situation.

Situationist position. Approach to understanding communication that emphasizes the impact of situational variables.

Small band-width. A term from language expectancy theory that reflects when people have a smaller variety of persuasive linguistic strategies that will be seen as appropriate or within an expected range.

Small group communication. Communication in gatherings that vary in size from three to about fifteen persons.

Small group. Group of fewer than 20 people who develop regular patterns of interaction and share a common purpose; members influence and are influenced by each other.

Social assertiveness. A dimension of assertiveness that reflects an individual being able to start conversations with strangers, feel comfortable around a wide variety of people, and is generally able to initiate desired relationships.

Social composure. A dimension of communicative adaptability that reflects the degree to which a person is calm, cool, and collected in social situations.

Social confirmation. A dimension of communicative adaptability that reflects the degree to which a person can affirm or maintain the other person's face or self-image while interacting.

Social experience. A dimension of communicative adaptability that reflects the degree to which a person actually experiences, or is willing to experience novel situations.

Social information. Processing theory (SIPT). A theory that explains how people get to know one another online, without nonverbal cues, and how they develop and manage relationships in the computer mediated environment.

Social learning. Cause of verbal aggression brought about by direct reinforcement of verbally aggressive behavior or by modeling the behavior after an esteemed person.

Social proof heuristic. A compliance gaining strategy that assumes that we determine what is correct by finding out what other people think is correct.

Social scientific approach. An approach to theory building that provides prediction, explanation, description, and control for communication behavior and follows the scientific method.

Social scientific method. A concept of systematic thought and the application of scientific principles specific to the social world.

Sociocultural tradition. A tradition of theory building that views communication problems as problems as diversity and relativity as well as cultural change.

Sociological information. Communication characteristics of impersonal communication and is comprised of information such as age, sex, and race.

Sociopsychological tradition. A tradition of theory building that assumes communication is a process of social interaction and can reveal cause and effect relationships.

Soldiering. The assumption that workers purposely work below their capacity.

Solution multiplicity. The number of possible, effective solutions to a problem.

Source credibility hypothesis. Hypothesis that asserts television news is a powerful agenda setter because people perceive the news to be credible and authoritative (see agenda setting).

Source credibility. Set of attitudes toward a source's expertise, trustworthiness, and dynamism that influence response to the source's message.

Source. The originator of a message.

Speech act theory. Assumes that to understand language you must understand the speakers intention. Since language is intentional behavior, language should be treated as a form of action.

Speech act. Term used by Searle to refer to a statement designed to perform some specific function (for example, to give a command or to ask a question).

Spiral of silence. A theory about how minority viewpoints disappear from public awareness. People remain silent because of the fear of being different and isolated. The media play a major role in informing people what is normative.

Spontaneous cooperation. The fostering of relationships and teamwork among work-group members.

Spouse subsystem. Involves achieving complimentary and mutual support among the spouses.

Stability-change dialectic. This tension takes the form of predictability/novelty within a relationship; the public form is stability-change.

Stagnation stage. A stage in the relationship interaction stages model and reflects the boredom experienced in a relationship

Stakeholder theory. A theory that assumes the sole responsibility of an organization is to those people who own the instruments of production.

State behavior. Behavior that varies from one situation to another within the same context.

Statistical hypothesis. Statement of a research hypothesis in mathematical terms.

Statistical significance. The magnitude of results from a study, of a mathematical nature, that are not the result of chance.

Stereotypes. Beliefs about members of a group based on learned opinions rather than information about a specific individual.

Stimulating further research function. A function of communication theory that reflects the degree to which the theory contributes to the development of new experiences that need to be organized and understood.

Strangers. Concept in AUM theory representing people whom we do not know and who are themselves in an unfamiliar environment.

Stratified sample. Partitioning a population and then drawing a random sample at each level of stratification.

Stress reaction. A dimension of taking conflict personally and reflects the level of physiological response one has when in a conflict episode.

Strong cultures. In Deal and Kennedy's theory of organization culture, a characteristic of successful organizations. In organizations with strong cultures, employees are aware of and support the organization's values, heroes, rites and rituals, and the organization has networks for communicating its culture.

Strong link. Communication link that is frequently used.

Structural functionalism. Form of systems theory such as the communication systems theory developed by Farace, Monge, and Russell that stresses the structure and functions of systems.

Structural model. A model that examines the social organization of the family.

Style approach to leadership. A leadership approach that focuses on the different ways or styles people use to lead others.

Style-specific theories. Also known as special theories. A group of theories which deal with the specific communication practices or styles of particular groups or rhetorical communities.

Subjective experience. Individual's unique experiences and perceptions of reality.

Subjective norm. The pressure a person feels to conform to the will of others to perform or not perform a behavior.

Subsequent conditions. Events occurring later in time that are related to some earlier (antecedent) conditions or effects.

Subsystems. Smaller units within a larger system.

Suprasystems. Larger units that make up a system; suprasystems are composed of subsystems.

Surveillance. A dimension of the functional theory of mass communication and is the information and news providing function of mass communication.

Survey research. Interviews and mail surveys.

Suspicion. A dimension of hostility that is reflective of expressing an unjustified distrust of people, expecting that others do not have goodwill, believing that others are planning to harm you, and treating people as if their characters are flawed.

Syllogism. Method of reasoning that consists of a major and minor premise and a conclusion.

Symbol. Type of sign that is created to stand for something else.

Symbolic activity. How people use symbol systems to relay meaning to one another.

Symbolic convergence. How people unite through sharing symbol systems, including group fantasies. The way people try to unite their own symbol systems to achieve a "meeting of the minds."

Symmetrical link. Communication link used equally by two organization members; i.e., each initiates communication with the other.

Symptom. Type of sign that bears a natural relation to an object.

System 4 management approach. A human resource approach to management that ranges from depersonalization of employees to the full integration of employee input and potential.

System perspective. Based on general systems theory of biologist Ludwig von Bertalanffy, a theoretical paradigm that assumes the true nature of reality is contained in systems-interdependent units that work together to adapt to a changing environment.

System. Set of interdependent units that work together to adapt to a changing environment.

Tactic rules. Rules used to achieve some type of personal or interpersonal objective.

Tag questions. A question added to the end of an assertion or statement that asks for agreement with the speaker (for example, "that's a beautiful dog, isn't it?").

Taking conflict personally (TCP). A communication trait that reflects the degree to which we have a negative emotional reaction to participating in a conflict.

Talk is action. A component of conversational analysis theory that in order to understand interpersonal interaction, we must have the understanding that talk is something people do.

Task activity track. A decision making track in which the group engages to accomplish its task.

Task area of group communication. Communication behaviors that include contribution, seeking ideas, evaluating ideas, asking others to evaluate ideas, and fostering understanding of ideas.

Task demands. The degree to which the conversation is mentally and/or emotionally involved for the participant.

Task leadership behaviors. Part of the functional approach to leadership that includes initiating ideas and procedures, coordinating member contribution, summarizing to let the group know its progress, and elaborating on ideas.

Task manager. A management style that indicates a low concern for worker and a high concern for task.

Task-oriented groups. Groups that have a job or task to accomplish.

Team manager. A management style that indicates a high concern for worker and a high concern for task.

Teleological. Property of open systems that indicates systems are designed to meet specific end states or goals.

Tell style. Reflects that workers have a high task focus and a low relationship focus.

Temperaments. Traits with a biological basis that differentiate people based on behavioral tendencies.

Termination stage. A stage in the relationship interaction stages model reflecting the ending of a relationship.

Territoriality. Claiming that one has rights to a given area; responding to boundary violations.

Testable. A necessary criterion for a theory to be considered scientific. The theory must be subject to empirical testing.

Theoretical significance. The magnitude of the empirical findings in either supporting or not supporting the theory.

Theory in use. The actual behaviors that a manager engages in with employees that exposes the manager's ethics, management style, and management philosophy.

Theory of independent mindedness. A communication based organizational theory that advocates cultural congruity between the organization and the larger culture within which it operates. Based on the three communication traits of argumentativeness, verbal aggressiveness, and communicator style.

Theory of interpersonal communication motives. The goal of the theory is to identify reasons (or motives) for why people initiate and engage in interpersonal communication.

Theory of linguistic relativity. Assumes that all higher level of thought depend on language and the structure of language and the structure of the language we use influences the way we understand our environment.

Theory of planned behavior (TPB). An extension of the theory of reasoned action and is based on the premise that the best predictor of an actual behavior is a person's behavioral intention.

Theory of reasoned action. A theory of persuasion that is based on attitudes, belief strength, and the evaluation of the meaning of the belief.

Theory X approach. A management approach that assumes workers are lazy, have little ambition, and are motivated by coercion and threats.

Theory Y approach. A management approach that assumes workers are motivated by an internal need to excel and actively pursue responsibility.

Theory Z approach. An approach to management that advocates matching the organization's culture to that of the larger society and assumes that involved workers are the key to increased productivity.

Theory. Group of related propositions designed to explain why events take place in a certain way.

Therapy groups. A group that seeks to help people solve personal problems.

Throughputs. Partially modified products that are passed from one subsystem of an open system to another during the process of being transformed into outputs.

Time-motion study. A process used in scientific management theory that reflects the analysis of any given task in an effort to make that task optimally efficient.

Tolerance for disagreement. A communication trait that reflects the amount of disagreement a person can tolerate before he or she perceives the existence of a conflict in a relationship.

Topical activity track. A decision-making track made up of the content of the issues and arguments of concern to the group at various times in the discussion.

Topoi. Lines of argument developed by Aristotle.

Traditional couple type. A couple who have traditional views about marriage (for example, women use husbands' surname), demonstrate interdependence, and describe their communication as non-assertive.

Training in critical methods. Advocates that when people are taught to think critically and identify fallacies in reasoning, they will become difficult to persuade.

Trait approach to leadership. Assumes that leaders have traits that distinguish them from followers. Leaders are more likely than followers to be high on traits such as self-esteem, extroversion, open-mindedness, aggression, achievement motivation, analytic thought, sociability, and argumentativeness.

Trait approach. Approach to communication that maintains there are broad predispositions that account for behavior.

Trait behavior. Behavior is assumed to be consistent across contexts and specific situations within particular contexts.

Trait position. Approach to communication that maintains there are broad predispositions that account for behavior.

Transactional process. People sending each other messages that reflect the motivations of the participants.

Transcribing. A data gathering method of conversational analysis that involves using conventional symbols to indicate the verbal and vocal characteristics of the conversation.

Transference. Cause of verbal aggression that involves using verbal aggression against people who remind one of unresolved sources of conflict and pain.

Transformational leadership theory. A theory of leadership that focuses on the empowerment of individual workers and aiding the organization in adapting to change in both internal and external environments.

Transition relevance places (TRPs). Those places in a conversation where a change of speaking turn is possible.

Transparent structure. An ethical perspective that assumes every practice the organization engages in should be up front and open.

Trust. A dimension of the interpersonal dynamics model that requires both members of a relationship to be trusting and trustworthy.

Turn-taking. An exchange of speech and listener roles. Turns are viewed as "opportunities at talk" into which utterances are slotted.

Two-step flow. Theory that asserts information from media is processed first by opinion leaders who then pass it along via interpersonal channels.

Type A organizations. An organization that uses typical American management style of individuality, short-term employment, and rapid advancement.

Type J organizations. An organization that uses typical Japanese management style of collectivism, long-time employment, and non-specialized career paths.

Typology of couple types. A way of characterizing (married) couples. A traditional couple holds more conventional values about marriage; independent couples value individual freedom and subscribe less to conventional male/female roles; separate couple types are more conventional than independents on marital and family issues but maintain individual freedom and communicate assertively.

Uncertainty management theory. A theory that explains how people react to health-related uncertainty.

Uncertainty reduction theory. A theory that explains and predicts interpersonal communication during the beginning of an interaction. A core assumption of this theory is that when strangers meet, they seek to reduce uncertainty about each other.

Uncertainty. When you are unsure about something. In information theory, when you do not know exactly what will happen in a situation. Also related to the concept of predictability and a component of AUM theory.

Underload. Communication underload occurs when the flow of messages is too slow; workers are able to manage more information than they receive.

Unitary sequence model. Model of group decision making that suggests groups pass through certain stages as they move toward a decision.

Unobtrusive control. In Tompkins and Cheney's theory, the process organizations use to control workers by providing premises (through workers' identification with the organization) that subtly influence the decisions made by employees (see identification).

Unpredictable behavior. A motivation associated with uncertainty reduction theory that assumes when communication behavior deviates from our expectations, we monitor the communication of others more closely to get additional information.

Unreciprocated link. Communication link reported by only one organization member. If one person reports frequently using the link and the other says that no communication took place, the link is unreciprocated.

Unwillingness to communicate. Tendency to devalue and avoid communication; the more global of the apprehension traits.

Upward communication. Messages that flow from the worker up to the supervisor.

Uses and gratifications theory. A theory of mass communication that attempts to explain the uses and functions of the media for individuals, groups, and society in general. This theory attempts to explain how individuals use mass communication to gratify their needs and to discover the underlying motives for individuals' media use.

Utilitarian ethical perspective. Assumes that ethical behavior is based on outcome as opposed to intention.

Utterance acts. A speech act where a person utters a string of words.

Valance. Term used to describe the evaluation of behavior. The evaluation can range from negative valence to positive valence.

Validity. Ability of a scale, test, or instrument to measure what it says it does.

Variable-analytic. Approach to studying persuasion that focuses on analyzing important variables rather than developing theories.

Variable. Characteristics of the unit being investigated.

Variety. Part of the evolution of ideas that requires freedom of speech.

Verbal aggressiveness. Tendency to attack the self-concept of people instead of, or in addition to, their positions on issues in order to inflict psychological pain.

Verbal codes. The process of humans manipulating verbal symbols to stimulate meaning in other humans.

Verbal intensifiers. Adverbs that moderate, decrease intensity, and reduce the strength of an utterance.

Verbal plan. What a speaker plans to say in a specific or general communication situation.

Verbal qualifiers. Expressions such as "possibly," and "perhaps," which modify and reduce the strength and impact of an utterance.

Vertical chain of communication. Communication between members of different levels of the organizational hierarchy; i.e., between managers and subordinates.

Vocalics. Study of how we use our voice to communicate.

Weak link. Communication link used only occasionally.

Wide band-width. A term from language expectancy theory that reflects when people have a greater variety of persuasive linguistic strategies that will be seen as appropriate or within an expected range.

Wit. A dimension of communicative adaptability that reflects the degree to which a person utilizes humor in appropriate situations to diffuse escalating aggressive communication exchanges.

Working class climber. A lifestyle type primarily consisting of males, lower in education and income, middle-aged, and married. These people do not use the mass media for intellectual stimulation and enjoy cable television more than any other lifestyle type.

XY management theory. A theory of management that contains bi-polar assumptions about employee behavior. Theory x contains three assumptions whereas theory y contains six assumptions about human behavior.

References

Adorno, T. W., Frenkel-Brunswik, E., Levinson. D. J., & Sanford. R. N. (1950). *The authoritarian personality.* New York: Harper & Row.

Afifi, W. A., & Matsunaga, M. (2008). Uncertainty management theories: Three approaches to a multifarious process. In L. A. Baxter & D. O. Braithwaite (Eds.), *Engaging theories in interpersonal communication: Multiple perspectives* (pp. 117–132). Thousand Oaks, CA: Sage.

Ajzen, I. (1985). From intentions to actions: A theory of planned behavior. In J. Kuhn & J. Beckman (Eds.). *Action-control: From cognitions to behavior* (pp. 11–39). Heidelberg: Springer.

Ajzen, I. (1988). *Attitudes, personality, and behavior.* Chicago, IL: The Dorsey Press.

Ajzen, I. (1991). The theory of planned behavior. *Organizational Behavior and Human Decision Processes, 50,* 179–211.

Ajzen, I. (2001). *Constructing a TpB questionnaire: Conceptual and methodological considerations.* Retrieved May 17, 2002 from http://www.unix.oit.umass.edu/~ajzen/tpb

Ajzen, I., & Fishbein, M. (1980). *Understanding attitudes and predicting social behavior.* Englewood Cliffs, NJ: Prentice-Hall.

Alberti, R. E., & Emmons, M. L. (1974). *Your perfect right: A guide to assertive behavior* (2nd ed.). San Luis Obispo, CA: Impact.

Andersen, J. F. (1979). The relationship between teacher immediacy and teaching effectiveness. In B. Ruben (Ed.), *Communication yearbook 3* (pp. 543–559). New Brunswick. NJ: Transactions Books.

Andersen, K., & Clevenger, T., Jr. (1963). A summary of experimental research in ethos. *Speech Monographs, 30,* 59–78.

Andersen, P. A. (1985). Nonverbal immediacy in interpersonal communication. In A. W. Siegman & S. Feldman (Eds.), *Multichannel integrations of nonverbal behavior* (pp. 1–36). Hillsdale, NJ: Lawrence Erlbaum.

Andersen, P. A. (1987). The it debate: A critical examination of the individual differences paradigm in interpersonal communication. In E. Dervin & M. J. Voigt (Eds.), *Progress in communication sciences* (Vol. 7, pp. 47–52). Norwood. NJ: Ablex.

Andersen, P. A. (1991). When one cannot not communicate: A challenge to Motley's traditional communication postulates. *Communication Studies, 42,* 309–325.

Andersen, P. A. (1998). The cognitive valence theory of intimate communication. In M. T. Palmer & G. A. Barnett (Eds.), *Progress in communication sciences, Vol. 14: Mutual influence in interpersonal communication theory and research in cognitive affect and behavior* (pp. 39–72). Norwood, NJ: Ablex.

Andersen, P. A. (1999). *Nonverbal communication: Forms and functions.* Mountain View, CA: Mayfield Publishing Co.

Anderson, C. M., & Martin, M. M. (November, 1995a). *Communication between mothers and their adult children: The path from motives to self-disclosure and satisfaction.* Paper presented at the annual meeting of the Speech Communication Association. San Antonio, TX.

Anderson, C. M., & Martin, M. M. (1995b). Communication motives of assertive and responsive communicators. *Communication Research Reports, 12,* 186–191.

Anderson, C. M., & Martin, M. M. (1995c). The effects of communication motives. interaction involvement, and loneliness on satisfaction. *Small Group Research, 26,* 118–137.

Anderson, C. M., & Martin, M. M. (1995d). Why employees speak to co-workers and bosses: Motives, gender, and organizational satisfaction. *The Journal of Business Communication, 32,* 249–265.

Anderson, C. R., & Schneier, C. E. (1978). Locus of control, leader behavior, and leader performance among management students. *Academy of Management Journal, 21,* 690–698.

Anderson, L. (1994). A new look at an old construct: Cross-cultural adaptation. *International Journal of Intercultural Relations, 18,* 293–328.

Argyris, C. (1965). *Organization and innovation.* Scarborough, Ontario, Canada: Irwin.

Argyris, C. (1985). *Strategy, change, and defensive routines.* London, England: Pitman.

Argyris, C. (1993). *Knowledge and action: A guide to overcoming barriers to change.* Hoboken, NJ: Jossey-Bass.

Argyris, C., & Schon, D. (1978). *Organizational learning: A theory of action perspective.* Boston: Addison-Wesley.

Arntson, P. (1985). Future research in health communication. *Journal of Applied Communication Research, 13,* 118–130.

Arntson, P., & Droge, D. (1988). Addressing the value dimension of health communication: A social science perspective. *Journal of Applied Communication Research. 16,* 1–15.

Aronson, E., & Mills. J. (1959). The effect of severity of initiation on liking for a group. *Journal of Abnormal and Social Psychology, 59,* 177–181.

Auter, P. J. (1992). TV that talks back: An experimental validation of a parasocial interaction scale. *Journal of Broadcasting and Electronic Media. 36,* 173–181.

Avtgis, T. A. (2002). Adult-child conflict control expectancies: Effects on taking conflict personally toward parents. *Communication Research Reports, 19,* 226–236.

Avtgis, T. A., & Myers, S. A. (1996, November). *Perceived control and communicative adaptability: How outlook on life influences ability to change.* Paper presented at the annual meeting of the Speech Communication Association, San Diego, CA.

Avtgis, T. A., & Rancer, A. S. (2007). The theory of independent-mindedness: An organizational theory for individualistic cultures. In M. Hinner (Ed.), *The role of communication in business transactions and relationships: Freiberger beitrage zur interkulturellen und wirtschaftskommunikation: A forum for general and intercultural business communication* (pp. 183–201). Frankfurt, Germany: Peter Lang.

Avtgis, T. A., & Rancer, A. S. (2003). Personalization of conflict across cultures: A comparison among the United States, New Zealand, and Australia. *Journal of Intercultural Communication Research, 33*, 109–118.

Avtgis, T. A., West, D. V., & Anderson, T. L. (1998). Relationship stages: An inductive analysis identifying cognitive, affective, and behavioral dimensions of Knapp's relational stages model. *Communication Research Reports, 15*, 280–287.

Babrow, A. S., Black, D. R., & Tiffany, S. T. (1990). Beliefs, attitudes, intentions, and a smoking-cessation program: A planned behavior analysis of communication campaign development. *Health Communication, 2,* 145–163.

Ball-Rokeach, S. (1973). From pervasive ambiguity to definition of the situation. *Sociometry, 36,* 378–389.

Ball-Rokeach, S. J.. & DeFleur, M. L. (1976). A dependency model of mass-media effects. *Communication Research, 3,* 3–21.

Ball-Rokeach, S. J., Power. G. J., Guthrie. K. K., & Waring, H. R. (1990). Value-framing abortion in the United States: An application of media system dependency theory. *International Journal of Public Opinion Research, 2,* 249–273.

Baran, S. J., & Davis, D. K. (1995). *Mass communication theory.* Belmont. CA: Wadsworth Publishing Company.

Barbato, C. A., & Perse, E. M. (1992). Interpersonal communication motives and the life position of elders. *Communication Research, 19,* 516–531.

Barbato, C. A., Perse, E. M., & Graham, E. E. (1995, Nov.). Interpersonal communication motives and family communication patterns: Interfacing mediated and interpersonal communication. Paper presented at the annual meeting of the Speech Communication Association, San Antonio. TX.

Barge, J. K., Downs, C. W., & Johnson, K. M. (1989). An analysis of effective and ineffective leader conversation. *Management Communication Quarterly, 2,* 357–386.

Bargh, J. (1989). Conditional automaticity. In J. Uleman & J. Bargh (Eds.), *Unintended thought* (pp. 3–51). New York: Guilford.

Barnlund, D. (1962). Toward a meaning centered philosophy of communication. *Journal of Communication, 2,* 197–211.

Barnlund, D., & Haiman. F. (1960). *The dynamics of discussion.* Boston: Houghton Mifflin.

Baseheart, J. R. (1971). Message opinionation and approval-dependence as determinants of receiver attitude change and recall. *Speech Monographs, 38,* 302–310.

Basen-Engquist, K., & Parcel, G. S. (1992). Attitudes, norms, and self-efficacy: A model of adolescents' HIV-related sexual risk behavior. *Health Education Quarterly, 19,* 263–277.

Bass, B. M., & Stogdill, R. M. (1990). *Bass & Stogdill's handbook of leadership: Theory, research, and managerial applications* (3rd ed.). New York: Free Press.

Bate, B. & Bowker, J. (1997). *Communication and the sexes* (2nd ed.). Prospect Heights, IL: Waveland Press.

Bateson, G. (1972). *Steps to an ecology of the mind.* New York: Ballantine Books.

Baukus, R. A. (1996). *Perception of mediated social conflict: Media dependency and involvement.* Unpublished manuscript, the Pennsylvania State University.

Bavelas, J. B. (1990). Behaving and communicating: A reply to Motley. *Western Journal of Speech Communication, 54,* 593–602.

Bavelas, J. B., & Segal, L. (1982). Family systems theory: Background and implications. *Journal of Communication, 32,* 99–107.

Beatty, M. J., & McCroskey, J. C. (1997). It's in our nature: Verbal aggressiveness as temperamental expression. *Communication Quarterly, 45,* 446–460.

Beatty, M. J., & McCroskey, J. C. (1998). Interpersonal communication as temperamental expression: A communibiological paradigm. In J. C. McCroskey, J. A. Daly, M. M. Martin, & M. J Beatty (Eds.). *Communication and personality: Trait perspectives* (pp. 41–67). Cresskill, NJ: Hampton Press.

Beatty, M. J., Marshall, L. A., & Rudd, J. E. (2001). A twin study of communicative adaptability: Heritability of individual differences. *Quarterly Journal of Speech, 87,* 366–377.

Beatty, M. J., McCroskey. J. C., & Heisel, A. D. (1998). Communication apprehension as temperamental expression: A communibiological paradigm. *Communication Monographs, 65,* 197–219.

Beatty, M. J., Valencic, K. M., Rudd, J. E., & Dobos, J. A. (1999). A "darkside" of communication avoidance: Indirect interpersonal aggressiveness. *Communication Research Reports, 16,* 103–109.

Beck, K. H., & Davis, C. M. (1978). Effects of fear-arousing communications and topic importance on attitude change. *Journal of Social Psychology, 104,* 81–95.

Beebe, S. A., & Masterson, J. T. (2003). *Communicating in small groups: Principles and practices* (7th ed.). Boston: Allyn & Bacon.

Beisecker, A. E. (1991). Interpersonal communication strategies to prevent drug abuse by health professionals and the elderly: Contributions of the health belief mode. *Health Communication, 3,* 241–250.

Bell, R. A., & Daly, J. A. (1984). The affinity-seeking function of communication. *Communication Monographs, 51,* 91–115.

Bellefontaine, A., & Florea, J. (1983, March). *The effect of unemployment on family communication: A systems examination.* Paper presented to the DePauw University Communication Honors Conference, Greencastle. Indiana.

Benne, K. D., & Sheats, P. (1948). Functional roles of group members. *Journal of Social Issues, 4,* 41–49.

Berger, C. R. (1979). Beyond initial interaction: Uncertainty, understanding, and the development of interpersonal relationships. In H. Giles & R. N. St. Clair (Eds.), *Language and social psychology* (pp. 122–144). Oxford: Basil Blackwell.

Berger, C. R. (1986). Uncertainty outcome values in predicted relationships: Uncertainty reduction theory then and now. *Human Communication Research, 13,* 34–38.

Berger, C. R. (1991). Communication theories and other curios. *Communication Monographs, 58,* 101–113.

Berger, C. R., & Calabrese, R. J. (1975). Some explorations in initial interaction and beyond: Toward a developmental theory of interpersonal communication. *Human Communication Research, 1,* 99–112.

Berger, C. R., & Chaffee, S.H. (Eds.). (1987). *Handbook of communication science.* Newbury Park, CA: Sage.

Berkowitz, L. (1962). *Aggression: A social psychological analysis.* New York: McGraw-Hill.

Berlo, D. K. (1960). *The process of communication.* New York: Holt. Rinehart & Winston.

Berlo, D. K. (1977). Communication as process: Review and commentary. In B. D. Ruben (Ed.), *Communication yearbook 1* (pp. 11–27). New Brunswick, NJ: Transaction Books.

Berscheid, E. (1966). Opinion change and communicator-communicatee similarity and dissimilarity. *Journal of Personality and Social Psychology, 4,* 670–680.

Berscheid, E., & Walster, E. H. (1978). *Interpersonal attraction* (2nd ed.). Reading, MA: Addison-Wesley.

Bertalanffy, L. von (1968). *General systems theory.* New York: Braziller

Blake, R. R., & Mouton, J. S. (1964). *The managerial grid.* Houston, TX: Gulf Publishing.

Blake, R. R., & Mouton, J. S. (1978). *The new managerial grid.* Houston, TX: Gulf Publishing.

Blake, R. R., & Mouton, J. S. (1982). A comparative analysis of situationalism and 9.9 management by principle. *Organizational Dynamics, 24,* 20–43.

Blumler, J. G. (1979). The role of theory in uses and gratifications studies. *Communication Research, 6,* 9–36.

Bochner, A. (1976). Conceptual frontiers in the study of communication in families: An introduction to the literature. *Human Communication Research, 2,* 381–397.

Bochner, A. R. & Eisenberg, E. M. (1987). Family process: System perspectives. In C. R. Berger & S. H. Chaffee (Eds.). *Handbook of communication science* (pp. 540–563). Newbury Park, CA: Sage.

Bormann, E. G. (1972). Fantasy and rhetorical vision: The rhetorical criticism of social reality. *Quarterly Journal of Speech, 58,* 396–407.

Bormann, E. G. (1980). *Communication theory.* New York: Holt, Rinehart & Winston.

Bormann, E. G., Kroll, B., Watters, K.. & McFarland, D. (1984). Rhetorical visions of committed voters: Fantasy theme analysis of a large sample survey. *Critical Studies in Mass Communication, 1,* 287–310.

Boster, F. J., & Levine, T. (1988). Individual differences and compliance-gaining message selection: The effects of verbal aggressiveness, argumentativeness, dogmatism and negativism. *Communication Research Reports, 5,* 114–119.

Boster, F. J., & Mongeau, P. (1984). Fear-arousing persuasive messages. In R. N. Bostrom (Ed.), *Communication Yearbook 8* (pp. 330–375). Beverly Hills: Sage.

Boster, F. J., Levine, T., & Kazoleas, D. (1989, November). *The impact of argumen*tative*ness and verbal aggressiveness on strategic diversity and persistence in compliance-gaining.* Paper presented at the meeting of the Speech Communication Association. San Francisco.

Bostrom, R. N. (1980). Altered physiological states: The central nervous system and persuasive communications. In M. Roloff & G. R. Miller (Eds.), *Persuasion: New directions in theory and research* (pp. 3–8). Beverly Hills, CA: Sage.

Bostrom, R. N. (1983). *Persuasion.* Englewood Cliffs. NJ: Prentice-Hall.

Bostrom, R. N., Baseheart, J., & Rossiter, C. (1973). The effects of three types of profane language in persuasive messages. *Journal of Communication, 23,* 461–475.

Bowers, J. W. (1963). Language intensity, social introversion, and attitude change. *Speech Monographs, 30,* 345–352.

Bowers, J. W., & Osborn, M. (1966). Attitudinal effects of selected types of concluding metaphors in persuasive speeches. *Speech Monographs, 33,* 147–155.

Bradac, J. J. (1988). Language variables: Conceptual and methodological problems of instantiation. In C. R. Tardy (Ed.), A *handbook for the study of human communication: Methods and instruments for observing, measuring, and assessing communication processes* (pp. 301–322). Norwood. NJ: Abler.

Bradac, J. J., Bowers, J. W., & Courtright, J. A. (1979). Three language variables in communication research: Intensity, immediacy, and diversity. *Human Communication Research. 5*, 257–269.

Brannigan, A., & Zwerman, W. (2001). The real "Hawthorne effect." *Society, 38*, 55–61.

Brashers, D. E. (2001a). Communication and uncertainty management. *Journal of Communication, 51*, 477–497.

Brashers, D. E. (2001b). HIV and uncertainty: Managing treatment decision making. *Focus: A guide to AIDS research, 16*, 5–6.

Brashers, D. E., Goldsmith, D. J., & Hsieh, E. (2002). Information seeking and avoiding in health contexts. *Human Communication Research, 28*, 258–271.

Brashers, D. E., Hsieh, E., Neidig, J. L., & Reynolds, N. R. (2006). Managing uncertainty about illness: Health care providers as credible authorities. In B. LePoire & R. M. Dailey (Eds.), *Applied interpersonal communication matters: Family, health, and community relations* (pp. 219–240). New York: Peter Lang.

Brenders, D. A. (1987). Fallacies in the coordinated management of meaning: A philosophy of language critique of the hierarchical organization of coherent conversation and related theory. *Quarterly Journal of Speech, 73*, 329–348.

Brenders, D. A. (1989). Perceived control and the interpersonal dimension of health care. *Health Communication, 1*, 117–135.

Brooks, R. D. (1970). The generalizability of early reversals of attitudes toward communication sources. *Speech Monographs, 37*, 152–155.

Brooks, W. D. (1970). Perspectives on communication research. In P. H. Emmert & W. D. Brooks (Eds.), *Methods of research in communication*. Boston: Houghton Mifflin.

Brown, R. W., & Lenneberg, E. H. (1954). A study in language and cognition. *Journal of Abnormal and Social Psychology, 49*, 454–462.

Brown, W. J. (1991). An AIDS prevention campaign. *American Behavioral Scientist, 34*, 666–678.

Buller, D. B., & Aune. R. K. (1988). The effects of vocalics and nonverbal sensitivity on compliance: A speech accommodation theory explanation. *Human Communication Research, 14*, 301–332.

Buller, D. B., & Burgoon, J. K. (1986). The effects of vocalics and nonverbal sensitivity on compliance: A replication and extension. *Human Communication Research, 13*, 126–144.

Buller, D. B., & Burgoon, J. K. (1996). Interpersonal deception theory. *Communication Theory, 6*, 203–242.

Buller, D. B., Burgoon, J. K., White, C., & Ebesu, A. S. (1994). Interpersonal deception: VII: Behavioral profiles in falsification, equivocation, and concealment. *Journal of Language and Social Psychology, 13*, 366–396.

Buller, D. B., Strzyzewski, K. D., & Hunsaker, F. G. (1991). Interpersonal deception: II. The inferiority of conversational participants as deception detectors. *Communication Monographs, 58*, 40.

Buller, M. K., & Buller, D. B. (1987). Physicians' communication style and patient satisfaction. *Journal of Health and Social Behavior, 28,* 375–388.

Burgoon, J. K. (1978). A communication model of personal space violations: Explication and an initial test. *Human Communication Research, 4,* 129–142.

Burgoon, J. K. (1983). Nonverbal violations of expectations. In J. M. Wiemann & R. P. Harrison (Eds.), *Nonverbal interaction* (pp. 77–111). Beverly Hills. CA: Sage.

Burgoon, J. K. (1985). Nonverbal signals. In M. L. Knapp & G. R. Miller (Eds.), *Handbook of interpersonal communication* (pp. 344–390). Beverly Hills: Sage.

Burgoon, J. K., & Buller, D. B. (2004). Interpersonal deception theory. In J. S. Seiter & R. H. Gass (Eds.), *Perspectives on persuasion, social influence, and compliance gaining* (pp. 239–264). Boston: Allyn & Bacon.

Burgoon, J. K., & Buller, D. B. (2008). Interpersonal deception theory: Purposive and interdependent behavior during deception. In L. A. Baxter & D. O. Braithwaite (Eds.), *Engaging theories in interpersonal communication: Multiple perspectives* (pp. 227–239). Thousand Oaks, CA: Sage.

Burgoon, J., & Burgoon, M. (2001). Expectancy theories. In W. P. Robinson & H. Giles (Eds.), *The new handbook of language and social psychology* (2nd ed., pp. 79–102). Sussex, UK: Wiley.

Burgoon, J. K., Buller, D. B., & Floyd, K. (2002). Does participation affect deception success? A test of the interactivity effect. *Human Communication Research, 27,* 503–534.

Burgoon, J. K., Buller, D. B., Guerrero, L. K., Afifi, W., & Feldman, C. (1996). Interpersonal deception: XII: Information management dimensions underlying deceptive and truthful messages. *Communication Monographs, 63,* 50–69.

Burgoon, J. K., Coker, D. A., & Coker, R. A. (1986). Communicative effects of gaze behavior: A test of two contrasting explanations. *Human Communication Research, 12,* 495–524.

Burgoon, J. K., & Ebesu Hubbard, A. S. (2005). Cross-cultural and intercultural applications of expectancy violations theory and interaction adaptation theory. In W. B. Gudykunst (Ed.), *Theorizing about intercultural communication* (pp. 149–171). Thousand Oaks, CA: Sage.

Burgoon, J. K., & Hale, J. L. (1988). Nonverbal expectancy violations: Model elaboration and application to immediacy behaviors. *Communication Monographs, 55,* 58–79.

Burgoon, J. K., & Jones. S. B. (1976). Toward a theory of personal space expectations and their violations. *Human Communication Research, 2,* 131–146.

Burgoon, J. K., LaPoire, B.A., & Rosenthal, R. (1995). Effects of preinteraction expectancies and target communication on perceiver reciprocity and compensation in dyadic interaction. *Journal of Experimental Social Psychology, 31,* 287–321.

Burgoon, J. K., Pfau, M.. Parrott, R., Birk, T., Coker, R., & Burgoon, M. (1987). Relational communication, satisfaction, compliance-gaining strategies, and compliance communication between physicians and patients. *Communication Monographs, 54,* 307–324.

Burgoon, J. K., & Walther, J. B. (1990). Nonverbal expectancies and the evaluative consequences of violations. *Human Communication Research, 17,* 232–265.

Burgoon, M. (1989). Messages and persuasive effects. In J. Bradac (Ed.), *Message effects in communication science* (pp. 129–164). Newbury Park, CA: Sage.

Burgoon, M. (1990). Language and social influence. In H. Giles & P. Robinson (Eds.), *Handbook of language and social psychology* (pp. 51–72). London, UK: Wiley.

Burgoon, M. (1995). Language expectancy theory: Elaboration, explication, and extension. In C. R. Berger & M. Burgoon (Eds.), *Communication and social influence process* (pp. 29–52). East Lansing, MI: Michigan State University Press.

Burgoon, M. H., & Burgoon, J. K. (1990). Compliance-gaining and health care. In J. P. Dillard (Ed.), *Seeking compliance* (pp. 161–188). Scottsdale, AZ: Gorsuch Scarisbrick.

Burgoon, M., & Bettinghaus, E. P. (1980). Persuasive message strategies. In M. E. Roloff & G. R. Miller (Eds.), *Persuasion: New directions in theory and research* (pp. 141–169). Beverly Hills: Sage.

Burgoon, M., Cohen, M., Miller, M. D., & Montgomery, C. L. (1978). An empirical test of a model of resistance to persuasion. *Human Communication Research, 5,* 27–39.

Burgoon, M., Denning, V. P., & Roberts, L. (2002). Language expectancy theory. In J. P. Dillard & M. Pfau (Eds.), *The persuasion handbook* (pp. 117–136). Thousand Oaks, CA: Sage.

Burgoon, M., Jones, S. B., & Stewart, D. (1975). Toward a message centered theory of persuasion: Three empirical investigations of language intensity. *Human Communication Research, 1,* 240–256.

Burke, K. (1950). *A rhetoric of motives.* New York: Prentice-Hall.

Burke, K. (1966). *Language and symbolic action.* Berkeley, CA: University of California Press.

Burleson, B. R. (1984). Role-taking and communication skills in childhood: Why they aren't related and what can be done about it. *Western Journal of Speech Communication, 48,* 155–170.

Burleson, B. R. (1992). Taking communication seriously. *Communication Monographs, 59,* 79–86.

Burleson, B. R. (2003). Emotional support skills. In J. O. Greene & B. R. Burleson (Eds.), *Handbook of communication and social interaction skills* (pp. 551–594). Mahwah, NJ: Erlbaum.

Burleson, B. R. (2007). Constructivism: A general theory of communication skill. In B. B. Whaley & W. Samter (Eds.), *Explaining communication: Contemporary theories and exemplars* (pp. 105–128). Mahwah, NJ: Erlbaum.

Burleson, B. R., & Caplan, S. E. (1998). Cognitive complexity. In J. C. McCroskey, J. A. Daly, M. M. Martin, & M. J. Beatty (Eds.), *Communication and personality: Trait perspectives* (pp. 233–286). Cresskill, NJ: Hampton Press.

Burrell, N. A., & Fitzpatrick, M. A. (1990). The psychological reality of marital conflict. In D. D. Cahn (Ed.), *Intimates in conflict: A communication perspective* (pp. 167–185). Hillsdale, NJ: Lawrence Erlbaum.

Byrne, D. (1971). *The attraction paradigm.* New York: Academic Press.

Byrne, D., Griffitt, W., & Stefaniak. D. (1967). Attraction and similarity of personality characteristics. *Journal of Personality and Social Psychology, 5,* 82–90.

Cacioppo, J. T., Petty, R. E., Feinstein, J. A., & Jarvis, W. B. G. (1996). Dispositional differences in cognitive motivation: The life and times of individuals varying in need for cognition. *Psychological Bulletin, 119,* 197–253.

Cahn, D. D. (1981, May). *A critique of Bertalanffy's general systems theory as a "new paradigm" for the study of human communication.* Paper presented to the

International Communication Association, Minneapolis, Minnesota. Cambridge University Press.

Campbell, D. T. (1957). Factors relevant to the validity of experiments in social settings. *Psychological Bulletin, 54*, 297–312.

Campbell, D. T., & Stanley, J. C. (1963). Experimental and quasi-experimental designs for research on teaching. In N. L. Gage (Ed.), *Handbook of research on teaching* (pp. 171–246). Chicago: Rand McNally.

Cappella, J. N. (1984). The relevance of the microstructure of interaction to relationship change. *Journal of Social and Personal Relationships, 1*, 239–264.

Cardello, L. L. Ray, E. B., & Pettey, G. R. (1995). The relationship of perceived physician communicator style to patient satisfaction. *Communication Reports, 8*, 27–37.

Carmichael, C., & Cronkhite, G. (1965). Frustration and language intensity. *Speech Monographs. 32*, 107–111.

Cathcart, R., & Gumpert, G. (1983). Mediated interpersonal communication: Toward a new typology. *Quarterly Journal of Speech, 69*, 267–277.

Cattell, R. B. (Ed.). (1966). *Handbook of multivariate experimental psychology*. Chicago: Rand McNally.

Caughlin, J. (2002). The demand/withdraw patterns of communication as a predictor of marital satisfaction over time. *Human Communication Research, 28*, 49–86.

Caughlin, J., & Afifi, T. (2004). When is topic avoidance unsatisfying? Examining moderators of the association between avoidance and dissatisfaction. *Human Communication Research, 30*, 479–513.

Cegala, D. J. (1984). Affective and cognitive manifestations of interaction involvement during unstructured and competitive interactions. *Communication Monographs, 51*, 320–335.

Cegala, D. J., & Lenzmeier-Broz, S. (2003). Provider and patient communication skills training. In A. M. Dorsey, T. L. Thompson, K. I. Miller, & R. Parrot (Eds.), *Handbook of health communication* (pp. 95–120). Mahwah, NJ: Erlbaum.

Cegala, D. J., Savage, G. T., Brunner, C. C., & Conrad, A. B. (1982). An elaboration of the meaning of interaction involvement: Towards the development of a theoretical concept. *Communication Monographs, 49*, 229–245.

Chaffee, S. H., & Rogers, E. M. (Eds.). (1997). *The beginnings of communication study in America: A personal memoir by Wilbur Schramm*. Thousand Oaks, CA: Sage.

Chase, S. (1956). Forward. In J. B. Carroll (Ed.), *Benjamin Lee Whorf: Language, thought and reality* (pp. v–x). Cambridge, MA: The M.I.T. Press.

Cheek, J. M., & Buss, A. H. (1981). Shyness and sociability. *Journal of Personality and Social Psychology, 41*, 330–339.

Chesebro, J. L., & Martin, M. M. (2003). The relationship between conversational sensitivity, cognitive flexibility, verbal aggressiveness, and indirect interpersonal aggressiveness. *Communication Research Reports, 20*, 143–150.

Chew, F., Palmer, S., & Kim. S. (1998). Testing the influence of the health belief model and a television program on nutrition behavior. *Health Communication, 10*, 227–245.

Cialdini, R. B. (1987). Compliance principles of compliance professionals: Psychologists of necessity. In M. P. Zanna, J. M. Olson, & C. P. Herman (Eds.), *Social influence: The Ontario symposium* (Vol. 5). Hillsdale, NJ: Erlbaum.

Cialdini, R. B. (1988). *Influence: Science and practice* (2nd ed.). New York: Harper Collins.

Cialdini, R. B., & Ascani, K. (1976). Test of a concession procedure for inducing verbal behavior and further compliance with a request to give blood. *Journal of Applied Psychology, 61*, 295–300.

Clark, R. A., & Delia, J. G. (1976). The development of functional persuasive skills in childhood and early adolescence. *Child Development, 47*, 1008–1014.

Clark, R. A., & Delia, J. G. (1977). Cognitive complexity, social perspective-taking, and functional persuasive skills in second- to ninth-grade children. *Human Communication Research, 3*, 128–134.

Cline, R. J., & Cardosi, J. B. (1983). Interpersonal communication skills for physicians: A rationale for training. *Journal of Communication Therapy, 2*, 137–156.

Cobb, S., & Rifkin, J. (1991). Practice and paradox: Deconstructing neutrality in mediation. *Law and Social Inquiry, 35*, 35–62.

Cody, M. J., & McLaughlin, M. L. (1980). Perceptions of compliance-gaining situations: A dimensional analysis. *Communication Monographs, 47*, 132–148.

Cohen, B. (1963). *The press and foreign policy.* Princeton: Princeton University Press.

Colbert, K. R. (1993). The effects of debate participation on argumentativeness and verbal aggression. *Communication Education, 42*, 206–214.

Cole, J. G. (2000). A temperament perspective of nonverbal immediacy. *Communication Research Reports, 17*, 90–94.

Conger, J. A., Kanungo, R. N., & Associates. (1988). *Charismatic leadership: The elusive factor in organizational effectiveness.* San Francisco: Jossey-Bass.

Conlee, C. J., Olvera. J., & Vagim, N. N. (1993). The relationships among physician nonverbal immediacy and measures of patient satisfaction with physical care. *Communication Reports, 6*, 23–33.

Conley, T. M. (1990). *Rhetoric in the European tradition.* New York: Longman.

Cooley, C. H. (1902). *Human nature and the social order.* New York: Scribners.

Costello, D. E. (1977). Health communication theory and research: An overview. In B. Ruben (Ed.). *Communication Yearbook 1* (pp. 557–567). New Brunswick, NJ: Transaction Books.

Courtright, J. A. (1978). A laboratory investigation of groupthink. *Communication Monographs, 45*, 229–246.

Cragan, J. F., & Wright, D. W. (1999). *Communication in small groups* (5th ed.). Belmont, CA: Wadsworth.

Craig, R. T. (1993). Why are there so many communication theories? *Journal of Communication, 43*, 26–33.

Craig, R. T. (1999). Communication as a field. *Communication Theory, 9*, 119–161.

Craig, R. T. (2006). Communication as practice. In G. J. Shepherd, J. St. John, & T. Striphas (Eds.), *Communication as . . . Perspectives on theory* (pp. 38–47). Thousand Oaks, CA: Sage.

Craig, R. T. (2007). Pragmatism in the field of communication theory. *Communication Theory, 17*, 125–145.

Craig, R. T., & Muller, H. L. (2007). *Theorizing communication: Readings across traditions.* Los Angeles, CA: Sage.

Crockett, W. H. (1965). Cognitive complexity and impression formation. In B. A. Maher (Ed.), *Progress in experimental personality research* (Vol. 2, pp. 47–90). New York: Academic Press.

Cronen, V. E., Pearce, W. B., & Tomm, K. (1985). A dialectical view of personal change. In K. Gergen & K. Davis (Eds.), *The social construction of the person* (pp. 203–224). New York: Springer-Verlag.

Cronkhite, G. (1969). *Persuasion: Speech and behavioral change.* Indianapolis: Bobbs-Merrill.

Cronkhite, G. (1976). *Communication and awareness.* Menlo Park, CA: Cummings.

Cronkhite, G. (1986). On the focus, scope, and coherence of the study of human symbolic activity. *Quarterly Journal of Speech, 72,* 231–246.

Cronkhite, G., & Liska, J. R. (1980). The judgment of communicant acceptability. In M. E. Roloff & G. R. Miller (Eds.), *Persuasion: New directions in theory and research* (pp. 101–139). Beverly Hills: Sage.

Daly, J. A. & McCroskey, J. C. (1984). *Avoiding communication.* Beverly Hills: Sage Publications.

Dansereau, F., Cashman, J., & Graen, G. B. (1973). Instrumentality theory and equity theory as complementary approaches in predicting the relationship of leaders and turnover among managers. *Organizational Behavior & Human Performance, 10,* 184–200.

Dansereau, F., Graen, G. B., & Haga, W. J. (1975). A vertical dyad linkage approach to leadership within formal organizations: A longitudinal investigation of the role making process. *Organizational Behavior & Human Performance, 13,* 46–78.

DeFleur, M. L., & Ball-Rokeach, S. (1982). *Theories of mass communication* (4th ed.). New York: Longman.

Delia, J. G. (1976). A constructivistic analysis of the concept of credibility. *Quarterly Journal of Speech, 62,* 361–375.

Delia, J. G. (1987). *Communication research: A history.* In C.R. Berger & S.H. Chaffee (Eds.). Handbook of communication science (pp. 20–98). Newbury Park, CA: Sage.

Delia, J. G., & Clark, R. A. (1977). Cognitive complexity, social perception, and the development of listener-adapted communication in six-, eight-, ten-, and twelve-year-old boys. *Communication Monographs, 44,* 326–345.

Delia, J. G., Crockett, W. H.. Press, A. N., & O'Keefe, D. J. (1975). The dependency of interpersonal evaluations on context relevant beliefs about the other. *Communication Monographs, 42,* 10–19.

Delia, J. G., O'Keefe, B. J., & O'Keefe, D. J. (1982). The constructivist approach to communication. In F. E. X. Dance (Ed.), *Human communication theory* (pp. 147–191). New York: Harper & Row.

Denton, R. E., Jr., & Woodward, G. C. (1998). *Political communication in America* (3rd ed.). New York: Praeger.

DePaulo, B. M., Kashy, D. A., Kirkendol, S. E., Wyer, M. M., & Epstein, J. A. (1996). Lying in everyday life. *Journal of Personality and Social Psychology, 70,* 979–995.

DeVito, J. A. (2001). *The interpersonal communication book* (9th ed.). Boston: Allyn & Bacon.

DeVito, J. A. (2002). *Human communication: The basic course* (9th ed.). Boston: Allyn & Bacon.

Dillard, J. P. (Ed.) (1990). *Seeking compliance: The production of interpersonal influence messages.* Scottsdale, AZ: Gorsuch Scarisbrick.

Donohew, L., & Ray, E. B. (1990). Introduction: Systems perspectives on health communication. In E. B. Ray & L. Donohew (Eds.), *Communication and health* (pp. 3–8). Hillsdale, NJ: Lawrence Erlbaum.

Donohew, L., Palmgreen, P., & Rayburn, J. D. (1987). Social and psychological origins of media use: A lifestyle analysis. *Journal of Broadcasting and Electronic Media, 31,* 255–278.

Drew, P., & Chilton, K. (2000). Calling just to keep in touch: Regular and habitualized telephone calls as an environment for small talk. In J. Coupland (Ed.), *Small talk* (pp. 137–162). Harlow, UK: Pearson Education Limited.

Drew, P., & Heritage, J. (1992). Analyzing talk at work: An introduction. In P. Drew & J. Heritage (Eds.), *Talk at work* (pp. 3–65). Cambridge, MA: Cambridge University Press.

Duck, S. W. (1985). Social and personal relationships. In M. L. Knapp & G. R. Miller (Eds.), *Handbook of interpersonal communication* (pp. 655–686). Beverly Hills: Sage.

Duck, S., & Barnes, M. K. (1992). Disagreeing about agreement: Reconciling differences about similarity. *Communication Monographs, 59,* 199–208.

Duran, R. L. (1983). Communicative adaptability: A measure of social communicative competence. *Communication Quarterly, 31,* 253–258.

Duran, R. L. (1992). Communicative adaptability: A review of conceptualization and measurement. *Communication Quarterly, 40,* 253–268.

Duran, R. L., & Kelly, L. (1985). An investigation into the cognitive domain of communicating competence. *Communication Research Reports, 2,* 112–119.

Duran, R. L., & Zakahi, W. R. (1984). Competence or style: What's in a name. *Communication Research Reports, 1,* 42–47.

Duran, R. L., & Zakahi, W. R. (1988). The influence of communicative competence upon roommate satisfaction. *Western Journal of Speech Communication, 52,* 135–146.

Eadie, W. F. (1990, November). Being applied: Communication research comes of age. *Journal of Applied Communication Research,* Special Issue, 1–6.

Edwards, A. L. (1972). *Experimental design in psychological research* (4th ed.). New York: Holt, Rinehart, and Winston.

Edwards, J. L. (1998). The very model of a modern major (media) candidate: Colin Powell and the theory of reasoned action. Communication *Quarterly, 46,* 163–176.

Ehninger, D. (1968). On systems of rhetoric. *Philosophy and Rhetoric, 1,* 131–144.

Eiser, J. R. (1980). Prolegomena to a more applied social psychology. In R. Gilmour & S. W. Duck (Eds.), *The development of social psychology* (pp. 271–292). New York: Academic Press.

Ekman, P. (1985). *Telling lies.* New York: Norton.

Ellis, D. G. (1992). *From language to communication.* Hillsdale, NJ: Lawrence Erlbaum.

Erdogan, B., Liden, R. C., & Kraimer, M. L. (2006). Justice and leader-member exchange: The moderating role of organizational culture. *Academy of Management Journal, 49,* 395–406.

Ewing, D. (1982). *"Do it my way or you're fired": Employee rights and the changing role of management perspectives.* New York: John Wiley & Sons.

Fallows, D. (2004). *Many Americans use the Internet for everyday activities, but traditional offline habits still dominate.* Retrieved August 12, 2008, from http://www.pewinternet.org/pdfs/PIP_Internet_and_Daily_Life.pdf

Fast, J. (1970). *Body language.* New York: Pocket Books.

Fayol, H. (1949). *General and industrial management.* New York: Pitman.

Feezel, J. D. (1974). A qualified certainty: Verbal probability in argument. *Speech Monographs, 41,* 348–356.

Festinger, L. (1957). *A theory of cognitive dissonance.* Stanford: Stanford University Press.

Fiedler, F. E. (1972). How do you make leaders more effective? *American Behavioral Scientist, 24,* 630–631.

Fishbein, M., & Ajzen, I. (1975). *Belief, attitude, intention and behavior: An introduction to theory and research.* Reading, MA: Addison-Wesley.

Fisher, B. A. (1970). Decision emergence: Phases in group decision making. *Speech Monographs, 37,* 53–66.

Fisher, J. Y. (1974). A Burkean analysis of the rhetorical dimensions of a multiple murder and suicide. *Quarterly Journal of Speech, 60,* 175–189.

Fitzpatrick, M. A. (1977). A typological approach to communication in relationships. In B. Ruben (Ed.), *Communication Yearbook 1* (pp. 263–275). New Brunswick, NJ: Transaction Books.

Fitzpatrick, M. A. (1983). Predicting couples' communication from couples' self reports. In R. N. Bostrom & B. H. Westley (Eds.), *Communication Yearbook 7* (pp. 49–82). Beverly Hills: Sage.

Fitzpatrick, M. A. (1984). A typological approach in marital interaction: Recent theory and research. In L. Berkowitz (Ed.). *Advances in experimental social psychology* (Vol. 18, pp. 1–47). Orlando: Academic Press.

Fitzpatrick, M. A. (1988). *Between husbands and wives: Communication in marriage.* Newbury Park, CA: Sage.

Fitzpatrick, M. A., & Ritchie, L. D. (1994). Communication schemata within the family: Multiple perspectives on family interaction. *Human Communication Research, 20,* 275–301.

Fitzpatrick, M. A., & Wamboldt, F. S. (1990). Where is all said and done? Toward an integration of intrapersonal and interpersonal models of marital and family communication. *Communication Research, 17,* 421–430.

Flew, T. (2002). *Newmedia.* Melbourne, Australia: Oxford University Press.

Florence, B. T. (1975). An empirical test of the relationship of evidence to belief systems and attitude change. *Human Communication Research, 1,* 145–158.

Floyd, K., & Burgoon, J. K. (1999). Reacting to nonverbal expressions of liking: A test of interaction adaptation theory. *Communication Monographs, 66,* 219–239.

Floyd, K., Ramirez, A., Jr., & Burgoon, J. K. (1999). Expectancy violations theory. In L. K. Guerrero, J. A. DeVito, & M. L. Hecht (Eds.), *The Nonverbal Communication Reader* (2nd ed., pp. 437–444). Prospect Heights. IL: Waveland Press.

Floyd, K., & Voloudakis, M. (1999). Affectionate behavior in adult platonic friendships: Interpreting and evaluating expectancy violations. *Human Communication Research, 25,* 341–369.

Foss, S., Foss, K., & Trapp, R. (1991). *Contemporary perspectives on rhetoric* (2nd Ed.). Prospect Heights, IL: Waveland Press.

Frank, J. D., & Frank, J. B. (1991). *Persuasion and healing: A comparative study of psychotherapy*. Baltimore: The Johns Hopkins University Press.

Franke, R. H., & Kaul, J. D. (1978). The Hawthorne experiments: First statistical interpretation. *American Sociological Review, 43*, 623–639.

Frey, L. R. & Botan, C. H. (1988). The status of instruction in introductory undergraduate communication research methods. *Communication Education, 37*, 249–256.

Friedman, M. (1970, September 13). The social responsibility of business is to increase its profits. *The New York Times Magazine*.

Fromm, E. (1947). *Man for himself*. New York, NY: Rinehart & Winston.

Galvin, K. M., & Brommel, B. J. (2000). *Family communication* (5th ed.). Boston: Allyn & Bacon.

Gerbner, G., & Gross, L. (1976a). Living with television: The violence profile. *Journal of Communication, 26*, 172–199.

Gerbner, G., & Gross, L. (1976b). The scary world of TV's heavy viewer. *Psychology Today*, pp. 41–45, 89.

Gerbner, G., Gross, L., Morgan, M., & Signorielli, N. (1980). The "mainstreaming" of America: Violence profile no. 11. *Journal of Communication, 30*, 10–29.

Gerbner, G., Gross, L., Morgan, M., & Signorielli, N. (1986). Living with television: The dynamics of the cultivation process. In J. Bryant & D. Zillmann (Eds.). *Perspectives on media effects* (pp. 17–40). Hillsdale, NJ: Lawrence Erlbaum.

Gergen, K. J. (1980). Toward intellectual audacity in social psychology. In R. Gilmour & S. W. Duck (Eds.). *The development of social psychology* (pp. 239–270). New York: Academic Press.

Gibbs, J. L., Ellison, N. B., & Heino, R. D. (2006). Self-presentation in online personals: The role of anticipated future interaction, self-disclosure, and perceived success in Internet dating. *Communication Research, 33*, 1–26.

Giffin, K., & Patton, B. R. (1971). *Fundamentals of interpersonal communication*. New York: Harper & Row.

Giles, H., & Wiemann, J. M. (1987). Language, social comparison, and power. In C. R. Berger & S. H. Chaffee (Eds.), *The handbook of communication science* (pp. 350–384). Newbury Park. CA: Sage.

Giles, H., Mulac, A., Bradac, J. J., & Johnson, P. (1987). Speech accommodation theory: The first decade and beyond. In M. McLaughlin (Ed.), *Communication Yearbook 10* (pp. 13–48). Newbury Park, CA: Sage.

Glynn, C. J., & McLeod, J. M. (1985). Implications of the spiral of silence theory for communication and public opinion research. In K. R. Sanders, L. L. Kaid, & D. Nimmo (Eds.), *Political communication yearbook 1984* (pp. 43–65). Carbondale, IL: Southern Illinois University Press.

Glynn, C. J., Hayes, A. F., & Shanahan, J. (1997). Perceived support for one's opinions and willingness to speak out: A meta-analysis of survey studies on the "spiral of silence." *Public* Opinion *Quarterly, 61*, 452–463.

Goffman, E. (1959). *The presentation of self in everyday life*. Garden City, NY: Anchor/Doubleday.

Goffman, E. (1967). *Interaction ritual: Essays on face-face behavior*. Garden City, NY: Anchor Books.

Golden, J. L., Berquist, G. F., & Coleman, W. E. (1978). *The rhetoric of Western thought* (2nd Ed.). Dubuque, IA: Kendall/Hunt Publishing Co.

Gonzenbach, W. J., King, C., & Jablonski. P. (1999). Homosexuals and the military: An analysis of the spiral of silence. *The Howard Journal of Communications, 10,* 281–296.

Gorden, W. I., Infante, D. A., & Braun, A. A. (1986). Communicator style: Is the metaphor appropriate? *Communication Research Reports, 3,* 13–19.

Gouran, D. S., & Hirokawa, R. Y. (1986). Counteractive functions of communication in effective group decision making. In R. Y. Hirokawa & M. S. Poole (Eds.), *Communication and group decision making* (pp. 81–90). Beverly Hills: Sage.

Graham, E. E., Barbato, C. A., & Perse, E. M. (1993). The interpersonal communication motives model. *Communication Quarterly, 41,* 172–186.

Grant, A. E., Guthrie. K. K., & Ball-Rokeach, S. J. (1991). Television shopping: A media system dependency perspective. *Communication Research, 18,* 773–798.

Griffin, E. (2006). *A first look at communication theory* (6th ed.). Boston: McGraw-Hill.

Gruner, C. R. (1965). An experimental study of satire as persuasion. *Speech Monographs, 32,* 149–154.

Gruner, C. R. (1970). The effect of humor in dull and interesting informative speeches. *Central States Speech Journal, 21,* 160–166.

Gudykunst, W. (1985). A model of uncertainty reduction in intercultural encounters. *Journal of Language and Social Psychology, 4,* 79–98.

Gudykunst, W. (2005). An anxiety/uncertainty management (AUM) theory of effective communication: Making the mesh of the net finer. In W. Gudykunst (Ed.), *Theorizing about intercultural communication* (pp. 281–322). Thousand Oaks, CA: Sage.

Gudykunst, W., & Hammer, M. R. (1988). Strangers and hosts. In Y. Y. Kim & W. B. Gudykunst (Eds.), *Cross-cultural adaptation* (pp. 106–139). Newbury Park, CA: Sage.

Gudykunst, W. B., & Nishida. T. (1984). Individual and cultural influence on uncertainty reduction. *Communication Monographs, 51,* 23–36.

Gulley, H., & Berlo, D. (1956). Effects of intercellular and intracellular speech structure on attitude change and learning. *Speech Monographs, 23,* 288–297.

Gumpert, G., & Cathcart, R. (Eds.). (1986). *Inter/Media: Interpersonal communication in a media world* (3rd ed.). New York: Oxford University Press.

Hackman, M. Z., & Johnson, C. E. (2000). *Leadership: A communication perspective.* Prospect Heights, IL: Waveland Press.

Hamilton, M. A., Hunter, J. E., & Burgoon, M. (1990). An empirical test of an axiomatic model of the relationship between language intensity and persuasion. *Journal of Language and Social Psychology, 9,* 235–255.

Hample, D. (1977). Testing a model of value argument and evidence. *Communication Monographs, 44,* 106–120.

Hample, D. (1979). Predicting belief and belief change using a cognitive theory of argument and evidence. *Communication Monographs, 46,* 142–146.

Hample, D. (1981, May). *Models of arguments using multiple bits of evidence.* Paper presented at the annual meeting of the International Communication Association, Minneapolis. MN.

Hample, D. (1999). The life space of personalized conflicts. In M. E. Roloff (Ed.), *Communication yearbook 22* (pp. 171–207). Thousand Oaks, CA: Sage.

Hample, D., & Dallinger, J. M. (1995). A Lewinian perspective on taking conflict personally. *Communication Quarterly, 43,* 297–319.

Hart, R. P., Carlson, R. E., & Eadie, W. F. (1980). Attitudes toward communication and the assessment of rhetorical sensitivity. *Communication Monographs, 47,* 1–22.

Hatfield, E., & Rapson, R. L. (1992). Similarity and attraction in close relationships. *Communication Monographs, 59,* 209–212.

Hawes, L.C. (1975). *Pragmatics of analoguing: Theory and model construction in communication.* Menlo Park, CA: Addison-Wesley Publishing Co.

Hawking, S. (1996). *The illustrated a brief history of time* (Updated and expanded ed.). New York: Bantam Books.

Hawkins, R. P., & Pingree, S. (1982). Television's influence on social reality. In D. Pearl, L. Bouthilet, & J. Lazar (Eds.), *Television and behavior: Ten years of scientific progress and implications for the eighties: Vol. 2. Technical reviews* (pp. 224–247). Washington. DC: U.S. Government Printing Office.

Heider, F. (1958). *Psychology of interpersonal relations.* New York: Wiley.

Heims, S. J. (1991). *The cybernetic group.* Cambridge, MA: MIT Press.

Hempel, C. G. (1965). *Aspects of scientific explanation and other essays in the philosophy of science.* New York: The Free Press.

Henderson, S., & Gilding, M. (2004). "I've never clicked this much with anyone in my life": Trust and hyperpersonal communication in online friendships. *New Media & Society, 6,* 487–506.

Heritage, J. (1984). *Garfinkel and ethnomethodology.* Oxford, UK: Polity Press.

Hersey, P. (1984). *The situational leader.* Escondido, CA: Center for Leadership Studies.

Hersey, P., & Blanchard, K. H. (1977). *Management of organizational behavior: Utilizing human resources* (3rd ed.). Englewood Cliffs, NJ: Prentice Hall.

Herzberg, F. (1968). One more time: How do you motivate employees? *Harvard Business Review, 46,* 53–62.

Herzberg, F. (1982). *Managerial choice: To be efficient and to be human.* Provo, UT: Olympus.

Hiers, J. M., & Heckel, R. V. (1977). Seating choice, leadership, and locus of control. *Journal of Social Psychology, 103,* 313–314.

Hinkle, L. L. (1999). Nonverbal immediacy communication behaviors and liking in marital relationships. *Communication Research Reports, 16,* 81–90.

Hirokawa, R. Y. (1985). Discussion procedures and decision-making performance: A test of a functional perspective. *Human Communication Research, 12,* 203–224.

Hirokawa, R. Y. (1988). Group communication and decision-making performance: A continued test of the functional perspective. *Human Communication Research, 14,* 487–515.

Hirokawa, R. Y., & Pace, R. (1983). A descriptive investigation of the possible communication-based reasons for effective and ineffective group decision making. *Communication Monographs, 50,* 363–379.

Hirokawa, R. Y., & Scheerhorn, D. R. (1986). Communication in faulty group decision making. In R. Y. Hirokawa & M. S. Poole (Eds.), *Communication and group decision making* (pp. 63–80). Beverly Hills: Sage.

Hirsch, P. (1980). The "scary world" of the nonviewer and other anomalies. *Communication Research, 7,* 403–456.

Hirschburg, P. L., Dillman, D. A., & Ball-Rokeach, S. J. (1986). Media system dependency theory: Responses to the eruption of Mount St. Helens. In S. Ball-Rokeach & M. G. Cantor (Eds.), *Media, audience, and social structure* (pp. 117–128). Newbury Park, CA: Sage Publications.

Hofstede, G. (2001). *Culture's consequences* (2nd ed.). Thousand Oaks, CA: Sage.

Hoover, K. R. (1992). *The elements of social scientific thinking* (5th ed.). New York: St. Martin's Press.

Hopper, R.. Koch, S., & Mandelbaum. J. (1986). Conversation analysis methods. In D. G. Ellis & W. A. Donohue (Eds.). *Contemporary issues in language and discourse processes* (pp. 169–186). Hillsdale, NJ: Lawrence Erlbaum.

Horner, W. B. (Ed.). (1990). *The present state of scholarship in historical and contemporary rhetoric* (Rev. ed.). Columbia and London: University of Missouri Press.

Horton, D., & Wohl, R. R. (1956). Mass communication and parasocial interaction: Observations on intimacy at a distance. *Psychiatry, 19,* 215–229.

Hovland, C. (1948). Social communication. *Proceedings of the American Philosophical Society, 92,* 371–375.

Hovland, C. I. (Ed.) (1957). *The order of presentation in persuasion.* New Haven: Yale University Press.

Hovland, C. I., & Janis, I. L. (Eds.) (1959). *Personality and persuasibility.* New Haven: Yale University Press.

Hovland, C. I., Janis, I. L., & Kelley, H. H. (1953). *Communication and persuasion.* New Haven: Yale University Press.

Hughes, M. (1980). The fruits of cultivation analysis: A reexamination of some effects of television watching. *Public Opinion Quarterly, 44,* 287–302.

Hullman, G. A. (2007). Communicative adaptability scale: Evaluating its use as an "other-report" measure. *Communication Reports, 20,* 51–74.

Hunter, J. & Boster, F. (1987). A model of compliance-gaining message selection. *Communication Monographs, 54,* 63–84.

Infante, D. A. (1973). Forewarnings in persuasion: Effects of opinionated language and forewarner and speaker authoritativeness. *Western Speech, 37,* 185–195.

Infante, D. A. (1975a). Differential functions of desirable and undesirable consequences in predicting attitude and attitude change toward proposals. *Speech Monographs, 42,* 115–134.

Infante, D. A. (1975b). The effects of opinionated language on communicator image and in conferring resistance to persuasion. *Western Journal of Speech Communication, 39,* 112–119.

Infante, D. A. (1975c). Richness of fantasy and beliefs about attempts to refute a proposal as determinants of attitude. *Speech Monographs, 42,* 75–79.

Infante, D. A. (1976). Persuasion as a function of the receiver's prior success or failure as a message source. *Communication Quarterly, 24,* 21–26.

Infante, D. A. (1978). Similarity between advocate and receiver: The role of instrumentality. *Central States Speech Journal, 24,* 187–193.

Infante, D. A. (1980). Verbal plans: A conceptualization and investigation. *Communication Quarterly, 28,* 3–10.

Infante, D. A. (1987a). Aggressiveness. In J. C. McCroskey & J. A. Daly (Eds.), *Personality and interpersonal communication* (pp. 157–192). Newbury Park, CA: Sage Publications.

Infante, D. A. (1987). Enhancing the prediction of response to a communication situation from communication traits. *Communication Quarterly, 35,* 305–316.

Infante, D. A. (1987, May). *An independent-mindedness model of organizational productivity: The role of communication education.* Paper presented at the annual meeting of the Eastern Communication Association, Syracuse, NY.

Infante, D. A. (1987b, July). *Argumentativeness in superior-subordinate communication: An essential condition for organizational productivity.* Paper presented at the American Forensics Summer Conference of the Speech Communication Association, Alta, UT.

Infante, D. A. (1988). *Arguing constructively.* Prospect Heights, IL: Waveland Press.

Infante, D. A. (1995). Teaching students to understand and control verbal aggression. *Communication Education, 44,* 51–63.

Infante, D. A., Anderson, C. M., Martin, M. M., Herington. A. D., & Kim, J. (1993). Subordinates' satisfaction and perceptions of verbal aggressiveness and style. *Management Communication Quarterly, 6,* 307–326.

Infante, D. A., Chandler, T. A., & Rudd, J. E. (1989). Test of an argumentative skill deficiency model of interspousal violence. *Communication Monographs, 56,* 163–177.

Infante, D. A., & Gorden, W. I. (1981). Similarities and differences in the communicator styles of superiors and subordinates: Relations to subordinate satisfaction. *Communication Quarterly, 30,* 67–71.

Infante, D. A., & Gorden, W. I. (1985). Superiors' argumentativeness and verbal aggressiveness as predictors of subordinates' satisfaction. *Human Communication Research, 12,* 117–125.

Infante, D. A., & Gorden, W. I. (1987). Superior and subordinate communication profiles: Implications for independent-mindedness and upward effectiveness. *Central States Speech Journal, 38,* 73–80.

Infante, D. A., & Gorden, W. I. (1989). Argumentativeness and affirming communicator style as predictors of satisfaction/dissatisfaction with subordinates. *Communication Quarterly, 37,* 81–90.

Infante, D. A., & Gorden, W. I. (1991). How employees see the boss: Test of an argumentative and affirming model of supervisors' communicative behavior. *Western Journal of Speech Communication, 55,* 294–304.

Infante, D. A., & Grimmett, R. A. (1971). Attitudinal effects of utilizing a critical method of analysis. *Central States Speech Journal, 22,* 213–217.

Infante, D. A., Parker, K. R., Clarke, C. H., Wilson, L., & Nathu, I. A. (1983). A comparison of factor and functional approaches to source credibility. *Communication Quarterly,* 31, 43–48.

Infante, D. A., & Rancer, A. S. (1982). A conceptualization and measure of argumentativeness. *Journal of Personality Assessment, 46,* 72–80.

Infante, D. A., & Rancer, A. S. (1996). Argumentativeness and verbal aggressiveness: A review of recent theory and research. In B. R. Burleson (Ed.), *Communication Yearbook 19* (pp. 319–351). Thousand Oaks, CA: Sage Publications.

Infante, D. A., Sabourin, T. C., Rudd. J. E., & Shannon, E. A. (1990). Verbal aggression in violent and nonviolent marital disputes, *Communication Quarterly, 38,* 361–371.

Infante, D. A., Trebing, J. D., Shepherd, P. E., & Seeds, D. E. (1984). The relationship of argumentativeness to verbal aggression. *Southern Speech Communication Journal, 50,* 67–77.

Infante, D. A., & Wigley, C. J. III. (1986). Verbal aggressiveness: An interpersonal model and measure. *Communication Monographs, 53,* 61–69.

Iyengar, S., & Kinder, D. R. (1985). Psychological accounts of agenda-setting. In S. Kraus & R. M. Perloff (Eds.), *Mass media and political thought* (pp. 117–140). Beverly Hills: Sage.

Jablin, F. M. (2001). Organizational entry, assimilation, and disengagement/exit. In F. M. Jablin, L. L. Putnam (Eds.), *The new handbook of organizational communication: Advances in theory, research, and methods* (pp. 732–818). Newbury Park, CA: Sage.

Jablin, F. M., & Putnam, L. L. (Eds.). (2001). *The new handbook of organizational communication: Advances in theory, research, and methods.* Newbury Park, CA: Sage.

Jacobs, S. (1980). Recent advances in discourse analysis. *Quarterly Journal of Speech, 66,* 450–472.

Jacobs, S. (1988). Evidence and inference in conversation analysis. In J. A. Anderson (Ed.), *Communication Yearbook 11* (pp. 433–443). Newbury Park, CA: Sage.

Janis, I. L. (1972, 1982). *Groupthink: Psychological studies of policy decisions and fiascoes* (2nd ed.). Boston: Houghton Mifflin.

Janis, I. L., & Feshbach, S. (1953). Effects of fear-arousing communications. *Journal of Abnormal and Social Psychology, 48,* 78–92.

Jefferson, G. (2004). Glossary of transcript symbols with an introduction. In G. H. Lerner (Ed.), *Conversation analysis: Studies from the first generation* (pp. 225–256). Amsterdam: John Benjamins.

Jeffres, L. W., Neuendorf, K. A., & Atkin, D. (1999). Spirals of silence: Expressing opinions when the climate of opinion is unambiguous. *Political Communication, 16,* 115–131.

Johannesen, R. L. (1996). *Ethics in human communication* (4th ed.). Prospect Heights, IL: Waveland Press.

Johnson, A. (1990). Trends in political communication: A selective review of research in the 1980's. In D. L. Swanson & D. Nimmo (Eds.), *New directions in political communication* (pp. 329–362). Newbury Park, CA: Sage.

Johnson, D. W., & Johnson, R. T. (1979). Conflict in the classroom: Controversy and learning. *Review of Educational Research, 49,* 51–70.

Johnston, J., & Ettema, J. S. (1986). Using television to best advantage: Research for prosocial television. In J. Bryant & D. Zillmann (Eds.), *Perspectives on media effects* (pp. 143–164). Hillsdale, NJ: Lawrence Erlbaum.

Kanter, R. M. (1977). *Men and women of the corporation.* New York: Basic Books.

Kaplan, A. (1964). *The conduct of inquiry: Methodology for behavioral science.* San Francisco, CA: Chandler Publishing Company.

Kassing, J. W., & Avtgis, T. A. (1999). Examining the relationship between organizational dissent and aggressive communication. *Management Communication Quarterly, 13,* 100–115.

Kato, T. (2001). The end of lifetime employment in Japan?: Evidence from the national surveys and field research. *Journal of the Japanese and International Economies, 15,* 489–514.

Katz, E., & Lazarsfeld, P. F. (1955). *Personal influence: The part played by people in the flow of mass communication.* New York: Free Press.

Keltner, J. W. (1970). *Interpersonal speech-communication: Elements and structures.* Belmont. CA: Wadsworth.

Kennedy, G. (1963). *The art of persuasion in Greece.* Princeton, NJ: Princeton University Press.

Kerlinger, F. N. (1986). *Foundations of behavioral research.* New York: Holt, Rinehart, and Winston.

Kiesler, C. A., & Kiesler, S. B. (1969). *Conformity.* Reading, MA: Addison-Wesley.

Kiesler, C., Collins. B., & Miller, N. (1969). *Attitude change: A critical analysis of theoretical approaches.* New York: John Wiley.

Kim, Y. Y. (1988). *Communication and cross-cultural adaptation: An integrative theory.* Clevendon, UK: Multilingual Matters.

Kim, Y. Y. (2001). *Becoming intercultural: An integrative theory of communication and cross-cultural adaptation.* Thousand Oaks, CA: Sage.

Kim, Y. Y. (2005). Adapting to a new culture: An integrative communication theory. In W. B. Gudykunst (Ed.), *Theorizing about intercultural communication* (pp. 375–400). Thousand Oaks, CA: Sage.

Kitcher, P. (1982). *Abusing science: The case against creationism.* Cambridge, MA: MIT Press.

Knapp, M. L. (1978). *Social intercourse: From greeting to goodbye.* Needham Heights, MA: Allyn & Bacon.

Knapp, M. L. (1984). Forward. In M. L. McLaughlin. *Conversation: How talk is organized.* Beverly Hills: Sage.

Knapp, M. L., & Comadena, M. E. (1979). Telling it like it isn't: A review of theory and research on deceptive communications. *Human Communication Research, 5,* 270–285.

Knapp, M. L., Hart, R. P., Friedrich, G. W., & Shulman, G. M. (1973). The rhetoric of goodbye: Verbal and nonverbal correlates of human leave-taking. *Speech Monographs, 40,* 182–198.

Knapp, M. L., & Vangelisti, A. L. (2005). *Interpersonal communication and human relationships.* Boston: Allyn & Bacon.

Knower, F. R. (1935). Experimental studies of attitude change I: A study of effect of oral argument on changes of attitude. *Journal of Abnormal and Social Psychology, 6,* 315–347.

Koenig, F., & Lesson, G. (1985). Viewers' relationship to television personalities. *Psychological Reports, 57,* 263–266.

Koermer, C., Goldstein, M., & Fortson, D. (1993). How supervisors communicatively convey immediacy to subordinates: An exploratory qualitative investigation. *Communication Quarterly, 41,* 269–281.

Kotter, J. P. (1988). *The leadership factor.* New York: Free Press.

Kreps, G. (1979). *Human communication and Weik's model of organizing: A field experimental test and revaluation* (Vol. 40): Dissertation Abstracts International.

Kreps, G. L. (1988). The pervasive role of information in health care: Implications for health communication policy. In J. Anderson (Ed.). *Communication Yearbook 11* (pp. 238–276). Newbury Park, CA: Sage.

Kreps, G. L., & Atkin, C. (1991). Introduction: Current issues in health communication research. *American Behavioral Scientist, 34,* 648–651.

Kreps, G. L., & Thornton, B. C. (1992). *Health communication: Theory and practice.* (2nd ed.) Prospect Heights, IL: Waveland Press.

Kreps, G. L., Frey. L. R., & O'Hair. D. (1991). Applied communication research: Scholarship that can make a difference. *Journal of Applied Communication Research, 19,* 71–87.

Krupat, E. (1986, November). A delicate imbalance. *Psychology Today,* 22–26.

Kuhn, T. S. (1970). *The structure of scientific revolutions* (2nd ed.). Chicago, IL: University of Chicago Press.

Lakoff, R. (1975). *Language and woman's place.* New York: Harper & Row.

Lane, S. (2002). *National magazine letters to the editor post-Columbine: Did a spiral of silence occur among those who hold pro-gun opinions?* Unpublished master's thesis, University of Akron, Akron. OH.

Langer, E. (1989). *Mindfulness.* Reading, MA: Addison-Wesley.

Lannutti, P. J., Laliker, M., & Hale, J. L. (2001). Violations of expectations and socio-sexual communication in student/professor interactions. *Communication Education, 50,* 69–82.

Lasagna, L. (1964). *Hippocratic Oath-Modern Version.* Retrieved March 14, 2008, from http://www.pbs.org/wgbh/nova/doctors/oath_010315.html

Lasswell, H. D. (1927). *Propaganda technique in world wars.* New York: Knopf.

Lasswell, H. D. (1948). The structure and function of communication in society. In L. Bryson (Ed.), *The communication of ideas (pp.* 37–51). New York: Harper.

Lazarsfeld, P. F. & Stanton, F. N. (1944). *Radio research 1942–1943.* New York: Duel, Sloan, and Pearce.

Lazarsfeld, P. F., Berelson, B. R., & Gaudet, H. (1944). *The people's choice: How the voter makes up his mind in a presidential campaign.* New York: Columbia University Press.

Lefcourt, H. M. (1981). *Research with the locus of control construct: Vol. 1: Assessment methods.* New York: Academic Press.

Lefkowitz, M., Blake, R. R., & Mouton, J. S. (1955). Status factors in pedestrian violation of traffic signals. *Journal of Abnormal and Social Psychology, 51,* 704–706.

LePoire, B. A.. & Burgoon, J. K. (1994). Two contrasting explanations of involvement violations: Expectancy violations theory versus discrepancy arousal theory. *Human Communication Research, 20,* 560–591.

Levy, M. R. (1979). Watching TV news as parasocial interaction. *Journal of Broadcasting, 23,* 69–80.

Levy, M. R., & Windahl, S. (1984). Audience activity and gratifications: A conceptual clarification and exploration. *Communication Research, 11,* 51–78.

Likert, R. (1932). A technique for the measurement of attitudes. *Archives of Psychology* (No. 140).

Likert, R. (1961). *New patterns of management.* New York: McGraw-Hill.

Likert, R. (1967). *The human organization: Its management and value.* New York: McGraw-Hill.

Lin, C. A., & Salwen, M. B. (1997). Predicting the spiral of silence on a controversial public issue. *The Howard Journal of Communications, 8,* 129–141.

Lippman, W. (1922). *Public opinion.* New York: Macmillan.

Loevinger, L. (1979). The ambiguous mirror: The reflective-projective theory of broadcasting and mass communication. In G. Gumpert & R. Cathcart (Eds.), *Inter/Media: Interpersonal communication in a media world* (pp. 234–260). New York: Oxford University Press.

Loftus, E. F. (1979). *Eyewitness testimony.* Cambridge: Harvard University Press.

Loftus, E. F. (1980). *Memory.* Reading. MA: Addison-Wesley.

Loges, W. E., & Ball-Rokeach, S. J. (1993). Dependency relations and newspaper readership. *Journalism Quarterly, 70,* 602–614.

Lord, R. G., Phillips, J. S., & Rush, M. C. (1980). Effects of sex and personality on perceptions of emergent leadership, influence, and social power. *Journal of Applied Psychology, 65,* 176–182.

Lori, M., & More. W. W. (1980). Four dimensions of assertiveness. *Multivariate Behavioral Research, 2,* 127–135.

Lowery, S., & DeFleur, M. L. (1995). *Milestones in mass communication research: Media effects* (3rd ed.). New York: Longman.

Lull, J. (1982). A rules approach to the study of television and society. *Human Communication Research, 9,* 3–16.

MacKay, A. L. (1977). *The harvest of a quiet eye: A selection of scientific quotations.* London: Institute of Physics.

Madlock, P. E., Martin, M. M., Bogdan, L., & Ervin, M. (2007). The impact of communication traits on leader-member exchange. *Human Communication, 10,* 50–64.

Magnusson, D., & Endler, N. S. (1977). Interactional psychology: Present status and future prospects. In D. Magnusson & N. S. Endler (Eds.), *Personality at the crossroads: Current issues in interactional psychology* (pp. 3–35). Hillsdale, NJ: Erlbaum.

Mandelbaum, J. (2008). Conversational analysis theory. In L. A. Baxter & D. O. Braithwaite (Eds.), *Engaging theories in interpersonal communication: Multiple perspectives* (pp. 175–188). Thousand Oaks, CA: Sage.

Marcoux, B. C., & Shope, J. T. (1997). Application of the theory of planned behavior to adolescent use and misuse of alcohol. *Health Education Research, 12,* 323–331.

Markus, H. R., & Kitayama, S. (1991). Culture and self: Implication for cognition, emotion, and motivation. *Psychological Review, 98,* 224–253.

Markus, H. R., & Kitayama, S. (1998). The cultural psychology of personality. *Journal of Cross-Cultural Psychology, 29,* 63–87.

Marris, P. (1996). *The politics of uncertainty.* New York, NY: Routledge.

Martin, M. M., & Anderson, C. M. (1995). The father-young adult relationship: Interpersonal motives, self-disclosure, and satisfaction. *Communication Quarterly. 43,* 119–130.

Martin, M. M., & Anderson, C. M. (2001). The relationship between cognitive flexibility and affinity-seeking strategies. *Advances in Psychological Research, 4,* 69–76.

Martin, M. M., & Anderson, C. M., & Sirimangkala, P. (1997, April). *The relationship between use of organizational conflict strategies with socio-communicative style and aggressive communication traits.* Paper presented at the annual meeting of the Eastern Communication Association, Baltimore, MD.

Martin, M. M., & Rubin, R. B. (1995). A new measure of cognitive flexibility. *Psychological Reports, 76,* 623–626.

Martin, M. M., Anderson, C. M., & Thweatt, K. S. (1998). Individuals' perceptions of their communication behaviors: A validity study of the relationship between the Cognitive Flexibility Scale and the Communication Flexibility Scale with aggressive communication traits. *Journal of Social Behavior and Personality, 13,* 531–540.

Marwell, G. & Schmitt, D. (1967). Dimensions of compliance-gaining behavior: An empirical analysis. *Sociometry, 30,* 350–364.

Maslow, A. H. (1943). A theory of human motivation. *Psychological Review, 50,* 370–396.

Mattson, M. (1999). Toward a reconceptualization of communication cues to action in the health belief model: H1V test counseling. *Communication Monographs, 66,* 240–265.

May, S. (2006). Ethical perspectives and practices. In S. May (Ed.), *Case studies in organizational communication: Ethical perspectives and practices.* Thousand Oaks, CA: Sage.

Mayo, E. (1933). *The human problems of an industrial civilization.* New York: Macmillan.

McClelland, D. C. (1962). Business drive and national achievement. *Harvard Business Review, 40,* 99–112.

McClelland, D. C. (1975). *Power: The inner experience.* New York: Irvington.

McCombs, M. E., & Shaw, D. L. (1972). The agenda-setting function of mass media. *Public Opinion Quarterly, 36,* 176–187.

McCroskey, J. C. (1968). *An introduction to rhetorical communication.* Englewood Cliffs, NJ: Prentice-Hall.

McCroskey, J. C. (1969). A summary of experimental research on the effects of evidence in persuasive communication. *Quarterly Journal of Speech, 55,* 169–176.

McCroskey, J. C. (1970). Measures of communication-bound anxiety. *Speech Monographs, 37,* 269–277.

McCroskey, J. C. (1977). Oral communication apprehension: A summary of recent theory and research. *Human Communication Research, 4,* 75–96.

McCroskey, J. C. (2006). Tolerance for disagreement. In A. S. Rancer & T. A. Avtgis, *Argumentative and aggressive communication: Theory, research, and application* (pp. 244–245). Thousand Oaks, CA: Sage.

McCroskey, J. C., Larson, C., & Knapp, M. L. (1971). *An introduction to interpersonal communication.* Englewood Cliffs, NJ: Prentice-Hall.

McCroskey, J. C., Richmond, V. P., & Daly, J. A. (1975). The development of a measure of perceived homophily in interpersonal communication. *Human Communication Research, 1,* 323–332.

McCroskey, J. C., Sallinen, A., Fayer, J. M., Richmond, V. P., & Barraclough, R. A. (1996). Nonverbal immediacy and cognitive learning: A cross-cultural investigation. *Communication Education, 45,* 200–211.

McCroskey, J. C., & Wheeless, L. R. (1976). *An introduction to human communication.* Boston: Allyn & Bacon.

McCroskey, J. C., & Wright, D. W. (1971). A comparison of the effects of punishment-oriented and reward-oriented messages in persuasive communication. *Journal of Communication, 21,* 83–93.

McDonald, D. G., Glynn, C. J., Kim, S., & Ostman, R. E. (2001). The spiral of silence in the 1948 Presidential election. *Communication Research, 28,* 139–155.

McGregor, D. (1960). *The human side of enterprise.* New York: McGraw-Hill.

McGregor, D. (1966). *Leadership and motivation.* Cambridge, MA: MIT Press.

McGuire, W. J. (1964). Inducing resistance to persuasion: Some contemporary approaches. In L. Berkowitz (Ed.). *Advances in experimental social psychology* (Vol. 1, pp. 191–229). New York: Academic Press.

McGuire, W. J. (1969). The nature of attitudes and attitude change. In G. Lindzey & E. Aronson (Eds.), *Handbook of social psychology* (Vol. 3, pp. 136–314). Reading, MA: Addison-Wesley.

McGuire, W. J. (1996). The Yale communication and attitude-change program in the 1950s. In E. E. Dennis & E. Wartella (Eds.), *American communication research: The remembered history* (pp. 39–60). Mahwah, NJ: Erlbaum.

McLaughlin, M. L. (1984). *Conversation: How talk is organized.* Beverly Hills: Sage.

McLaughlin, M. L., & Cody, M. J. (1982). Awkward silences: Behavioral antecedents and consequences of conversational lapse. *Human Communication Research, 8,* 299–316.

McLaughlin, M. L., Cody, M. J., & O'Hair, H. D. (1983). The management of failure events: Some contextual determinants of accounting behavior. *Human Communication Research, 9,* 208–224.

McLaughlin, M. L., Cody, M. J., & Robey, C. S. (1980). Situational influences on the selection of strategies to resist compliance-gaining attempts. *Human Communication Research, 7,* 14–36.

McLaughlin, M. L., Louden, A. D., Cashion. J. L., Altendorf, D. M., Baaske, K. T., & Smith, S. W. (1985). Conversational planning and self-serving utterances: The manipulation of topical and functional structures in dyadic interaction. *Journal of Language and Social Psychology, 4,* 233–251.

McQuail, D. (1984). With the benefit of hindsight: Reflections on uses and gratifications research. *Critical Studies in Mass Communication, 1,* 177–193.

Mehrabian, A. (1971). *Silent messages.* Belmont, CA: Wadsworth Publishing Co.

Mehrabian, A. (1981). *Silent messages: Implicit communication of emotions and attitudes* (2nd ed.). Belmont, CA: Wadsworth.

Mehrley, R. S., & McCroskey, J. C. (1970). Opinionated statements and attitude intensity as predictors of attitude change and source credibility. *Speech Monographs, 37,* 47–52.

Millar, F. E., & Rogers, L. E (1976). A relational approach to interpersonal communication. In G. R. Miller (Ed.), *Explorations in interpersonal communication* (pp. 87–103). Beverly Hills: Sage.

Millar, F. E., & Rogers, L. E. (1987). Relational dimensions of interpersonal dynamics. In M. E. Roloff & G. R. Miller (Eds.), *Interpersonal processes: New directions in communication research* (pp. 117–139). Newbury Park, CA: Sage.

Miller, G. R. (1963). Studies on the use of fear appeals: A summary and analysis. *Central States Speech Journal, 14,* 117–125.

Miller, G. R. (1966). On defining communication: Another stab. *Journal of Communication, 16,* 88–98.

Miller, G. R. (1978). The current status of theory and research in interpersonal communication. *Human Communication Research, 4,* 164–178.

Miller, G. R., & Baseheart, J. (1969). Source trustworthiness, opinionated statements, and response to persuasive communication. *Speech Monographs, 36, 1–7.*

Miller, G. R., & Berger, C. R. (1978). On keeping the faith in matters scientific. *Western Journal of Speech Communication, 42,* 44–57.

Miller, G. R., Boster, F., Roloff, M., & Siebold, D. (1977). Compliance-gaining message strategies: A typology and some findings concerning effects of situational differences. *Communication Monographs, 44,* 37–51.

Miller, G. R., Burgoon, M., & Burgoon, J. K. (1984). The function of human communication in changing attitudes and gaining compliance. In C. C. Arnold & J. W. Bowers (Eds.), *Handbook of rhetorical and communication theory* (pp. 400–474). Boston: Allyn & Bacon.

Miller, G. R., de Turk, M. A., & Kalbfleisch, P. J. (1983). Self-monitoring. rehearsal, and deceptive communication. *Human Communication Research, 10,* 97–117.

Miller, G. R., & Lobe, J. (1967). Opinionated language, open- and closed-mindedness and responses to persuasive communications. *Journal of Communication, 17,* 333–341.

Miller, G. R., & McReynolds, M. (1973). Male chauvinism and source competence. *Speech Monographs, 40,* 154–155.

Miller, M. D., & Burgoon, M. (1979). The relationship between violations of expectations and the induction of resistance to persuasion. *Human Communication Research, 5,* 301–313.

Miller, V. D., & Jablin, F. M. (1991). Information-seeking during organizational entry: Influences, tactics, and a model of the process. *Academy of Management Review, 16,* 92–120.

Mischel, W. (1968). *Personality and assessment.* New York: John Wiley & Sons.

Mitchell, T. R. (1984). *Motivation and performance.* Chicago: Science Research Associates.

Moine, D. J. (1982, August). To trust perchance to buy. *Psychology Today, 16,* 50–54.

Monge, P. R. (1973). Theory construction in the study of communication: The systems paradigm. *Journal of Communication, 23,* 5–16.

Mongeau, P. A. (1989). Individual differences as moderators of persuasive message processing and attitude-behavior relations. *Communication Research Reports, 6,* 1–6.

Mongeau, P. A., & Carey, C. M. (1996). Who's wooing whom II?: An experimental investigation of date-initiation and expectancy violation. *Western Journal of Communication, 60,* 195–213.

Mongeau, P. A., Hale, J. L., Johnson, K. L., & Hillis, J. D. (1993). Who's wooing whom?: An investigation of female initiated dating. In P. J. Kalbfleisch (Ed.), *Interpersonal Communication: Evolving Interpersonal Relationships* (pp. 51–68). Hillsdale, NJ: Lawrence Erlbaum.

Mongeau, P. A., & Johnson, K. L. (1995). Predicting cross-sex first date sexual expectations and involvement: Contextual and individuals factors. *Personal Relationships, 2,* 301–312.

Montgomery, B. M., & Norton, R. W. (1981). Sex differences and similarities in communicator style. *Communication Monographs, 48,* 121–132.

Morrison, E. W. (1993a). Longitudinal study of the effects of information-seeking on newcomer socialization. *Journal of Applied Psychology, 78*, 173–183.

Morrison, E. W. (1993b). Newcomer information-seeking: Exploring types, modes, sources, and outcomes. *Academy of Management Journal, 36*, 557–589.

Morrison, J. (1997). *Enacting involvement: Some conversational practices for being in relationships.* Unpublished doctoral dissertation, Temple University, Philadelphia, PA.

Motley, M. T. (1990a). On whether one can(not) not communicate: An examination via traditional communication postulates. *Western Journal of Speech Communication, 54*, 1–20.

Motley, M. T. (1990b). Communication as interaction: A reply to Beach and Bavelas. *Western Journal of Speech Communication, 54*, 613–623.

Motley, M. T. (1991). How one may not communicate: A reply to Andersen. *Communication Studies, 42*, 326–339.

Mulac, A., Bradac, J. J., & Gibbons, P. (2001). Empirical support for the gender-as-culture hypothesis: An intercultural analysis of male/female language differences. *Human Communication Research, 27*, 121–152.

Murphy, J. J. (1974). *Rhetoric in the Middle Ages: A history of rhetorical theory from Saint Augustine to the Renaissance.* Berkeley and Los Angeles: University of California Press.

Murphy, J. J. (Ed.). (1992). *A synoptic history of classical rhetoric.* New York: Random House.

Myers, S. A., Zhong, M., & Mitchell, W. (1995). The use of interpersonal communication motives in conflict resolution among romantic partners. *Ohio Speech Journal, 33*, 1–20.

Nelson, G. (1988, November). *Oliver North's testimony before the U.S. Congress' Select Committee on secret military assistance to Iran and Nicaraguan opposition: A fantasy theme analysis.* Paper presented at the meeting of the Speech Communication Association. New Orleans, LA.

Nemeth, C. J. (1986). Differential contributions of majority and minority influence. *Psychological Review, 93*, 23–32.

Nicotera, A. M. (1995). The constructivist theory of Delia, Clark, and associates. In D. P. Cushman & B. Kovacic (Eds.), *Watershed research traditions in human communication theory* (pp. 45–66). Albany: State University of New York Press.

Nimmo, D., & Combs, J. E. (1982). Fantasies and melodramas in television network news: The case of Three Mile Island. *Western Journal of Speech Communication, 46*, 45–55.

Nimmo, D., & Combs, J. E. (1983). *Mediated political realities.* New York: Longman.

Nimmo, D. D., & Sanders, K. R. (1981). Introduction: The emergence of political communication as a field. In D. D. Nimmo & K. R. Sanders (Eds.), *Handbook of political communication* (pp. 11–36). Beverly Hills: Sage.

Nisbett, R. E., & Norenzayan, A. (2002). Culture and cognition. In D. L. Medin (Ed.), *Stevens' handbook of experimental psychology* (3rd ed., Vol. 2, pp. 561–597). New York: John Wiley & Sons.

Noelle-Neumann, E. (1984). *The spiral of silence: Public opinion—Our social skin.* Chicago, IL: University of Chicago Press.

Nofsinger, R. E. (1976). Answering questions indirectly. *Human Communication Research, 2,* 171–181.

Nofsinger, R. E. (1991). *Everyday conversation.* Newbury Park, CA: Sage.

Noll, A. M. (2007). *The evolution of media.* Lanham, MD: Rowman & Littlefield.

Norton, R. W. (1978). Foundation of a communication style construct. *Human Communication Research, 4,* 99–112.

Norton, R. W. (1983). *Communicator style.* Beverly Hills, CA: Sage.

Oetzel, J., & Ting-Toomey, S. (2003). Face concerns in interpersonal conflict: A cross-cultural empirical test of the face-negotiation theory. *Communication Research, 30,* 599–624.

O'Hair, D. (1989). Dimensions of relational communication and control during physician-patient interactions. *Health Communication, 1,* 97–115.

O'Keefe, B. J., & Delia, J. G. (1979). Construct comprehensiveness and cognitive complexity as predictors of the number and strategic adaptation of arguments and appeals in a persuasive message. *Communication Monographs, 46,* 231–240.

O'Keefe, D. J. (1990). *Persuasion: Theory and research.* Newbury Park, CA: Sage. Park, H. S. (1998). The theory of reasoned action and self construal in predicting intention of studying among Korean college students. *Communication Research Reports 15,* 267–279.

Osgood, C. E., Suci, G. J., & Tannenbaum, P. H. (1957). *The measurement of meaning.* Urbana: University of Illinois Press.

Ostroff, C., & Kozlowski, S. (1992). Organizational socialization as a learning process: The role of information acquisition. *Personnel Psychology, 45,* 849–874.

Ouchi, W. G. (1981). *Theory Z: How American business can meet the Japanese challenge.* Reading, MA: Addison-Wesley.

Parks, M. R. (1994). Communication competence and interpersonal control. In M. L. Knapp & G. R. Miller (Eds.), *Handbook of interpersonal communication* (pp. 589–620). Beverly Hills, CA: Sage.

Parks, M. R., & Adelman, M. B. (1983). Communication networks and the development of romantic relationships: An expansion of uncertainty reduction theory. *Human Communication Research, 10,* 55–79.

Pearce, W. B. (2005). The coordinated management of meaning (CMM). In W. Gudykunst (Ed.), *Theorizing about intercultural communication* (pp. 35–54). Thousand Oaks, CA: Sage.

Pearce, W. B., & Cronen, V. E. (1980). *Communication, action, and meaning.* New York: Praeger.

Pearce, W. B., & Cushman, D. P. (1977). *Research about communication rules: A critique and appraisal.* Paper presented at the annual meeting of the Speech Communication Association, Washington, D. C.

Pearce, W. B., & Wiseman, R. L. (1983). Rules theories: Varieties, limitations, and potentials. In W. B. Gudykunst (Ed.), *Intercultural communication theory* (pp. 79–88). Beverly Hills, CA: Sage.

Pearson, J. C. (1995). *Gender and communication* (3rd ed.). New York: McGraw-Hill.

Perse, E. M. (2001). *Media effects and society.* Mahwah, NJ: L. Erlbaum.

Perse, E. M., & Rubin, R. B. (1989). Attribution in social and parasocial relationships. *Communication Research, 16,* 59–77.

Peters, J. D. (1989). John Locke, the individual, and the origin of communication. *Quarterly Journal of Speech, 75,* 387–399.

Peters, T., & Waterman, R. (1982). *In search of excellence.* New York: Harper & Row.

Petronio, S. (2002). *Boundaries of privacy: Dialectics of disclosure.* Albany: SUNY Press.

Petronio, S., & Braithwaite, D. O. (1993). The contributions and challenges of family communication to the field of communication. *Journal of Applied Communication Research, 21,* 103–110.

Petronio, S., & Durham, W. T. (2008). Communication privacy management theory: Significance for interpersonal communication. In L. A. Baxter & D. O. Braithwaite (Eds.), *Engaging theories in interpersonal communication: Multiple perspectives* (pp. 309–322). Thousand Oaks, CA: Sage.

Petronio, S., Jones, S. S., & Morr, M. (2003). Family privacy dilemmas: A communication privacy management perspective. In L. Frey (Ed.), *Bona fide groups* (pp. 23–56). Mahwah, NJ: Erlbaum.

Pettegrew, L. S., & Logan, R. (1987). The health care context. In C. R. Berger & S. H. Chaffee (Eds.), *Handbook of communication science* (pp. 675–710). Newbury Park, CA: Sage.

Petty, R. E., & Cacioppo, J. T. (1986). *Communication and persuasion: Central and peripheral routes to attitude change.* New York: Springer-Verlag.

Philipsen, G. (1995). The coordinated management of meaning theory of Pearce, Cronen, and Associates. In D. P. Cushman & B. Kovacic (Eds.), *Watershed research traditions in human communication theory* (pp. 13–43). Albany: State University of New York Press.

Plax, T. G., Kearney, P., McCroskey, J. C., & Richmond, V. P. (1986). Power in the classroom VI: Verbal control strategies, nonverbal immediacy, and affective learning. *Communication Education, 35,* 43–55.

Polya, G. (1945). *How to solve it: A new aspect of mathematical method.* Princeton, NJ: Princeton University Press.

Poole, M. S. (1981). Decision development in small groups I: A comparison of two models. *Communication Monographs, 48,* 1–24.

Poole, M. S. (1983a). Decision development in small groups II: A study of multiple sequences in decision making. *Communication Monographs, 50,* 206–232.

Poole, M. S. (1983b). Decision development in small groups, III: A multiple sequence of models of group decision development. *Communication Monographs, 50,* 321–341.

Poole, M. S., & Roth, J. (1989). Decision development in small groups IV: A typology of group decision paths. *Human Communication Research, 15,* 323–356.

Popper, K. (1963). *Conjectures and refutations.* London, UK: Routledge.

Popper, K. (1996). *The myth of framework: In defense of science and rationality.* New York: Routledge.

Potter, W. J. (1986). Perceived reality and the cultivation hypothesis. *Journal of Broadcasting and Electronic Media, 30,* 159–174.

Pritchard, M. (1991). *On becoming responsible.* Lawrence, KS: University of Kansas Press.

Pugh, D. S., & Hickson, D. J. (1997). *Writers on organizations* (5th ed.). Thousand Oaks, CA: Sage.

Purcell, W. M. (1992). Are there so few communication theories? *Communication Monographs, 59,* 94–97.

Putnam, L., & Wilson, C. E. (1982). Communicative strategies in organizational conflicts: Reliability and validity of a measurement scale. In M. Burgoon (Ed.), *Communication yearbook 6* (pp. 629–652). Beverly Hills, CA: Sage.

Rancer, A. S., & Avtgis, T. A. (2006). *Argumentative and aggressive communication: Theory, research, and application.* Thousand Oaks, CA: Sage.

Rancer, A. S., & Avtgis, T. A. (2009). Communication theory and research: Bridging the chasms of controversy. In J. W. Chesebro (Ed.), *A century of transformation: Studies in honor of the 100th anniversary of the Eastern Communication Association.* New York: Oxford University Press.

Ratzan, S. C. (1994). Education for the health professional. *American Behavioral Scientist.* 38, 361–380.

Ratzan, S. C., Payne, J. G., & Bishop, C. (1996). The status and scope of health communication. *Journal of Health Communication, 1,* 25–41.

Ray, E. B., & Miller, K. I. (1990). Communication in health-care organizations. In E. B. Ray & L. Donohew (Eds.), *Communication and health* (pp. 92–107). Hillsdale, NJ: Lawrence Erlbaum.

Raymond, G., & Heritage, J. (2006). Physicians' opening questions and patients' satisfaction. *Patient Education and Counseling, 60,* 279–285.

Redding, C. W. (1972). *Communication within the organization.* New York: Industrial Communication Counsel.

Reicher, S., Spears, R., & Postmes, T. (1995). A social identity model of deindividuation phenomena. *European Review of Social Psychology, 6,* 161–198.

Richmond, V. P., & McCroskey, J. C. (1979). Management communicator style, tolerance for disagreement, and innovativeness as predictors of employee satisfaction: A comparision of single-factor, two-factor, and multiple factor approaches. In D. Nimmo (Ed.), *Communication yearbook 3* (Vol. 3, pp. 359–373). New Brunswick, NJ: Transaction Books.

Richmond, V. P., & McCroskey, J. C. (1985). *Communication: Apprehension, avoidance, and effectiveness.* Scottsdale, AZ: Gorsuch Scarisbrick. Publishers.

Richmond, V. P., & McCroskey, J. C. (2000a). The impact of supervisor and subordinate immediacy on relational and organizational outcomes. *Communication Monographs, 67,* 85–95.

Richmond, V. P., & McCroskey, J. C. (2000b). *Nonverbal behavior in interpersonal relations* (4th ed.). Needham Heights, MA: Allyn & Bacon.

Richmond, V. P., McCroskey, J. C., & McCroskey, L. L. (2005). *Organizational communication: Making work, work.* Boston: Pearson.

Richmond, V. P., Smith, R. S., Jr., Heisel, A. D., & McCroskey, J. C. (2001). Nonverbal immediacy in the physician/patient relationship. *Communication Research Reports, 18,* 211–216.

Roberson, D., Davies, I., & Davidoff, J. (2000). Color categories are not universal: Replications and new evidence from a stone-age culture. *Journal of Experimental Psychology: General, 129,* 369–398.

Roberto, A. J., Meyer. G., & Boster, F. J. (2001). Predicting adolescents' decisions about fighting: A test of the theory of planned behavior. *Communication Research Reports, 18,* 315–323.

Roethlisberger, F. J., & Dickson, W. J. (1949). *Management and the worker.* Cambridge, MA: Harvard University Press.

Rogers, E. M. (1994). *A history of communication study*. New York: The Free Press.

Rogers, E. M. (1995). *Diffusion of innovations* (4th ed.). New York: Free Press.

Rogers, E. M., & Bhowmik. D. K. (1970). Homophily-heterophily: Relational concepts for communication research. *Public Opinion Quarterly, 34,* 523–538.

Rokeach, M. (1960). *The open and closed mind*. New York: Basic Books.

Roloff, M. E. (1980). Self-awareness and the persuasion process: Do we really know what we're doing? In M. E. Roloff & G. R. Miller (Eds.), *Persuasion: New directions in theory and research* (pp. 29–66). Beverly Hills: Sage.

Rosenstock, I. M. (1974). Historical origins of the health belief model. *Health Education Monographs, 2,* 354–385.

Rosenthal, R., Hall, J. A., DiMatteo, M. R., Rogers, P. L., & Archer, D. (1979). *Sensitivity to nonverbal communication*. Baltimore, MD: Johns Hopkins University Press.

Rotter, J. B. (1966). Generalized expectancies for internal versus external control of reinforcement. *Psychological Monographs, 80* (Whole No. 609).

Ruben, B. D. (1983). A system-theoretic approach to intercultural communication. In W. B. Gudykunst (Ed.), *Intercultural communication theory: Current perspectives* (pp. 131–145). Beverly Hills, CA: Sage.

Rubin, A. M. (1979). Television use by children and adolescents. *Human Communication Research, 5,* 109–120.

Rubin, A. M. (1983). Television uses and gratifications: The interactions of viewing patterns and motivations. *Journal of Broadcasting, 27,* 37–51.

Rubin, A. M. (1984). Ritualized and instrumental television viewing. *Journal of Communication, 34,* 67–77.

Rubin, A. M. (1985). Uses and gratifications: Quasi-functional analysis. In J. R. Dominick & J. E. Fletcher (Eds.), *Broadcasting research methods* (pp. 202–220). Boston, MA: Allyn and Bacon.

Rubin, A. M., Perse, E. M., & Powell, R. A. (1985). Loneliness, parasocial interaction, and local television news viewing. *Human Communication Research, 12,* 155–180.

Rubin, A. M., & Rubin, R. B. (1985). Interface of personal and mediated communication: A research agenda. *Critical Studies in Mass Communication, 2,* 36–53.

Rubin, A. M., & Windahl, S. (1986). The uses and dependency model of mass communication. *Critical Studies in Mass Communication, 3,* 184–199.

Rubin, R. B. (1982). Assessing speaking and listening competence at the college level: The Communication Competency Assessment Instrument. *Communication Education, 31,* 19–32.

Rubin, R. B. (1985). The validity of the Communication Competency Assessment Instrument. *Communication Monographs, 52,* 173–185.

Rubin, R. B., & Martin, M. M. (1994). The interpersonal communication competence scale. *Communication Research Reports, 11,* 33–44.

Rubin, R. B., & McHugh, M. P. (1987). Development of parasocial interaction relationships. *Journal of Broadcasting and Electronic Media, 31,* 279–292.

Rubin, R. B., Fernandez-Collado, C., & Hernandez-Sampieri, R. (1992). A cross-cultural examination of interpersonal communication motives in Mexico and the United States. *International Journal of Intercultural Relations, 16,* 145–157.

Rubin, R. B., Perse, E. M., & Barbato, C. A. (1988). Conceptualization and measurement of interpersonal communication motives. *Human Communication Research, 14.* 602–628.

Rubin, R. B., & Rubin, A. M. (1992). Antecedents of interpersonal communication motivation. *Communication Quarterly, 40,* 305–317.

Ruechelle, R. C. (1958). An experimental study of audience recognition of emotional and intellectual appeals in persuasion. *Speech Monographs, 25,* 49–58.

Sacks, H. (1992). Lectures on conversations: Volumes 1–2. In G. Jefferson (Ed.). Cambridge, MA: Blackwell.

Salmon, C. T., & Glynn, C. J. (1996). Spiral of silence: Communication and public opinion as social control. In M. B. Salwen & D. W. Stacks (Eds.), *An integrated approach to communication theory and research* (pp. 165–180). Mahwah. NJ: L. Erlbaum.

Salmon, C. T., & Moh, C. Y. (1992). The spiral of silence: Linking individual and society through communication. In J. D. Kennamer (Ed.), *Public opinion, the press, and public policy* (pp. 145–161). Westport, CT: Praeger.

Sanders, J. A., Gass, R. H., Wiseman, R. L., & Bruschke, J. (1992). Ethnic comparison and measurement of argumentativeness, verbal aggressiveness, and need for cognition. *Communication Reports, 5,* 50–56.

Sanders, J. A., Wiseman, R. L., & Gass, R. H. (1994) Does teaching argumentation facilitate critical thinking? *Communication Reports, 7,* 27–35.

Sapir, E. (1958, 1964). In D. G. Mandelbaum (Ed.), *Selected writings of Edward Sapir in language, culture and personality.* Berkeley: University of California.

Satir, V. (1972). *Peoplemaking.* Palo Alto, CA: Science and Behavior Books.

Scandura, T. A., Graen, G. B., & Novak, M. A. (1986). When managers decide not to decide automatically: An investigation of leader-member exchange and decision influence. *Journal of Applied Psychology, 71,* 579–584.

Scheidel, T. M. (1963). Sex and persuasibility. *Speech Monographs, 30,* 353–358.

Schegloff, E. A., Jefferson, G., & Sacks, H. (1977). The preference for self-correction in the organization of repair in conversation. *Language, 53,* 361–382.

Schein, E. H. (1989). *Organizational culture and leadership.* San Francisco: Jossey-Bass.

Schein, E. H. (1992). *Organizational culture and leadership* (2nd ed.). San Francisco: Jossey-Bass.

Scheufele, D. A., & Moy, P. (2000). Twenty-five years of the spiral of silence: A conceptual review and empirical outlook. *International Journal of Public Opinion Research, 12,* 3–28.

Scheufele, D. A., Shanahan, J., & Lee, E. (2001). Real talk: Manipulating the dependent variable in spiral of silence research. *Communication Research, 28,* 304–324.

Schifter, D. E., & Ajzen, I. (1985). Intention, perceived control, and weight loss: An application of the theory of planned behavior. *Journal of Personality and Social Psychology, 49,* 843–851.

Schneider, B. (2000). The psychological life of organizations. In N. M. Ashkanasy & M. F. Peterson (Eds.), *Handbook of organizational culture and climate* (pp. 18–21). Thousand Oaks, CA: Sage.

Schoening, G. T., & Anderson, J. A. (1995). Social action media studies: Foundational arguments and common premises. *Communication Theory, 5,* 93–116.

Schramm, W. (Ed.). (1954). *The process and effects of mass communication.* Urbana: University of Illinois Press.

Schramm, W., Lyle, J.. & Parker. E. (1961). *Television in the lives of our children.* Palo Alto, CA: Stanford University Press.

Schrodt, P., & Wheeless, L. R. (2001). Aggressive communication and informational reception apprehension: The influence of listening anxiety and intellectual inflexibility on trait argumentativeness and trait verbal aggressiveness. *Communication Quarterly, 49*, 53–69.

Schrodt, P., Wheeless, L. R., & Ptacek, K. M. (2000). Informational reception apprehension, educational motivation, and achievement. *Communication Quarterly, 48*, 60–73.

Scott, M., & Hurt, T. (1978). Social influence as a function of communication and message type. *Southern Speech Communication Journal, 43*, 146–161.

Searle, J. R. (1969). *Speech acts: An essay in the philosophy of language*. Cambridge: Cambridge University Press.

Seligman, M. E. P. (1990). *Learned optimism: How to change your mind and your life*. New York: Pocket Books.

Seligman, M. E. P. (1992). *Helplessness: On development, depression, and death*. New York: Freeman.

Sereno, K., & Bodaken, E. (1972). Ego-involvement and attitude change: Toward a reconceptualization of persuasive effect. *Speech Monographs, 39*, 151–158.

Severin, W. J., & Tankard, J. W. (2001). *Communication theories: Origins, methods and uses in the mass media* (5th ed.). Boston: Allyn & Bacon.

Sharf, B. F. (1993). Reading the vital signs: Research in health care communication. *Communication Monographs, 60*, 35–41.

Shaw, D. L., & McCombs, M. E. (1977). The emergence of American political issues: The agenda-setting function of the press. St. Paul, MN: West Publishing Co.

Shaw, M. E., & Costanzo, P. R. (1970). *Theories of social psychology*. New York: McGraw-Hill.

Sheer, V. C., & Cline, R. J. (1995). Testing a model of perceived information adequacy and uncertainty reduction in physician-patient interactions. *Journal of Applied Communication Research, 23*, 44–59.

Sherif, C. W., Sherif, M., & Nebergall, R. W. (1965). *Attitude and attitude change: The social judgment-involvement approach*. Philadelphia: Saunders.

Shibutani, T., & Kwan, K.M. (1965). *Ethnic stratification: A comparative approach*. New York: Macmillan.

Shields, D. C. (1981). A dramatistic approach to applied communication research: Theory, methods, and applications. In J. F. Cragan & D. C. Shields (Eds.), *Applied communication research: A dramatistic approach* (pp. 5–13). Prospect Heights, IL: Waveland Press.

Shimanoff, S. B. (1980). *Communication rules*. Beverly Hills, CA: Sage.

Smith, B. L., Lasswell, H. D., & Casey, R. D. (1946). *Propaganda, communication, and public opinio*n. Princeton, NJ: Princeton University Press.

Smith, M. J. (1982). *Persuasion and human action*. Belmont, CA: Wadsworth.

Snyder, M. (1974). Self-monitoring of expressive behavior. *Journal of Personality and Social Psychology, 30*, 526–537.

Snyder, M. (1979). Self-monitoring processes. In L. Berkowitz (Ed.). *Advances in experimental social psychology* (Vol. 12, pp. 85–128). New York: Academic Press.

Spillman, B. (1979). The impact of value and self-esteem messages in persuasion. *Central States Speech Journal, 30*, 67–74.

Spitzberg, B. H., & Cupach, W. R. (1984). *Interpersonal communication competence.* Beverly Hills: Sage Publications.

Stachel, J. (1989). *The collected papers of Albert Einstein, Vol. 2. The Swiss years: Writings 1900–1909.* Princeton, NJ: Princeton University Press.

Staub, E. (1989). *The roots of evil.* New York: Cambridge University Press.

Stefanone, M. A., & Jang, C. Y. (2007). Writing for friends and family: The interpersonal nature of blogs. *Journal of Computer-Mediated Communication, 13,* 123–140.

Steinfatt, T. M. (1977). *Human communication: An interpersonal introduction.* Indianapolis, IlN: Bobbs-Merrill.

Steinfatt, T. M. (1987). Personality and communication: Classical approaches. In J. C. McCroskev & J. A. Daly (Eds.). *Personality and interpersonal communication* (pp. 42–126). Newbury Park. CA: Sage Publications.

Stephen, T. (1990, June). *Research on the New Frontier: A review of the communication literature on marriage and the family.* Paper presented at the meeting of the International Communication Association. Dublin, Ireland.

Stevens, S. S. (1950). A definition of communication. *Journal of the Acoustical Society of America, 22,* 689–690.

Stewart, C. J., Smith, C. A., & Denton, R. E., Jr. (1994). *Persuasion and social movements* (3rd Ed.). Prospect Heights, IL: Waveland Press.

Stewart, L. P., Stewart, A. D., Cooper, P. J., & Friedley, S. A. (1996). *Communication and gender* (3rd ed.). Scottsdale. AZ: Gorsuch Scarisbrick.

Stewart, R. A., & Roach, K. D. (1998). Argumentativeness and the theory of reasoned action. *Communication Quarterly, 46,* 177–193.

Stiff, J. B. (1986). Cognitive processing of persuasive message cues: A meta-analytic review of the effects of supporting information on attitudes. *Communication Monographs, 53,* 75–89.

Stogdill, R. M. (1948). Personal factors associated with leadership: A survey of the literature. *Journal of Psychology, 25,* 35–71.

Stogdill, R. M. (1974). *Handbook of leadership: A survey of theory and research.* New York: Free Press.

Stogdill, R. M., & Bass, B. M. (1981). *Stogdill's handbook of leadership: A survey of theory and research.* New York: Free Press.

Stotland, E., & Patchen, M. (1961). Identification and change in prejudice and authoritarianism. *Journal of Abnormal and Social Psychology, 62,* 250–256.

Straus, M. (1974). Leveling, civility, and violence in the family. *Journal of Marriage and the Family, 36,* 13–30.

Street, R. L., Jr., & Buller, D. B. (1987). Nonverbal response patterns in physician-patient interactions: A functional analysis. *Journal of Nonverbal Behavior, 11,* 234–253.

Street, R. L., Jr., & Buller, D. B. (1988). Patients' characteristics affecting physician-patient nonverbal communication. *Human Communication Research, 15,* 60–90.

Street, R. L., Jr., & Giles, H. (1982). Speech accommodation theory: A social cognitive approach to language and speech behavior. In M. Roloff & C. R. Berger (Eds.), *Social cognition and communication* (pp. 193–226). Beverly Hills: Sage.

Suedfeld, P., Bochner, S., & Matas, C. (1971). Petitioner's attire and petition signing by peace demonstrators. *Journal of Applied Social Psychology, 1,* 278–283.

Sunnafrank, M. (1983). Attitude similarity and interpersonal attraction in communication processes: In pursuit of an ephemeral influence. *Communication Monographs, 50,* 273–284.

Sunnafrank, M. (1985). Attitude similarity and interpersonal attraction during early communicative relationships: A research note on the generalizability of findings to opposite-sex relationships. *Western Journal of Speech Communication, 49,* 73–80.

Sunnafrank, M. (1986). Predicted outcome value during initial interactions: A reformulation of uncertainty reduction theory. *Human Communication Research, 13,* 3–33.

Sunnafiank, M. (1992). On debunking the attitude similarity myth. *Communication Monographs, 59,* 164–179.

Sunnafrank, M. J., & Miller, G. R. (1981). The role of initial conversations in determining attraction to similar and dissimilar strangers. *Human Communication Research, 8,* 16–25.

Sussman, L. (1973). Ancients and moderns on fear and fear appeals: A comparative analysis. *Central States Speech Journal, 24,* 206–211.

Swanson, D. L. (1981). A constructivist approach. In D. D. Nimmo & K. R. Sanders (Eds.), *Handbook of political communication* (pp. 169–191). Beverly Hills: Sage.

Sypher, H. E., Davenport-Sypher, B., & Haas, J. W. (1988). Getting emotional: The role of affect in interpersonal communication. *American Behavioral Scientist, 31,* 372–383.

Taylor, F. W. (1911). *The principle of scientific management.* New York: Harper and Brothers.

Teven, J. J., McCroskey, J. C., & Richmond, V. P. (1998). Measurement of tolerance for disagreement. *Communication Research Reports, 15,* 209–217.

Thistlethwaite, D. L., Kamenetsky. J., & Schmidt, H. (1956). Refutation and attitude change. *Speech Monographs, 23,* 14–25.

Thompson, T. L. (1986). *Communication for health professionals.* New York: Harper & Row.

Thompson, T. L. (1990). Patient health care: Issues in interpersonal communication. In E. B. Ray & L. Donohew (Eds.), *Communication and health* (pp. 27–50). Hillsdale, NJ: Lawrence Erlbaum.

Thweatt, K. S., & McCroskey, J. C. (1998). The impact of teacher immediacy and misbehaviors on teacher credibility. *Communication Education, 47,* 348–357.

Tichy, N., & Devanna, M. A. (1986). *The transformational leader.* New York: Wiley & Sons.

Ting-Toomey, S. (1988). Intercultural conflicts: A face negotiation theory. In Y. Kim & W. Gudykunst (Eds.), *Theories in intercultural communication* (pp. 213–235). Newbury Park, CA: Sage.

Ting-Toomey, S. (2005). The matrix of face: An updated face-negotiation theory. In W. Gudykunst (Ed.), *Theorizing about intercultural communication* (pp. 71–92). Thousand Oaks, CA: Sage.

Ting-Toomey, S., & Kurogi, A. (1998). Facework competence in intercultural conflict: An updated face-negotiation theory. *International Journal of Intercultural Relations, 22,* 187–225.

Tjosvold, D. (1984). Effects of leader warmth and directiveness on subordinate performance on a subsequent task. *Journal of Applied Psychology, 69*, 222–232.

Tominaga, J., Gudykunst, W. B., & Ota, H. (2003, May). *Perceptions of effective communication in the United States and Japan.* Paper presented at the annual meeting of the International Communication Association, San Diego, CA.

Tompkins, P. K., Fisher, J. Y., Infante, D. A., & Tompkins, E. L. (1975). Kenneth Burke and the inherent characteristics of formal organizations: A field study. *Communication Monographs, 42*, 135–142.

Triandis, H. C. (1995). *Individualism and collectivism.* Boulder, CO: Westview.

Trost, J. (1990). Do we mean the same by the concept of family? *Communication Research, 17*(4), 431–443.

Tubbs, S. (1968). Explicit versus implicit audience conclusions and audience commitment. *Speech Monographs, 35*, 14–19.

Turner, J. R. (1993). Interpersonal and psychological predictors of parasocial interaction with different television performers. *Communication Quarterly, 41*, 443–453.

Vangelisti, A. L. (1993). Communication in the family: The influence of time, relational prototypes, and irrationality. *Communication Monographs, 60*, 42–54.

Walther, J. B. (1993). Impression development in computer-mediated interaction. *Western Journal of Communication, 57*, 381–398.

Walther, J. B. (1996). Computer-mediated communication: Impersonal, interpersonal, and hyperpersonal interaction. *Communication Research, 19*, 50–88.

Walther, J. B. (2008). Social information processing theory: Impressions and relationship development online. In L. A. Baxter & D. O. Braithwaite (Eds.), *Engaging theories in interpersonal communication: Multiple perspectives* (pp. 391–404). Thousand Oaks, CA: Sage.

Walther, J. B., & Bunz, U. (2005). The rules of virtual groups: Trust, liking, and performance in computer-mediated communication. *Journal of Communication, 55*, 828–846.

Watzlawick, P., Beavin, J. H., & Jackson, D. D. (1967). *Pragmatics of human communication: A study of interaction patterns, pathologies, and paradoxes.* New York: Norton.

Weaver, D. (1987). Media agenda-setting and elections: Assumptions and implications. In D. L. Paletz (Ed.), *Political communication research* (pp. 176–193). Norwood, NJ: Ablex.

Weaver, D. H., Graber, D. A., McCombs, M. E.. & Eyal, C. H. (1981). *Media agenda setting in a presidential election: Issues, images, and interest.* New York: Praeger.

Weber, M. (1947). *The theory of social and economic organization* (A. M. Henderson & T. Parsons, Trans.). New York: Oxford.

Weick, K. E. (1979). *The social psychology of organizing* (2nd ed.). Reading, MA: Addison-Wesley.

Weick, K. E. (1995). *Sensemaking in organizations.* Thousand Oaks, CA: Sage.

Weiner, N. (1948). *Cybernetics.* New York: John Wiley.

Welch, S. A., & Rubin, R. B. (2002). Development of relationship stage model. *Communication Quarterly, 50*, 24–40.

Wellmon, T. A. (1988). Conceptualizing organizational communication competence: A rules-based perspective. *Management Communication Quarterly, 1*, 515–534.

Wheeless, L. R. (1975). An investigation of receiver apprehension and social context dimensions of communication apprehension. *The Speech Teacher, 24,* 261–265.

Wheeless, L. R., & Schrodt, P. (2001). An examination of cognitive foundations of informational reception apprehension: Political identification, religious affiliation, and family. *Communication Research Reports, 18,* 1–10.

Wheeless, L. R., Eddleman-Spears, L., Magness, L. D., & Preiss, R. W. (2005). Informational reception apprehension and information from technology aversion: Development and test of a new construct. *Communication Quarterly, 53,* 143–158.

Wheeless, L. R., Preiss, R. W., & Gayle, B. M. (1997). Receiver apprehension, informational receptivity, and cognitive processing. In J. C. McCroskey, J. A. Daly, J. Ayres, T. Hopf, & D. M. Ayres (Eds.), *Avoiding communication: Shyness, reticence, and apprehension* (2nd ed., pp. 151–187). Cresskill, NJ: Hampton Press.

Wheeless, V. E. (1984). A test of the theory of speech accommodation using language and gender orientation. *Women's Studies in Communication, 7,* 13–22.

White, C. H. (2008). Expectancy violations theory and interaction adaptation theory: From expectations to adaptation. In L. A. Baxter & D. O. Braithwaite (Eds.), *Engaging theories in interpersonal communication: Multiple perspectives* (pp. 189–202). Thousand Oaks, CA: Sage Publications.

White, C. H., & Burgoon, J. K. (2001). Adaptation and communicative design: Patterns of interaction in truthful and deceptive conversations. *Human Communication Research, 17,* 3–27.

White, R. K. & Lippett, R. (1968). Leader behavior and member reaction in three social climates. In D. Cartwright & A. Zander (Eds.), *Group dynamics: Research and theory* (3rd. ed., pp. 318–335). New York: Harper and Row.

Whorf, B. L. (1956). In J. Carroll (Ed.). *Language, thought and reality: Selected writings of Benjamin Lee Whorf.* Cambridge, NIA: Technology Press, MIT.

Wiemann, J. M. (1977). Explication and test of a model of communication competence. *Human Communication Research, 3,* 195–213.

Wigley, C. J. (2006). Verbal triggering events. In A. S. Rancer & T. A. Avtgis, *Argumentative and aggressive communication: Theory, research, and application* (pp. 243–244). Thousand Oaks, CA: Sage.

Wilkie, W. H. (1934). An experimental comparison of the speech, the radio, and the printed page as propaganda devices. *Archives of Psychology, 25,* No. 169.

Windahl, S. (1981). Uses and gratifications at the crossroads. In G. C. Wilhoit & H. deBock (Eds.), *Mass Communication Review Yearbook* (Vol. 2, pp. 174–185). Beverly Hills: Sage.

Witte, K., Stokols, D., Ituarte, P., & Schneider, M. (1993). Testing the health belief model in a field study to promote bicycle safety helmets. *Communication Research, 20,* 564–586.

Wright, C. R. (1960). Functional analysis and mass communication. *Public Opinion Quarterly, 24,* 606–620

Yerby, J., Buerkel-Rothfuss, N., & Bochner, A. R. (1990). *Understanding family communication.* Scottsdale, AZ: Gorsuch Scarisbrick.

Zaidel, S. F., & Mehrabian, A. (1969). The ability to communicate and infer positive and negative attitudes facially and vocally. *Journal of Experimental Research in Personality, 3,* 233–241.

Zakahi, W. R. (1985). The relationship of assertiveness to communicative competence and communication satisfaction: A dyadic assessment. *Communication Research Reports, 2*, 36–40.

Zillmann, D. (1972). Rhetorical elicitation of agreement in persuasion. *Journal of Abnormal and Social Psychology, 21*, 159–165.

Zuckerman, M., DePaulo, B. M., & Rosenthal, R. (1981). Verbal and nonverbal communication of deception. In L. Berkowitz (Ed.), *Advances in experimental social psychology* (pp. 1–59). New York: Academic Press.

Subject Index

Experimental operational definitions, 428–429

Experimental paradigm, 89, 424

Experimental research designs, 433, 441
  completely randomized factorial design, 441–442
  randomized blocks/mixed design, 442
  repeated measures design, 442–443
  See also Nonexperimental research designs; Research design

Experimenter effects, 439
  biological characteristics of experimenters and, 439
  blind contacts and, 440
  control strategies for, 440
  experimenter expectancy and, 439–440
  experimenter modeling and, 439
  masking research hypotheses and, 440
  multiple experimenters and, 440
  personality traits of experimenters and, 439
  training for experimenters and, 440
  written/recorded instructions and, 440
  See also Communication research methods; Research design

Experimenting stage, 263, 264, 424–425

Expertise dimension, 157, 173, 175

Explanation, 85
  stimulus-response perspective and, 337–338
  See also Explanation goal of theories

Explanation goal of theories, 41–42

Exploiting orientation, 20

Exploitive-authoritative type management, 305

Extension process, 38–39, 40, 172

External locus of control, 390

External validity, 436

Eye behavior, 221, 226, 236

F

Face, 128, 181, 404

Face gain, 404

Face loss, 404

Face negotiation theory (FNT), 404, 411
  ambivalent orientation and, 409
  avoiding conflict style and, 411
  avoiding facework and, 406
  biconstrual orientation and, 409

compromising conflict style and, 411
  conflict styles and, 409–411
  cultural factors in, 406–408
  dominating conflict style and, 411
  dominating facework and, 406
  face and, 404
  face gain and, 404
  face loss and, 404
  face moves, conflict situations and, 406
  face threats and, 404, 406
  facework and, 404, 406, 407–408
  high power distance and, 407
  independent orientation and, 409
  independent self-construal and, 408–409
  individual factors in, 408–409, 410
  integrating conflict style and, 411
  integrating facework and, 406
  interdependent self-construal and, 408, 409
  low power distance and, 407
  model of face negotiation and, 406, 407
  mutual face obliteration moves and, 406
  mutual face protection moves and, 406
  obliging conflict style and, 411
  other-face and, 406
  other-face upgrading moves and, 406
  out-group relationships and, 409
  power distance and, 407
  relational/situational factors in, 409, 410
  self-construal and, 408–409
  self-face and, 406
  self-face defensive moves and, 406
  See also Intercultural communication

Face threats, 404, 406

Face-to-face (FTF) interaction, 6, 12, 366, 367–368

Facework, 404
  avoiding facework, 406
  cultural factors in, 407–408
  dominating facework, 406
  integrating facework, 406
  utility of, 406
  See also Face negotiation theory (FNT)

Factor model of credibility, 157–158

Factorial design. *See* Completely randomized factorial research design

Falsification, 35–36

Familiar situations, 16–17

Family communication, 10, 28, 374
  abusive behaviors and, 384–385
  argumentative skill deficiency model and, 384–385
  commitment/intimacy and, 375, 376
  communication context, characteristics of, 375–376
  communication privacy management theory and, 379–384
  content dimension of communication behavior and, 377
  couple types, typology of, 378–379
  dialectical tensions and, 376, 379–380
  dysfunctional consequences of interaction and, 377
  equifinality concept and, 377
  family, conceptualizations of, 42, 374–375
  family rules, media use and, 99–100
  family secrets and, 380
  family systems, 103–105
  functional consequences of interaction and, 377
  independent couple type, 378–379
  interactional complexity and, 376, 378
  interactional model of family processes and, 378
  interdependence principle, 377
  longevity of influence and, 375, 376
  mixed-type couples and, 378
  nonsummative system of, 377
  nonvolition and, 375, 376
  relationship dimension of communication behavior and, 377
  self-concept, development of, 375, 376
  separate couple types, 379
  sibling subsystem and, 378
  spouse subsystem and, 378
  structural model of family processes and, 378
  subsystems, individual family members and, 377–378

reflective-projective theory of mass communication, 336–337
resonance and, 356
restrained activists and, 352–353
ritualized use of television and, 349, 351, 352, 353
social information processing theory and, 367–369
spiral of silence theory and, 357–361
surveillance dimension and, 340–341
symbolic convergence theory and, 416–417
two-step flow theory, decision process and, 338–339
two-way communication potential, 335–336
uses and gratifications theory and, 348–354
working class climbers and, 353
Maximum threshold for anxiety/uncertainty, 402
McCroskey model of communication, 65–66
Meaning, 273
connotative meaning, 187–188
culture, learned system of meaning and, 407
denotative meaning, 187
group fantasies and, 78
information theory and, 73
language and, 187–188
shared meaning, 10, 50
symbolic convergence and, 77–78
See also Coordinated management of meaning (CMM) theory; Symbols; Verbal behavior approaches
Measured operational definitions, 428
Measurement, 427–428, 446
behavioral observation, 449–450
content analysis, 450–451
interval data and, 446–447
Likert scales and, 448, 449
linear scales and, 448–449
nominal level of, 446
ordinal level of, 446
physiological measures, 451
pretest/posttest effects and, 437
rank order data, 446
rating scales, 447–449
ratio data and, 447
reliability of, 450

semantic differential scales and, 447–448
validity, threat to, 437
See also Communication research methods
Media
family rules on, 99
mass media, 24
social action media theory, 49
See also Mass media contexts; Media dependency theory
Media dependency theory, 361
assumptions of, 362–363
audience-media relationship and, 362
continuum of dependency and, 363
dependency, definition of, 362
disaster/emergency reporting and, 363–364
media influence and, 362–363
media information sources and, 362, 363–364
media selection, information goals and, 364, 365
parasocial interaction theory and, 364
societal complexity and, 364
society-audience relationship and, 362
society-media relationship and, 361–362, 363–364
uses and dependency model and, 365
See also Mass communication; Mass media contexts
Mediated communication, 38–39, 335–336
Mediated interpersonal communication theory, 336, 365–366
Internet use and, 366
mediated technology and, 366–367
pervasiveness of media and, 367
social networking sites and, 366, 369
teleparticipatory media and, 367
See also Mass communication; Mass media contexts
Memoria/memory, 61–62
Mentation function, 19
displacement, development of, 19
See also Cognitive function; Communication
Messages, 63, 64
accuracy of, 6, 7

channel of conveyance, 5–6
communication plans and, 16, 146–147
communication traits and, 111
decoding process and, 6, 7
definition of, 5
encoding process and, 6
evidence in, 155–156
existence of, 12, 13
fear messages, 148, 149, 152–155
feedback and, 7
forewarnings, 196
information reception apprehension and, 39
intentional message, 1, 9, 11
interpretation of, 63, 68–69
message exchange patterns, 276
noise and, 6
nonverbal messages, 5, 6
perception and, 12
receivers of, 6, 7, 11
redundancy in, 6
reinforcement and, 73
source of, 5, 6, 7, 14
transmission of, 67
verbally aggressive messages, 136
verbal messages, 5, 6
See also Communication; Compliance-gaining message selection; Ideas; Message variables; Persuasion approaches; Yale communication research program
Message variables, 110, 152
evidence in messages, 155–156
fear appeals and, 152–155
See also Messages; Persuasion approaches
Metatheory, 44
Mindfulness concept, 403, 405
Mindlessness concept, 17, 403
Minimum threshold for anxiety/uncertainty, 402
Minority groups, 4
Mobilization dimension, 342
Model I/model II approaches, 309–310
defensive routines and, 309
double-loop learning and, 310
Espoused Theory and, 309
generative learning and, 310
learned helplessness and, 309
manager training and, 310

Name Index